THE STEVENSONS

*A Biography of an American
Family*

THE STEVENSONS

A Biography of an American
Family

JEAN H. BAKER

W. W. NORTON & COMPANY
New York London

The text of this book is composed in Berkeley Old Style Medium
with the display set in Mona Lisa Recut and Copperplate Gothic.
Composition and manufacturing by
The Maple-Vail Book Manufacturing Group.
Book design by Charlotte Staub.

Library of Congress Cataloging-in-Publication Data

Baker, Jean H.
   The Stevensons: a biography of an American family / Jean H. Baker
      p.   cm.
   Includes bibliographical references and index.
   1. Stevenson, Adlai E. (Adlai Ewing), 1900–1965—Family.
   2. Stephenson family.   3. Statesmen—United States—Biography.
   I. Title.
E748.S8B35   1996
973.921'092—dc20   95-5823

ISBN 0-393-03874-2
ISBN 0-393-31598-3 pbk.

W. W. Norton & Company, Inc.
500 Fifth Avenue, New York, N.Y. 10110
W. W. Norton & Company Ltd.
10 Coptic Street, London WC1A 1PU

1 2 3 4 5 6 7 8 9 0

*This book is dedicated to
the next generation.*

CONTENTS

Introduction

INTRODUCTION

THIS BOOK TELLS the story of four generations of an American family and especially of its most celebrated member—Adlai Ewing Stevenson II (1900–1965). It is also a book about the relationship of a family to its times. Like all families, the Stevensons elaborate various issues and themes central to our history and culture, though they are by no means typical Americans. In broad terms their lives illustrate important social facts about the American past: like thousands of other Scots and Irish, they migrate to North Carolina in the eighteenth century, in generational sequence moving westward into Kentucky and finally into central Illinois by the middle of the nineteenth century. By the twentieth century, again like many Americans, they exchange small-town life in Bloomington, Illinois, for that of metropolitan Chicago and its suburbs. Viewed over time, their collective existence becomes a prism through which to observe the shrinking of families, increases in divorce, patterns of child raising, and changes in housing and education.

Yet the Stevensons are a special American family. Because holding public office became an inherited business passed on from son to son until Adlai Stevenson II acknowledged his "bad case of hereditary politics," any history of the Stevensons is necessarily one of politics and party. Unlike the Adams and Kennedy families of Massachusetts, the Stevensons have no single running theme in their chronicles—no descent from glory or ascent to the presidency. Like the town named Normal and the flat expanse of the Illinois prairies where they lived for so long, the annals of the Stevensons, if less melodramatic, reveal continuities that display the family's success in delivering its convictions. The Stevensons came to repeat themselves and their ideas. Among their inherited beliefs was the increasingly anachronistic understanding that politicians must be interested in principles and programs and not driven by personal ambition.

More often losers than winners, like other also-rans, the Stevensons reveal possibilities of what might have been. Their accomplishments were great, but they will be remembered primarily not for what they did but for what they said and for their persistent engagement in public affairs. What the poet Archibald MacLeish said of Adlai Ewing Stevenson II stands for generations of the family: "His great achievement was not political triumph or, indeed, triumph of any kind. His great achievement was the enrichment of his time by the nature of his relationships with his time."

No doubt every American family reflects some historical themes. As a school of mirrors filled with reflections of an older generation and therefore tending to promote custom, not innovation, all families serve as historical agents. Standing at the center of our national life, families provide an opportunity for historians to view the sweep of American history. In that nexus of past, present, and future lies the significance of family history, and few have understood this point as profoundly as the Stevensons. Families pass on, along with shared genetic material, acquired characteristics and kinship traits that shape both the course of individuals and the future of the family. With a view of their exceptionalism that matched that of their nation, the Stevensons preserved their past and prepared young male Stevensons for political life—training that the women of the family fostered. "The Stevensons," complained the family's outstanding dissident Ellen Borden Stevenson, "must be Chinese, they worship their ancestors so much."

The Stevensons reveals the ways in which family members transmitted special Stevenson attitudes about public life. Like those of all politicians, the private lives of the Stevensons—the way they were raised, their education, their wealth, and even their parents' relationships—shaped their public intentions and behavior. In fact, any separation of public and private is a connivance which family biography breaks down. The politics the Stevensons practiced drew on emotions and attitudes formulated in childhood. This interrelation of personality and political styles was never incidental to their individual losses or victories. Nor was the fact that, in the way of family businesses, they learned—and retained—the blueprints of a previous generation, making it difficult to adopt new practices and, in the end, impossible for them to see the constantly changing politics of their times as anything but an ordeal. Viewed over several generations, the Stevensons straddle a party system that has now so deteriorated that nearly half of all Americans support the idea of a third party.

While there are many notable Stevensons, one stands out. Just as every family produces a dominant representative of its collective culture, so for the Stevensons that person was Adlai Ewing Stevenson II. Organized in three parts around the critical episodes of his life, *The Stevensons* begins with Adlai Ewing Stevenson II's campaign for governor of Illinois in 1948, followed by his governorship and his decision to run for president in 1952. "What my brother became," his sister, Buffie Ives, maintained, "was the result of the influences in this house."

Following these decisive moments is a flashback to the Stevenson migration and Adlai Ewing Stevenson I's (1835–1914) various occupations as a lawyer, state's attorney, congressman, first assistant postmaster, vice president of the United States, and perennial candidate, along with his wife Letitia Stevenson's (1843–1913) public career in various organizations of the Progressive period. It was from his grandparents that Stevenson II learned about politics, and the location of these chapters in a section entitled "Journeys" is intended to reveal the heritage that propelled a reluctant candidate into a partisan arena he often disdained.

The second part of this book is entitled "Opportunities." It covers the lives of neurasthenic Helen and Lewis Stevenson and their son Adlai II's early years in small-town America, his education in the East, and his marriage and career in Chicago. The section ends with Stevenson's losing presidential campaigns of 1952 and 1956. In recent years Stevenson's reputation has declined, but after his death one admiring biographer believed that he would have a greater influence on American history than Dwight Eisenhower, who defeated him twice for the presidency. Some of his proposals did influence John F. Kennedy, but he is remembered mostly by a few influential Americans who cite Adlai Stevenson as the reason they entered public service. And Stevenson still survives in the fantasies of older Americans as an expression of a different kind of politics—nobler, more issue oriented, less compliant to the greedy ambitions of modern politicians, and less driven by the media. "Remember if I die to tell my children about Adlai Stevenson," implores a character in the comic strip *Doonesbury*.

However admired, Stevenson lacked the fierce ambition that is a requirement for high-level contemporary politics. Passion was forever modulated by his personality and his upper-class status. The final section, entitled "Echoes," covers Stevenson as an enigmatic possibility for the 1960 Democratic nomination won by John Kennedy, and his life in the shadows as the American ambassador to the United Nations from 1961 until his death in 1965. By that time the family baton had been grasped by a third Adlai Ewing Stevenson (1930–). The last chapter tells the story of Stevenson III's family life and later political career as an Illinois delegate and state treasurer in the 1960s, as U.S. senator in the 1970s, and his (and possibly the family's) last hurrah as a two-time Democratic candidate for Illinois governor in 1982 and in 1986 during a time of disillusionment among Americans—including the Stevensons—about politics in the United States.

Politics, along with the entertainment industry that it today resembles, is the most public of our national pursuits; yet the Stevensons are the most private of families. While they do not approve of what follows—indeed they do not accept the proposition that the telling of the private lives of public figures is inextricably mixed with "the issues," which they prefer to separate from personalities—they have been generous with their time and, for the most part, forthcoming with information. From the moment that I arrived in Bloomington in the summer of 1988 to begin a series of interviews with then ninety-one-year-old Buffie Stevenson until a recent folder of letters between father and son arrived from Adlai Ewing Stevenson III, they have been gracious and helpful.

This book could not have been written without the historical sense that has impelled them to preserve the records of their ancestors' past, though they have never tried to interfere with my interpretation of their lives. My thanks to the late Buffie Stevenson Ives, her son Tim Ives, Borden Stevenson, Nancy Anderson Stevenson, and Adlai Ewing Stevenson III.

Most of the vast Stevenson archive is in two libraries: the Illinois State Historical Library, where there are several Stevenson collections, including the Ives Family Collection and the papers of Adlai Ewing Stevenson III and Adlai Ewing Stevenson II, the latter primarily gubernatorial papers. I am grateful to its chief archivist, Cheryl Schnirring, for her assistance. The bulk of Adlai Ewing Stevenson II's correspondence is in the Seeley Mudd Library in Princeton University, presided over by the efficient and helpful Ben Primer and his assistant Monica Ruscil. Smaller Stevenson collections are housed at the Milner Library of the Illinois State University in Normal, Illinois, in the McLean County Historical Society, where Greg Koos has shared his insights about McLean County and the Stevensons, and in Buffie Ives's home in Bloomington.

Many Goucher students—Michelle La Penna, Forrest Norlin, Paul Tanner, and especially Oona Schmid—have helped with both the research and the preparation of this manuscript. As always, my colleagues in Goucher College's History Department—Julie Jeffrey, Peter Bardaglio, and Kaushik Bagchi—have assisted in various ways, and I am grateful as well to the Goucher College librarians, who never flinched at my requests for materials. Colleagues at the Newberry Library in Chicago, class of 1991–92, where I spent a fellowship year, were discerning critics. Steve Forman of W. W. Norton has been a perceptive and gently encouraging editor. Finally, while I studied the Stevenson family, my own family has provided a loving sanctuary.

THE STEVENSONS

William (Little Gabriel) Stephenson ——— m. 1754 ——— Mary McClelland
(1725–1809)   (1730–1811)

James Bell Stevenson ——— m. 1793 ——— Nancy Brevard
(1768–1850)   (1774–1841)

John Turner Stevenson ——— m. 1832 ——— Elizabeth Ann Ewing
(1808–1857)   (1809–1899)

Adlai Ewing Stevenson ——— m. 1866 ——— Letitia Barbour Green
(1835–1914)   (1843–1913)

William O. Davis ——— m. 1863 ——— Eliza Fell
(1837–1911)   (1842–1900)

Lewis Green Stevenson ——— m. 1893 ——— Helen Elizabeth Davis
(1868–1929)   (1868–1935)

Elizabeth Davis Stevenson (Buffie)   Adlai Ewing Stevenson II ——— m. 1928 ——— Ellen Waller Borden
(1897–1994)   (1900–1965)   (1907–1972)

John Fell Stevenson   Borden Stevenson   Adlai Ewing Stevenson III ——— m. 1955 ——— Nancy Anderson
(1936–)   (1932–)   (1930–)   (1934–)

Adlai Ewing Stevenson IV ——— m. 1991 ——— Barbara Ann Lisner
(1956–)

Adlai Ewing Stevenson V
(1994–)

PART ONE

JOURNEYS

CHAPTER ONE

POSTWAR DILEMMAS

1

ON A BITTER, windy morning in late December of 1947—the kind of day for which Chicago is notorious—Adlai Ewing Stevenson II had fifteen minutes left to decide. The clock was running out on this grandson and son of Illinois politicians who, after fifteen years of intermittent public service in appointive federal jobs, wasn't certain he wanted the nomination. "If you don't run when they want you, they won't take you when you are ready," cautioned his Republican friend Hermon Smith, while the Democrat who thought he wanted to be a U.S. senator made up his mind about the Illinois governorship. A few blocks away, Jack Arvey was waiting.

Colonel Arvey, as he was known from his rank in the Illinois National Guard, needed recruits for his partisan battles, new men to be slated for high state offices by the Democratic State Central Committee and the Cook County Democratic Committee, which he controlled. Returned from four years in the U.S. Army, the bald, fifty-three-year-old son of Jewish immigrants from Poland was uncertain of his recently attained political power. As he probed the changing contours of American politics, Arvey needed winners. Independent candidates occasionally challenged the organization's choice in the spring primary, but rarely did the disciplined ranks of the Illinois Democrats break to nominate an insurgent. If Stevenson accepted, he would lead the Democratic ticket in next year's election. And if he won, Arvey's clout was assured.

Among its legacies World War II had shattered the certainties of domestic politics. The great Democratic general Franklin Roosevelt was dead; no one knew whether the voting coalition that had sent him to the presidency for four terms could survive under Harry Truman's leadership. Wars often converted loyal followers into restless idealistic independents searching for leaders capable of avoiding the catastrophes of their predecessors. The Chicago machine was already challenged by reformers who disliked the exchange features of an organization that traded jobs and economic support for votes. Civil servants overseeing federal programs increasingly controlled jobs that in the past had tied voters to the boss's choice. Moreover, the fading reputation of President Truman, whose administration sagged under the weight of the "mess" in Washington, eroded Arvey's authority.

A Chicago precinct captain and alderman of twenty years' duration, Arvey detected the emergence of a bloc of voters who differed from the faithful of his inner-city wards. These middle-class Democrats opposed patronage, believed in participating in politics not for gain but for good government, measured their votes according to the man and the issues, and proclaimed their pursuit of the public interest. In the Fifth Ward, near the University of Chicago, the newly organized Independent Voters of Illinois (whose name alone upset a party man like Arvey) seemed more concerned with the importance of transforming practical politics into a noble moralizing influence than with the concrete considerations of Arvey's world.

Before the war Americans had accepted politics as a profession, dispensing to its practitioners money, power, and the pleasure of playing the nation's greatest sport. But this new group of amateurs scorned such personal rewards. Unlike the elites who had served in top-level appointive positions during the New Deal and, when duty called, as dollar-a-year men in Washington's wartime agencies, they expected to contribute to the humble routines of local elections, from licking stamps to answering phones. As the partisan winds shifted toward the Republicans, Arvey understood that victory in the 1948 election might come to blue-ribbon candidates who could appeal to such citizens. The colonel intended to slate men "without any scars," men of reputation, unsullied by previous office holding, who could make the abstractions of peace, prosperity, and democracy credible not because of what they promised but because of who they were.

In the past, partisan Horatio Algers had scrambled up the ladders of office holding. Now neither they nor the ethnic representatives of precinct politics, the men whom the newspapers dismissed as party hacks, suited. Jack Arvey had already replaced Chicago's wartime mayor Edward Kelly with Martin Kennelly, a silver-haired insurance man lacking political experience but full of high-sounding platitudes. And with nearly a third of Cook County's votes now housed in suburban communities ringing the city, the standing decision for the Democrats that had made the city a customary party fiefdom was weakening. Richard Daley had lost the sheriff's office, and in the midterm elections of 1946 the Republicans had won a disproportionate twenty of Illinois's twenty-six congressional seats, a political shift reflected at the national level, where, for the first time since 1932, the Democrats had lost control of Congress. In 1947 Arvey placed his hopes on a possible ticket led by the returning war veteran and former alderman Paul Douglas for U.S. senator and the novice Adlai Stevenson for governor.

Still Stevenson hesitated. Before the war he had sought out appointive positions in the federal government. Understanding his veiled ambitions, his friends had urged his candidacy for the U.S. Senate in 1942, although he had never run for any public office. When the Democrats chose instead a party man with more political experience, Stevenson was undismayed: "I never fancied myself as a combatant politico. . . ." Now he did, but for the Senate. As he paced back and forth across his law office muttering, "I am bothered, I am bothered," he wanted assurances that the mayor would support him with the get-out-the-vote passion that commanded the six-figure majorities necessary to offset downstate Republicanism. Arvey's offer was not a surprise, but Stevenson wanted more time to decide.

From his family's experience, Stevenson knew that Illinoisians rarely sent Democrats to the governor's mansion in Springfield. Only three had been elected since the Civil War, and his grandfather Adlai Ewing Stevenson I, who had run a strong campaign in 1908, had not been among them. He did not intend to be Arvey's sacrifice to the two-term Republican governor Dwight Green, or part of the purge of liberal New Dealers intended by conservative Democrats in a Republican year. Nor was he convinced that he wanted to be in electoral politics at all, remembering, as he said to an aunt, "father's admonition to keep out of politics."

By his reckoning of elections as educational debates over past policies and future intentions, Stevenson believed that as a senator he could inform Americans on national and international issues. Like many Americans, Stevenson had never engaged state issues. In Washington, however, he could contribute his accumulated experience from appointive positions in the Navy and State Departments as legal counsel and personal assistant to the secretary of the navy, and after the war as adviser and alternate delegate to the U.S. delegation to the United Nations, positions that his wife mordantly characterized as indistinguishable and unmemorable. "Poor Adlai," Ellen said more than once, "he seems destined to be someone's assistant forever."

Even as the Republican incumbent Senator C. Wayland Brooks waved his bloody shirt from World War I (once disrobing to show a startled audience where a German bullet had entered his back as he recounted the story of winning a Croix-de-Guerre), Stevenson wondered why the Democrats must truckle to such demagoguery by also nominating a veteran, in this case the former Marine private (later lieutenant colonel) Paul Douglas. Douglas did not even have to undress to show his wounded arm, a recent battle scar from his service as a fifty-two-year-old combat Marine on Okinawa. But Douglas preferred to be governor, although party gossip held that the Marine veteran was too independent to defer to Arvey on patronage matters. Did this mean that Stevenson must cater to Arvey and his machine? If so, he wanted no part of such an arrangement.

There was uncertain personal business as well. Several months after he returned from his post as alternate delegate to the United Nations, on February 5, 1947, Stevenson had taken stock in the diary he kept mostly on trips: "Why don't I do what I want to do and like to do and is worthwhile doing? . . . Am 47 today—still restless; dissatisfied with myself. What's the matter? Have everything. Wife, children, money, success—but not in law profession. Too much ambition for public recognition; too scattered in interests; how can I reconcile life in Chicago as lawyer with consuming interest in foreign affairs—public affairs and desire for recognition and position in that field? Prospect of Senate nomination sustains & at same time troubles, even frightens me. Wish I could at least get tranquil & make Ellen happy and do go[od] humble job at law." The malaise continued: "Is it political stature I need or professional?" Or was it family serenity? And was the latter possible?

In 1947 Ellen Borden and Adlai Stevenson had been married for nineteen years. In 1941 Ellen Stevenson had threatened a divorce when her husband left Chicago on one of his wartime missions abroad. Bitterly she complained of incompatibilities and absences that had begun in the 1930s. After the war Ellen's sister had demanded a conference with Stevenson to talk about his "situation with Ellen." But just as Adlai avoided his wife's threats (sometimes considering them no more than late evening whiskey talk), so he told everyone who would intrude on his personal affairs that "all was well."

It wasn't. At some point in the 1930s, possibly while his wife was having an affair, Stevenson had revived a friendship with Alicia Patterson Guggenheim, the publisher of *Newsday*, the Long Island daily. Patterson, the tiny red-haired daughter of a newspaper family, had exchanged Chicago's debutante ballrooms for the frenzied press rooms of *Newsday*, the paper she and her husband Harry Guggenheim had founded in 1940 to service the burgeoning Levittowns of Suffolk and Nassau Counties. As politics ran in Stevenson's blood, so journalism ran in hers—her great-grandfather Joseph Medill had bought the *Chicago Tribune* before the Civil War; her aunt Cissie published the *Washington Times-Herald;* her cousin "Uncle" Bertie McCormick the *Chicago Tribune;* and her father, Joseph Medill Patterson, the New York *Daily News.* By the 1930s Alicia, who had lasted only one year in boarding school, had been married three times, had learned her trade as a reporter, and had fallen in love with Adlai Stevenson—a relationship he recalled in 1949 as ten years of all he'd "known of love and genuine personal concern."

Stevenson admired the forty-four-year-old Alicia Patterson's direction: "I marvel at you more and more. You've made a great success—in the very field I had once dreamed of working." But this relationship was more than the mutual professional attraction of an ambitious newspaperwoman and an emerging politician. Stevenson was smitten. "I don't suppose love and envy can meet. Maybe I'm confused with wanting any direction. Or perhaps it's wanting you rather than your objective. Anyway the love is hard enough without the other, whatever it is."

If Adlai Stevenson was bored by the law, uncertain about his future, and available to other women, and if Ellen Stevenson was isolated from the Chicago arts world she craved as her place of distinction and ambivalent about her marriage, the couple still shared their three sons, along with the pleasures of their country estate in Libertyville, with sheep and horses on seventy-two acres of soybeans, pasture, and lawn. Nearby in the living rooms of Lake Forest, they both starred in the social life of Chicago's premier suburb.

In a few of these living rooms and on Stevenson's own tennis court, his friends had become excited about his candidacy, a campaign from which he had kept a discreet distance. Even before its enthusiasts had officially organized as the Committee to Elect Adlai Stevenson U.S. Senator, they had never mistaken his self-described "casual indifference" for noncompliance, and had worked on. Lou Kohn, the lawyer whom Stevenson acknowledged as his "most ardent backer for the Senate," told everyone who would listen how during his service as a naval officer in the South Pacific he had concluded that the United States must lead the postwar world in order to prevent another war. Returned to Chicago, Kohn remembered Stevenson from the Chicago Council on Foreign Relations and found one answer. Led by Kohn, the eager band of Stevensonites sought out Arvey, who in 1945 had never heard of Adlai Stevenson. Arvey also noted the Republican backgrounds of his promoters and, among the group's few Democrats, the lack of any previous "party activity."

Some of Adlai's blue-blooded amateurs did not know any Democrats (and were proud of it) besides the partisan who had so gracefully assimilated into their circle as a congenial friend and whom they now zestfully touted for public office. Adlai's Amateurs had other attributes, including money, time, and links to other rich Americans. With admirers like these, Stevenson hardly needed an apprenticeship in some lesser office to attract independents and Republicans.

As noon on December 29, 1947—the hour of Arvey's deadline and the moment of Stevenson's destiny—approached, Adlai Ewing Stevenson measured his fate: the certainty of the 1948 Democratic gubernatorial nomination against a remote future chance for a senatorial nomination; the focusing of his scattered public ambitions against his marriage and the unfettered pleasures of private life in Libertyville; his obligation to friends whose efforts on his behalf he had never discouraged, and had sometimes encouraged, against an established career as a partner in a well-known law firm and a reputation as a Chicago civic leader; the influence of party leaders over his future against his autonomy as a government in-and-outer; his uncertainty about his ability to be a successful governor against past successes; and finally the Stevenson heritage of public service against the anonymity of a private citizen.

At five minutes before twelve, Adlai Stevenson gave his answer. Later he provided a more memorable explanation. Now he simply said as he picked up the telephone, "Well, I guess you're right. It's now or never. I'll do it." Although he called Arvey, the circumstances of Stevenson's selection confirmed his belief that he had been chosen to run. He had not insinuated himself into electoral politics. "Well, the fact of the matter is, I didn't seek the job," he informed McLean County Democrats a few weeks later, attempting to establish his independence and difference from greedy politicians twice in this speech and often in the early days of the campaign. "I didn't ask to be put on the ticket." To Ellen's uncle he wrote that he had "finally surrendered to the blandishments of the politicians and agreed to run."

That night on the train to Lake Forest, there was jubilation among the commuters. The news had traveled quickly along La Salle Street, from Arvey's law office at One La Salle to Democratic headquarters, on the third floor of the Morrison Hotel, and upward through the glass-encased corporate and legal offices in the skyscrapers straddling Chicago's main commercial boulevard. At home when neighbors and friends gathered, Ellen Stevenson stayed apart from the celebration but came downstairs to read her poems to those assembled to congratulate her husband, not listen to her poetry. In a later conference with Arvey, she agreed not to divorce her husband until the campaign was over. "I am in it after several dreadful days of indecision and stalling," Stevenson acknowledged to his sister, Buffie Ives. "Whether I've the strength, thick skin & capacity to at least make a good race I don't know, but at least I've got to try now for 10 fearful months. . . . I don't feel very gay this New Year's Day."

It was now Arvey's turn to worry. In the calendar of Illinois politics, candidates came to be slated before the state central committee, itself chosen by elected delegates from county conventions. At this meeting party lieutenants talked patronage and Democratic politics. Here Paddy Bauler, who ran a tavern in the Forty-third Ward and who believed everlastingly that "Chicago ain't ready for reform," gossiped about the Democracy's future with Paul Powell, corn farmer from downstate Johnson County who held gubernatorial aspirations and who, after a lifetime in Illinois politics, left a cash estate of $800,000 in shoeboxes and his bowling bag. In early January, Stevenson appeared before what he called "the politicians." Arvey feared his reluctant amateur would be too removed, too highbrow, and too much the novice.

But it was not the Lake County socialite or chagrined senatorial hopeful who appeared that night. Instead, a smart campaigner conveying integrity and conviction laid out the nonpartisan terrain on which he intended to fight. From the beginning Stevenson separated himself from the endeavors of party members, at the same time praising the professionals with characteristic sensitivity and paternalism. "I have a bad case of hereditary politics, and I hope by associating with veterans like you to contract an equally bad case of practical politics!" Despite his unearned prize, he acknowledged that he was not one of "the organized, militant shock troops of the Democratic party in Illinois who have carried the standards of the people's party for so long in adversity as well as triumph." Then, with a touch of the heretical candor that forever marked his political style, Stevenson implied that he would campaign in the name of nonpartisan efficiency—for good men who might not be Democrats in state office, for a new constitution that might not protect the organization, and for the civil service cloture of patronage jobs that formerly bound the "shock troops" to the Democratic party. Campaigning for the Illinois Senate seat, Paul Douglas complained that Stevenson's message was no more than "noblesse oblige on the part of the privileged. This did not appeal to the miners and hard-scrabble farmers who were having trouble getting enough to wear."

Stevenson's campaign for the governorship began in the dark and cold and snow of an Illinois winter, with his chances as dismal as the weather. By spring when the planting began and the long horizons held a mist of color, and he had received a good turnout in the uncontested primary, his chances for election had improved. The Republican incumbent, Dwight Green, felt it necessary to shorten his Florida vacation to respond to Stevenson. By summer when a withering hot dry spell set in and the bookies in Mason County, in central Illinois, were giving seven-to-five odds on Green, the two candidates were providing Illinois voters, as is the way of American politics, mirror images of themselves and their concerns. With tireless public ebullience, the bald-pated, rumpled, self-proclaimed amateur in Brooks Brothers button-down shirts talked and talked, worried about contributions, and sometimes helped install the red, white, and blue Stevenson banners at the county fairs and courthouse squares where he spoke. "Four counties a day is a fine education," he informed Alicia Patterson in September, "but I don't recommend it for human beings."

Unknown to most Illinoisians, who had forgotten his family, Stevenson squirmed when after his calls for better government the first question was how to pronounce his first name. In Lincoln, a small town in central Illinois, he spoke of ending corruption and especially gambling, before an audience that couldn't hear him for the shouts from the racetrack in the background. Some days Stevenson suffered six catfish dinners, and on others went unfed. Once he confused local sentiments on alcohol and had to be routed out of bed to visit Nauvoo's five taverns. At one county fair the banner across Main Street read "Evening Program-Band Concert / Parade of Prize Swine—Adlai Stevenson, Democratic Candidate for Governor." In

Paddy Bauler's Forty-third Ward, in Chicago, when some of the faithful could not understand the candidate, Bauler yelled from the rear, "Attaboy, Professor, give us some more of those words!" Paul Douglas's campaign symbol this political season was a basket of food to show the necessity for postwar price controls; Adlai Stevenson's was a yellow legal pad, which thereafter became the insignia of his public career and on which he scribbled his good-government messages to the people.

Meanwhile Stevensons's opponent looked like the professional politician he was. With the abundant, well-groomed silver hair that Americans craved in their officials and a round handsome face unfurrowed by any state problems even after seven years as governor, Green reminded audiences of his crusading past as a U.S. attorney responsible for the conviction of Al Capone. By 1949 Green needed to cloak himself in reform clothes to offset criticism that members of his administration had ties to Capone's successors. The governor said nothing of the angry veterans who had picketed the state house for better housing and more benefits. Nor did he discuss the disastrous explosion at Centralia, in southern Illinois, where just a year earlier over a hundred miners had died. During the campaign Stevenson made a charge he later regretted: "Green promised to protect the lives and safety of the miners at Centralia and he let 111 of them die. He ignored the appeals of miners for protection while his mine inspectors collected campaign funds from the operators."

Green had no Stevenson record to attack; instead, he tied his opponent to the national Democratic party of Truman administration scandals, bigspending New Deal programs, and softness on communism. He excoriated the United Nations and called his opponent a "striped pants diplomat," a charge that backfired when the *Chicago News* printed a picture of the governor in the striped pants of the male aristocracy's haute couture. Green's issues were not especially Illinois concerns, since this governor had vice-presidential ambitions. He had been chosen to give the keynote address at the Republican convention, which instead chose two other governors for its national ticket, Thomas Dewey of New York for president and Earl Warren of California for vice president.

While the handsome incumbent who knew state and local affairs talked dully of national budgets and foreign policy, "Stevie" (the nickname the downstate politicians preferred to the unpronounceable, uncommon Adlai) concentrated on Illinois. The veteran of six years of federal and international service now talked about the state affairs he had long avoided. With an eloquence that soon gained national attention, Stevenson offered a model for good government. He attacked the corruption of Green's administration; he promised more efficient state government, better and fewer officials, higher pension and welfare payments, and a new constitution; he inveighed against the citizenry's sins of indolence, self-interest, and excessive partisanship. Throughout he grounded his campaign in the sentiments of his hero Woodrow Wilson, who, in his 1910 campaign for the New Jersey governorship, had also tried to raise state affairs to a compelling level of moral regeneration. And like Wilson, who had also been chosen to bring respectability to a state ticket, Stevenson declared his independence from both party and politicians.

On some social issues Stevenson ran slightly behind the Democratic platform, though the differences were hard to detect from his adjective-filled, value-laden speeches. To a black audience he committed himself to a state Fair Employment Practices Act, "to make our righteous proclamations of economic equality of opportunity something more than pious words"; he promised a civil rights division in the Attorney General's Office. But he dismissed the need for any new civil rights laws, urging only enforcement of the old ones, and his FEPC lacked any powers to ensure compliance. Along with most northern Democrats in 1948, Adlai Stevenson stood staunchly and rhetorically against racial discrimination in education, an end that did not yet require a statement on implementation. To the women of Illinois he offered equal pay for equal work, and a gentleman's paternalism conveyed in his acknowledgment, as if he were speaking to foreigners, that his wife and mother were women.

Throughout the campaign, Stevenson one-liners stung: we will clean house of "Greed, Grime and Green and the state house gang." He called the governor dirty names: "Bertie's Boy," "McCarthy" Green, and "Governor Greed." He coined a new word, "plunderbund," to describe Green's malfeasance. He filled a black notebook with alliterative slams—"perfidious Pete," "Dwight the blight," "Pete—the man who never said no to a payroller and never said yes to honest government." He was funny, self-deprecatory, and, especially in the beginning, long-winded and long-worded. His comment that Illinois had game wardens who had never been closer to a quail than "Ananias to the truth" sent some listeners to their dictionaries and others to an understanding that this candidate was not one of "the boys." Later the gibe reappeared in a more populist form as more "game wardens than rabbits."

Stevenson listened, learned, and improved. In these days before political consultants, his tiny campaign staff included mostly journalists, who, with the cynicism of their trade, recognized his weaknesses: his voice was too high and too patrician. He sounded, one decided, like the movie actor Ronald Coleman with the tinge of a midwestern accent. He paused in the wrong places and lost his punch lines. And he was, according to one reporter, "too painfully eager."

When even his admiring sister, Buffie Ives, told him that he had put a Pontiac audience to sleep, Stevenson shortened his words and paragraphs and eventually his speeches. "Keep your talks down to fifteen minutes," advised his campaign manager, Jim Mulroy, "and always end optimistically." Yet the jokes and the silver-tongued self-derogation remained a graceful contrast to Green's sober self-congratulation. If he was Green's nameless member of the left-leaning, striped-pants brigade of diplomats who had given Eastern Europe away to the Communists at Yalta, the governor was for him "the third-term candidate of the Greed Gang."

As Stevenson labored over his talks in the backseat of the car that bumped along the roads of Illinois (which he promised to improve), he worried about philosophical issues that few candidates ever considered. To an audience in Peoria, he contemplated the nature of the electoral process and "the illusive business of finding [his] way to the heart of the average man—when there is no such thing—and . . . the human heart is often encased in a pocketbook." Always an ardent self-critic, Stevenson decided that he could impress his listeners, but not excite them. Nor was he pleased with his radio performances, which at $525 for fifteen minutes outraged his frugality. In his promotional films the lights bounced from his unpowdered forehead like the headlights of a car off a water slick. In profile, his prominent nose overwhelmed his other features until his managers advised confronting the cameras full-face.

And all the while, as politicians do, Stevenson reassured his private self publicly. For personal reasons he had nearly deferred his candidacy. But now life in the public eye had become the central endeavor of a man later described by his son Borden as "enormously insecure." His messages spoke to his dilemmas. Supported by the most notorious machine in American history, Stevenson threw vitriol on his opponent's statehouse gang and its connections to the remnants of Capone's organization. Chosen by the boss of the Cook County Democratic Committee, who gave office for favors, he criticized his opponent's version of the same process. Engaged in winning the people's favor in a process that exhausted and irritated him, Stevenson reflected on civic virtue. His was the high road: "Those who treat politics and morality apart will never understand the one or the other." Yet it was hard for Stevenson to keep these two together while a political mendicant on a campaign marked by sharp, denigrative attacks on the vulnerable Green.

In his distaste for the exchange aspects of the American electoral system, which traded political promises (and sometimes jobs, contracts, and even money) for votes, Stevenson the Democrat emerged as Stevenson the nonpartisan, concerned, do-gooding progressive. Whatever he was, he was not a politician. "The good of the whole sometimes transcends normal party allegiance," he declared, appealing to his fellow voters "not so much in the name of a Democratic candidate but as just another citizen." But as that private citizen, he sometimes acted as if he was "off-duty" as a politician, forgetting to pick up restaurant checks or greet the people with the camara-

derie of most seekers of office, who so easily established commonality with
the voters.

Nor was Adlai Stevenson comfortable with the attention given to personal matters: "the way I tie my necktie, whether I prefer jelly or jam. . . .
A few weeks ago some very political gentlemen took my manager aside
downstate and asked him a little sheepishly if he had objection to suggesting to me in some delicate, inoffensive manner that I wear a different
hat." Hoping to retain his privacy, Stevenson preferred discussion of the
issues along with criticism of his opponent's record as he tested his virtue
in a potentially corrupt endeavor. Such a public style was good politics in
a Republican state, but it was also a private comfort.

As his marriage collapsed, Stevenson narrated the cautionary tale of his
life. This political campaign, he told listeners in Waukegan, was a discussion of "our intimate family problems in Illinois." He mixed public and
private worlds: "I can readily understand why [the people of Illinois] want
a *new* Governor, but I am compelled to confess that my wife can't understand why they should want me!" "You can't have everything you want,"
he warned voters growing accustomed to expansive promises from their
leaders.

Adlai Stevenson was advising himself because, as a married man who
had been taught that marriage was forever, he had fallen in love with Alicia
Patterson. Laboring over his speeches, Stevenson introduced his dilemma
with dark images of illness and pessimism that hedged his political promises and that conveyed his family problems: "Our nation is very sick in the
very large and very important part known as Illinois." "The world is troubled and frightened as never before." His distress was obvious in a speech
to the Chicago Immigrants Protective League: "Must we forever foul our
own nest; must we forever corrupt the mind and the spirit to serve personal
ends?" At the end of the campaign he promised a victory or a broken heart
in the attempt.

In the private life that extended into his public affairs, though he wished
to separate the two, Adlai Stevenson found purpose. One night from a third-
rate hotel in Urbana, he "toppled" into bed after the "last of the politicians
and professors" had left and wrote Alicia Patterson of the rigors of campaigning: he would leave for Danville in the morning "and so on and on to
the end of time or until my sins are expiated—I wonder what the hell I'm
doing and why and then I think of you and that you think it's good and
worthwhile and wouldn't love me if I didn't behave this way and then I get
up and go at it again."

In mid-September the campaign came to Bloomington, the central Illinois town that had been home to five generations of Stevensons. Stevenson
had opened his quest for the governorship there in February. Now, seven
months later, an old-fashioned torchlight parade with floats and speeches

in the courthouse square was planned. In a modern resurrection of the partisan ritual that had been the culmination of nineteenth-century campaigns, horse-drawn wagons had been replaced by the vintage Model T's, "Hummers," and Reos that Stevenson's parents and their generation had driven along the shady, sometimes muddy streets of Bloomington in the first decade of the twentieth century. The chamber of commerce financed a float; so did the railroad shop workers. The Bloomington Women's Club featured a member dressed in the wedding dress of the candidate's mother, an ornate affair of ivory satin with the elaborate puff sleeves and pinched waist of Helen Davis Stevenson's time. Someone counted fifteen floats, sixty horses, twenty-five antique cars, thirty-seven motorcycles, and one hundred homemade torchlights of kerosene in beer cans.

But no one wore the Democratic uniforms that had been such an essential part of the nineteenth-century understanding that partisans were an army en route to do battle against an enemy. Nor did the crowd of eighteen thousand line up as a military division with its officers directing the order of march, its soldiers singing campaign songs, as they had to Adlai Stevenson I. Instead, there was a languid rendition of "If you knew Stevie, like we know Stevie /Oh! Oh! Oh! what a man / He so outclasses his opposition / Who is just another politician / Stevie's a statesman." When Stevenson spoke, the crowd listened passively without the noisy exchanges that characterized the partisan involvement of the witnessing crowd of an earlier public culture.

However forced, the connection of past and present, family and community, was apparent. Even Ellen Stevenson, who had made few appearances after she informed a luncheon meeting of the Democratic women of Illinois that she was and would remain a Republican, had agreed to come and to dress in the bonnet and ankle-length dress of some imprecise earlier age. Before the parade made its way from Grandfather Adlai Stevenson's former house in Franklin Park to the courthouse square in the center of town (Ellen's Model T broke down in an explosion of steam, and she had to walk), a crowd of neighbors overflowed onto the sidewalk of 1316 East Washington Street. This was the house and lawn of Buffie Stevenson Ives, the candidate's sister—and the place where Adlai Stevenson had lived from 1907 until 1916, when he went to boarding school in the East.

Returned from Europe in 1939 after her husband's retirement from the consular service, Elizabeth Ives (whose nickname, along with so much in her life, had been bestowed by her younger brother) had bought the house from her parents' estate. Thereafter she kept what family members called "1316" as it had been during the Bloomington childhood she had shared with her brother. Her mother's soothing lavender still decorated one of the four upstairs bedrooms, and in the front living room and side porch, shaded now by the oaks, pines, and a gingko planted by Helen Stevenson before

World War I, the furniture and the royal red damask upholstery were identical to those her mother preferred. For Buffie 1316 represented a tangible link to a past that she also preserved in the letters of previous generations now carefully typed and elegantly bound. In the attic and the back room on the second floor, manila folders and file cases overflowed with earlier chapters of a family story of which she was this generation's archivist. On this day dressed in a Quaker bonnet and the dress of her maternal grandmother, and holding the sign "Pioneer 1830," Buffie intended to play a supporting role in the future chapters of the Stevenson story.

Amid the tradition some innovations were apparent—a popular radio host circulated through the crowd on the lawn interviewing those who had known the candidate in his youth. To save time the candidate had temporarily abandoned his slow-moving automobile caravan for the train. He arrived from Chicago with an entourage that included influential leaders of the Democratic party. At first they had written off as a loser this candidate who disarmingly characterized his efforts as "an amateur's pilgrimage through the political jungle of Illinois." But now the politicians suspected an upset and wanted to see for themselves.

Most of the local well-wishers were Republicans; McLean County rarely deviated from its almost century-long attachment to the Republican party. Its prosperous farmers had refused even the New Deal appeals of Roosevelt, though Bloomington had gone Democratic in 1932 and 1936. Still, the Stevensons were well known in this community. A few members of the crowd could remember the parades and rallies held sometimes to honor and sometimes to promote the various candidacies of Stevenson I. Some could dimly recall his losing campaigns for the vice presidency in 1900 and for the Illinois governorship in 1908. More remembered when the current candidate's father, Lewis Stevenson, campaigned for secretary of state in 1916. Still others connected the candidate to the region's most influential newspaper, the Bloomington *Pantagraph,* a maternal legacy from the Republican side of the family that had, just this time, put blood before party habit by endorsing Stevenson for governor and, to the irritation of Paul Douglas, no one else on the Democratic ticket.

To this audience, as he stood on the wooden platform that commanded the courthouse square, Adlai Stevenson described the virtues of heartland America with its ideals of "friendliness, belief in the Republic, trust in the democratic principle—faith in the future—respect for the past—progress along the path that our ancestors blazed." It was the kind of political sermon at which Bloomington's favorite son excelled. Stevenson would never be more eloquent than he was that afternoon as he gave the sentimental lesson of his childhood to his former neighbors: "that in quiet places, reason abounds; that in quiet people there is vision and purpose; that many things are revealed to the humble that are hidden from the great." Through words and delivery, he conveyed what modern politicians in an age without the compass of parties must: a superior character who deserved office. Without artifice, private sentiment merged with public intentions, however vague, in the self-revelation that postwar politics increasingly required. Stevenson concluded humbly by expressing the hope that he could measure up to the Bloomington-instilled virtues of "self-respect, humanity and friendliness." Nowhere did he mention the Democratic party. Nor did he mention that this particular son of the prairie had left for Chicago as soon as he could.

The Bloomington rally was the turning point of Adlai Stevenson's 1948 gubernatorial campaign. The Chicago Democrats who had traveled to Bloomington now untied their purse strings to support a candidate most had earlier dismissed. Along with four-figure gifts from several Chicago wards, the Democratic Central Committee contributed $10,000, which disturbed Adlai's Amateurs, though Stevenson's campaign fund of $175,000 was much less than that of Green. "You are asking the independent voters of Illinois to vote for you because there is a corrupt machine," complained Jane Dick, a Lake Forest confidante who questioned the candidate's independence after accepting such "dubious" support.

This was neither the first nor the last advice Jane Dick would deliver to Adlai Stevenson. As wealthy, blond Jane Warner, she had danced with Stevenson in the debutante ballrooms of Chicago in the late 1920s; after her marriage to Edison Dick, heir to the A. B. Dick Company, makers of business machines, she had dined with him in the chic North Shore Casino Club in the 1930s. Unlike most society women, Dick had worked at the city's legendary Hull House, where Stevenson was on the board. Preferring politics and Adlai Stevenson to bridge and garden clubs, she had become a charter member of Adlai's Amateurs, with an official role during the campaign as cochair of the women's division.

The hardworking Stevenson took the money and gained in the polls, even though Truman's support against the Republican candidate, Thomas Dewey, remained fixed at a mere 30 percent. By November the gamblers whom Stevenson had vowed to put out of business were offering even odds on Green and Stevenson. But the national press, including the *New York Times*, predicted the Republicans would retain the governorship, just as it believed, along with most observers, that Dewey would beat Truman. Yet all were impressed with the man *Newsweek* described as "the friendly, earnest candidate [who] visited almost every lunch wagon and curbstone from little Egypt in Southern Illinois to the North Shore along Lake Michigan, making as many as a dozen speeches in a single night."

On November 2, 1948, Adlai Stevenson was elected governor of Illinois by what was at that time the largest margin in the state's history. On election night, when the press finally caught up with the victor and asked whether he thought the returns were going well, Stevenson responded that he had been out to dinner and out of touch. "Is it going well?" he inquired of an astonished reporter, revealing again that nonchalance so foreign to most politicians. With 58 percent of the total vote, he led the Democratic ticket, as Illinois Republicans abandoned their party and voted for the man, not the organization. Stevenson carried Bloomington by 2,000 votes, and in a familiar pattern of postwar voting, the citizens split their ballots to favor Dewey over Truman by nearly the same margin. The winner was especially proud of his downstate showing, although the disciplined soldiers of Arvey's machine had provided 60 percent of his statewide vote. In Arvey's Twenty-fourth Ward, which had earned a reputation as the Gibraltar of the Democracy, 99 percent of the 28,000 voters cast their ballots for the man Arvey touted as our "golden nugget in the backyard." Stevenson was not surprised that he had failed to carry his home county of Lake; as Arvey had predicted, suburban voters were Republicans. Stevenson hardly noticed what later came to concern him: a declining turnout, which, despite population increases, was less than in 1940 and 1944.

In a corollary to the presidential coattail, Stevenson served as a political front-loader, bulldozing Truman before him. The president's statewide margin was a skimpy 33,000 votes; Stevenson's was an abundant 570,000 on a ballot that did not include this presidential year's minor parties: Henry Wallace's Progressives, Strom Thurmond's Dixiecrats, and Norman Thomas's Socialists. Stevenson's majority was enough to earn a congratulatory note from Harry Truman, who recognized in the new Illinois governor the vote-getting ability that, especially after his startling defeat of Dewey, the president respected. Stevenson answered with the earnestness that sometimes overrode his worldliness: "Command me if I can ever be of any service."

Green's record helped Stevenson to the extent that elections are referendums on past policies and administrations; so too did the two-term governor's ambitions for the third term, for which Republicans despised Franklin Roosevelt. Stevenson did especially well in the downstate counties whose support acknowledged his small-town, Protestant background, though by 1948 he had lived twice as long in Chicago as he had in Bloomington. Republicans did not feel as if they were voting for a Democrat, so effective was Stevenson's pledge as "just another citizen" that party politics and good government were divisible. He benefited as well from the suspicions of downstate farmers who heard Dewey's tepid endorsements of farm supports. Stevenson also won because of his tireless campaign and his reform message. "He might have been reluctant to go for it at first," one reporter commented, "but once committed, he fought as if his survival depended on the outcome."

In one year the self-proclaimed good citizen preoccupied with international affairs and ambivalent about his future had lost his status as an occasional visitor to public service. As governor of the fourth-largest state in the union, he would over the next four years exchange questions about the United Nations and deteriorating Soviet-American relations for considerations of roads, mental health, pensions, and coal mines. As an elected official, he would also surrender his privacy for public scrutiny, and he would lose his wife.

The hundreds of postelection messages included one from Alicia Patterson, who was in Germany. Sending her love and congratulations, she wanted introductions to European leaders whom Stevenson knew from his work at the United Nations. The new governor responded with exuberance and a characteristically plaintive note: "I carried Ill. by 565,000 plus—never anything like it in history—515,000 ahead of Truman and 180,000 ahead of the closest man on the Democratic ticket. Now I'm really in trouble."

Rashly the governor-elect considered visiting Alicia Patterson in Paris, where she was covering international events in a tumultuous year marked by the American airlift to Berlin and a national debate over postwar aid to Europe. Discretion held the day. Instead, after a short holiday with his sister and brother-in-law in North Carolina, covered, to his chagrin, by the press, Stevenson acknowledged both the joy in his fulfilled "dream of this Gov. business" and the tedium of the "exacting preparations . . . staff, research, conferences, appointments to major jobs, patronage."

He showed no ambivalence about what he felt for Alicia. After three husbands she had declared that she had never loved anyone but him. "Is it really true my angel—or was it just a girlish explosion that you might have better spared a sensitive passionate governor. We must talk of that and ten thousand other things that seem more important than cabinet appointments in Illinois. . . . Somewhere the sun is shining—and you're in it—a pool of bright light, your hair is glistening and reddish and tumbling all about your shoulders, your delicate little face serene and your eyes half shut in reverie. And in a moment I'm going to kiss you and you're going to be all alive again." In this letter the newly elected governor offered a hopeful motto for the challenges of his private and public life: "There's nothing we can't do if we want to enough and we are wise enough."

2

AT HIS INAUGURATION in January 1949, Ellen Stevenson sat in the front row with her sons Adlai III, a freshman at Harvard, and twelve-year-old John Fell, a sixth-grader at the Lake Forest Country Day School. Borden, the often overlooked middle son, stayed at boarding school in the East, as relatives flooded into Springfield. So too did a trainload of Adlai's Amateurs, the proud neighbors and friends from Lake Forest and Chicago who mixed uneasily with the professional politicians. Ellen Stevenson had suggested a black jazz ensemble for the inaugural ball rather than five hours of dance music by Newt Perry's twenty-piece local swing band. So Dizzy Gillespie and Duke Ellington shared the bandstand with another orchestra.

A talented pianist, Ellen Stevenson might have joined them on the piano. Her one successful campaign appearance had been in a black ward on Chicago's South Side, where she ended up at the piano entertaining a delighted audience. This night, elegant as usual in the cool colors that conveyed her glacial nonchalance about her husband's public career, she wore a gray, off-the-shoulders, floor-length ball dress of satin—and a petulant expression. To the reporters who asked intrusive questions about her clothes, she abruptly responded that expensive fabric was the key to style. Husband and wife danced stiffly and distantly in a small, cordoned-off area in the huge Springfield Armory.

Ellen Stevenson spent that night in the governor's mansion (John Fell spent some of it stuck in the elevator) and left the next day for Libertyville. She joined her husband on a trip to Harry Truman's inauguration later in January and came to Springfield only three more times, presiding over the governor's traditional dinner for the legislators in March. The last time she came with her mother to discuss a divorce.

Meanwhile her husband ran the state of Illinois from what he called his "cell" and "this dungeon." "I am marooned in Springfield," lamented the governor to his brother-in-law Ralph Hines. During one hectic period the governor did not leave the mansion for two weeks. In his downstairs study he worked long hours poring over budget and employment figures, composing the speeches that took too long and eroded an already spacious schedule, greeting humble and mighty visitors, reading the reports from legislative and department heads, and making the patronage appointments that, without the encumbrance of previous promises, he insisted could be given to the best men. As with all executives, his personality stamped the kind of leadership he provided.

With a natural frugality primed by his public position, Adlai Stevenson turned the lights off in the thirty-room mansion, ordered rubber bands put around the flags on state limousines so that the tiny emblems would not wear out so quickly, and at night answered the telephone himself. (News of this soon leaked out, and state residents began calling Springfield 6064 after ten.) When, to balance his budget, he demanded a 10 percent reduction in all departmental budgets and found that the mansion's had little slack, the grocery bills were scrutinized and gubernatorial entertainments postponed.

Reflecting his dismissive attitude toward professional politicians, he spent little time in his office in the Capitol Building. Since its completion in 1876, most governors had worked in the Victorian setting of a domed statehouse with its 361-foot cupola of glistening metal visible for miles above the flat prairies of Sangamon County. There, in a second-floor office with no exit except through a waiting room usually filled with lobbyists, reporters, and the public, previous Illinois governors had run the state, buttonholing legislators for the exchanges that led to support of their programs, discussing appointments with party leaders, and meeting with department heads. Stevenson preferred the seclusion of the nearby mansion. His wry acknowledgment that his beloved Dalmatian Artie was better known than he on Springfield's streets revealed as much about his style as about Artie's wandering.

To be sure, Stevenson fulfilled the necessary social obligations. Without a wife, he turned to Buffie and her husband, Ernest Ives, who were well acquainted with matters of protocol from their years overseas in the consular corps. Even with his gregarious sister at the foot of the table, his dinners were universally acknowledged to be short and dry. More than one legislator complained that the hospitality was grudging—"only one drink before we sit down and then after eating out the door." Old-timers remembered the conviviality of the Green regime, when the cigars and after-dinner drinks signaled the beginning of a late evening. In the spring, when the governor scheduled the annual press dinner for the St. Nicholas Hotel, a reporter warned him that gossip in the press rooms and legislative halls held him a snob "who considered us a drunken gang of uncouth slobs." His response was to offer catfish in the mansion.

On weekends Adlai Stevenson sometimes flew home to Libertyville in the twin-engine Illinois National Guard Beechcraft that became his sole gubernatorial extravagance. Restless wherever he was, the governor was lonely enough to offer the empty bedrooms of the mansion to members of his staff, who shared his table and his geniality but not his inner life. "Work has been my refuge for many years," he wrote Patterson, "and now it will be for many more years." Quick to offer overnight accommodations to celebrities like Lily Pons and Alben Barkley who traveled to the prairies, he often organized house parties, reminiscent of college weekends, for his Lake Forest friends.

Some visitors were dismayed by the bleakness of his life. The poet Archibald MacLeish, who came to the mansion the first year of his governorship, recalled, "I found Adlai at the end of a big reception room with obviously political types who were haranguing him. Adlai was looking forlorn and lost and miserable. . . . The whole evening left me with an impression of forlornness and misery. I had a dreadful feeling that even more than resentment of Ellen he felt a longing for her—he still loved her. If ever a man needed a wife, Adlai did."

A man with a splintered family, Adlai Stevenson served intermittently as a companion to his sons, once this first year taking John Fell canoeing on the Des Plaines River, which bordered his property in Libertyville. "I love him so much it hurts," he wrote the childless Alicia, who had become the recipient of his paternal reports. "And I think he really loves me . . . he and you and who else?" In the summer young Adlai joined him at the governor's conference in Colorado Springs and at a friend's ranch. In the winter Buffie Ives organized a Christmas dance for the boys and their friends, as his intimates came to understand that their invitations must include his sons. But Stevenson worried about his role as a father, despairing to Alicia, "Did I ever tell you that I'm a sickly sentimentalist and that I love my boys so that it literally hurts. Perhaps that's why I haven't been a better father." At least in the early days of the separation, the children, according to John Fell, spent more time with their mother, who believed, as she rebuked her busy husband, "that the boys should come and go as they please, as it fits their schedules, not ours."

Alicia Patterson came to the governor's mansion too, although as publisher, editor, and occasional columnist of *Newsday* she was busy. "100,000 circulation," the governor marveled in the spring of 1949: "So you've made it—you indomitable little tiger. I could bite your ears with savage joy. I know what it means to win, when people smiled and had no faith—just damnable courtesy. But why this Napoleonic—'I'll found an empire?' Must Caesar forever gather laurels to be happy. Is this father jealousy-love healthy? Profit my heart, profit from the lessons of your inheritance. The stuff of greatness is goodness, serenity, wisdom—not conquest. I *know* you're a hard little empire builder—but I *love* a woman—a gentle, wise, compassionate woman—not a mighty, ruthless, determined conqueror! Or do I?"

Throughout their affair, Stevenson shared a private self rarely on view for others. In a confessional style reserved for his female companions who responded in kind, he admired Alicia's discipline and "self-management," remarking, "Maybe it comes from greater self-confidence or at least better perception of what's important and what isn't. To me everything seems to be of the same dimension—serious, important, worth the best until there is no best or even good." Such nonselective diligence made his work as governor exhaustingly ceaseless.

Early in 1949 Alicia Patterson and Adlai Stevenson considered marriage, though neither was legally free at the time. In the first weeks of his lonely governorship, as he struggled to learn his new job, Stevenson used the salutation "Dearly beloved" and closed his letters with the schoolboy's fervent expectation of the "way things will be." But in February they clashed. "I think I behaved well. Dictated a little longer and took the elevator upstairs," he wrote in the aftermath of one disagreement.

They fought over the future, for Alicia declined the role of first lady in Springfield, just as Ellen had. "Very well, Alicia, I guess I didn't understand well. Maybe we are cut out of different clothes. I'm not resentful. I'm deeply grateful for even a few months of what was to be forever and don't worry about me." Later their positions reversed. By 1950 it was Alicia who contemplated a divorce. Now Stevenson urged caution, patience, deliberation, and an ambiguous future. "Certainly to seek a divorce impetuously would be, I should think, a great mistake . . . and your last recourse. Three [divorces] is quite a lot—even for a brave free spirit!" In the coming years other women discovered that Adlai Stevenson did not intend marriage and that the best way to his heart was to be married.

By 1950 the governor was also involved with unmarried Dorothy Fosdick, who had misread his amatory cues and believed that he might marry her. An earnest, hardworking State Department assistant secretary, Fosdick shared an interest in international affairs with the governor as well as some physical attention. "Nobody's ever kissed me like that before," wrote Fosdick after a visit to the mansion in 1950. While Patterson and the governor gaily signed their correspondence with drawings of rats and lice, Fosdick used an angel. Then Patterson heard rumors of the governor's new relationship. Questioned, Stevenson gave a misleading response: "Donald Duck what libel. Fosdick's a bright little lass of 35–40 who worked for me in England. What have you heard? I'm bewildered."

Never were the perplexities of Stevenson's life as sundering as in his love affairs, especially that with Alicia. For Alicia Patterson was rich, attractive, energetic, and successful, and like other men of his class and generation, he was unfamiliar with such females. Alicia was like a man; she knew public affairs and could survey the prospects of the Soviets in Eastern Europe as easily as she could dissect the postwar strategy of the Democratic party. She had flown in the American planes that were supplying West Berlin during the Soviet blockade. "How can you be so many things—lovely and feminine, businesslike and brisk, precise and persistent? . . ."

After Alicia was featured in a *Saturday Evening Post* article that rankled her husband, Adlai took Harry Guggenheim's side, wondering how a proud male could "bear to be obscured by his wife? Is the answer to happiness and compatibility dull and balanced mediocrity? It sounds a little like my latter years with Ellen." Yet Patterson's career and her interest in public affairs made her "half-man, half-woman" to a man who believed in the abstractions of equal pay for equal work and the Equal Rights Amendment but who was enmeshed in conventional attitudes about female behavior. "You are like a guy," the governor marveled, thereby resolving the dilemma.

Separated by schedules, distance, ambition, and the uncertainties of their careers, Alicia Patterson and Adlai Stevenson never married. Their life together became one of poignant anticipation of times to come and nostalgic remembrance of times past—an affair of separation. For a public man with a long-distance, severed family and the politician's distaste for intimacy, Patterson became a discreet confidante of private matters that could not be shared with others. In time she also became a symbol of Adlai Stevenson's other world of leisure, privacy, and serenity, far from his maddening life in politics. Alicia's Georgia plantation on a river made black from the roots of the ancient mangrove trees represented a mythic place of release from an overcrowded life—"the fairy land of the Black River . . . with the forest and solitude and you."

For the next fifteen years, until Alicia Patterson's death in 1963, they saw each other fleetingly—at her plantation, in Chicago, in Springfield, in New York, at her home in Port Washington, Long Island, on overseas trips, and even in Libertyville. They were always greeting and leaving each other, only to exert the necessary energy to find another place in the schedule for a vacation or even a dinner together. They required mutual itineraries: "I will be in Chicago July 16 and 17. On July 21 I go to Seattle but I will be in Ill. no later than the 27th when I have a speaking engagement in the evening and another at St. Anne on the afternoon of the 28th, but I will be back in the evening," advised Adlai in 1951. Sometimes they conspired to shake off friends with thin excuses so that they could be alone. Accustomed to being apart, Adlai wondered whether more companionship would make Alicia's heart grow less fond of this "soft, fat and bald old man."

In an age of telephones they wrote letters. At times Patterson was indiscreet; a secretary at the statehouse opened one of the "tell-tale" blue envelopes. "Write guarded letters for a while until I get the secretarial situation down there under control," cautioned a "horrified" governor. Once Stevenson rebuked his house guest about "that strong scent . . . the place reeked the next morning and the maids must have been slightly confused or not confused at all."

Often he used religious references in his love letters. Usually from Psalms or the Book of Common Prayer, these quotations had been learned during his childhood Sundays in the Unitarian and Presbyterian churches of Bloomington and later at boarding school and college. "Oh Lord," he wrote in February of 1949, "let me be an instrument of thy peace. Where there is injury, let me sow pardon. Where there is doubt, faith." As Alicia learned, psalms and proverbs such as "I glory in tribulation" and especially the Twenty-seventh Psalm, with its beginning lines "The Lord is my light and salvation; whom then shall I fear," summarized the conflicted, uncertain, perpetually seeking side of a man who mixed gloom with gaiety and morality with sin. Later the governor engraved thoughtful quotations on his Christmas cards as their recipients marveled at the sensitivity of this man. "I stood at the gate and asked one who stood there to give me a light so I shall see my way," went the inscription on the governor's card in 1950. And it was on the editorial page of *Newsday* that he found a useful proverb from the Old Testament: "Where there is no vision, the people perish."

3

As Patterson became a central part of his private life, Stevenson discussed with her what he called, with characteristic evasion, "this Ellen business." His friends, at least one of his children, and his sister heard from others about the breakup of his marriage. Borden was at Choate when the headmaster drew him aside to deliver the news; later a telegram from his father confirmed, "Mother has been unhappy and feels we must be divorced . . . you boys will divide your vacations with mother and me and I will keep the farm. Everything is all right."

Alicia Patterson could have told his relatives that he was upset about his divorce and a financial arrangement he considered unreasonable, especially when he had to sell $32,000 worth of stock for a settlement. "Ellen is getting very demanding about money and in her present abnormal, irrational state of mind I suppose she could be very difficult which would mess things up not only for us but for years to come," he advised Alicia. Two weeks later, he grumbled, "I don't know how much I can pay her for a divorce *she* wants."

In the first summer of his governorship, Adlai and Ellen Stevenson bickered through their lawyers. One July morning the governor detailed their differences. "Ellen wants," he recorded, "custody of John Fell—me to pay the school expenses; use of house until she makes final living arrangements, $4,000 a year—total $75,000 as settlement not alimony, and [acknowledgment] that I have forced her to get divorce—I am at fault." By the fall the couple had resolved most differences in the governor's favor, but not before Ellen Stevenson's lawyer had complained about Adlai's unfairness and "light provision . . . in view of her interest in her husband's property and her contribution to the marriage over a long period of years." Later Ellen Stevenson accused her husband of undervaluing his assets of over half a million dollars as well as the Libertyville house (which he kept) and especially her financial contributions to their marriage. But this was an age before divorce courts placed price tags on the substantial endowments that women made to the home, and given her ignorance of financial matters and her husband's power, Ellen Stevenson was poorly equipped for any contest.

When the arrangements were complete in the fall, Ellen Stevenson left for Las Vegas, where the six-week residency for uncontested divorces attracted rich women who did not want to wait the longer periods required in Illinois and most other states. She was not alone. Like many of the 15,000 other women who received a Nevada divorce in 1949, she had waited until the war ended. As divorce skyrocketed to over 600,000 in 1946 from a prewar annual total of 251,000 in 1939, continuing to rise at an annual rate of 2 to 3 percent, a severed marriage became, almost, a customary procedure. Raised in a family where enduring domestic arrangements were considered the strength of the Republic, Adlai Stevenson believed divorce a moral failure.

Most women—and women were the plaintiffs in over four-fifths of all divorce proceedings—could not afford Las Vegas or Reno, where the grounds for divorce included the nonspecific, uncontestable modern complaint offered by Ellen Stevenson of mental cruelty. The latter was legally defined in Nevada as "misconduct calculated to render the life of the other as miserable." While promising speed and convenience and agreeable surroundings, Nevada divorces did not require the presence of the respondent, only his lawyer. Nor were any potentially embarrassing cross-examinations required. Testimony was taken in private and then sealed from public scrutiny, although the reporters were on hand when Ellen Stevenson left the courtroom on December 12, 1949.

Earlier the press had asked Stevenson to comment. Overnight the Illinois governor who preached high public virtue had become the most prominent official in the United States to bear the private stigma of a divorce. Like many men of this generation, the governor would have preferred to keep his marriage, though Ellen could have challenged his fidelity to it. In a week that included problems over his appointments, a speech to the National Council of State Governments, and several appearances around the state, Stevenson issued an adroit statement: "I am deeply distressed that due to the incompatability [*sic*] of our lives, Mrs. Stevenson feels a separation is necessary. Though I do not believe in divorce, I will not contest it. We have separated with the highest mutual regard."

In the gossip columns of Chicago newspapers and the living rooms of Lake Forest the incompatibility was explained as Ellen's refusal to accept her husband's career and take up her assigned duties in Springfield. "Your wife," wrote Ellen's aunt, "must be crazy not to want to share your brilliant public life." Ever after the Stevensons indicted Ellen for jealousy of a man whom she had, Pygmalion-style, escorted into the highest circles of Chicago society, but who, to Ellen's distaste, had left far behind the murmured identification "That's Ellen Borden's husband." Buffie Ives regarded her brother's fate as a time of "trouble and triumph. . . . Ellen had not understood" the long-standing Stevenson tradition that the women of the family served their husbands' political careers. Her brother must not blame himself—"We can't punish ourselves for others' folly or faults."

Viewing the matter differently, Ellen Stevenson had refused to exchange privacy, home, and independence for her husband's career. After twenty years of domesticity organized mostly on his terms, she declined to move to Springfield. She also suffered from the postwar system of female subordination and dissatisfaction recognized a decade later in Betty Friedan's *Feminine Mystique*. According to Friedan, "the problem" had lain "buried and unspoken ... in the minds of American women" who suffered boredom and seclusion in their suburban homes, where the tasks of homemaking frustrated and stultified them. Like many of these women, Ellen was restless. Certainly she was more isolated than most, in a country house ten miles from Lake Forest. And while her divorce was hardly remarkable by 1949, Ellen's wealth, age—she was forty-one and her husband forty-nine—and the length of her twenty-one-year marriage set her apart from other discomfited women.

For years incompatibilities had seared the relationship of Ellen and her husband. Ellen was tardy, Adlai punctual; Ellen was rich and extravagant, Adlai wealthy and frugal; Ellen was interested in art and poetry, Adlai in national and international affairs. Ellen was fey, sophisticated, tasteful, and elegant; Adlai earnestly diplomatic, with the provincial stamp of Bloomington not entirely faded; Ellen lacked discretion, and Adlai had an abundance of manners. Ellen was a stern disciplinarian who sometimes smacked the children and who singled out her second son for angry attacks; Adlai was permissive with the children, demanding with his wife, and accustomed to attention from his adoring mother and sister; Ellen was self-absorbed; Adlai, often a domestic absentee, was concerned with causes that overrode attentive solicitude to a wife who drank too much. Some of these contrarieties had been recognized by his parents, who on their first meeting with Ellen judged her "not the girl" for their son.

Ellen Stevenson had the misfortune to arrive on the fringes of public life at precisely the time when Americans were demanding information about the private lives of their candidates—from dogs and children to wives and houses. Like her husband, she detested such intrusions on her private affairs and, also like him, considered politics to be the work of plebeians. Meanwhile the electorate was replacing partisanship with a nosy personalism that included the scrutiny of political families, who must corroborate the postwar ideal of the husband breadwinner, the homemaking wife, and the well-balanced and maternally attended children—a world soon to be portrayed on television's *Donna Reed Show.*

The Stevenson model was skewed, although this was not apparent in the governor's campaign literature, which placed Ellen in her home and garden, raising the children and baking her famous cherry pies. Only in the mention of her talents as a singer and piano player did she achieve any individuality, although her poetry and her fights with the domestic servants were omitted from the campaign material on the Stevenson family.

Also left out was Ellen's considerable experience with divorce. At an earlier time in American history, when divorce was a social stigma of unforgivable proportions, her father, John Borden, married three times—the last time to a woman younger than Ellen—and her mother twice. Such a family heritage eased the road to Las Vegas, as did Ellen's dissatisfaction with a husband who from her perspective offered her few possibilities for independence and feelings of self-worth.

With his friends the governor remained silent about the end of his marriage. What had seemed unthinkable had gradually become unexpected and then unmentionable in the long-instilled Stevenson manner of overlooking personal problems. Carl McGowan, an adviser living at the governor's mansion, was astonished when the story broke in September. He had heard nothing from a man whom he saw daily. When McGowan expressed his shock and sorrow, Stevenson explained that he didn't know what the trouble was. "She apparently feels that her life is overshadowed and constricted and she can't express herself the way she wants to in this relation since I've become governor. I don't understand but that's the way she feels."

Instead, Alicia Patterson and Jane Dick heard the governor's pain and self-vindication. "I really never thought anything could hurt quite so much as this has," he wrote when the divorce had become unavoidable, perhaps protesting too much, given his passionate love affair with Alicia Patterson. He accepted the separation, he said, in fairness to Ellen. Still, the divorce was, Adlai Stevenson lamented to Alicia Patterson, the end "of the first volume of two lives that could have been rarely happy & successful. Why did it end in Greek ghastliness? I don't know, in spite of borrowed hours of prayer & search. Am I mad? Is she?" In fact, he had already decided that it was she who was mentally unbalanced. By this time Adlai Stevenson had established his diagnosis, reading his sons the *Encyclopaedia Britannica*'s sketchy description of paranoia. "You have just heard a description of your mother," he informed them.

In time justification by reason of Ellen's irrationality consoled him, though he would always be ambivalent about the destruction of a relationship he believed should be enduring. Two days after the divorce the governor informed Alicia Patterson that it was "the end of what might have been, should have been and was a good chapter in the myriad annals of American families. I am a little bruised, but utterly emancipated."

In December, her six-week residency in Nevada complete and her divorce in hand, Ellen Stevenson returned to Chicago and confronted a battery of reporters, whose notebooks she filled with extraneous information. When asked about the settlement, she demurely replied that she could not talk about it. Instead, she offered details of her solitude at the El Rancho Motel, a large postwar creation on the south side of Las Vegas with a pool and small cottages. The weather had been beautiful. She had played the piano, had read at least twenty books, had written fifty letters (including several to her soon-to-be ex-husband), and had walked two miles a day to keep her figure. "I'm just an old has-been. I'm not in the news anymore.

After I get over the embarrassment of being a divorcee, I will try to organize my future. All questions between my husband and myself have been amicably resolved."

Meanwhile her ex-husband disliked the sympathetic tone of the newspaper accounts: "Perhaps Ellen thinks they've made her look like the shy, modest retiring little wife who can't bear publicity and me as an ambitious, ruthless politician." He was reassured by his sister, who was convinced that Ellen wanted only "attention and the limelight [while] your personal happiness is tangled up in your service to mankind."

Although the divorce seemed to bring to an end his perplexing relationship with his wife, in fact it was an additional dilemma for a man whose life incorporated many contradictions. One night after she had served as a hostess for one of her brother's gubernatorial functions, Buffie Ives went down to the basement office, where a light still burned. And there, after a day that had begun with breakfast conferences and had continued with business unabated through a supper for the Illinois judiciary, Adlai Stevenson was still working. When she pleaded with him to go to bed and added the Stevenson imperative that he would ruin his health, Adlai Stevenson refused. "I've failed as a husband," he sighed. "I've failed as a father. I will succeed as governor!"

CHAPTER TWO

CLEANING HOUSE

1

ON HIS INAUGURATION in January 1949, Adlai Stevenson became only the fourth Democratic governor of Illinois since the Civil War, thereby installing his family name in the pantheon of Democratic heroes. Besides his partisanship and the size of his majority, his reform intentions and his eloquence quickly established his conspicuous exceptionalism. In fact, he was an advanced version of the better-trained, postwar governors who were replacing the indolent, back-slapping, good-time Charlies of the past in state capitals across the United States. Ambitiously, Adlai Stevenson called for a new constitution, more aid to education, a state Fair Employment Practices Act, and better men in government, in an inaugural address that was not finished in time for the printers. "I will have no reluctance to break boldly with the complacent, quiet past," he announced.

The disparate specifics of his intentions were woven into a domestic image: "We can set our own house in order." As he struggled to modernize both the structure and the workings of an archaic state government, this humble image of Illinois as a home—the place his ancestors had settled—animated his leadership. During Stevenson's four-year administration, cleaning up became the organizing principle from which the specific initiatives of his regime flowed.

Earlier he had compared the governor's duties to the tasks of a housewife: "I want to do the job you do regularly and it is to give the house a little attention. . . . You sweep and dust and vacuum the corners and wash the dirt off the floor. You open the windows to let in fresh air. You give the children a chance to grow up healthy and wise, decent and respectful. You budget wisely not neglecting essentials and not spending on the trivial, and you treat your family with understanding and kindness. As I see the job of governor, that's it." Inspired, Stevenson supporters had adopted brooms as a symbol, and with their help he had indeed swept out his predecessor, although, as the new governor cautioned, some "Green slime" remained.

Once elected, a man who had home and family on his mind retained the image that linked his public and private lives. After his decision to run for office had, for the time being, resolved a chronic struggle between duty and desire, purification appeared as the central image of Stevenson's initiatives—from the necessity for a tighter mining code to fighting gambling, from raising some nuisance taxes to ending the notorious Illinois "lug," which required state workers to contribute to political campaigns or lose their jobs. For the new governor, good government was a series of moral choices—of honesty over corruption, of involvement over indifference, and of duty over irresponsibility. "Good government is not a matter of party, it's a matter of will."

Some legislators in the Republican-controlled Illinois senate were insulted by such nonsense, believing their new chief executive "a curiosity." Accustomed to the rhetorical flings required on state occasions, they were nevertheless offended by this neophyte's lofty misunderstanding of the realities of partisan life. The new governor, they complained, sounded more like a preacher than a politician, and they were not of his religion. "It is," grumbled one, "a good program that will be impossible to enact."

Even Democrats, as they gathered in the Tavern Room of the Leland Hotel and the downstairs bar of the St. Nicholas Hotel, dismissed Stevenson's message as far removed from the world of legislative trading. Controlling the assembly, these Democrats were dismayed by the casual references to party by a man who, on assuming the governorship, had become their state leader. No sooner inaugurated, the governor had even announced uncertainty about what kind of Democrat he was, explaining, "I am not one of those who believes we should have a Democratic regime because it is good for the Democratic party. If the Democratic party is not good for Illinois and the nation, it is not good for me, and for Democrats." Professional politicians and patronage holders who held the opposite—that what was good for the Democratic party was good for Illinois—predicted Adlai Stevenson would be a one-term governor. Most of these men (there were only two women in the Sixty-sixth Illinois Assembly) were lawyers, businessmen who sold insurance and real estate, and farmers who came to Springfield for six months every other year, earning for their service $6,000—and the incalculable benefits of influential contacts.

Under Stevenson's administration legislators worried that certain prerequisites of their tenure—the use of state police cars to drive home on weekends, the patronage assignments to friends that helped business at home, and even the convenient connections to well-placed officials—might disappear. In their place loomed, if they heard the governor correctly, the twin vultures of electoral disaster—higher taxes and, under a new constitution, legislative reapportionment. Either could close off the political aspirations closely linked to their economic self-interest.

"The house" of Illinois that Adlai Stevenson would set in order had changed during the tumultuous decades of the New Deal and World War II. Nowhere were these transformations more obvious than in Springfield, where Adlai Stevenson lived for the next four years and where he had briefly attended school when his father served in state government. The capital had always represented a middle place between the urban concentrations of Chicago, East St. Louis, and even Peoria, with its population of 111,000, and the isolated rural checkerboard of corn and hog farms. Having grown up in Bloomington, Stevenson knew this small-town culture, just as having lived in Chicago and suburban Lake County, he understood the diversity that made statewide legislation difficult to enact.

Along with other cities and towns in Illinois, Springfield emerged from the war years as what one critic called "an overgrown prairie village" of 86,000 residents. The small-town world of one-story white clapboard cottages that stretched north and south from the downtown political and commercial center now pressed into adjacent farmlands. Building had been postponed during the war, at a time when a new population, attracted by opportunities in state government and jobs in light industry, had flooded into town. Migrants—some from the South, some from Appalachia, and still others from no farther away than Egypt, the sixteen southern counties of Illinois below the Baltimore and Ohio railroad line—found few places to live.

After the war, with a rapidity that astonished old-timers, empty lots gave way to apartments and motels on Highway 66. As the city filled in, a new development was planned for the affluent west side. Chain stores replaced family businesses, and a fifteen-story building gave rise to jokes that Springfield's skyscrapers would soon match those of Chicago and New York. Behind the graceful elms in the southern and western parts of the city, nineteenth-century Victorian homes still survived, though many had been turned into multiple-dwelling units during World War II. A city that had prided itself on being typical still had more middle-class residents with incomes of $3,500 (for a family of four in 1949) than most places in the United States.

Town boosters rarely included another statistic: that Springfield, according to one reporter, contained the "largest collection of taverns, joints, and low dives functioning in any American city of less than 100,000 population." The Lincoln legend survived in the names of some of these bars and businesses. "In Springfield you are bound to get mixed up with Abraham Lincoln," concluded a writer from the *New Yorker*.

The state's new governor already was. His maternal great-grandfather Jesse Fell had encouraged Lincoln to run for public office; his great-aunts treasured a signed copy of Lincoln's brief autobiography until they ran out of money and contemplated its sale. Stevenson himself often took visitors to the Lincoln home at Eighth and Jackson Streets and to the restoration of nearby New Salem, all the while contemplating the capital's strange mix of moral elevation through its historical association with Lincoln, immorality through its attachment to gambling, drinking, and prostitution, and civic endeavor through its status as capital of the nation's fourth-largest state.

When Adlai Stevenson took up residence in the twenty-eight-room, painted-brick mansion in the middle of town, postwar prosperity had engulfed a community that wanted to forget the strictures of gas and food rationing. Most residents considered price controls a barely tolerable form of wartime socialism. Like middle-class Americans everywhere, the citizens of Springfield flocked to the glass showcase windows on Washington Street to gaze at—and sometimes buy on the installment plan—fin-tailed, low-slung Hudsons and Frazers. Derivatives of the car culture, new forms of shopping and eating emerged, as young and old used their "purchased-on-credit" automobiles to travel to the stores, diners, and barbecue pits that welcomed drive-in customers.

Across the railroad tracks in east Springfield, the economic contrasts between whites and blacks were sharp. Residentially segregated but politically gerrymandered into white districts, the city's blacks found their political power diluted among the city's all-white aldermen, at the same time that custom and white authority restricted them to the poorest neighborhood in town. Nor did the community's African-Americans have equal access to jobs, despite the wartime migration that pulled southern blacks northward into cities and smaller towns like Springfield. Forgotten amid postwar expectations of the late 1940s, some blacks sought opportunity in larger cities and moved on to South Chicago and East St. Louis. What they left behind was a segregated city. In 1947, when the African-American lawyer Cecil Partee came to Springfield to be sworn in as an assistant state's attorney, he could neither eat nor sleep with his white colleagues at the Abraham Lincoln hotel.

Never limited by his immediate surroundings and especially not by the parochialism of heartland America (in his downstairs office Stevenson worked with his back to the window), the new governor looked beyond Springfield to the world, continuing to give speeches about international issues. His sense of language, along with his thoughtful commentary on Cold War issues, struck a response in an uncertain postwar generation anticipating affluence and national power, but encountering inflation and the Russians. The more speeches Stevenson gave, the more he was asked to give.

Stevenson rarely declined. In 1950 the governor of Illinois delivered nearly ninety speeches, three-quarters either to national organizations, or outside of Illinois, or about international affairs. Before an audience expecting a speech on crime, the state penal system famed for its rigorous discipline, or possibly juvenile delinquency, the governor talked instead about the Berlin airlift. At the dedication of a building at Southern Illinois University in Carbondale, he discussed Soviet totalitarianism; to a group of veterans on Veterans' Mental Health Day, he spoke on "the conduct of foreign policy." After dedicating a new chapel at a boys' correctional camp, Stevenson considered the emerging national policy of containment and America's place in the world. In a speech to the Illinois Secondary Principals' Association, he linked education to a free society and the battles of the Cold War. "Our foreign policy has taken a seat at the family table," he said, using one of the resonant, domestic metaphors that made him a popular speaker.

Affairs of Illinois—the need for higher taxes on trucks and a revenue system less dependent on property taxes, the need for a new constitution, even what he called "the moral tone of government"—became part of world politics. "Total diplomacy and total effort in the cold war can't be effective abroad if they are ineffective at home." What happened in Illinois under his leadership now determined the future of democracy in its struggle with the Soviets. Even Lincoln was reevaluated by the governor as a man who understood the "global dimensions of the Civil War."

Already burdened by his meticulous attention to the details of running a state with a half-billion-dollar annual budget and 32,000 state employees, the governor sought additional staffing to help with his speeches. As he explained to Porter McKeever, whom he considered hiring from the United Nations before his staff convinced him of the impolitic overtones of such an appointment, "As I have said before, writing—good writing—and saying something thoughtful and coherently is my greatest problem. I simply *can't* use the conventional banalities of politicians, even if I should." In this process of presenting a bifocal perspective on issues near and far, Adlai Stevenson created, by the time his four years in Springfield ended, another painful dilemma for himself.

2

STEVENSON'S FUTURE PREDICAMENT was not apparent as he began his crusade for a new Illinois constitution. At a time when the contours of state governments were changing, their constitutions remained antiquated—according to later observers, "grotesque parodies on modern government." Certainly the Illinois charter, which had been passed by the legislature and approved by voters in 1870, when the entire population of the state was less than Chicago's in 1950, was such an archaic example.

Virtually impossible to amend, the Illinois constitution required, for any changes, not only the legislature's approval, but that of two-thirds of the voters at any election. The constitution had passed in an era of party ballots, but in the twentieth century amendment after amendment had fallen before this requirement. Rarely did even a third of the Illinoisians who voted for candidates bother to vote on proposed reforms that Stevenson believed crucial for good government in Illinois: more taxing authority to local subdivisions, yearly meetings of the legislature, and less dependence on the property tax. All were unconstitutional under the 1870 constitution. Nor had the legislature been redistricted since 1920. With farmers' traditional animus toward the city, Chicago was especially underrepresented.

In the midst of his battle for the most central of his programs to clean up Illinois, the governor discovered an ally. Forty years before, in his final campaign for public office, Grandfather Stevenson had predicted that a time would come when the constitution must be rewritten. "In the remote or near future," the first Adlai Ewing Stevenson had argued in 1908, "it may be that a new constitution will be formulated. It will be strange indeed if changing conditions, augmented population, the growth of cities especially our great city, and commercial development does not render some alteration of our organic law of the state necessary. No state can expect to be permanent unless it guarantees progress as well as order."

With Grandfather on his side, Stevenson began his campaign for a new constitution. First he must persuade two-thirds of the legislature to pass a resolution calling a convention. Then a convention call must be approved by two-thirds of those voting in a special election. Next a convention, composed of elected delegates, must meet to rewrite the old constitution, after which a majority of voters must approve the final document. It was a daunting undertaking for a man who did not know the names of most legislators.

Other states had initiated similar procedures in the postwar era, and with state pride on his side, the governor compared laggard Illinois with neighboring Missouri, where the process of constitutional reform was further advanced. But where Stevenson saw better government, state legislators glimpsed, if a new constitution was adopted, the perils of redistricting and taxes. And they balked. So he turned to the voters who had delivered his handsome majority in the recent election. In his first radio address, he spoke to "the people [who] helped me get my job; now I want you to help me to do the job. I am not asking you to approve anything; all I am asking is that the legislature give you a chance to decide in 1950 whether a constitutional convention should be held." Promptly the amateurs mobilized into blue-ribbon commissions lobbying the legislature. More quietly, the governor depended on Jack Arvey to contact the members of the Democratic-controlled house on his weekly visits to Springfield.

Many assemblymen and senators were more comfortable with the boss of Cook County than with the governor. While his admirers praised his touch with the people, Adlai Stevenson did not like most of the politicians he encountered in his public life. Privately he divided them into two groups—"the rationals," who might listen to sensible propositions for better government, and the "pols," who saw politics, as Stevenson never did, as a means of making their living and acted accordingly. Never reconciled to the cajoling that was part of any system of shared powers, Stevenson grumbled when he had to give up conversation with the witty columnist Marquis Childs for that with "the likes of Botchy Connors," the three-hundred-pound Democratic floor leader from Chicago's Twenty-ninth Legislative District. Abraham Lincoln Marovitz, a state senator, cited the governor's unwillingness to talk to legislators as an impediment to his program. "Stevenson was not naturally at home with the average guy in politics. He'd try but it was difficult. He had a facial reaction, a forced smile." Whenever he did have a good time with the pols, it was sufficiently unusual to merit comment.

Mary Jane Masters, a friend in Springfield, observed the same behavior: "He was not an old-shoe and was more at home with his own social and economic class than he was the people in general." As Stevenson sought the most basic and enduring reform that any governor can accomplish, what was needed, according to his lieutenant governor, Sherwood Dixon, was "a legislative liaison man who has had experience in either house, who has some native shrewdness and diplomacy, and who wears a celluloid collar and a made up tie and who reeks of the barnyard." Instead, William McCormick Blair, a well-born Chicago aristocrat who when asked to work for Stevenson in the primaries had confessed he did not know any Democrats, served as the governor's chief of staff.

Then, in March 1949, Chicago's so-called West Side bloc of legislators, notorious for their supposed links to the Chicago syndicate that had replaced Al Capone and Frank Nitti, proposed a deal: their votes for the constitutional convention resolution in exchange for the governor's quashing the anticrime bill. It was the kind of arrangement familiar to most American governors and presidents, but it tortured Stevenson. "How," he complained to his Lake Forest friends Ellen and Hermon Smith, "am I going to do anything useful? Maybe it's better to go ahead and make deals like that." But of course it wasn't, at least not for Adlai Stevenson. As the governor had suspected, he lost both the anticrime bill and any prospects for a new constitution, though both parties approved a bill to make the process of constitutional amendment easier.

This new arrangement would later become a much touted example of Stevenson's gubernatorial success, though the Gateway amendment, which permitted three amendments to be voted on in a single election, served to chill the movement for a new constitution until 1970. Stevenson himself acknowledged that it was a stop-gap measure, and some observers were convinced that the governor could have obtained broader amending powers, if he had worked harder with legislative leaders. Somehow he never shaped a coalition-building strategy for dealing with legislative inertia. Instead, in a radio broadcast he saw the issue as a moral choice: "If I had been willing to trade off other desirable legislation, it would have passed, but I don't think that is right and I don't believe you think so either." Principles, it was becoming clear, carried a price tag for a governor who, because of his personality and his attitude toward political parties, lacked the ability to take a disparate group of individuals with varied interests and pull them together around a common purpose.

At the same time that he struggled for a new constitution, Stevenson crusaded for "good" men to run "this enormous business." "We need more responsible people—perhaps more insurance men—to know, explore and understand our state government," he told the Insurance Federation of Illinois in 1950. "You will only get good government from good people." The governor was never precise about the specific ingredients of such virtue. Rather, he carried to the selection of his administration's personnel the understanding of nineteenth-century mugwumps and twentieth-century Progressives that decency was a transcendent given, understood in the beholding and mostly bestowed on wealthy, well-educated white males. Thus the governor's descriptions for both his staff and the key administrative jobs of running Illinois departments were characterological: these "honorable" men must be honest, intelligent, hardworking, and more endowed with judgment and "savvy" than with technical knowledge and previous political experience—"really high class" men. Honest government would subsequently descend in a trickle-down arrangement, as good men in turn chose upstanding subordinates.

For the top jobs party designation rarely mattered. To the chagrin of professional Democrats, the governor included in his first ten high-level appointments three Republicans. Later he maintained that he got rid of "incompetent" Republicans as quickly as any executive, but he still deserved his reputation for nonpartisan appointments. Sensitive to the issue, he ordered his staff to keep count of the replacements. Only after recruiting Willard Wirtz for a position designated by law for a Democrat did the governor inquire about Wirtz's partisan habits, which the new liquor commissioner promptly agreed to change. Nor did large contributions to Stevenson's campaign carry weight in his choices, although at least two members of his inner circle were political legacies—Richard Daley, the former minority leader of the Illinois senate, came from and returned to the Cook County machine and Frank Annunzio, the director of labor whom Stevenson later fired after some unsavory conflicts of interest, was the chairman of the CIO political action committee that had contributed $1,500 to the campaign.

Sometimes good men proved hard to recruit, and usually they were difficult to keep. Like Stevenson himself, they had to be lured from more lucrative endeavors: indeed, it was their accomplishments in other fields that established their eminence and suitability in the first place. "My misgiving is that I can't induce the kind of people I want to leave private affairs to serve with me. It's all very well to talk about inferior people in government. The problem is how to induce superior people to make the sacrifice that entails." One difficulty emerged from the patronage system, which as employed by politicians, according to Stevenson, "louses up this political business and freezes the bright young hopefuls out."

When Walter Fisher, a Chicago lawyer, finally accepted the chairmanship of the Illinois Commerce Commission, he was the eighth man to whom Stevenson had offered the job. Only because the governor talked so compellingly about citizen responsibility did Fisher succumb. Suspicious of lobbying and reluctant to solicit others, Stevenson avoided using his clout to place his men in the Democratic hierarchy.

His chief administrative aide, Walter Schaefer, became an exception when an Illinois supreme court justice died and Stevenson appointed Schaefer to fill the vacancy, prodding Daley to slate his friend over some of the organization's "unqualified" candidates. After pushing *his* guy for a Cook County post against the choice of the machine, Stevenson acknowledged the inevitable compromise: "Who am I to be complaining about machines and bosses?—me the creature of Kelly, Nash, Arvey, et al." By 1951 the governor exaggerated that he was becoming something of a boss himself, though his interventions were rare. But he continued to insist that virtuous public servants, intent on reform, manage the big business that government in Illinois had become.

In time Adlai Stevenson surrounded himself with likes—men like Carl McGowan, William McCormick Blair, and Edward Day, the son-in-law of his former law partner, with whom he was congenial and who inhabited the highest corporate, legal, and social circles in the state. "Business and government are the gainers," Stevenson exhorted, "when the best among us will make the sacrifice if need be." With the charm and good humor that made him so beloved by his staff and cabinet, he preached service in state government as a painful obligation. "The public takes a lot out of you. . . . A politician pays a frightful price for all he does," he told a group of law clerks. In return, his men received, as they replaced his family as companions, a solicitude that made working for Adlai Stevenson an exhilarating adventure. "We had a good time," remembered William Blair. "He was a wonderful boss, never impatient and angry, no matter what," his secretary agreed.

In his inaugural address Stevenson had argued for higher salaries for senior state officials. Along with low pay, "too often . . . the reward for sacrifice in public service is not gratitude in lieu of dollars, but abuse, criticism and ingratitude." Those in government must wear, as he did, a hair shirt, though they gained in return a moral elevation grounded in the contemplation of their unselfishness. Of course they were underpaid (Stevenson himself earned only $12,000); of course they worked harder than any ambitious La Salle Street lawyer for one-third the salary; and of course they got little recognition, because most Illinoisians were profoundly uninterested in the affairs of their state.

Stevenson supplemented what he considered the meager salaries of his staff and department heads from a private fund. Collected by his friend and early supporter Hermon Smith, the money had originated in the campaign's surplus. Even after the election, wealthy acquaintances like John Murray of the Murray Supply Company and organizations with state contracts like the Peabody Coal Company continued to contribute until donations reached over $21,000. Six months after he had taken office, Mrs. Emmons Blaine, who admired Stevenson for his work on the United Nations, sent the governor a check for $2,500, intended "for some small service of work for you and therefore for Illinois." On the same day that the governor sent his broker a check for $2,500 to cover various personal transactions, he thanked Mrs. Blaine: "I find that for almost ten years I have been earning little and spending much on a large and expensive family. That seems, however, to be the unhappy plight of public servants generally, and I suppose it is my own fault!"

Stevenson used these donations at his discretion, investigating the possibilities of a tax-deductible Illinois fund. Over $18,000 of his Stevenson fund went to supplement the salaries of eight members of his inner circle. James Mulroy, his campaign manager and executive secretary, received $100 in 1949; Carl McGowan found his salary increased by Christmas bonuses of $3,000. Edward Day, an administrative assistant and later the state's director of insurance, received a total of $2,000. The largest gift, of $7,900, went to William Flanagan, his press secretary. Some recipients declared these supplements as income and paid taxes on them; others like Day insisted that they had made great sacrifices to be in government and that the bonuses were gifts, "neither contracted for nor counted on." As the governor later rationalized, "None ever asked me for help, and none could have been improperly influenced by these gifts, because I gave them and I appointed them to their jobs and I could have discharged them at any time." Blinkered by self-righteousness, Stevenson overlooked any possibility of influence peddling on him.

Even with the inducement of his fund, he spent too much time on the appointments of his cabinet amid increasing impatience at party headquarters on the third floor of Chicago's Morrison Hotel about less exalted positions. After eight years out of the statehouse, partisans like Paul Powell had "smelt the meat cooking" since Stevenson's victory in November. Meanwhile Jack Arvey intended that loyal Democrats receive the spoils of office. By the governor's calculations, of Illinois's 30,000 employees 10,000 to 15,000 were his "so-called personal appointees. . . . That is the area known as: Patronage, which is the curse of all public officials, so far as my experience extends, and which has been my principal obstacle and difficulty to date and will be as long as I endure in this office."

Stevenson was not interested in using the patronage to create an adhesive personal following. In 1951 he gave desultory attention to recommendations for convention delegates and confessed to the more attentive U.S. senator Paul Douglas that he hadn't followed the slating personally. Later his son Adlai III acknowledged, "If [Dad] had had more experience in politics and he had better understood the dimensions of his power, he might have done more to reform the government and the party. He didn't discover the real dimensions of the office in time. The Governor is the most powerful man in the state of Illinois. I mean favors, patronage, press, all the rest. . . . There's a great opportunity there for any Governor—to get patronage into the hands of his friends, to get better candidates and a better legislature. If he had been a politician he'd have been more than a match for the Eddie Barretts and Paul Powells."

Of course, Stevenson expected his high-class appointees to be incorruptible. In time he found otherwise. Professional politicians expected a little misdoing, now and then, and did not torture themselves over its appearance. Because he had promised something different, Stevenson's piety made him, like the embezzling preacher or the tippling temperance advocate, a tantalizing target for criticism. By the end of 1951 the columnists had plenty of ammunition.

Jim Mulroy, his executive secretary, had purchased 1,000 shares of stock in the racetrack Chicago Downs for ten cents a share. In a few months, along with several members of the legislature, Mulroy received dividends of $1.75 a share. Far worse were the rumors from federal inspectors that state employees in the Illinois Department of Agriculture were being bribed to accept horsemeat as cow meat. "Adlaiburgers" became a state joke. "I'll be on a steady diet of horsemeat from now until November," the governor tried to joke, although according to his friends and advisers, he was "heartbroken." He moved quickly to fire the corrupt, but his administration was forever flawed by the horsemeat scandal and the sale of counterfeit cigarette stamps. Ruefully Stevenson acknowledged the "pain and grief" from several instances of malfeasance by members of his staff. If his administration could not be, like Caesar's wife, above suspicion, whose could?

In Washington another politician struggled with the problem of dishonesty in public service. Like Stevenson, President Truman had ridden a machine to power; like Stevenson's, his subordinates sometimes violated his trust. But unlike the Illinois governor, the president refused to fire what some Americans contemptuously called his cronies. When Truman's military aide Harry Vaughan was implicated in kickback scandals, the word "five-percenters" entered the nation's vocabulary. When officials in public agencies like the loan-giving Reconstruction Finance Corporation and the tax-taking Internal Revenue Service played favorites, Truman was finally forced, after a series of damaging congressional investigations, to fire his appointees. What came to be known by the Republicans as Democratic corruption shocked Stevenson, who never hesitated in his choice of the public's interest over personal loyalty.

The president and the governor were confronting habitual political behavior. Wars often engendered a peacetime nonchalance about public activities unsupervised for the duration. In an economic society that valued wealth and a political system that created the means of its attainment, corruption in office was an American constant. What was unique was Stevenson's attitude. Enclosed by self-imposed absolutes and new to practical politics, the governor was devastated by the gap between his intentions and the actions of men he trusted. At the end of his administration, he had improved what he labeled "the moral tone of Illinois government." But when asked his greatest problem as governor, he invariably replied graft, explaining that "corruption is treason. The greatest weapon we have in the [Cold War] struggle is public and private morality. Anything that dulls the edge of that weapon weakens our cause."

In December of 1952, at the end of Stevenson's administration, another form of corruption cast a shadow on his public performance when an explosion in West Frankfort, Illinois, killed 119 miners, more than had lost their lives in the Centralia tragedy of Green's governorship. Throughout his campaign Stevenson had implied that such a disaster would never occur in his administration, because he would remove the politically appointed "pay-rollers" who neglected their inspections. In southern Illinois, the center of the state's mining industry, Stevenson had promised to protect miners as Green had not.

In response to the greatest catastrophe of his administration, Stevenson flew to the mining community in southern Illinois and observed what he described as "about the most distressing experience [he had ever seen] in war and peace." Immediately he ordered an investigation; he encouraged the mining commission to hold hearings; he cooperated with federal investigators and hurried to Washington for consultation with federal authorities and the president of the United Mine Workers, John L. Lewis.

No one knew the cause of the fire and the explosions, although several survivors remembered smelling coal gas just before a cloud of smoke filled the underground tunnels. Ignited coal dust could easily account for the disaster. Indeed, the point of inspections was to monitor the accumulations of the lethal dust. In Green's administration miners had complained of the operators' failure to consider their safety, while state inspectors failed to provide the washings of the tunnels required by state and federal law, but enforceable only by the state government. Centralia became, to Stevenson and many Illinoisians, what John Bartlow Martin, a future Stevenson speech writer, dubbed "the Mine Disaster No One Stopped."

Now Stevenson faced similar charges. Federal investigators soon discovered that one of the state's inspectors had relied on a visual inspection of the mine's walls instead of taking actual samples, as required by law. A reporter mindful of the governor's earlier pledges found that the mine inspector was a Democrat, that he had contributed to a Democratic campaign fund at the request of the director of his agency, and that he saw nothing wrong with his contribution. While Stevenson explained that mine safety could never be an absolute, his opponents held him responsible for the languid progress of a mine safety bill through the state legislature. The resistance of operators and union alike had made passage impossible, the governor insisted. Having declined the forceful cajoling that pushes legislation forward, he suffered the consequences of the gap between the politics of worthy intention and customary practice, between proximate solutions and insoluble problems. "What a job," he despaired to Alicia.

In his continual search for good men to clean up Illinois and end disasters like that in West Frankfort, Stevenson did not entirely destroy the party patronage. To lesser jobs he appointed Democrats over Republicans, all things being equal, and he set up a screening committee to review the candidates. As he struggled over the lists, spending hours weighing choices that sometimes included over one hundred applicants for one position on the court of claims, Stevenson tried to reduce the number of patronage jobs and place them under civil service. His answer to the spoils was not so much to prevent the victors from having some as to have less of it and to encourage good men to enter politics. "Nothing has exasperated me more than to be told that I ought not consider appointing a particular person to a particular job solely because he has been active in a political party." To the Richard Daleys of his administration, such a position threatened party suicide.

Stevenson's first attack on the patronage shocked the politicians, although the governor had been clear about the need for state troopers "of character, discipline and undiluted loyalty" in his inaugural address. But few legislators expected that he would so promptly follow his promises about cleaning house with a proposed bill to remove the state police, nearly all of whom were Republicans, from the governor's pleasure and place them under a merit system. In what later became the act that Illinoisians would most often associate with the Stevenson governorship and that Stevenson himself would cite as a major contribution, he made appointment to the state police depend on age, skill, and education.

Adlai Stevenson had lived in Chicago long enough to be impressed by the professionalism of Eliot Ness and his FBI untouchables. Removing the state police from politics became the best example of his attempts to modernize the Illinois government by creating a state administration with professional bureaucracies operating on standardized procedures. Armed with the understanding that modern problems demanded the knowledge of professionals, he traveled to Washington to ask an expert how to transform the patronage-riddled Illinois Highway Maintenance Police into a modern police force.

By 1950 J. Edgar Hoover was at the height of his forty-eight-year reign as head of the Federal Bureau of Investigation. The director had already opened a file on Adlai Stevenson that would eventually expand to over nine hundred pages and that would take its place in the notorious cabinets in his private office holding what Hoover called his Official and Confidential Files. Like those of Martin Luther King Jr. and John F. Kennedy, Stevenson's FBI file contained irrelevant, often erroneous reports of his political and sexual activities.

The first meeting of the governor and the director was cordial, as Hoover instructed Stevenson in modern police techniques and even volunteered the names of appropriate candidates for the position of director of Illinois public safety. But Stevenson had no intention of appointing an FBI man the head of his state agency. The governor's preference for "savvy," "high-class men" over functionaries with "technical knowledge," along with his perpetual struggle for independence, precluded such an appointment.

Returned to Chicago, the governor said so and added, "FBI men are not renowned for their ability as administrators." The quotation from John Dreiske's column in the *Chicago Sun Times* was on Hoover's desk the next day, and a man who held on to his grudges as if they were life supports never forgot. With the defensiveness that marked his reaction to criticism and that became a hallmark of the bureau as an institution, Hoover retaliated.

When Stevenson asked for another interview, Hoover was unavailable. When the governor invited the director to Springfield for the signing of the bill that would make the state police a professional force, the FBI director suddenly had another engagement. Thereafter Hoover scribbled on several gubernatorial requests: "This is the governor who had negative things to say about the Bureau." "Keep this [Stevenson's attitude towards the Bureau] in mind." Soon Illinois police were not admitted to the FBI Academy; Stevenson could not get an appointment with the director, and two years later he became the target of a malicious FBI crusade to make him into something that he was not.

Along with his energetic efforts for a new constitution, good men in office, and an expanded civil service, Adlai Stevenson undertook a campaign against gambling. This crusade emerged from his belief that government must improve the ethical tone of Illinois life; it flourished as well in the moralism that merged his private and public identities. For a man who named his dogs King Arthur, Sir Launcelot, and Merlin, a war against gambling held appeal. Not only was gambling the most visible form of sin, but it was a nearly universal failing. Community leaders who gambled at night in private lodges and country clubs held forth in daytime about the poor people's gaming and the interlocking directorates of criminals and gamblers.

Here was an evil that could ignite a statewide renaissance. Here was a redemptive cause that could lead to what Stevenson christened the state's "rediscovery." Those who had been indifferent to government might be mobilized to fight "a vexatious problem." And the governor himself could teach the reasons why, as he explained in an article published in *Harper's*, "the dropping of a fifty-cent piece in a slot machine is too often not merely a matter between you and your conscience." But even in this campaign there were dilemmas, contradictions, and uncertainties, and victory proved elusive, though in an echo of other gubernatorial battles, improvement prevailed.

Governor Stevenson could not begin immediately, having neither the legal authority nor the will to invade the local responsibility of counties and municipalities. He had always believed that local governments were the wellsprings of the American system, standing in somewhat the same relation to the state as states to the federal government. For years he had warned of government's "heavy hand" and of the individual "beneath a monster state that loves him but doesn't know him." And until the state police were independent, he did not have any untouchables under his command.

Meanwhile powerful members of the legislature and his party opposed his efforts. In Springfield politicians and lobbyists were accustomed to doing business at the Lake Club, entertained by stars like Mel Torme and Rudy Vallee and, in between shows, by the largest roulette wheel south of Chicago. Like drinking, gambling, they insisted, was a human activity beyond the reach of statute law. Of all Americans, those in Illinois best understood how ineffective government-mandated prohibition had been in the 1920s and how illegal drinking had linked gangsters and politicians in an unholy alliance.

Several legislators advised the governor that his programs for increased school spending and the consolidation of school districts would be imperiled by his attack on gambling. Donald O'Brien, a Democratic state senator from Cook County, warned that any antigambling initiative would be "a terrible mistake. The people are not going to forget it." To this an angry Stevenson responded that he had been elected by a majority of over 500,000 votes. But O'Brien had the last word: "Governor, you weren't elected by 500,000 votes because of raiding places. . . . You couldn't stand on the corner of State and Madison [in Chicago] and call one hundred people by their first names. You were elected governor because fellows like me and some more of us carried wards for you by fifteen, twenty, twenty-five and thirty thousand votes."

O'Brien was protecting one of the state's biggest businesses. For years, but especially during the 1940s, bookie joints, punchboard emporiums with their bingo-like betting devices, dice games, and slot machine clubs had proliferated until it was a rare veterans organization, fraternal lodge, country club, and even barbershop that did not have some method of wagering. Chicago had become the center of the nation's gambling industry, producing more punchboards, roulette wheels, and slot machines than any other city in the United States. Sales from the Taylor Manufacturing Company, which was owned by the successors to the Capone syndicate, to just one casino in Madison County amounted to over $75,000 a year. So entrenched were some forms of betting that owners of gambling machines paid federal taxes for an activity that was illegal in Illinois. Owners casually paid off members of the Chicago crime syndicate and the smaller downstate Shelton gang as well as local sheriffs, mayors, even state's attorneys, and, in the past, the state police.

During the second year of his governorship, Adlai Stevenson initiated raids on the most notorious gambling clubs in the state—outside of Chicago. From the Hyde Park Club in Madison County to Fat's Rendezvous in Sandoval, from the tavern in which, according to one gambling widow, the milk money disappeared on policy wheel bets to the basement of the Bloomington Country Club, where the governor's family were members, the state police gathered up the paraphernalia of the most popular illicit activity in Illinois. Immediately local police noted an increase in robberies of those facilities that hadn't been raided as gamblers, hardly intimidated by this first skirmish, replaced their confiscated goods. But outside of Chicago, Adlai Stevenson persisted.

In his radio messages the governor dramatized his war, offering to the "good" citizens of Illinois "seizure" counts: 152 slot machines in Madison County, 75 slot machines in McLean County along with 109 pinball machines, sixty-three punchboards from Sangamon County, 2,765 fewer federal licenses; seventy-five towns raided; 300 gambling houses closed, and so on throughout his term. "Since the state police began their raids on commercial gambling at my direction in May 1950," he reported, "there has been a tremendous drop in slot machines in the seventy-six counties . . . in southern Illinois." Privately the governor admitted to Alicia Patterson, "I may skin my nose. 'Stevenson Threatens Gambling Crackdown.' I think I hear a muffled hollow laugh from Cicero to Wisconsin." Despite his uncertainty, few clubs outside of Chicago were immune to an unannounced raid by the newly reorganized police, who swept into taverns and grocery stores, gambling and singing clubs to haul off the instruments of crime in state-owned snow removal trucks.

Along the way the governor's mood changed. He was depressed by "public indifference and cynicism," and what had begun as a triumphant reform ended as a lesson in the breakdown of decency in government, and merely the enemy's retreat: "In ordering these raids I did not feel the joyful exhilaration of a knight in shining armor tilting against the forces of darkness. I felt like a mourner at a wake. For something had died in Illinois," the governor informed the annual meeting of the American Bar Association in Washington.

Then, in 1951, Estes Kefauver came to Chicago. Like Stevenson, the senator from Tennessee had embarked on a crime crusade, and the investigating committee of which he was chairman had been gathering testimony in the crime capitals of the postwar United States. Kefauver's televised hearings, with their tales of murders and gambling and their firsthand views of gangsters with nicknames like Buggsy and Fats, titillated large audiences. But the Chicago hearings were closed, its conclusions supposedly secret. Stevenson testified and was lauded by Kefauver. Within weeks, however, an article in *Collier's* made clear that gambling—at least Chicago style— still flourished.

Complaining of inaccuracy, Stevenson denied having promised an end to gambling; his program was to sever the connection between the state government and gambling. Louis Ruppel, the editor of *Collier's* and a disaffected Stevenson campaign worker, responded that he had evidence for his charges, especially those relating to gambling in Chicago. Wrote Ruppel to Stevenson, "You knew gambling existed when you ran for governor, you know gambling has gone on since you have been governor, and you know gambling will go on until as promised you clean it up. . . . The point of the article is that you should do more. It is better for you to turn the state police loose than try to discredit a *Collier's* article. You simply can't look at this on a personal basis."

Later Kefauver's committee backed Ruppel's assertions: "No major efforts to break up Chicago's huge policy operation have been undertaken, shocking evidence of ineffective or dishonest law enforcement is apparent [Chicago boasted the richest cop in the world, a Democratic candidate for sheriff, famous for his successful gambling, outrageous graft, and sparkling diamond rings]; and wide-open conditions in Madison and St. Clair counties [continue] because pay-offs still exist."

In the final accounting, Stevenson's efforts to stop gambling had charted a new course for Illinois, though in the context of national efforts they were neither as unusual nor as successful as he and his supporters believed. Again the gap between reach and grasp made the governor an easy target for his own low threshold of self-criticism and outsiders' faultfinding. Like the knights of the round table, he had tilted against ferocious enemies, leaving gambling in Chicago untouched, in part for jurisdictional reasons. If his moral crusade had not ended in victory, he had at least challenged the casual acceptance of an activity to which, in the final irony, Illinois and other states would soon give their official imprimatur by organizing legitimate forms of gambling in order to increase tax revenues.

In his motives Stevenson differed from many postwar politicians who, after placing anticrime crusades in an electoral calculator, were beginning to see that such endeavors appealed to voters. The governor did not think in such terms. Like many reformers, he was finding diagnosis easier than cure. For him "the morality of government is, like the law, a seamless garment, and it cannot be rent in one small place without endangering the whole fabric." Yet in this image, which had a domestic parallel in the severing of his family after the divorce, the remaining tears threatened the whole cloth. Public life became a harrowing personal battle with defeats and victories, not just improvements and reverses. When the time came to assess the major contributions of his administration, Stevenson did not include his multifaceted war on immorality but mentioned instead practical improvements in schools and highways, increases in trucking fees and gasoline taxes, an amendment of the revenue article in the constitution, and increased workmen's and unemployment compensation, all accomplished without any alteration in the general tax rate by a parsimonious governor. "If we can do a better job of domestic housekeeping, we will have more confidence in ourselves, to say nothing of the confidence of others in our wisdom and purpose," he wrote in an article in the *New York Times*.

3

IN THE SUMMER of 1949, during Stevenson's first year in office, a U.S. commissioner came to his office to take a deposition. Throughout the United States, the specter of anticommunism had become its own perversion. Even guilt by association had emerged as a means of protecting the most powerful nation in the world as political parties, pressure groups, and national leaders combined with different branches of government to create a domestic Red scare. In 1947 President Truman had launched a program of loyalty tests for government employees; the House Un-American Activities Committee (HUAC) was in full chase after Hollywood stars suspected of being Red during the 1930s; the FBI, zealous in its surveillance of suspected internal enemies, had installed in its Washington headquarters on Pennsylvania Avenue a map of the world with countries under socialist, Marxist, and Communist regimes displayed in vivid red. And Senator Joseph McCarthy of Wisconsin faced a difficult reelection campaign.

Illinois was not immune. The state legislature had already passed a bill authorizing an investigation of Communists on the campuses of the University of Chicago and Roosevelt University, a bill Stevenson had allowed to become law without his signature. A senate committee officially designated as the Seditious Activities Investigation Commission, under Paul Broyles of Jefferson County, was hard at work writing a bill to require state employees to take a loyalty oath, to establish a state seditious activity committee, and to outlaw membership in the Communist party. Scourged by a similar committee, the playwright Lillian Hellman labeled these years "scoundrel times," as a rights-denying, anti-Communist mentality settled onto America. Connecting his public and private worlds, Adlai Stevenson used a different description. "This is the Anxious Age," he declared.

After a few preliminary questions, the commissioner asked two critical questions of the governor: "How long have you known Mr. Alger Hiss, the defendant?" and "Can you state what the reputation of Alger Hiss is for integrity, loyalty, and veracity?" At the time Hiss was on trial in New York on charges of perjury. The former State Department official had denied knowing his accuser Whittaker Chambers before a Senate investigating committee, just as he had denied any complicity in a spy ring. Amid titillating charges of passed documents, secret papers hidden in a pumpkin on a Maryland farm, and a typewriter with a defective letter, Hiss's lawyers believed that the best means of convincing a jury of their client's loyalty was to produce character references. If Americans could be tarnished by guilt by association, perhaps they might be redeemed through innocence by companionship. And Alger Hiss had indeed been a friend and associate of the most influential men in America.

Unlike the Supreme Court justices Felix Frankfurter and Stanley Reed, Stevenson refused to give his testimony in the New York courtroom where Hiss's perjury trial was taking place, pleading the pressure of work. Instead, his deposition was taken, duly recorded, and entered at the trial. In it he acknowledged that he had known Hiss since 1933, "when we served together in the Legal Division of the Agricultural Adjustment Administration." Hiss's reputation for integrity, loyalty, and veracity was "good."

Later that summer a New York jury failed to reach a verdict. At a second trial Alger Hiss was convicted of perjury and sentenced to five years in prison. But Adlai Stevenson's trial by association with Hiss never ended. It began with the *Chicago Tribune*'s editorial "The Party of Acheson and Stevenson and Hiss" and continued with Senator Joseph McCarthy's purposeful confusion of the two names Alger and Adlai during the 1952 presidential campaign. Stevenson's tarring also included the widely held slander that the Democratic governor of Illinois held the convicted perjurer and Communist Hiss in high regard when, in fact, Stevenson had attested only to Hiss's reputation.

For Stevenson the issue was one of decency—his own. He could not, he insisted, have refused Hiss's lawyers on either legal or moral grounds, though at least one of his advisers thought he should have declined to answer the questions, possibly avoiding a subpoena. But for Stevenson deposition giving was a fundamental obligation of all Americans, especially of lawyers. Later he shared the aggravation of the misunderstood with Alicia: "To damn and impugn a man for telling the truth, rather than taking the easy, timid way out by refusing to testify," was wrong.

With his virtue and patriotism at issue, the governor personally responded to the rabid editorials in the *Chicago Tribune* through the paper's letters-to-the-editor column. Ever prepared for battle, Colonel Robert McCormick's *Tribune* printed all with relish, even reviving the canard that Stevenson's grandfather, as a member of a disloyal Civil War association called the Knights of the Golden Circle, had also been a traitor. In high dudgeon the governor of normal wit and whimsy wrote, "I can hardly believe the *Tribune* is recommending that politicians protect themselves in unpopular situations by lying. Nor can I believe that you would discourage citizens from testifying honestly in a criminal case for fear the defendant might later be convicted." As for Grandfather Stevenson, the *Tribune* had lied.

In 1951 the legislature passed the Broyles bills, the Illinois version of the antisubversion statutes that were sweeping the country. Stevenson responded with a veto that placed him among only a handful of governors who were willing to oppose their state legislatures on these popular efforts to define loyalty and outlaw so-called un-American activities. "I know full well that this veto will be distorted and misunderstood, even as telling the truth of what I knew about the reputation of Alger Hiss was distorted and misunderstood." Acknowledging "this period of grave anxiety," the governor argued that state laws were superfluous and imperiled "the reputations of innocent people. . . . Does anyone seriously think that a real traitor will hesitate to sign a loyalty oath?" Even in the age of anxiety, "We must not burn down the house to kill the rats." Meanwhile the Republicans tried unsuccessfully to override his veto, though only three gubernatorial vetoes had been overturned in nearly one hundred years. For the governor, this veto became a crucial element in his future career, for it extended his reputation among an influential group whose hero he became—the academics and intellectuals of the Democratic party. But the veto also made him an easy target for rabid Republicans of the 1950s.

An advocate of retaining civil liberties, Stevenson was less interested in the civic purification that advancing civil rights represented. In fact, the Stevenson vision of a cleaner, better house of Illinois was limited to whites. In this oversight the governor was no different from most Democrats, most Illinoisians, and certainly most white Americans of his time. Like theirs, his responses to the aggrieving postwar problems of segregation and police brutality were shallow, at least as viewed from a later perspective. "He felt," according to his principal adviser, Carl McGowan, "that the kind of good-will and lack of prejudice that he felt would sort of generally spread and increase and that racial problems would work themselves out." Still, his reputation as an enlightened governor revealed the limitations of the liberal agenda in postwar America.

While the 1948 national Democratic platform opposed lynching and the poll tax and called as well for a federal Fair Employment Practices Act, Stevenson insisted that federal intervention was not the answer. Like all Democrats, he was well aware that even this program had led to the Dixiecrat walkout at the 1948 convention and the formation of the Southern Rights party, which had captured the electoral votes of four states in the subsequent election. Not only would a federal Fair Employment Practices Commission (FEPC) violate the proper relation of state and federal governments, but the Illinois governor judged that such a regulation would interfere with the rights of businessmen and force social change too quickly.

Stevenson pleaded for a recognition of the special circumstances of the South, by which, of course, he meant the white South. The man who rarely met blacks as neighbors, classmates, colleagues, clubmates, or friends, but knew them well as domestic servants and delivery boys, supported a state FEPC without sanctions and a civil rights section in the Illinois Attorney General's Office. He made little effort to appoint blacks (or women) to his administration. Instead, in a new administrative age of commissions and investigating committees, he relied on the Illinois Commission on Human Relations for recommendations to end discrimination at a time in which five other states had already passed employment practices statutes.

Like Truman, who invested few executive resources in a federal FEPC, Stevenson did not lobby the legislature for his state version with the same intensity that he reserved for his good-government programs. Nor was the FEPC passed in either session of the legislature, although it was approved by the Democratic assembly in 1949. In the state senate when the FEPC failed by two votes, Stevenson did not pressure either the Democratic defectors or the progressive Republicans whose votes might have changed. Like Truman, the governor remained an infrequent, uncertain advocate of racial justice, as he preached the litany of words without actions to already persuaded audiences such as the Human Relations Commission and the Urban League. At a national meeting of the latter, Stevenson spoke with the eloquent vagueness that characterized his rhetoric on civil rights: "Whatever our personal prejudices and shortcomings, problems in human relations must not be solved by violence. . . . The answer to communism is democracy; not less democracy, or just enough, but more. And democracy is color blind."

Before such groups the governor recited his excellent credentials in race relations. As an assistant to Secretary of the Navy Frank Knox during World War II, he had encouraged efforts to integrate naval units, male and female, and to give blacks the opportunity to become naval officers. Stevenson also recalled that, as a delegate to the 1948 Democratic convention, he had voted against seating the Mississippi delegation that had denied blacks participation in the process of delegate selection. But Stevenson's past did not lead to present and future commitments or instrumental policies, though he did order the desegregation of the Illinois National Guard, at a time when General Eisenhower suggested withholding federal support from integrated state units. Somehow a concern that a later generation would frame in ethical terms escaped, in Adlai Stevenson's otherwise active conscience, the constraints of right and wrong.

Instead, for Stevenson and many other Democrats, race relations remained mostly a pragmatic matter of the reputation of American democracy in the Cold War. "We have learned from the past, and more recently in the bitter experience of two World Wars, that today human freedom is indivisible. We have come to know that the most basic human rights we cherish are linked with the fate of even the most humble and remote peasant. Whenever fundamental human rights are denied, freedom everywhere is threatened, whether it be in far off Korea or in Cicero, Illinois," he explained in 1951 to the Illinois Commission on Human Relations.

Cicero was in fact embarrassingly nearby, and it was there, in July of 1951, that the festering antagonisms that made postwar America so dangerous for blacks erupted. Earlier Chicago blacks who crossed the residential Jim Crow line had been attacked by crowds without reproof from public officials. Casual acceptance of race-baiting was the public order of the age. Several bombs had destroyed the homes of African-Americans with no consequences for the criminals. Nor did local officials in Springfield or Chicago favor an ordinance that would have banned racial discrimination in the selection of tenants for any publicly financed urban development, an attitude in keeping with the national standards of the Federal Housing Administration.

Still, the Chicago chapter of the NAACP was hopeful that an African-American population that had increased by 80 percent in the 1940s would soon be permitted to break free of its ghetto, which stretched southward from the central business section of Chicago for seven and a half congested miles. In 1948 the Supreme Court had ruled that racial covenants were unenforceable. Now at least suits against whites who rented or sold to blacks had no standing in law, though the National Board of Realtors still prohibited realtors from "introducing into a neighborhood members of any race or nationality whose presence will be detrimental to property values." Neighborhood associations stood on alert to protect the apartheid of their communities and to insist that a black in the neighborhood would depress property values.

In 1951 Johnetta and Harvey Clark, she a housewife and he an Army veteran, bus driver, and graduate of Tennessee's Fisk University, heard of that postwar rarity—a reasonably priced apartment, at $60 a month, with four rooms for their family of three children. But the Clarks were black, and the apartment was in Cicero, a working-class city of 60,000 populated mostly by second-generation Czechs, Hungarians, and Poles, seven miles west of downtown Chicago. As word spread in the summer of 1951 that a black family might move into the neighborhood, Clark was assaulted by cries of "No Niggers in Cicero." Protected by a court injunction, the couple paid a month's rent and moved into the third-floor walk-up. The next day a mob of 4,000 hissing and howling whites—a community of children and rock-heaving adult arsonists—burned the building. Earlier—and some said none too soon—the Clarks had been hustled from the building by a police-man who, in Clark's sworn testimony, ordered them at pistol point "to get out of Cicero and stay out."

The local police remained impervious to any sense of responsibility to keep the peace and to provide equal protection of the law. Some, in fact, joined in the bonfire; others stood with their backs to the crowd. Finally the sheriff and the state's attorney requested assistance, and in Springfield, Governor Stevenson called out the National Guard, which restored order within hours but which had to remain in angry Cicero for over a month. For his actions the governor received praise from black civil rights leaders, including Ralph Bunche.

Stevenson hardly believed Cicero a cause for congratulation. For him the episode was not a racial incident but rather a defeat for law and order as well as a setback for the international competitiveness of democracy. Rarely did Stevenson refer to blacks in his public statements on the Cicero attack. "Deep beneath the Cicero disorders and the breakdown of local law enforcement, lie the fears, the alarms, the pressures, and tensions of the continuously critical housing shortage." Rather than a lynch mob of whites whose actions revealed a tradition of American violence, Cicero held global implications for the governor because it reflected a local failure of democracy in his domicile. The Clarks, he informed the Illinois Commission on Human Relations, had tried "to break through the *iron curtain* which con-fines so many of our fellow citizens." "Large numbers of the low income groups, and among these large numbers of the *so-called minority groups*, are inadequately housed, rigidly segregated and confined to slums and deteriorated residential areas. The demoralizing effects of overcrowding, of sub-standard housing, inadequate sanitation, illegal building conversions, and a host of resultant social evils, are placing a severe strain upon the whole range of state and municipal welfare services."

On his monthly television and radio show in November 1951 (Stevenson did not mention the riot in his September or October appearances), the governor decried the unfortunate publicity that Cicero had brought the United States. "I need not tell you these stories have served the purposes of Communist propagandists." His solution was more housing and "an honest and expert diagnosis" by a representative group of private citizens from the Chicago metropolitan area.

Later when a local grand jury exonerated the leaders of the mob and instead indicted Clark's attorney for destroying property values, the attorney general of the United States, not the governor of Illinois, intervened by initiating another investigation. Private outrage eventually forced the local officials who had maliciously sought legal penalties against the Clarks' lawyer and the owner of the apartment to drop the charges against the victims. In his private letters of the time, Stevenson reflected on "the restraint and constructive attitude of the Negro leaders," which he found "one of the most encouraging and hopeful aspects of the Cicero affair." "I get frightfully irked by wild men like Congressman Powell," he maintained, in a reference to the New York congressman Adam Clayton Powell. And while he did not mention the NAACP organizers active in Illinois, he often complained of Thurgood Marshall's trying "to stir things up."

4

DURING HIS FOUR YEARS as a governor, Adlai Stevenson learned that he could not "live by a calendar" but was instead controlled "by events and spacing." He called this his fate, though often the disturbing events were man-made disasters like the West Frankfort mine explosion and the Cicero disorders. Occasionally his overloaded schedule was interrupted by ceremonial affairs such as the arrival in the spring of 1951 of the defrocked General Douglas MacArthur, whose Illinois supporters organized a parade. With calculated disobedience MacArthur had called for total victory in Korea—the war that had begun during the second year of Stevenson's governorship—and Truman had removed him. Asked for a statement, Stevenson produced an adroit comment: "No one has done more than MacArthur to preserve and protect our system of government—but it is a system in which civilian control of the military is basic. As a great military leader his apparent departure from the fundamental principle of obedience is hard to understand."

Lamenting the interruption, the governor still had to fly to Chicago for the parade.

The "spacing" that burdened his schedule also featured the political events that Stevenson disliked—the biennial sessions of the state legislature, the discussions with county leaders about their organizations, and even the off-year elections of 1950, when he had campaigned vigorously but unsuccessfully for Democratic candidates for the U.S. Congress and Senate. In 1952 another political interval arrived, and Adlai Stevenson had to decide about a second term. On the one hand he was tired of the "publicness" of his job, complaining to Buffie that his life was "controlled": "I live in a gold-fish bowl and have no freedom of anything."

Exhausted by self-imposed standards of diligence and principles that made good government everlastingly unattainable, Stevenson was unable to shed failures as malfunctions of the system. Unlike those of other politicians, his disappointments remained personal transgressions. "I'm alone, utterly alone . . . brooding over this appalling pile of papers . . . gloating in self-pity, oppressed with forebodings of disaster and dishonor. Surrounded with everything for happiness and usefulness, I'm desolate and destitute— and think of nothing except the creeping morrows," he wrote Jane Dick.

Publicly, at least, he retained a sense of humor bequeathed by his grandfather. When the legislature tried to embarrass him with a specious cat bill—an act to protect "insectivorous" birds by restraining cats—Stevenson earned an enduring place among cat lovers and the good-humored with his veto. "I cannot agree," he wrote, "that it should be the declared public policy of Illinois that a cat visiting a neighbor's yard or crossing a highway is a public nuisance. It is in the nature of cats to do a certain amount of unescorted roaming. . . . The problem of cat versus bird is as old as time. If we attempt to resolve it by legislation who knows but what we may be called upon to take sides as well in the age-old problem of dog versus cat, bird versus bird, and even bird versus worm. . . ."

At Buffie's urging, after an episode of kidney stones and a siege of insomnia, the fifty-two-year-old governor went to his doctor—"for the works, barium both ends, fluoroscopes for two days . . . . what a horror." To Stevenson's chagrin Dr. Emmet Pearson discovered "no good and sufficient reasons to thumb my nose at the pols for keeps." Even without a medical discharge, one side of his divided self craved freedom, the mythic existence of the Black River or perhaps a job in the State Department, about which he had already inquired through Dorothy Fosdick and other well-placed friends.

But the dutiful side of Adlai Stevenson knew that there was much left to do and knew as well that he was acclaimed, beyond his state, for efforts at cleaning up Illinois that elevated him, in several polls, to the ranks of the best governors in postwar America. Despite his achievements, his highly tuned ethical sense continued to fashion perplexing quandaries, and as he often did at the choice points of his life, he provided Alicia, his "beloved and hot-tempered publisher," with a balance sheet of his self-examination. "I've been in fiendish travail trying to decide what to do. The party wants and needs me desperately this time. But where does it all lead? Four more years and if I'm still alive, where am I? 4 years older, feebler, completely out of touch with the international field, no job, no security (damnable word) and no use, except in politics for 'higher office' which I don't want. In short it would seem to me that now is the time to get out and during the remaining year of my term when my availability would be known look about for something else to do. However I'm sure to succumb to the immediate I suppose." At the same time he informed his cousin Letty Bromwell that he would like to get out of "combat politics."

In a manner that neither his grandfather nor his father could have fathomed, Adlai Stevenson consulted his private feelings rather than his party's needs. Characteristically his public comments testified to his dilemmas. "Our society," he told the members of the Illinois Retail Equipment Association in Peoria, "is becoming increasingly complicated. Life is becoming so complex that the average individual finds far greater difficulty in adjusting himself to proper living than did our fathers and grandfathers." Other Americans felt similar confusions in their personal lives, and so were attracted to a man who translated into politics a view of human nature as irrational, uncertain yet redeemable, though not, in the classic dichotomy of political philosophers, evil. Concerned with individual rights, liberals appreciated a man whose personal decisions were more wracking than those about public issues. The latter Stevenson resolved promptly, but often with an attendant sense of guilt that he had not done better; the former became tribulations.

In January 1952 the governor made one of the choices of this crowded year: "After long and prayerful consideration I have decided to be a candidate for re-election as Governor in 1952." His statement was typically self-effacing and shockingly unambitious for partisan politics: "I invite the Republican party to nominate the best man it can find. It is of little importance whether the next Governor of Illinois is named Adlai Stevenson; but it is of the highest importance that he finish what we have started. No matter then who loses, the people will win."

Like many Americans in 1952, Stevenson also speculated about the presidential candidates with Alicia Patterson and his gubernatorial advisers. For the Republicans there was, in Stevenson's view, the insider Robert Taft, whose opposition to the New Deal and to Truman's containment policies placed him to the right of most Republicans. Stevenson believed that the nomination of the Ohio senator would force American voters to make a choice between isolationism and the global engagement he favored. While Taft had supported American military action in Korea, he opposed Truman's aid programs to Europe.

And then there was Eisenhower, although no one knew the general's party preference. With his taste for winners Jack Arvey had unsuccessfully promoted Eisenhower for the Democratic nomination in 1948. By February 1952 the leader of the Allied victory in Europe had emerged from his closet partisanship: he was a Republican who would not seek the nomination but who would accept a draft. By April, Stevenson liked Ike and devised a strategy for the Republican. "If I were Ike and wanted the nomination I would stay in Europe, keep up the impression that Taft can't win & hope the hungry leaders would ditch Taft at the convention," concluded Stevenson.

For the Democrats there was the incumbent Harry Truman, who, deciding not to run the year before, had kept the secret of his retirement so that he could oversee the passing of the New Deal–Fair Deal torch to a successor. As early as January the president had found his indispensable man in Adlai Stevenson. By March, Truman and Stevenson had met three times, twice secretly as Truman offered his support to the "flabbergasted" and unwilling governor of Illinois. Stevenson was not Truman's first choice, but once he had selected him, the president worked hard to recruit the candidate whose reluctance was incomprehensible to a man who campaigned with the zest of a sportsman playing his favorite game. He's too "coy and backward," said Truman, among other things, of Stevenson.

At the end of March over five thousand faithful Democrats, attired in tuxedos, black ties, and stiff collars dined together on beef and shrimp at the party's annual $100-a-plate Jefferson-Jackson Day celebration in Washington. Truman gave the partisan speech that he had delivered in different places and in slightly revised versions ever since his surprise victory in 1948. At the end, without changing the midwestern monotone that sometimes accented third syllables in a strange cadence, the president shocked his audience with the news that Stevenson had known for months. Declining another nomination, Truman noted his long service to party and public. Then came the words that caused Adlai Stevenson to bury his face in his hands: "I shall not be a candidate for re-election. I shall not accept a renomination. I do not feel that it is my duty to spend another four years in the White House." Despondent cries of "Oh No, Oh No" echoed in the smoke-filled National Guard Armory, though with his approval ratings at under 30 percent, the despair was short-lived.

Many of the contending crown princes—Vice President Alben Barkley, New York's Averell Harriman, and Senator Richard Russell of Georgia—were present. Even the one announced candidate, Senator Estes Kefauver of Tennessee, had come, though he was out of favor after embarrassing the president by winning the New Hampshire primary and thereafter using his popularity to gain support from the party leaders who controlled nominations. Stevenson was there, too, for he was everywhere this political season. After Truman's announcement a crowd gathered around the Illinois governor, who was heard to say in a revealing refrain, "Get me out of here." For the rest of the spring and early summer, two Adlai Stevensons struggled for primacy.

The more visible one established his position on the presidency in a March letter to Charles Murphy, Truman's special counsel. "I do not want to be a candidate for the nomination. I do not want to run for President, and I do not want to be President at this time. I have been in politics only three years; while I have learned a great deal, I have a great deal more to learn. . . . That I am, aside from the President, the best available man to assume this monstrous task seems to me grotesque. . . ." To Jane Dick he described a conversation with his youngest son, John Fell. Asked by the sixteen-year-old what he had told "the men," Stevenson replied that he "had wriggled out again. In his simple direct way [John Fell] said you did the right thing for *us,* but the wrong thing for the country."

In April, after the gubernatorial primary in Illinois, the beehive of journalists provided a new conundrum for the governor to consider: if he would not campaign for the nomination, was he available for a draft? To Alicia, who liked ambitious men, he wrote, "I can't or don't want to tell them if Taft yes, if Ike no?," though after Eisenhower was nominated, he did not change his position. In the first of several statements, Stevenson announced that he had made a prior commitment to the voters of Illinois, that he had unfinished work in the state, and that he could not accept the nomination for any other office "this summer." "Illinois," he repeated, "has been very good to me and my people for a century and a half. I have a large debt to discharge if I can."

Along with his commitment to Illinois, Stevenson's view of the presidency bridled his limited ambitions for power. To him, though not to the postwar aspirants to the office, the presidency was an impossible job whose attainment required the distortion of issues, moral compromise, and partisan intemperance. Could a man be true and just and be president? In any case, "I'm not qualified to be President, or equipped." Asked who was, he responded, "Nobody but God is really equipped to be President." In fact, Stevenson remained suspicious of anyone who sought the office. "Beware of too much success," he had learned from his mother. "Pride goeth before a fall . . . so we must exercise self-discipline and humility." To those who distrusted such modesty, the governor offered the additional reason of his "limited capacity." "I never overestimate my abilities or prospects and I hate to fail in anything. I undertake measured objectives one at a time and conservatively."

To his friends and to Truman, he gave the further excuse that his children (now twenty-one, nineteen, and sixteen) seemed to him "altogether too young and undeveloped to subject to the pityless exposure of a national campaign, let alone the Presidency. Nor do they have the security and advantage of a stable family life." Like his much publicized unwillingness to be a candidate, the family pretext was unique in American history, having been forged in the unusual ancestry and private life that made him the kind of politician he was. Other public men—William McKinley, whose epileptic wife detested Washington, Harry Truman, whose wife preferred the couple's shaded Victorian home in Independence, Missouri, to the White House, even his own grandfather—had pulled protesting family members along the road to power and almost never considered declining a post for family reasons.

But Stevenson believed he had failed as a father, and his divorce proclaimed a bankrupt marital relationship, no matter who initiated its legal dissolution. As one Illinois woman inquired, "Women don't leave good husbands. Why did the governor's marriage fail?" As a second-term governor he might "find a little time for the boys," although he had not found much in his first term. As president, he knew, he would find less. Still, the Stevenson sons were hardly boys needing to be shielded from campaigning. In fact, their participation might nurture in them the sense of public service important for all Stevensons. Adlai III, who had graduated from Harvard in 1952 and was in Marine boot camp, surely needed no protection. Nor did nineteen-year-old Borden, who had dropped out of Harvard to join the Army, while the youngest, John Fell, was a senior in boarding school. Only Stevenson's nostalgia for lost time with his children returned these adults to boyhoods a busy father would share in his dreams and use as a pretext not to run for president.

Stevenson did not mention his wife as a reason for not seeking the Democratic nomination, although privately he described Ellen as "on a rampage in the East." He exaggerated, but his growing notoriety impinged on his former wife's fragile esteem. After the divorce she had lived quietly, though affluently, for she was an active exponent of the nation's postwar consumerism, renting apartments on Chicago's Astor Street and near Libertyville. Freed from the frugality of her husband and his perpetual dark-hued Buicks and Studebakers, she now drove a yellow Cadillac convertible and surrounded herself with poets and artists, who provided the congeniality that for years had been missing from her marriage.

By 1952 Ellen Stevenson was a board member and principal fund-raiser of *Poetry,* and she had expensive plans for a Chicago arts center in her ancestral home, the grand Victorian palace of the Borden family at 1020 Lake Shore Drive. The prospects of a campaign in which her sons provided the family cover necessary for a divorced candidate aggravated her. Angrily, she described her sons' "exploitation" and her own supporting role as a termagant establishing sympathy for her husband. Characterized as a selfish woman who refused to serve as a political wife, Ellen began to tell her side of things.

As July and the moment of decision at the Democratic convention approached, Adlai Stevenson issued three statements, held four press conferences, and told anyone who asked either by letter or by phone (and at least fifty a day did) that he was not a candidate for president and wanted only to be a second-term governor. With an informality soon to be forgotten in more imperial regimes, Harry Truman called, too, sometimes waiting on the line until the governor's secretaries found Stevenson.

Certainly the Illinois governor did not sound like a presidential candidate. He told the Illinois delegation to the Democratic convention, which hoped for a moment in the spotlight when they nominated their governor, that he was "mentally, temperamentally, and physically" unfit to be president. In an interview with the Truman adviser James Loeb, a charter member of the newly formed Americans for Democratic Action, the governor outlined his considerable differences with the liberals who were so attracted to him: he was against national health care for the aged; he was not in favor of the repeal of labor's nemesis, the Taft-Hartley Act; he believed that states should be left in control of civil rights and that the activities of the NAACP did more harm to race relations than good. "You know, I've got southern blood in me," he explained, after which Loeb labeled Stevenson "a Northern Dixiecrat" and encouraged the ADA to find another candidate.

Stevenson also ordered his advisers to desist from assisting any of the proliferating Stevenson for President committees, although he had no authority over the Independent Voters of Illinois, who were raising money in his name and had used some of it on a full-page Stevenson for President advertisement in the *New York Times*. Nor could the governor forestall the energetic efforts of the amateurs who had stimulated his ambitions for public service in 1948 and who in their campaign without a candidate expected to propel their beloved "Guv" to Washington. Meanwhile, in Washington, Stevenson's friend George Ball opened a Stevenson information bureau. No matter what Stevenson said, his supporters remembered his agonies in 1948 and believed, like Jack Arvey, that he would "ultimately be available."

Stevenson had said no to a campaign for the presidency, but would he, insisted reporters, friends, liberals, party leaders, and independent Democrats, accept a draft at the Democratic convention in July? Stevenson dismissed such a prospect as remote: "I refuse to speculate. . . . I had better wait until the improbable arrival of that situation before I comment." To Alicia he explained that he could not issue a "General Sherman," a reference to the Civil War general William Tecumseh Sherman, who in 1884 declared he would not run if nominated nor serve if elected. In Stevenson's view such a forthright disclaimer would be "a cocky, distasteful thing to do and

I hate to earn a place in the History books by saying I won't do something honorable that has come to few people." Meanwhile his friends asked this anomalous politician to avoid a straightforward renunciation.

And so, like a "naked runner amid spears," he suffered, while the other hopefuls vented their ambitions in more traditional ways by rounding up delegates, talking to the favorite sons who would control first-round votes, and trying to get a pledge of support from Truman, the wounded, though still powerful, Democratic lion of this year's partisan jungles. In these pre-convention days Stevenson's exaggerated imagery revealed his distaste for the process that Porter McKeever crudely described as "rape." "If one has to be raped," advised McKeever, "there is no point in struggling too violently. . . . One's moral position is better if there is at least a convincing demonstration of resistance up to the moment the inevitable is obvious."

Stevenson's "appalling" prospects were to him like "a holocaust"; "a torture chamber"; his "Golgotha"; "a noose . . . tightening." In June, at an Illinois National Guard outing, the governor was asked what would happen if he was drafted, and he answered, "I'll shoot myself." To Jane Dick, who complained that he protested too much, he revealed his turmoil: "Do you really think I magnify my misfortunes when there are none—or very few? I want so much to be worthy, to earn, to keep, all the things I have to be thankful for. I feel so inadequate, so unworthy. I really want so hard to do the right thing, the wise thing, God's work, if you please. . . ."

Dismissed by some of his advisers as more posture than conviction, the hyperbole in fact revealed an internal struggle. From the Book of Psalms he drew consoling thoughts shared with Jane Dick: "We glory in tribulations, knowing that tribulations maketh patience, and patience, experience, and experience, hope. Hope in His good time." For at the same time that the governor made known his desire to remain in Springfield—"the full measure of my strength and capacity"—he was also at work improving his national reputation and expanding the domain of his ambitions.

In an overcrowded public schedule a less bashful Adlai Stevenson found time to write two articles for important national journals—*Harper's,* where his piece on gambling was published in February, and *Foreign Affairs,* where, in the April 1952 issue, he supported Truman's Korean policy. Stevenson was not too busy, this spring of 1952, for long interviews with reporters from the *Saturday Evening Post, Harper's, Time,* the *Reader's Digest, Newsweek, Life, Collier's,* and *Look.* In favorable articles that included governor-approved family pictures, these national magazines, with a combined circulation of over twenty-three million, spread the word about the "dark horse" from Illinois.

The governor who wanted to serve Illinois for another term also traveled across the Mississippi, the Wabash, and the Ohio Rivers to speak in California, Oregon, Colorado, New York, Virginia, Texas, Pennsylvania, and Washington, D.C. Both at home and abroad his topics were as varied as a national candidate's and as broadly international as a modern president's must be during the Cold War. Three times he appeared on national radio and television shows; on his monthly Sunday afternoon television series, "From the Governor's Office," on which he answered letters from the people, he selected the query of a nine-year-old from Peoria who wanted him to run for the presidency, to which he responded with classic Stevenson whimsy that perhaps he would when she was ready to vote.

Thirteen times in May alone he stepped onto podiums to deliver major speeches. Although he complained about "dodging around to hotels to clubs to homes to avoid my dear old friends of the press," in fact several times he initiated calls to the columnists James Reston and Joseph Alsop. He gave unlimited time to the journalist Noel Busch, who was writing an admiring biography with a publication date two weeks before the Democratic convention. Yet the governor insisted that the frontispiece of *Adlai Stevenson of Illinois* carry the disclaimer "This book is not an authorized biography and should not be construed by any stretch of the imagination as any sort of political gesture on the part of the subject."

This other Stevenson who needed to be needed also refused to employ the kind of denial that would have immediately ended speculation about his presidential ambitions. "Nothing," he said, "could keep me from the governorship except health, death, or higher office." Having opened the door with his joke, he promptly shut it: "And I have no ambitions for the latter save the governorship." In the early spring the governor set his staff (as well as some friends, including Jane Dick and Jack Arvey) to work drafting statements about his intentions. Carl McGowan produced the unequivocal "I would not accept a nomination." The governor never used it. In Stevenson's revision the critical verb became a more compliant "could," a variation not lost on the press. In the difference between a "could" and a "would" lay Adlai's dual world.

In one of his own undated statements, parentheses displayed his ambivalence: "I would not accept the nomination if offered to me. . . . I feel (do not feel) that I have the strength the wisdom, or the (reverence) (grace) (courage) (self-confidence) (resources of the spirit) (serenity) (goodness) (virtue) (divine guidance) to (lead the way) (guide us) to coexistence with an inscrutable hostile and *equal* power in the world. (I marvel that anyone does) (has such self-confidence.)"

Nor did he work for other candidates, choosing to support Averell Harriman, who had never held elective office. As the convention approached, he refused repeated requests to nominate Alben Barkley. Although he impeded the chances of other contenders, there were explanations that delivered Adlai Stevenson from the charge of hypocrisy. Most dealt with his gubernatorial campaign, even though never before had a candidate for state office voluntarily spent so much time out of the state speaking about national and international affairs. He wrote Alicia, "If there's a touch of destiny about the draft business, I don't want to thwart it and make a tragic mistake."

In one of his meetings with Stevenson, Truman encouraged the governor to run because of, not despite, his family. "I had thought," wrote the president in his *Memoirs*, "that some solid political instincts had filtered down to him from his very astute grandfather of the same name." Truman was not alone in placing the governor's choice in a family context. Earlier his wife had also recognized the importance of the Stevenson heritage: "The Stevensons must be Chinese they worship their ancestors so much," she complained.

On one of his frequent out-of-state appearances during the spring of 1952, the governor appeared on the popular television program *Meet the Press*. Dexterously he sidestepped questions about the nomination and tangled with the feisty May Craig of the *Portland* (Maine) *Press-Herald* about corruption in the Truman administration and the long period of Democratic control of the presidency. Toward the end of the program, Ed Leahy of the *Chicago News* asked Stevenson again about his intentions; in the fencing that followed, Leahy finally exploded: "Governor Stevenson, wouldn't your grandfather twirl around in his grave if he saw you running away from a chance to be the Democratic nominee in 1952?" To which a chagrined Stevenson responded, "I think we will have to leave grandfather lie."

Grandfather stayed where he was—buried in the Bloomington cemetery—but he remained very much alive in the memory of his namesake and grandson. As "the shadows gathered" and the moment of decision approached, excited Democrats began appearing in Chicago for the nominating convention the third week of July. During that week the Illinois governor so acclaimed for his oratory was scheduled to deliver the welcoming address. For the first time since 1936, the party had no incumbent president to return to the White House. Its convention of 1952 promised a great melodrama for the nearly two thousand delegates.

Meanwhile a tormented Adlai Ewing Stevenson wondered what he would say and what he would do and how he would resolve his dilemma. Four years after he had accepted the Democratic nomination for governor, the stakes had been raised, though the conflicts were similar—this time between his commitment to cleaning up his house of Illinois and the party's nomination for the presidency, and between his sense of self and the ghosts of generations past.

CHAPTER THREE

"OUR FATHERS IN THEIR GENERATIONS"

1

THE GENIAL GRANDFATHER whom Adlai Stevenson II remembered so often during the spring of 1952—Adlai Ewing Stevenson the First (1835–1914)—was a family man, a storyteller, and a politician. In all three endeavors he was encouraged by relatives and especially by his wife, Letitia. Mostly these passions melded harmoniously, although occasionally his ambitions and the labor-intensive demands of party politics strained his desire for privacy. Yet neither politics nor storytelling was a reliable means of supporting a family, and like other nineteenth-century breadwinners who did many things rather than one, Adlai Stevenson also made his living as a lawyer, the operator of several farms, a banker, and the part-owner of a coal company.

In his later years Stevenson liked to gather the family around the dining room table or, if the weather was good, on the porch overlooking Bloomington's Franklin Park. There, settled in a rocking chair with an unlit cigar or a ring of keys available for punctuation, he told the legends of the politicians along with the jokes and yarns he had learned in public life. Even after he became vice president of the United States and a celebrity who dined with kings and prime ministers, the favorite souvenirs bestowed on his offspring were family stories, especially the great saga of the Stevenson migration.

As Adlai Stevenson recounted this chapter of family life in the accents of a Kentucky native, he had arrived in the central Illinois town of Bloomington with his mother, his sister, and four of his younger brothers at exactly six o'clock on the searingly hot afternoon of July 7, 1852. At the time it seemed as if the bells of the First Presbyterian Church tolled to acknowledge the successful termination of a difficult 430-mile, month-long journey. The family had delayed its start from Christian County, Kentucky, when the spring rains turned the roads into a sticky morass. Then, in early June, family members had loaded the two canvas-covered caravans, placed eight-month-old Thomas Stevenson's cradle under the wooden seats, and set the oxen into their heavy harness.

Like all uprootings, it was a bittersweet occasion. The Stevensons would leave behind the relatives, friends, and neighbors, who in the braided kinship arrangements of this family, were usually the same. But Adlai's father, John Turner Stevenson, and his younger brother, William Washington Stevenson, had left the year before. And after the family had sold its farm in southwestern Kentucky, valued at $2,634, and leased its nine slaves to relatives and after Father bought part of a sawmill in Bloomington, it was time to go.

A cautious, sickly man, Turner Stevenson (who used his middle name to distinguish himself from five other related John Stevensons) had sent back word about the safest route to Illinois. Because the roads were so poor, the members of the family began their journey in the opposite direction from their destination, as travelers of this time were accustomed to doing—first south to Clarksville, Tennessee, and from there along the Cumberland River east to Pineville or Cumberland Ford, where the Old Wilderness Road arced north and west through central Kentucky to Hazel Patch and Logan's Station, and finally to the falls of the Ohio at Louisville. There they loaded the wagons onto one of the new Ohio River steamships that connected Kentucky's river towns to the Mississippi. At Alton they traveled the Illinois River route to Pekin, where the road was wide and smooth enough for the weekly stagecoaches to the towns of central Illinois. Disembarking, they journeyed the last thirty-five miles eastward across Illinois to McLean County, sometimes at night because of the omnivorous greenhead flies. An axle had broken in Kentucky, where the main road was so rutted that Adlai's mother, Eliza Ewing Stevenson, preferred walking to the bumping that passengers of this generation suffered as "a bad case of the jolts." With his father already in Bloomington, sixteen-year-old Adlai had been in charge.

They left, Adlai and his mother forever claimed, because an August frost in 1850 had destroyed the tobacco crop that was the family's source of income. Of this catastrophe there is no official record in the chronicles of southwestern Kentucky, though in the family's fervent attachment to that state only a calamity justified the abandonment of what was and would remain "homeplace." There had been a hailstorm in 1851, and that same year a late spring frost had blackened the tiny, slow-maturing tobacco plants before they could be set out in the fields. But these were the vicissitudes that farmers expected.

In fact, the weather was an excuse, and there was another reason. The Stevensons were a restless, migrating clan that moved every generation in search, like thousands of others in a vast tide of eighteenth- and nineteenth-century voyagers, of better, cheaper land, of more certain titles to their property, of cleaner water, and, always, of improving their circumstances. Some family members had already settled in Bloomington and sent back word of inexpensive fertile land in surrounding McLean County and commercial prospects in town. Earlier the family had begun to listen to the stories about Illinois, had reconnoitered, had decided in a family conference who would go, and then had procured the wagons and supplies needed for the move. The latter was a process, for the Stevensons and other families, that often took as long as two years, but when they left, the Stevensons reenacted a family tradition.

2

STEVENSON MIGRATIONS had begun in the Scottish lowlands of Roxburgh-shire, a region of rocky, impoverished soil along the English border fit mostly for sheepherding but angrily and bloodily contested by the highland clans, the belligerent MacDonnels and Campbells, and later by the armies of the Scots and the English. The Test Oath of 1703 had installed a new oath to the Church of England, and four years later the Act of Union, which joined Scotland and England administratively, scarcely quieted the tumul-tuous course of local affairs. Many Scots feared that unification would bring a more implacable supervision of the Anglican Church's required ortho-doxy. In the popular warning of the time,

> Instead of asleep in your pews,
> You'll be vexed with repeating the creed
> You'll be dunned and demurred with their views,
> If their damned project succeed.

In 1715 an effort to restore the Catholic Stuarts brought more armies tramping through the countryside, plundering the farms, killing the sheep, and rendering perilous the practice of Presbyterian beliefs. Earlier, during a period known as "the hungry years," the region's already limited economic prospects had been dimmed further by seven years of rainy sunless sum-mers, bitter frosty autumns, and deep snowy winters. By the 1730s a migrant population of 200,000 hungry Scots roamed the countryside, and in Roxburghshire Officer George Stephenson was paid extra for digging "poor folks graves."

Sometime after 1700, perhaps after the English government put down the Jacobite uprising of 1715, the Stephenson family moved to County Antrim, in northern Ireland. What they gave up is uncertain, although a private chapel in the diocese of St. Andrews that carried the family name suggests the prominence of some relatives as well as their commitment to Presbyterianism. They may have been encouraged by the British govern-ment's efforts to transplant its citizens to the lands of insubordinate Irish natives. They may have felt the pressure of an expanding population in the

Scottish lowlands that made visitors of the time wonder "how so small a bounds can contain so very many people."

In the early eighteenth century prices and rents had risen sharply, and there were reports of better opportunities in northern Ireland. Several land-lords near Roxburgh had already become "undertakers" in that two-way process whereby Scots replaced what the English considered their unruly, pope-loving Irish tenants. Randal MacDonnel, whose family had dominated Roxburghshire for generations, had taken title to a vast tract of land along the coast and the fertile valley of the Bann River where the fish and forests provided a bounty unusual in Scotland. MacDonnel had encouraged some of his tenants to leave the hardscrabble life on the lean, barren lands of Scotland, where trees were rare, harvests uncertain, and politics oppressive.

Like many Scots, the Stephensons were familiar with the northern and eastern counties of Ireland—the region known as Ulster. Trade and an infor-mal commerce across the Irish Sea made northern Ireland better known to lowland Scots than the English capital of London. Under the plantation sys-tem of the late seventeenth century, a steady exodus of Scots had already occurred, some to Ireland and others to America. On a trip to Scotland in 1773, Dr. Samuel Johnson and his loyal companion James Boswell observed a local dance called America. By the end of the reel all the partners had pledged to leave the old country. Some like the Stephensons made an inter-mediate stop in Ulster, where, by 1672, about 100,000 Scots already lived.

Yet only a thin strip of land along the northern coast of Antrim was suit-able for the gray oats that sustained the poor and that even for more prosper-ous families like the Stephensons served as a nutritional insurance policy. In other parts of the county, the land was as rocky and barren as Scotland's. The Stephensons chose the area near the port of Belfast, where sixteen-year-old William apprenticed to a tailor who also made hats. Years later his grand-child to the fifth degree Adlai Ewing Stevenson II recalled his ancestor as a hatter. Meanwhile William's brother Robert was already in service to a "gen-tleman." Under such arrangements an apprentice was bound to a master for seven years, while he learned his trade and received in return "meat, drink, clothes and apparel and all other necessities fitting for an apprentice of pro-fession and faculty." After his service William was assured a position in the tightly controlled guilds, but by that time he and his brother had other plans.

In the 1730s William's father died, and his mother, whose family lived in Antrim, remarried, possibly to a younger son of the prominent White family. Simultaneously pushed from Ireland by high rents, crop failures, taxes for a state church that was not theirs, political discrimination against Presbyterians, and prohibitory English tariffs on Irish textiles, these volun-tary refugees were pulled to America by praise of its plenty from relatives who had gone before. And so the Stephensons moved again—this time across the Atlantic Ocean to Pennsylvania.

In doing so, they became part of the fourth migration of English-speaking peoples to the New World. Journeying from Belfast, they joined a vast flood of emigrants from the border counties of England and Scotland and the six counties in the north of Ireland. They traveled as families, but there was no interest in holy experiments or cities on the hill or even the establishment of a religious community purified by the isolation of the New World. Instead, the Stephensons came for land and an end to the insecurity that plagued their lives in the borderlands of Great Britain. To be sure, the departure of like-thinking and -acting neighborhoods and clans diminished their sense of exile. For they carried—along with their wooden chests filled with blankets and pewter—habits, opinions, and ways of living to be transplanted to a new environment that, in turn, would mold their culture.

No one knows exactly how many of these border people emigrated in the eighteenth century. During the years from 1718 to 1775, there were probably as many as 300,000, half of them from northern Ireland. By 1736 over a thousand families were waiting in Belfast for ships to carry them to America, and in some estimates the Scottish and Irish emigration into Pennsylvania between 1730 and 1775 exceeded 10,000 persons annually. For most of these travelers the passage across the Atlantic, now organized as a business by agents who searched the towns and countryside for possible prospects, was a dangerous undertaking marked by overcrowded ships, insufficient food, and high shipboard mortality.

The arrival of the border peoples in colonial America tested the tolerance of the Quakers who had come to the middle Atlantic region a century before. Soon there was opposition to the influx in Philadelphia and Newcastle, the other major port of entry in nearby Delaware. One Philadelphia Quaker complained that the streets had filled with "a swarm of people . . . strangers to our Laws and customs." Others argued for laws to restrict immigration.

The Stephensons did not stay in Philadelphia; instead, they headed west, like many Scots before them, into the counties outside the city, only to find that the good land had already been surveyed and "taken up," language that suggests the indeterminacy of this generation's land titles. What remained, mostly at fifteen pounds for a hundred acres, cost so much that by 1750 one-half of the farmers in Chester County rented. So the clan continued on to a region claimed by the colonies of Pennsylvania, Maryland, and Virginia. In an area then part of Pennsylvania's Lancaster County where the foothills of the Blue Ridge Mountains were reminiscent of the Cheviot Hills of their native Scotland, they settled—briefly.

Young William had stayed in Ireland to finish his apprenticeship, but now twenty-three, he joined the family in 1748. It was the year in which the Iroquois Confederacy signed, at gunpoint, one of several treaties with the English. In response to the white man's voracious appetites for the possession of the land, the Six Nations agreed to give up their claims to land south and east of the Allegheny River, thus opening the way for more European settlement in the backcountry. So too did a treaty signed that same year by the English and French that ended the two-continent conflict known as King George's War.

Several years later Mary McLelland, of an Antrim family, who had moved to Lancaster County and who would also transplant in North Carolina, married William Stephenson. By 1759 the Stephensons and McLellands (in a common practice William's two brothers "Carpenter" John and Robert married two of Mary's sisters, and Mary's brothers through their marriage connected the family to Nesbits and Osbornes) along with a network of other interrelated families were ready to move again. In family tradition a diaspora that resembled the rooting of a forest from a few trees recurred. Some members, including William's mother, remained in Pennsylvania, just as some had stayed in Roxburghshire, Scotland, and County Antrim, Ireland. Thereafter biographies of well-known citizens in all these areas included Stephensons, Ewings, and McLellands. Other branches of the kinship, often daughters married to younger sons or widows and widowers, moved on. Some went first to establish beachheads in the new community. Others, following the paths of Native American traders, surveyed land or investigated the Scots' settlements in the backcountry. These latter numbered, by the time of the American Revolution, over 130 in Pennsylvania and Maryland and perhaps as many as 50 in North Carolina. By 1800 over a quarter of North Carolina's population was Scottish born, and in the western counties of the state the proportion was higher.

Even as the Stephensons changed locations, their remembered attachments to kin served as a protective shelter in the boundless terrain of their new country. They were a clan, and they carried with them to America an inherited sense of blood relatives—past and present—as a "derbfine," an ancient arrangement recognized in the laws of northern Britain and Ireland that "encompassed all kin within the span of the last four generations." They referred to themselves as "our people" and meant by that an extended family whose younger generations carried the names of their forebears and whose dead were remembered in story and legend.

At some point in the 1750s, the agents of the Carolina proprietor John Carteret, the earl of Granville, brought word to western Pennsylvania of cheap grazing land in the Carolinas. It was even rumored that Governor Tryon had promised one hundred acres free of surveying fees as an inducement to settlers who would venture away from the coast. William, now in his thirties and the father of two sons, traveled to North Carolina, where after a month's exploration he entered a request for a survey in Rowan County on land that was part of a vast royal grant in the western Carolinas to Lord Granville.

As the British government moved to place proprietary colonies under royal control, of eight proprietors in the Carolinas only Granville had refused to sell his land back to King George, although in 1744 he had surrendered to royal authority any political control over its inhabitants. In the meantime he adopted the model of the English plantation of Ulster for his property, setting up land offices to encourage sales. When he died in 1763, his heirs hoped for profits from rents and sales of his 20-million-acre holdings. In fact, the land was sold at low prices, and settlers who brought others established their traditional headright claims to more land. A family of four could take up as much as 640 acres for three shillings in the area between the Catawba and South Yadkin Rivers, although thereafter annual rent to the proprietor might rise to twenty-five shillings.

But the frontier was aflame for the next seven years, as an alliance of Iroquois, Cherokee, Creek, and French contested English hegemony in the Shenandoah valley. The peace after King George's War had lasted less than a decade, as settlers continued to push on to the lands of the Native Americans where French traders had already established their posts. It was too dangerous for the Stephensons to travel at a time when most of Rowan County's fifteen hundred families had fled eastward across the Yadkin River. The remaining few huddled in the tiny stockade of Fort Dobbs for the duration of the French and Indian War, or the Cherokee War, as it was known in this region. They traveled only in armed groups to till fields and feed cattle. By 1762 the English had prevailed in an expensive conflict that led to increased taxes and embittered relations between the colonists and the English government. Even before the final treaty extinguishing French claims east of the Mississippi was signed in Paris in 1763, the clan—sixty-five families of McLellands, Ewings, Osbornes, McKenzies, Sherrills, and Stephensons, mostly Scots and mostly Presbyterians—was ready to transplant again.

Sometime in 1762 the clan members left southern Pennsylvania in an ox-drawn caravan, crossing the Susquehanna River at Wright's Ferry and pressing on toward Lancaster, where they joined the Great Philadelphia Wagon Road. Here they turned south for their journey of over 450 miles, traveling through western Maryland to Winchester, Virginia, and then down the Shenandoah valley west of the Blue Ridge Mountains, where the towering deciduous oaks, hickories, and chestnuts surprised even those who had lived in wooded Pennsylvania. They stopped in Staunton and then forded the headwaters of the James River, passing by the salt deposits that gave Big Lick its name. Then they moved across the still-contested boundary from Virginia into North Carolina. Finally they arrived in Salisbury, the county seat of Rowan County, with its new courthouse built after the war, its eight dwellings, and the pillory post that symbolized, amid the wilderness, its expectations of law and order.

This caravan of Stephenson kin was not alone. During the exodus after the French and Indian War, as many as a thousand wagons came through Salisbury. In fact, the transplanters were so numerous that no one was ever isolated for long on the Great Philadelphia Wagon Road. Some wagons continued south through Charlotte into South Carolina and Georgia. Instead, turning westward, the Stephenson clan used the south branch of the Yadkin River as its route into Rowan County. Here, in what early settlers called "a delicious country" of fertile undulating plains, they located in the piedmont area between the Catawba and the South Yadkin Rivers in what became Iredell County after the American Revolution and what today is the area slightly south of Statesville, North Carolina.

Some of the clan would remain here forever, to be buried in the Fourth Creek graveyard closest, in the custom of the day, to the tiny church that was the center of their community. Here in 1876 Adlai Stevenson I found family tombstones that dated from 1765, three years after their arrival. Others would stay for a time and then migrate again, this time to Kentucky, while another branch of the family moved westward into Texas.

William and Mary Stephenson settled on 339 acres on the north side of the unpredictable Third Creek, whose fresh water, despite occasional floods, was essential for their survival. Later they surveyed and claimed another 500 acres. Throughout their lives they were well known for "always taking up land," and by 1790, after they had given farms of over 500 acres to each of their nine surviving children, "Home Plantation" included 788 acres, a barn fifty-four by eighteen feet, and a house worth $200. At their death, the Stevensons—the family name respelled during the American Revolution to delete the Englishness of its "ph" and for easier pronunciation—owned over 3,400 acres and nine slaves.

Near the source of a spring, Mary and William built a simple cabin whose logs came from the nearby forests of ash, oak, and maples. Probably they used the notched horizontal log construction adopted by people of the backwoods, and undoubtedly they were helped by their relatives. Later the couple built a larger frame house in the Scots-Irish style—a plain, rectangular two-story structure, not unlike the houses in Ulster. But when Adlai Stevenson searched for his grandfather's birthplace in 1876, even the road and chimney, usually the most durable physical remnants of a colonial past, had disappeared. As he described it with characteristic nostalgia to his mother, "the house is gone, but the old trees still stand, silent witnesses that beneath their shade two generations of our kindred have lived and Gone!" Nor did the Fourth Creek church, which had also originated as a log structure in 1751, survive, although on its original site stood, by the end of the nineteenth century, a larger, more substantial brick replacement.

The clan had hoped to settle on lush pasture land such as that found in the Kentucky and Virginia bluegrass meadows, described by an early surveyor as "a pleasant savanna ground, high and dry." Instead, they found a terrain of rolling ridges and plateaus traversed by streams over nine hundred feet above sea level. Earlier settlers had designated these streams by numbers. Having no desire to use Scottish and Irish place-names—for they expected better things in their new world—they used simple descriptive titles: Hunting Creek, where the Catawba Indians killed deer, Camp Creek, where the evangelists of the Great Awakening preached, and Buffalo Branch, where the soon-to-be-extinct buffalo gathered.

Because the sandstone soil resisted the successful production of grasses and nitrogen-fixing legumes, the Stevensons became, like thousands of others in the backcountry valleys that stretched from the Carolinas to Pennsylvania, corn and wheat growers who grazed cattle and sheep on the tallgrass of the unclaimed ridges and whose hogs rooted on mast and cut timber. Corn proved their most versatile product. They roasted its ears, made hominy, pone, and bread from its kernels, and when their Presbyterian commitment to temperance wavered, alcoholic beverages. Its sheaves they fed to their animals in winter. Generations before, the Indians had burned the tough scrub, and by the eighteenth century livestock could forage in the less dense, replacement vegetation. For a time the clan hoped that timber could be marketed, as was the case in eastern North Carolina. But they needed roads to get their products to market, and the absence of transportation would become one of the reasons the clan moved again.

Mostly the Stevensons were self-sufficient, at first raising what they needed to eat and bartering for salt, finished cloth, and a few other luxuries. Eventually Mary became the head of a system of household production that fed and clothed her family. As a result they needed to buy only a few commodities. Later calculations place the cash value of her industry at $5.37 per capita in North Carolina in 1800—which for her family of nine children and three slaves amounted to over $70 a year.

At first only the need to register their livestock brands required a trip to the distant county seat of Salisbury. Isolated from outsiders, the clan in time replaced its nonspecialized farming with the labor intensive, market crop of tobacco, which yielded a greater money return per acre than did corn. The family's slaves increased in number, as did their neighbors' until by 1800 a quarter of the Iredell County population was slave. While the clan never became dependent on one crop, it nonetheless participated in the irresistible southern process that required masters to support their dependence on slaves by growing cash crops and then demanded intensive labor to produce those crops. In the backcountry of North Carolina, cured tobacco, with its high value in proportion to bulk along with its durability, was packed into hogsheads and pulled by oxen to the warehouse in Salisbury or farther eastward along primitive roads cut through forests, eventually to be sold in an international market.

The clan grew and prospered, and was misnamed Scotch-Irish, though in fact they were Scots Presbyterians who had spent thirty years in Ireland. In the process of serial migration, more relatives joined the community between the Yadkin and the Catawba Rivers. Living in what demographers have called "an open-field arrangement," they did not cluster in villages, but instead in land-rich America kept their bonds with other family members through marriage and the church. Families intermarried—the Osbornes and the Hamptons, the Stevensons and the Brevards, the Ewings and the Stevensons, and the Stevensons and the Stevensons. This practice of cousin marriage was a familiar one; in some parish registers in England and Scotland over a quarter of the brides and grooms had the same last name. The Nesbit family built a storehouse, the first in Iredell County, where they sold groceries, finished cloth, and the fermented apple cider called the ardent. The Morrisons improved their grist mill on Gardner stream, where the power of the water turned the large wheels attached to grinding presses that pulverized kernels of grain. William was called for jury duty: Mary was busy with the children.

In the inexorable twenty-four- to thirty-month cycle of conception, pregnancy, birth, nursing, weaning, and conception, Mary McLelland Stevenson delivered twelve children in twenty-four years. Her first child, Thomas, was born in Pennsylvania before the migration to North Carolina. Betsy, her last, arrived in 1780, just as the British general Cornwallis was preparing to invade North Carolina. Because this generation did not rationalize the process of reproduction and knew little of the sequences of fertility, Mary's childbearing was not remarkable. During the fourteen-month period in which she nursed her babies, Mary Stevenson most likely did not ovulate, but as soon as they were weaned, she lost her infertility and became pregnant again in a routinized process that defined the lives of women of this period and place. Given the size of the Stevenson farms, children were welcomed as little units of productivity, not, as would later be the case, as expensive items requiring capital investment.

The couple named their children after relatives—James, David, and Nancy from the McLelland side of the family; John, William, Robert, and Elizabeth from the Stephensons. Two daughters christened Mary died as infants, and the name, thereafter considered a curse, disappeared from family annals. When the clan needed to differentiate their sons and daughters from cousins, the Old Testament provided Moses, Joseph, Lamech, and, in the Osborne family that lived nearby, Adlai. The latter, the name of the son of King David's sheepherder, appears in the Book of Chronicles. Later generations of the family enthusiastically fastened on to its translation from Hebrew as "Seeker of Justice," though it may have meant "the Strong" or "My Ornament."

Then, one Sunday in June of 1780, the routine of private lives so lightly touched by public events was interrupted by the American Revolution. The Reverend James Hall, a Princeton-trained minister of the Fourth Creek church who was given to such brooding introspection that some of his congregation believed him deranged, had just begun services when a courier from the American commander Richard Caswell interrupted to announce an invasion by the British army. Citizens must now become soldiers and serve the cause; General Rutherford depended on local militia units to deny the British control of the interior, said the officer as he unwrapped the primitive maps that showed the route of Cornwallis's forces from Charleston, South Carolina, to Camden and Charlotte. In the backcountry the English expected to organize a Loyalist army of the highland Scots clustered in southeastern North Carolina.

Of course, the congregation knew about the Revolution. Although without newspapers and far from the seaboard capital of New Bern, the clan had heard of the resolves of nearby Mecklenburg County. Circulated as broadsides, these propositions served as North Carolina's version of the Declaration of Independence. "We resolve," Ephraim Brevard and others had agreed in Charlotte in 1775, "that all commissions granted by the king in the colonies are null and void" and that the people "now free and independent should hold their power independent of Great Britain."

Soon after, Rowan County's Committee of Safety affirmed that the "cause of Boston [the port had been shut down by the British in 1774] is the common cause of all communities" and that "the African trade is injurious to this colony and obstructs the population of it by freemen and prevents manufactures and other useful emigrants from settling among us." Such a condemnation of the African slave trade was unusual, although it did echo Thomas Jefferson's similar complaint, the latter omitted in the Declaration of Independence because of substantial opposition from most southern colonies.

The signers of the Mecklenburg resolutions included the Brevards and the Osbornes, who were neighbors of the clan, soon to become relatives through marriage in the next generation. Later the Brevards were acknowledged as a family of Revolutionary heroes. In fact, so many of John Brevard's eight sons served in North Carolina regiments that Loyalists burned his home in the kind of guerrilla action that disrupted the backcountry. News of this had spread to Fourth Creek, where the lowland Scots heritage of immemorial antagonism to the English had made it easy to resist Governor Josiah Martin's appeals to support the crown.

Seventeen-year-old Thomas volunteered when the first call of the Continental Congress came, in 1775. Initially North Carolina's quota had been set at nine regiments, though there would be subsequent calls for more troops. Once enrolled, Thomas fought in Virginia and then in 1777 at the Battle of Brandywine, in Pennsylvania. Wracked by dysentery, he returned home to die, like so many other soldiers, not from a British bullet but from a lethal microorganism.

After Thomas's death, for a time the American Revolution remained remote to the clan. But then British forces took Charleston, South Carolina, in the winter of 1780, and after a brief interlude Cornwallis, their new commander in the south, marched in a northwesterly direction toward Rowan County in order to join up with the local Tories and, in a grand campaign intended to end the rebellion, split the southern colonies of Georgia, South Carolina, North Carolina, and Virginia from those in the north.

Alerted to the danger in 1780, the Reverend James Hall barely hesitated before taking the pulpit to preach what this generation of Americans came to know as a "war sermon." First he exhorted the people to take up arms and fight for their liberties, and then, in the connection that reverberated from pulpits throughout the colonies, he linked the mustering of the militia against the British to God's will, a command, as it were, from providence. At the end of the service, with Hall in the lead, ten members of the congregation, including fifty-five-year-old William Stephenson and two of his sons, rode off to Ramsour's Mill, where they joined a militia unit that included nearly one hundred men from the area. Later, for like most endeavors this was a family affair, twelve-year-old James Bell Stephenson drove his father's wagons filled with provisions for the militia to the battlefront at Guilford Court House, where Cornwallis expected to gather supplies and weapons at nearby Hillsborough.

Ramsour's Mill, Cowan's Ford, and Guilford Court House were neither the most nor the least significant of Revolutionary battles. The outnumbered North Carolina militia temporarily stopped the forward advance of the British, and the Americans retained territory, resources, and morale. Still, these engagements were bloody enough: thirteen men from the Statesville region were killed at Ramsour's Mill. Young William was wounded, but he recovered in time to fight at Cowan's Ford and again in the spring of 1781 at Guilford Court House, this time as part of General Nathanael Greene's army.

The latter was hardly a triumph for the Americans, for in the ancient reckoning of victory the British retained the battlefield. Still, the British commander Cornwallis recognized that such victories were destroying his army, and in Carolina legend he was quoted as saying that he had never seen such fighting since "God made me. The Americans fought like demons." Later that year Cornwallis surrendered his army to George Washington at Yorktown, and the Revolution ended for most Americans. There were still confrontations in the backcountry, but in time the clan celebrated peace and the assurance of independence from the British. No matter what the importance of the clan's contributions to the military, in their carefully crafted family history the Stevensons were at the center of the essential public episode of their generation.

Gradually national events receded in importance in the area between the Creeks. Private matters such as land purchases and the children's marriages replaced public issues for the Stevensons of newly created Iredell County. The only one of their sons to attend college, William and Mary's sixth son, Robert, enrolled in the faraway College of New Jersey in Princeton, where Presbyterian doctrines prevailed in a curriculum designed to train ministers. James Bell, the fourth son, and his younger brother Joseph married the Brevard sisters of nearby Burke County and, adopting familiar routines, supported their families by farming.

By 1800, when only thirty farms in Iredell County comprised over a thousand acres, the Stevensons—father and sons—owned three of them. At a time when two-thirds of the landowners in the county owned less than four hundred acres and only 16 percent owned slaves, the Stevensons owned twelve slaves and thousands of acres in a tricounty area. Their circumstances belie the traditional view that frontier life in the new Republic created a rough economic equality in the backcountry. Members of a wealthy elite, they measured themselves against the largest property owners of North Carolina. And because they were never the richest of these, in what became a family practice, they held fast to their sense of themselves as simple, middling farmers. Nor in this age of patrician leadership based on political deference to the "best men" did they challenge other leading Iredell County families such as the Osbornes and Nesbits for the elective positions of county clerk, state representative, or sheriff. The male members of the clan did accept appointive positions, and for a time James Bell Stevenson was the local tax collector.

Instead, it was the Fourth Creek church, where William was elected an elder, rather than the courthouse in Statesville that was the focal point of their public lives. Before the Revolution a census located 196 families within ten miles of the church, nearly one-half of whom had the same surnames. By the 1790s the radius of congregants had widened. There was talk of building a new church to accommodate the families whose trip to services now took almost a day. To those who no longer attended, William recounted the story of his own flagging spiritual zeal, and its renewal after he heard George Whitefield's gospel preaching at a camp meeting outside of Philadelphia and later in North Carolina.

The peripatetic English-born missionary Whitefield was on his way to Georgia from Pennsylvania on his sixth visit to the colonies when he came through western North Carolina, bringing his evangelical message of God's grace. For years Whitefield, who intended to make the world his parish and whose sermons were available even in the backcountry, had spread similar doctrines in informal out-of-door meetings to Christians in England, Ire-

land, and Scotland. Now ranging up and down the frontier from New
England to Georgia, the charismatic preacher offered stirring possibilities
of redemption and reaffirmation for lapsed Christians. William Stevenson
was attracted by Whitefield's advocacy of a faith that had grown cold and
remote to some in the Fourth Creek parish.

When Whitefield died in 1770, he left behind a religious tradition of
camp meetings in Iredell County. In 1801 William was one of hundreds
who gathered during a spring snowstorm at Camp Creek, where a clearing
in the woods served as an outdoor amphitheater. As described a century
later by his great-grandson Adlai, "first there was the discovery of a convenient spot near a spring or brook, then the making of a rude pulpit and for
many miles around and even from neighboring counties the people came
on horseback, in wagons and on foot. Each family furnished its own tent,
the needed bed clothing, cooking utensils and abundant provisions for their
temporary sojourn in the wilderness."

Warmed by the preaching of fourteen Presbyterian ministers, three
Methodist ministers, and one Baptist minister, the assembled throng listened to the nondenominational word of God delivered from a six-foot
stand to a "number of exercised persons." Some came forward to be rebap-
tized; others discovered the presence of the Holy Ghost; all accepted an
emotional religion that rejected the dour message of inherited sin and predestination and instead emphasized personal salvation.

These camp meetings of the Second Great Awakening divided the family
and split the Fourth Creek congregation. William, a "Blue-Stocking" Presbyterian who prayed five times a day, said grace before each meal, and
spent his Sundays in solemn devotions that prohibited any secular activity,
including cooking, feared the religious "backsliding" that the frontier
encouraged. Having conquered his doubts, he argued against what he and
others called the "Dry Bones" Presbyterianism of textual exegesis, formal
service, and tedious "manuscript" sermons. Supporting the impassioned
search-for-soul revivals, he emerged as a religious leader in the clan.

Although Presbyterians often held services outdoors, Mary Stevenson's
brother John McLelland detested what he considered the frenzied displays
of camp meetings. His faith, as he argued to his brother-in-law, was more
than recurring conversion experiences intended to stamp out sin, retrieve
the faith of the wavering, or even improve behavior. Like many other Presbyterians, the brothers (who disdained the distancing refinement of adding
in-law to their relationship) disagreed over a vital community issue of their
time and place until, like a summer storm that moves on, the great revivals
disappeared from the community after 1805.

In the meantime, when the Reverend Hall could not preach (for the
reverend was often distracted, rendered speechless by what the congregation called "the deaf and dumb devil," or leading services at another

church), William Stevenson, acknowledged as "gifted in prayer" by the clan, took the pulpit to deliver impassioned, two-hour sermons to the Fourth Creek congregation. In his family's biblical reference he became "Little Gabriel"—the founding father of one branch of the clan in America, a storyteller of short stature and resonant voice, whose parables of restlessness, of fierce ambition, and of strong faith in family and God were offered as directives to his children. He had acceded to a status known in the borderlands of Britain as the rule of the thane, whereby authority "was conferred . . . upon the eldest and worthiest among the surviving kinsmen."

In the will that William Stevenson wrote four years before his death in 1809, along with the division among his wife and children of property that included slaves, he left his Bible and prayer book to his youngest son, Moses. He also left a prayer that "my children and my children's children to the last generation may be followers of my master and when the time shall be no more may we all be united in Thy Heavenly Kingdom."

He did not expect his children to be followers in Iredell County, for like family and farming, religion was movable. And while William Stevenson's will favored his sons, his three surviving daughters were not omitted. Nor, in contrast to English practice, where patterns of dynastic discrimination encouraged deference to a father's authority and guaranteed entailed estates and the primacy of the eldest son, did the division of his property require his offspring to stay in the county to inherit his farms. Instead, the land that comprised his legacy had become a commodity of exchange in the marketplace, not, as it had been in Scotland, an ancestral patrimony.

Only two Stevensons of the nine who survived into adulthood—William (called Young Billy by the clan) and John, the eldest of his surviving sons, remained in the community throughout their lives. Generations later, when Adlai Stevenson of Bloomington was tracing his roots in western North Carolina, he came to Statesville, the town closest to the Third Creek community of the eighteenth century. "Getting out of the omnibus at the tavern door, I saw a man leaning against a store door upon the opposite side of the street. I inquired who he was and was promptly told Adlai Stevenson. I thought from his appearance, he was a relation, but I had no idea it was myself!"—though of course "myself" was the grandson of his great-uncle John Stevenson, who had remained in North Carolina.

3

ATTRACTED BY NOTICES of better land, James Bell and Nancy Brevard Stevenson and their nine children made plans to join a pilgrimage of kin headed toward Kentucky, where the clan intended to reestablish a colony of relatives. In their forties, James and Nancy might have remained sheltered during their old age by the established family community in which both had been born and raised, and where in 1800 they owned 709 acres, a barn thirty-four by sixteen feet, and a house valued at $115. But they were Stevensons accustomed to the family practice of migration. The same restlessness and desire for better land that had propelled their ancestors across the Irish Sea and the Atlantic Ocean and through the forests to North Carolina now impelled them to move.

Like their ancestors, they had economic reasons to do so. After a half century of steady cultivation, their lands were declining in fertility. Meanwhile the persistent pleas of backcountry politicians for better roads had gone unanswered for decades in the state legislature at Raleigh, at the same time that the economics of slavery required that they produce marketable agricultural products. By no means were the Stevensons unique. Between 1790 and 1815, some 200,000 other North Carolinians left the state, nearly all headed westward.

In an established pattern of family movement, scouts went first to explore Kentucky, the state that some called an "American Eden" and where a population of 73,000 in 1790 burgeoned in twenty years to 400,000. From other North Carolinians they heard of the bluegrass meadows around Lexington and the central counties where lush, cleared land for the raising of the market crops of tobacco and hemp was available. But at fifteen dollars an acre the price was too high. Instead, the clan chose the Pennyrile region (named for the fragrant wild mint along its streams) in southern Kentucky along the Tennessee border, where the Cumberland River promised good transportation.

As their grandfathers had a half century before, they waited until the frontier was quiet. Again the English and Americans were fighting, and the War of 1812 made travel uncertain. Some fighting had already taken place in the backcountry, and there had been reports of attacks by the followers of the Shawnee Prophet and Tecumseh. In nearby Rowan County supporters of the war had called for volunteers; in Salisbury the community had hastily built a barracks. Some clan members had signed up. By 1813 one of Adlai Osborne's sons had been killed, defending Alabama's Fort Mimms from a British attack.

In 1816, two years after the Treaty of Ghent, ending the war, had been signed and five years after General William Henry Harrison had destroyed Tecumseh's fort at Tippecanoe, Indiana, the Stevensons posted notices that their North Carolina "property of wheat, oats, rye, corn and some fattening hogs, beef cattle and household furniture" was for sale. Their seven slaves they took with them. In the midst of a postwar depression, two Ewing, one Sherrill, two McKenzie, and three Stevenson families undertook the long journey—led by Moses.

For eighty miles and nine days, they traveled along "the Western Path," which had earlier served as a route for those trading with the Catawba and Cherokee Indians. The clan followed this familiar path—though it was no more than an animal trace—to its intersection with the French Broad River, where the families moved slowly along the river banks. In summer when the water was low, the cobbled river bed was easily forded, and the caravan tracked it to the Holston River and the Old Wilderness Road that became a highway for thousands of Americans during the great tobacco rush into Kentucky. Here the corrugated hills and ridges to which they were accustomed gave way to the low mountains of the southern Appalachians. Thick brush and vegetation—a tangle of canebrake, honeysuckle, rhododendrons, and scrub pines—barred the way. As these land pilgrims moved into the Blue Ridge Mountains, the forests of hickory, chestnut, and oaks with thirty-foot diameters described by Daniel Boone as "so wild and horrid that it is impossible to view without terror" were replaced by stony ledges, gorges, and water falls. Some of the horses went lame; all suffered from a lack of forage. "One nag got a little lazy in crossing the Blue Ridge Mountains," reported James Stevenson.

They forded the Powell and Clinch Rivers before this fork of the Wilderness Road reached the renowned Cumberland Gap, the great portal through the Appalachians. What had been no more than a path had been improved, but even after the Kentucky legislature provided state funds for its widening in 1795, the Wilderness Road—named for its absence of houses and its association with the children of Israel—remained rocky, rough, and narrow. Here, more than 1,600 feet above sea level, the clan gazed westward on the rolling mountains covered by pine trees that seemed, to many travelers of this generation, to extend forever.

As they climbed down the mountains onto the Kentucky plateau, the families still had to travel more than two hundred miles to their destination in Christian County. Most settlers—and as many as 200,000 came through the gap between 1790 and 1820—took the northern branch of the Wilderness Road leading to Danville and Harrodsburg and then to the river port of Louisville. Too early for the steam-powered boats that transformed Kentucky travel, the clan members instead floated down the Ohio and then the Cumberland River on a barge, disembarking at Clarksville, Tennessee, where they followed either the Cumberland Lake Falls Trail or an Indian path to Russellville. In either case the final part of the overland trip passed through a menacing wilderness before they reached their new home outside of Hopkinsville, Kentucky, the county seat of Christian County.

"We arrived in good health," wrote Annie Ewing Stevenson in 1817, displaying the sanguine spirit necessary to sustain such an enterprise, "with as much safety as traveller that ever travelled." Not everyone was as pleased as Annie and Moses Stevenson after months of living in wagons and canvas tents. Cousin Sally, Annie Stevenson reported, seemed unable to forget

North Carolina, and the often sickly and sometimes morose James Bell Stevenson struggled with a series of infirmities.

For at least a year they rented a plantation, waiting for prices to fall in the depression of 1819 and wanting to find adjacent farms for the individual families of the kinship. They had intended to exercise a claim on cheap government lands, using their dead brother Thomas Stevenson's veterans claims, but the bounty land was too marshy. Eventually they bought one thousand acres from Judge Broadnax—choice tobacco and grazing land, Annie reported, at three dollars an acre "with every necessity, buildings and an excellent spring handy . . . a half mile east of Brother Stevenson, ten miles from town." Seeking to persuade those who had stayed behind to join them ("come along now" was the constant refrain), the Kentucky kin emphasized the availability of the "fresh land" that no longer existed near Third Creek in North Carolina.

In the letters that served as a counterpart to the "America letters" encouraging overseas immigrants to come to the United States, the Stevensons wrote of "more bags of coffee and barrels of sugar than you have pounds of either in Iredell and plenty of everything to use with it (thanks to the Giver of all good for it)." They celebrated "friendships among neighbors here that the people in Carolina know nothing about. May it ever be a fresh spur to move you to Kentucky if you ever intend coming as land is rising fast in this country." They advertised mills, constant money-makers available in the Pennyrile for $2,000. Mostly they boasted about the land that had been the principal motive for their migration: "I would not begrudge 5 dollars if you could see my corn fields this day," wrote one of the clan to a relative still in North Carolina.

For the next thirty-six years members of the Kentucky branch of the family moved from log cabins to clapboard houses, married, went to church and school, disciplined and trained their slaves, grew the gummy, heavily nicotined tobacco of the Pennyrile along with some corn, took the former to the Clarksville warehouse for shipment to Louisville and tried to sell the latter in town, bore children, ran their households, got sick and died, some of old age and others from accidents like that of James Stevenson's brother-in-law Andrew McKenzie, the husband of Betsy, who drowned in a flood. Still its own little commonwealth, the family supported its needy widows, Sophia Ewing and Betsy McKenzie, and their children. "These of our kindred," Adlai Stevenson wrote in 1876, "have dwelt upon the same spot, tilled the same old fields, drunk from the same spring, and worshipped in the same church their fathers and our fathers did. . . ."

Theirs were the repetitive task-oriented rural routines of most early-nineteenth-century Americans, whose lives were framed by the turn of the seasons rather than the clocks that were beginning to toll the quarter hours in the towns of America. The Stevensons and Ewings prospered, and by

1850 they were among that third of the county with personal property valued at over $2,000. Yet even with slave labor, the work was hard and complicated, as they followed the annual toil of plowing, transplanting and setting the tobacco plants, topping the blossoms, harvesting, hanging the sheaths in the barns to cure, and finally stripping the leaves for marketing.

A few relatives ran for public office. James and Nancy Brevard's son John Turner Stevenson served as the constable and major of the county militia and was in charge of the lackadaisical and infrequent muster drills of farmers in the Hopkinsville courthouse square; Young Ewing (there were so many Ewings with the same first names that further description was necessary to distinguish among them) and Cousin James Stevenson were elected to the Kentucky legislature; a few relatives joined the westward tide rushing northward into Illinois. But most stayed for a generation.

On Sundays they practiced their Presbyterianism in the log cabin Blue Water church and later at the Old Lafayette church, where the familiar service, even without Little Gabriel's sermons, provided continuity amid new surroundings. Because their church government required the election of governing elders along with trials for misbehavior, their religious life mimicked the self-governing procedures of the local, state, and national governments, which only rarely touched their lives.

The Stevensons brought with them, in addition to their religion, their family remembrances. On some days, as Adlai I later described, "memory was busy," serving as a means of finding coherence amid their displacement. To keep their history, the Stevensons filled letters with stories of births, weddings, sicknesses, and deaths and made sure that anyone traveling within miles of homeplace in Iredell County carried their news. Incorporating their past into vivid stories, they kept alive their family history.

After six years in Christian County and the death of her husband, Adlai, Sophia Ewing wrote such a kinship letter to her sister who had stayed in North Carolina. "Death has made wide breeches since we left our native land," she grieved, using an image that conveyed her sense of family as a fortress against misfortune. Her father had died, so had her husband and several cousins. Then "the bilious fever" had struck her young children, including thirteen-year-old Eliza. As Eliza lay near death, in the story her mother created of this deathbed scene, the young girl had suddenly rallied and provided her kin with a dramatic "near view of death," the kind of glimpse of the world beyond promised to faithful believers of the resurrection and most often delivered by expiring females to relatives gathered around the deathbed. "I am happy. I shall see my savior. He smiles, he bids me come. I shall see Pop and brother," Eliza had gasped.

Eliza recovered, and in a ceremony ten years later, in the spring of 1832, at her widowed mother's home she married a Stevenson, as did on other occasions her elder brother and younger sister. Such a process of sibling exchange knit closer the bonds of family already tightly fastened in this clan. At twenty-three Eliza was slightly older than the typical Kentucky bride, but on her wedding day she wore a white knitted snood on her head, the traditional garb of a Scottish bride.

Eliza had picked John Turner Stevenson without the interference of her relatives, who no doubt approved anyway. In the United States freedom over the choice of a husband had transformed marriage from an occasion in which parental considerations of a groom's resources and status held primacy into a personal event in which mutual attraction was important. But in the small community outside of Hopkinsville most of the boys Eliza knew were relatives or fellow pilgrims from North Carolina. Twenty-four-year-old John Turner, the fifth child of James Bell and Nancy Brevard Stevenson, was both: his uncle Moses had married Eliza's aunt, and as young children Eliza and John had traveled together to Kentucky in the family caravan of 1816—along with the slave boy Maddison, whom Eliza had inherited from her grandfather.

After her wedding, in the familiar ritual of married female life, Eliza was almost immediately pregnant. In time she bore seven children at mostly two-and-a-half-year intervals, naming them after family—first Sophia, her eldest and only daughter after her mother, and then the six boys. Adlai Ewing carried her father's name, and he was followed by James, William, Fielding, John, and Thomas, all familiar Stevenson and Ewing names carried to America by ancestors. For second names Eliza and Turner used patriotic titles like Washington and, to mark their religious preference, Calvin. Fielding, the exception, was a Ewing name. Celebrating the popular English novelist of the eighteenth century, it conveyed the literary tastes of a family that would hold education as one of its essential values.

After each birth—though she had little spare time and though there was no postal service—Eliza Ewing Stevenson wrote the clan about its newest member. In 1837, after the birth of her second son, she entrusted a letter to a stranger to be delivered to Cousin Jane Stevenson, who had married a first cousin, Joseph Stevenson, and "removed" to Illinois. Like many nineteenth-century Americans, Eliza applied the recursive prefix "re" to a process that was indeed repetitive. She had been sick, Eliza wrote, and her hand still trembled from the remnants of the fever. The year's peach crop was plentiful; her eldest son, Adlai, was a white-headed blond boy who at two could say "anything he pleases." And then, because her cousins were so far away, she ended with the plaintive motto of the clan's growing dispersion: "Time nor distance can not lessen you in my estimation."

While her husband, John Turner, oversaw the fields and worried about the fluctuating price of tobacco, along with the weather and the insects, Eliza, with the help of five slaves, ran the household inside the two-story, white-washed rectangular frame house. A traditional division of labor held her responsible for the garden around the house and the milk cows as well as the domestic production of boiling, baking, washing, furnishing home-spun cloth, and child raising. Sometime in the 1840s, with both her mother and his widowed father (Nancy Brevard Stevenson died in 1841) living in the house along with the children, Eliza Ewing and John Turner Stevenson added an extension to the home they had inhabited since their marriage. What had been the front now became the back of an L-shaped clapboard house, sheltered from Kentucky's harsh summer sun by fruit trees and a giant oak and well known among the clan for its large log-finished upstairs rooms and barrel-ripened cider in the root cellar.

Later, when her grandchildren asked how she had managed this large household, Eliza, a wiry short woman with a complexion like a porcelain doll's and cheeks as ruddy and round as plums, replied with the noncha-lance of slave owners, "All I had to do was give each a little nigger his own age to pick up his things." These owned humans were also "her children" in the cruel patriarchal understanding of slaveholders of her time and place, and they lessened the family's dependence on the labor of its children, free-ing the Stevenson young for more schooling.

Still, there were times when the tobacco crop required the labor of the children, and Adlai worked on the farm with the same distaste as many other nineteenth-century boys did. Later he appropriated an oft-told Lin-coln tale to convey his displeasure when his father sent him out to the fields. In both the Lincoln and Stevenson versions, the fathers tied long strings from the plow in order to assure their sons' industry. Like Lincoln, Adlai instead fastened the string to his toe, intermittently giving a few con-vincing tugs to the line as he engaged in the sedentary pleasure of reading.

This generation of the Kentucky-born clan grew up in a seamless arrangement where community, family, church, and school fused together. The family had little contact with government officials, who in any case were usually cousins. Nor were there many outsiders. The tiny civil estab-lishment in Hopkinsville intruded only to take the census and make peri-odic tax assessments. Even the traditional nineteenth-century emblem of public life—the post office—was for years located on John Turner Steven-son's farm. For the Stevenson children kinship blurred any division between public formality and private intimacy, making politics a natural activity. Not only did the family run the school and the church, but most of the Blue Springs community, including for a time the minister and the teacher, were imports from Iredell County. There was no need to hide spon-taneous feelings or to resist the kind of self-disclosure that would soon overtake nineteenth-century public life. As a young boy Adlai Stevenson wore no masks, for everywhere he was at home, surrounded by relatives.

In church Cousin William McKenzie, whose first wife was a Stevenson and whose second was a Ewing, "lined" the hymn, using his strong baritone voice as a cantor to rehearse the melody before the congregation joined in. This same "Squire McKenzie" officiated at family weddings before these rituals became church affairs in the 1840s. Using a cardboard-backed version of "The Missouri Harmony," young Adlai learned harmony in the singing school held in his uncle Jakie's house, where for a time he boarded—though in the understanding of this family living with a relative was no different from living at home.

Fifty years after his grandfather James Bell Stevenson's death in 1850, Adlai Stevenson remembered the funeral text of family preference: "It is appointed unto men once to die." And he recalled as well two other favorite passages—the first from the New Testament Book of John, "In my father's house are many mansions," and the second, a reading from the Old Testament Book of Ecclesiasticus, chapter 44: "Let us now praise famous men." Not by chance did the kin respond to a biblical reading that recognized "our fathers in their generations—their bodies were buried in peace, and their name lives to all generations."

Meanwhile, in the local Blue Springs school where Adlai Stevenson spent much of his childhood, the stern schoolmaster Mr. Caskie, in the custom of the day, boarded with the parents of his students. Living first with the Stevensons, next the Ewings, and then other kin, Caskie presided over the same coeducational one-room classroom in the same shed-like building where Adlai's parents, John Turner and Eliza Ewing, had briefly gone to school. Here Adlai learned how to read, write, and do arithmetic at a time when less than a fifth of Kentucky's white children between five and fifteen attended school and when even in well-schooled Massachusetts only half the population under twenty was in school. And because schools do more than teach subject matter, he also learned American ways of power and authority—the latter essential aspects of the political career he would soon undertake.

At the Blue Springs school—itself a little government teaching civic postures—the schoolmaster sat on a "high perch near the spacious fireplace with his ever present symbol of authority, the rod" representing a supposedly unassailable governance. Years later Stevenson still carried the marks inflicted by Mr. Caskie's ruler, or so he joked when the old schoolteacher came to hear one of his star pupil's speeches fifty years later. Each morning they entered—"the boys making their manners scraped the right foot upon the floor and bowed low as they entered the schoolroom [while] the girls upon like occasion were equally faithful in the practice of a bewitching little curtsy" to their governor. Adlai Stevenson remembered that "the ways of the old field school [a reference to the placing of schools in unused fields] included for the act of omission as well as commission . . . the uncomfortable effect of a punishment delivered by the petty school room tyrant bestowed in the name of [doing] his duty by your parents."

Yet this despot did not have supreme authority, because the local families paid his salary. It was impossible for Mr. Caskie to be an absolute tyrant when the neighborhood controlled his housing, wages, and reappointment. No more than president to people could schoolteacher be martinet to his pupils, for it was their fathers who determined his future.

In Blue Springs as well as in other American schools, the boys sometimes barred out the schoolmaster, who, before being readmitted to the school, negotiated with student leaders about the issues—the length of the school day or perhaps the terms of punishment for delinquents. Several times during Stevenson's school years the boys had rushed to school before Mr. Caskie arrived. Piling benches against the door, they prevented his entry. Helpless before this collective form of rebellion (and with his future depending on his management of the issue), the aggrieved schoolmaster granted concessions. Power, as in the Republic at large, was limited and divided; sovereignty abided in the will of the ruled.

Like the larger community, the world of Adlai Stevenson's schoolroom consisted of a little tribe of all ages drawn from the neighborhood, although not everyone was included. None of the young Stevenson slaves attended school, in a state where teaching reading and writing to slaves had been illegal since the 1830s. Nor did the children of tenant farmers when their labor was required in the fields. Rather, Mr. Caskie's schoolroom consisted largely of young members of the clan. When he was fifteen years old, Adlai sat in the same schoolroom as his Ewing and McKenzie cousins along with his older sister, Sophia, and his younger brothers, twelve-year-old James and seven-year-old William. Of Adlai's thirty classmates, at least two-thirds were relatives.

In the 1840s these children, like others in the United States, learned a standard version of American history that celebrated the Revolution and, to a lesser extent, the War of 1812. Stories of the martial deeds of the founders filled the elementary readers and texts brought from home, for there was no budget for books in the early schools of the United States. The lessons to be learned beyond reading, writing, and arithmetic were those of patriotism and civic activism in a still-experimental political system. The heroes of the national past—and none more so than George Washington—appeared in the Blue Springs classroom, and elsewhere in the Republic, as models for a new generation of Stevensons. Recitations based on memorization of the details of Washington's military engagements marked a pedagogy that depended on a catechism to be memorized, not discussed. Lessons were repeated in unison, and when the wind blew, the students of this loud or "singing school of which we all were apart" could be heard for miles.

The Blue Springs school used monitors or special students to whom the master delegated tasks, thereby teaching the lessons of leadership to the worthy. Years later Adlai Stevenson remembered making quill pens and hearing the lessons of a younger group; he recalled as well the special favors of an orange and a new book bestowed by Mr. Caskie as rewards to his monitors. Such a process of delegating authority to pupils who exercised temporary power as preceptors inspired an understanding of shared office holding, rotation in office, and representation by untrained leaders—the same procedures that American men practiced in public life.

In 1851, when Adlai was sixteen, the Stevensons decided, again, to "remove." The reasons are uncertain, though the clan's—and the nation's—incessant mobility made it easier to consider another resettlement. Possibly the frequent cholera epidemics in Kentucky provided one propellant; rumors held that the adjacent states of Illinois, Ohio, and Indiana were healthier. More likely the depressed tobacco prices of the 1840s along with an outbreak of local violence that included battles between debtors and creditors, defective land titles, horse stealing, and several lynchings in Christian County also encouraged the family's departure. And too, the now staunchly Democratic Stevensons felt themselves outsiders in what had become a Whig party stronghold.

Like other emigrants from the Pennyrile area, the Stevensons also resented a steady transformation in which an earlier community of family farms where raising livestock and corn was mixed with tobacco production changed into a region of thousand-acre plantations worked by gangs of fifty slaves or more. By 1860 wealth and power had become concentrated among the 145 slave owners (of 979) who owned 63 percent of the slaves. Half a century earlier, land had been more equitably, though not equally, divided: 20 percent of the population owned a half of the wealth, though, as in 1850, a third of the households held no assets. As a result of the size and number of tobacco plantations, land prices rose, making it harder for the Stevenson family to buy land as their sons reached maturity and needed to purchase their own farms. The proportion of blacks to whites—10 percent in 1817—quadrupled, to 42 percent, in the 1850s, partly because of the slow growth of the white population, which had not even doubled in forty years, a figure attained by most American counties in twenty years.

To make matters worse, in 1849 the Kentucky legislature repealed an earlier prohibition on the importation of slaves. Trafficking in human beings promised to be a major enterprise as slave hunters scoured the state for prospects. By the time the Stevensons left Christian County, the popular conviction that white labor was degraded in a slave society had taken hold. To move north across the Ohio River was to leave a society that, in the thinking of many Kentucky emigrants, was polluted not only by the competition of black labor but by the very presence of African-Americans. The slogan later adopted by the Republican party—"Free Men, Free Labor, and Free Soil"—conveyed to emigrants like the Stevensons the possibility of whites living and working on soil "free" from blacks.

The Ewings—Eliza's brother John and his family—left in 1835, and other scouts had gone as well. So numerous was the clan's proposed migration that the *Hopkinsville Gazette* felt it necessary to advertise the virtues of the county in a series of editorials: "We are surprised so many citizens should come to the conclusion that their interests require them to move to other states. Call in your roving thoughts. Permit your affection to rally. No milder sky hangs over any region, no sweeter zephyr blows, no soil more kindly repays the laborer's toil where there is elbow room for a population of 14,000 in 700 square miles. Is it wealth only that lies amid a more densely settled population?"

Then, in 1850, Adlai's eighty-two-year-old grandfather James Bell Stevenson died, and another tie that kept the family in Kentucky snapped. Meanwhile the Ewings, those double cousins bound to the Stevensons through sibling exchange, sent word of McLean County's attractions. After living in several towns, including Metamora, the Ewings had settled in the central Illinois town of Bloomington, where John Ewing ran the National Hotel on Front Street and worked in a sawmill. "Tell the boys it would make their eyes dance to look over the prairies," enthused Albert Ewing. The next year the frost withered the tobacco plants, and rather than moving to the newly opened and immensely profitable cotton lands of the Southwest, the clan went north. It was a decision that for future generations would be as significant as that of their ancestors to cross the Atlantic.

4

WHEN SIXTEEN-YEAR-OLD Adlai Stevenson arrived that hot July afternoon of 1852, Bloomington was the noisest, busiest, and most crowded place he had ever been. Its population was also the most homogeneous, for the community's one hundred African-Americans were invisible as laborers, artisans, and domestic servants who supported their own African Methodist Church and lived north of town. The unnamed "Indian family" located on early maps had disappeared. Day after day the sound of hammering, the shouts from the brick and sawmills, and the repetitive clanking from spikes being driven into iron rails filled the ears of a country boy more accustomed to nature's sounds. Unlike many new Bloomington residents in the boom days of the 1850s, the Stevensons already had a place to live and a church in which to worship.

They joined relatives in the area of town known as the Kentucky district, near the grove of trees cherished on the unforested prairies. Across town lived the northerners from Massachusetts, Pennsylvania, and Ohio, who clustered in an area of town called Bloomington Junction and later after the teachers college located there, Normal. On Sundays the Stevensons walked the few blocks to the First Presbyterian Church, where Uncle Fielding Ewing was the minister. Later, when a defiantly proslavery minister replaced him, they helped organize the Second Presbyterian Church.

On the side of the only hill in town, a diminished clan now reconstituted itself in a four-block area bounded by Grove and Albert Streets and intersected by Kentucky Alley. In a small frame house next to the Ewings, Adlai Stevenson accomplished the second part of his migration. For he had not only left the slave state of Kentucky for free Illinois, but he and his family, like thousands of other Americans of this generation, had exchanged the physical labor and isolation of open-country farm life as a clan for new arrangements as individuals in a community of strangers. The Stevensons had come to town.

Outside of large cities over 50,000, the most rapid growth in the United States was taking place in villages and towns like Bloomington of fewer than 10,000 residents, and it was on farms or in such communities that most Americans lived until the twentieth century. Towns and cities accounted for nearly 75 percent of the doubling of the national population every fifteen years. Modeling these trends, Bloomington's population increased eightfold in the 1850s. By 1855 the town's first directory listed the specialists who attended its growth: three dressmakers, four cabinet-makers, a daguerrotype "artist," a clockmaker, several marble dealers, a pastry cook, and a bookseller, along with the traditional blacksmiths, grocers, and surveyors. A visitor of the time described Bloomington as "overcrowded with emigrants, land-buyers, railroad construction workers and laborers"—a place where the only public buildings remained the one-story clapboard courthouse and three churches. Even the town's several meeting halls were privately owned, though available for rent for community affairs.

In order to navigate the uncharted economic and social waters of this society, most families adapted their rural ways to the novel demands of town life. Such transformations became especially important for the young men of middle-class ambition who would no longer be farmers but who would want to know different things—how to be bankers, lawyers, doctors, and shopkeepers and "how to manage labor, manipulate credit, and set prices in such a way as to outdo . . . competitors." Adlai would require training different from the kind that had served his father, John Turner, his grandfather James Bell, and his great-grandfather William, all of whom had absorbed the necessary knowledge for farming through observation and apprenticeship to their fathers. Adlai had to support himself by providing a service grounded in an acquired skill.

The town of Bloomington—its population of 1,168 in 1850 made it no more than that—had just celebrated its twentieth birthday when the Stevensons arrived. At first the place amounted to nothing more than expectation: a survey on paper with the traditional grid arrangement of intersecting parallel streets separated by blocks of unsold lots. Earlier the Northwest Ordinance of 1785 had established an arrangement of six-mile-square townships with one subdivision reserved for schools. For twenty years a nonelected, self-perpetuating board of trustees, which in recent years included Adlai's uncle John Ewing, had run town affairs.

Before the white man came, the powerful Kickapoo nation had dominated the unending plains of central Illinois, where the grasses often reached ten feet in height. As whites encroached on their lands, the Kickapoos at first defended themselves by setting fire to the prairie grass, nourished by ancient glaciers that had flattened the land but also made it rich. During the War of 1812 Major Zachary Taylor had been driven back by just such a tactic, for once ignited, the fires rushed uncontrollably across the flat terrain. But the Kickapoo success was temporary, as the settlers wore down Indian resistance by disease, by guns, and by agreements that promised to be the whites' final claims but never were. A year after Illinois became a state, in 1818, the Kickapoos signed a treaty with the United States. And after centuries in central Illinois some were forced onto a reservation in Kansas, while a second group, refusing to recognize the sovereignty of the U.S. government, migrated to Mexico.

After the depression of 1837 several of Bloomington's promoters had gone bankrupt, and the town had barely survived as a tiny cluster of houses. Then, in 1838, with the boosterism necessary in a society in which villages rose, flourished, and vanished in three decades, what had been Blooming Grove ("Walnuts, burr oak, white oak, it looks blooming here!") renamed itself and became, as it was already known in the state legislature, Bloomington, the county seat of McLean. Town fathers anticipated that politics would enhance development, drawing judges, lawyers, clients, and private citizens to town when the courts were in session. Similarly, farmers in the surrounding area would drive their wagons to Bloomington to pick up mail, register land surveys, pay taxes, talk politics, and, if the town could attract a printer and a press, buy a newspaper.

Even after it became a county seat, Bloomington's future was not secure. There were already pleas by rival villages to take its place. With disastrous results, Vandalia in Fayette County had lost the state capital to Springfield, and if Bloomington's population did not increase, land speculators like Jesse Fell and Asahel Gridley would move on to more flourishing towns. Out-of-state speculators had already formed land companies to transplant entire colonies of easterners to nearby areas like Hudson, where a share of stock purchased for $235 entitled its owner to 160 acres of prairie land, 20 acres of timberland, and four lots in the proposed town.

To compete with such towns and to combat the open-country residence patterns that, in fertile McLean County, sprinkled a population of 10,000 in 1860 over a vast territory of over a thousand square miles, Bloomington's founders began an advertising campaign in eastern newspapers as well as in the foreign-language pamphlets circulated by agents in Germany and Ireland. Their town, the advertisements boasted, was the seat of justice of McLean County, was located near fine prairie land and good timber, with good water, and overall was "among the most beautiful towns in Illinois." But no matter what its self-proclaimed virtues, everyone knew that the future of landlocked Bloomington depended on the railroads. And on some maps the route first proposed to Congress in 1848 showed the line connecting Galena in the north to Cairo in the south of the state passing a ruinous ten miles northwest of town. Then, in 1851, after the Whig state senator who had defeated Uncle John Ewing—Asahel Gridley—had harangued the legislature, that body approved a route through Bloomington.

Less than a year after the Stevensons' arrival, two railroad lines were completed through town, and there was talk of another, which would connect the emerging rail center of Bloomington to Kankakee, on the Indiana border. For months residents had ridden out to observe the progress of the Irish laborers, who earned $1.25 a day and lived in tents alongside the wooden ties that they arranged by hand on a roadbed smoothed by horse-drawn barrels rolled over the line. The iron rails and track came from the East, as did the original investors, who, within the year, received a 7 percent return on their investment in the state-chartered Illinois Central Railroad. When the line was complete, in May 1853, a community celebration inaugurated Bloomington's growth insurance. Nearly the whole town gathered for a public ceremony at the depot, the latter a place of excitement where residents gathered for years to look at the huge clock that now measured their waking hours and to listen for the whistles that seemed to bring messages of faraway places. The most courageous male citizens (for the railroads would for many years remain public terrain forbidden to respectable females traveling alone) rode the horseless cars at twenty-five miles an hour to the next station of La Salle, amid whistles, bolting horses, and the flag-waving usually reserved for the Fourth of July.

Turner Stevenson already knew the importance of the railroads. The sawmill in which he was a partner furnished railroad ties "of good white or burr oak" to the Illinois Central as well lumber to the railroad repair shops, which, accompanying the railroads, soon employed 150 men "out west of Bloomington." With the population of the town doubling every two years and 250 houses under construction by 1855, the Stevenson-Flagg sawmill made additional profits by selling finished boards for the houses that filled in the empty squares created by the parallel arrangement of streets; these were named in Bloomington and elsewhere on the prairies like a crossword puzzle, presidents' surnames on the east–west axis and trees on the north–south axis.

More original than most, Bloomington's trustees included directions as names for their future thoroughfares. Somehow the vast homogeneity of the flat prairie expanse demanded spatial definition. Accordingly Center, East, North, and West Streets intersected with those bearing presidents' names, at first only Washington, Jefferson, Madison, and Monroe, but later, and out of order, also Jackson and Taylor. Honoring the American political system that furnished a stable mechanism for the creation of new communities with rights equal to those in the East, town fathers recognized another critical resource. Streets that remained muddy, impassable byways until the twentieth century thus bore the names of trees such as Grove, Olive, Locust, and Chestnut.

For a time during the summer and fall of 1852, Adlai Stevenson worked at the sawmill, lugging boards to huge piles of cut lumber and loading others on a wagon that carried them to a nearby shingle factory. He hated this work as much as he had despised tobacco cultivation, and the family's new-monied prosperity permitted him to return to school again.

In the fall Adlai Stevenson entered his brother-in-law Reverend McCaughey's school, at the corner of Monroe and Oak. The next year his parents paid the impressive annual tuition of twenty dollars (five dollars a quarter for the special college preparatory classical course) at Lemuel Foster's new Presbyterian academy. He attended with his double first cousin and next-door neighbor James Stevenson Ewing, but for the first time most classmates were not members of the clan. Nor were they of Scots or Irish or Presbyterian or even southern background; instead, because Bloomington was a crossroads, the classroom brought together the children of the pioneers, along with the offspring of mid-Atlantic Congregationalist and Quaker families that were marching across Ohio and Indiana into central Illinois. Diluted at school, some folkways of the clan's southern heritage were reaffirmed in the after-school sessions at Dr. Hobbs's dancing academy where, attired in vest and tailcoat, the Virginia-born dentist taught dance steps, manners, and the perpetuation of the soft viscous accents that southerners like the Stevensons had brought with them to Bloomington. (When Hobbs died, he left, according to one obituary, "no enemies, many debts and twenty-seven satin vests.")

Along with the novelties of dancing class, a music emporium, and a barbershop, Adlai Ewing Stevenson discovered politics in Bloomington. In the partisan realignment of the 1850s, American men surrendered their twenty-year attachments to the Whigs and Democrats and, in a process of reshuffling, joined new organizations like the anti-Catholic, anti-immigrant Know-Nothings. So many Illinoisians shifted their support to temporary coalitions that the Illinois legislatures in the 1850s included an unpredictable array of self-designated Know-Nothings, Anti-Nebraska Democrats, Free-Soilers, Temperance and People party's advocates as well as Whigs and Democrats.

In this new political world familiar disagreements over tariffs and internal improvements were replaced by debates over the extension of slavery into the territories, the practicability of the Illinois senator Stephen Douglas's plan for popular sovereignty, and a legitimate constitution for the Kansas territory. Political differences also featured topics such as drinking and religion. In Bloomington the Catholicism and national origins of the Irish and German workers who lived on the west side of town, and who by 1860 represented a quarter of Bloomington's population, came under fire from the Know-Nothings, who called for longer naturalization periods for immigrants and an end to the pope's suspected efforts to dominate the American Republic.

In Christian County, Adlai had lived too far in the country to observe the excitement of campaigning and voting, but in Bloomington during the 1850s "politics was in the air everywhere." Not only had young Stevenson arrived during the presidential campaign between the Democrat Franklin Pierce and the Whig Winfield Scott—just in time to hear Abraham Lincoln's speech favoring the Whigs—but his father ran and was defeated and ran again and was elected to the Bloomington town council. Then Uncle John Ewing was successful in his campaign for mayor of Bloomington in 1854, and in that year and again in the presidential year of 1856 two of the greatest American politicians of this age—Abraham Lincoln and Stephen Douglas—addressed crowds outnumbering Bloomington's population. Adlai Stevenson and his ever-present companion James Ewing listened from a second-story railing, and later they eavesdropped on the first convention of the Illinois Republican party, which met in Bloomington in May 1856. In John Ewing's hotel they heard the partisan debates that accompanied the lawyers of the Eighth Judicial Circuit to town, and several times Stevenson called on his hero Stephen Douglas for advice about a career in public life, imagining that he too might become a political hero from central Illinois.

Enveloped by public affairs, Stevenson came of age in an active political culture that offered elections as the best entertainment in town. In Bloomington, as elsewhere in the United States, established partisan routines began with ratification meetings after the nomination of a candidate, progressed during the late summer and fall with pole raisings (in 1856 the 112-foot Democratic pole with a Buchanan banner on top soared over the countryside until the Republicans found it untended one night and cut it down), and culminated with serenades, picnics, barbecues, and mass rallies. The climax occurred during election week when the faithful paraded as an army to the courthouse in symbolic prediction of their forthcoming victory. Such festivities underwrote the huge turnouts of between 80 and 85 percent of the electorate who cast ballots in the incessant campaigns for local, state, and national office. Politics in Bloomington was not only everywhere in the community; it also went on all the time.

In 1854 nineteen-year-old Adlai and James enrolled in another family-influenced institution—Illinois Wesleyan University. Uncle John Ewing had helped to organize the college whose name, at least in the 1850s, reflected its aspirations rather than its reality. Yet it provided an essential tool for young men like Stevenson. Along with academic subjects necessary for further professional training, Illinois Wesleyan offered the handful of male scholars who gathered in the basement of the Methodist church the basic rudiments of middle-class manners. As an investment in Adlai Stevenson's future, his schooling was worth the tuition, some of which he earned himself by "boarding around" as a teacher for twenty-five dollars a semester.

Earlier Stevensons who expected little change in their lives hardly needed the kind of education advertised by the university. "We urge it upon parents, to send us their sons," advised a Wesleyan circular, ". . . better forego their help upon your farms, and in your shops, and hire the necessary labor . . . and bear the expense of their labor than when you leave the world leave them uneducated and unqualified to manage your estates, or accomplish your incomplete plans and purposes of life. Better that you should spend the half of your estates that they may the more advantageously manage when you are gone." Initially too few parents heeded the warning, and in 1855 a bankrupt Illinois Wesleyan temporarily closed.

Before it did, Adlai Stevenson wrote an essay on the visit to the United States of the Hungarian rebel Louis Kossuth, "the great Champion of freedom who has come to ask our aid in a great and noble cause." Kossuth, forced into exile after his uprising had been crushed by the Russian and Austrian monarchs in 1849, had come to the United States for money to revive his independence movement. Throughout Illinois, citizens used the occasion to resolve that "any people have the right to throw off the existing government." Kossuth's cause was a popular one, especially praised by Democrats, despite some sentiment that Americans should remain apart from European squabbles.

Young Adlai felt no such reservations, and on lined paper in careful slanting script that later became illegible, he encouraged support for the Hungarians in their efforts to win independence. With what became an enduring enthusiasm for democracy, its heroes and its practices, he spoke of "the need for the United States to help others and send money for the glorious cause of human liberty and man's redemption. If it be asked what right have we to interfere with the affairs of other nations, we could ask if France hadn't a right to assist us in gaining our liberty which we probably never could have gained without her interference. Besides this we hold to be the model nation of the earth. . . . Would the Father of our country look down from Heaven and behold his countrymen engaged in extending the work of human liberty, methinks he would have shed tears of joy."

After Illinois Wesleyan shut down, Adlai's parents made the unusual decision to send their son to faraway Centre College, a Presbyterian college in Danville, Kentucky, where he might gain the necessary entry card into a profession and simultaneously retain some of his Kentucky heritage. In the fall of 1856 Adlai Stevenson left Bloomington with his cousin James Ewing. Obediently he wasted no time sending word to his parents of his safe arrival: "It gives me great pleasure to inform you that I am at last safely established in Danville." He shared the embarrassment that, at twenty-one, he was the oldest in his class and had failed the Latin and Greek reading and translations for entry into the junior class. Still, he assured his parents that the other students treated him "kindly and courteously." And he had passed the orals on Caesar's *Commentaries* and Virgil's *Eclogues* necessary for enrollment in the sophomore class of an institution that advertised "standards as high as those of the oldest and most flourishing institutions of the east." Later Adlai Stevenson would be remembered by a classmate as bright, handsome, and "inclined to frolicsome [activities] and giving no promise of any particular prominence," the last an assessment that haunted his grandson as well.

The Presbyterians had chartered Centre College in 1819, during a time when only those intending to enter the ministry bothered with higher learning. But the white-collar jobs and professions in midcentury towns required more schooling, and an increasing number of Centre's alumni (of whom there were 572 by 1860, including 145 ministers) were no longer ministers but earned their livings as lawyers, planters, judges, physicians, or business men. Sensitive to the change, the college instituted a practical science and mathematics program for future businessmen that did not concentrate, as did the traditional curriculum intended to cultivate gentlemen, on Greek and Latin.

For all its prestige, the college's future was never assured, because its enrollment oscillated dangerously. In the 1820s some classes registered two and three students. But Adlai's class of 1859 included 44 undergraduates, who, along with 143 classmates, studied the standard classical curriculum of Horace, Homer, Virgil, and Plato's *Gorgias,* along with trigonometry, nautical astronomy, and, in an acknowledgment of the importance of practical subjects, surveying—all taught by a faculty of six professors. Required to study seven of every twenty-four hours, Adlai and his classmates memorized their readings and repeated them in formal class recitations held in the college's only building, a sturdy brick Greek Revival edifice whose Ionic columns replicated the curriculum's preoccupation with the classical period.

At Centre, Adlai joined one of the debating societies that, like American political parties, divided the college into two competing parts. Now began a career in public speaking that lasted throughout his life, as he argued in the required oratorical style such nonpartisan matters as "Should women receive the same amount of education as men?" and "Are republican governments more favorable to the cause of learning than monarchies?"

Most of Adlai's classmates were from the South, most were Presbyterians, and all had come to an institution that promised effective discipline. This last was not the case, according to Centre's catalogs, "in many institutions. Three and four years have passed without the necessity of any exercise of discipline beyond the admonition of one or two students." Such claims of law and order were notable, for increasingly American college students rebelled against college authorities in acts so organized as to merit names. Graduates of Harvard distinguished between the Great Rebellion of 1832 and the Uprising of the Rotten Cabbage. Those at Yale spoke of the Bread and Butter Riot. Few colleges managed to avoid some form of the collective disobedience that had its roots in the efforts of students of this generation to attain more professional training for the jobs required of middle-class breadwinners. Latin may have stretched the minds and sensibilities of students as well as provided background for future ministers, but it was increasingly irrelevant for a new generation of American men who sought commercial and business careers.

Adlai Stevenson had completed only two semesters at Centre when forty-nine-year-old Turner Stevenson died suddenly in the spring of 1857, perhaps from cholera, the dreaded bacterial intestinal disease haunting Bloomington that year. Or perhaps his father's death was the result of the anxiety of running a sawmill when the trees required for his business were rapidly disappearing from his grove and a depression had settled onto Bloomington and the nation. Evidently Turner's partnership in the sawmill ended with his death, and the family provider left no provisions for the continuing education of his sons. Suddenly widowed, Eliza could no longer afford either her eldest son's absence or his yearly tuition and boarding bill of seventy dollars.

Like many men of this generation, John Turner Stevenson left all his assets to his wife and did not, as both his father and grandfather had done, divide them differentially among his sons and wife. But unlike the land and slaves of his ancestors, his sole asset—the house on Albert Street and its middle-class furnishings, including a map of the world, a hatrack, a parlor carpet, a looking glass, four stoves, and ten cane-back chairs—produced no income. He had foreseen the possibility of his widow's having to move in with the relatives who, in Illinois as in Kentucky and North Carolina, provided a shield against misfortune. "If rents, interest and profits are not enough for comfortable support, you can sell the homestead where we now live," he advised in his will.

Leaving James Ewing to graduate, Adlai returned home to become the head of a family of five younger brothers, none of whom would attend college. The abrupt termination of his college years instilled a lifelong nostalgia for the classics and the carefree life of students. But his father's death left him searching for paternal figures, some of whom he located among the leading politicians of his time. Lacking any familial model, he had to find something to do, which would amount to what he would be. In the East another young man provided the motto for Stevenson's predicament: "What a tremendous question it is! What shall I be?" wondered Charles Eliot about a question that Adlai Stevenson of Bloomington had to answer quickly.

5

IN 1859 BLOOMINGTON'S grandly and classically named newspaper the *Pantagraph* listed fourteen lawyers who competed for the insufficient business of the Eighth Judicial Circuit. There, near the top, appeared the card of Adlai Stevenson. Influenced by Lincoln and Douglas, he had chosen his future and in just a year had read enough Blackstone and Chitty under the supervision of his mentor and future partner Robert Williams to qualify, after an informal oral exam before several attorneys, as a lawyer. In this period the law was still a craft handed down from one practitioner to another. It would be another thirty years before the American bar, controlling admission to the profession, developed schools for specialized training and codes of ethics.

Now entering a professional community, he hosted the traditional supper for his future colleagues and competitors, and advertised a practice before the circuit court in the county seats of Bloomington, nearby Metamora, in Woodford County, and more ambitiously, before the federal courts in Chicago and Springfield. The camaraderie and conviviality of lawyers was well established among members of the bar, who possessed a sense of themselves as a special group, bound together by their work and knowledge. Good-fellowship extended beyond the courtroom, where, in their abundant free time (for clients were sometimes hard to come by), lawyers listened to each other's passionate summations and furious cross-examinations. After hours they traded stories and political tales in the local hotel where plaintiff, defendant, judge, prosecutor, and defender often shared beds as well as dinner plates, all the while complaining of bad food and greasy tablecloths.

Sometime during 1858 Adlai Stevenson moved with his twenty-five dollars' worth of lawbooks, four pairs of socks knitted by his mother, two shirts, a change of clothes, and a tin shingle to Metamora, the tiny community whose prospects he and its population of nine hundred expected to rival those of Bloomington, that is, if the railroad came. In a town where several cousins had already settled, Adlai Stevenson lived for the next decade, first in Mrs. Whitmire's boardinghouse for $2.50 a week (laundry included) and later in a brick home, near the courthouse where he argued about the ownership of cows and the details of property lines, negotiated the claims of contesting spouses, defended clients from the complaints of their neighbors and the charges of the sheriff, and bargained over the proper compensation for personal injuries. When his practice flagged, he served as a claims agent who managed freight deliveries. He also engaged in the popular activity of speculation, buying and selling nearby land. In the large second-floor room of a still-surviving porticoed Greek Revival courthouse in Metamora's town square, Adlai Stevenson heard the illustrious circuit riders of the law, his heroes (for he was always an admiring man)—Abraham Lincoln, David Davis, Leonard Swett, and Samuel Treat. He found time to listen to Abraham Lincoln's and Stephen Douglas's political speeches during the senatorial campaign of 1858. Following their example, he began his own political career, running for town council unsuccessfully in 1858.

Like Lincoln and Douglas, Adlai Stevenson intended to be a political lawyer who filled his time and pocketbook with the sometimes meager proceeds from appointive and electoral politics. Indeed, he had settled in Metamora—along with two male cousins—because the county's attachment to the Democratic party made it more congenial than Republican McLean County. In 1859, just one year after his arrival, Stevenson ran as the Democratic candidate for state's attorney of his judicial district. Thus began a public career that lasted for forty-one years, until in 1908, as the seventy-three-year-old Democratic nominee for the governorship of Illinois, Adlai Stevenson promised voters that he would never seek office again—if they would just elect him this last time. Throughout this extraordinary political life campaigning came easily to a practiced storyteller. So did the formation of an inner circle of political managers and advisers recruited from his clan. In time politics merged with family affairs, and the Adlai Stevensons of Illinois became a public family.

Having caught the eye of prominent Democrats, he was appointed to his first patronage job as master of chancery. In this position he represented the court's interests, selling land on which taxes were unpaid (buying some of it for himself), and acting as the legal deputy of orphans. As he traveled to the dusty county seats of central Illinois, he met the public men of his time and place until it was gossiped, in the way of small towns, that "young Stevenson has the acquaintance of everyone." Then, in 1864, he was elected state's attorney for his judicial district and was also chosen, by a local convention of delegates, as a Democratic presidential elector committed to the election of George B. McClellan, Lincoln's failed general.

In the spring of 1861, just after Adlai Stevenson had begun his duties as a master of chancery, the Civil War suddenly, though not unexpectedly, began. For months newspapers in central Illinois had chronicled the events that foretold its coming—first the candidacy of Lincoln, the resident of nearby Sangamon County whose election on November 4, 1860, proved intolerable to southerners, then the secession of seven states and the formation of the new nation of the Confederate States of America in February of 1861, followed by the unsuccessful Union attempt to provision Fort Sumter, in Charleston Harbor, and on April 14 the firing by Confederates on Fort Sumter and Lincoln's subsequent call for 75,000 militia to put down the "insurrection." "War," proclaimed the Bloomington *Pantagraph* three days later, "is upon us at last. The rebels of Charleston have opened fire upon Fort Sumter, and the garrison have responded like brave men who know their duty and dare to perform it 'in the throat of death.' By the act of traitors themselves the slaughter has been begun. Shoulder to shoulder let all citizens stand in defence of the Government of our country."

And so they did in most parts of Illinois, a state that throughout the war was credited with sufficient volunteers to keep its quotas low after the enrollment act of 1863 established a draft. Not until 1864 were any Illinoisians drafted into the Union Army, and in all only 3,538 of them served as draftees, though some avoided service by paying a $300 commutation fee or finding a substitute. In Bloomington the first call for volunteers, in 1861, produced an outpouring of young men, mostly in their twenties; in nearby Normal, where the state university had opened in 1857, overnight the college president, Charles Hovey, became Colonel Hovey, as he marched a company of teachers and college students to a hastily arranged training camp on the Springfield fair grounds. Officially known as the Thirty-third Illinois Regiment, Hovey's troops soon bore the nickname "the Teachers' Regiment," and it was said that they practiced their Latin verbs along with the arms manual as they marched off to the Battle of Fort Donelson, in Tennessee.

These spontaneous, community-organized decisions to volunteer characterized the first days of the war in both the North and the South. In central Illinois hundreds of young men answered the drum taps for national duty, as volunteering revealed a spiraling process of allegiance, from familiar local connections and associations to an unfathomable dedication to the abstraction called the United States of America. In central Illinois, as elsewhere in the Union, young men were attached to family, town, county, and state—the institutions that created the wellsprings of patriotism in lightly governed nineteenth-century America.

In 1862, when Lincoln appealed again—this time for 300,000 more soldiers—over 1,200 McLean County men volunteered in less than ten days. No doubt the bounties of over $500 provided by private citizens like James Stevenson Ewing and Jesse Fell, and by the county and state governments, spurred this third harvest of recruits. A man might march off to war with three times his annual peacetime wages in his pocket, and in the process lessen the number of his neighbors who might be forced to do so. Aided by such incentives, in four years of war, an astonishing 4,325 men, or over 80 percent of McLean County's available male population between twenty and forty, signed up. In Illinois as a whole 259,000, or over 90 percent of the same age group, served, thus making a young man who did not a rarity.

In Adlai Stevenson's new home of Metamora and its surrounding county of Woodford, the reservoirs of patriotism, lower to begin with, dried up quickly. The first of Woodford County's soldiers had volunteered after a mass meeting in the courthouse square in 1861, but unable to form even a company of a hundred recruits the men had become part of a Bloomington regiment, the Illinois Ninety-fourth, and later the Illinois Forty-fourth and Seventy-seventh. Most were farm boys from surrounding Woodford County, though their ranks also included some of Metamora's gentry: a merchant, eight teachers, three clerks, a broom maker, and a butcher.

From the beginning, Woodford was less friendly to the war than the adjacent counties were. No one was surprised when McClellan won 56 percent of its votes in his presidential campaign in 1864 against Lincoln. Earlier, after the Emancipation Proclamation of 1863, the *Woodford County Sentinel*'s tepid Unionism was transformed into vehement opposition to what Democrats in the area magnified into the president's tyrannical violations of the Constitution and his "black abolitionism." Considering Lincoln a tyrant and the draft a violation of the individual liberties of Americans, the Democrats of Woodford resented the army officials who appeared in their community. Meanwhile forty miles away Republicans promoted dissent into disloyalty and held every Democratic stronghold to be the hotbed of virulent antiwar conspiracies organized as the Knights of the Golden Circle, the Order of American Knights, and the Sons of Liberty.

Twenty-five years old when the war started, Adlai Stevenson never served in the Union Army or Navy. In 1861 he was enrolled as a member of the Woodford County militia, where his status was listed as a "second-class reserve, available for service if needed." In the summer of 1863, when the Union Army desperately needed more men, having already swept up those who initially volunteered for patriotism, or to end their boredom, or to please their relatives, or to seek adventure at a time in their lives when they were still immune to any sense of mortality, an assistant provost marshal came to Metamora to enroll all men between twenty and forty for the federal draft. From these names the Illinois quotas would be drawn, and predictions were that as many as 30 percent of the list would be conscripted. In the thick leather ledgers of the Eighth District of Illinois under Class A men—that is, unmarried males between twenty and forty—the name of Adlai Ewing Stevenson, lawyer, appears.

But after the draft ended that fall (there would be three more drafts to fill the county's assigned quota of 1,655), Stevenson's name disappeared from official records, though at least one resident remembered "being with

Stevenson when his name was called." There is no official evidence that his was one of the 908 names picked from a glass bowl by a town official, or that he hired a substitute, or that he paid the blood money of $300 required for a commutation, as his younger brother William did. Nor was he exempted for medical reasons, as nearly a third of all those enrolled were, on the grounds that they had bad teeth (recruits needed strong teeth to tear the paper off the gunpowder containers used to load their rifles), or hernias, or undescended testicles.

Most likely after his enrollment Stevenson applied for an exemption on the basis that he was his mother's sole support, even though he did not live with her in Bloomington and he had five brothers. According to the law, the only son of a widow dependent on his labor for support was exempt from military duty. But there is no record of the disposition of Stevenson's case or his wartime status. Nor did he ever discuss it. The Civil War, such a full episode in so many family histories, disappeared in the Stevenson-created archive, where the unpleasant was often omitted. Still, as a public man after the war Stevenson must have regretted his choice, for he lived the rest of his life as an outsider to the political and moral touchstone of his generation.

Later Adlai Stevenson was accused of having joined the Knights of the Golden Circle, a group whose members, exaggerated in numbers and influence by the Republicans, supported the Confederacy and opposed the draft. In one affidavit signed by a neighbor, he and his invariable companion James Ewing were said to have discouraged volunteering as they rode through a country town on their way to a knights meeting, an offense punishable by imprisonment. William Whiffen, the influential editor of the *Woodford County Sentinel,* also charged Stevenson with both antiwar activities and sentiments. In other hearsay evidence after the war, when he had become a prominent Democrat, Stevenson was accused of having sold pistols to draft resisters. Yet a Union officer affirmed the young lawyer's loyalty and his support of the Union, if not of the Lincoln administration. During his political campaigns when he had to answer these indictments or risk the label Copperhead, Stevenson defended himself with circumstantial evidence by noting that he had been elected state's attorney during the war by the votes of some Republicans, who, in his logic, would never have supported a traitor.

In fact, Adlai Stevenson was a Union Democrat who had accepted Stephen Douglas's wartime division of the Union into traitors and patriots. Of course he was the latter, a member of the loyal opposition, whose service in the military was not required, given his personal circumstances. In demonstration of his loyalty, he pledged five dollars bounty money in one Woodford County rally, an act of self-interest as much as patriotism, because high bounties encouraged others to volunteer. Later in the war, according to one officer, he encouraged all men to serve, enthusiastically beseeching his neighbors to sign up and do as he said and not as he did.

Often overlooked in the attention bestowed on those who fought the Civil War were thousands of young, healthy stay-at-homes like Adlai Stevenson. In Illinois this group represented between 10 and 15 percent of the unmarried males between twenty and thirty. All had different but broadly similar reasons. And those like Adlai Stevenson who became prominent after the war passed on the stigma of noninvolvement as angry veterans charged they had stayed at home to make money. Nearly a century later, when Adlai Ewing Stevenson II was running for president, the rumors about his grandfather surfaced again. And his aunt Julia Stevenson Hardin in a letter to Buffie Ives noted "how cleverly Adlai evaded [his questioner] by citing James Polk's campaign when his enemies brought out that his grandfather was a Tory, and it had no effect on the election."

Like many other stay-at-homes, Adlai Stevenson wanted to get ahead in the perplexing competitive arena of town life. Even with the most generous bounty, a private in the Army earned $156 a year at a time when Stevenson's income was probably over $500 (though less than $600, for he paid no income tax). In Woodford County, and throughout the North, Democrats claimed that "the war was a rich man's war and a poor man's fight," though today's refined statistical analyses reveal that, in the aggregate, Civil War soldiers matched the occupational classifications of the day.

Instead, Adlai Stevenson's case was that of an ambitious young lawyer, politician, and head of family who declined to serve in order to help his mother and possibly to pay his younger brother's commutation fee. In the ancient understanding of his kin now removed to town, Adlai Stevenson had become the patriarch—the thane of the Stevensons. "Now Tommy," Stevenson advised his youngest brother in 1865, as the war was ending, "I want you to be a good boy to your mother. You are the only one left at home. Take good care of mother. If you will only be a good boy and study well, I will do all I can to make a man of you."

Stevenson was also inclined to civilian life because of his affiliation with a party whose Unionism was more conditional than that of the Republicans, because of the political culture of recusant Woodford County, which sent less than half of its available men to war, and because of his Kentucky slave-holding heritage. So Adlai Stevenson stayed in Metamora, learning his craft as a lawyer, moving into the inner circle of county Democrats, buying land, and considering marriage. To the extent that his status was the result of family responsibilities, he had resolved his dilemma by placing personal affairs before public duty. Yet the result would be an additional spur to an already well-developed appreciation of politics. Throughout his life Adlai Stevenson's insatiable public spirit could be assuaged only by the gratification of office holding, but the stories he told so well always omitted the Civil War.

CHAPTER FOUR

CALLINGS

1

WHEN LETITIA GREEN STEVENSON (1843–1913) came home to Bloomington in 1897 after four years in Washington, she began to write her autobiography. Such an undertaking was a bold endeavor for anyone. For a married woman of Letitia Stevenson's generation, it was an audacious enterprise. Certainly in the well-tended family archive, there was no lack of material. For years, as Mrs. Adlai Stevenson, she had collected notices of her husband's public life. And after his election to Congress in 1874, Adlai Stevenson had begun subscribing to the Argus Press Clipping Bureau, one of the new services that surveyed newspapers and magazines across the United States for customers who paid five dollars for every one hundred clippings about themselves.

Carefully the couple pasted these notices, along with their favorite poems and stories, into large, marble-papered, cloth-backed scrapbooks inscribed to their children. "To my son Lewis," wrote Adlai in the front of one album, "from his affectionate father, 1879," and in another, "From Adlai Ewing Stevenson to my children, Lewis, Mamie, Julia and Lettie." Letitia dedicated a volume "To my beloved daughters, from their adoring mama." Fastened with colored laces and ribbons, scrapbooks of every size accumulated in the upstairs hall bookcase.

By the 1890s when reporters interviewed Letitia about her family life and her public activities, she enthused, "I love my scrapbooks. Like a magician's wand, they transport me back to dear old scenes. . . . It is my honest belief that our keenest joys come in remembering and not in realizing the things that we hoped for. So I tell my friends to keep a scrapbook. I have one, a big bulky volume which would be a blot on the landscape in a well-appointed library but which I consider among my genuine treasures." Available for the nostalgic perusal in which Letitia and Adlai delighted, this biographical archive served as a reference book to the couple's public life and the historical source for what Granddaughter Buffie Stevenson Ives described as "the great legend of the grandparents." For the couple's four children, the scrapbooks served as unforgettable textbooks of parental achievement.

Letitia Stevenson began her life's story with that of her father, Lewis Green, a Presbyterian minister who had also been the president of Transylvania College, in Lexington, Kentucky, and later of his alma mater, Centre College. A well-known scholar descended from a collateral relative of George Washington's who, it was said, could trace his lineage to a favored bodyguard of the Plantagenet kings of England, Lewis Green was widely admired for more than his ancestry. He had conquered an inhibiting stutter to become an effective speaker, mixing college teaching and administration with his ministry. Letitia's mother, the aristocratic, twice-married Mary Peachy Fry, traced her lineage to Joshua Fry, a famous professor of classics at William and Mary. "Ah," George Washington was reported to have lamented, in the oft-told family anecdote, when Fry died on his way to battle in the French and Indian War, "under this tree lies the body of the good, the just, and the noble Fry."

Letitia also described her unusually long and rigorous education at Lexington's Walnut Hill Female Institute, a self-proclaimed "academy of the highest standing," and later in Miss Haynes's fashionable school on New York's East Twentieth Street, where the girls paraded two by two through Gramercy Park. Here she and her older sister, Julia, absorbed the contradictions of the nineteenth century's "Ladies Curriculum"—manners, sociability, and Latin. The Green sisters were commended for their aptitude in the classics, and they understood that only a handful of American women were as well educated as they. But both also knew that their foremost skill must be in finding a good husband, for the choice of a bad mate irrevocably blighted a woman's life.

In 1861 when the Civil War began, eighteen-year-old Letitia hurried home from New York to Hillcrest, the president's house shaded by elms on a slope dominating the Centre College campus. A year later Union and Confederate troops fought a great battle at nearby Perryville, Kentucky. Overnight the college became a military hospital. One day a sniper's bullet ripped through Letitia's window, scattering goose feathers from her pillow in a display of the meaningless violence that summarized the war for the Greens of border-state Kentucky. The next year Lewis Green died of natural causes, though his family forever insisted that he had succumbed from heartbreak at the disruption of his country.

With neither income nor home (for Lewis Green had saved no money and as a minister and college president had had little enough to save), Letitia and her mother traveled north to the tiny Illinois town of Chenoa, in McLean County, where Julia Green had settled after her marriage to the Kentucky-born land speculator Matthew Scott, who had also been educated at Centre College. Mother and daughter believed themselves wartime refu-gees, though their displacement reflected the perpetual uncertainties of females dependent on a male breadwinner. Rueing her exile from Kentucky, Mary Peachy Green forever blamed the Yankees. Letitia promptly forgot.

Soon she and Adlai Stevenson were courting on the Scotts' porch. In the formal letter of intention that he wrote to Mrs. Green asking for her daughter's hand, Adlai Stevenson acknowledged the Kentucky roots of his romance: "I have loved [your daughter] almost from the time I first met her. To secure her happiness will be the object of my life."

There is no record of Mary Peachy Green's response. In better days she might have wished for her younger daughter a suitor as rich as her son-in-law Matthew Scott or as pedigreed as a Kentucky Breckinridge, but her circumstances as an impoverished widow ended such pretensions. In this era only foolish parents interfered with a child's choice of mate, though according to the established rituals of Victorian courting, Letitia could not accept her suitor immediately. Instead, she must furnish some hurdle for Adlai to overcome so that he might demonstrate, along with his words of love, the strength of his attachment. Only if he passed some test could the relationship of Letitia Green and Adlai Stevenson move beyond the tempo-rary state of falling in love to the permanent condition, in this age without established divorce procedures, of marriage.

Often such obstacles included a jealous charge of a suitor's attention to another woman, perhaps after his wistful gaze at a presumed rival, or as in Letitia's case, a test of time. She had not, as she would tell her children and the inquiring reporters who later found her ideas noteworthy, accepted Adlai Stevenson "at once, but he had had to prove his constancy by waiting, for three years." Letitia also followed established courting conventions by displaying her irritation at Adlai's presence at a Lexington party where other aspirants claimed her attention. Adlai had to suffer these premarital insults during a time when Letitia exerted an authority that, after her mar-riage, would be diminished by laws rendering her civilly dead and economi-cally invisible. Later the family's generational memory included an embellished story, as told by Adlai Stevenson II, that his grandfather courted and won the hand of the daughter of the college president—"always a sound policy for a struggling student." In fact, Adlai had returned to Bloomington before Lewis Green became president of Centre.

On December 22, 1866, Letitia Green married Adlai Stevenson in her sister's front parlor in Chenoa under the handsome ceiling molding, which hinted at Julia Green Scott's expensive tastes and her husband's wealth. The bride was surrounded by Stevensons. Invited by her husband, the clan had arrived from North Carolina, Kentucky, and Illinois for a long Christmas visit. "This is to invite you and Cousin Amelia," Adlai wrote one set of relatives, "to my wedding on December 20. Though there will be a formal invitation, come and spend a few weeks with us." Adlai's uncle Fielding Ewing read the Presbyterian "words," so called because home ceremonies were not considered religious services. To friends in central Illinois the Scotts sent official notice that they were at home after eight o'clock, following the ceremony. In the custom of the day, they enclosed the engraved calling cards of Adlai Ewing Stevenson and Letitia Green.

At thirty-one Adlai was five years older than most American grooms. Like many ambitious exiles from the country, including Abraham Lincoln and Stephen Douglas, who were both married in their thirties, Stevenson's migration to town had lengthened the time before he could afford a wife. His forebears had married in their midtwenties because the means of their breadwinning already existed in the fields beyond the family homestead. But no such ready-made resource was available for Stevenson, who competed for business in tiny Metamora with seven other lawyers. As for the twenty-three-year-old bride, her age was typical, although the eight-year gap between the couple was unusually large.

Still, the similarities between the bride and groom promised the kind of congenial marriage sought by young Americans, who married now for love and not, as in earlier times, for considerations of land, cows, and parental choice. Both were Presbyterians; both were exiles from Kentucky and Centre College to central Illinois; both were fatherless; both were well schooled; both had been raised in ambitious families that self-consciously embraced the exceptional in their ancestry; and both were poetry-loving sentimentalists who believed in the kind of all-suffusing, breathtaking romance that became the idealized reason for marriage in nineteenth-century America.

Only in their physical appearance did they differ, for Adlai was a broad-shouldered, sandy-haired man of what the newspapers called "superb mold." His physique was already a notable asset at political meetings, where, six feet tall and weighing two hundred pounds, he stood out among the crowd as a presumptive leader. On the other hand, Letitia was short, brunette, and plump. Throughout her life, though women's fashions changed, she parted her hair in the middle and pulled it tightly around her ears, in a style that emphasized the angularity of her face, highlighted her imperious chin, and set off an exquisite pink complexion compared by one admirer to the inside of a seashell. And because Adlai believed that a woman who ventured outside her home without gloves and a hat was as undressed as one without stockings, Letitia was seldom seen in anything but an elegant dress, usually of moiré or watered silk, with muttonchop sleeves and a cinched waist.

In her description of the wedding, Letitia concentrated on the weather and the catering: "It was the coldest day of the winter and the cakes, sandwiches and salads ordered from St. Louis arrived frozen." With this account of a grand, city-catered wedding in a tiny town on the prairie, Letitia Stevenson ended her autobiography. Although she would write newspaper articles, complete a history of the Daughters of the American Revolution, and deliver speeches to large audiences, the sensibilities of her class and sex, along with the deliberate wall of secrecy imposed by Victorians around their intimate relationships, closed off any exposure of the private affairs that she and Adlai now shared. Henceforth the story of her life dwindled into what she called, with a perceptive understanding of the fragmentation of female lives, "Sketches."

Nor did the routinized daily tasks of domesticity offer much dramatic substance for a personal narrative. Like most women, Letitia Green Stevenson did not see her parallel life with Adlai as an individual journey or even as a story in which she played a leading role. No longer the author of her own life, she now became the creator of a family. And so she ceased writing her autobiography, in symbolic recognition of the end of her autonomy as Letitia Green and the beginning of her existence as Mrs. Adlai Stevenson.

2

FOR THE NEXT twenty years Letitia disappeared into the clapboard, unshuttered house on the corner of Bloomington's Charles and Albert Streets into which she and Adlai moved in 1869. Young, ambitious, and energetic, the couple had not stayed long in Metamora. Adlai's land speculations had soured; the acres that looked so flourishing when covered by prairie grass in the summer did not drain properly in the spring. When the population of Metamora declined from eight to five hundred, Stevenson could not even sell his lots in town. After her first child was born—most likely under the supervision of the village midwife and in the comforting surroundings of her sister's home in Chenoa, where her mother still lived—the Stevensons moved to Bloomington. Soon Adlai and his cousin James Ewing had begun a durable law partnership that was evaluated a few years later by the investigators of the national credit agency of R. D. Dun as "standing 1" in the community.

Before their move Adlai Stevenson began a family tradition that lasted for three generations. On one of many absences (like Lincoln and other ambitious lawyers, he followed the convening of the county courts through central Illinois), Stevenson addressed a letter to his newborn son. "If all goes well, we will move to the East side of Charles street in the house where I spent the happy hours of my early manhood. Here we can enjoy a large amount of happiness." Then, remembering the toil of his early years on a Kentucky farm, Adlai offered some gratuitous advice: "Remember chores is a miserable Yankee word."

In a home that frequently included her mother-in-law, Eliza Ewing Stevenson, her mother, Mary Peachy Green (called behind her back for her aristocratic ways "the Queen" and "the Duchess of Buccleuch"), her five brothers-in-law, and her own children, Letitia now did woman's work, the invisible, unrecognized, essential toil of the female. "The welfare of the household depends on the wife's guiding the family," she once explained after she had become something of an authority on the family. "Woman's first and highest mission as a wife is to share in her husband's honors as well as be his comfort and solace in times of trial. She should prevent the distractions of family life from interfering with his affairs." And so she cooked, sewed, cleaned, washed, raised the children, and served as "Adam's rib" to a husband who was a chronic absentee.

When he was home, "Papa" was not expected to do women's work, although in this new age of domesticated masculinity, he consulted with his wife about household furnishings, the raising of the children, and the family's finances. Companionate marriages were not based on any symmetry of household responsibilities, but rather on emotional warmth. Years later one of the revealing family stories about Adlai concerned his visit to the butcher when his wife was sick, a shopping expedition so unusual as to be memorable. He proudly purchased a beefsteak that was adjudged monstrously tough by the women of the household, who could not permit such a trespass onto their preserve. "He has," observed his wife, "never had the care of his home or family, though he is devoted to both."

Sometimes Letitia had help, live-in or daily, from the Swedish, German, and Irish wives and daughters of the railroad shop workers and coal miners on Bloomington's west side. Like many middle-class women who tried to make fancy serving maids of immigrants who knew nothing of the genteel customs of late-nineteenth-century dining and drawing rooms, she found the supervision of these domestic servants a tedious burden. According to the census, in the 1880s two Swedish maids lived in the household, though by 1890 they had been replaced by day workers from the Hungarian community. Earlier an Irish cook from the oldest of Bloomington's ethnic groups presided in the kitchen. Always Letitia depended on her sister Julia Scott, who, in recognition of the bonds of sisterly affection, named her daughters Julia and Letitia.

In this feminized household, Letitia trained her daughters for their domestic futures. "By a fair division of labor much exhausting fatigue may be avoided and decided benefit to all concerned [will] result," Letitia believed, for she was an efficient woman who understood the lessons of American industry and their application to the emerging science of home management. Later, when interviewed about running a home, Letitia described her own progression toward middle-class domesticity: "But establishing a home doesn't mean that the woman shall forever cook, sweep, darn stockings, sew on buttons and play general ladies maid." Still, "all of this may be necessary under certain financial conditions"—as it had been for her.

Letitia and Adlai's children arrived at intervals that suggest family planning. When she became a public figure, Letitia boldly supported birth control or what her generation proposed as "voluntary motherhood." Scornful of "the mother suicide" of too many children, she advocated "the deeper sense of personal responsibility for the presence of children. No thoughtful woman can support larger families with no reference to the health or life of the mother." In 1905, when President Roosevelt called those American women who avoided having children "criminals against the race . . . the objects of contemptuous abhorrence by healthy people," Letitia objected. "I was one of those who took issue with former President Roosevelt in urging this delicate theme before the public for general discussion. I do not recall one word on the ability of the parents, morally, spiritually and financially, to rear a large family of children." Similar sentiments led Margaret Sanger to challenge the blackout on birth control information and the definition of contraceptive material as obscene matter. Letitia Stevenson was publicly attacked "for her preference of women's clubs to the ownership of a half dozen children. She finds bridge more interesting than babies."

Letitia Stevenson's convictions emerged from her personal experience. Like other immigrants to town, the Stevensons understood that children no longer represented cheap labor, available to help with planting and harvesting at critical periods during the agricultural season. Instead, town children drained resources. They must be educated and launched, as well provisioned as possible, onto the uncharted waters of late-nineteenth-century urban life. In Washington and Bloomington, Letitia observed the plight of abandoned, abused children, whom she would protect by premeditated reproduction and by the establishment of children's nurseries and the recent import from Germany—kindergartens.

Unlike wives of an earlier generation who might have wished to control their fertility but who had neither information nor contraceptives, Letitia Stevenson lived in a community where the newspapers often advertised abortifacients and where by 1874 Dr. Ellen Ferguson offered medical advice to women too embarrassed to discuss matters of reproduction with a man. Although as a congressman her husband once supported a more stringent version of the federal prohibitions on mailing information about contraceptives, everyone in Bloomington knew that the brown-wrapped packages that arrived in the post office on Main Street with no return addresses contained marriage manuals, along with what the restrictive Comstock law of 1874 termed the "obscene material" of douches, condoms, and information about family planning.

In Letitia's life with Adlai, there is a hint of enjoyed sexuality that may have made her receptive to issues of female reproduction. Throughout their lives the Stevensons affectionately greeted each other as "my beloved husband," "my darling loving wife," and "my adored." Victorians veiled their intimacies—which is not to say that they did not enjoy sex. Nearly all the marriage manuals of this generation, even those of conservatives, accepted sexual passion as natural and healthy.

Evidently the Stevensons agreed. Thirty years after their marriage, when sixty-two-year-old Adlai was sitting for the bust that would eventually fill a vice-presidential niche in the U.S. Senate, a lump of red clay began to look like him. Or so he thought, and wrote to his wife, "I have no doubt you would feel like putting your arms around it if you could see it." Still, he was a modest man, embarrassed when women were not properly clothed. Once seated before the sculpture of a nude female at a Washington dinner party, he was sufficiently mortified that he could not look. Bending his head to his plate, he ate so many oysters that his amused hostess had to send out for more.

In the spacing and number of her children, Letitia was typical, producing the national average, for her generation of native-born urban white women, of four children. Her first child and only son arrived nearly two years after her marriage. She named him—for naming was generally a mother's perquisite—Lewis Green after her father. Then, after a four-year gap, at two-year intervals three daughters were born, always, it seemed, during the summers of their father's ceaseless election campaigns—Mary Ewing in 1872, Julia Scott in 1874, and Letitia Green in 1876. Like her son, Letitia's daughters carried Green names, perhaps to recognize the superior social class of that family stem, perhaps to keep the faith with distant Kentucky relatives (for her husband was still surrounded by many kin, while she had only her sister and mother on the Illinois prairies), but certainly to indicate Letitia's importance in their upbringing. Her influence over the children's naming displayed her domestic authority, and as a result the name Adlai Ewing Stevenson skipped a generation.

A busy man of public affairs, Adlai Stevenson acknowledged his wife's primacy in the matter of child raising. His role was one of indulgent paternalism, encouraging obedience and for the children's serious transgressions threatening, but rarely delivering, a spanking. "I suppose Papa applied his sovereign remedy and threatened to whale the Ange," wrote Julia of her younger sister. Papa's spankings were rare, and the couple's affectionate attachment to each other and their children undermined any possibility of a stern authoritative role for a man who was forever "dear old Dadder."

Like many American fathers who were out of the house most days and, in Adlai Stevenson's case, also nights, weekends, and during his congressional terms over half the year, he intended that the children obey their mother. "The home is the woman's kingdom where her influence, the most sacred in life, will support the very foundation of the state," Stevenson advised the mostly female graduating class of the Bloomington High School in 1901. To his son, Lewis, he quoted Robert E. Lee's command to his son Rooney: "Never let your mother wear one gray hair from lack of duty on your part," adding his own prescription, "Would you have no unkind word to your mother and grandmother pass your lips." Other members of the family employed the same system of injunctive child raising. Stevenson's brother-in-law Matthew Scott once wrote his daughter Letitia that he expected her "to gratify mama and myself by determining that you will hear or read and heed these suggestions so spoken or written to you touching the character of the thought and conduct which are to shape your course in life—no unworthy conduct, self-discipline, reputation and character."

To his son Stevenson also preached the importance of hard work, along with the lessons that he had learned as a county courthouse lawyer familiar with bankruptcy. "Opportunity," Lewis heard often from his father, "rarely seeks a man. People have to make an effort. Children can be born into families that have attained greatness, but by their own efforts must the reputation be maintained. Great competition should be a spur in every phase of life."

Yet both parents adopted the contradictory tactic described by Letitia as "making home a place of great freedom in order to be worthy of the sacred name. Here the children should be made to feel that they may do as they please, providing they do not please to do wrong, of which there is little danger. It is only by allowing this liberty that the parents can learn the dispositions of their children. . . . Home should be a place of mirth and merriment. Blessed is the boy who feels that home is a jolly place. . . ."

Certainly the Stevenson household was such a place. "Do you remember your old Father?" worried Adlai when he had been away from home only a few weeks. Because he wanted his only son, Lewis, to emulate a success requiring frequent absences, he mixed instruction with affection. "Do you remember your old father's job? Do you remember when Papa used to chase you around the house and you would get on his back like a horse and we would gallop over the house?" wrote a homesick Stevenson from Washington in the 1870s. "I am thinking about the times when I chased Bessie around the table and through the nursery into Grandma's room." Declining the role of a patriarch like many fathers of his time, Stevenson approached his children's merriment as an equal participant.

Years later, as the sixty-year-old vice president of the United States, he was still, according to a young visitor to Bloomington, "an active member of the throng who participated in our games, playing croquet, beanbag, drop the handkerchief. One day Uncle Adlai was 'it,' and he slipped and fell. His hat went one way and he the other. We all laughed, he as heartily as the rest. His brother was looking from the verandah, with not even a smile. He didn't approve of the Vice President making a fool of himself. The Vice President only laughed and said, 'You know, I'm only a barefoot boy at heart.' "

To maintain their identity as a family in an age of incursions by outside agencies such as schools, which mandated attendance until the age of fourteen, baseball leagues, and bicycle clubs and, in Bloomington as elsewhere, boys' clubs like the "East Side Gang" and the "Main Street Hellions," the Stevensons created pet names to establish a privileged relationship among themselves: "My precious JuJu, Angie, and Bessie"; "dearest Ange and Minna." Only Lewis was denied an enduring pet name, though as a young child he was briefly Bub. Instead, for Lewis would have to make his way in competitive arenas beyond family parlors and playgrounds, his father sent him descriptions of the U.S. Capitol and encouraged him to relate to the family circle the story of George Washington and his cherry tree.

When he was an old man given to remembering things past, Adlai Stevenson acknowledged his "darling wife's" domesticity in an affectionate letter of farewell that suggested the strain of Letitia Stevenson's circumstances in this seemingly placid, overtly loving, usually extended family household: "Never forget how I love you. For whatever I have achieved in this life I am indebted to you. God bless you for all you have been to me and to our dear children and for a lifetime of tender devotion to my angel mother. Remember everything that I have achieved I owe to you." Julia, the third child, was more forthright about her mother's tribulations as Letitia struggled to live up to happiness, the meaning of her name: "What a wonder our mother was, frail and burdened with the care of two delicate children and two boisterous ones, and [keeping] those two old ladies happy and reasonably pleasant."

Just as her husband made a career of political compromise, trying to synchronize the discordant strains of the divided Democratic party and the tensions between the easy life of a small-town lawyer and businessman set against his public ambitions, so in the Stevenson home his wife smoothed over the disagreements between the two mothers. Her mother, "the Duchess," stayed in bed reading all morning, never buckled her own shoes, insisted on having tea delivered to her bedroom, and sometimes refused meals until "when papa talked of skeletons one of her granddaughters referred to the one we have upstairs." Invariably dressed in a black silk dress, rose point lace collar, and seed pearls, she appeared for lunch to amuse the children with tales of the thwarted dreams of the fictional characters that represented the real-life disappointments of this exile from Kentucky. "She was not of a domestic nature. Her small shapely hands were seldom used except to play the piano and hold a book," explained her granddaughter Julia.

Meanwhile the other widow of the household, the storytelling Eliza

Ewing Stevenson, "the encyclopedia of Kentucky history," gave too much domestic advice to her daughter-in-law, passing the days in a leisurely fashion that contrasted with Letitia's modern schedules. Eliza, though she lived to see the establishment of time zones in 1883, never wore a watch. With only the turn of the seasons as her clock, she claimed disproportionate hours of her busy son's time in order to recount the tales of the North Carolina clan. Meanwhile busy, clock-watching Letitia tried to save minutes and hours in order to apply them to another task.

Her daughter Julia recalled, "My grandmother and Papa spent hours telling the stories of the past on the back porch. Her major regret was that he had not been born and lived in North Carolina at homeplace." Even in her old age Eliza Stevenson continued to preserve the family heritage, informing her son when he was vice president and she in her eighties about her recent discovery that his grandmother Sophia Wallis had died, in a shining example of the clan's early religiosity, while taking communion.

Two invalids in the household on Charles and Albert Streets tested Letitia's maternal diligence and skill as a nurse. Sweet Mary, "the home-daughter" of her father's adoration, seldom went to school, and after a series of broken bones, high fevers, and one episode of cholera, "Bessie" died in 1895 from tuberculosis. Although the Stevensons' only son, Lewis, lived to be sixty-one, he never recovered from a hunting accident. A shadowy episode in family annals—like many Victorians, the Stevensons were adept at the omissions that masked their turmoils—Lewis had been shooting on a forbidden Sunday. The gun recoiled into his shoulder, perhaps from a double charge, and he kept silent about the bruise. "A few days afterwards," according to his father, "taken with scarlet fever which it now seems selecting the weakest point settled in his shoulder joint and resulted in an abscess." Eventually the infection was removed, along with his pectoral muscle, by Dr. Edmund Andrews, a Chicago surgeon who had learned about infection on the Civil War battlefields. For nearly a year after his operation, fourteen-year-old Lewis was kept inside, away from the suspected lethal vapors and miasmic gases—for this was before the doctors properly understood germ theory—that the specialists feared would reinvade his maimed shoulder. Having learned disease, Lewis for the rest of his life would search, attired in custom-made suits tailored to obscure the hole in his shoulder, for an ever-elusive health.

Like many mothers of this generation, Letitia Stevenson shared the nursing of her two invalid children with outsiders. In Bloomington doctors still used heroic doses of calomel, tartar emetic, Peruvian bark, and an occasional bloodletting to treat most illnesses, just as mothers like Letitia continued to rely on traditional remedies like egg lemonade, beef tea, and, for her own migraine headaches, a tincture of opium rubbed behind the ears. Like most of her neighbors, she also used Dr. Wakefield's locally manufactured, all-purpose Family Remedy, with its characteristic cherry taste and high volume of alcohol.

Yet it was to Chicago that Letitia Stevenson took Lewis for consultation and surgery. Mother and son also traveled to the popular citadels of health such as Western Springs, outside of Chicago, and John Harvey Kellogg's Battle Creek Sanitarium, in Michigan, both of which promised relief from her son's persistent neurasthenia through rest, quiet, and nutrition. But in this transitional era between dependence on the experts and the primacy of maternal care, mothers were still held accountable for their children's illnesses. In popular thought and private conscience, a neglectful, uninformed mother created the opportunities for family sickness. In response to expectations that tied the success of a child's course to the quality of his mothering, Letitia did not abandon her authority readily.

In the beginning of her son's lifetime quest for good health, Letitia Stevenson accompanied him to the spas and sanitariums, usually taking up her post in a nearby boardinghouse. Her letters served as progress reports for the rest of the family: "Lewis is about the same. I have not seen him since Monday but the Dr. said he would be able to go downstairs soon." And during another treatment: "Lewis is exhausted. I have not seen him often as he can not stand anyone in his room more than a moment at a time." And the same year: "Lewis is not feeling quite so strong—the effect of a little over effort." In 1895, when Mary Stevenson died, she was a patient in an Asheville, North Carolina, sanitarium, where the mountain air and bedrest were considered therapeutic by several experts who had established clinics there.

In time Letitia Stevenson's maternal responsibilities lessened. Lewis married and no longer needed her constant surveillance. Her husband's income increased. There was more money for cooks and maids; the crowd of relatives and political friends at the dinner table diminished. Her mother died in 1885, and her mother-in-law, Eliza Ewing Stevenson, lived for part of the year with her other sons' families. Her daughters Julia and Letitia went to boarding school, and Julia was gone for a semester at college.

Two seasons in Washington—where respectable women, some even smoking cigars, went unchaperoned at night and where leaders of the suffrage movement like Susan B. Anthony displayed female autonomy—revived a sense of independence sometimes smothered by family duties. In her forties Letitia began the public activities that made her a famous American woman. For years she had listened to her husband's calls for reform—messages that during the Progressive period concentrated on finding solutions to dirty streets, neglected children, miserable sanitation, and ineffective local government. Letitia's private world of motherhood furnished a bridge into concerns affecting women and children, just as her family ties convinced her of the importance of preserving a national past based on the primacy of the Anglo-Saxon heritage. By the time her husband was nominated for the vice presidency in 1892, Letitia was even ready to campaign.

3

IT ALWAYS SURPRISED Adlai Stevenson that he reached national prominence. Although he sought political positions avidly, running five times for Congress, twice for vice president, and once for governor of Illinois and in between soliciting patronage appointments, his expectations were limited. In fact, he retained such a childlike astonishment about his notoriety that, like a traveler unfamiliar with the landscape ahead, he bulged his eyes to scrutinize more closely the unexpected terrain he was traversing. "He expands and contracts his eyes," wrote one reporter in the kind of personal observation that Stevenson found distasteful. Always the same man—whether in Bloomington or in Washington, at a public meeting or in his children's nursery—he rarely masked his private self except in photographs, where he put on a stern face. Consequently in the competitive world of late-nineteenth-century politics, he was adjudged compliant, too full of geniality to be a true political man in a partisan arena that demanded bold combatants, not storytellers.

In 1908, after his wife abandoned her autobiography and after his last campaign, Stevenson began writing his life story. Entitled *Something of Men I Have Known* and graced with an expansive subtitle characteristic of this age—*With Some Papers of a General Nature, Political, Historical and Retrospective*—the five-hundred-page reminiscence was not about himself at all. Instead, it included anecdotes, observations, and profiles of "great statesmen." Reviewers criticized the book's mixing of generations, parties, and topics—"from Henry Clay to James Blaine in a few pages," complained one. Some critics called the book an example of an outmoded genre in which public men wrote long-winded memoirs of a best-forgotten period of corruption. Others commented that the author was too preoccupied with trivia and that important issues were obscured by descriptions of men admired for their stories, occasionally for their speeches, and, in the case of his special heroes Lincoln and Douglas, for their success. In judgments that mirrored the modest approval Stevenson himself received as a public figure, many readers enjoyed the book's amiable nostalgia. "A valuable contribution to the last 70 years," wrote Champ Clark in a letter to the author.

Never confident of his ability as he edged up the political ladder, Stevenson revealed himself through his reverence for public figures whom he acknowledged as more forceful and talented and even more gifted storytellers (though few were that) than he. After his political defeats ended any pretensions, Stevenson fathomed his dependence on the great men whom he cheerfully courted and whose biographies, as he explained of Stephen A. Douglas, were "the history of their country." As a "witness following at a great distance and along a humbler path," Stevenson produced a memoir that was the antithesis of self-glorification.

Of course Stevenson included his favorite stories, the more than twice-told tales whose protracted and repeated telling made his colleagues squirm. The politicians of the post–Civil War generation had no time for swapping anecdotes as they rushed about Washington attending to affairs of state. Yet Stevenson, no matter what his job, always found time for Kentucky hospitality. "The latch-key," he was fond of saying when he was first assistant postmaster and later vice president, "will always be on the outside of my office door." As a result his office overflowed with friends, acquaintances, and favor seekers. In the tradition of unhurried rural life, as many as a hundred men a day paused to talk and swap jokes. "Contrary to all precedents, his policies of receiving all callers at all hours has already turned my office into a beer-garden," complained one official in the 1880s.

Stevenson's comic treatment of sober matters of state disclosed lessons not so much about the specific partisan issues of his day as about human foibles. The pride and long-windedness of politicians, the relation of man to God, the ignorance of voters, the underdog's protection through sharp riposte to an opponent's attack—all appeared as the point of his parables. In this impersonal way a politician who, according to one of his opponents, "stayed awake nights thinking up ways not to hurt people's feelings," responded to slights accumulated during a lifetime in public life. Despising personal attacks, he replaced vituperation with irony and parable.

And so he told a story on William Springer, another Illinois Democrat of his generation, who, having pompously repeated Henry Clay's maxim "I'd rather be right than President," was informed by the Speaker of the House, "You'll never be either." Another tale, directed at the Bloomington neighbors who didn't have the sense to vote for him, described a local citizens "indignation" meeting called to discuss improvements in the schools. When addressed by a compelling orator on another subject, the assembly promptly forgot about education.

Stevenson also revealed a disdain for the sovereign people in the story of a voter's confusion between Jefferson Davis, the president of the Confederacy, and David Davis, Adlai's Bloomington neighbor and a member of the Supreme Court. Jokes such as the one about the politician "who never took a drink of water without serious meditation as to how it would affect his political prospects" or the candidate who asked a scarecrow to distribute his bills testified to his own ambitions. So too did Cousin James McKenzie's wry comment, when this Kentucky cousin along with John W. Stevenson was in Congress with Stevenson, "How strange it is three cousins in Congress and *ours not an officeseeking family either!*"

Through his seemingly artless stories he obliquely displayed the equivocation that remained his principal tactic. He often repeated the story of Zebulon Vance, the North Carolina governor and later U.S. senator, who forgetting the denomination of the congregation to which he was speaking, instead reminded the audience, "My sainted grandfather was a Presbyterian, my father an equally devout Methodist and myself I'm an old Baptist." Stevenson remembered the politician who, asked whether Macbeth or Hamlet was the better, shilly-shallied: "My district is equally divided. Hamlet has his friends down there and Macbeth too." Or his own contribution, which his grandson repeated more than sixty years later, during the 1952 presidential campaign: when traveling in Oregon, Stevenson was confronted with a disagreement between two towns over what to name a nearby mountain, a controversy he avoided by delaying his choice until the train started, and then in synchrony with its piercing whistle he said in a voice no one heard, "Its name should be . . ."

Especially useful as guides to his politics were the "darkey tales," which he delivered in dialect and which established his reputation as a northern politician sensitive to southern white interests at a time when the former Confederate states were becoming a one-party fiefdom of the Democrats. Later he admired the nostalgic stories of an unchanging Old South written by his friend Thomas Nelson Page, whose vision of ignorant, subservient, ever-loyal African-Americans coincided with Stevenson's own perceptions.

Modestly Stevenson included in *Something of Men I Have Known* only fragments of his own life—his migration from Kentucky, his arrival in Bloomington and return to college in Kentucky, his early years in Metamora followed by his move to Bloomington, his two terms in Congress, his appointive position as first assistant postmaster from 1885 to 1889, his four years as vice president during Grover Cleveland's second administration, his selection in 1900 as William Jennings Bryan's running mate, and his final campaign for the Illinois governorship in 1908. He wrote nothing of his disappointments. Instead, with the innocent optimism that got him where he went but then prevented him from going farther, he told the good and trivial about himself and others. Nevertheless, he liked to recall the tale, as it displayed his relationship to the Democratic party, of "the negro who, when told by his parson that the Lord had been very good to him, replied: 'Yes sah; but den you see I'se been berry good to de Lawd.' "

Adlai Stevenson included nothing about his wife and children. Although he dedicated *Something of Men I Have Known* to his wife, "the patient listener of these twice-told tales," like most men of his generation Stevenson separated his public from his private affairs. In this distinction he failed, continually carrying to politics a sensitivity better reserved for personal affronts. His children observed his frequent humiliations. "Father had a dual nature and in his extreme sensitiveness and over-delicacy of feeling and emotion was exactly like his mother. . . . He suffered extreme pain under adverse criticism and [his personality was] almost that of an 18th century mystic, so did he shrink from enduring slight pain," explained his daughter Julia.

When the newspapers published a family letter full of characteristic foolishness, Adlai was angered by the intrusion into his private life. Thereafter his envelopes carried the warning "Personal and Private," and he ended his nonsensical messages to "Bessie, the Duchess and JuJu." The publication of a letter about Lewis's health made him more suspicious. "Father didn't write to the children often after he had been saddened and angered by a personal letter printed in a paper," explained Julia. Ever a traditionalist, he objected to the emerging view expressed by a contemporary that "a public man can have no private correspondence."

Sheltering his private life, Stevenson cheerfully applied himself to public affairs, recognizing "good fortune" as essential to his and other political careers. Because he lived in the Republican party stronghold of McLean County in a Republican state in a period of that party's control of the presidency and the Congress, his chances of election were limited. To overcome the odds, he relied on his private assets—his personality, his family connections, and eventually the friends who found him so congenial. Living in Bloomington, he could never attract the electoral following that the Chicago mayor Carter Harrison achieved by using municipal jobs as incentives for support. Nor, given his amiability, could he create an inner circle devoted to him for his potential, as Governor John Altgeld of Illinois did in the 1890s.

Some ambitious Democrats, faced with such depressing prospects after the party realignment of the 1850s, fled to more congenial neighborhoods in order to improve their prospects of winning office. Samuel "Sunset" Cox, a congressman from Ohio, moved after his district's shift to the Republicans closed off any chance of his election. In 1869 a triumphant Cox returned to Congress as the representative of New York City's dependably Democratic Sixth District, which he represented until his retirement in 1885. But such raw, single-minded purpose was impossible for Stevenson, a family man attached to community and local party.

Politicians who did not change their residence sometimes switched parties to conform to the partisan choice of their neighborhoods. But Stevenson's attachment to the Democracy represented an ancestral preference carried to Bloomington in the ox-drawn wagons of 1852. To give up such a heritage would be an act of cultural surrender, like exchanging Presbyterianism for Congregationalism or forgetting Kentucky and the Stevenson-

Ewing heritage. Nor by the 1880s could Stevenson expect the kind of kinship migration to Democratic territory that had brought his mother and
father to Bloomington. No longer seeking the common goal of better land
but instead divided in their individual aspirations of running a hardware
store and a coal mine and selling real estate and insurance, the clan members could not pick up and move as they had in other centuries. Rather,
Adlai had somehow to accommodate his political ambitions through different means.

4

IN 1874 THE DEMOCRATIC CONVENTION of the Thirteenth Illinois Congressional District needed a candidate, in a district that had not sent a Democrat
to Congress since 1863, and nominated Adlai Stevenson. As the delegates
agreed, there were few more deserving activists in the five-county area of
Tazewell, De Witt, McLean, Mason, and Logan than the thirty-nine-year-
old Stevenson. Well liked by Republicans for his geniality, the director of
the People's Bank and the part-owner of the McLean County Coal Company
might appeal across party lines.

An enthusiastic joiner, Adlai Stevenson was also a Mason who had met,
in the Monday night meetings of his Bloomington lodge, influential men
from both parties. He had joined a local literary club and good-naturedly
performed in the town's amateur theatricals, getting good reviews for his
spirited portrayal of Mr. Justice Stareleigh in the hilarious production of
The Trial of Bardwell versus Pickwick, the adaptation from Charles Dickens
of a breach-of-promise suit. Stevenson had even participated in community
spelling bees, his mistakes coming at the proper point of commonality with
his neighbors, who might miss, as he did, "ecstasy," but who knew "representative" and "receive" and who were put off by pedants who correctly
spelled four- and five-syllable words like "idiosyncrasy."

Every lawyer in the district—and beyond—knew Adlai Stevenson from
the bar's charivari when lawyers satirized themselves and then repaired to
the local hotel for lengthy dinners full of toasts and jolly fraternizing. In
one mock trial Stevenson served as the judge dismissing petitions for more
alms for the town's underemployed lawyers. Once during an orgmathorial
court (a tribunal where lawyers jokingly tried other lawyers), he was
charged with writing under a pseudonym "which he palmed off as an argument in a case and fooled the Supreme Court."

Rarely had this friendly, civic-minded man ever refused an invitation
for an address. With patriotism worthy of the event and the durable voice
essential for a generation lacking microphones, Stevenson had several times
delivered two Fourth of July addresses on the same day. He began in Clin-

ton or Farmer's City in the morning and then, riding hard thirty miles back to town, spoke at dusk to his "neighbors and friends" from the bandstand in Bloomington's new Miller Park.

Despite such recognition, in an age of party ballots when only the brave and seriously disaffected "scratched a ballot" and crossed party lines to vote for the candidate of the other party, no one expected Adlai Stevenson to win in the Thirteenth District. Certainly his Republican opponent was not an easy mark, for New York–born John McNulta had been the colonel of the Bloomington regiment during the Civil War.

But Stevenson had also been nominated by a new political organization—the Independent Reform party, whose call had gone out to "farmers, mechanics and other citizens." This third party had burst on the scene, emerging from over a thousand Patrons of Husbandry and Grange organizations that sought to alleviate the psychological isolation and economic distress of farmers. Hard times during the depression of 1873, when prices for wheat and corn dropped by nearly a third, had led desperate farmers to extend their social solidarity into politics.

The target of this first of several third parties (variously known during the next two decades as the Anti-Monopolist, the Farmer's, the Greenback, the Greenback-Labor, and the Populist parties) was the economy and especially what this generation of Democrats labeled the "Crime of '73." The latter referred to a bill passed by a Republican Congress and signed by the Republican president Ulysses Grant that ended the coinage of silver dollars. Angry at such a deflationary change, farmers believed that less money in circulation would further depress already disastrous prices for their wheat, corn, and hogs, even as intermediaries seemed to absorb larger proportions of their profit. Relief seemed possible if the currency could be expanded by the inclusion of silver, which until 1873 had backed the nation's paper currency.

In 1875 another assault on the money supply became national policy. Officially known as the resumption of specie bill, this legislation would prohibit, beginning in 1879, the use of the Civil War paper currency nicknamed "greenbacks" for payments of debt, interest on bonds, and custom duties. In the view of sad-faced, pinched midwestern farmers and demoralized Democrats who hoped to replace the popular Republican issue of waving the Civil War's bloody shirt with the showing of a depression's empty purse, such a policy would accomplish a devastating contraction of the money supply. But easterners—for the monetary issue of the postwar generation divided sections as well as parties—sought deflation and the stabilization of the amount of currency in circulation in order to bring American prices in line with those of Europe.

Convinced that prosperity depended on inflation, central Illinois farmers—the instinctive monetarists of this period—located another enemy in the railroads that controlled the cost of transporting their crops. Earlier these same corporations had been wooed by communities like Bloomington and Chenoa with offers of land, bonds, and tax breaks. The editors of the *Metamora Sentinel* had placed the twin symbols of their society on the masthead of their paper—an etching of a cow and a train. By the 1870s the train had demonstrated its power, by charging higher rates for shorter rather than more-distant hauls and splitting markets by pooling routes, which promptly became noncompetitive. Supporting state regulation, farmers' conventions sought government intervention. An Illinois state commission had recently brought suit in the McLean County courts against the Chicago and Alton Railroad for a rate schedule that charged less for a run from Chicago to Springfield than for the shorter distance between Chicago and Bloomington. To many central Illinois voters, what their parents had avidly pursued had become a powerful monopoly that could be tamed only by a new political organization.

Still, these reformers were realists who understood the partisan clasp of the traditional two parties on the affections of voters. Many had grown up during a period of high turnouts and intense interest in parties as a public force. Loyalty to the Republicans and Democrats stamped their understanding of American democracy, and voting by handing a party-printed ballot to an election judge symbolized the power of the established political organizations. With such a system as their model, the disaffected Independent Reformers of 1874 saw the benefit of nominating the Democrat Adlai Stevenson on a fusion ticket.

Immediately Stevenson's prospects improved, particularly if this new organization could draw off enough votes from the Republican's natural majority of three thousand and simultaneously gain the support of first-time voters whose allegiances were not fixed. In an off-year without the presidential campaigns that habitually lured nearly a quarter more Republicans to the polls, the decline in voting might permit an upset, especially if the young contender could make a case that the Republicans were corrupt, favored business at the expense of the farmers, and had been in office too long.

Ever a traditionalist, Stevenson disliked the new style of politics that viewed campaigns as educational, and he apologized to voters for "some statistics to which your careful attention is called. Figures are dry and many times uninstructive, but in the discussion of this financial question which is now paramount and above all others in American politics today it is necessary to refer to data." In 1874, and then again in 1876, 1878, 1880, and 1882, traveling by horse and buggy and increasingly by train through his largely rural district—the lopsided parallelogram nearly one hundred by sixty miles, stretching from Chenoa in the north to Pekin in the west, from Belleflower in the east to Mount Pulaski in the south—he preferred to tell stories to Illinoisians gathered in county seats and crossroads, the basements of village churches, even the edges of cornfields, where there were often more scarecrows and meadowlarks than voters.

As every politician does, Stevenson created in his imagination a view of the people, whom he ambiguously believed to be loyal partymen available to cast a Democratic ballot if his speeches were successful, his personality sufficiently engaging, and his character revealed as stalwart and honorable. At Centre College he had imbibed the Ciceronian notion that only a man of virtue could be a true orator, and so his personal morality must ineffably fuse with his public self. But Stevenson also held to the ancient "republican" view of himself as a mute tribune who had yielded reluctantly to the call of duty and who did not speak for himself but rather felt the party speaking through him. Holding to the fiction that he had been solicited by his party, chosen by its adherents (hence his enduring surprise) and then offered to the men of the Thirteenth District without any self-promotion, he was convinced that good Americans must vote without the manipulations of demagogues, even as he campaigned with the endorsement of two political organizations.

The clan, his brothers, brother-in-law, Ewing cousins, and especially his law partner and political manager, James Stevenson Ewing, campaigned as well. In the final torchlight parade in Bloomington, the five Stevenson brothers provided several floats, some designed to appeal to the growing enclaves of Irish and Germans on the west side, and others, such as the one on which a white-robed Mrs. Jacob Stonebrunner portrayed the Goddess of Liberty, created for the entire community.

Such ceremonies acted out the meanings of nineteenth-century politics, with Stevenson riding in the front of the parade either on a large white horse or in a carriage that separated him from his followers, who marched in organized ranks resembling an army on its way to battle. From the backs of the people, he was lifted onto platforms, from which as a leader he looked down on those below. Politics was war carried out by other means, intended to mobilize the electorate and get the boys to the polls. Fittingly Bloomington's Butler cannon, a relic from the Civil War, was fired twenty-five times after one of his rallies.

The candidate got no money from the national Democratic Congressional Committee. The latter, a loosely organized, Washington-based association of Democrats from each state, depended on an assessment of 2 percent on appointed party officeholders earning under $1,000 and 3 percent on those making over $1,000. In these Republican times the committee raised little money, since there were few Democrats in patronage jobs available for kickbacks either in Illinois, where the practice became institutionalized as "the lug," or in Washington. In Chicago, Cyrus McCormick had just begun the organization of a state Democratic machine, and the millionaire manufacturer of reapers made personal contributions to congressional races, mostly to pay for printing the campaign documents needed for the new-style "politics of education." In the absence of other sources, the candidate depended on his family for campaign funds, especially his wealthy brother-in-law, Matthew Scott, who donated $25 to Stevenson himself, and gave additional gifts of $8 for the torchlights and $25 for the uniforms proudly worn by Stevenson's Democratic army.

Like most office seekers, Adlai Stevenson concentrated on his opponent's mistakes, in speeches that sometimes lasted over two hours. In 1874 McNulta's transgressions consisted of support for high tariffs, high spending, and hard money as well as his vote for retaining what Democrats christened the Salary Grab Act—by which members of the Forty-third Congress had raised their salaries from $5,000 a year to $7,500. Stevenson spent little time offering his own correctives and prescriptions for the future, although on the salient local issue, like his opponent, he favored railroad regulation. In the way of partisan politics that often limits voter choice, the candidates' agreement was obscured by Stevenson's reliance on a class-based rhetoric that separated the "Republican monied interests of this country and their conspiring bondholders" from "the impoverished and overtaxed people." Sometimes—for he never left home without his stories—the candidate ended his speeches with the tale of the convicted murderer who awaited his hanging on the same platform as a local politician waiting to speak. Asked what his last wish was, the prisoner demanded to be hanged before the politician began his stump speech.

Waving the bloody shirt of wartime memory, the Republicans charged that Adlai Stevenson had been a member of the Knights of the Golden Circle. Once, when a heckler called out from the back of a hall, "You were a Confederate sympathizer and a knight of the Golden Circle, Stevenson," the candidate replied defiantly, "My friend, you are a liar. I want you to understand me. Any one else who makes that statement is a wilful and a deliberate liar." But like his grandson who could never shake the libel of his supposed friendship with the convicted perjurer and suspected Soviet spy Alger Hiss, Adlai Stevenson was forever tarred as a traitor. The charge was false, but because he had never served in the Union Army, his perennial quest for office became a substitute for the military duty he had avoided.

On November 4, 1874, Adlai Stevenson and his mostly Kentucky-born male neighbors marched to the polls at Stump and Coons' blacksmith shop. A new state law required that they earlier register and swear that they had lived in Bloomington for three months, McLean County for six months, and the state of Illinois for a year. Outside the polls temperance advocates demanded that the candidate sign a pledge opposing the selling of liquor in Bloomington. "Down with the Dramshops," they cried. Stevenson, a teetotaler who once offered the alcoholic Ulysses Grant his choice of lemonade

or water, brushed them off, with his inveterate response to this local issue—
"Let every man be his own judge." Then he took the Democratic ballot and
handed it to the election judge. Late that night Adlai Stevenson learned of
his election to Congress with 52 percent of the vote in a three-candidate
race. To his chagrin, he had not carried Bloomington, nor in eight other
campaigns for various offices would he ever do so.

As the new congressman from the Thirteenth District, Adlai Stevenson
had achieved a notable victory, for himself, for the Democrats, for the Independent Reformers, and, not least, for his family. Following the election in
the bipartisan understanding of his nation that losers accept winners and
behave as a loyal opposition, Stevenson organized a bipartisan "Jubilee"
and promised, for he now represented everyone in his district, "that all men
have won." By his victory he became part of the "Overturn of '74," a historic
return to power by the Democrats in the Forty-fourth House of Representatives, the first since 1861 to be under Democratic control.

5

ADLAI STEVENSON HAD never been to Washington, but the city where he
lived intermittently from 1875 to 1897 was no longer the sleepy southern
town of the prewar period. That earlier District of Columbia had been dismissed as nothing more than a provincial village by Europeans, who disdained its empty spaces, scavenging pigs, muddy streets, and modest
buildings, which included, until 1863, the unfinished Capitol. After the
war, reflecting the expansion of the federal government, Washington's population had grown to 140,000. Under the direction of an ambitious developer, Alexander Shepherd, who served as president of its Board of Public
Works and as its territorial governor until both he and the District went
bankrupt, the hills and valleys to the north and west had been flattened,
the stagnant malaria-breeding pools drained, sixty thousand trees planted,
and attractive parks planned.

By the 1870s the growing prestige of the United States, the appearance
of a sizable diplomatic corps, and the mild climate were attracting wealthy
Americans who sought high society during the winter season. The Beales
of California refurbished Decatur House on Lafayette Square, adding a par-
quet floor in an upstairs parlor with a 22,000-piece mosaic of the seal of
California; Larz and Catherine Anderson of Cincinnati were making plans
for their Romanesque castle designed by Henry Hobson Richardson on K
and Sixteenth Streets; the bonanza kings of mining wealth—California's
Senator George Hearst and Nevada's Senator William Stewart—were erect-
ing five-story mansions garnished with elaborate towers, splendid interiors,
and turrets of dubious aesthetic distinction.

Grand public buildings matched the pretentiousness of private dwellings. In the 1870s the State Department, with its huge granite-faced wings for the Army and Navy Departments, was still under construction. So was the Naval Observatory and an addition to the Government Printing Office. There was talk of a new building for the Library of Congress on Capitol Hill. All were needed for the burgeoning force of over thirteen thousand federal employees. Even the city's best-known symbol—the Washington Monument—was finally dedicated in 1884. Most of these buildings bore the architectural mark of this generation—the cascades of columns, the overladen decoration, and the heaviness of the eclectic Romanesque–French Empire style, whose extravagant dimensions suited the spirit of a Gilded Age given to seven-course banquets, fifty-inch male girths, and, in affairs of state, lengthy orations.

Adlai Stevenson found such grandeur beyond his budget. After a long search he rented rooms in a cheap boardinghouse five miles north of Capitol Hill on Missouri Avenue that charged three dollars a week, laundry and breakfast included. He took his main meal downtown in the National Hotel, where he met the great men of his party in its crowded lobby and billiard rooms. Like nearly half of the congressmen of this period, he could not afford the travel and board for his family, completed in June 1876 with the birth of his third daughter and fourth child, Letitia Green. Riding the three-penny horse-drawn cars to the Capitol, the freshman congressman discovered that the casual schedule of a small-town, lawyer-businessman did not suit the capital.

Soon he knew most of his congressional class of 174 Democrats, 107 Republicans, and 10 Independent Reformers, the latter all from farming states. The contingent included an unusually large percentage of first-time congressmen, 100 of whom were Democrats and one-third of whom had served in the Confederate Army. Among the representatives were five African-Americans, the largest group of blacks to sit in the House until the 1960s. Similar in its composition to that of other states, the Illinois delegation of 19 included 14 freshmen and 16 lawyers, who, like Stevenson, practiced as much politics as law. Most, however, were older than Stevenson, having long ago begun their political careers in the state legislature. The Republican James Garfield disdained the newcomers as undistinguished: "Nothing is more striking than the difference in appearance between a Republican and a Democratic crowd. The class of men scattered at hotels has not been seen in Washington for many years."

A loyal Democrat despite his association with the Independent Reformers, Stevenson attended the Monday night Democratic meetings, where leaders sought support for the party's program. Unaccustomed to such efforts at discipline, Congressman Garfield condemned these meetings as "tyranny," adding, "The Democratic caucus acts as a kind of moral duress which governs both the Chairman and members of the committee and makes this House not a legislative body but one to register the dictates of a caucus." But the result was a party cohesion well above twentieth-century levels, though never so tidy as to make it possible for voters to identify promises with programs and, in the next election, use their ballots to reward and punish. Come to Washington to spend less money and to reverse Republican policies toward the South, the Democrats had limited success.

After a Christmas adjournment during which Stevenson traveled home to Bloomington, the House remained in session from March to August 1875 and, in its second session, from December 1875 until March 1877, refusing to adjourn during the presidential-succession crisis of 1876. Mornings were spent in the committee meetings crucial for an overburdened assembly whose output of 739 bills, nearly evenly split between public and private legislation, had dramatically increased from that of prewar Congresses. Appointed to two minor committees—those of the District of Columbia and Territories—Stevenson spent afternoons and sometimes evenings in the handsome chamber where the elegance of the room's magnificent ceiling with its glass panels decorated with the states' coats of arms belied the foul air that led this session to form a special committee to deal with air circulation.

Advised Congressman William Kelly of Pennsylvania in a statement that drew bipartisan applause, "We have a murderous ventilation . . . draughts of hot and cold air . . . smells from the water-closets below . . . turpentine and resin ooze out from the floor timbers . . . there is not enough oxygen." Congressmen complained that the stagnant air brought on headaches, pneumonia, nonspecific vapors, hallucinations, and long-windedness, any of which might require a visit to the soothing bathtubs in the basement or the Hole in the Wall, where brandy and wine were available.

Attendance was mandatory in a body that defied the growing refinement of social Washington. Members carried flasks onto the floor, picked their fingernails, spit constantly into the cuspidors arranged around the hall that cost the government over $4,000 a year to maintain, and rested their feet on their desks as they read the mail from home. Stevenson, who in Bloomington had shed the linsey-woolsey denim overalls of a farmer's son for a professional's high stiff collar, white shirt, black tie, and broadcloth Prince Albert coat, discovered that Alabama's Jeremiah Williams attended to the Republic's business attired in blue jeans. Lobbyists circulated on the floor, exchanging stock in new ventures for votes, although corruption was more widespread in the Senate, where the persuasion of a few members could more easily change the course of legislation. Senators Nelson Aldrich and James Blaine grew rich from bribes, while in the House during debate on the sugar tariffs, H. O. Havemeyer, the president of the American Sugar

Company, presented little bags of sugar, and some said more, to lawmakers.

Several times during this session the doors were locked, and absent members not paired or excused were fined. Never did the diligent Stevenson miss a roll call, except when he was out of town on House business, once for the funeral of a colleague and once as a member of a delegation investigating corruption in the Republican-controlled New Orleans customhouse. Voting the Democratic program of retrenchment in federal spending, expansion of the money supply by issuing silver-backed currency, and accommodation with, and amnesty for, the white South, from his seat on the front row (as he explained to his family, "seat assignments are put in a box and picked out by a blind-folded nigger"), Stevenson rarely spoke. The new congressman found, like many freshmen, that it was hard to get the Speaker's attention in a body that understood, as Woodrow Wilson later warned, "the terrible possibilities of perfect freedom to debate." "You had to," according to Congressman Henry Dawes of Massachusetts, "watch for your opportunity, be instantaneous, and with eyes on the clock say what was possible."

Finally, with the apologetic tone that would be one of his legacies to his son and grandson, he spoke. "It has been my intention," Stevenson acknowledged after three months, "rather to listen than to take part in these solemn ceremonies." Only at the request of a friend was he taking up the time of the House, to offer an obituary for a recently deceased representative.

Later Congressman Stevenson decided that the House of Representatives was like a schoolhouse with its repetitive routines, suffocating lectures, and all-day vigils at desks that served as offices. In the Forty-fourth and Forty-sixth Congresses, Stevenson learned the expansive range of the Republic's curriculum—disagreements over moving the Bureau of Indian Affairs from the Department of Interior to the War Department, divisions over pork barrel allocations, discussions on appropriations that took up nearly a third of the session, arguments over the tariff, and the increasing preoccupation with currency. Internal matters took time as well. In the Forty-fourth Congress, Stevenson heard angry debate over prohibiting lobbyists from the floor, outlawing the party assessments exacted on office-holders, and, on a hot July day in 1875, appropriating money for lemonade. Throughout, the claims of private citizens were an essential part of the legislature's business. Stevenson introduced his share of private bills, mostly for constituents' pensions.

To the House of Representatives, Stevenson brought good humor, humility, conscientiousness, jokes, loyalty to party, and surprise and pleasure that he was a member. He was by no means a leader or even a petty baron like Illinois's William Morrison and William Springer. Unlike many representatives from marginal districts, he did not use the system of pairing or abstention to avoid unpopular votes useful to an opponent in the next election. In every session he managed one political speech for home consumption—in 1876 comparing the desolate territory of New Mexico currently seeking statehood "with its indigent Indians, Mexicans and greasers" to Illinois, with its prosperous farms, towns, and cities, and well-educated population of three million.

In 1877, during the controversial negotiations over the presidential election of Samuel Tilden and Rutherford Hayes, Stevenson spoke as a conciliator. Arguing in his longest speech (and the only one that was printed in the appendix of the *Congressional Record*), "The time, sir, for angry discussion has passed. In this hour of public peril patriotism has higher demands upon us than party. For myself I declare that I have no theories upon this subject, that I am unwilling to relinquish in the interest of a fair and peaceful adjustment of the question. . . . Civil war is a remedy for no evil." Typically—for his sentimental nature craved the heightened expression of poetry—Stevenson ended with a quotation:

> Peace in the quiet dales
> Made rankly fertile by the blood of man
> Peace in the woodland and the lovely glen
> Peace, God of Peace, Peace in all our homes
> And all our hearts.

In August 1876 the session finally adjourned, and Stevenson hurried home to campaign. In the recursive schedule of congressional politics, he was running again, having been nominated this time by the Democrats and the Greenback party. The latter supported an expanded currency of greenbacks and silver to pay off the principal from maturing Civil War bonds, but its name masked other, more progressive intentions—the direct election of senators, an eight-hour day, an income tax, and women's suffrage. As a result of accepting this nomination, Stevenson was forever tainted in the minds of conservatives, while from the Greenback dissenters came complaints that the congressman was too much the "Mossback Bourbon Democrat" to satisfy farmers and mechanics. "Who will Mr. Stevenson vote for?" taunted the Republican Bloomington *Pantagraph* in reference to the national election, "the Greenback candidate Peter Cooper or the Democrat Tilden?"

Incumbency assured little. At least a fifth of the congressmen in the Forty-fourth Congress did not return, as the political tides endlessly washed ambitious men in and out of Washington. In presidential years more Republicans voted in his district, and Stevenson had somehow to appeal across the well-tended corrals of Democrats into the larger one of Republicans to attract either some strays or new voters. In 1876 Stevenson's

Republican opponent was Thomas Tipton, well known for his service as a states's attorney, a circuit court judge, and, like more than a third of the House during the 1870s and 1880s, a veteran of the Union Army.

The challenge was too great. Stevenson lost in 1876, but was reelected in 1878. His defeat by 250 votes in 1876, his close victory in 1878, and his loss in 1880 and in 1882, by 620 votes of 14,000 cast, demonstrated the competitive party politics in an era when even presidential elections were determined by a few percentage points. Now Stevenson advised his friends, "I will pillow my head consoled by the thought that no act of mine has made the poor man's burden heavier."

But he had politics in his blood. An expectant party man as his friends were hopeful capitalists, he kept campaigning, always allied to a third party and always with the personal style that drew fire from his opponents. "Mr. Stevenson," complained the *Pantagraph,* "takes refuge in his character. No one has drawn the line of demarcation more clearly and strongly between private morals and political candor and integrity. The public aren't just interested in Mr. Stevenson's life and character and to save time we will stipulate in advance that Mr. Stevenson's private life is pure and spotless. What the public are now concerned with is his political positions." Solicited for an endorsement by Stevenson, David Davis concurred, describing the politician Republicans called "the Great Straddler" as a man "of large *liberal and conservative* views."

The indefatigable Stevenson tried for the nomination in 1884, although by this time a Republican legislative gerrymander made any Democrat's chances remote. The replacement of Mason and Tazewell Counties by rabidly Republican Macon and Piatt created what the *Pantagraph* celebrated as a safe seat. These were odds that even Stevenson declined. In 1886, after a decade of Stevenson for Congress campaigns, the party searched for another candidate to contest a district that would send Republicans to Congress for another four terms. At a crossroads Adlai Stevenson either had to remain a small-town businessman and lawyer (for he had no interest in serving in the state legislature) or to find another route to public life.

6

BETWEEN HIS TERMS in Washington, Adlai Stevenson returned to Bloomington, a village become a town in the 1850s and by the 1880s a town of 18,000 that was almost a city. Ever a Bloomington booster, he retrieved the law practice and money-lending operation, appraised at $60,000 to $70,000 in 1873, along with his directorships of the People's Bank and the family-owned and managed McLean County Coal Company. In his second-story office above Bunn's Bank overlooking Front Street, a striped awning sheltered him from the sun but not the passersby who stopped to exchange stories with Uncle Adlai. Available for community service, he was elected to the school board and became the grandmaster of his Masonic lodge and a trustee of the Second Presbyterian Church.

As a party leader, he understood the power of the press and organized a Democratic newspaper to counter the *Pantagraph*. Bankrolled by Stevenson's rich brother-in-law, Matthew Scott, the clan established the *Bloomington Daily Bulletin* in 1881 and then waited in vain for its loud partisan voice to cure the district of its implacable Republicanism. "Mr. Stevenson and his brothers and his cousins and his aunts are all out for him in the new paper," derided the *Pantagraph* after his endorsement in the *Bulletin*. "He is not in private life and we will evaluate him accordingly." Soon the *Pantagraph*'s columns were filled with criticism of Stevenson's inflationary, prosilver stands, his failure to support appropriations for the Michigan and Illinois Canal, and his bank directorship, which struck his opponents as inconsistent with his attacks on a national banking system.

Meanwhile, never certain when destiny might sweep him back into public office, Adlai and his brothers developed Stevensonville, the clan's smaller version of George Pullman's paternalistic community in Pullman, Illinois. On forty-six acres west of Main Street near the McLean County Coal Company's two mine shafts, the brothers built three-room, one-story cottages, intended for sale to their 250 employees for $800—$100 down and $10 a month, six years to pay. The family considered these terms liberal, though layoffs, slowdowns, and an uncertain average annual wage of $300 made it impossible for most mining families to move from renting to homeowning. After a decade only fourteen had done so. While the Stevensons never ran a company store in what they called "our little suburb," they did expect the miners of the McLean County Coal Company to support any Stevenson running for office. Several times workers complained that they had been fired after voting Republican during an election in which Adlai Stevenson was running for Congress.

Besides his economic ventures, Stevenson was always available for speeches and storytelling. When Bloomington needed a booster's enthusiasm for the new business association that was trying to attract companies to town, or a law-and-order speech, he spoke for a civic capitalism in which class conflict and lack of cooperation (such as going out on strike or buying clothes from the new mail-order house of Montgomery Ward rather than in local shops) were submerged in the spirit that would assure Bloomington's future.

In 1881, after Stevenson had returned home from his second term in Congress, a mob of enraged Bloomington citizens lynched a white man for the murder of a popular sheriff. For a day the man's body, maimed from the crowd's physical beating and with a cigar hanging ignobly from its mouth, swung from the large elm on Market Street. The manner of the victim's death symbolized growing community fears. The supposed lawlessness of striking workers (even the usually obedient miners of Stevenson's McLean County Coal Company had twice walked off their jobs and been promptly replaced by imported strikebreakers), of angry farmers, and of disorderly tramps threatened Bloomington's tranquillity at the end of the nineteenth century. A seething McLean County recalled a number of supposed criminals who had been let off by lenient courts, sometimes, it was said, because underemployed lawyers with too few clients "pitched into the defense to make a reputation."

Stevenson thought otherwise. When the reporters came to him for a statement, Bloomington's most accomplished peacemaker quieted his neighbors with a law-and-order speech: "This act of lawlessness is a blight upon this city . . . [and is] the most outrageous affair that has ever occurred in McLean County. I have no respect for the men who were prominent in the mob. There is no excuse for it. There is no county in the Union where the law is more faithfully carried out."

Despite his interest in local matters, Adlai Stevenson still yearned for a larger political stage, tolerating contradictions that might have exhausted or embittered another man. A local notable but an also-ran nationally, he was a private man who wished to quarantine information about his personal affairs even as he took to public life the amiability others left behind in their parlors. A lawyer, he made more money from signing notes, real estate investments, and profits from the coal company than from his practice. A faithful Democrat in Republican Bloomington who accepted nominations from every third party in central Illinois except the Prohibitionists, he was a popular man of the people who talked the populist language of class difference but who was also a wealthy businessman, investor, and ruling father of his town. A man of humility and gracious warmth at his dining room table, he pursued a career in a field notorious for corruption and guile, held positions on the issues of the day and yet spent much of his time telling tales that seemingly had nothing to do with public concerns.

With prospects as dim as his party's, Adlai Stevenson needed a sponsor and found one in Wisconsin. Like other middle-class families, the Stevensons left Bloomington during the suffocating prairie summers. Letitia and the children usually went first, in June after school was over, their departure chronicled in the new personal columns of the *Pantagraph* and the *Bulletin.* Sometime in August, Adlai joined them at the lake resorts with Indian names near Minnetonka, Waukesha, and Mackinaw. Some families, like that of William O. Davis, the editor of the *Pantagraph*, settled on one location, such as Lake Michigan's Charlevoix, and purchased a summer cottage, but the peripatetic Stevensons went to many places. Everywhere the head of the family made friends.

At one of the lakes Stevenson met William Vilas, a lawyer, businessman, friend of Grover Cleveland's, and leader of the midwest Democrats. The friendship flourished. Soon Stevenson requested a photograph and promised that to be of service he would let "no question of conscience" stand in his way. In 1884, at the Democratic presidential nominating convention in Chicago (where Stevenson briefly backed a dark horse Illinoisian rather than the party's first-ballot choice, Governor Grover Cleveland of New York), the delegate from Bloomington took the floor to recommend Vilas as the head of a committee that would travel to New York to inform the nominee of his selection.

With the grateful Vilas's help, Stevenson in turn was chosen to be a member of this committee, carrying the news to Cleveland, who had heard by telegraph two weeks earlier and whose manager, William Whitney, had been working for months to gain the support of state leaders. Outdated and unnecessary, the notification ceremony survived as a mechanism to enact the national understanding that in a democracy the people are sovereign. Through their delegates they choose a man who must be sought rather than seeking, pursued rather than pursuing.

After accepting a nomination he considered "a dreadful self-inflicted penance for the good of my country," Cleveland did little more. He believed that campaigning was a repulsive act "of self-assertion." Instead, loyal Democrats like Stevenson did the work of educating voters, armed with their own speeches and the new *Democratic Textbook* sent from Washington. Especially the tariff issue suited Stevenson's conciliatory instincts, and he concentrated on its possibilities to please everyone, by supporting tariffs for revenue on some items and protective tariffs on others. The customary four-thousand-item tariff statute of the late nineteenth century was a compromiser's haven, which is why Congresses of this period spent so long deliberating tariff bills and why Adlai Stevenson relied on the issue.

During the campaign of 1884 Stevenson said nothing about the bribe taking of the Republican candidate, James Blaine, though it was widely known that the Maine senator had accepted stock in a railroad company in return for his vote. For their part, the Republicans did not mention Cleveland's illegitimate child or the complaints of the child's mother, Maria Halpin, about his neglect. Believers in a double sex standard, most Americans blamed Halpin. In any case, such transgressions of the moral code were private matters, deemed irrelevant to a politician's performance by a generation that, like Adlai Stevenson, separated public and private behavior.

Elected in November 1884 by less than a percentage point of the popular vote, Cleveland was the first Democrat to win the presidency since James Buchanan in 1856. In Bloomington, his horizons now widening, Adlai Stevenson exaggerated the result into "the greatest moral victory of the age," though Cleveland had carried neither McLean County, nor Bloomington, nor the new Fourteenth Congressional District. Still, Stevenson hoped for an appointment despite the new president's pledge that no "partisan zeal should lead to the arbitrary dismissal for party or political reasons of those . . . who have not engaged in party service." Even amid reformers' talk of merit appointments based on civil service exams, the Democrats now controlled 125,000 nonmilitary federal jobs, most in the hands of the Republicans; 96,000 were in the post office.

In time—for the 280-pound president nicknamed Jumbo moved slowly—Cleveland chose William Vilas as his postmaster general, and Stevenson hoped for a place. Twice he hurried to New York and sent James Ewing to Wisconsin for a conference with Vilas. But Cleveland was reluctant to appoint a man who had dallied with greenbacks and silver, and chose another to be first assistant postmaster. Again it seemed that Stevenson had to surrender his public ambitions. But after a few months in office Cleveland's first choice became ill—some said from the constant harassment of office seekers. Now Vilas proposed the man from Bloomington, and in the summer of 1885 an exuberant Adlai Stevenson, for the annual wage of $4,000, took charge of 55,000 fourth-class post offices stretching across the United States. "It is," Senator David Davis of Bloomington advised him, "a better consignment with the public than almost any other in Washington—almost the grade of a cabinet minister . . . and you have plenty of executive ability and common sense and are a natural politician."

The tiny sinecures of the fourth class—dispensed to party loyalists as the rewards of party virtue—were worth less than a thousand dollars. But as command posts of nineteenth-century rural politics, they were beyond the surveillance of the postmaster general and the president, who had time to attend to only the larger plums of office. In these offices farmers, separated by the vast acreage that was at once the source of their individual livelihood and the destroyer of their civic life, found relief from their isolation.

Often after the talk of crop prices and the weather flagged, discussions around the stove in the local post office turned to politics. Party newspapers were read. Issues and candidates were discussed, and during election time a man might find, if his politics differed from the postmaster's, that his circulars and papers had mysteriously disappeared. Knowing the preferences of the neighborhood, the local postmaster served as a partisan informant, drawing up lists of the faithful who might be solicited for their vote. Around election time an energetic postmaster was, some said, worth more than a good stump speaker. "Therefor I say to the Dimocrisy, be uv good cheer. We have the Post Offsis and nothing short uv impeachment can take 'em from us," applauded the political humorist Petroleum Nasby, who knew the power of these "rewards of virtue."

In the summer of 1885, when Stevenson took over his duties in the corner office of the U.S. Post Office, with its classical Corinthian columns an external sign of civic probity no matter what happened inside, he immediately controlled the largest patronage system in the United States. Unlike the mugwumps who would outlaw the spoils system and the president who was so outraged by insistent office seekers that he ended the traditional Friday morning appointment hours for those he disparaged "as begging like dogs," Stevenson treasured the visits of those who wished a friend or relative appointed. Congressmen, lobbyists, Illinoisians, and casual visitors crowded into his office, where they enjoyed what his daughter Julia Stevenson Hardin called "Father's lambent humor . . . never bitter or exercised at the expense of others or to hurt the soul, but instead playing like light over the ordinary interaction of daily living." So great was the clamor that Cleveland mistook the storytelling and camaraderie for a possible conspiracy by Stevenson and his silverite friends.

Like his predecessors (the previous postmaster had left Washington with the nickname "the Headsman"), Stevenson had no scruples about the necessity of replacing Republicans with Democrats. Soon he earned notoriety as Adlai the Axeman, "a man who uses the guillotine freely and is decapitating thousands," complained the Republican *New York Herald*. The Republicans kept count: "Stevenson Removes 100 in Two Weeks"; "The First Assistant Postmaster Has Decapitated 14,000"; "Sixty-five Removed in Two Minutes," raged the Republican press. In fact, Stevenson's record of removals was not exceptional and was exceeded by his Republican successor. Firmly he believed, even as a new generation was replacing his partisan traditionalism with a modern bureaucracy run by trained civil servants, that the patronage bound Democrats to the party and that, as Andrew Jackson had said, all citizens were competent to serve.

Thereafter caricatured with an ax in hand chopping away at marble columns labeled "reform" and "good government," Stevenson became a national figure and the delight of political poets: "I fear the whizzing of the ax, Adlai's ax / What a world of misery it is working with its whacks / How it slashes, slashes, slashes / Through the officeholder's neck." Democrats shortened his title to general, a partisan rank that no doubt Adlai Stevenson earned, although he never explained its origins. Unsuspecting Americans outside of Illinois usually associated "General" Stevenson with the Civil War, not the patronage battles of the post office, where the commander insisted, with irony, that "great attention would be given to qualifications."

Professing that he removed only "offensive partisans," Stevenson replaced the ins with the outs. Sitting on rolling chairs at their long high desks, the female clerks who had come to Washington for government jobs during the war and stayed to support their families on a clerk's annual wage of $900 transcribed his official decisions of removals and replacements. Yet the first assistant postmaster could never be a bureaucrat of the new order.

Adlai Stevenson arrives in his hometown of Bloomington for a parade during the 1948 gubernatorial campaign. By this time many Democratic leaders thought that their throwaway amateur might win. (Courtesy of Buffie Ives)

Wherever Stevenson campaigned in Illinois, images of his grandfather, seen here with Cleveland and Bryan, accompanied him. Here a group of young supporters ride to an evening rally during the 1948 campaign. (Courtesy of Buffie Ives)

During the 1948 campaign Stevenson appealed across party lines to the increasing number of independents in Illinois. Here he pats an Illinois cow at the McLean County fair, in the kind of politicking he disliked. (Courtesy of Buffie Ives)

Governor and Mrs. Stevenson attend an inaugural ball after his surprise election in 1948. Directly behind are Stevenson's sister, Buffie, and her husband, Ernest Ives. (Courtesy of Buffie Ives)

Stevenson signs a bill making the formerly partisan-ridden Illinois State Police a more professional organization in which officers were appointed by merit. This reform became his best-known initiative. (Illinois State Historical Library)

Ellen and Adlai Stevenson meet with legislators in Springfield. Ellen Stevenson rarely came to the Illinois capital and in 1949 divorced her husband. (Courtesy of Buffie Ives)

One of the earliest photographs of Bloomington shows the town and its planked sidewalks before the Civil War. (McLean County Historical Society)

When they moved to Kentucky in 1816, the Stevensons lived in this house, which they added to as time went on. (Illinois State Historical Library)

The fire of 1900 burned most of Bloomington's downtown area. Note the courthouse in the background. (McLean County Historical Society)

Stevenson's political and legal career was aided by his family. Here he sits as the eldest, in the middle of his five younger brothers James B., William, Thomas, Fielding A., and John Calvin. (Illinois State Historical Library)

Letitia Green Stevenson met Adlai Stevenson in Kentucky in the 1850s. After their marriage, she became an active participant in public life. (Illinois State Historical Library)

Among Letitia Stevenson's public roles was her participation on the board of the National Congress of Mothers, which later became the PTA. Here she sits in the first row, second from left, next to Alice Birney and her sponsor Phoebe Hearst. (Illinois State Historical Library)

The four Stevenson children pose—Letitia ("the Lily"), Julia ("the Rose"), Lewis Green, and Mary, who died of tuberculosis in 1895. (Princeton University Libraries)

Adlai Stevenson was nominated for vice president at the so-called wig-wam in Chicago, where Democrats gathered in 1892. (Smithsonian Institution)

Grand Democratic
RALLY,
Friday, Nov. 4th, 1892, 4 P. M.

Tariff for Revenue!
Down with the Robbers!
Down with the Monopolists!
Down with the Millionaires!
Down with the McKinley Bill!
Down with the Force Bill!

Government for the People and not for the Benefitted.

CLEVELAND and STEVENSON.
Ruth and Letitia.

Down with Baby McKee!
Down with Grandfathers!

BROOM PROCESSION---Line of March:

Democrats will assemble in the Boiler House armed with Brooms. The steam will be run up to 260 lbs. In this explosive state the column will march, yelling all the way, to the evergreens; from thence to Porte Cochere; from thence to front gate; from thence to Tennis Court; from thence to Dining Room entrance. (If any Democrat in line SEES DOUBLE let her pass to the rear.)

P. S.—Ambulances ready on line of march for any Democrat out of Plumbline. Colored people will sit on the fence while the procession passes.
Don't forget Boiler House, at 4 sharp. Bring brooms, and come level-headed. Right angel at the center.
Refreshments free in the Dining Room (no drinks). Leave despair at the door. We are on the top wave. Keep sober and we WILL SHOUT VICTORY.

Among the posters and broadsides in the election of 1892 was this call for a Democratic rally, in which the major themes of the campaign were turned into slogans. The broom is a traditional emblem symbolizing the need for Democrats to sweep out the Republicans. (Illinois State Historical Library)

In the summer of 1900, after Stevenson I's nomination for vice president, two Adlai Ewing Stevensons were photographed. (Courtesy of Tim Ives)

The Stevenson home in Franklin Park, Bloomington, represented a grand style of town living at the end of the nineteenth century. (Princeton University Libraries)

Four generations of the family. *From left,* Eliza Fell Davis, Buffie Stevenson, Helen Davis Stevenson, and Hester Brown Fell. (Illinois State Historical Society)

Gubernatorial candidate Adlai Stevenson I puts on a serious face during the campaign of 1908. (Collection of the Library of Congress)

When the Paddy's Run post office in Kentucky requested a change of name, Stevenson declined. "It is," he wrote on St. Patrick's Day, "a reflection on St. Patrick himself. Paddy's Run is a landmark. Within the decade Lick Skillet and Hog Wallow and Hell's Bend have gone the way of all flesh. . . . I choose to draw the line at Paddy's Run."

Throughout his tenure Stevenson hoped for higher office—first to be postmaster general when Vilas was elevated to the position of secretary of the interior. But Cleveland chose another and with exasperation supposed "that he [Stevenson] might think he ought to be chosen except for some reasons which he couldn't be made to understand connected with the number of places Illinois already has."

Then, just before Cleveland left office in March of 1889 (Cleveland had lost the electoral vote to Harrison despite winning the popular vote by nearly 100,000 votes), the first assistant postmaster prevailed upon the president to nominate him to the District of Columbia federal court, a position that would not, as did the federal courts in Illinois, require the approval of the state's two Republican senators. "Father," explained Lewis to his future wife, "is infatuated with Washington." But the District of Columbia bar was disgusted by the midnight appointments to its bench of displaced officials who had no experience in their codes. One hundred and twenty members of the District bar signed a petition opposing "political appointments of those unfamiliar with local laws." By the time the president forwarded the name of Adlai Stevenson to the Senate Judiciary Committee in February, it was too late for action in a session awaiting a party change. Again humiliated (his friend William Springer called it a "severe blow"), the first assistant postmaster lamented, for neither the first nor the last time, that his life in public affairs was over.

When Adlai Stevenson came home to Bloomington in the fall of 1889 (he had not come immediately but had gone to Mexico on business), Letitia Stevenson was relieved. She had lived for a time in Washington during his tenure as first assistant postmaster, but she preferred Bloomington to a lifetime in Washington on a federal judge's skimpy salary of $5,000. Active in Bloomington's clubs, she worried about her children, who disliked uprooting, though she had valiantly tried to make their rooms in the home they rented for the winter season on fashionable K Street replicas of those in Bloomington.

Letitia also liked her new home. Eight blocks from downtown Bloomington, the three-story, twelve-room Italianate brick mansion faced Franklin Park, the city's fashionable square. Called a villa by its builder, it featured on its exterior the kind of mass-produced wooden trim popular in this era. Inside, the new home was nearly twice as large as the old clapboard structure on Albert Street. For the first time Letitia had a place of her own and one that displayed wealth and status.

Like thousands of other Americans at the end of the nineteenth century, the family joined an exodus from the center of the city. The Stevensons left behind their old Kentucky neighborhood, now three blocks from the Lake Erie and Western passenger depot on Main Street, and a block from the commercial and industrial hub of what in 1880 was the seventh-largest city in Illinois. Removed from the dirt and noise of the railroad shops, the stench of the new beer factory and Dr. Schroeder's vinegar factory, and especially the corner of Grove and Main, where the rowdies gathered under the newly installed electric lights before they headed off to the Button Hole Bouquet Saloon (the latter, scorned by the *Pantagraph* as "a resort for lascivious women, its backrooms devoted to ungodly practices"), the Stevenson's new residence on the corner of McLean and Chestnut was imposing. It had an entrance hall, a large carpeted parlor and dining room for entertaining, a winding walnut stairway, individual rooms for Letitia, Julia, and Mary, who had earlier shared the nursery, a stained-glass skylight over the second-floor landing, a chandelier, and what the builders of the late Victorian age promoted as "father's study."

Here Adlai Stevenson kept a cabinet full of mementos from his public life. Here along with the indispensable Shakespeare and Burns, he shelved useful reference volumes of stories and jokes such as *The Merry Heart* and *The Wit and Wisdom of the Ages,* and the political writings of Burke, Jefferson, and Gladstone and the state papers of Grover Cleveland. Never one to forget his roots or his ambitions, he hung Joaquin Miller's popular sentimentalized sketch of a man sitting in front of a log cabin—the kind of dwelling he remembered from Kentucky—next to the mark of his ascent, an oil portrait of himself. The latter, he amiably noted, "was sometimes replaced by that of a stag at bay when I was not in favor at home."

In their twenty years on Albert Street, the Stevensons had been surrounded by their Kentucky friends and relatives now dispersed through the northern and eastern sections of the city, and increasingly to other parts of Illinois. James Ewing no longer lived next door but had built a vast Italianate mansion on East Street. James Stevenson was over a mile away on Olive Street. Fielding Stevenson and his family had moved to a farm in Downs Township. The clan members saw less of each other, replacing daily intimacy with more formal interchanges at birthdays, anniversaries, and weddings. Instead of visits, they relied on telephone calls. Typically Adlai Stevenson had a story about this new invention, telling and retelling how the first time he talked to a woman on the phone he took his hat off.

In their selection of a home, Adlai and Letitia Stevenson achieved only limited privacy. Surrounded by a quarter acre of grass and elms, protected from outsiders by a porch and heavily curtained windows, they had left downtown Bloomington. But they remained in a public area. Not by chance did another politician, Joseph Fifer, who was elected the Republican governor of Illinois in 1888, choose a house down the block from the Stevensons, where he too appreciated, as private families might not, a mixed setting of isolated grandeur near a public park. From the Stevenson porch—called a piazza to confirm its Italian origins—the family observed the community activities that took place in Franklin Park: the erection of an obelisk to honor the state's Union troops, the public concerts by De Molay's Marching Band, the night dancing, and the speechmaking by political partisans and leaders of the temperance movement. In turn they were observed. On the special occasions of Stevenson's triumphs, crowds of neighbors and friends marched through the park on their way to serenade Bloomington's most famous resident. But most days were more routine. As he walked to his downtown office, Stevenson met the community, jovially offering the youngest of them "taffy for revenue only," with the tariff, according to his daughter Julia, a kiss or handshake.

Then, just as their lives settled into the humdrum routines of small-town life, though unexpectedly Mary's cough was worse, and Lewis had survived only a few months at Washington and Jefferson College in Pennsylvania, and Adlai's new venture the Bloomington Interstate Building and Loan Association was having trouble finding investors, just as it seemed Bloomington held their future and that of their twentieth-century descendants, the most astonishing chapter of the Stevenson's family life unfolded.

CHAPTER FIVE

LEGACIES

1

ON JUNE 23, 1892, the Democratic National Convention nominated Adlai Ewing Stevenson for vice president. He was not Grover Cleveland's first choice, though a presidential candidate's desire for a compatible running mate was not considered in this era of party primacy. Cleveland's first two running mates—Thomas Hendricks of Indiana in 1884 and Allen Thurman of Ohio in 1888—met the more critical requirement of balancing the ticket regionally and of choosing vice presidents from states with high electoral counts that a native son might carry. In Cleveland's time, with the South suspect and the West feeble, midwesterners had become popular choices.

Stevenson was lucky. A split in the Democratic party undermined better-known leaders. Several possible candidates disdained the vice presidency, believing it a final resting place for has-beens and never-wases. Even after four vice presidents had inherited the presidency, public men still believed that the founding fathers intended, in the case of a president's death (disability was hardly considered), that the vice president should serve as chief executive only until a special election could be held. Before vice presidents emerged as senior advisers to the president, such views did little to elevate a ceremonial post. Ambitious men of the Gilded Age preferred senatorships, and accepted Mississippian Lucius Lamar's dismissal of the position as "four years of rest and a good income and (for the children) a fine time."

The location of the Democratic convention in Chicago boosted Stevenson's chances. His relatives had rushed to the city, soliciting influential party leaders gathered in the smoke-filled mezzanines of Chicago's hotels—the massive Palmer House, the new Grand Pacific, and, for those on lower budgets, Burke's Hotel or one of the city's five thousand boardinghouses. Here, to the leaders of the state parties who commanded their delegations as colonels a regiment, his cousins—James, Whig, and Adlai Ewing—and his brothers—James, Fielding, and William—along with the leaders of Chicago's Iroquois club headed by the city's grandly mustachioed mayor, Carter Harrison, made the case for their man in Bloomington: he was, they pleaded, a popular Illinoisian who, as a nearly native son, could attract enough votes to win the state from the Republicans; he was a well-known midwestern supporter of silver who would balance any ticket led by the eastern, progold Cleveland; he had been born in Kentucky and still celebrated his family ties to the South. Above all, he was General Stevenson, the loyal Democrat who had fearlessly removed thousands of Republicans from their post offices. No one doubted that the perpetually available, irresistibly likable Adlai Stevenson would accept.

After a raucous disagreement over the specifics of its low-tariff platform, the convention selected Grover Cleveland on the first ballot. The former president remained a popular figure among this generation of Democrats. Elected president in 1884, he had won the popular vote in 1888, only to lose the electoral vote and the election to Benjamin Harrison. "Give us Grover Cleveland again," shouted one delegate. "We're in the clover with Grover," sang others. James McKenzie, Adlai's first cousin from Kentucky, seconded the nomination with a flourish: "Mr. Cleveland is the honest, earnest, persistent, defiant, and relentless opponent of that axiom of the Republican party that announces that in the sweat of the hired man's face thou shall eat bread."

Turning to the selection of a running mate, Democrats listened to an Illinois delegate characterize Adlai Stevenson as "a man that is known by every woman, child, and voter that ever licked a stamp, in every village and hamlet in the land." A member of the delegation, Stevenson had remained discreetly in his hotel room during the nominations and did not hear himself described as "big-boned, big-headed, and big-brained." Others—the governor of Iowa, a Michigan judge, and Henry Watterson, Stevenson's friend from Kentucky—were nominated in a series of "the man who" speeches. Then, amid thunder, lightning, and a torrential rain that poured through the roof of the insubstantial wigwam-shaped building located beside Lake Michigan, Adlai Stevenson, "a man of commanding presence and dignified mien, a man whose courtesy in his everyday manners is rarely equalled and never excelled, a man who like his great leader believes that a public office is a great trust, but that the Democrats are the best trustees of this public trust," was chosen on the first ballot amid the cheers of the assembled throng of 15,000, fewer than 900 of whom were voting delegates. For the first time neither candidate had served in the Civil War.

One of Stevenson's friends, the newspaper reporter Henry Clendenin, braved the storm to carry the news to the Palmer House, where he greeted "Mr. Vice President" so clamorously that the corridors filled with well-wishers, who "had a jolly good time." Later, in his letter of acceptance, Stevenson announced his gratitude, his astonishment, and his uncertainty of his "capacity fully to meet the expectations of those who have honored me by their confidence." This last sentiment became one of several legacies to his grandson.

Soon after this unexpected marvel, the next family surprise occurred when fifty-year-old Letitia decided to campaign with her husband. At the time it was a rare presidential candidate who traveled to meet the voters. Instead, most stayed at their desks writing diplomatic responses to inquiries about their position on the issues. Stevenson's counterpart—the Republican vice presidential candidate Whitelaw Reid—declined political rallies, calling them "unnecessary appointments." He advised, "After accepting the nominations and defining their position, the candidates would do well not to be too active in the progress of the canvass." Like many older politicians, Reid feared that active campaigning "converts one warm supporter into a lukewarm one and makes nine others discontented."

In a political style associated with its best-known practitioner, William McKinley, candidates sat on their front porches and discussed the issues with party notables, curious citizens, and inquiring newspaper reporters. No one was concerned with their personal magnetism. Instead, their opinions, usually presented in the vaguest manner, were flashed across the United States on the half million miles of telegraph wire that were transforming presidential elections from a community affair into a national event. No one, and certainly not candidates' wives, embarked on cross-country pilgrimages.

Rather, as Cleveland believed, the party must let its "opinions be known. . . . The campaign is one of information and organization. Every citizen should be regarded as a thoughtful, responsible voter, and he should be furnished the means of examining the issues involved in the pending canvass for himself." While such an understanding explained the flood of documents printed by the new Democratic Literary Bureau and mailed to party members identified by local postmasters, it obviated any need for personal appearances by the candidate. "I can not bring myself to regard a candidacy for the place as something to be won by personal strife and active self-assertion," wrote Cleveland. With the royal disdain of which he was capable, Cleveland denounced the Frankie clubs that bore his wife's nickname so that "a name now sacred in the home circle as wife and mother may well be spared in the organization and operation of clubs created to exert political influence." He disclaimed the Baby Ruth mementos, even the candy bars, that carried his first legitimate child's name. In such a partisan environment, any appearance by Mrs. Adlai Stevenson was extraordinary.

Letitia Stevenson went first to New York in July, where the Democrats planned a rally in Madison Square Garden. Only reluctantly had Cleveland acceded to the pleas of his advisers that the electorate deserved at least one personal appearance. The notification ceremony of twenty thousand cheering partisans, with Letitia seated in the female gallery, where the ladies waved handkerchiefs in their traditional display of approval, was as close to the people as the former president got. Both he and Stevenson delivered acceptance speeches heard by almost no one in the auditorium, but later printed as campaign documents.

By August, Republican charges of Stevenson's support of inflationary greenbacks demanded a firmer commitment to gold. Stevenson reinforced his reputation as a straddler when he obediently pledged his support for gold, using its cue words "a sound honest money and a safe circulating medium." While the Madison Square Garden rally marked Cleveland's last personal appearance, despite pleas that he come down from his Buzzards Bay retreat to lead the people "like Moses from his mountain," it was only the first of Letitia and Adlai's appearances.

They traveled by railroad, and although Letitia did not go on every political trip during the summer and fall of 1892, she did join her husband in his journeys to Alabama, Virginia, North Carolina, and Kentucky. Among Cleveland's advisers were the new species of press agents—men of modern instincts who understood that candidates might be advertised. "Politics," wrote one, "I believe to be like any other business, a matter of careful detailed and persistent work," and, of course, money, a resource more easily obtained by the Republicans, who in the last two elections had outspent the Democrats by three to one.

George Parker, a Cleveland adviser who later started a publicity agency, sent Stevenson south to counter, by means of personal appearances, the Populist party's growing support in the South and the West. Party strategists feared that the former Confederate states might defect to an organization promising the direct election of senators, government ownership of the telegraph and railroads, and economic changes that included an income tax and a currency backed not just by gold but by silver. Especially in Virginia, Tennessee, North Carolina, and Kentucky, pockets of Republicans remained to divide the vote three ways. "The one point of danger," Stevenson acknowledged, "is the Farmer's Alliance or People's Party. It draws mostly from us."

With his Kentucky drawl, his mannerisms of a courtly antebellum southern planter, his storytelling, and his regional roots, the Democratic candidate for vice president might help hold the South. Some party members joked that Stevenson's office-holding cousins, ten of whom held influential positions in states ranging from Texas to Virginia, were sufficient to turn the balance in evenly divided states below the Mason-Dixon line; others believed that the mere appearance of a candidate for national office would impress southern voters.

While Letitia charmed the local ladies and sometimes talked politics, Adlai delivered rousing campaign speeches about the need to end the high tariffs that unfairly created, and then protected, American monopolies from European competition. To southern audiences accustomed to hearing about the iniquity of the tariff since the 1830s, Stevenson used "this unfair tax" as an example of the government's interference in the lives of Americans—in this case, through the protective schedule of the recently passed McKinley Tariff, which helped the rich and the bondholders but hurt the poor by raising prices. "Protection for the masses, not the classes" read the banners in Birmingham, Alabama, as the candidate, in his appeals to voters as consumers, flourished a three-dollar tin plate costing five dollars, he claimed, after Republican tariffs had created the monopoly of the American Tin Company.

To those who wearied of the tariff—though Americans of this generation held an insatiable interest in an easily understood topic that satisfied their demand for an economic palliative in hard times—Stevenson played the racial card. He approached the subject of race relations obliquely, opposing what the Democrats had labeled the force bill and what the Republicans had written as the federal elections bill of 1890. Defeated by the Senate in the last Congress, the measure sought to protect the Republican constituency of southern black males who, as the region returned to white one-party rule, were disenfranchised, despite the Fifteenth Amendment, by registration procedures, poll taxes, and violence. To prevent this noncompliance, the bill would require the monitoring of elections by federal registrars in electoral districts that prevented blacks from voting.

In language that would reappear seventy-three years later in the South's opposition to the Voting Rights Act of 1965, Adlai Stevenson told cheering crowds, "Men of Alabama, men of the South, the force bill is aimed at you. . . . Have you forgotten the sad lessons of the past? Such legislation will bring thousands of supervisors and deputy marshals and canvassing boards to your neighborhood whose business it will be to stir up ignorant negroes. The force bill will disturb harmonious relations between blacks and whites and create the old race prejudice so bitter under carpet bagger regimes." Stevenson never began with race, but by the time he had finished, white southerners knew where he stood when he spoke of the purity of the ballot and the sanctity of their homes.

In the North the chairman of the Democratic National Committee continued to worry that the vice-presidential candidate was too old-fashioned and not sufficiently businesslike. "I fear [Stevenson] is talking too much but in this I may be wrong. I have no fear for his record, but we are living for today and the future and not for twenty years ago." In response, Stevenson advised Cleveland that he was doing all in his "power to bring the Democrats back."

Wherever the couple went, their visits were followed by a gracious acknowledgment written in Letitia Stevenson's elegant hand. To Frances

Cleveland, Letitia explained her role in biblical terms. "You will play the beauty part and I will be the mother in Israel," she wrote, referring to Deborah of the Old Testament, who had inspired the Israelites. A frequent speaker at the Bloomington women's clubs, Letitia Stevenson had grown accustomed to taking positions on public issues, announcing boldly in North Carolina that the force bill would bring unqualified voters to the polls. What methods, she inquired in Kentucky, could be used "to manage the colored voters"? And in Alabama she was "disgusted" to hear that Republicans gave blacks circus tickets in exchange for their votes.

In September the Stevensons, along with several cousins and the candidate's brother William, arrived by train in Herndon, Kentucky, the tiny community near Blue Springs where Adlai had lived for sixteen years before the family migration to Illinois. After a mutton and shoat barbecue of 150 sheep and a hundred hogs, the candidate addressed a crowd of thirty thousand, the largest ever assembled in Christian County. Stevenson delivered his speech first from a rustic log stand too low and distant from the crowd for it to hear and then from a farm wagon, which, according to the local newspapers, he used as his rostrum, though most of the audience still could not hear him.

As public men everywhere reveal their private selves through their speeches no matter how seemingly impersonal the topic, so Stevenson displayed his different sides—first the sentimental, childlike popular fellow who was always telling stories until his friends declared that the least important thing about Uncle Adlai was his public career. But he also showed off his serious official demeanor, thereby encouraging his critics, in a purposeful age when rural ways were being overturned by city culture, to believe that "heavy responsibility might develop in [Adlai Stevenson] unforeseen traits of seriousness and caution."

In Herndon, Stevenson spoke nostalgically about the past, his forebears, and the boyhood he never surrendered: "With my eyes resting upon the spot where stood the old schoolhouse, within little more than a stone's throw of my earliest home, within a little distance of the sacred place where sleep the dust of three generations of my kindred, it would be passing strange if I were not overwhelmed with the recollections of the past." Overcome by sentiment, he could not trust himself "to recall the memories of those who are gone," concluding the first half of his speech with an applause-getting story about the minister who "wound up a description of heaven with the exclamation, 'The fact is, it is a regular Kentucky.' "

At the same time Adlai Stevenson was not just a casual emigrant home for a visit. As a national figure he had to present the issues to voters, even if they were relatives and acquaintances from the past. In the second portion of his two-hour speech, a more formal, professional Adlai Stevenson—the man whose gray eyes bulged and whose face straightened when he took up his roles as a public man from Bloomington rather than a country boy from Blue Springs—inveighed against the tariff that "taxed for the purpose of building up and enriching, year after year, the manufacturers of this country who are thus made a privileged class." As a result farmers and mechanics (Stevenson was never comfortable with the term "workers") bought necessities at inflated prices.

Stevenson's speeches were widely admired, and not just in Herndon. Some liked his voice and his endurance; "he can do two-three hours simple," marveled one reporter. According to Champ Clark, an authority on stump speaking, "he always spoke right out in meeting and did not mince his words . . . his information was wide and varied . . . his voice [was] musical and far-carrying, his elocution good, and he was not afraid." Voters appreciated his physical mannerisms, especially his stretching over the platform to get closer to his audience and sometimes even to touch an outstretched hand in the symbolic understanding that leaders must be in contact with the people. Southerners, in particular, were impressed by his reputed ability to spin tales for two weeks without repetition.

Stevenson was also praised for the way he shook hands. He seemed not to have any "airs"; though never completely beyond artifice, he relied on a relative to whisper the names of approaching friends in Herndon so that he could greet them by name. On the other hand, those few who approached Cleveland complained that the president did not so much shake as grab and cover a voter's hands, as if he were enclosing a squirming cod fish from his beloved Buzzards Bay.

Laden with adverbs, double negatives, and participial phrases, Stevenson's sentences were long and, to a modern ear, overloaded. "Should it please my countrymen to call me to this office, the high appreciation of its dignity and of its responsibilities—as expressed in the utterances and illustrated in the public life of the eminent statesmen whom I have mentioned—will be a light to my own pathway." At the time such ponderousness was a familiar political counterpart to the bloatedness of Gilded Age culture. Lacking self-awareness and cynicism, the candidate's exhortations to duty, virtue, and morality were not poses, though what Stevenson meant by these platitudes was often as lost to the moment as the details of his extemporaneous speeches.

Nor were the ambivalent intentions of Stevenson's stump speaking unusual. Just as Victorians refused to acknowledge sexual ardor, even as they experienced it, so Stevenson denied any intention to appeal to "the partisan passions of the people rather than to [their] sober judgment." But he followed such disclaimers with energetic attacks on the Republicans. In his indictment the opposition party was guilty of egregious sins: the unnecessary intervention of federal troops during Reconstruction, the stealing of the election of 1876 from Samuel Tilden, and the support of deflationary policies helpful to eastern "bondholding conspirators." These charges, often accompanied by fist pounding, finger shaking, and a desire to have his "lips touched with a live coal," were meant to inspire Democrats to the partisanship that Stevenson decried when he appealed "to the judiciousness and reason of Americans." Like many office seekers, he tailored his messages to his audiences—once in Peoria affirming his Irish heritage in a working-class district and in California supporting the popular policy of restricting Asian immigration.

At the end of a campaign in which Adlai Stevenson had delivered fifty-three speeches, Letitia and Adlai returned home for an election eve, torchlight serenade organized by the clubs that now served as political counterparts to Bloomington's social organizations. Replacing the Democratic army of past elections that had marched undivided by profession or age or ethnic background, the supporters of "Cleve and Steve" now came to Franklin Park and the Stevenson home as segments of the Democracy, first the German Democratic Club, then the Miners for Stevenson, followed by the Old Democrats, and finally, in their snappy blue blazers and white caps led by their president, Lewis Green Stevenson, the First Time Voters Club.

The next day Adlai Stevenson and James Ewing walked to the polls together. Letitia stayed home, although this year for the first time in Illinois history women could vote, but only with a special ballot and only for candidates for school board and University of Illinois trustees. Perhaps in honor of its local hero, the city had replaced its old ballot boxes with sturdy oak ones two feet square. In a familiar procedure shortly to give way to the secret ballot, Stevenson gave his name to an election judge, who then checked the registration lists, after which he placed his Democratic ballot in the voting box. Within hours of the polls' closing, the special telegraph wire installed in his home (first refused by the candidate as an undemocratic and expensive gimmick) brought the news of victory. "Cleve and Steve" had carried all the former Confederate states, along with the middle Atlantic states (except Pennsylvania), California, Indiana, Wisconsin, and Illinois and had won 46 percent of the popular vote to Harrison's 43 and the Populist James Weaver's 8.

That night over half the population of Bloomington surged through Franklin Park singing "Our fellow citizen, Oh! Ad, Ad, Ad." Persuaded to say a few words amid the bonfires, calcium lights, and Roman candles, Stevenson exchanged his partisanship for unity as he saluted his community in remarks that avoided the divisiveness of party competition: "I remember Bloomington from the time it was but a village without a railroad and a telegraph. I rejoice with you in its growth and prosperity. . . . Until this mortal pilgrimage is over, Bloomington will be my home." And then the vice president–elect closed with a Jeffersonian plea for cooperation: "We are all Americans. We have one country, one destiny," after which so many neighbors surged forward to greet Bloomington's most famous citizen that his front porch collapsed.

2

WHEN THE TIME CAME for Stevenson's inauguration in March 1893, Letitia and the four children went too, but eighty-four-year-old Eliza Ewing Stevenson stayed behind in Bloomington. As the city's first family departed from the depot, someone took a photograph. Collected on the rear car of the Hummer, the Chicago and Alton's fastest train, which would carry them to Chicago in four hours for their thirty-six-hour journey to Washington, the Stevensons, joined by Aunt Julia Scott and her children, might have been going to a funeral. Only Letitia, with her natural sense of diplomacy and her intentions for a substantial public life in the capital, was smiling; her husband was wearing his public face. No doubt the children's seriousness reflected sadness at parting from their Bloomington intimates— Lewis left behind his future wife, Helen Davis, and the Stevenson daughters their classmates and neighbors. Familiar with Washington and Chicago, they did not look, these Stevensons, like small-town provincial Americans.

Signaling their public status, the adults as well as the children were in full dress—the girls, their mother, and Aunt Julia Scott in the dark Victorian clothes that made it so hard for women of this generation to move— wide broad-brimmed hats decorated by the artificial flowers crafted by Italian women in the East and the popular ostrich feathers (Letitia's flowers rose nearly a foot over her hair), fox tails around their dark coats, long dresses enhanced by layers of petticoats and, no doubt underneath, the girdles and waist cinchers that left skin marks on this tight-laced generation. Shy Mary had dipped her face so that this most anonymous of Stevensons could barely be seen, while the two men of the family, Lewis and his father, Adlai, wore top hats.

In the style of military men, the vice president–elect had placed his right arm on his heart, perhaps to signify his forthcoming service to the Republic. To the rear, in another car, the members of the hundred-man Stevenson Escort Club leaned out the train windows to wave a boisterous goodbye. This group of enthusiasts intended to see the sights of Washington and to march in the inaugural parade, attired in their silk hats and carrying an American flag fitted conveniently on top of their umbrellas.

Two days after their arrival in Washington, the Stevensons began their social duties with a reception in the parlors of the fashionable Victorian Ebbitt House, one of three Washington hotels owned by the Willard brothers. Later they lived in a four-room suite and parlor in the recently completed Normandie Hotel, with its highly praised plumbing and $10-a-day rooms, located on McPherson Square, six blocks from the White House. At some point the family began another scrapbook to hold the tales of their Washington adventures: Father's induction to the vice presidency and his speech to the Senate, over which he presided, the parade from the Capitol down Pennsylvania Avenue on a snowy March inaugural day in 1893, the inaugural ball that followed in the Pension Building, whose interior court-yard and massive columns had been transformed into a court decorated with fountains, palms, and pineapples in this time of growing interest in Cuba and Hawaii, and along with these events, clippings about Letitia's increasing activity in female associations.

Soon the private doings of the family appeared in the gossip columns of Frank Carp and Kate Field's "Capital Chatter," where by the 1890s "a man's domestic and private life become objects of rare interest." The Stevensons' official status guaranteed their inclusion in Washington's highly permeable society, where they danced in embassies, presided at White House recep-tions because the Clevelands preferred quiet evenings at home, took tea in the mansions of the rich, and ate the salads and cakes of perfection at lunches organized by the bored wives of congressmen. Affable, pleasant, and unassuming, the Stevenson women behaved like good republican citi-zens, with manners poised somewhere between the extremes of plebeian vulgarity and snobby pretense that, according to Jane Keim's *Handbook of Official and Social Etiquette,* "were antagonistic to the spirit of liberty."

Miss Julia Scott Stevenson, discovered one reporter, "is a brunette and the only one of dark complexion in the family. . . . Mary Ewing Stevenson is the lily. Her manner is most gracious, her face most regular and bewitching." In time compliments turned to criticism, as reporters held Julia's nose to be too big; Mary too pale, and Mrs. Vice President Stevenson "a little plump but well-proportioned." "Not one of the girls is as handsome as their mother," sniffed one reporter. "They seem to take after the rugged Stevenson side of the family. Mary's nose is too large for beauty," com-mented another, thereby identifying the most prominent facial characteris-tic of generations of Stevensons. Even the results of Stevenson's phrenology exam—in the popular fad his skull and brain lobes had been measured—were published, and Americans learned that their vice president's head revealed him, fittingly, as "lofty, earnest, loyal, with social feeling and able to do his best in a partnership." The vice president had expected some intrusion into his personal affairs, but was chagrined to find in the gossip columns intimate details of family life such as his refusal to allow his daughters to ride bicycles, which were all the rage.

In time the new family scrapbooks included accounts of Vice President and Mrs. Stevenson's reception for Julia and Letitia at the Normandie Hotel, with the music of the Tuxedo Blues; Lewis's service as his father's $2,200-a-year secretary and his efforts to get a patronage job in the army; the all-pink luncheon given in honor of the new "Second Lady" by the outgoing vice president's wife; and before their return to Bloomington, Julia's marriage in 1896 to a Presbyterian minister with Kentucky roots, Martin Hardin. Like the rich residents of the Midwest who used Washington as the theater for their social aspirations, the Stevensons had become members of high society.

Asked if he did not tire of parties, Stevenson jovially replied, "I can't shake hands enough with Democrats of either sex." His wife was diplomatically nonpartisan: "People love to say they have shaken the hands of those in high office. Some people treasure such a memory as rich women do their jewels and I am happy to give them pleasure. . . . There is not much fatigue in receiving the American people. The American people enjoy meeting their leaders, and if I can, I will do it. At my last reception people came in the hundreds."

By this time Letitia had been elected president of the newly formed Daughters of the American Revolution, a post to which she was reelected twice. Organized in 1890 by a handful of wellborn Washington women, the DAR formed an elite national association of patriotic intention. Among its goals was "the promotion of education, especially the study of history and the enlightenment of our foreign population." Disgusted with what Mary Desha of Kentucky described as "being limited for so long to orphan asylums and hospitals," the Daughters proposed to support public endeavors, in fact "all that makes good citizenship."

In these intentions there was, at least for Letitia's generation, a feminism of the elite, for though Daughters were not citizens—at least not voting citizens—their patriotic models included Revolutionary heroines like Hannah Arnett, who had sternly exhorted her husband and sons to take up arms against the British. Disdaining absorption into several male counterparts, the DAR remained part of the separatist tradition of female organizations, thereby providing women like Letitia Stevenson with experience in speaking in public, traveling without a male chaperon, raising money, and managing an organization that by 1900 numbered 23,000. "It became apparent if women were to accomplish any distinctive patriotic work, it must be within their own circle and under their own leadership," argued Letitia.

With membership restricted to those women whose ancestors had "rendered material aid to the cause of independence," the DAR simultaneously excluded latecomers while denying any aristocratic pretensions. Still, its chapters quickly filled with well-dressed, prosperous, dignified, and snooty middle-class, middle-aged women with the leisure and education to research the genealogies necessary for inclusion in this tribe of quality. The stern injunction "Do not fail to arouse a genuine devotion to your ancestors" took time and money and, once accomplished, encouraged a self-satisfied nativism and family worship.

With a discernment that led to the location of their national headquarters three blocks from the White House, the founding mothers persuaded Caroline Scott Harrison, the wife of Benjamin Harrison, to serve as their first president. When the Democrats came to town, they turned to Frances Cleveland, but now the mother of a small child and pregnant with a second daughter, the first lady declined. Next in line was Letitia Stevenson, who became the second president of an organization whose ideals of flag-waving patriotism, reconciliation with the white South, and exclusionism on the basis of ancestry reflected a national malaise at the end of the century. Many native-born Americans believed, along with the Daughters, that the nation's Anglo-Saxon heritage was being diluted by immigrants from southeastern Europe "who have never read the first letter of the spirit of Americanism."

When Letitia Stevenson was elected president, she had been a member for only a few weeks, having established her pedigree through Joshua Fry. Later both she and her sister Julia Scott claimed the most exalted lineage available in republican America: collateral descent from the family of George Washington, though the claim was not verified and led Julia Scott to argue the complex matter of Henry Willis's second wife's birth name with the august genealogist Mrs. Watson. "My ancestors had always stated that the first wife of Dr. Walker was the granddaughter of Laurence Washington," insisted Julia incorrectly. "If you do prepare another edition, I hope you will do our family the justice to correct and erase the statement [that we are descended from Mary Taliaferro]."

In this investigation of their lineage, the sisters joined other Americans who discovered in the worthies of their past a status threatened by change. The 1890s became the time in which, along with the nativist American Protective Association, Americans created, according to the new *Patriotic Review*, over fifty national hereditary and historical associations. To accommodate such interest, public libraries in cities from New York to Chicago opened search rooms for family history.

Not everyone approved. Jane Addams spoke for those who found the exclusionary criteria that limited membership to the descendants of early settlers repugnant. The Chicago reformer preferred the type of inclusiveness she was promoting at Hull House. Noting Letitia Stevenson's election to the Daughters of the American Revolution, the *Charlotte Observer* was offended by her membership in an organization designed "to build up a sort of American aristocracy based on the idea that an aristocracy based on blood is better than one based on money. But Adlai is a plain man and we cannot believe that he takes any stock in this sort of business. He was sprung from the loins of the common people and he bears the traits of his ancestry. Imagine him at a 'function.' Imagine him living in a house with a poodle dog with a blue ribbon around its neck."

On the other hand, Letitia's prominence in a patriotic organization served to offset persistent rumors of her husband's disloyalty during the Civil War. It also verified her family's distinguished heritage as the descendants of Mary Peachy Green—an American Duchess of Buccleuch. When her husband began his service as the vice president of the United States, she took up equivalent duties as the president-general of the Daughters of the American Revolution (the double title a legacy from George Washington's career). Mrs. Vice President Stevenson presided over the Daughters at their national meeting held on George Washington's birthday, raised money to buy land near the White House, rendered a decision as to whether members of the DAR could claim descent through mothers of revolutionaries and collateral relatives, learned Robert's *Rules of Order,* and underwent a humiliating attack in the newspapers that she had been in the chair during her contested reelection in 1896. "Ladies," Letitia warned more than once, "there is too much personality in your remarks. We will have quiet."

In 1904 Letitia's sister, Julia Green Scott, followed her to the presidency-generalship, presiding over the ground breaking for Continental Hall, the vast white-marbled headquarters of the DAR. And in Bloomington the Letitia Green Stevenson Chapter of the Daughters flourished. Eventually the portraits of the two sisters, looking like the twins that they were emotionally and physically, attired in dresses of the blue and white hues favored by the Daughters because they were the colors of Washington's uniform, gazed at each other near the Illinois Room in Constitution Hall.

Letitia found time and energy for another cause. When Phoebe Hearst, the rich widow of the mining magnate and California senator George Hearst, invited her to become a board member of the National Association of Mothers, a precursor of the Parents and Teachers Association, she accepted. There she joined five other reformers with the similarly spacious intentions of "inculcating the love of humanity and love of country, encouraging closer relations between home influence and school life, and working for life development from the standards of knowing truth and harmony."

Letitia had begun her journey to the Association of Mothers in the Bloomington Women's Club. There, surrounded by other women whose conversations often turned to their children, she came to consider motherhood as a self-conscious profession, a part of the new social sciences that, from a variety of perspectives and disciplines, sought to improve the nation. Like economists and political scientists, mothers must study their specialty—evaluating kindergartens, absorbing data from child-raising manuals, and undertaking what Letitia called the "scientific study of child nature." There was patriotic significance in such a view, for according to Letitia Stevenson, in an address to the National Conference of Mothers, "it is to the mothers of this country, America's greatest resource today, that we must look to for a better, stronger and more churched mankind."

Along with thousands of American women, Letitia Stevenson linked improved mothering to social reform. Thereby she sculpted a public, though not necessarily political, role for herself that left undisturbed her traditional domesticity, but that nonethless bestowed an invisible, ephemeral power, a dominion within the male empire. "The hand that rocks the cradle rules the Empire" was the motto of the Association of Mothers, which was boldly expanded into the conviction that "the destiny of nations lies far more in the hands of mothers than in the possessors of power."

As the battle for suffrage engaged others, Letitia Stevenson disclaimed any identification with women as a sex, only with woman's role as nurturer of the young. "I am not impressed with those who make speeches on the downtrodden sex," she said, even as her daughters began to speak out for women's suffrage. Instead, she made her cause that of improved maternalism.

Good mothering meant, in Letitia's definition, "less need of jails, prisons, the industrial and reform schools." But it required government policies to protect children, such as raising the age of marital consent and the passage of child labor laws. Of course the message held a contradiction. To be a good mother required staying at home; to be an expert demanded public activities. To do their job, mothers must know when to call the new specialists called pediatricians, and they must, above all, influence the schools that claimed their young for increasing periods of time. Hence the association of mothers supported a national training school for women to learn sanitation, the prevention of illness, and nutrition. Young women, according to Alice McClellan Birney, a president of the National Association, must train for at least a year "for their future vocation of mother." And although there was a vague hope that the education of boys would include something to make them better fathers, parenthood remained a female vocation.

While Letitia came to the DAR through the family remembrances of the aristocratic heritage of her Virginia and Kentucky forebears, her passage to the National Association of Mothers was more calculated. To be sure, the goals of the two organizations were fused through their mutual belief that, as Letitia claimed, "the supremacy of the Anglo-Saxon" was the result of "love of home." Still, Letitia had also joined the board because Phoebe Hearst was an influential, wealthy philanthropist who promised a job in one of her western silver mines to her son, Lewis. She became a member because she might redeem her own, necessarily flawed mothering. "The most wonderful achievement in all nature is the perfect child," she exulted to a meeting of mothers in Chicago, but she knew how unattainable this goal was.

Letitia's dilemma involved Mary and Lewis, her two sickly children, neither of whom was able to finish school, much less the colleges that by this period assured status and employment in a nonmanual trade. Letitia did not limit the advantages of higher education to her son. Instead, she believed that young women should have the benefits of college, and she rejected the doctrine of the eminent Harvard physiologist E. H. Clarke that young women placed their motherhood at risk through study, which forced blood to their brains and away from their reproductive organs. If too much energy was spent on Algebra or Greek, irreparable harm occurred in their uterus, according to Clarke.

Letitia focused on practicalities: "Every woman ought to be able to support herself. . . . I was brought up in an atmosphere where it was thought very unwomanly to do anything but keep house and make home attractive. When I grew older and saw more of the world, I began to realize there was a vast difference between theory and fact. It is all very charming to rhapsodize about the refining influence of a woman upon a home. What if she has no home? . . . A girl who is self-reliant is in no haste to choose a husband or, shall we say, let a husband choose her. She doesn't get married because she doesn't know what else to do."

Yet none of her daughters ever held jobs, and Julia, the only Stevenson to attend college, lasted just a semester as a special student at Wellesley. Red-haired Letitia, the beauty of the family, never married, and in the calculus of American success, Lewis was a failure, undertaking many jobs, succeeding at none, and holding only the least of these—as the farm manager for his aunt Julia Green Scott's extensive properties—for more than two years.

Letitia Stevenson had not caused her children's problems—though her success in public life may have sharpened her son's awareness of his shortcomings—but it was the woman's lot, a legacy of conscious motherhood, to absorb guilt for the imperfections of children who, as human beings, were inevitably flawed. "Motherhood is the only relationship which can know no separation. All others can be broken. . . . There may be estrangements but these are rare, especially on the side of the mother." Yet if good mothering shaped successful, morally correct children, then irresponsible mothering created inferior offspring. So Letitia suffered Lewis's angry outbursts and uncontrollable temper, Mary's illness and death, and her daughter Letitia's spinsterhood.

Through their public activities—hers of atonement, his of salvation—the Stevensons became celebrities. She traveled through the country to local chapters of the DAR, encouraged membership and, once on a steam launch in Lake Michigan, persuaded the wife of a territorial governor to become an organizing regent, gave speeches on the restoration of decaying monuments and the building of new ones to honor George Washington, and promoted the National Association of Mothers; he presided over the Senate, and in his abundant free time attended social occasions in Washington and journeyed through the country to give gracious nonpartisan speeches.

In these years Letitia and Adlai complemented each other—she a gracious and able administrator involved in the good works for which she had trained during her husband's absences; he an amiable, amusing, and conscientious public servant who, like his wife, was engaged in ceremonial tasks and duties. Adlai recognized the benefits of their partnership, while Letitia developed a theory about the importance of symmetrical marriages grounded in a wife's "thorough knowledge of her husband's business" and the husband's commensurate understanding of his wife's "occupations." Even when Letitia might have retired from the presidency of the DAR—for by 1895 she used braces for legs twisted by arthritis—her husband urged her to continue what she endured as "fatigues and excitements."

In the spring of 1893 the public lives of Letitia and Adlai Stevenson converged in Chicago at the Columbian Exposition, the world's fair that marked the quadricentennial celebration of Columbus's discovery of America. To Illinoisians like the Stevensons the event signified the coming of age of their region and their nation. Not by chance did the historian Frederick Jackson Turner, a midwesterner by birth, use the forum of the Columbian Exposition for his breathtaking analysis of the end of the frontier as concluding an epoch in American history. Surrounded by evidence from a city of over a million that had restructured the credit, agriculture, commerce, and industry of hinterland communities like Bloomington, Turner was not alone in his belief that the United States had become an urban society. Nor was he the only visitor among the twenty-five million fairgoers to fear the effects of the disappearance of free land on individualism, liberty, and democracy.

In Chicago in 1893 the evils of the city were juxtaposed to the progress symbolized by the fair. Everyone who came to the white fantasy world built in the swampland by the lake traveled through the dirt and noise of the city, cautioned to beware pickpockets and tramps. Those who intrepidly rode the marvel of the midway—the 250-foot Ferris wheel—viewed the hovels that led women like Jane Addams to organize Hull House in the city's First Ward. By this time Chicago had acquired a taint of radicalism as the home of the International Working People's Association, which had elected four assemblymen and several aldermen. In 1877, striking workers had closed down the national railway system, and nine years later as workers rallied, someone, perhaps an anarchist, perhaps a police provocateur, threw a bomb. Seven policemen were killed, hundreds of citizens were wounded, and the Haymarket Riot became a symbol of unrest in the Republic. Thereafter when papers like the Bloomington *Pantagraph* referred to Chicago as a metropolis, the word conveyed danger.

Among the white-stuccoed edifices at the Chicago fair was the porticoed three-story Women's Building, distinctive for its spacious loggia, colonnades, graceful round arches, and Italian Renaissance style. Smaller than the massive Transportation, Industry and Manufacturing Buildings, it had been designed by Sophia Hayden, a recent graduate of the Massachusetts Institute of Technology, who had won the competitive commission for a structure that cost $200,000. Within were displayed not only the new irons and washing machines expected to liberate women from domestic work but also their artistic achievements. Considered more delicate than (and therefore inferior to) the heavy Beaux Arts Administration Building, with its white and gold trim, and the massive neo-Renaissance temples that held displays ranging from a map of the United States made of pickles and a Krupp cannon from Germany to Gobelin tapestries and, in the Illinois Building, a sample of the state's precious dark loamy soil, the Women's Building expressed transformations in the attitudes of, and about, women. "This is the first time in the history of the Republic," proclaimed Mrs. Potter Palmer, "that woman has been recognized as competent to attend to any sort of public business by the national government."

Letitia Stevenson came to the great rotunda of the Women's Building in the spring of 1893 to address an assembled throng on motherhood and its role in reform. She avoided the suffrage issue, disavowing any "mission to discuss at length and in brief the many abstruse subjects which now agitate the female minds . . . nor whether woman shall have a voice in the councils of the nation or hold her peace forever." Like her husband, she offered words of harmony, ending with a gentle threat: "I feel assured that the women of the day and of this congress will leave an impress upon the time and nations that our honorable husbands, brothers and friends will never be able to efface—be they ever so much inclined."

Her theme was as old as the American Revolution, when mothers had been assigned the role of creating virtuous republican citizens in their homes. In the 1890s Letitia Stevenson argued for an extension of enlightened domesticity into municipal housekeeping. A variant of the domestication of politics, her ideas were intended to achieve the public benefits of a better (Letitia substituted "more moral" in her speech) society accomplished by professional child raising. Now, instead of patriots, mothers must raise law-abiding sons. In the fall Letitia Stevenson returned again to the great hall decorated by the artwork of women to give another speech on the importance of motherhood and to strike three times a huge replica of the Liberty Bell donated by the DAR.

At the same time that his wife was addressing the women, the vice president, who had lobbied for the exhibition's national appropriation, also visited Chicago's fair and was attracted to the gondolas that, gliding through the lagoons, carried passengers from one event to another. In his ceremonial capacity as vice president, Adlai Stevenson came several times during

1893, first accompanying the president when, during the singing of Handel's Hallelujah chorus, Cleveland opened the fair by turning an electric key that simultaneously lit 10,000 lights, turned on 500 fountains, and started the fair's machinery, a technological feat that the crowd of 300,000 appreciated as the type of modern marvel anticipated at world's fairs.

To the amusement of reporters, Adlai forgot his free pass. Refusing to pay the half-dollar admission fee, the vice president hiked back to the Palmer House, displaying the thrift, according to a *Chicago Journal* reporter, of "an old-fashioned man." On another occasion the vice president invoked the platitudes he always carried with him and spoke of American progress and virtue to an audience in the Illinois Building.

3

FROM THE RECORD of their years in Washington, the Stevensons expunged their tragedies—Mary's death in 1895 from tuberculosis; Lewis's restlessness and bad health; Father's failure to win the Democratic presidential nomination in 1896, after the question "Why not Stevenson?" became "What's the matter with Stevenson?"; the disturbing challenge to Letitia's third term and the controversy over omissions in the DAR minutes. Even the widening distance between the president and vice president disappeared from a Stevenson past that was not so much glorified as one-dimensionally portrayed. In a family that labored to place descendants in touch with ancestors by keeping scrapbooks and telling tales of bygone days until its heroic vision became success in public life, the official Stevenson history contained no chapters on thwarted expectations. Deprived of lessons on surmounting disappointments, the children lacked instruction on the uses of failure to accomplishment.

The depression that sharpened the differences between president and vice president had begun just after the inauguration, although there had been earlier signs of an overextended economy. Farm prices had dropped. Even the prosperous farmers of McLean County were pinched by a market that offered only forty-two cents a bushel for wheat and for corn, hardly enough to return costs. Then, as in the recession of 1873, a few railroads went bankrupt, and the stock market collapsed. Banks called their loans; European investors dumped their securities; and Americans hurried to exchange paper money for gold. The National Cordage Company failed, followed by fifteen thousand other businesses. By the summer of 1893 the unemployment rate had risen to 20 percent; in Chicago, estimates of those out of work ranged from 72,000 to 181,000. The economic ripples reached Bloomington, and a run on deposits nearly forced the People's Bank to close. Across the United States over five hundred banks did fail, as the national gold reserves dipped under $100 million and by 1895 were under $42 million.

Cleveland, relying on a precedent established during the Civil War, turned to the private investment company of J. P. Morgan to sell $193 million of gold bonds that would return specie to the Treasury. No one in the administration considered the modern palliatives of increased government spending, or aid to the unemployed, or adjustment in interest rates. Such initiatives were foreign to late-nineteenth-century suspiciousness about the federal government's role in the economy.

In his inaugural address the president had announced his position: "The lessons of paternalism ought to be unlearned and the better lesson taught that while the people should patriotically and cheerfully support the government, its functions do not include the support of the people." The vice president especially applauded these lines, for he believed that the least government was the best. Yet from this catastrophe the house of Morgan grew rich, while the president who had earlier vetoed a bill giving free seeds to Texas farmers did nothing. The people responded by naming their soup kitchens "Cleveland's Cafes." The president's girth, an earlier symbol of national prosperity, now seemed an insult to starving workers who, in Bloomington as elsewhere, scavenged for food.

Cleveland was not without ideas on how to treat the economic crisis. He looked to changes in the tariff and the repeal of the Sherman Silver Purchase Act. Passed in 1890, this act had been a compromise measure to accommodate the growing clamor to expand the amount of money in circulation by authorizing the Treasury's purchase of a minimum of 4 million ounces of silver a month. In two years the government had bought more than 147 million ounces of silver, and the notes based on this, redeemable in gold, caused a drain on specie reserves. Stubbornly committed to a gold standard that he believed would stabilize the American economy in international markets just as silver corrupted and debased it, Cleveland considered calling Congress into special session to repeal the silver act.

The president did not discuss his plans with Stevenson. The latter, ensconced in the vice president's room in the U.S. Capitol with its Adams mirror, Minton floor tiles, and former Vice President Henry Wilson's desk (nearly a century later Richard Nixon mistook the desk for Woodrow Wilson's, moved it to the White House, and cut holes in it for his electronic devices), said nothing about his solution for hard times. In fact Stevenson supported a national currency backed by both silver and gold in a fixed ratio of sixteen ounces of silver to one of gold. Keeping silent, the vice president joked with reporters about past days in the post office: "You boys will be just as welcome as in the old days. [There are] no sentries standing in front of the vice president's room. You won't have to dive in your pockets and pull out a card to be transmitted to me on a salver. You will walk right in and if I'm not there, you'll send for me. I am the vice president and the people are entitled to know what I'm doing."

The first spring of the depression, prior to the special session of Congress, the Stevensons traveled to the West on the kind of ceremonial visit at which the family excelled. They left just after a handsome yacht raised anchor and glided slowly from New York's East River through Hell's Gate and into Long Island Sound. For hours the *Oneida* cruised about as if on a Fourth of July outing. Below decks in the main salon, seated in a huge wicker chair strapped to the mast, was the president. A week earlier he had discovered a rough lump in the roof of his mouth. Deeply suspicious of Stevenson and "Adlai's silver cabinet," Grover Cleveland believed that any news of his bad health and the attendant possibility of Stevenson's becoming president would drastically shake the financial markets. Gold reserves already under pressure would be hoarded or would flee to Europe. Hence the president's cancer operation had to take place secretly on the *Oneida;* his difficulty in speaking with a vulcanized rubber jaw had to be disguised as trouble with his dentures. Years later, when the story of Cleveland's operation and his artificial jaw became known, a reporter asked Adlai Stevenson's two surviving daughters whether the vice president had known about the operation. Testifying to an incident that revealed Cleveland's hostility toward Stevenson, both replied no.

When Stevenson came back to town after his trip to the West, Congress convened to repeal the Sherman Silver Purchase Act. Besides the parties and storytelling, the vice president now had something to do. What he called "the office of dignity" featured presiding over the Senate and, in cases of a tie, voting—an opportunity that in Stevenson's tenure occurred only twice, on relatively minor procedural motions. As one congressman put it, "He is to preside over the Senate, simply enforcing the rules, as silent as a sepulchre unless in a tie vote. How meagre are his duties! . . . His absolute inherent powers are not the equal of a baliff. Still he is an heir expectant—a contingent remainder man."

Stevenson didn't mind. Day after day he rode the little green street cars that passed by the Ebbitt House and, after the family moved, two blocks from the Normandie. Arriving in his office an hour before the Senate convened, he took his place in the Empire-style chair on the raised marble dais that provided a splendid view of the most powerful chieftains of the three parties—Republicans, most of whom supported gold and a protective tariff, Democrats, split between the silverites and goldbugs and divided as well on the specifics of tariff schedules, and Populists, committed to coining silver in a ratio of 16 to 1 and to the popular election of U.S. senators. Unlike the House of Representatives, the Senate had no rules for limiting debate. The filibuster had become a sanctuary for its minorities. The senators from silver states, whose mines produced over fifty million ounces of silver a year, used the technique lavishly. Senator John Jones of Nevada spoke for five days against the repeal, filling one hundred pages of the *Congressional Record.*

Both sides worried about Stevenson's impartiality, though there was no cause. By nature he temporized; by training he conciliated; by residence and circumstance he was a middling man. Mute, like the disabled who hear but cannot speak, he intended to follow the precedent of unlimited debate unless the body by a two-thirds vote agreed to change its own rules. He would not, he told the senators who flocked to his office, pass over the silver senators who employed endless speeches to prevent the roll call that would result in repeal. Nor would the vice president extend the debate if the filibuster showed signs of ending. To his wife he explained, "We are in the midst of one of the most important and desperate struggles ever known to the Senate or to any legislative body. . . . I know the rules pretty well. I have been sustained in every decision. I do not write this in an egotistical spirit at all, but I know how interested you are."

But the possibility of Stevenson's—or anyone's—neutrality seemed preposterous. To be on the wrong side of the currency issue was to be liable to removal even from college presidencies, as Brown University's Benjamin Andrews was by trustees who found his support of silver so outrageous that they forced him to resign. William Allen White, the editor of the *Emporia* (Kansas) *Gazette,* compared the fanaticism over silver to that of religious crusaders of the eleventh century. In the West even fairy tales drew on the quarrel. The Nebraska Populist Frank Baum created Dorothy, a fictional character in *The Wizard of Oz* who wore silver shoes as she fended off the wicked witch of the East, walked the perilous yellow-brick road, and sought the key to a return to her past.

When a group of repeal senators presented Stevenson with their arguments for ending the filibuster, he refused and thereby earned the disdain of several influential Democrats: "Stevenson," concluded one observer, "lacked the courage to refuse dilatory motions . . . day after day helpless in his chair, unable to preserve more than a semblance of order and decorum." Amid passion foreign to his temperament—at a time when gold and silver were no longer economic abstractions but hovered in the air like storm clouds—the Senate finally repealed the silver measure.

Its effect was limited. In the spring of 1894 Coxey's army—a tattered band of five hundred protesters led by Jacob Coxey, a former businessman from Ohio, his daughter attired in red and blue astride a white horse, and his wife carrying their son Legal Tender—arrived in Washington to see the vice president. At the time Coxey's army was only one of several "living petitions" sent to lawmakers. As similar bedraggled groups moved across the United States, the comfortable classes feared a revolution. "Hark, Hark, the dogs do bark / Coxey's army is coming to town" went the rhyme of apprehension used to frighten children into silence.

Coxey had a solution for the hard times that involved neither violence nor the currency. Carrying from Ohio an idea whose time arrived during the New Deal, Coxey wanted the government to underwrite public works and hire the unemployed to work on them. After its arrival, his "army" milled about the U.S. Capitol, intending to make its case to the vice president. But the available man was not to be found this May day. The senate had chosen this moment to honor a colleague, dead for weeks, and Adlai Stevenson, who, unlike modern vice presidents, customarily presided, was neither on the floor nor in his office. The next day Coxey was arrested not for attempting to overthrow the U.S. government (as some had hoped) but for destroying the grass and shrubbery of the Capitol grounds. Of this matter Stevenson said nothing.

Before his term as vice president was over, there was talk of Stevenson for president. After two terms Cleveland intended to end his penance and retire to the pleasures of family and fishing. Yet the president had dominated Democratic politics for so long that there was no obvious replacement, and the controversies engendered by the titanic congressional battles over the currency and the tariff left a disgruntled, immobilized party.

To further his chances, Stevenson mailed his speeches to party leaders around the country, along with discreet solicitations to help through chain letters. Predictably the clan was active, though the success of Stevenson's patronage efforts had removed his closest advisers—his cousins James and Adlai Ewing—to diplomatic posts overseas. The candidate couched his requests for support in the mildest of appeals, for in his understanding of politics, he must not assert himself for a nomination. Such backdoor ambition irritated some. "If Adlai Stevenson took the presidential talk more seriously, he might have a chance," chided the *Pantagraph*. Reporters in Washington complained that "a good many people entertain some hesitation as to the mental, moral and social fitness of Adlai Ewing Stevenson." "There is no mark on anything he does or says. For some reason he doesn't seem to be in the running." Shelby Cullom, an Illinois governor and Republican leader, found the vice president an unlikely politician for the times: "He always left the impression that whatever you happen to do is just the thing that suits him."

On July 3, when the delegates to the 1896 Democratic National Convention assembled, again in Chicago, Stevenson stayed away. Associated with Cleveland, he was no longer favored by Illinois Democrats, who despised the president for sending federal troops to their state to end a railway strike in 1894. At the direction of the Democratic governor, John Altgeld, party regulars had even omitted Stevenson from the list of regular delegates, all of whom, like a majority of the convention, were silverites. Sensitive to

such stings, Stevenson was embarrassed to find himself an alternate delegate to his party's national convention. Still, he did not stay in Washington,
but traveling to Illinois, remained available in nearby Bloomington.

Like those from Illinois, most delegates supported silver, patrolling
hotel lobbys wearing silver asters (South Carolinian Ben Tillman's version
had three goldbugs impaled on a silver pitchfork), and to them the Stevenson lobby emphasized their man's inflationist credentials. He had been a
Greenback-Labor congressman and, as an independent Democrat, they
said, had voted the silver program of the 1870s; he had talked silver quietly
while vice president. To the eastern Democrats the Stevenson supporters
offered the vice president as a loyal member of Cleveland's administration,
and he became a man for both sides during a storm in party history that
required a fixed rudder rather than trimmed sails to catch every wind. "The
Vice President," according to the New York Times, "says nothing but imma-
terial pleasantries. He could be readily adjusted to a sound money plank or
a declaration for free silver. He would feel quite as much at home with one
position as the other."

If the vice president was bound by his old-fashioned notions of nominations as gifts of the people, thirty-five-year-old William Jennings Bryan was
not. A congressman from the small Republican state of Nebraska, Bryan
had worked to become what he called "the logic of the situation," traveling
during the 1890s on the Chautauqua circuit for one hundred dollars a
speech and tirelessly meeting with state leaders. To the latter he cast his
partisanship in polarized rhetoric that placed "the moneyed interests of
aggregated wealth and capital, imperious, arrogant, compassionless" at war
with "the work-worn, dust-begrimed . . . unnumbered throng who gave the
Democratic party a name and for whom it has assumed to speak." Chosen
to present the controversial silver platform for the free and unlimited coinage of silver in the ratio of 16 to 1, the ambitious Bryan grasped his opportunity.

Tossing aside the lemon he habitually sucked to prepare a voice practiced in sessions with his wife, according to the Springfield poet Edgar Lee
Masters, he sprang from his seat, "slim, tall, raven-haired, beaked of nose
. . . full of statuesque poses . . . [wearing] a black sack suit of alpaca and a
low cut vest and trousers that bagged at the knees." Watching him, Stevenson's friend William Vilas, who spoke earlier for gold, wondered if he was
hearing Robespierre.

When Bryan finished, no one doubted that he was silver's champion or
that his battle would pit, as sharply as any presidential campaign in American history, poor farmers and workers against the rich. In a memorable
political speech "the Boy Orator of the Platte" combined an appeal for silver
as "the cause of humanity" with a ferocious attack on those "who come
before us and tell us that we shall disturb your business interests. . . . We

reply that you have disturbed our business interests." Galvanizing delegates into the kind of floor demonstrations that were beginning to influence other delegates, Bryan first broke down class differences, making all those who worked with their hands into producers: "The man who is employed for wages is as much a business man as a farmer." Then Bryan separated these "struggling masses" from the parasitical "idle holders of idle capital." Raising the battle over money to a spiritual consideration—silver is "a cause as holy as the cause of liberty and the cause of humanity"—he made sinners of those who supported gold. Finally, separating farm and city, he ended, arms outstretched as if his body were a cross, with an unforgettable political irrelevancy:

"Burn down your cities and leave our farms and your cities will spring up again as if by magic. But destroy our farms and grass will grow in the streets of every city in this country. . . . Having behind us the producing masses of this country and of the world supported by the commercial interests and the toilers everywhere, we will answer their demand for a gold standard by saying to them 'you shall not press down upon the brow of labor this cross of thorns, you shall not crucify mankind upon a cross of gold.' "

The next day the Democratic convention chose William Jennings Bryan on the fifth ballot, with Adlai Stevenson receiving only a few scattered votes on each roll call. Later the Populists took a step back to the two-party system by also nominating Bryan. Not content with front porch conversations or letter writing, the Great Commoner (Bryan was the kind of politician who collected dramatic labels) visited twenty-seven states, traveled a record 18,000 miles by train, and on some days delivered more than two dozen speeches. Using the powerful, resonant voice that carried to the back row no matter how large the crowd, he concentrated on silver, the summary issue for the Democrats.

In October, Bryan came to Bloomington. At a Democratic rally at which Adlai Stevenson presided, the candidate spoke to his central theme: "The question of silver involves the welfare of our nation, it involves humanity, it involves civilization." Appealing both to farmers from McLean County and to workers from Bloomington, he took time to praise Adlai Stevenson, who had remained loyal to the party and who had not, like the prodigal son Cleveland now supporting a gold Democrat, "gone to feed the hogs of the enemy." When the former president heard about the Bloomington rally, he ridiculed "our friend Stevenson who introduced Bryan as the foremost statesman of the age."

Politics, it now seemed to Stevenson, required treachery. Sadly he noted that even close friends had deserted. "I am grieved beyond words at attacks on me. Control of the party [is now] in the hands of those hostile to me." A letter to the chairman of the Democratic National Committee had gone unanswered for weeks; he hoped that another friend would return a message he had written in a fit of pique. But he was not a man to hold a grudge. When the time came to write about Cleveland, the glory of close association with a president and Stevenson's natural goodwill erased any ill feeling. And Stevenson acknowledged the man who never forgave him as "a representative of the democracy of the highest type . . . [a man] with a kind heart who was ever generous in his dealings."

In this season of disappointments, the results of the election in November provided no consolation. In a realigning vote that, like a sculptor's mold, established for the next decades a pattern for partisan choices, McKinley won by 5 percentage points over Bryan, and easily carried the electoral vote by taking the North, the border states, and the Midwest, leaving for Democrats the less populated South and West, except for California and Oregon. In an improving economy McKinley had successfully dangled the promise of a full working pail and the stability of gold-backed currency before eastern workers. Remembering the depression of 1892 as a Democratic catastrophe, many American men to whom Bryan had appealed as dispossessed instead supported the Republicans. Thus the prospects for a coalition of workers and farmers were postponed for another three decades.

In Illinois, where 40 percent of the population now lived in communities of over 8,000, the Republicans carried Chicago, the northern and central counties, including McLean, leaving for Bryan only the southern counties in Egypt and along the Mississippi, where residents of southern birth and heritage provided the Democrats' core of supporters. Stevenson, who might have had a cabinet post if Bryan had won, mourned the end of his public life. "My political career has closed," he lamented to a friend. To his mother he repeated, "My public career will now be closed." "What remains of my life shall be devoted to my children and grandchildren," he advised his son, Lewis.

When the time came in 1897 for Stevenson to surrender his office to Teddy Roosevelt, who had at first resisted the possible sacrifice of his political career in what he called "that singular office" (though it gained him the "bully pulpit" after McKinley's assassination in 1901), the Senate, as it customarily did, bestowed praise on its presiding officer for his "prompt decision, dignified bearing, just enforcement of the rules of this body" in the great silver repeal and tariff fights. Stevenson also was rewarded with a handsome silver desk set, which, representing the highest and emptiest office of family attainment, became a celebrated and contested object among four generations of Stevensons.

Like other vice presidents, Stevenson was also honored with the traditional bust to be placed in a niche around the Senate floor. During the Gilded Age vice presidents had expensive tastes. Chester Arthur had wanted the famous sculptor Augustus Saint-Gaudens to have the commission for his bust, but the government refused the necessary $800. Stevenson was more easily satisfied and proudly informed his mother that his would be the twenty-fourth. "First it was a block of marble, then it assumed the shape of a human head and finally the features of the vice president. Everyone pronounces it perfect."

4

IN 1897 THE STEVENSON FAMILY returned to Bloomington. Like their public careers, the town seemed to have stalled, its population of 23,000 only a few thousand larger than that of 1890. But Bloomington continued to serve as a commercial center for McLean County's 70,000 residents, who shopped every Saturday in the stores around courthouse square. When the buying was over, farmers disappeared into the corner saloons with shellacked chest-high counters, leaning on the bronze rails to call their orders for the locally brewed Meyer's beer (the temperance movement had never won Bloomington, though Normal remained chastely dry), while the women had nowhere to go until a lunch counter allowed them to sit and use the facilities.

Bloomington remained a railroad town, with its twin city Normal the intersection point of five lines. The Chicago and Alton Shops employed over fifteen hundred workers, maintained a daily payroll of $60,000, and completed six to eight new railroad cars each day. Local factories depended on freight trains to carry their hams, stoves, bricks, and patent medicines to Chicago and St. Louis, and awaited their return with raw materials and a growing variety of both consumer goods and factory parts purchased from wholesale establishments in Chicago. To help with sales, dozens of "commercial travelers" employed by the town's larger firms rode the trains beyond the county to promote hometown products.

Shortly after her return, Letitia Stevenson was elected president of the Bloomington Women's Club, and she rejoined the History and Art Club. With a diminished household—she had gone to Washington with four children and returned with none living at home—she had begun writing, first the never completed autobiography and then a history of the Daughters of the American Revolution. Active in her sister Julia's election as president-general of the Daughters ("the highest honor that can come to any woman in the country") and insistent on the need for day nurseries in Bloomington, fifty-four-year-old Letitia grew more outspoken on the issue of scientific motherhood. "There is no thoughtful woman in America," she informed the McLean County chapter of the Federated Clubs of Illinois, "who has not been more than startled by the gospel for large families." Mute on women's suffrage with its possible embarrassments for her husband's career, she had few inhibitions about discussing family planning.

Community improvement had replaced an earlier focus on self-improvement; still, she declined the label club woman: "I am not a club woman as the term goes, but I belong to a number of clubs and I think they have a splendid mission which should in no way conflict with home-duties." Indeed, it was these organizations that provided women like Letitia Stevenson with an informal liberal arts education. Though she held herself to be "unprogressive" because she did not read modern literature, in fact Letitia delivered lectures on a variety of subjects. Asked once what she was reading, Letitia replied that along with the obligatory Bible and Shake-speare, her bedside table held Hamilton Mabie's didactic essays, which encouraged readers to "strive not to enjoy but to comprehend," and, inexplicably, Sir Isaac Walton's *The Compleat Angler*.

By this time elegance had overtaken the Stevensons and their neighbors; handsome three-story houses of granite and brick that cost over $10,000 were transforming the eastern and northern parts of town. Inside, these mansions were decorated with bric-a-brac, gilt mirrors, heavy velvet hangings, frescoed walls, and elaborate furniture. More than furnishings, it was the dining room that stamped a family as middle-class. Such a room displayed the owner's wealth and leisure time to have conversations with wife, children, and friends around the table, indulging, as Adlai Stevenson often did, in the intimacies that separated private life from the harsher world of public affairs.

Such grandiosity was part of the conspicuous consumption practiced first in American cities, and at the end of the century come to Bloomington, where millionaires like David Davis, Asahel Gridley, and Matthew Scott toured Europe, supported a country club, and in their homes displayed the grand style of the late Victorian age. Cousin Spencer Ewing, whose grandparents had come to Illinois in an ox-drawn cart, gloried in his fancy carriage complete with a matched team of black thoroughbreds and two "black boys gotten up in livery." Soon Adlai bought Letitia a snappy black brougham, but with the plebeian sense that led him to gaze in horror at the knickers required for an audience with Queen Victoria, he refused to allow any initials or crest on its enameled doors. "Father disdained this as too aristocratic," explained Julia.

By 1900 the rough egalitarianism of Stevenson's early years in Bloomington had disappeared. No longer did the entire community enjoy picnics and watermelon sociables organized in the nearby groves, meet in Major's Hall to consider some local concern, or enjoy private hospitality such as that extended by the Crawfords in 1874 when they set up a 100-foot-long table in their backyard and invited everyone in Bloomington for a barbecue "in gratitude for saving our property from a fire." Responding to the change, the *Pantagraph* divided its local news into two columns: "Town Talk," which carried news of the middle-class north and east sides, and "West Side Notes," which covered the working class.

In the summer of 1900 a great fire destroyed the center of Bloomington, including the courthouse, the popular Windsor Hotel, and the highest building in town—the supposedly fireproof six-story Griesheim "skyscraper," which contained the offices of Stevenson's Interstate Building and Loan Association. High winds were responsible, but the fire was also fueled by the new balloon frame houses and shops with their supporting studs that provided air space and no firebreaks between floors and their wooden roofs and cornices. Along with every building in four downtown blocks, the courthouse was ruined, as the city lost the official symbol of its public life.

Anxious about its future at a time when towns throughout central Illinois were losing population, a community that a few weeks before had congratulated itself on fifty years as "no mean city" pondered its future. Built by man and his machines, Bloomington had grown without any advantage from nature. Citizens understood that their community would never be a great city; instead, as James Ewing instructed them on Bloomington's fiftieth birthday, they traded size for morality, excitement for law and order, and a simpler life for the metropolitan Sodoms and Gomorrahs of small-town imagination. The fire's destructiveness drew attention to other changes: the end of the easy patriotism that previously had made the Fourth of July the most important day in the year, the rapid increase in immigrants from unpronounceable places in Hungary and Slovakia, the battle over whether working-class Stevensonville would become part of Bloomington, and the decline in the number of citizens who bothered to vote.

Stevenson promptly entered the campaign to rebuild the city's commercial center, a task eventually accomplished through county bonds. In 1907 the former vice president, in an address in Miller Park, called for "the return of all McLean's children, all its sons and daughters" who had left for larger cities. No doubt he thought of his own scattered family—one brother in California, another in northern Illinois, a sister in Iowa, one daughter in the East, another in North Carolina, and his only son in California. "No man can ever get wholly away from his ancestors. Once a Bloomingtonian, always a Bloomingtonian, and no art of the enchanter can dissolve the spell. . . . On occasions like this the spirit of the past comes over us with its mystic power. The years roll back, and splendid farms, stately homes, magnificient churches and the marvellous appliances are for the moment lost to view. Instead we see the blooming prairie, the log cabin, nestling near the borderline of the grove or forest, the old water mill, the cross-roads store, the flintlock rifle, the mould-board plough, the dinner-horn. . . ." Such sentiments were marooned in the past; what the town fathers intended was a celebration of the future.

A few months after the fire, Stevenson celebrated his sixty-fifth birthday, having now lived longer than 90 percent of his generation. In the birthday letter he wrote his son, he described himself as living on borrowed time, though the economic allusion was at odds with what he usually likened to "crossing the dark river." The year before his mother had died, at ninety-one; only then had he been released from the childhood roles he played with her. Like many Victorians who were fascinated with death as an occasion for high emotion, he and his wife now filled the family scrapbooks with death's aphorisms and mourning's poems.

Stevenson's frequent appearances at the funerals of acquaintances—some of whom he barely knew—made him a professional pallbearer. "The tender grace of a year is gone never to return," he reminded his children each December. With his wife he reread family letters with their "mementoes of long ago of loved ones gone from us," pondering the scattering of the clan that made his children's life so different from his own. From his family he received compensation for his removal from public life. By 1900 Julia Hardin had delivered his first grandchild, a daughter named Letitia Stevenson, and her second son was christened Adlai Stevenson.

Then, in February of 1900, a grandson and namesake was born in Los Angeles, where Lewis Stevenson was the business manager of the Hearst-owned *Los Angeles Examiner*. The birth of the child at the beginning of a new century and on February 5, just seven days before the birthday of Stevenson's hero Abraham Lincoln, seemed a portent—of what he did not know. When the child visited Bloomington with his mother, Helen Davis Stevenson, the proud grandfather rushed to Fenwick's photo gallery for a picture of the two Adlai Ewing Stevensons, grandfather and grandson. For this occasion, the white-haired mustachioed Stevenson put on his stern unfathomable public face and the baby, also bald, looked straight at the camera.

5

THAT SUMMER OF 1900 the Stevensons rented a cottage at Lake Minnetonka, Minnesota, with their daughter Julia and son-in-law, Martin Hardin. There, on a placid day in July, Adlai Stevenson learned that he had again been nominated for the vice presidency. Hearing the news from a reporter, Stevenson denied that he had expected his name to be mentioned: "I am much surprised that it was. I did not seek the nomination, but I will not reject it." The inquiring reporter understood: "A presidential campaign for Mr. Stevenson would not be at all disagreeable."

In Kansas City, the day before, the Democrats had again nominated William Jennings Bryan as their presidential candidate. Earlier a huge plaster of Paris bust of the Nebraskan wrapped in an American flag had been rolled down the aisle of the convention hall amid tumultuous cheering nearly matching that after his "cross of gold" speech four years before. An erroneous expectation—"the Democratic party is stronger than it was in 1896; it is mightier than ever before in its glorious history"—had swept over the delegates.

The drama, delegates anticipated, would come over the choice of a vice president. The popular New Yorker David Hill declined despite a fifteen minute demonstration; the former Republican Charles Towne, Bryan's choice, was considered an inappropriate selection. Now Stevenson appealed for the reasons he had not suited in 1896. Unlike those who had joined Cleveland to support an insurgent movement of gold Democrats, he had been loyal. And by serving as a McKinley appointee on a bimetallic commission to Europe after his term as vice president had ended, Stevenson emerged as a solvent for Bryan's extremism on the currency issue. "He [Stevenson] is a man," shouted a Georgia delegate, "that belongs to no wing or faction of his party. . . . He is a conservative man, . . . an old-time simon-pure Jeffersonian Democrat." Adlai Stevenson is "a typical American and a great Democrat," proclaimed another.

Replacing the regional imperative that prohibited a ticket of two mid-westerners with a supposed balance on the fading concern of the currency, the Democrats of 1900 looked past Stevenson's Illinois roots (Bryan had been born in Illinois as well), revived his southern ones, and offered him as an average American who had served his country and party. "He is the most available man for the place," concluded one party leader, though "available" meant serviceable as much as obtainable.

Never identified with any ideology or conviction, Adlai Stevenson of Bloomington now represented the small-town citizen to whom the Democrats must appeal in order to increase the six and a half million votes they had received in 1896 and thereby defeat William McKinley. Consistently his positions had been conservative—from his opposition to internal improvements in the Forty-fourth Congress to his slow acceptance of a silver-backed currency and later a bimetallic currency and his opposition to federal intervention in the South during Reconstruction. Above all, he held that governments should be light and simple, though he opposed the concentration of wealth in which he personally participated and which in the coming years the government would struggle to control. As younger Democrats moved toward an acceptance of the authority of the central state as an instrument of reform to tame the savage inequalities of late-nineteenth-century society, Stevenson quoted Alexander Pope's couplet "How small a part of all mankind endure / That part that kings can cause or cure."

While Bryan continued to run on the silver issue, which was as dead as the Populists, Stevenson concentrated on foreign policy. The treaty ending the three-month Spanish-American War had been signed the preceding winter. After a military adventure—for it was hardly a conflict—that saw Admiral George Dewey steam from Hong Kong and take Manila with the loss of one sailor, the United States had control of Cuba, Puerto Rico, and the Philippines. Charging imperialism, Stevenson walked the narrow line between support of the Spanish-American War and opposition to the nasty guerrilla conflict developing in the Philippines between American troops and the followers of the Filipino nationalist leader Emilio Aguinaldo.

Such a stance proved hard to clarify in an election campaign where simplicities drove out complexities. In any case, the Democratic position was not popular, as Americans came to believe the war as splendid and painless as Teddy Roosevelt, their new hero from the charge at San Juan Hill, told them it was. Only 385 American soldiers had died in action, though another 5,806 succumbed from disease, most in Florida's unsanitary training camps. Bloomington had organized three companies of volunteers, but when the Caribbean heat began to take its toll, a call had come back for black troops, considered better able to withstand the tropical heat.

Well-financed Republicans hammered at the Democratic confusion on expansion during the campaign of 1900. "If you want to see the U.S. flag hauled down in the Philippines and the victory of Admiral Dewey brought to nought, j'ine the Democracy," taunted the *Pantagraph*. Did the Democrats, asked Republicans, intend to give Puerto Rico back to Spain? Or forget that American lives had been lost in the Philippines? Weren't Democratic anti-imperialists like Stevenson, as President McKinley asked, similar "to guerrillas who shoot at American soldiers"?

Sensitive to the concentration of power that accompanied war, Stevenson informed Bryan that imperialism must remain the central issue of the campaign. His constant subject, after his brief complaints about high tariffs, "which secure unjust advantages for the few," remained "the greedy spirit of commercialism which has embroiled our government in an unnecessary war, sacrificed valuable lives and placed the American Republic in deadly antagonism to our former allies in their effort to secure their liberties. For the first time in our history we are boldly confronted with the question of imperialism—the spirit of empire."

Expansionism also summoned Stevenson's belief in a racial hierarchy that placed Filipinos outside of democracy because of their skin color. While territory acquired during Democratic administrations had been climatically "fit for men of our own race," Asians living in the tropics lacked "civilization." And though the Constitution followed the flag (never, in Secretary of War Elihu Root's witticism, catching up to it), the islands must be held "permanently as conquered provinces." Because the United States could have no subjects, and Filipinos were dark-skinned residents of an island seven thousand miles away that few Americans, including the president, could locate before 1898, the United States must leave the Philippines. To do otherwise, according to Stevenson, was to abandon "the sure pathway in which past generations have found prosperity and happiness and embark upon that of aggression and conquest against which we are warned by the wrecks that lie upon the entire pathway of history. . . . 60,000 soldiers are now in the Philippine Islands. How much more will be the sacrifice of treasure and life before the conquest is completed. And when completed, what next?"

Sixty-five-year-old Stevenson carried this anti-imperialist message to only half the states he had visited in 1892. Neither well-organized, nor well-funded, nor well-advertised, the Democratic campaign of 1900 did not grip voters. Champ Clark, the Missouri Democrat and longtime Speaker of the House, reported a conversation with a farmer during the election. After Clark proclaimed the evils of imperialism, the man replied, "I guess I can stand it as long as beef cattle are 7 cents a pound on the hoof," which in 1900 they were.

In November the election results confirmed electoral patterns established in 1896, as McKinley increased both his popular vote and his electoral vote. The prediction that Stevenson would swing his state to the Democrats proved false. Neither Illinois nor McLean County, nor Bloomington, nor even the family's home ward voted for its native son. More voters had vanished from what had been, when Adlai Stevenson began his political career, a well-attended civic event. No one raised a liberty pole with a Bryan-Stevenson banner. Now laced with streetcar tracks, the city's arteries made parading difficult. Voters had other diversions. For Stevenson there was one consolation. Lewis had come from California for the campaign and had delivered a speech at the national meeting of Democratic clubs in Indianapolis. He was now thirty-two years old, and perhaps this was the inauguration of another Stevenson's political career.

6

EIGHT YEARS LATER, seventy-three-year-old Adlai Stevenson ran for the governorship of Illinois. Lewis was aghast: "I should have kept Father out of politics," he wrote his wife. "I shall never forgive myself for not ignoring everything and everybody and persisting 'till I stopped it. Don't know where it will end." But Adlai Stevenson could never refuse an opportunity to repair a sense of public duty damaged when he had stayed at home during the Civil War. Besides, he loved politics for the sociability of campaigning and the prestige of office holding. During campaigns he encountered the great men of the day and saw, as he bulged his eyes, the distance he had traveled from a farm in Christian County to the dais of the U.S. Senate.

For a time after his losing campaign in 1900, Stevenson had disavowed his vocation, complaining with an old man's discomfiture that he lost money in public life. He lamented the decline of politics: "old times are changed, old manners gone"; "men pursue politics for what there is in it," not as he believed he had done, as a service to the people. Stevenson had even criticized the indispensable endeavor of his life for its failure to develop into a respected profession like law and medicine, and he had praised the British parliamentary system, which would have permitted him to run from a safe Democratic congressional district. Still, when the opportunity came, his objections were easily brushed aside. Despite Illinois's new primary system, which required 10,000 signatures to get on the ballot, and despite the rumors that he was in bad health, Adlai Stevenson was soon in the field, "riding in the common cars, in autos and in a horse and buggy, making quick jumps from town to town." With a recognizable name and reputation, he won easily over four other Democrats, including the swashbuckling, red-sideburned Chicagoan James Hamilton Lewis, in a primary that, to his horror, cost four thousand dollars.

The family campaigned as well—Lewis, now living in Bloomington after the failure of several ventures in Michigan and California, helped manage his fathers' campaign, though by the twentieth century running for the governorship of Illinois could no longer be an informal family affair. Two experts from Chicago—Roger Sullivan and Francis Peabody, both representatives of a new political culture based on planning and advertising—traveled to Bloomington. Sipping Letitia's lemonade on the lawn, they plotted strategy. His wife handled the correspondence, made campaign appearances, and turned up throughout the state at meetings of the Illinois women's clubs and the DAR. Asked by a reporter whether the family approved of their patriarch's latest venture into politics, Letitia described a "conference" in which there was support for the campaign. "I've never been so ready to help. A political contest appeals to me. He's on the warpath again," she said with practiced enthusiasm.

After the August primary, during one of the hottest, driest fall seasons in Illinois history, Stevenson began the general campaign against the incumbent Republican governor, Charles Deneen, who was half his age. Ever the chameleon, Stevenson disguised his partisanship in order to gain the votes of an increasing number of ticket splitters in Republican Illinois. "I stand as a nonpartisan. If elected I will represent the whole people and I will never run again," he said, attempting to convert age and experience into an advantage.

To make his claim authentic, Stevenson described the governorship as an office that was public but not partisan, that was concerned with charities and institutions but not political parties or patronage, and that was, by the twentieth century, an administrative structure. Republicans remained suspicious. Remembering his previous association with the Greenback-Laborites and Anti-Monopolists and his support of Bryan, who was running for the third time for the presidency, Stevenson's opponents called him "a political Hessian"—for hire, as the Germans had been during the American Revolution.

No longer the Democrat he had been throughout his life, Adlai Stevenson appeared as a genial, fun-loving private man—a man who loved family and friends and was the best storyteller in Illinois. "He does not need the office of governor. He can get along better [without it] than the people of Illinois can get along without him," claimed his supporters, though they exaggerated, for he craved a public position. Refusing to be labeled ambitious like other party men, he explained that he had been urged to run by numerous Illinoisians. Avoiding contemporary political issues—for how else could he take advantage of his nonpartisanship?—Stevenson discussed the U.S. Constitution and the Northwest Ordinance and, in Pekin, the Illinois constitution of 1870. He said nothing about the recent race riot in Springfield where blacks in Lincoln's hometown had been assaulted and two had been lynched after false rumors of a white woman's rape.

Nor, to the frustration of the Republicans, did Stevenson discuss the state's labor turmoil, forcing Deneen to satirize as hopelessly archaic his old-fashioned, do-unto-others-as-you-would-have-them-do-unto-you attitude toward unionization, strikes, and the use of Pinkertons and strikebreakers. In one satiric pamphlet, Stevenson and a miner engaged in an imaginary dialogue: "I am told, Mr. Stevenson, you claim to be the special friend and champion of labor," to which Stevenson replied, "You indeed touch a tender place in my heart when you speak of the poor downtrodden workingmen. I rarely see a blacksmith or a mechanic without feeling a strong impulse to embrace him." Stung—for he considered himself a friend of labor—Stevenson recalled his invitation to give the first Labor Day speech in Bloomington, his hospitality to the miners who came, especially during election years, to his home, his "sincere convictions" in favor of unions, and his election eve endorsement by John McBride, the president of the mine workers.

As the gap closed between the two candidates, a frustrated Deneen posed some questions to the man who was running on his winning personality: How did Stevenson stand on the primary law? How could the owner of a coal mine present himself as a friend of miners? Hadn't the McLean County Coal Company, like others, blacklisted its union members? Why had its employees struck three times in the last twenty years? What position did the axman of the 1880s take on the new system of civil service protection for state employees? And of course, hadn't Stevenson been a Copperhead during the Civil War?

Everywhere, Adlai Stevenson had an appreciative following, though the "political whirlwind" was so strenuous that Lewis worried about his father's health. In the tiny town of Mt. Sterling, the local paper reported a well-attended rally where the candidate spoke of Abraham Lincoln, the Lincoln-Douglas debates, and the pioneers who fashioned the first water mill and crossroads store in the county. Though he talked about the past, politics, it seemed, kept him young. "He appeared," according to the *Democratic Messager,* "as a man of 60—of robust health, nearly 6 feet, straight and erect with short gray hair and mustache, the brightness of youth still in his eyes and his tone of voice clear and resolute."

Stevenson lost the election in November, though the margin of Deneen's victory was only 22,000 of over a million votes cast. Not ready to surrender the ambitions of a lifetime, amid rumors of Republican "manipulation" in Chicago, Stevenson took his case for a recount to the Republican legislature, which ruled against him, on the basis of the expense of a recount as well as the size of Deneen's majority. In its selective memory, the clan transformed his loss into a victory and remembered that he had carried Cook County and run 100,000 votes ahead of Bryan and that only the coattails of the winning presidential candidate, William Howard Taft, had swept Deneen to victory. No one paid much attention to the difficulties of voting a long ballot that stretched over three feet, contained 347 names, including 8 for president and 6 for governor, and took some voters forty minutes to complete, as the steady demobilization of the Illinois voters continued along with the party-ravaging split-ticket voting.

Four years later Adlai Ewing Stevenson tried again, this time for a Democratic nomination for the U.S. Senate. In a quiet campaign that split the family (Stevenson's nephew-in-law Carl Vrooman was one of his competitors), he and Lewis worked to line up supporters in the legislature. Despite his age and ill health, despite his family's reservations he had, according to Lewis, never been "quite so anxious for anything and his friends seem to think he could land it without much effort." But the Democrats chose a younger man. After fifty-four years in politics, seventy-seven-year-old Adlai Stevenson's political career ended, though his was no voluntary retirement.

At the end of his life, surrounded by relatives during Sunday lunches of fried chicken, salt-rising bread, ham, beaten corn dodgers, and cucumber pickles, with Hunter's ice cream the only Yankee innovation, Adlai Stevenson told the story of the man who had a brilliant future behind him. After a review of the sermon in Bloomington's Second Presbyterian Church, which he and Letitia attended, when the conversation turned to politics, Stevenson reminisced about a career that had taken him on an American pilgrimage—from farm to town, from plow to lawbooks; from the district attorney's office to the vice presidency and eventually to an appointment on one of the new fact-finding commissions; from old-fashioned stump speeches to the strategic plans of campaign managers and interviews with newspaper reporters; from conventions to primaries; from loyal yellow-dog Democrat to a candidate with a winning personality. For the grandson who bore his name and sometimes tried to snap his butterball onto the ceiling during these Sunday lunches, Grandfather's odyssey was an informal course in American history.

On Christmas Day 1913, seventy-one-year-old Letitia Green Stevenson died at her home in Bloomington. Among the sympathy notes to her husband was one from William Jennings Bryan, who, like most of those who knew this couple, acknowledged "the comradeship" between husband and wife and "how her life intertwined with your own." Within weeks Stevenson himself was ill, suffering, according to a Chicago specialist, "a nervous breakdown after his wife died and complications set in." Wearing a catheter for the last six months of his life, Adlai Stevenson suffered from prostate cancer as well as an unusual skin disease. Six months later, on June 14, just two weeks before the assassination of Archduke Francis Ferdinand of Austria led to the world war that forever separated Stevenson's small-town innocence from a harsher time, seventy-nine-year-old Adlai Ewing Stevenson died in a Chicago hospital. He was remembered as a guileless, unaffected man "with the gentle virtues of private life."

To his three surviving children in the will that he wrote shortly before his wife died, Adlai Stevenson left assets carefully divided into equal shares: the shares of stock in the People's Bank, McLean County Coal Company, Galena lead and zinc mine, and Interstate Savings and Loan Association, along with his home on Franklin Park and farms in Downs Township. The silver pen set from the Senate and the framed senatorial resolution of praise, he left expectantly to Lewis. With these material assets—and he died a wealthy man—went the intangible legacy described by his daughter Julia that "we were part of a link in this living chain of family and fast-moving events . . . that we had been born in Kentucky in 1809 when his mother had been and that we were part of a stream of history." "I've always had that mysterious feeling that my personal life began in 1809."

His fourteen-year-old grandson, Adlai Ewing Stevenson II, had already learned some of these lessons. He learned more of them the following November, when at a ceremony at the Bloomington library, dressed in knickers, he stepped forward and slowly pulled a cord that unveiled a portrait of his grandfather, after which he listened to his great aunt Julia Scott remind the audience that "if the sons asked how to honor the dead, they must imitate the ancestors." That lesson would, as it turned out, skip a generation.

PART TWO

OPPORTUNITIES

CHAPTER SIX

AFFLICTIONS AND AFFECTIONS:
Helen Davis Stevenson and
Lewis Green Stevenson

1

LEWIS GREEN STEVENSON, the son of Letitia and Adlai Stevenson, married Helen Louise Davis in 1893—on a late November day with snow and rain in the morning, clouds in the afternoon, and by night, in an inaccurately favorable omen of the couple's future together, clearing skies as the bride and groom stepped from Bloomington's Second Presbyterian Church. Their long courtship had been a troubled one, interrupted by illness and separation. Now this public confirmation of a mutual attachment was a private triumph for the couple, both of whom were twenty-five.

It was also a public occasion, given the prominence of the groom's parents. For the nearly one thousand invited guests, the wedding was more than a personal matter or even the premier social event in Bloomington's history. The merging of a Republican, Unitarian, Pennsylvania-rooted family with the Democratic, Presbyterian, Kentucky-bred Stevensons suggested the end of the community's persistent cultural divisions, an amiable American version of Romeo and Juliet at a time of national uncertainty.

From such a perspective the wedding of a Davis and a Stevenson heralded the emergence of a new midwestern regionalism. "Love in the prairies hath levelled all," proclaimed the *Daily Bulletin,* the Democratic newspaper that supported the Stevensons. "No politics in romance," agreed the Republican *Pantagraph,* which was published by Helen's father, William O. Davis. Normal, the traditional seat of the Davises, joined Bloomington at the altar; the wealthy family that owned the influential *Pantagraph*—a paper that had never supported a Stevenson or a Democrat—now embraced as kin a central Illinois Democratic dynasty. Romance had conquered partisan difference, though the disenfranchised bride announced that she would become a Democrat. And the groom acknowledged that he might surrender his lightly embraced Presbyterianism.

Reinforcing the sense of assimilation, the marriage ceremony was grandly secular. During the service six bridesmaids in white and seven groomsmen in cutaways arranged themselves in a tableau adopted from the bridal scene in Richard Wagner's opera *Lohengrin,* which Helen had admired during a trip to Vienna. The bride wore white, as was customary by the 1890s, and a veil that symbolized her retirement into the invisible world of domesticity. Organ and trumpet accompanied several soloists, and the traditional Presbyterian service, celebrated by two ministers, ended with the Mendelssohn recessional from *Midsummer Night's Dream,* as the bridal party marched gaily down the nave.

By the 1890s America's Protestant churches had taken title to what in the past had been informal civic arrangements celebrated in the bride's front parlor by a justice of the peace. In Lewis and Helen's day weddings mixed the spiritual and the worldly. Rings were exchanged, secular music was performed, and attendants dressed in expensive outfits shared the spotlight with the principals. No longer a family matter, a daughter's wedding emerged, in towns and cities throughout the United States, as an expensive showpiece of parental status. With nosy, small-town inquisitiveness, the *Pantagraph* and *Bulletin* had even provided their readers with descriptions of the silver, porcelain, and cut-glass wedding gifts sent to Helen and Lewis, along with the names of their donors.

To accommodate the guests—some high-ranking members of the Cleveland administration were expected along with Governor and Mrs. John Altgeld of Illinois—the Unitarian convictions of the bride's family gave way to the need for a bigger church. While Eliza and W. O. Davis hastily enlarged the dining room of their Chestnut Street home for the reception, Vice President and Mrs. Stevenson, with their capacious public talents, had organized a party at their Franklin Park home for local Democrats to pay their respects to Secretary of Navy Hilary Herbert, who had come all the way from Washington for the occasion.

At the end of the reception, the bride and groom were exhausted when they finally left for Chicago and their honeymoon. In earlier days brides and grooms stayed home and entertained, as Letitia Green and Adlai Stevenson and William and Eliza Fell Davis had, visiting relatives who traveled long distances under difficult conditions to attend their nuptials. By the 1890s better transportation, especially on the railroads, along with a growing sentiment for privacy had established the honeymoon as a necessary ritual for middle-class couples. Helen and Lewis planned to spend theirs in southern France. Before embarking on a steamship to Le Havre, however, they consulted Dr. S. Weir Mitchell, the well-known Philadelphia neurologist, at his home on Walnut Street. With its legitimation of a sexual relationship, marriage would place new demands on the delicate nerves from which both had suffered for most of their lives.

Helen Davis and Lewis Stevenson had known each other since childhood. Though they never attended the same school, they were the same age, came from two of the richest, most powerful families in the community, and shared their generation's coeducational recreations—the dancing and card parties, the ice skating, tobaggoning, picnics, and railroad excursions. Too young for the automobiles that soon revolutionized courting, they had instead flirted on the Davis's front porch, and for privacy had taken rides together in horse-drawn buggies and walked along the shaded dirt roads of Bloomington and Normal—activities described by Lewis as "Maple Lane's lover lanes and old-time talk." Like other Bloomington couples, they sought out the hollow at Miller Park and talked for hours, in the way of courting couples, of their families and friends, their hopes and expectations, and, as often as not, their ill health. Several times they argued and parted. But after Helen's parents moved to a house three blocks from Lewis's home, they could hardly avoid each other.

The two families shared the status of Bloomington's privileged. In the 1890s the Davises and the Stevensons joined the new country club, where Helen's older brother, Hibbard, played golf, tennis, and baseball with the "very best fellows," whose fathers had been sorted through a restrictive membership process affirming Bloomington's stratifications of race, religion, class, and gender. A shoulder injury at fourteen limited Lewis's participation in organized sports, though he continued hunting—the activity that caused his impairment after a defective gun recoiled into his armpit and the resulting bruise became infected. Since their frequent contact was guaranteed, the acquaintance of the tall, angular, olive-skinned, fashionable Helen, who so resembled her adored (and adoring) father, William O. Davis, and the slight, 126-pound, balding Lewis, whose most prominent characteristic was his long forehead and who favored neither his father nor his mother, ripened into friendship and eventually, to the delight of the Stevensons and the displeasure of the Davises, romance.

In 1885 Lewis accompanied his father, who had been appointed first assistant postmaster, to Washington, and Helen went east to the Dean Academy, a coeducational, Universalist boarding school in Franklin, Massachusetts, where she ate cod fish cakes and boiled New England dinners, wore brown uniforms, sought to improve a dull roommate from Nebraska, and received constant reminders from Bloomington that "overdoing brings nervousness." Romance became a long-distance epistolary affair, with Helen ever on the alert for Lewis's frequent spelling errors and Lewis complaining of his health and her absence.

For a time Lewis stayed in the East at Exeter Academy ("a dandy place," he wrote in his first enthusiasm), one of the most celebrated and expensive boarding schools in the United States. Ambitious parents of the heartland like the Stevensons and the Davises understood the social uses of education in an economic and political society that was hardly egalitarian, and sent their children across the prairies to meet the offspring of America's eastern aristocracy in a reversal of Horace Greeley's dictum to go west. In a preview of his lifetime role as a transient, Lewis lasted only a semester, disappearing without explanation from the school roster in April 1886. After his abrupt departure he was again absent from Helen during his half-year employment in 1887 as a rod and chain man on one of John Wesley Powell's expeditions to Colorado and Montana.

The geologist-explorer Powell, a friend of the family's from Bloomington, who often hired the sons of congressmen for his expeditions, was indebted to Adlai Stevenson for his sponsorship of a resolution funding the printing of his surveys of the Colorado River Basin. As a Union soldier, Powell had lost his arm at the Battle of Shiloh in 1862, but his injury was neither a catastrophe nor the occasion for alibis. Instead, his zest for adventure and activity contrasted with the often demoralized, always restless Lewis, who seemed unable to forget his own, less severe injury.

By the time twenty-year-old Helen left for an eighteen-month European trip in 1888 with her aunt Fanny Fell, who kept her watch on Bloomington time no matter where she was, Lewis and Helen had created a lovers' long-distance world of private codes, endearments, present giving, and bickering. "You say you will do anything to make me happy and you know what you can do to make me the happiest and proudest boy on earth. I would feel then as if there was something worth studying and being good for," Lewis plaintively advised the young woman who was so sympathetic to his struggles and whom he wished to marry.

Like other young men of his generation, Lewis Stevenson was searching for an endeavor worthy of his status—a business or a profession so that he could support a wife as society expected, gain the respect of family and friends, and display a manly competence in some field, as his father and Helen's father had done. Trained to politics and public life as his father's secretary and campaign manager, Lewis had already served an apprenticeship in partisanship, but such training did not assure him any standing in work that required flexibility, determination, popularity, a sponsor, and luck. Lewis could not simply *be* a politician, though like most Americans he considered holding office an honorable career.

The grandson of a Presbyterian minister after whom he was named and the son of a college-educated lawyer, Lewis had not been able to complete high school at a time when educational credentials had become entry cards to the professions. By the 1890s fifty-one law schools in the United States were transforming legal education from an informal apprenticeship spent reading with a prominent lawyer into a formal inquiry organized around case law. In Lewis's day more emphasis was placed on training in the statutes and torts than on reading texts like Blackstone and Chitty or developing the oratorical skills so critical to his father's success. While only a tiny fraction of his generation of males had even high school diplomas, among lawmakers and politicians on every level, the proportion rose. If he was to make his way in the uncertain world of elective politics, Lewis Green Stevenson needed an alternative income such as the law practice that had sustained his father.

Closed off from other forms of institutionalized masculinity such as athletics, fraternities, and even the brotherhood of the bar, which served middle-class men of Bloomington as levers of identity and useful sources of social contact, Lewis considered himself an invalid and came to depend on his family and Helen for reassurance. At the end of his life, he acknowledged that he had few friends, but this was the result, he claimed, of his hard work. In another family he might have tried acting, for he loved to mask himself in the roles of amateur productions of school and community, and like his father he was a practiced storyteller. In middle age he indulged himself by directing the plays of the Bloomington community theater. But the professional theater was deemed an illicit activity by most Americans, and so he became, in this as in other arenas, a member of the audience rather than a player.

His contemporaries dismissed him as a spoiled only son. More sympathetic, his family attributed his difficulties to his maimed shoulder and the migraine headaches inherited from his mother. For whatever reason, Lewis lacked the determined persistence and good-humored equanimity necessary for politics at any level, though he could be affectionate and fun loving and, according to Helen, "hilarious." Throughout his life anger was his abiding companion, and a short temper, remembered years later by his neighbors, became his most prominent characteristic. Once Helen's brother, Bert, complained to his sister, though he knew of her affections, about Lewis's calling his Bloomington friends who did not support his father for vice president in 1892 "hypocrites. He flew off the handle. . . ." "Lou is very vindicative [sic] and unreasonable, but I won't allow myself to get mad at him unless he compels me to." Meanwhile after every election campaign Lewis held his Bloomington friends who refused to vote for his father in the "most intense hatred."

To his confidante Helen, Lewis wondered if "other boys suffer like I do and have feelings like mine." "I think of how happy I should be and am in one or two ways, but what am I to do, that is the question making life miserable." Offered a permanent position by John Wesley Powell if he studied two years and got "down to hard work, went in with a determination to win and study [topography and civil engineering] under his guidance," Lewis declined. "I prefer business to a profession," he decided, though when he tried a clerkship in Chicago in 1889 "sorting tariff rates and finding references" and then worked in New York for a railroad, his arm and joints and head promptly ached so much that he soon left. Finally he comforted himself with the conviction, seconded by his father, that he "had better take [his] time," though such indecision was not considered good for the nerves.

Meanwhile Helen suffered boredom and the trivial existence of young middle-class women awaiting their mandatory change in status to wife and mother. Returned home after her trip to Europe, she read, took a few courses at Bloomington's Wesleyan University in English literature and chemistry (the latter considered a vocational benefit for her future family's nutrition), and complained. "Bloomington," she informed Lewis, "grows more and more stupid every day." "Bloomington continues in a state of semi-slumber which only the Johnston flood would awake," she advised in the year in which a catastrophic tunnel of water had destroyed the mining town of Johnstown, Pennsylvania. Like thousands of other young Americans, she was kept in her hometown only by her close ties to her family and her inability to be respectably self-supporting.

Helen derided as pointless her sole public activity—membership in the King's Daughters, a social association of young women. In this she was unusual, for many women of her generation were finding companionship and importance in clubs and civic endeavors. "There is scarcely anything more amusing than to attend a meeting exclusively of women. They as a general thing know nothing about parliamentary rules nor legal business and it is either a grand hubbub or a dead silence," concluded a scornful Helen. Nor did she enjoy soliciting subscriptions for the local day nursery that Lewis's mother had founded.

Decades later she would have gone to college, but in her generation only three thousand American women a year received bachelor's degrees. Intelligent and intellectually curious, she vowed that she would "retire within [herself] again this winter and study real hard" in the sporadic non-credit courses she took at nearby Wesleyan.

Along with her status as Lewis's "dearest darling," Helen also became his "little adviser," full of suggestions about whether he should accept Uncle Matthew Scott's offer of a job in the McLean County Coal Company. Years before, Julia Green Scott had named her only son Lewis Green, just as her sister Letitia had, in order to sustain family ties. When Lewis Green Scott died as an infant, she and her husband, Matthew, had transferred their affection to Lewis Green Stevenson. As Lewis continued without a job, the offers from the Scotts came often. Would Lewis consider employment in Uncle Matthew's new enterprise, the Tennessee Iron Company, which had the potential to move the Scotts from the very wealthy into a tiny circle of the richest Americans? Lewis remained uncertain, sighing to Helen as he reconsidered the offer: "If you were here we could give and receive lectures." Still, as he recounted his tribulations, he wanted more of Helen's cheerleading and fewer of her spelling corrections, which "only take up space."

Helen was accustomed to practicing self-improvement under the watchful eye of her father. As she became more involved with Lewis, she extended this approach to a young man who was exactly her age. For years the punctilious William O. Davis had corrected his daughter's spelling mistakes, had ordered her to date her letters (as Lewis rarely did), and had encouraged her to add phosphorus to her diet, from eggs and oysters. Davis also had organized her trips abroad to the smallest detail of sightseeing and advice about where, when, and with whom to practice the French that was the "regular program" of the European tour that she, along with 25,000 other Americans a year, took in the late 1880s. One such journey was enough for most Americans, but in 1892 Helen traveled again to Europe. Davis held his eldest daughter responsible for writing a letter every Sunday, and if the description of her travels was sufficiently interesting, it appeared in the *Pantagraph*. When Helen reached Paris with her sister, Jessie, Davis applauded his daughters' decision to board on separate floors of a Paris pension, all the better to resist the temptation of speaking English to each other.

Raised in such a household, Helen believed that Lewis enjoyed her lectures and so continued (for a lifetime) to pass along reading lists and the rules of grammar. With Yankee reformism more than a misty memory from her ancestral past, Helen intended to improve her "dear invalid" and to lay the foundation, as a mother might, for a respectable man. It was a familiar role for many American girls, who, more likely to finish high school than boys, often served as teachers of the liberal arts to their boyfriends during their courtships. Few were as demanding as Helen.

Soon after Helen returned from her second trip to Europe, Lewis suffered the first of many nervous breakdowns (or "brain-collapses," as they were known at the time) that made his life a perpetual pilgrimage to the medical meccas of Europe and the United States. The symptoms of neurasthenia, the nerve disease of end-of-the-century, upper-class Americans, had no physical specificity. Instead, it raged from the head to the toe joints, from genital organs to the scalp.

Lewis was at risk for several reasons. He had no profession and no training that would assure his entry into respectable work. There was no family business, and although his father had appointed him to several patronage positions, the most famous family name was not his. Even in his seventies, Adlai Ewing Stevenson I continued to run for office and eclipse his son's opportunities. Only in 1914, after his father's death, could the forty-six year-old crown prince try to claim his birthright, though by that time he was too neurotic to use the magic of the Stevenson name with much effect.

Unlike his father, who was known throughout the state, Lewis found himself frequently confused with Robert Louis Stevenson and was omitted from a list of Bloomington's "special men" when he was nearly fifty. The editors of his future father-in-law's paper sometimes misspelled his first name, and his nickname Lewie (he preferred Lew) signaled not so much affection as insignificance. Agitated and insecure, displaying the personal discounting that is a common legacy of prominent men to their sons, Lewis needed some more permanent endeavor outside of politics. Ceaselessly he worried about what it might be and recruited Helen in his search.

His circumstances were further complicated by the hunting accident that made him a lifetime casualty and placed him under the experts' care at precisely the moment when these new specialists were defining what George Beard described in his classic texts *American Nervousness* and *Sexual Exhaustion*. Beard, a New York neurologist, related neurasthenia—this peculiarly American disease—to national progress and the effects on individual nerves of jarring technological advances and rapid societal changes. Telephones, automobiles, and large cities, with their labor unrest, rising crime rates (in Bloomington on the day of Lewis and Helen's wedding ten houses had been burglarized), and large numbers of immigrants—all afflicted the anxious. On the one hand a mark of society's advancement and American exceptionalism, neurasthenia was also related to the strain of survival in an imperfect society where the nervous system, like a telephone switchboard sending messages to too many places, was in danger of a short-circuit from overuse.

Meanwhile Helen was at risk because of her sex, because of her education, and because of her class. In the age of American nervousness, she was held—and came to accept the diagnosis—as susceptibly "fine," a description that conflated highly strung nerves and upper-class status. Already the number of leisured ladies who had succumbed made the disease as familiar as tuberculosis. Some commentators accepted the novelist William Dean Howells's diagnosis "that America seems little better than a hospital for invalid women." Helen was all the more vulnerable to neurasthenia because, it was supposed, her nerve-filled uterus drained a system already overloaded by the special demands imposed by her temperament. From such a perspective women were prone to bouts of nervousness.

The malady of nerves transformed the body into a reflection of the psyche at a time when Americans were preoccupied with economic issues. Those who suffered were believed to have overtaxed themselves and to have drawn down their neural savings, some to the point of bankruptcy from too much brainwork. Waste and repair, use and replenishment—in Beard's explanation, "nervousness is really nervelessness"—followed economic understandings of cash flow. What was needed for recovery, in this analogy, was self-discipline and prudence—the preservation of resources. Meanwhile the sexual manifestations of neurasthenia were so commonly interpreted as the results of too much sexual spending that Sears, Roebuck advertised in its popular catalogs electric belts with genital attachments for restimulation.

A more respectable illness than syphilis or tuberculosis, nervous exhaustion was sometimes associated with the effects of a trauma sustained in the dangerous mechanical world of the late nineteenth century. In the medical literature its onset frequently involved a railroad accident. Lewis's injury from the explosion of a gun perfectly fitted the kind of neurological shock that might deplete a nervous system, as a sudden panic might drain the gold reserves of the American economy.

Although Helen and Lewis were both neurasthenics throughout their lives, at first Lewis suffered the more severely. The shocking event of his boyhood had sent him to bed for a yearlong contemplation of his weakness. "My arm hurts," complained Lewis, who understood the connection of his shoulder injury to his entire being, "my poor disabled member . . . at times it feels as if I am hurting myself." He had contracted a class-biased sickness, for only those of sufficient "civilization" suffered. Beard's studies revealed that the majority of his patients were doctors, businessmen, and wealthy women. Thus Lewis's abiding affliction, which outfitted him for failure in the public world, simultaneously granted him status, offered an explanation for his periods of unemployment, and, when he did work, provided a convincing reason for resigning. "I wonder," he complained with amplified self-pity in his Valentine's greeting to Helen in 1904, "if there is anyone who gives himself up to business to the extent I do, neglecting family, self, health, and everything else. It isn't right and I'll not do it any more." But within the month he had given up this job in a mining firm in Colorado.

Before his marriage twenty-two-year-old Lewis entered Western Springs, a sanitarium for "the scientific and sympathetic care of the sick and weary" located outside Chicago, where for a time he remained secluded. Restricted to complete bed rest and later three nap periods during the day, he recovered. But in the summer he suffered a relapse and turned to Dr. Hiller's new regimen in Sheboygan, Wisconsin. It was from there that his sister Julia informed Helen in July of 1891 that Lewis's attempts to write had all "resulted in headaches and Dr. Hiller the young physician under whose charge he is thinks he had better not tax his strength . . . though he doesn't want his not being able to write to affect your letters. . . ."

Hiller had studied with the legendary S. Weir Mitchell, absorbing his mentor's view that nervous disorders required bed rest and privacy. But Mitchell's famous rest cure was a passive treatment generally delivered to women who spent as long as six weeks in bed, forbidden paper, pen, and printed word and, in the ultimate process of infantilization, spoonfed a milk diet by a nurse. When Lewis was finally permitted newspapers and writing materials, he complained to Helen about this "house of horrors surrounded by every imaginable disease." Like Lewis, most were sufferers from the pervasive disability of nervous exhaustion that, left untreated, could progress, it was believed, from sick headache to sleeplessness, through spinal and sexual exhaustion to, eventually, brain collapse and insanity. Meanwhile Helen consoled herself with visits to his mother and, when permitted, wrote peppy letters to "my dear boy."

There was a masculine corollary to the rest cure, and it was to its therapy of exercise that Lewis turned next. Convinced by two Washington doctors that his salvation lay in what Theodore Roosevelt popularized as "the strenuous life" that washed away "black care," Lewis went west, first to a ranch in Montana and then to California. He expected that physical activity would strengthen his wasted nerves and make him fit for the competitive work world he must now enter. To be a man he must not shrink from physical danger or be at the mercy of anything so intangible as his nerves. For a time the treatment worked: "I haven't felt so well in years. I have put in three solid miles and a half," he reported to Helen. Yet such improvement proved temporary, and a few months later, when Lewis rode horseback less than a mile and walked a shorter distance, he relapsed into exhaustion.

Torn between an inherited desire for prestige as a public figure and the need to support a family, battered by an inability to stick to anything, Lewis felt his nerves straining his system. Yet whenever he made a decisive commitment to any endeavor the hard work entailed placed its own stress on his psyche. "I believe," Lewis concluded before he was twenty-five, "that I am not capable of anything but light work. I'll worry along, get as much sleep and rest as possible and do the best I can." It was Helen's mother who noticed that Lewis's most complete cures took place during the political season. The son of Adlai and Letitia was seldom too nerve exhausted to write and talk about politics or to manage one of his father's campaigns.

When they finally married, the mutual attraction of Helen and Lewis was that of two neurotic Americans in search of sympathy and understanding, a relationship strained by their competing claims for bad nerves. In an alternation of pain they took turns with illness, as the well-being of their bodies and the calculations of their nervousness became a lifetime preoccupation. Acknowledging her "failing always to overdo things," Helen found purpose in her children, though when they became independent, her neurasthenia deepened. Raised at a time when praise came to those women who nurtured and sacrificed, Helen even in moments of her misery thought of how Lewis "suffered the same ordeal" and her heart went out to him "as it never had before." Meanwhile Lewis's roller coaster of illness and health leveled in late middle age when his contemporaries no longer worked.

The pursuit of quiet nerves filled this couple's lives, closing off any public commitments, though Lewis did serve a few years in state government and Helen was briefly a member of the Bloomington Women's History

Club and the Art Association, and once worked to improve Bloomington's roads. Their own welfare, especially as it related to their bodies and souls, demanded such close attention that there was no room for the public affairs that engaged Adlai and Letitia Stevenson. Life was a personal matter. And so a formerly civic family emerged in its twentieth-century form as a reactive, self-absorbed group, whose public ethic was leached out by the prevalent American disease of self-contemplation.

In the beginning Helen was the more stable. She had grown up in a household with W. O. Davis, whose bureau drawers were so neat that "even the collar buttons had their place and . . . his high black-laced boots stood in an even, neat row in the closet and on the night table the pencils had freshly made points and his beautiful gray waving hair showed brushing." Davis often sought health cures himself, carrying his own food when he traveled south. With the fluid metaphor of a newspaperman and the natural hyberbole of a hypochondriac, he described "the frigid state of [his] system wrapped in a light overcoat of malaria, an attenuated smile and an anguished disposition." But Davis never let any illness interfere with his thirty-six-year tenure as the publisher and owner of the *Pantagraph,* which he developed into one of the most important Republican papers in Illinois.

Helen had recognized in Lewis a peculiarity first observed in her father. In time she found her father's nervousness no match for her husband's impairment—or her own. Meanwhile Lewis discovered in Helen a caretaker who appreciated his ailments and applauded his efforts to overcome what had originated, ineffably, with his temperament, with his place in a prominent family as an oldest child and only son, and with the boyhood accident that he could neither forget nor permit others to overlook. "You are better and there is no denying it . . . have patience, suffering is bound to end," Helen inveighed when Lewis refused improvement, as he often did. Illness became the unsuitable grounds for an attraction that led to marriage.

The politics of this relationship at first required of Helen health and cheerfulness. She could not be too sick, for this unhinged Lewis's levers of empowerment, and so in 1888 Lewis sternly rebuked a trespass on his territory: "You are not an invalid, far from it, but we are all liable to become [so] and we must make preparations to fight such troubles off. . . ." And after their marriage he pleaded, "You simply must not be sick. . . . You can't be. Please please my lover you have great work to perform," by which he meant raising the children and running the house. Before long Lewis admonished Helen for any neglect that might bring on a headache on his "weary days" or one of the nervous debilities that lay in wait for him, perhaps a dyspeptic stomach or the ache in his knees, which Lewis believed "the dangerous beginning of stiff joints everywhere."

Chastised for delinquency as a correspondent, Helen capitulated: "But how selfish I am to think of my trouble when yours is so much greater. . . .

I feel so so sorry for you, dearest, and would sacrifice anything to alleviate your sufferings." Then Lewis extorted a visit with an irresistible plea: "Knowing the great love you have for me, I am confident that if you understood the circumstances you would change your plans, come here and add this sacrifice to those you have already made for me. I don't see Helen how I can get along without you. . . . This nervousness and depression isn't caused by temporary homesickness from you. . . . If you are with me the despondency and depression which with the continual state of anxiety are my principle [sic] drawbacks would disappear. . . ."

Such appeals alternated with his anger. When Helen left for a second trip to Europe, in 1892, this time to join her younger sister, Jessie, Lewis was immediately afflicted with a "strain headache," a dyspeptic stomach, and rage. "You have caused us enough trouble," he objected. And later, when Helen failed to send her address as she traveled through Europe, an outraged Lewis complained, "It's hard for me to keep up with your excuses."

In 1893, when these two married, what the community and their families celebrated in Bloomington's Second Presbyterian Church as a symbolic merging of public differences over matters of religion, politics, and culture, the newlyweds understood differently. For Lewis and Helen carried to the altar the similarities of a private distress sanctioned by the mentality of their times. Mutual affection was based on the dangerous proposition of, as Lewis put it, "devot[ing] ourselves to getting strong together." Their honeymoon visit to Dr. S. Weir Mitchell, when the newlyweds spent an afternoon with the craggy-featured, eagle-eyed, goateed neurologist, whose bangs made him appear like a predatory bird swooping to pick at the details of anxiety and nervousness in his patients' lives, served as a hallmark of their marriage. "I was never more interested than meeting him. . . . We talked for some time. He told me not to pay any attention to Lewis's ailments and I need have no anxiety," wrote Helen.

2

TWO YEARS LATER Lewis and Helen Stevenson separated. Lewis, who earned a clerk's salary of $2,200 as his father's secretary during the latter's vice presidency, abruptly left for Japan eighteen months after the couple's return from an eight-month honeymoon. Some presumed he went as an aspiring journalist for *McClure's* to investigate Japanese culture and politics in the aftermath of the recent Sino-Japanese War. The latter had pitted an unprepared China against Japan for the booty of Korea. The rapidity of the Japanese victory in a war fought mostly in Korea and on the sea piqued American interest in an emerging power. More Americans were now traveling across the Pacific. Some were attracted by Japan's politics and government; others found in the Orient an exotic flavor that stimulated jaded end-of-the-century sensibilities.

Although many tourists recounted their experiences, Lewis did not. Instead, he told the reporters who clustered around him before he set sail from San Francisco for his eighteen-day crossing on a mail steamer that he had become "run down" and sought rest. Returned six months later, Lewis acknowledged the Japanese as "wonderfully progressive and courteous to foreigners," though he disliked the female custom of blackened teeth. He indicated, too, that acupuncture in Canton had brought him no relief for an unspecified illness.

While Lewis detailed his infirmities to outsiders, in his letters to Helen he angrily asserted "our troubles" as another reason for his trip. Their short marriage, he complained from Yokohama, had been one "of blissful happiness and sickening misery . . . petty fault findings, and bickerings. I would come back at once in response to a cable or letter from you indicating that the past is to be left severely alone. I trust that you are improving and in a better frame of mind than I am." Only then, he concluded, would the terrible neuralgia in his head disappear and their lives progress with "entire confidence, peace and harmony."

In time Lewis and Helen reconciled, though harmony was forever elusive, confidence fleeting, and peace fugitive. In the next decade the couple ranged like nomads through the West. They lived in Grant County, New Mexico, where Lewis was the superintendent of the Santa Rita copper mines, and then in Berkeley, California, when Lewis was briefly the business manager of William Randolph Hearst's *Los Angeles Examiner.* Next they rented a house in Denver, where the impetuous Lewis was employed in an oil venture for which he unsuccessfully sought capital from his father-in-law. Then they moved back to Santa Cruz. When another venture collapsed, Lewis remained unemployed for months. At some point they were in Phoenix and then in Detroit, where Lewis was chosen as a Michigan delegate to the 1904 Democratic nominating convention. The next year Lewis required institutionalization and entered Dr. Harvey Kellogg's huge sanitarium in Battle Creek, Michigan. There, with over a thousand other neurasthenics, he disdained meat and became enamored with Postum. Released from the hospital, he briefly tried to manufacture a similar health product, named Javril. In 1905 the transients returned to San Francisco, where Lewis's principal sponsor, Phoebe Hearst, the widow of George Hearst, lived.

A lonely Helen acknowledged to her parents that Lewis was "gone again," to everywhere—California for three weeks, Phoenix "with poor results," Mexico for two months, Boston in the hope of a newspaper job and for treatment of a sore throat, and Missouri on unexplained business.

"Perhaps, my own darling," a self-described "well-isolated" Helen wrote to Lewis in 1899, when Buffie was two and her husband was investigating future prospects as a journalist in the East, "when you are with [Little Elizabeth] more, she will make life more precious to you." In these years Lewis missed his daughter's first four birthdays and saw his children most often in his "mind's eye."

In 1906 Lewis, again requiring institutionalization, left for a cure at a health colony in Summit, New Jersey, favored by leisured middle-class Americans. Later he traveled to a German sanitarium and then to a similar institution in Switzerland where the doctors were well known for their treatment of sexual and stomach nerve-related disorders. Lewis, who did everything temporarily, returned to Bloomington in 1907, after nearly nine months away. Years later, when his daughter, Buffie, tried to reconstruct this ten-year family odyssey, the task of remembering so many places proved impossible. In 1952, when Adlai Stevenson became the Democratic candidate for president, the exact location of his birthplace in Los Angeles had long ago been erased by a blur of family homes.

Frequently unemployed in his pathological version of American mobility, Lewis implored both his father and his father-in-law to find him a patronage job—even, perhaps, in the lowly position of an Army paymaster, which he held to be, though Lewis was always an enthusiast at the beginning, "more congenial" than his superintendence of the copper mine. "Lewis," Helen told her father, "can hardly stand this rough life." Meanwhile he supported his family from the interest on his father's wedding gift of $10,000, the rent from Helen's five-hundred-acre farm in Indiana, and subsidies from Helen's father.

As credentials for his desperate efforts at worthy and lasting employment, Lewis offered his "good business ability, employment with the Hearst estate in several positions, and absolute honesty." Still, as he wrote his Republican father-in-law, "you know as well as I that a man's fitness for a position is not as much weight with a President as the backing he has." In the Republican times of William McKinley, Teddy Roosevelt, and William Howard Taft, his father-in-law's Republican contacts counted for more than his father's Democratic ones.

At first Helen enjoyed her wandering. She had been raised in a pioneer family that celebrated mobility as a way to get ahead. Her grandfather Jesse Fell had walked to Illinois from Pennsylvania, stopping on his two-year journey in the 1830s to teach school and read law before settling outside of Normal. Her father, a migrant from Pennsylvania a generation later, often used the *Pantagraph* to prick the complacency of his Bloomington neighbors who never looked beyond their front porches. "We live," Davis wrote in the *Pantagraph*, "in a flat monotonous country with never a hill or river in sight. If we would teach children proper ideas about the earth's circumference, then we must take them away from home." The Fells and Davises took this advice to heart. Two of Helen's unmarried Fell aunts homesteaded for a time in a sod house in Nebraska, and Davis was forever taking and sending his family on journeys.

In the spring of 1898, when Helen boarded the Santa Fe and Southern Pacific for her thousand-mile trip to the southwestern corner of New Mexico by way of St. Louis, Santa Fe, and then a change in Deming for Silver City, the closest town to the copper mine where Lewis was then employed, her sense of adventure won out, for a time, over the depressing circumstances of her life. "I never was in better condition in my life because I am in my own house and have no outside demands and I needed it," she advised her parents.

Helen Stevenson brought with her an eight-month-old daughter named Elizabeth Davis after her mother, Eliza Fell Davis, along with a nurse from Bloomington. She had left the West to deliver her firstborn in her parents' home in Bloomington, and Buffie had arrived in her childhood bedroom with its iron bedstead and blue curtains. In the huge steamer trunks accompanying her back to one of the most remote corners of the United States, she placed consumer goods—bottles, a box of nipples, books, canned goods, and a good side of bacon unavailable in "ugly, third-rate" Silver City or the general store in tiny Hanover, the closest village to the mines.

At the time the Stevensons were living in a four-room red shanty, originally built for railroad workers near the Santa Rita mines. Their dwelling was, Helen gaily informed her mother, who was uncertain about the location of Silver City, like a yacht. The house featured no shades, only tiny slit-like portholes for windows, and no cellar for storage of the trunks and boxes piled in the kitchen. "Up the road through the gulch are many miserable Mexicans," wrote Helen. Soon her enthusiasm waned: "It is a horrible task with the care of a baby and a strange girl." When Helen's mother came to help, she recognized the problem. "Helen does not want to live around the mines and of course little E. [Elizabeth] must have better care than she can hope to get there. Lewis cannot long endure the hardships and severity of mining life." Later the family moved to a sand-blocked adobe and, when smallpox broke out among the miners, to several rooms in Fort Bayard, the military post used to direct operations against the Apaches.

For the next ten years as Lewis changed jobs, Helen measured her life by rented houses: the New Mexican clay huts near "the miserable Mexicans," the stucco home rented from Phoebe Hearst in Los Angeles, the shingled bungalow three blocks from the ocean on Santa Cruz's Third Avenue, and the agreeable cottage in Battle Creek, where she and Lewis became fervent practitioners of Dr. Harvey Kellogg's vegetarian diet of granola, cereals, and yogurt. Such a vagabond existence made her yearn for a home of her own.

Finally, far away in Bloomington, William Davis sat down at his huge rolltop desk and erupted in a letter to his daughter. At the time Helen was alone in California; Lewis was in Switzerland exhilarated by Dr. Roger Vittoz's training of the will through mental exercises called "brain-jogging" and the prospects for "attaining the joy of life we have never known" through mind control of his "subjective" brain. For years Davis had diplomatically praised his son-in-law's efforts; Lewis needed such constant assurance. At the same time Davis made clear his conviction that the best way to get ahead was to make "continued effort in one line. . . . Perseverance accomplishes wonders in a settled business." Only then could "sunshine" come to two lives he saw being overtaken by illness and his son-in-law's self-indulgent wanderings. "Sickness is part of your daily life," cautioned Davis.

Dubious that Lewis would progress beyond chronic invalidism and that his beloved daughter would ever leave what he scorned as "hired houses," father counseled daughter: "I doubt if Lewis is ever any better in health. My acquaintance with him shows no improvement. I think he will gradually become more helpless—it would be well for you to bear this in mind and watch your family affairs accordingly. Politics has been his life and he will never give up his interest therein. . . . Lewis has inherited a delicate constitution with a highly nervous temperament and headaches. . . . I expect you to take the cottage [in Charlevoix] as I have said it will suit you better, for I do not think you can count on Lewis."

It was good advice, but even before Lewis's pilgrimage to Germany, Helen had begun shaping her family into a feminized unit that, when completed by the arrival of her son, Adlai Ewing, in 1900 and the inclusion of her widowed father that same year, proved a network of intense affiliation. In time this family, which she first dubbed the quartet and then, after her father's death, "our trio" (always without Lewis), became the center of an existence that crumpled only when some domestic change—a fight with her sister, her mother's death, or even her children's departure for school—interfered. Her son, Adlai, provided the focal point for this unit of affection, and Lewis came to resent the alliance of mother and children. He wrote his wife, "You must recall you were completely dependent upon [the children]. . . . I counted for little as your thoughts seemed to repulse me rather than encourage our trying to get closer which I have always longed for. . . ."

Adlai had been born in Los Angeles, California, two weeks after Helen's mother died of breast cancer. His birth so soon after her mother's death made this child a special talisman of emotion and affection. In a choice made well before his birth (though many parents in the twentieth century were adopting the patronymic "junior" for their firstborn sons), he bore his grandfather's rather than his father's or even his maternal grandfather's name. Yet Adlai Stevenson I was a famous man whose standing in the Dem-

~~ocratic party,~~ while not included in his partible goods, remained a family asset. "Producing an heir for the House ~~of Stevenson was the effort of my~~ life and I tell Lewis that any more that may be coming in the future will be Davises," Helen confessed to her father, who had written to congratulate her "on the successful launching of this little presidential craft."

Soon the attentions that led Helen Stevenson to a suffocating involvement with her children began. Lewis noted immediately that "a young father's life [is] full of joy and humiliation—there is a conspiracy to keep me away from the baby and daily insults about my ability to care for it." In time he and others would recognize in Helen's hypervigilant mothering an exaggerated emotional dependence on her offspring. After his father-in-law died in 1911, Lewis acknowledged his wife's primary attachments: "Your father is gone now. . . . He loved you more than any of his other children. I cannot hope to take his place in your affection, but my fondest hope is that now I can get closer to you."

Helen's fervid attachments to the children were encouraged by the isolation of her early married years when she lived temporarily in places where she had neither father nor mother nor friends nor often husband, only the children and the nurses sent from Bloomington as mother's helpers. Wherever she was, Buffie and Adlai filled the life of a lonely woman who even when apart from them, as increasingly she had to be, sought to shape their health and habits.

"Take a pint of cream every day," went a typical injunction. Often she mixed such practical advice with maxims for proper behavior. "Forget every ugly and fearful thought." "You must conquer pride and give up struggling. Of course I don't mean losing all ambition." "Failure is better than nerve symptoms." "Words that need the light of the dictionary: descended, successive, fray (not frey)," she wrote to her misspelling son. "Use your atomizer and gargle." "Keep the body free of blockages," and so on through a life's course of imperatives for right thinking and acting from Helen Stevenson's personal child-training manual.

Neither socialite nor clubwoman, Helen Stevenson found that domestic duties did not absorb the hours of the day, though she was an avid housecleaner and a stylish dresser. Like nearly all married middle-class mothers, Helen stayed home, the embodiment of those females who even during the great suffrage battles of the early twentieth century were engrossed in domestic affairs. Helen worried about the proper color for the handsome cloth covering for the living room walls at 1316 East Washington, and when to mark the seasons by changing to the chintz slipcovers for Bloomington's hot summers, and whether the design of her gray outfit with the moleskin cloche broadened her long face, and always she worried over Adlai and Elizabeth.

In an exaggerated, privatized version of the civic maternity promoted by her mother-in-law, Letitia Stevenson, Helen Stevenson came to love too much. A comprehending Lewis soon changed his insistence that his wife could not be sick because he was, to the plea that she must not be sick because the children depended on her, and she on them. Years later the neighbors remembered Helen Stevenson's overzealous maternity, and even Buffie acknowledged her mother as a "home creator," adding, "If mother had had a job and interests, she wouldn't have become so possessed with herself and us. She always thought she was ill and felt the loneliness so acutely."

After her mother's death Helen and the children began to travel with her father—to the Charlevoix cottage for the summer, to Florida, to New Orleans, and to California in the winter. Some years the children missed months of school, as one of Buffie's abiding childhood memories became that of trunks being carried up and down the twisting stairs at Washington Street. Soon the children were calling their seventy-year-old grandfather William Davis "Daddy," reserving for Lewis the more formal and distant "Father." Meanwhile their mother revealed her unequally distributed affection in the nicknames she applied to her children even in adulthood: "dearest Laddie," "angel boy," and "my darling boy" for Adlai; "dearest angel," "my beloved," and "most precious" for Buffie, and for Lewis "my dear" or simply "Lewis."

In October of 1906 with Lewis in Switzerland, Helen Stevenson came home to dependable, predictable, nerve-settling Bloomington and bought a house for $8,500, using the $4,500 she had inherited from her mother's estate and some cash from her father. She did not include her husband's name on the deed of a home located in the new suburbs where the city stretched away from the industrial, working-class west side and the noisy, commercial center of town toward the quiet countryside on its eastern perimeter. Number 1316 East Washington Street was a square, clapboard, pitch-roofed structure set back from one of Bloomington's main arteries now linked to Main Street by an electric trolley. In time Helen Stevenson made improvements—exchanging the wood clapboards for stucco, adding a tiny half porch whose size suggested that the public front porch conviviality of earlier generations had been replaced by backyard living, planting the gingkos and elms and pines that provided privacy as they thickened and branched. She did not have to add the modern conveniences of inside plumbing, central heating, and electricity; these were already standard features of suburban houses in Bloomington.

The interior design of her new house expressed the American conviction that love of home represented one of the deepest feelings of nature. Orderly attractive surroundings, it was supposed, provided the proper structure for rearing good children. Downstairs three public rooms with sliding doors and curtains opened off the entrance hall in a more informal arrangement than prevailed in the houses of either Letitia Stevenson or Eliza Davis. In their homes stout doors secluded the parlor and gentleman's library.

Instead, Helen's dining room, nearly as large as the living room, signaled the emergence of mealtime family communication established around, in this case, an oak table, while the butler's pantry, a mark of gentility, shielded the preparation of food in a household that depended on domestic servants. What had for earlier generations been called the parlor became in language and practice a living room, where Helen Stevenson played the Baldwin piano for the children and sang the sentimental songs she had learned in the 1880s at the Dean Academy—"Darling Clementine," "Bicycle Built for Two," "Angel Gabriel," and "The Young Lover." In the library, an intimate room ten by fifteen feet warmed by a fireplace, Helen read aloud from Markham's *History of the United States* and the works of Sir Walter Scott.

Upstairs four bedrooms, three bathrooms, and, after 1912, a healthful sleeping porch with the oxygen-laden, blood-purifying ventilation that responsible mothers insisted on for their children, provided the privacy surrendered downstairs to family togetherness. But Helen was too fearful of germs to permit a dog or cat to complete the domesticity featured by similar families of the new century.

This home was a substantial one, displaying the family wealth of the Davises and Stevensons. Unlike the inhabitants of the mixed neighborhood of Lewis's childhood, where within a mile lived a washerwoman, a miser, a lawyer, a struggling widow, and a tenant farmer, the Stevenson's neighbors on Washington Street were a collection of well-off professionals—a group that included a banker, the manager of the McLean County Coal Company, a lawyer, and Helen's sister Jessie, who had married the owner of a commercial laundry.

On the other hand, "1316" was not a lavish residence like the local mansions owned by David Davis, Uncle Matthew and Aunt Julia Scott, and Asahel Gridley. Later Helen came to dislike its Victorian gingerbread and depressing brown stucco, complaining as well of the poor materials used in its construction. Still, even the owning of a home placed Helen Stevenson in a small group of privileged townspeople and almost alone among married women whose husbands' names were routinely placed on financial documents, no matter which partner had provided the resources. Less than half of Bloomington's families owned their homes in 1900, and of these, fewer than a quarter lived in single-family, free-standing dwellings with lots.

For Helen such calculations were irrelevant to the purpose of her home. "With the home begins and depends the salvation of the race and its evolution," she once declared. Finally she had the setting to expose the children to culture amid books, music, and her tasteful decorations—the Tiffany window on the landing, the rich red fabrics of the living room, and the handsome sturdy chests and tables of her Davis and Fell ancestors. Home became a place for the children to learn manners, moral uprightness, responsibility (no wet clothes or rubbers in the front part of the house), and the frugal restraint of a family that found conspicuous ornamentation a sign of decadence. "Do not spend time with the mediocre," Helen Stevenson enjoined her children. The corollary—"Do not be extravagant"—was also displayed in her home.

After fifteen years of wandering, the thirty-nine-year-old self-confessed "doting Mother" had found "Home Sweet Home" in the peaceful surroundings of Bloomington's suburbs. Here she raised and educated Buffie and Adlai in an atmosphere of predictability, comfort, complacency, and conformity. Here among neighbors whose houses and values resembled hers, Helen Stevenson tried to establish continuity for the children and mental health for herself.

3

WHEN, IN 1907, LEWIS returned to Bloomington from Germany and his rest cure, he had neither job nor prospects. He worried, as he always did, about his reputation and how his wife had explained his long sojourn in Europe to nosy neighbors. But in the next year his father ran for governor, and with his perpetual enthusiasm for the partisan politics that served him as well as galvanized-current or water cures, Lewis traveled about Illinois campaigning.

Then, in 1910, after unsuccessful efforts to begin a business school, run the family coal company, and set up a dairy farm, forty-one-year-old Lewis went to work as the manager of his aunt Julia Scott's farms in Iowa, Indiana, and Illinois, signing a formal agreement with his mother's sixty-six-year-old widowed sister. Finding his life's work on the fertile prairies of the Midwest, Lewis became a throwback. His grandfather John Turner Stevenson had abandoned a Kentucky farmer's life for that of Bloomington, and his father, Adlai, had been interested in land solely as an investment. Both men had been active promoters of Bloomington and had been at the center of the creation of a civic culture. Lewis was not.

By 1900 the ambitious young men of Lewis's generation had moved to cities like St. Louis or Chicago where the concentration of economic power enhanced opportunities for employment. Some worked for corporations, many as salaried workers in the mammoth Illinois steel, meat-packing, and railroad companies, or in the adjuvant commercial enterprises like banks and insurance companies that clustered in the nation's fifty-one cities with populations of over 100,000 in 1910. Lewis, on the other hand, stayed in

Bloomington, though even there he was never a member of the local elite or a messenger of the values of the town. Sleeping with a pistol by his side, ever on the alert for imagined tramps and burglars, frequently crying "Who's there—I'll shoot" from his second-floor window, he patrolled his house, remaining an outsider in the town his family had done so much to establish.

For the next twelve years, until Julia Scott's death in 1922, three times a year—in the critical planting season of early spring, in the mandatory weeding times of summer, and in the expectant harvesting period of autumn—Lewis left Bloomington to oversee work on the farms, sometimes by railroad, sometimes in the luxury Locomobile that Aunt Julia bought for him, a routine interrupted by several incapacitating breakdowns. To his children he exaggerated both the importance and the stamina necessary for his work. Short of men during one harvest season, Lewis had put up hay and "for three full days driven a mowing machine." Because he could never resist self-congratulation, he added, "And [I] stood the work splendidly."

To his employer Julia Scott he wrote, "You would either laugh or cry to see me tonight while waiting here in the little store for a train. For the last five days I've been visiting the farms going over them, planning the work with new tenants and arranging the old. I am mud from head to foot and a bit battle scarred but still carrying the banner." The political imagery he used was not unusual, for his heart remained in the politics he craved, though eventually his career as a farmer became the most important part of his skimpy partisan credentials.

Lewis was occasionally described as a "practical farmer," but by no means was he typical of twentieth-century Illinois agricultural workers, a bare majority of whom now worked family farms of an average 127 acres. Instead, his job of overseeing—for which his wealthy aunt paid him expenses, $2,100 a year, and sometimes a percentage of the crop—placed him in touch with the darker side of American agriculture, that is, with the system of sharecropping tenancy choking off the aspirations of the farmers who worked Aunt Julia's nearly ten thousand acres.

By 1910, when land cost ninety-five dollars an acre and a family farm of one hundred acres was beyond the reach of most, over 40 percent of all Illinois farmers were tenants bound to prairie landlords through their labor. In the next decades the proportion of tenants rose, as prime agricultural land in central Illinois became scarce and expensive. Riding an economic roller coaster driven by weather patterns, international trade, and the resulting variations in corn and wheat prices, many farmers had been unable to avoid foreclosures during the agricultural depression of the 1880s and 1890s and had slid into renting and cropping; others had bought too much farm equipment or land and had been foreclosed; still others were sons unable to afford a farm, though some families used their collective resources—including the profits from working tenant farms—to buy available acreage for their sons. At least one-tenth of the tenants moved every year, seeking better land or housing. Ever the prey of drought and grasshoppers and, if not these, overproduction, they were rarely able to climb the ladder (unless their fathers owned farms) from dependency to the private ownership that Franklin Roosevelt later linked to democracy and the American "family dream."

When Aunt Julia's husband, Matthew Scott, and his brothers had begun buying up land warrants bestowed by the government on veterans and purchasing vast tracks in central Illinois in the 1840s, first for pennies and then for five dollars an acre, they had built cottages for agricultural workers. Like the coal miners of Stevensonville, these men were expected to make extra payments through their crops to pay off their contract and become homeowning proprietors. Yet farming remained as uncertain and low paying as mining, and that made it impossible for many Illinoisians to become independent. Instead, the plantations of the Scotts grew larger, until by 1850 they controlled 34,700 acres worked by tenants. Like Adlai Stevenson's miners and in almost identical proportions, only a quarter of the Scott agricultural workers had purchased homes by the twentieth century. The rest—their sons and grandsons—were tenants, living without electricity or plumbing though, after 1896, enlightened by the free delivery of the mail.

Lewis Stevenson despised most of the thirty tenants he oversaw. As a group "the boys" were "shiftless and utterly without ambition," he complained to Aunt Julia. Nor did they adhere to the clause in their contracts to find and employ the latest and most effective methods of scientific farming. James Hokes's place in Livingston County was overgrown with weeds in the potato patch and vegetable garden that members of his family were supposed to use to supplement their income. George Parke of Vermilion County in Iowa had cheated, giving some oats to his brother on the sly. (Lewis made Parke sign an admission of guilt, which ended with the promise that he would keep his son in school rather than working him on the farm.) "I must let these fellows understand from the start that the old slipshod methods are no longer in vogue and that the place is to be conducted properly from now on. . . ."

At a time in Illinois history when both Democrats and Republicans remembered the Populist complaint that one-year contracts increased dependency and destroyed any interest in improvements, Lewis insisted on such short-term arrangements so that, like other managers, he could remove those tenants he believed lazy and dishonest. It was part of his arrangement with Aunt Julia "to secure better tenants and to see that all the tenants subscribe to a good farm journal." Most of the annual sharecropping contracts Lewis wrote were standard ones, requiring the tenants, after the harvest, first to pay their rent to Aunt Julia of one-half the shelled corn and wheat grown on her land, one-half the oats and hay, and ten dollars for grazing land for livestock; only then could they receive their personal share. Unlike many southern farmers with whom the system of cropping was most often identified, Illinois sharecroppers owned the plows, wagons, and animals they used, though not the houses, barns, and seed. Nor were they caught in the same treacherous merchandising arrangements that made credit so expensive in the cotton counties of the South. Still, by state law Illinois landlords had the power of the lien over possessions of reneging tenants.

Overall this system was supposed to provide incentive to farmers who would get more if they raised more, but its clear effect was also to lessen the landlord's risk. Even with the most delinquent of his tenants, Lewis rarely needed to go to court for a lien. Instead, he used his authority as the manager of the Scott farms to persuade the owners of grain elevators and warehouses to boycott the harvest of recalcitrant tenants.

Ensconced in his new job, Lewis remained a traveling man gone from Bloomington, as he evidently preferred, for long periods of time. Though failed as an entrepreneur, businessman, and journalist, he had found opportunity as a manager. He made the most of it, sending tenants to agricultural school at Urbana, spending Aunt Julia's profits for improvements such as sheds and barns, searching for the cheapest pulverized manure, studying the markets, and occasionally working the threshers himself. Yet he had not surrendered his lifelong ambition for a successful venture of his own and tried to lease two thousand of his aunt's best acres to set up a dairy operation with several partners. But Julia Scott wanted "no partnership with cows" and demanded cosigners on his note. Soon the enterprise floundered.

As an overseer, Lewis expected an autonomy lacking in his other jobs; instead, he got the affectionate paternalism of an aging aunt who had run things for twenty years without him. She knew the Chicago grain markets as well as he, and they argued ceaselessly over the best time to sell. She read the Chicago papers with their reports on the futures. She understood the effect of international events on corn prices, calculating, on her seventy-fifth birthday, the influence on the grain markets of the closing of the Dardanelles in 1915 and the rumored switch of English importers to Argentinian sources. For years in the early spring, she had sent stamped self-addressed postcards to her tenants with convenient boxes for them to list the acreage they expected to plant in corn, wheat, and oats. From this she calculated how many bushels to anticipate in the fall.

Inevitably Lewis Stevenson and Aunt Julia Scott quarreled. "I begin to realize your lack of confidence in my judgment and loyalty is going to be a serious barrier in our doing business," Lewis complained after suggesting that she had not invested enough of her profits in farm improvements. "You can't have tenants without providing houses, barns, cribs, and keeping them in repair. . . . You have let things go," he impertinently declared in the first year of his management. When Aunt Julia responded by pointing to the farms' profits "under my hard work when I was stupid enough to manage my own affairs" and by comparing her son-in-law Carl Vrooman's forty-six-bushel-an-acre harvest to Lewis's thirty-five-bushel one, Lewis lost his temper.

At the time he was also engaged in a bitter controversy over the future of the McLean County Coal Company. A minor stockholder, Lewis believed the flagging company a Scott-Stevenson enterprise, though it was now owned and managed by his neighbor Lyman Graham. With the help of some "capitalist partners" from Decatur, Lewis presented Graham with a contract of sale, according to Graham and several other businessmen, "so utterly preposterous and ridiculous that it didn't seem worth making any reply to it [because] it was so favorable to the buyers and unfavorable to the stockholders." When Graham refused to sell, Lewis threatened to go to court and, in the recollection of several observers, "was so angry he was like a madman."

Unlike Graham and most of Bloomington's business community, Aunt Julia understood her nephew's tribulations and encouraged him to put aside his "restlessness and nervousness." "You are very much a boy just to fly off the handle like that," she consoled. Still, the differences and tempers persisted, with Lewis complaining, "It seems no matter how hard I work and plan there is some misunderstanding between us." A stranger would have found another manager, but Aunt Julia was family. And so their relationship survived, with Lewis needing constant approval and Aunt Julia insisting her manager supply more accurate forecasts of necessary capital needs, whether for draining, fencing, or new storage cribs.

In 1913, as the international turmoil preceding World War I began to choke off grain shipments from European farmers, Lewis felt its effects when corn prices doubled to $1.38 and wheat to almost $2.00 a bushel. For a time the profits on Aunt Julia's farms ended the conflict between the aunt and the nephew she would help while "he was rising." These were the golden years of American agriculture; in 1933, when the issue of the equitable ratio between what farmers paid as consumers of goods and what they were paid as producers of food reentered national politics, the resulting parity price formula was based on the prices paid from 1909 to 1914. It was a federal entitlement program supported by Lewis's son, Adlai Stevenson, in both of his national campaigns.

Pleased with her profits, Julia Scott listened sympathetically, as Helen often did not, to the continuing litany of Lewis's medical problems—the headaches, the nervousness, the bad stomach and sore throat, and even the accidents—one caused by a fall and one by a runaway horse. She sympathized with his need to "take the cure" and "tonic up," encouraging his departures for various sanitariums in 1913, when he again traveled east to consult with S. Weir Mitchell, in 1916, and in 1920, when he traveled to Germany for his health and to promote a venture with the Germans to land dirigibles at Chicago's Municipal Pier. Aunt Julia's standing in Lewis's hierarchy of affections was high: "Please just believe this," he appealed in 1915, after an angry exchange of letters. "I know you love me, you have shown it since my earliest memory and I do [love] you only second to Buffie and Adlai." Perhaps embarrassed by the exclusion of his wife, Lewis had omitted the word "love" in his letter, but the ranking was accurate.

4

NOTHING—NOT mining, not journalism, not business—ever diverted Lewis Stevenson from politics. Farming proved no exception. During his years as Aunt Julia's manager, he still yearned to be a public man, though a third-rate political temperament hampered him in work demanding an ego strong enough to withstand the insults of partisan battle. Over the years Lewis had developed neither persistence nor equanimity. Nor did he have the raw ambition that brought men to contest the places he sought in order to bolster, not endanger, a fragile self. Still, like his father he had a vast store of stories, was enthusiastic, knew many state and national leaders, attended nearly every Democratic National Convention, carried a respected name, and hungered for a role in politics.

In 1912 both factions of the Illinois Democratic party offered Lewis Stevenson their support for the party's nomination to the state's lieutenant governorship, a position with few duties, resembling the vice presidency in its honorific emptiness. Startled and irritated that he had been given only a day to decide (for he was not the party's first choice), Lewis declined, giving as his reason illness in the family. No doubt he referred to his wife, who had taken refuge in an eastern sanitarium. Later he explained his "temptation" to a surprised Aunt Julia, who believed that he should accept: "It's just barely possible they wanted the Stevenson name as much as they wanted me personally. . . . I can't help regretting it a little bit, for it would have given me the recognition I crave."

In 1913 another chance arrived. This time Lewis accepted Governor Edward Dunne's appointment to one of the state's proliferating boards that, along with commissions and agencies, were transforming the relationship of the state to its citizens. Dunne, a second-generation Irish American mayor of Chicago, was a Progressive reformer elected to the governorship in 1912. That year two factions of Illinois Republicans, mimicking the national party split between Teddy Roosevelt and William Howard Taft that helped elect Woodrow Wilson, had splintered the state's normal Republican majority, making possible an unusual Democratic victory.

Elected on a platform calling for women's suffrage, workmen's compensation, direct election of senators, tighter controls on corporations, municipal ownership of transportation, and a new constitution, Dunne represented a generation of Democrats who sought to use the power of the state to correct political and economic abuses. Adapting to Illinois what Woodrow Wilson dubbed the "New Freedom," Dunne believed that "the government promoted the happiness and well-being of the people and helped the weak and helpless." At the state level this newly defined liberalism required the use of Chicago's political machine not only to provide the majorities necessary to offset downstate Republican domination of statewide offices but also to bring about the election of legislators who would support Progressive legislation as downstate assemblymen and senators did not.

Among the reforms Dunne sought was that of the prison system, and in the name of efficient, scientific government he used convicts, no longer attired in striped uniforms, to work on the state's inadequate roads. Intent on prisoner "regeneration rather than vengeance," Dunne was also an advocate of parole. At the turn of the century Illinois, like many other states and in 1910 the federal government, had installed an appointed part-time parole and pardon board to oversee arrangements that allowed conditional releases for "good time," along with revocations of violated paroles. In 1914 Dunne chose Lewis Stevenson to be the $2,000-a-year chairman of the Illinois State Parole and Pardon Board. But Lewis found it hard to make a mark during a time in which he was hospitalized in Chicago, Massachusetts, and New Jersey for throat, stomach, and liver disorders.

In 1914 Dunne, in grateful acknowledgment of the recently deceased Adlai Stevenson's downstate support, appointed Lewis to a more significant post, this time as a replacement for his secretary of state, who had committed suicide. A patronage post earlier held by the governor's closest advisers, the office of the Illinois Secretary of State had in 1870 become elective. By the twentieth century the secretary's responsibilities had expanded into the management of an increasing number of service bureaus that chartered and regulated corporations, licensed and regulated automobiles, and supervised the state's elections. The latter reflected the government's supervision of a process that political parties had earlier controlled.

To all these tasks Lewis energetically applied himself, though his scheme for voluntary neighborhood watches to write down speeders' license plates was the solution of a simpler small-town age. In any case he was now an important man with influence over others; even his brother-in-law Lou Merwin signed up for his auto safety crusade and then requested one of the low-numbered license plates that the secretary could dispense.

By law the secretary of state also presided over the Illinois House of Delegates until that body chose its speaker. Usually the secretary's role was limited to the routine task of calling the session to order and counting the ballots for speaker. Still, there had been rumors of a possible deadlock, and given their competitive party politics, most Illinoisians could remember long stalemates in the legislature. But when Lewis, who had watched his father preside over the Senate in Washington, took his place in the speaker's chair on a cold January day in 1915, he gloried in his role as presiding officer of the Forty-ninth Illinois General Assembly.

Seated in a gilt chair on a dais, he surveyed the entirely white male faces of the 153 representatives elected from fifty-one districts of Illinois. The 82-man Republican delegation held a majority of 12 seats, but like the Democrats the Republicans were on the issue of prohibition split into wets, who denied the state's authority to control personal habits, and drys, who wished to end the selling of liquor by using local referendums. Meanwhile a handful of socialists had already announced their "conscientious" refusal to vote for the spokesman of either party.

Sixty-eight roll calls later, an exhausted Lewis Stevenson gave the oath to a Republican wet. During this six-week period only a resolution to create a committee to investigate the ravages of hoof-and-mouth disease was passed. What Lewis Stevenson confronted was an important twentieth-century phenomenon that his son and grandson would also detest—the power of the single-issue lobby. Assemblymen (of both parties) who were members of the growing Anti-Saloon League—which no longer concentrated on temperance as a personal failing but instead sought to end the sale of liquor—held this issue as their preeminent concern, to the point of refusing to support a wet of their party for speaker.

For a time Lewis hoped, and there were rumors that this might break the impasse, that he would be chosen as a compromise candidate for speaker. In the traditional manner of aspiring politicians, he sent letters of solicitation asking his friends to write their assemblymen. But no wet Democrat could win; besides, he was not an elected representative. Instead, after he was coached on parliamentary procedure, his pipe dream faded and he began to show his fatigue during what he called "the legislature's low-down wrangling," which included drunks on the floor, name-calling, and several fistfights.

For Lewis Stevenson presiding over the legislature was the most continuous labor of his life. Even as a farm manager he always had time for rest and long vacations. "I'm too sick to finish this letter," he advised Julia Scott as he struggled with constant headaches. On the weekends Lewis retired to bed to prepare himself for the turbulence of the next week. Wearily he wrote in the guest register in his Bloomington home that sometimes he felt like a stranger. Still, there was some solace in the clippings he forwarded to Aunt Julia Scott. "I just sent that article so you could see some compliments my friends had paid me," he grumbled when Aunt Julia misunderstood and thought he was boastful.

In 1916, another presidential year, Lewis ran for secretary of state on Governor Dunne's ticket, finding campaigning as "awful" as his son would. "One rotten hotel after the other," he complained, although his objections went beyond physical discomfort. "My experience has not been altogether a bed of roses. While I have been prompted by *really* the best of motives in everything I have done, I have had so much fault found with me by my political adversaries my life in some regards is miserable," he lamented. Scandalized by the "vicious fight" of the Chicago machine to put another Stevenson on the primary ballot to confuse voters, he hired private detectives to watch his opponents and "prevent the toughs from disrupting my rallies."

Lewis Stevenson ran on his record. "Use sense" and "Safety first" became his slogans to an electorate wedded to automobiles. Anger lay on the surface of his speeches: "No one is more in favor of efficiency and economy than myself. Anyone who states otherwise is guilty of misrepresentation." He borrowed one of his father's tactics, printing up postcards for Republicans to send to their friends identifying themselves as Charles Evans Hughes (the Republican presidential candidate against Wilson) supporters who nonetheless wanted other Republicans "to vote for my friend Secretary of State Lewis G. Stevenson." Fatigued after the primary, he retired to Lakewood-in-the-Pines; when he returned to Illinois, he became so exhausted that he disappeared for three weeks in October, at the climax of the campaign.

This campaign for the secretary of state was Lewis Stevenson's only attempt at elective office. He lost, though in his mind he won. "I want you to know the remarkable race I made here in Illinois," he exulted to the North Carolina Democrat Jonathan Daniels, recounting his success in carrying Cook County, in receiving 40,000 more votes than Governor Dunne, and in winning a greater percentage of the popular vote than Wilson, who lost Illinois but was reelected. Stevenson paid no attention to the fall-off of nearly 40 percent from the presidential vote to that cast for statewide offices, as Illinoisians showed declining interest in the local politics that had once been a catalyst for his father's career.

In family history Lewis Stevenson demonstrated his success by running ahead of the ticket. He was also memorialized in the carefully preserved clippings from local newspapers that hailed him as the best candidate. From Peoria to Chicago to Metamora, the latter the town where he had been born, newspapers proclaimed him "a naturally endowed candidate." He was described as a man who should not be forgotten when the Democrats looked around for a gubernatorial candidate in 1920. To his son, who was away at boarding school, he rationalized: "I was defeated as I told you all along I would be, but defeat in the nature of a victory in that I ran far ahead of any other Democrat." From New York, where Helen had taken sanctuary

in the Clifton Springs Sanitarium, came a gay rhyme: "However it be / It
seems to me / 'Tis better to have run and lost / Than never to have run at
all."

Lewis Green Stevenson made two final appearances in politics, both on
the party's fringes. In 1924, at the Democratic nominating convention in
New York City, he was not a delegate, but was allowed the floor, as a point
of personal privilege, to nominate for vice president David Houston, Woodrow Wilson's former secretary of agriculture; Houston lost the convention
vote to Governor Charles Bryan of Nebraska. Then, in 1928, he promoted
his own cause as a possible vice-presidential candidate. Spending hours
in the third-floor attic on Washington Street, he wrote family friends and
Democratic leaders. After thirty-five years of marriage, his wife was realistic
about his chances, informing Buffie "of father's vindication in this little
boom—good for him, but not of much ultimate value." She added, "I hope
to see him gaining daily in his own self-responsibility."

In the end his appeal, to a convention that met in Houston with
chicken-wire fences separating the few black delegates from whites, was as
a midwestern farmer representing the rural wing of the Democratic party
who might balance the wet, Catholic New Yorker Alfred Smith. But in a
final public humiliation Smith asked him to withdraw his name as a candidate. His own possibilities ended, Lewis now concentrated on his son,
arranging jobs at conventions and introductions to candidates.

5

WHILE HER HUSBAND oversaw Aunt Julia's farms, disappeared into institutions, and hungered for public office, Helen Stevenson lived a private life
with episodes of nerves aggravated by domestic crises. She too had the sanitarium habit. In the letters that she wrote her family, she disclosed her
thoughts. In 1913, after five months at Clifton Springs, she contemplated
her life:

> Miserable life! There is nothing holding me or the children in
> Bloomington now that Papa has died. Lewis is away on the farms and
> when he is here it's sometimes worse. He accused me recently of having
> an affair with Ledyard Horton at Charlevoix—where he never comes to
> share the summers with the children. Little Adlai spends half the sum-
> mer meeting the trains. Lewis has neglected me most of the summers of
> our married life. Now he has written that I went to the beach with
> Ledyard, but always had an excuse not to go with him. Doesn't he
> understand that I must put the children to bed?
>
> Ledyard and I were on the beach late that night because I was trying

to learn if hypnosis can help my blues. Though there was gossip about Lewis in California with that Hungarian woman, I have never deceived my husband. Nor will I. I go for months in good health, happy with the children and my life. Then some upset shatters my equanimity, as it did last year when Papa died and Adlai shot that Merwin girl.

With all these burdens coming at once, sometimes I have felt it easier to turn over and pass into the great beyond. I have told Lewis that I wished my love could compensate for all he feels he has lost in life—but it hasn't. He grieves and resents the years, while the children compensate for the disappointments I have had. I tell Lewis to look up and not down. Instead he finds his enjoyments in his doctors and health foods and now the new exercise machine he learned about from Dr. Kellogg. And the new Indian bar bells that he lifts to and fro in the yard.

I worry about the children. They crowd in too much in this fast-paced life. The important thing is to keep well. If Buffie allows herself spells of crying and killing disappointment, they will grow on her as they have on me. And if Adlai does not gauge his strength and allot his time and not give of both too carelessly he will be successful. Failure is better than bringing on nerve symptoms through too much activity. Adlai and Buffie must rest, drink plenty of water, eat only at meal time, chew every morsel forty times, walk slowly, go slowly up and down stairs, breathe deeply, and lie down even if it's for a moment. Oxygen is essential to life. They must take four-hundred breaths a day, lifting their arms and at the same time pulling in their diaphragm. I will not have Adlai go back to school after he comes home for a rest.

Last year after Papa died, I took the children to Europe for a diversion to restore my nerves and give the children a rest. We went to Switzerland and Montreux which I remembered, from my trips as a girl with Jessie and Aunt Fanny Fell, as a place of invalids with the streets full of nurses and rolling chairs. I wonder if years from now the children will remember and thank me for this winter so far from home and kin. Now after this dreadful accident with Adlai and the gun, I must do something. Adlai can not stay in town, though he bravely went back to school and faced the boys after that terrible weekend. But he needs to forget, and we will make a wall of silence, never to speak of it again.

Perhaps the trio will travel south; then I will take them to Dr. Jackson's health resort. Whatever happens, I will not be separated from my children. If they go to camp, I will find somewhere nearby; if they go to school in the east, I will follow. We can't be separated. Elizabeth will have a better time and Adlai will be safer if I am nearby.

Later that year from Dr. Jackson's health resort in Danville, New York, a sanitarium famous for its water cures, Helen wrote:

Life is necessary. I have been made ill by others but I must let nothing
hurt me but my own mistakes. Lewis resents my illness and says I forced
him away from his mother's death bed when she died in 1913 and I was
so sick. Now I think I am better. It is a marvel to watch the children. I
have written my husband that we can have such lovely times with the
children. Let's quit being intense and laugh at our malignancies. But last
month Lewis loaded his gun four times during the night believing robbers in the house and he accused a neighborhood boy of driving his car.
Now I sit in the chair outside looking at the mountains, reading what
my beloved Laddie has written: "Dear Father, June 24, I am sitting here
with mother trying to think what to say. Buffie has gone to chapel. We
have lots of cherries on the cherry trees and I have enjoyed picking
them. When are you coming east?"

And in Lakewood-in-the-Pines in 1917, Helen Stevenson wrote:

I am better. Just knowing I am near Laddie and Buffie in the east reas-
sures me though I had a slump when Laddie went to boarding school
in Connecticut and my precious Buffie was at Miss Wright's School in
Pennsylvania and Lewis took a war job in Washington as a special
inspector for the Navy Department though he won't last long there. I
don't think about the war much or for that matter other public things,
though I wish Papa were alive. Perhaps I am too sick to be interested in
the world. Papa would agree with me that Americans are drifting into a
state of extravagance and luxury and softness that will ruin us if not
curbed.

Now Adlai is not far away and I have spent every holiday with him.
I know he is overdoing at Choate with the play and his tennis. I have
written him to take intelligent care of himself, to write a little note to
the girl who invited him to a dance at Rosemary Hall, but he should be
careful that it is written well and properly spelled. He should practice it
in his room. It is glorious that my precious Laddie won both the singles
and the doubles! I would rather have him sound physically and morally
than president. Failure is better than nerves. And I have reminded him
of one or two changes in his behavior that he should make. He must
guard against a briskness of manner that gives the appearance of cold-
ness. That we have a genius in our midst is becoming more and more
apparent, though I worry about his equilibrium. Perhaps that is why his
grades in French were not so good. I do not approve of his taking Spanish as a replacement. Still there are no dark and muddy spots on his
career, for no one remembers the accident. Perhaps if he goes to
Princeton I will rent a house there and take Buffie with me. My greatest
desire is to be well so that I can be of help to Buffie and Laddie.

I have been reading William James. I need to do what he says and what I tell the children: believe in my free will and make my first act of free will the belief in it. If I have been mistreated by life, then I must not think of this any more than Adlai should contemplate his accident. I will think not on the wrongs and have a doleful state of mind. Instead I will by an act of will change my ideas and beliefs about life. Right thinking. Be always happy. Let go my hold. Resign my destiny to higher powers. Have faith that as I affirm so it will come to pass. The new book Lewis has recommended—Aaron Crane's *Why Worry?*—says the same thing—that our states of mind are never independent of our conceptions of them. Get rid of discordant thoughts. Uncover the good. So if I resolve by my will to change how I think, I can change my spirits. Lewis must do the same thing and perhaps we can finally come closer to each other. I always feel ashamed to quarrel with Lewis. Lewis is so frail and I admire his splendid will and humor—if only he had learned to control himself, how wonderful he would have been.

And in Princeton in 1918, 1919, and 1920 in a rented house within blocks of her son's dormitory, Helen Stevenson mused:

I wish angel boy would come to dinner more often, and next week his birthday, his blessed natal day, the anniversary of his precious life, so I have written again. Though he is only a mile away, I must not interfere. I left angel boy so beautiful and fine last night, but he must study. We must see Adlai through this dreary winter. I have met a few of his friends and so has Buffie. John Harlan seems captivated by her, and she will meet more Princeton boys, rather than some of those dreary fellows from Bloomington. We have a fine house on Library Place and I have even brought the silver service so that we can entertain. Teas, I think, are best. Adlai is with educated people and I am glad for that.

Adlai must not become an invalid like his father and like, I suppose, me—though I have always kept this family going through my ups and downs whereas Lewis' whole life has centered around his delicate condition. I have sent Adlai a thermometer, along with the instructions about oil in his nose and not to use his eyes too much and not to get overheated on the athletic field. I am fearful he will lose his hair, and he has agreed to have scalp treatments like his father. At least he does not need a mustache to make him look older like Lewis. I remember so well on our honeymoon how angry Lewis was when he couldn't even get into the gambling casino at Monte Carlo because he looked too young. I have warned Adlai about too much exercise and getting in the bad practice of going off weekends to debutante parties in Philadelphia.

How terrible it is to live a life without peace and harmony! Lewis has just written me a terrible letter about all the trouble I have caused by forgetting to send a bank draft to him in Germany where he is off again with another of the projects that never works out. He is angry because I complained to Buffie about one of his letters and how many mistakes there were. Now he says he was exhausted when he wrote it and that he will not write again. In the end he threatens and baffles me with the words *"There is to be no more punishment."*

And in Battle Creek in 1927 Helen Stevenson thought:

This Saturday my precious Buffie will be married in Naples to Ernest Ives, a man I have never met. I am too sick to be there. How alone I am, lying in this chair, though surrounded by doctors and nurses and nutritionists and masseurs in this vast atrium where we are wrapped in blankets and put out on chaise lounges like living sculptures to ponder—what? I have written Lewis with all the energy I possess not to insist on his way at the wedding (as he always does)—not to try and force things—not to have scenes or bring again to Buffie's poor tired memory the hideous past. He must control his irreliability at every cost and not talk health or give a negative suggestion, though he should get Ernest Ives's family history and urge him to give up tea, coffee, all liquor and careless eating. Habits and intellect make impulses.

I will think of the wedding. I will do more walking. I must remember Buffie's letter about letting the Divine Mind come into my darkened chamber and forget this terrible fight with my sister Jessie and Lou Merwin over Papa's will and the control of the *Pantagraph*. The Illinois Supreme Court has just decided in our favor, but what does it matter now? At first I thought the courts the best way to solve the disagreement over what Papa wanted, a friendly suit they called it. Who would have ever thought that my brother Bert and his two sons would die before Jessie and me, wiping out their entire family? Papa always wanted Bert to run the paper, though he was closest to me. I know he meant to divide the stock between Jessie and me. But the Merwins say he wanted the shares to go evenly to his grandchildren and since they have three children and we the two (Lewis says he would have had ten children if he had known the way the will would be interpreted), their family will control the paper. Of course they expect their sons Davis and Loring to manage the paper, but what of Adlai if he chooses to be a journalist? The Merwins say father's will was purposely confusing, because he wanted at all accounts to keep the paper from my husband. Now the court has ruled that we are right, but in the meantime through cunning and deceit those despicable Merwins have purchased the ten shares that Papa gave an employee, so they have control no matter what the next court says. By any moral law they have been unjust and unethical and have made a baghouse of family pride, loyalty and dignity. I will never speak to Jessie again.

I will not think of such things; it is better to remember my routine—

up at 8, drink cold water, a sponge bath and then my breathing exercises, then breakfast which I eat more slowly every day, next exercises and then resting until dinner at 1 and from 1:30 to 3:30 a nap and then a steam bath and massage and so on and on.

I have written Adlai that my whole married life centered on him and on Buffie . . . that no children had ever more devoted attention. I have told him that I have always held him to be a Moses come to bless and lead . . . and that he must abide always in consciousness and openness to opportunity unfailing. Let go your hold, says William James, and resign your destiny to higher powers and you will get perfect inward relief.

During the 1930s in sanitariums across the United States, in Takoma Park, Maryland, and Winter Park, Florida, in Battle Creek, Michigan, and the Riggs Hospital in Springfield, Massachusetts, and finally in the Milwaukee Sanitarium, in Wisconsin, Helen Davis Stevenson meditated:

I hate to write about myself, but I am in a new phase of my nerves. After Buffie and Brod left (I try to call him that now that he is an adult though he'll always be Laddie), I have gotten terribly excited and get no sleep or relaxation without medicine. I wonder if I'm ever going to get well. I am losing ground daily; I feel myself slipping away into melancholy and terrible negative mental feelings. The high feeling of last fall is gone. I am sinking into a stifling nothingness of despondency and sleeplessness. The Christian Science I learned under Miss Balch has not worked, though the idea of using the power of the spirit over mortal mind and healing myself through spiritual power by denying the matter of my body and casting out error to cure my problems helped for a while. God's presence is immanent and we are bound by spiritual not material laws. There is no sickness. Certainly the doctors haven't helped me much. Perhaps there is nothing apart from God and the infinite mind.

How I miss Buffie so far away in South Africa and Denmark, or is it Algeria now? She has written that I must take deep breaths of peace and memorize the 142nd Psalm and read the thanksgiving lessons of the fourth chapter of Ephesians. The summers when she comes home are never long enough. How I miss Adlai. Now that he is married and a father it can never be the same! And Buffie writes that it is the biggest struggle of her life to love Adlai's wife Ellen.

One of my nightmares is that my children will not find me the real thing, but I must know the truth of myself as well as others. I have written my sister Jessie that I want to be a true white light upon the path of my children, otherwise it had better be over. My faith in human nature hasn't improved with the years. I'm in a slump. The nurses are terrible, the doctors harsh and uncaring. They say I am self-absorbed

and sulking in the mind. The food and room are absymal. I have written
all this to Buffie and told Adlai when he visits—about the medicine I
take to sleep and my fears and anxieties and the unsuitability of this
place. Sometimes I think I would like to go home to Bloomington to the
house that I bought so many years ago.

Both Adlai and Buffie say I complain and talk too much of myself,
and they want me to stop what they call dull series of wailings. Buffie
has written that I am a spoiled lady and she wants me to begin each day
thinking of my blessings. But how can I? My whole married life has
centered on my children and they are gone. Some days I remember the
soft summers at Charlevoix when Buff and my precious lad climbed the
sheds, played golf, and pressed autumn leaves and spent the long cool
evenings in Papa's room and I read to them until I was blind and played
guessing games. And sometimes I sit by the window in the twilight
staring over the trees into the soul of night and I remember my wedding
vividly and my boy-like eager lover. I don't want to complain but this
place is too hot and the nurses uncooperative.

6

IN 1929 SIXTY-ONE-YEAR-OLD Lewis Green Stevenson collapsed at the
Bloomington Club from a heart attack and died three weeks later in a hospital. In family legend, at the moment of his collapse he was writing a letter
to the daughter with whom he often clashed. His wife was in Europe visiting Buffie and so, in the persistent reckoning of this family, husband and
wife were separated in death as they had been in life. Nor did Buffie attend
her father's funeral. Lewis Stevenson's will recognized the unbalanced
affections of this family. He left to his wealthy wife, Helen, only that part
of his estate "to which she is entitled by law." In his handwritten instructions to his son, he dictated his wish to be buried next to his father. "Your
mother should be buried in her father's lot," though through a series of
rearrangements by their children the couple were eventually reunited in the
Stevenson burial ground in Bloomington's Evergreen Cemetery.

In his careful instructions to his son about his estate of $174,000—
which consisted of real estate, mortgages and bonds, and a portfolio of
investments including ninety shares of now worthless McLean County Coal
Company stock—Lewis omitted the intangible legacies of his afflictions. He
was, acknowledged one obituary, a man with a nationwide acquaintance
with public men, though "death came before he had fulfilled the usefulness
of which his life gave promise." Lewis was more realistic in the bitter advice
he offered to his children the year before he died: "Observe your mother
and me and our unhappy lives as examples to be avoided. I struggled
against ill-health all my life and particularly in my young manhood, trying

to make a place for myself and save money. Your mother has made every sacrifice for you and Adlai . . . has neglected everything including me and our possible happiness largely for you. . . . You can give her with little effort what I am worn out trying to do."

Six years later, in November of 1935, after a severe nervous breakdown, sixty-seven-year-old Helen Stevenson died in the Milwaukee Sanitarium of "a fever of unknown origin perhaps acute endocarditis, with the contributory cause a manic depressive depression." Her inheritance to Buffie and Adlai was both tangible—in the form of the *Pantagraph* stock that would ensure the Stevenson's affluence—and intangible—in the form of an enveloping affection that both inspired and inhibited.

CHAPTER SEVEN

FAMILY CLAIMS:
The Obligations of Youth

1

IN 1906, WHEN HELEN STEVENSON returned to Bloomington and bought the house at 1316 East Washington Street, her six-year-old son, Adlai, was an experienced traveler. Already he had lived in four states, sometimes moving twice a year. Three times he had journeyed across the Rocky Mountains in the Union Pacific Railroad's elegant Pullman Palace sleeping cars, en route to Chicago and Bloomington for brief reunions with his Merwin, Davis, and Stevenson cousins and three surviving grandparents before boarding another train for "Daddy" Davis's summer cottage on Michigan's Lake Charlevoix.

Other children collected dolls, stamps, rocks, and coins; nomadic Adlai gathered baggage checks and railroad tickets in the pockets of his knickers. Rather than policeman or postman, the trainman served as his image of authority; movement became, and remained, his reality in a family that was always going somewhere. "He dogged the footsteps of every conductor and porter, pestering them with questions, and he hopped off at each stop, to consult with his friends the brakemen and bear up-to-the-minute reports to Grandfather," remembered his sister, Buffie. For Adlai Stevenson the haunting whistle of a train forever recalled his bittersweet childhood.

Adlai's father was usually away, and in a family that avidly posed for photographs, there were few of Helen, Lewis, Buffie, and Adlai together. Lewis Stevenson, whose collection of shoes from Japan, Holland, China, and Germany testified to his restlessness, disappeared for months on his perpetual search for another business opportunity or a more successful treatment for his nervousness and bad shoulder. Adlai's first letters reflected his father's absence: "I hope you'll come home soon"; "I hoped you will come home soon?" "I hope you'll soon homeward sail." In 1907, when Lewis had been in Europe for nearly a year, his son addressed a plaintive note in his childish script: "Come home, you've been gone a very long time and you can see the water works," the latter one of Bloomington's recent municipal improvements. Once, in a letter to his father, Adlai drew a picture of himself astride a cow with a ring in his nose, not the cow's. Growing up in a family that lacked a reliable breadwinner and that featured angry confrontations between his parents, Adlai commended himself as "Your loving, anxious little son."

Throughout these early years three women—his mother, his older sister, Elizabeth, renamed Buffie after her brother's youthful lisp, and his nurse, Codie—provided constancy. Before the return to Bloomington, the family had never stayed anywhere long enough for casual boyhood intimacies. In their place a lonely woman whose two children became her life's work offered an incessant maternalism. As Helen Stevenson grew older and sicker, this attention developed into demanding claims for reciprocity. "Remember," she reminded her daughter shortly before her death, "I have loved you [children] more than anything else in this world." To her son, who needed no reminding, she wrote, "Darling one, my whole married life has centered on you and [Buffie] ... No children ever had more loving devoted attention." And she signed herself "With all my heart, all my love, my darling, my darling."

Unique only because of Helen's exaggerations, such intense mothering expressed contemporary conventions of maternal intervention. Helen's mother-in-law, Letitia Stevenson, had organized a public version of these strategies in the civic associations that instructed the poor mothers of Bloomington in matters of child management, the term itself acknowledging a new approach to raising the young. In Bloomington and elsewhere conscientious mothers found their manifesto in Emma Marwedel's popular *Conscious Motherhood,* an assigned reading for the members of the Bloomington Women's Club in 1901.

In the early twentieth century only local volunteers were permitted to intrude in family affairs, a private arena mostly closed to government. Progressive reformers intended to end such prohibitions. In 1912 the federal government organized the Children's Bureau, devoted to the welfare of children, although for years its tiny budget restricted the agency to the publication of two pamphlets, *Prenatal Care* and *Infant Care.* At the state level under pressure from activists like Florence Kelley and Sophonisba Breckinridge, Illinois enacted school attendance and child labor laws. Yet the legislation was rarely enforced. In Bloomington as elsewhere in the United States, a quarter of all children under sixteen still worked long hours in nonfarm jobs that included the railroad shops and the Stevenson-owned McLean County Coal Company.

Never interested in public activities, Helen Stevenson applied middle-class maternalism in her home. She had absorbed these ideas from popular child-raising advice books like Felix Adler's *The Moral Instruction of Children* and Mrs. Emma Angell Drake's *Self and Sex* series. Providing "what every mother should know," such manuals prescribed new techniques of nursing, nutrition, and learning, "with the mother [as] the primary school responsible for what her children know and don't know." Mothers were also responsible for building character and developing a child's potential. On the one hand, women like Helen Stevenson applied what Mary Read's *Mothercraft Manual* called "the moral curriculum." On the other, they were encouraged to appreciate their children's innate characteristics.

As it had been during the nineteenth century, masturbation remained the great battleground, with mothers seeking to instill in their sons the practice of a euphemistic "clean manhood" achieved through self-control. Unlike their mothers and grandmothers, Helen and her generation did not believe that youthful violators risked insanity. But they did accept the view that such habits led to a range of illnesses and, most terrifying to a neurasthenic like Helen, nerve exhaustion. Mothers sought to compel obedience less through physical coercion than by means of conditional loving withdrawn for bad behavior.

By this time Sigmund Freud had undermined the nation's sexual taboos in lectures delivered at Massachusetts' Clark University in 1909, but his ideas on infant and child sexuality and the dangers of repression did not become well known until after World War I. Meanwhile mothers like Helen Stevenson continued to warn their young in coded language of the importance of "clean living habits and good hygenic habits early acquired." "Watch your impulses," Helen implored her obedient son. So well were the principles of continence instilled in Adlai Stevenson that years later he confided to a friend that only after he married did he have sexual intercourse.

Since the liability for bad children was theirs, mothers had a solemn responsibility to create proper homes and there devote themselves to becoming what one expert called "a soul gardener," nurturing their offspring in "the good soil of a worthy home." Such ideas had inspired Helen's solitary return to Bloomington and the purchase of her home. Similar convictions undergirded her domesticity in woman's "oldest, steadiest, most satisfying vocation," even at a time when many middle-class women were abandoning full-time homemaking for public activities, especially the fight for women's suffrage. Never a suffragist or an activist in one of Bloomington's associations, Helen instead believed that "history has never attempted to prove that the home is not the foundation of civilization. We home lovers do not need an argument to prove to us that with the home begins and depends the salvation of the race and its evolution."

To the conservative tendencies of this early-twentieth-century maternalism, Helen added neurotic intensity. Once settled in Bloomington, she applied the lessons of scientific management by adding a sleeping porch to the second floor of 1316 East Washington Street. Thereafter Buffie and

Adlai breathed fresh air when they were asleep at night or napping in the daytime. Even when her children were adults, Helen Stevenson was still offering a drumbeat of instructions, which included those for "fletcheriza-tion," a system of thorough chewing. "Get the right habits of thinking and living," she reminded Adlai when he was eighteen. Her directions always included correct spelling, and so she added, "You have misspelled definite in each letter." Until she became obsessed with her own illnesses in the 1930s, Helen Stevenson's letters remained abbreviated behavior and health manuals, singular for their didactic concentration on right acting and think-ing and for their neglect of local or family news. "Character is better than all success," she reminded her son in 1917. "It will bring success more certainly than friends, fortune or talent."

Helen's standards were high. Years later Adlai acknowledged that he felt inferior in intellect and moral understanding to the mother whose spiritual elevation (and spelling) he believed unattainable. Simultaneously suffocat-ing and uplifting, such vigilant management by an adoring mother both impeded his autonomy and made him cautiously fearful that he would not meet her expectations (and eventually his own); at the same time his moth-er's adoring surveillance enhanced his self-importance. Few sons received from their mothers the confident assertion extended to a mediocre student that the family had a genius in its midst. "How can you keep your equilib-rium with so much glory thrust upon you?" she inquired after her son had dropped algebra and moved into a lower section of Latin. Helen extended to Buffie the same enhancing devotion until the relationship between mother and daughter grew so intense that as a child Buffie denied herself an independent existence, believing that she would die when her mother did. "Our Mother," Buffie once informed Adlai, "is too wonderful to be our Mother."

Meanwhile Lewis remained a distant figure to a son who seldom talked about his father (what was there to say?) and who later told a friend that his father lacked the toughness for success. During a period of redefinition in which the father's role as a stern breadwinner and family protector was giving way to paternal involvement as an example of sociable masculinity, Lewis was neither breadwinner nor role model. When he was home, his erratic style of fathering wavered between hot-tempered demands for obedi-ence ("I will remove you from camp if you do not write twice a week and will write the headman to see that you do it") and warmhearted affection for the slender son he nicknamed, with a touch of irony, "Brute."

After the family's return to the Bloomington community, which Adlai Stevenson later characterized as "tranquil and phlegmatic" and which he worried would make him lazily parochial, the young traveler might have expected a routine existence. In this classically sized small city of 25,000 set in the middle of the best corn-growing counties in the United States, he might be everyboy—a latter-day Abraham Lincoln, learning the traditional virtues of integrity and responsibility and hard work associated with family-centered towns, making lasting friends and moving, as youngsters gradually did, beyond the orbit of his mother and sister. He could join a boy's culture, playing mumblety-peg with knives, rummaging in attics, exploring the meadows that still enclosed Bloomington, and entertaining himself in the prairie version of capture the flag, which pitted settlers against Indians, while his parents strolled under the elms in their placid universe, enjoying the small things that towns were famous for—neighborhood friendships, associations with kin, and the simplicities of an uncomplicated life. But as it turned out, the serenity of young Adlai Stevenson's external surroundings masked a hectic existence at home; independence proved the longest and most difficult journey of his youth.

2

FROM THE BEGINNING of their residence in Bloomington, both Buffie and Adlai were special. Grandfather Stevenson's notoriety as a Democratic politician and former vice president and Grandfather Davis's prominence as the editor and publisher of the *Pantagraph* assured their recognition and provided, in their mother's mind, an additional reason for good behavior. Adlai was instantly a celebrity when one of his first compositions—a rueful tale about a pet bunny that ran away—appeared in the *Pantagraph*. Both Buffie's and Adlai's accents also set them apart from local children, who spoke with the nasal midwestern twang later analyzed by Adlai as a "highly developed lingual peculiarity . . . an important contribution to the composite America." The Stevenson children, whose parents were considered snobs, talked like easterners with the broad *a*'s that led to derision by playmates, especially of Adlai, who until he was a teenager stammered, often starting his sentences over again. In Bloomington the Stevensons were well-known Democrats in a Republican town and county. Around election times the taunt "Stewed cats and pickled rats / Are good enough for Democrats" sometimes followed them home.

Remarkable in their lineage, speech, and politics, Buffie and Adlai soon became notable in their schooling. Neither received any formal instruction in California, Colorado, and Michigan, although the German-influenced kindergarten movement had by this time gone from idea to reality throughout the United States. By 1906 Bloomington boasted four private kindergartens and a new day nursery in a rented house on Mulberry Street. Some parents, rejecting the exaggerated mothering of women like Helen Stevenson, had came to accept a competing notion that children would be better prepared for school by attendance in some collective setting before first grade. About 10 percent of Bloomington's mothers had the most practical reason to support kindergartens—they worked full-time outside the home, most in the local candy factory and in domestic jobs.

Reluctant to relinquish Buffie and Adlai to outsiders, Helen did not immediately enter either in school, though Buffie was almost nine and Illinois law required schooling for children over six. Only in 1908 did they start at the local public school, walking most mornings with their mother the two long blocks down Washington Street—the grand boulevard of Bloomington—to the newly enlarged, handsome brick building on the corner of Washington and Towanda Streets. Years later Helen, whose emotional life was filled with more autumns and winters than springs and summers, remembered her son trudging through the fallen leaves on his walks to and from school. Even when her children were required to go to school, Helen "dreaded" sending them, believing that the schools would change their "natural currents." No match for her vigilance, these institutions in fact proved "not as influential" as she feared.

From its nineteenth-century origins as a district school without age-graded classes, the Washington Street School had expanded to four floors and eight grades. The school's massive building testified to the community's commitment to public education, as did the large proportion of the budget devoted to education. By 1910 there was talk of the need for a separate intermediate school before children entered the Bloomington High School, and several parents had complained that seventh and eighth grades repeated material learned in sixth grade.

Influenced by critics of American schooling like John Dewey and William Harris, who wanted to expand learning beyond books to experience and who encouraged curricular reforms designed to end mindless memorization, the newly organized Mothers Club of the Washington Street School was demanding more drawing, music, and nature study, along with a playground to replace the tiny yard outside the school. There a maypole provided the sole equipment, and recess was limited to a collective recreation called giant stride.

Some mothers were campaigning for a special school to "Americanize" the children of Hungarian and Bohemian immigrants who flocked to the west side for skilled jobs in the Chicago and Alton railroad shops. Others crusaded for an end to corporal punishment in the schools. In this they were following broad changes in the nation's emotional understanding, which held that fear, deemed so useful in controlling youngsters in the nineteenth century, impeded sensible behavior and the development of good character. Years later Buffie Ives remembered her mother and Aunt Jessie Merwin "grabbing their hats and flying out of the house" to protest a spanking not of their own children but of another child.

A rare event at the Washington Street School, the use of physical force was still accepted practice in other Illinois schools. Each year the emerging school bureaucracy documented between 125 and 150 instances of whipping inflicted on a school district population of over four thousand. Only the most intrepid educator would have spanked Buffie and Adlai. In any event, there was no occasion, for, as his sister remembered, "Adlai was a very good little boy."

For four years, along with more than two hundred other children, ranging in age from five to fifteen and arranged in eight grades, Adlai Stevenson intermittently attended school with his east side playmates. Wearing stiff Eton collars and bearing his all-too-starched manners, he and twenty-six classmates sat on the hard immovable seats at the fixed desks in the orderly rows of Miss Jennie Zolman's class and later those of Miss Elizabeth Garret and Miss Bessie Reynolds, learning through drill and repetition reading, writing, and arithmetic from an established curriculum. All of his teachers until he went to boarding school were women. The low pay and prestige of elementary teachers assured the feminization of the staff in the Bloomington schools, as elsewhere in the United States.

At home Buffie's and Adlai's formal lessons were supplemented by their mother's program of reading aloud. When her son's third-grade class began Rudyard Kipling's popular stories adapted for children, Helen Stevenson seized upon the advice given to Kim, as the young orphan searched for a mystical river in a faraway land. In this parable success came to those who persisted and who did something again and again "till it is done perfectly for it is worth doing. Mother always stressed the moral of this story— Observe. Persist. Learn."

Later Joe Bohrer, a classmate at the Washington Street School whose grandfather Joseph W. Fifer was a Republican governor of Illinois and a neighbor of Grandfather Stevenson's, recalled the friend he roller-skated with in Franklin Park as an average student—"very nervous [and] always charging around . . . [with] a runny nose." When young Adlai brought home his monthly grades, they were mediocre in spelling, arithmetic, writing, geography, and history, and he repeated part of the second grade. Yet he excelled in two categories: deportment and absence.

Adlai had just started the Washington Street School when his attendance was interrupted by a long winter's stay with his sister, mother, and Grandfather Davis in Winter Park, Florida, where he was enrolled in a local school. Thus began a pattern of intermittent attendance that influenced Stevenson's later work patterns. In 1909 absent forty-six days and present only forty, he spent half the year in California. In 1910 for several months he visited New Orleans. In the winter of 1911 he left Bloomington with his mother, sister, and a tutor on the *Lusitania* bound for an eight-month stay in Europe. Travel was education for the land-bound Stevensons, but this trip was so long that even Helen worried that her children would never forgive her for this prolonged tour of England, France, and Switzerland.

Adlai also missed school because of his health. Under his mother's protective eye he was kept home because of bronchitis, sore throats, and head colds, for which Helen Stevenson followed—there being few other therapies—time-consuming nursing regimens of special nutrition, sponge baths of chlorate of potash, ventilation, and bed rest. She also moved into his room and occasionally hired trained nurses, who tended the children in their blue-striped dresses and neat white caps. Another child might have found in such chronic, maternally encouraged absenteeism a reason to misbehave or to consider schooling unimportant, but young Adlai earned near-perfect scores in deportment—a 93 in 1909 and a 95 in 1912.

In the fall of 1912 Adlai Stevenson was in his last year at the Washington Street School. The next year he would follow his sister to the Metcalf School and then on to University High in nearby Normal, both attractive options for well-off, educationally ambitious Bloomington parents who could afford the tuition of twelve dollars a term. Classified as model schools, Metcalf and University High were part of the teachers training program at Illinois State University. In small classes students received instruction in more subjects than Bloomington High offered, and their teachers, supervised by seasoned professors, used the newest instructional methods. Whereas the Bloomington High School was a community school from which few students went on to college, Metcalf and University High offered, according to their catalog, "Latin and German for such students as expect to enter college, another [curriculum] designed for girls giving a large place to household economy. . . ."

For Helen Stevenson there was a further reason to send her children to school in Normal. In 1857 her grandfather Jesse Fell, armed with community pledges of financial support as well as a generous gift of his own land, had persuaded the Illinois legislature to locate a state teachers college, or "normal school," in the town that he had done so much to promote and where, forever planting trees, he had lived for so many years. By the twentieth century Illinois State Teachers College (today's Illinois State University) had become one of several family contributions to central Illinois.

Christmas vacation of 1912 was nearly over when gregarious fifteen-year-old Buffie persuaded her parents to entertain at a supper party for a visiting friend from Charlevoix. Buffie's group, a few now attending boarding schools, were home for the season, and Buffie had started University High. For all the reasons that habitually separated the Stevensons, the family had rarely been together that year. First Lewis had pursued one of his ventures in Michigan. Then in the spring Helen's severe case of nerves had required institutionalization in New York's Clifton Springs Sanitarium, where for several months Adlai and Buffie had also lived—their presence

considered therapeutic for their mother. Gradually recovering, she
remained depressed by her father's death the year before.

In the late summer family spirits improved when the doctors agreed
that Helen Stevenson could leave. Before the Stevensons returned to Illinois, Lewis arranged a family meeting with New Jersey's governor, Woodrow Wilson, who had just won a hotly contested Democratic nomination
for president in early June. For the rest of his life, Adlai Stevenson remembered this visit to Governor Wilson's summer home at Sea Girt, where a
long lawn sloped down to a New Jersey beach. There on a wide, Grecian-
columned porch, an impressionable twelve-year-old boy listened to the
man whose ideas and career influenced his own.

Returned to Bloomington, family members were soon caught up in the
election season. They heard Grandfather Stevenson introduce William Jennings Bryan at a rally for Wilson. In its new Hudson Super-Six the entire
family motored through the county hammering Wilson for President posters onto the telephone poles that old-timers believed a blight on the prairies. When Wilson was elected president, in a contest that returned the
Democrats to the White House for the first time since Grover Cleveland
and his running mate Adlai Stevenson had won in 1892, the Stevensons
celebrated, though the new president owed his election to a three-way contest in which the Republican vote was divided between Teddy Roosevelt
and William Howard Taft. Pleased about the results and their reunion during Bloomington's gayest season, the Stevensons looked forward to the new
year as they prepared for Buffie's guests on December 30.

Sometime after ice cream and cake had been served, Helen and Lewis
set off on a neighborhood walk, perhaps to visit the Merwins, who lived
next door. During a break in the dancing, games, and Victrola playing—
some of the more sophisticated guests were trying out a dance step new to
the prairies called the Lulu Fado—young Robert Whitmer, the son of a
neighboring banker, offered to demonstrate the manual of arms he had
learned at military school. More an observer than a participant at his sister's
party, Adlai hurried off to find a gun.

Several times Whitmer put the presumably empty .22-caliber rifle in
front of him. Lifting it from shoulder to shoulder in the traditional manual
of arms, amid applause, he proceeded to replace it with a flourish by his
side. Summoned to retrieve the gun, Adlai Stevenson mimicked the drill.
Then, apparently aiming the rifle from the landing, he squeezed the trigger
of a weapon he had every reason to expect was empty. Just at that moment
Buffie's friend Ruth Merwin moved from the library toward the hall.
Instantly, for the shot had been fired at close range, the fifteen-year-old
cousin of Adlai's Merwin cousins fell dead with a bullet in her head. Someone screamed; others wondered for a long moment why Ruth didn't get up.

Buffie remembered thinking that her classmate would never again wear her handsome red hat. Several guests were puzzled that there was not more blood, and a moaning Adlai rushed upstairs and flung himself onto his mother's bed. Returned to the house, his father's shout "What boy did this?" brought the agonized answer "I did."

By every measure an accident, this was the second tragedy with guns to afflict the Stevenson family in two generations. Apparently an old shell unseen when the chamber had been examined was dislodged by a rusty spring through a faulty mechanism. Moved into the firing chamber after the handling of the gun, the shell had ejected when Adlai pressed the trigger. According to the *Pantagraph*, "all due precautions had supposedly been taken, the gun cleared of all cartridges. . . . The accident can be accounted for only on the grounds that a rush spring kept one of the cartridges from being forced out [until] the continual forcing finally forced the cartridge into place."

Adlai Stevenson was not present at Ruth Merwin's funeral, "too prostrated by grief," according to the *Pantagraph,* to attend. Instead, Buffie and her father represented the family. Nor, in deference to his age (and perhaps his family's prominence), was he called to testify at the inquest, where the jury quickly returned a judgment of accidental shooting. Ruth Merwin's mother, along with his parents, provided the consolation that two lives must not be ruined. The week after the shooting twelve-year-old Adlai left town with his mother for Chicago. Later they would travel to Summerville, South Carolina, in a calculated strategy to obliterate the memory of the shooting. Only twice did he return to the Washington Street School to face his classmates. Thereafter a collaborative, protective curtain of silence descended upon the Stevensons, who lived as if the shooting had never occurred.

A letter revealed the event's rapid oblivion, as Adlai described to his father making "pop corn balls and had lots of fun in the attick. We had consibrel snow to day it is freezing so I think we will have some costing. . . . I made a big Wind Mill with my American Model builder, it works fine. I am going to attach my motor and see how fast the fan will go around. I am going to school to morrow and day after to morrow they have a Geography test and I dont have to go becuase I dont have to take it." He signed his note with the special family cue that was more than a cliché: "I hope you are well." Of his brief return to school, his father wrote Aunt Julia Scott that Adlai "was determined to face the boys and did it bravely. . . . He feels like a different boy."

Never mentioned in its consignment to his private demons, the memory of the accidental killing faded. Stevenson even extended the blackout to his wife and was surprised when Ellen Stevenson learned of it years after their marriage. Only during his presidential campaign did he discuss the shooting, and only when asked by a reporter from *Time* who had heard rumors in Bloomington. Then Stevenson told "the whole story in a quiet, matter-of-fact way" for the first time since his account to his parents forty years before. Despite his silence, in the Merwin shooting originated Stevenson's lifelong understanding that no matter how decent his motives, events flowed beyond his control. A man's character might not be his fate. Destiny, sometimes favorable, sometimes not, sometimes understood to be God's providence, sometimes considered to be random, directed his future. "Of course," he explained to a friend when his son was later in an automobile accident, "a thing like this, it leaves scars on the spirit." Buried, the tragedy retained its power to emerge as pain and humiliation.

As the Stevenson tragedy faded, accounts differed. There were disagreements about the gun, about young Adlai's role, and about the effect of the killing on his personality. For while the .22-caliber rifle ("a repeating rifle," according to the *Pantagraph*) was described as old and in the attic, like other boys on the prairie Adlai Stevenson hunted rats, ducks, geese, and rabbits. Once Lewis joked with his son that the rabbits were safer now that Adlai was away, and Stevenson remained a lifelong hunter of ducks, geese, grouse, and quail. The evidence suggests that the Stevensons owned several .22's as well as a shotgun and the revolver Lewis hid under his pillow in order to protect his household from robbers and tramps. One witness placed the faulty .22 in a downstairs closet, which removed any need for Adlai to stand on the landing. But it was unlikely that guns kept downstairs were old with rusty mechanisms. And if the weapon was in the attic, as Stevenson maintained, was it the weapon of double jeopardy—the faulty gun that had somehow misfired years before when Lewis and his cousin had been shooting rabbits on the prairie?

In Buffie's and Adlai's accounts—contradicted by one observer—the .22 "went off," somehow spontaneously discharging without Adlai's aiming or pulling the trigger, an unlikely occurrence, but an interpretation guaranteed to protect, as the Stevensons intended, a vulnerable boy from a lifetime of guilt over an irreversible tragedy. When the story became public knowledge, it rankled the family. After Stevenson's authorized biographer John Bartlow Martin wrote in the 1970s that Adlai had killed a girl, Buffie Ives angrily rejected this interpretation. "[My brother] had an accident and the girl who was struck by the bullet was no child. . . . You speak of a tragedy in a far too sensational manner."

Still, the shooting was important to an understanding of Adlai Stevenson. Some friends and biographers anchored the distinctive features of his personality—his reluctance to commit himself to the presidency, his diffidence and sense of unworthiness, which appeared to some as humility and to others as a pose, his oft-expressed uneasiness with things he had said and done, his avowed desire to be good, his determination to measure behavior, his own and that of others, on a self-constructed scale of morality, and even his dependence on written texts in order to avoid mistakes—in his need for expiation. He had, after all, taken another's life. Yet it is unlikely that a single unintended action could leave such an imprint.

At least superficially, the family therapy to make young Adlai forgive himself was successful. For Stevenson guilt emerged not as an emotional pastime but, as he once informed his mother, as a form of selfishness. However, the greatest significance of Ruth Merwin's death was to place Adlai Stevenson more completely in the dominion of a mother who hovered more closely than ever over "Laddie Boy." Just as he reached adolescence and its possibilities for independence, he had to make amends to his mother for an egregious violation of her directives to be good. He became self-deprecatory and less able to assert himself even as, in the wake of the shooting, Helen Stevenson became more anxious about her son. Her nerves rattled by the accident, in 1913 she suffered another depression, and Adlai spent several months in Las Encinas, California, where his mother was treated for a nervous breakdown.

In the fall of 1913, after his return to Bloomington, Stevenson attended Metcalf and then University High. His prominence as a Stevenson, his continuing absences from school, and the gossip about the shooting distinguished him, even as he appeared to be a typical teenager. He had no sooner started in Metcalf than he was again absent for a semester, attending the Springfield High School while his father was the Illinois secretary of state. Returning to University High, he made average grades and joined the debating club, where, once matched against a scion of the Funk family, he argued the negative on the question "Resolved, that the Senate of the United States should be elected by direct vote." This heated issue of the day, which later led to the Seventeenth Amendment, was being debated in Congress as one of Wilson's reforms, and young Adlai was practicing the debater's discipline of arguing against his personal preference.

During these prewar years, like other sons and daughters of Bloomington's upper class, Adlai Stevenson learned dancing at Miss Coleman's, where along with the waltz he tried out the new-fashioned one-step. In the manner of small-city boys, he went to roasts, joined a school fraternity, and enjoyed the five-cent silent movies. These included the weekly serial *Zorro*, the *Perils of Pauline*, and *Robin Hood*, along with W. D. Griffith's virulently antiblack *Birth of a Nation*, all shown at Bloomington's new Majestic Theatre, with its impressive organ and the largest screen in the state outside of Chicago. Years later he remembered watching the "girl in the pink tights" in the vaudeville show at the Majestic on Saturday nights and attending his mother's Unitarian church on Sunday mornings.

Like other boys and girls his age, Adlai tried to contest his parents' authority. In letters to Buffie he began calling his father "the old man" and irreverently joked about his need for a raise in his allowance. Heatedly, he denied to his mother that he was "overdoing," though when he finished classes and other boys ran to catch the five-cent streetcars for the thirty-minute ride to Bloomington, as often as not an embarrassed Adlai found the Stevenson Locomobile and his mother's driver waiting to take him home. Years later a classmate remembered him hiding from his mother under a bearskin rug. In the summer of 1915, when Helen Stevenson followed her son to summer camp in Maine, taking up her maternal station in a nearby town, he offered, as an excuse to keep her away, the mosquitoes and the bad weather. Once—though this was a rare act of disobedience—when his mother refused to consent to a hiking trip, he went anyway. Surrounded by the cold war marriage of sick parents, Adlai Stevenson sought harmony, not dissonance; compliance rather than rebellion; avoidance rather than confrontation.

Only politely and diplomatically did he dispute academic matters with his parents. "Please, Please! please! don't make me change [the English class]. . . . Am having a fine time except the thought of having to change hope I will not have to," young Adlai implored his mother in 1913. Forced to do so, he never sulked. To do otherwise might bring on another parental breakdown. Soon Adlai cheered his mother, who was still in the Clifton Springs Sanitarium, with a note that he had changed his studies—"so do not worry."

His father adjudicated athletic matters. In 1913 an anguished Adlai wrote his mother, who had already consulted several doctors about football injuries, "Please telegraph father to let me play football as you said you would. . . . You promised me . . . you would let me play this fall. All doctors haven't played it, and more than that they did not play it like we play at Normal. . . . Just because they have read of accidents in for instance a Harvard or Yale game this is a third Normal team." When Helen suggested less strenuous sports, her son, by this time a practiced negotiator, noted that "all the games you mencioned [*sic*] in your letter are out of season." As a compromise he ended up as a timekeeper.

3

IN THE FALL OF 1916 Adlai Stevenson left Bloomington for boarding school, a choice so painful for his mother that it was delayed until the last minute, leaving him without a roommate. But the necessity was plain; that spring Adlai had failed three college entrance exams. Immediately his parents made inquiries to several eastern boarding schools with better college preparatory programs than University High and with closer ties to the prestigious Ivy League colleges they expected their son to attend. With Buffie at Miss Wright's Boarding School in Philadelphia, the Stevensons had no intention of letting Adlai languish in a small town where their nightmare might come true: their exceptional child might marry a daughter of the prairies. "You are too fine to fall in the ways of the mediocre, that is not what you are," Helen advised Buffie, while Lewis told his daughter not to marry a Funk, of the wealthy seed-manufacturing family—or any other native son. Throughout the summer the search for a boarding school continued, until the choices narrowed to the Hill School in Pottstown, Pennsylvania, and Choate in the picture-book New England town of Wallingford, Connecticut. Finally they decided on Choate after Adlai, who spent the summer with a tutor, passed the entrance exams for admission to the sophomore class.

The Stevensons expected Adlai to enter Princeton after a year at boarding school, but Choate's headmaster, George St. John, cautioned that one year would not be sufficient: "With hard summer work in a year the boy could be prepared for Williams and some of the smaller colleges. I'm not sure I should advise trying to get the boy ahead in this way. For Harvard, Yale, or Princeton Adlai needs a two year prep."

Helen, remembering her own experience in an eastern boarding school and comforted by the presence of Adlai's cousin—her sister Jessie Merwin's son Davis—as a student at Choate, surrendered her son to outsiders. But her capitulation would never be complete, and she followed him east, entering the Clifton Springs Sanitarium in the fall. "It is clear," she warned her daughter, "that we can't be separated like this. . . . You can have a better time and Adlai is safer." For the next two years, while Adlai was at boarding school, his mother stayed nearby.

Several times she demanded his presence. "Let Adlai spend Saturday and Sunday with his mother. She is ill and needs him," telegraphed Lewis to St. John, who remained generally impervious to the cascade of parental advisements from the Stevensons. "It troubles [Adlai] to think of being away for so long on our busiest weekend," responded the headmaster, though attending his mother took priority. In 1917, after spending his entire spring vacation with his mother and her nurse, Adlai reassured her in polite, stilted prose, "My ten days with you all this Spring were the happiest of my life and it is certainly a great gratification to think that you enjoyed them."

The Choate to which Adlai Stevenson came as a sophomore in 1916 was neither the best-known, nor the most expensive (even with an annual tuition of $1,000), nor the most difficult of the fashionable boarding schools that emerged in the latter part of the nineteenth century as high schools for America's rich. Rather, Choate was typical of the nearly two dozen eastern institutions that by the turn of the century enrolled the sons of wealthy Americans. Eastern parents had discovered in boarding schools like Choate a means of stamping their sons as members of the upper class, even before the boys entered the Ivy League colleges that would reinforce shared affiliations. Such exclusiveness was attained by means of a snobby exceptionalism derived from Anglo-Saxon Protestant roots, private education, money, residence in suburbs like Chicago's Lake Forest and Baltimore's Roland Park, and the resulting membership in a transnational "high society" recognized in directories like the *Blue Book* and *Society Visiting List*.

Only a few sons of midwestern towns ventured across the prairies to boarding schools; there were only two in Stevenson's class of forty-three. By sending both children east, Lewis and Helen nurtured Buffie's and Adlai's understanding that they should avoid the banality of Bloomington. Exchanging the small-town midwestern world of Sinclair Lewis's fictional *Main Street* and *Babbitt* for the possibilities of sophisticated settings like F. Scott Fitzgerald's *Great Gatsby*, Adlai and Buffie now entered the East Coast establishment. Since childhood their father, the unsuccessful son of a famous father, had appreciated the importance of well-placed contacts, once advising his daughter that school was "a lot more than books. . . . It is coming in contact with people."

Lewis Stevenson also may have worried, like other turn-of-the-century fathers, about the subversive effects on his son of a doting mother and a leisured childhood. Stung by the vulgarity of American culture and by the claims of immigrant outsiders to national dreams of prosperity and liberty, families like the Stevensons located in the eastern boarding school an exclusive training ground for the characteristics necessary to compete in such a society: discipline, manliness, and self-reliance. They also expected an education that would set their Anglo-Saxon offspring apart from the nation's commoners through an appreciation of a culture based on English traditions. Such ideals were to be attained in the boarding school's unremitting dawn-to-moonlight schedule and through its English formulas symbolized by teachers called masters, classes named forms, and the dedication to God, country, and Choate by members of a future ruling class patterned after that of Great Britain.

In Adlai Stevenson's later assessment of his two years at boarding school, competition on the playing fields and in the classrooms of Choate had taught him "the capacity to distinguish the gods from the half-gods and to want what's worth having in life. . . . To think of schools as corridors to college is an unfortunate and improper emphasis. Boarding school is a boy's first impact with a compact social community of which he must at once become a self-reliant integral part. Mother isn't there to inflate his ego; father isn't there to help him with his lessons *even if he could.* There are big boys, little boys, school heroes, masters, discipline, work, play and every-thing is organized and all competing relentlessly for consideration and eval-uation by the astonishingly absorbent post-adolescent mind."

Omitting leadership and politics, he instead gave Choate credit for his transformation into an "accomplished actor, a promising writer and a pass-able athlete." Persuaded of Choate's benefits, when the time came in the late 1940s and early 1950s, Adlai Stevenson sent his three sons to New England boarding schools—Adlai III and John Fell to the Milton Academy in Massachusetts and Borden to Choate. Like their father, they would bene-fit from the boarding schools' privileged contacts with Ivy League colleges, along with the more intangible advantage of inclusion in an aristocracy whose references were available for most any endeavor.

Founded in 1896 by the prominent Connecticut judge William Choate and his wife, Mary, Choate had nearly floundered before the charismatic, Harvard-trained George St. John took over in 1908. An astute businessman as well as an ordained Episcopal minister, St. John proved adept at raising money and buying up property along the quiet streets of Wallingford. As the school expanded, its heart remained Hill House, the impressive Geor-gian-style, white-columned building that in Adlai's day (as well as in his son Borden's thirty-one years later) was a multipurpose space for eating, sleeping, studying, reciting, and playing. In its sovereign completeness Hill House displayed the seamlessness of the Choate experience—from its class-room recitations to its round tables where students ate with masters and their families to the extracurricular activities considered character building and value imparting.

By 1910 Choate's enrollments had increased to over two hundred boys, arranged in six "forms"; by 1916 besides its successful preparation of its students for Ivy League colleges (particularly nearby Yale, to which over three-fourths of every graduating class went), the school had found its mis-sion in instilling a sense of service for which school activities were a school-boy's surrogate. Such values were transmitted through the exhortation and example of Headmaster St. John and visiting clergymen who interpreted religion as right acting. Attendance in daily chapel and on Sundays at a Wallingford church of the parent's choice was required, and it was in these years that Adlai Stevenson absorbed the Protestant idiom he retained throughout his life. Especially from St. John but from all the masters, the boys heard the message of Christian stewardship. "We invite you to partici-pate with us in our common battle for a virile body, a vigorous mind and a genuine spirit . . . to maintain untainted the name and fame of Choate, to practice the art of living and the science of conduct, to lay the foundation of character as may be of real and great service to the world," St. John encouraged the new boys in 1916.

That same year, when the cheering and attendance at a football game slackened and St. John heard boys "just talking" rather than cheering the team, he provided the student body with his own exuberant example of service to school, to country, and to God. "I felt like going into the game myself," complained St. John to the blasé students he sometimes referred to as "muckers." Despising apathy, the headmaster intended that his charges train, through school activities, for their future as the nation's leaders. "If one has a vision of character which he wishes to attain, ambition and construction of purpose will bring him to it."

School had already started when Adlai arrived in September 1916, but having so often been the new boy in schools from Florida to California, he was accustomed to fitting in. Settled into his single room in Hill House, he embarked on the college preparatory course of English, French, history, plane geometry, and algebra (which he dropped in January, with his last mark a 44) and the essential Latin, in which he carried a yearly average of 56. But Adlai Stevenson's agreeable personality assured that he was never measured solely by his academic performance. Before long St. John had written his parents that he "is a delightful fellow to live and work with. We like him."

Such reports did not reassure either Lewis or Helen, and so began an extended correspondence between Headmaster St. John and the dissatisfied Stevensons. When their son joined the drama club and appeared in the student production of Richard Sheridan's *The Critic,* receiving good reviews for his convincing presentation of "the affected contempt and bored attitude of the character Sneer," both parents informed St. John that their son's energy would be better spent elsewhere. Lewis disapproved because of the disruption of his studies; Helen worried that the excitement of the performances would strain what she assumed was her son's limited stamina. Accustomed to parental oversight of offspring despite Choate's advertised "family atmosphere in an exceptionally healthful climate," St. John diplomatically reiterated, after the play, that "school life agrees with Adlai." But in June when Helen heard that Adlai was sick, she telegraphed St. John that her son needed a rest, should leave school immediately, and "not remain for examinations unless entirely well."

When Adlai finished the year, his mother was disturbed by his weight, eyesight, posture, listlessness, and nervousness. He was, she feared, "doing too much." When she heard that her son's day began with a rising bell at 7:00 and rushed along with no time for rest until 10:05 at night, Helen was convinced that the school threatened her son's well-being. Suspicious of athletics, which created school heroes, and even of the desks in the study hall where Carlotta St. Gaudens's huge oil painting of the Parthenon presided over boys hunched over their studies, Helen Stevenson demanded that Adlai undertake a special program of gymnastics and study in his room. "The boy should have a sufficient time to take a great deal of exercise.

He needs diversion in his routine and should drop algebra. Mrs. Stevenson thinks the long hours sitting at uncomfortable desks not properly adjusted is the reason for his stoop-shoulders," reported Lewis, who demanded "an outline of the way his time is proportioned in study, recreation, and extra work."

When there was no improvement, Lewis, ever inclined to bluster, informed St. John that "too little attention has been given him." Meanwhile Helen worried that her son was not getting enough fresh air. The next year Lewis repeated himself: "Frankly I am worried about Adlai and unless his appearance is better when he comes home for Christmas I shall feel obliged to take him out." Stung by Lewis's criticism ("It hurts me very greatly"), St. John was "at a loss to know what you mean that too little attention has been given him. Your criticism has no first-hand basis." There was, assured the headmaster, plenty of time for the individualized gymnastics that the Stevensons were demanding, for the careful chewing of food, for special help in Latin and mathematics, and even for a single room to protect young Adlai from the influence of an unsavory roommate. Only the most desperate appeals by Adlai made his mother honor his desire never "to room alone again."

Under such surveillance Adlai Stevenson emerged as the best of citizens. He became a member of the St. Andrew's Society, a religious group whose members contemplated the meaning of such concepts as sincerity, loyalty, and moral behavior. He was chosen the business manager of the *Choate News,* once asking his father to take out an advertisement so that he might succeed in the competition for a place on "the second biggest thing in school after football." When he wrote of his accomplishments on the tennis team, his mother exulted. "The news of your singles victories is indeed momentous—to think of your winning both singles and doubles. It's glorious!" Still, she advised that he be "careful about overdoing." At the end of his junior year, Adlai Stevenson had been elected vice president of his class, president of the St. Andrew's Society, and editor in chief of the *Choate News.* He was a self-described "pretty big dude." "It's nice to be in authority," he informed his mother.

In this dazzling display of school spirit, Adlai Stevenson took a different path from another of Choate's sons—Jack Kennedy, who came to the school in the mid-1930s and who was a charter member of the Muckers' Club of school bad boys. As the unavailable Rose and Joseph Kennedy furnished their son with benign neglect, sibling competition, and second-son status in a family characterized by one biographer as "an emotional wasteland," so Helen Stevenson created the opposite—a dispositional hothouse designed to shape a virtuous and temperate only son. Given their differences, when these two Choate graduates encountered each other in American politics, their distaste for each other was predictable.

Physically separated from his family, Adlai was never free of their presence. Other boys gained independence at boarding school. Adlai remained encircled by Lewis, Helen, and Buffie. When he decided, with the headmaster's approval, to substitute Spanish ("a coming Language," he advertised to his parents) in order "to get into Princeton without taking Physics, Solid geometry and trigonometry," a battle ensued. "Evidently you don't, yet, understand about my substituting Spanish. By taking Spanish I won't avoid taking Physics, Solid and Trig. because I will have to take them in my freshman year at college and won't have to take another modern language. It really is the best way to enter Princeton and Solid and Trig are worthless subjects anyway. Physics is very good but I will get plenty of that in college." Lewis, who had never finished high school, remained adamant, complaining to St. John that he was "unable to see how Spanish can be of much value in the way of mental discipline."

The headmaster joined the battle on his student's side. "Our conviction is that the theory of mental discipline that was the bulwark of old classical training cannot be successfully maintained. How a boy studies is more important than what he studies," responded St. John. A few weeks later Adlai's salutation "Dearest madre" celebrated a rare victory. Given the family's close supervision, it was not surprising that Adlai invited his sister to Choate's winter dance.

In early April 1917, as Adlai Stevenson was preparing for a round of midterm tests and a tennis match with the Taft School, his hero—a now troubled and weary Woodrow Wilson—walked down the aisles of Congress, climbed to the speaker's well, adjusted his monocle, and asked a joint session of Congress to recognize that a state of war existed between Germany and the United States. As the president informed his hushed audience, the purposes of a war he had earlier vowed to keep the United States out of, were to defeat "autocratic governments backed by organized force which is controlled wholly by their will, not the will of the people. . . . We have no quarrel with the German people, but with a Prussian autocracy waging war against mankind."

In the moralistic style that he bequeathed to Adlai Stevenson, Wilson pointed to German transgressions of the freedom of the seas and neutral rights, disruptions of American commerce by U-boats, and violations of human rights in the killing of innocent Americans. The resumption of unrestricted submarine warfare especially outraged Wilson. Congress agreed and four days later by an overwhelming margin voted, in Wilson's phrase, to make the "world safe for democracy."

That spring of 1917 the United States began preparing for war. In Bloomington, Company D of the Illinois National Guard had started drilling even before war was declared. By summer the superpatriots of the local Council of Defense, including Stevenson's cousin Spencer Ewing, ordered the *Bloomington Journal* to stop printing its German editions, while it considered "what to do with those who appear disloyal by their acts or refuse to contribute to war activities." In Franklin Park, where Letitia and Adlai Stevenson had lived for many years, the town fathers ripped out a cannon from the Spanish-American War and used the metal for a new generation of weapons.

War came as well to Choate. Overnight the school discovered in international conflict the moral equivalent of peacetime character building. Promptly the students exchanged their sports outfits for the uniforms of the Choate battalion. There was talk of a moratorium on all athletics, as the newly outfitted trainees with their khaki knickers, spiral puttees, and barracks caps resembling British uniforms drilled on playing fields earlier reserved for football and baseball. What had been teams now became regiments; what had been competition between schoolboys determined to be victorious over Hill or Taft or Pomfret was transmuted into anti-German spirit. In this spring of 1917, the sheltered period of national security ended—what the writer Max Eastman described as "the brief paradise of America. . . . We were children reared in a kindergarten and now the real thing was coming." It was, wrote Adlai Stevenson later, "our last time of daydreams before crisis made us face the dark ordeal of the twentieth century."

Editorials in the *Choate News,* some written by Adlai Stevenson, criticized Germany's "militarism and hate" and offered suggestions headed "How We Can Best Serve." Lectures on the military and political situation in Europe replaced discussions of classical Greece. On a quiet Sunday afternoon in the fall of 1917—one of the few hours of free time in the Choate schedule—students gathered in the great hall to hear William Lawrence, the Episcopal bishop of Massachusetts, link school values to those of war. Classifying the three essentials of patriotism as discipline, spirit, and noble sacrifice, Lawrence defined a national civic religion. "If a Christian is not a patriot, he is not following Christ. As Christ went through a period of self-discipline, so the essential element for us to have is discipline. It is the thrust of discipline that sends the football player through the line for a touchdown, the soldier over the top to conquer the opposing enemy. . . ."

Inspired by speakers with similar messages, Choate's students planted potatoes and surrendered their candy rations for war stamps. But it was the young masters who provided the best example of Choate's ethic of public service as they rushed off to volunteer, mostly in the Navy. A few like the science teacher Maurice Perry were accepted into the most glamorous service of all—the Royal Canadian Air Force. "Dearest Mum," Adlai proudly wrote, "we have 136 Choate alumni in the service and have lost 7." When school ended in June, St. John used a text from Saint Paul for his last remarks to the future Christian soldiers of the class of 1917: "I have fought a good fight; I have finished my course and I have kept the faith."

In the fall, when Adlai Stevenson returned as a junior, the first units had begun arriving in France, and by the end of the year 180,000 American troops were in Europe. Now his mother had an additional cause for alarm: "Also Dr. [St. John] we feel it is a great mistake to allow these young boys to think so much about the war and its horrors. I take it for granted that the discussion of the economy which we as a nation are obliged to have does not in the slightest way effect the diet of these growing boys." But as her son struggled with his junior-year courses of Latin, French, Spanish, algebra, and trigonometry, he added a new course entitled War History.

After his cousin Louis Davis joined the air force and was killed in a crash while training in Texas, Adlai's mind, like many of this boarding school generation, never left the Great War. To his mother he offered the consolation of a future warrior who might also succumb in the nation's service: "Once more I beg you not to grieve over Louis's death. In war one must not grieve but rejoice that a man can give his life for such a noble cause and pray for a speedy termination of the war."

No doubt his mother was more consoled by an editorial in the *Choate News* on the proper response of Choate boys to a war that had stalled in the twelve thousand miles of killing trenches that snaked from the North Sea coast of Belgium southward, bulged at Ypres in France, and then straightened near the Swiss border. "The country needs trained men now, but she will need them far more in a few years. Conscription was passed so that the Army and Navy could take the men it wanted, and it behooves us who are not yet of age to develop our mental powers to the fullest capacity of efficiency, and the nation will call us when we are needed," concluded the boy editors of the student-run paper.

In 1918 Adlai Stevenson reached draft age and registered with the Selective Service Board in Bloomington, where the *Pantagraph* printed the names of all 5,783 local registrants. Liable for a draft that enrolled three million American men from eighteen to thirty years old, Stevenson inquired of his father, now a naval inspector in Washington, how Cousin Davis Merwin had gotten into the air force. But it was a Choate faculty committee on military affairs that solved his dilemma with its recommendation that those students who "desire and are eligible to attend a training camp can take steps to do so by taking a preliminary exam and can go to Princeton." Promptly Adlai Stevenson seized a double opportunity: admission to Princeton and service to his country through a naval training program. After two years at Choate he surrendered his senior offices, studied all summer in Bloomington, and returned to the East in September of 1918 to take the dreaded, now mostly uniform college entrance exams.

4

THERE WAS NEVER any doubt where Adlai Stevenson would go to college, although he later told a friend that only after meeting Woodrow Wilson had he decided on Princeton. Like most choices in his early life, the decision was dictated by his parents, who considered Princeton a family tradition. Adlai's grandfather to the fifth degree, his grandfather Adlai's great-grandfather Adlai Osborne, had graduated in 1768 from what was then the College of New Jersey. In those days the institution's classes had been small, cupolaed Nassau Hall its only building, and its future uncertain. Entrance was guaranteed to any boy who could read Greek and pay four pounds a quarter. Pennsylvania-born Adlai Osborne passed on both counts. When Osborne moved to Kentucky, where his daughter married a Ewing and honored her father by naming her firstborn son Adlai, he joined a handful of colonists with college degrees. Three-quarters of a century later Adlai Stevenson's great-grandfather Lewis Green (Letitia's father) had renewed a family link by attending theological school in Princeton.

One hundred and fifty years after Adlai Osborne had graduated, the College of New Jersey had a new name (since 1896), a national reputation, a campus of twelve hundred acres, and twenty-one buildings, including a new commons completed in 1915. Its tuition and boarding costs had risen to over $1,200 a year, with laundry, heat, light, and chemical laboratory extra. The war had scuttled Princeton's earlier requirement that its freshmen read Greek "no more difficult than a sight translation of Xenophon's *Anabasis*." Instead, Adlai Stevenson took two sets of examinations— a physical required by the Navy and the math, Latin, and English tests for admission to the freshman class. Passing both, to his "surprise and satisfaction," he thanked his mother for her "unceasing care" of his health, noting that several friends had failed their physicals. Proudly he joined the 462-man class of 1922, along with the Navy cadets under the command of Admiral Caspar Goodrich, a family friend. Adlai Stevenson was eighteen and a half years old, five feet nine inches tall, weighed 131 pounds, and was pleased to be a "Princeton man" in the institution from which, eight years before, his hero Woodrow Wilson had resigned as president.

Immediately at home, Stevenson would never be otherwise in the institution that eternally summoned forth his nostalgic affection as "one of Princeton's children." His boarding school affiliation assured a network of friends and acquaintances that extended well beyond Bloomington. His roommate from New York knew the Clarks and the Thayers; several Princetonians had been to Charlevoix; his father's sister Aunt Julia Stevenson Hardin had a son, Parker, in his class. The commander of the naval unit and junior class president, John Harlan, who later became a Supreme

Court justice, had been courting Buffie after her recent debut in Washington. "There are quite a few fellows around here that I have seen or met before," the new freshman reassured his mother. There was even an unrelated Stevenson named William who became, in the short run, the better known of the two classmates.

Besides its rural beauty, its respected academic program, its sports teams that before the days of professional leagues received national attention, Princeton offered Adlai Stevenson his independence—or so he thought. John Harlan, who considered Stevenson a quiet, unassuming "slow developer with an inherent sense of modesty" remembered, "I thought he should be liberated from family obligations and the family entourage and get more into campus life." Recalling Stevenson as shy, one of his female friends described "his struggle against an overdevoted mother" amid the difficulties of "going to college with your family with you." For only grudgingly did Buffie and Helen surrender their claims on an essential member of the triumvirate.

Thoughts of his family were far from Adlai Stevenson's mind in September of 1918, when he arrived at Princeton Junction from New York. But he did not walk uncertainly up Prospect Street like Scott Fitzgerald's epic Princetonian of the 1920s, the fictional Amory Blaine, who tried to display a freshman's proper mix of nonchalant sophistication. Nor did Stevenson live off campus in a boardinghouse; instead, he joined one hundred other boys in the Gothic spires and towers of Little Hall, where he and three roommates shared two bedrooms and a large study. Unlike Amory Blaine, he cherished the hierarchical rituals of university life that required of freshmen black beanie caps and reserved for upperclassmen sidewalks, long white pants, and the local eatery Renwick's and for seniors their own courses.

Over 80 percent of his all-white classmates were Presbyterians or Episcopalians; there were no Jews, at least none were listed in the university's religious census, no blacks, and no women. Over 85 percent of this homogeneous class of 1922 were the products of private education, either of boarding schools or of country day academies. Almost immediately representatives of Princeton's Choate club (all the larger private schools had campus clubs) paid a call. So strong was the presence of prep schools on campus that they nominated freshmen officers, as Stevenson learned when the Choate club put his name forward as a candidate for freshman class secretary-treasurer. But the Hill School section was larger, and he lost.

At the beginning there was little time for anything besides academic work and the naval training unit's program of drilling, learning to tie knots, rowing on the placid waters of man-made Lake Carnegie, attendance in a required course on naval discipline and administration, and the mandatory letters to his mother. As it had at Choate, so the war intruded on the accustomed serenity at Princeton, where the same connection between school spirit and national service prevailed. In the words of the *Daily Princetonian*, after it had praised the bravery of a professor wounded in action whose leg had been amputated, "What we know as the Princeton spirit must be translated from the campus to the battlefield." By 1918 the marbled Greek temples of Whig and Clio Halls, where since colonial days words had served as weapons, housed army recruits and their guns; trenches could be seen on athletic fields; potatoes sprouted in vacant fields, and the rattle of machine-gun fire could be heard from nearby Potter's Woods.

Adlai Stevenson was technically a seaman second class, along with 250 others, some of whom were not regular Princeton students. "The difference between the regular Princeton men and the others is very obvious," he informed his mother with patent relief at his status. "Whenever 'Old Nassau' or any of the Princeton songs are sung the non-regular men are not allowed to sing and have to stand at attention." Since he was also enrolled in courses in Spanish, French, chemistry, and American history, Adlai's time was as controlled as it had been at Choate.

Awakened every morning before six by the ubiquitous Princeton bells tolling the quarter hour Westminister cadence, he marched to classes, a self-described "hot looking 'Jack'" in a store-bought $35 uniform "because the gov. stuff is not very good." Each day he attended chapel; twice a month he was required to attend Sunday services at a church in town. Like most of his classmates, Adlai Stevenson expected the war to continue, informing his mother in a letter full of the qualifying adverbs necessary to quiet her nerves and to rein in his hopes: "I'll probably have to work pretty hard but I won't be the only one. . . . This is certainly a great life but it will do me a lot of good. I'll probably stay here all year and then if I'm lucky I'll get sent to an officers material school, next summer. It's pretty hard to get an Ensign's commission I find."

Instead, the war ended two months after he arrived, and in January 1919 Adlai Stevenson was discharged from the Navy. Princeton reverted to civilian status, though the university retained its mission of trying to place its gentlemen-scholars in what Woodrow Wilson, class of 1879, called "Princeton in the Nation's Service." Yet in the postwar years, when the nation's patriotism evaporated, so did devotion to Princeton. Editorials in the *Princetonian* described a laxness of spirit. Where were the parades to the athletic fields before the brave heroes fought against Yale and Harvard? Why didn't the freshmen abide by the dress code? Some, wrote one outraged monitor of the university's established hierarchies, were even discovered sitting in sections of Palmer Stadium reserved for upperclassmen.

Princeton mirrored a nationwide cynicism. A world war with over 18 million casualties—116,000 of whom were Americans—had shaken the nation's faith in progress and reason. In the age of normalcy (as it was dubbed by Warren Harding), the university's emphasis wavered between a long-established mission to train national leaders—Wilson's "learned class"—and a more recent social culture that aped upper-class society shaped by a famously named white Anglo-Saxon Protestant establishment. Princeton was loved, wrote F. Scott Fitzgerald in *This Side of Paradise,* the novel that Stevenson read in the lilac-scented atmosphere of two May evenings in 1920, for "its lazy beauty, its half-grasped significance, the wild moonlight revel of the rushes, the handsome, prosperous big-game crowds, and under it all the air of struggle."

Though distinct, these two worlds of public duty and private pleasure were not mutually exclusive. During his four years at Princeton—and indeed for the rest of his life—Adlai Stevenson inhabited both. Wilson's Princeton of service and responsibility emphasized demanding tutorials with faculty, attendance at lectures by world-renowned figures such as James Bryce, Marshal Foch, the French hero who received an honorary degree in 1922, and Albert Einstein; hard work not just (as Wilson had differentiated) in classes or in courses but in learning a subject; downgrading of the exclusive eating clubs; public speaking honed in the debates of Whig and Clio Halls; and, especially, good works in extracurricular activities dedicated to the service of the university as a stand-in for the nation.

As at Choate, service to the university was best signified by earning a letter on the football or baseball teams. Was it more prestigious, wondered the *Daily Princetonian,* to win a letter for a major sport or earn a Phi Beta Kappa key? Even first-semester freshmen knew the answer after reading the *Princetonian*'s headlined, first-page coverage of sports events. And in the notoriously unpopular daily chapel Wilson's successor as president, John Grier Hibben, hammered on the university's mission to restless undergraduates who coughed too much: "Princeton provides moral and mental equipment of such a character that a man will speak and act with authority to command attention and respect—a new type of manhood—whose actions are guided by a sense of honor, alert but resourceful with the power of initiative. . . . To do so requires a spirit of adventure and a hopeful temperament." It was a description of the man Stevenson might become.

Fitzgerald's—and Stevenson's—other Princeton featured elegant dances where Paul Whiteman played the foxtrot to over five hundred couples, the special spring "house-party" weekend, and membership in the eating clubs arranged along Prospect Street like prosperous bankers' homes on large lots with handsome grounds and an occasional tennis court. Every spring, amid complaints about divisiveness, a select proportion of the sophomore class—in Stevenson's year about 60 percent—were invited to join the exclusive clubs that had begun innocently in the 1870s when student groups ate together before the university commons was completed. By Stevenson's day club membership marked a man for life, serving as a collegiate counterpart to the America of restricted neighborhoods, debutante balls, country clubs, and acceptance into the *Social Register*.

Enthusiastically Adlai Stevenson invested what he later called the "golden, irretrievable years" of his youth in "old Nassau." Speaking to undergraduates three decades later, he recalled his Princeton spirit of obligation, encouraging students of the 1950s to carry away with them what he had: "some of the wise serenity of the timeless courage, the unhurried objectivity which is the atmosphere of Princeton and which represents the collective imprint of its founders, students, and teachers who have gone before you." Although he remembered serenity, Adlai Stevenson felt anything but that during his four years at the university.

His friends early identified his perpetual motion and nicknamed him Rabbit. Through his ceaseless activity, Adlai Stevenson became a well-known Princetonian, not the class's most likely to succeed, an honor usually bestowed on a football or baseball hero with good grades, nor, in the class poll, the wittiest or even the biggest politician. But his ambitions evidently showed, for he was second in the voting for "thinks he is the biggest politician," a dubious honor he shrugged off as a joke. The man who eventually became the most famous member of the class of 1922 was not recognized as the most of anything by his classmates. Still claimed by his family, he was not the man he would become.

Too small for football, the sport described by Princeton's coach in 1921 as "more than a game, an American institution," Adlai Stevenson was cut from the tennis squad, and thus ended any hope of traveling the athlete's road to prominence. Still, by his sophomore year, he had competed (nearly all important positions at Princeton on and off the athletic field were competitive) and won his greatest prize. After heeling (getting news stories) for the *Daily Princetonian*, he was elected to its board over several others. By his junior year Adlai Stevenson was managing editor of an enterprise that besides its campus prestige held vocational possibilities for a young man who, after he inherited a quarter of the Bloomington *Pantagraph*, might become the managing editor of a newspaper valued at nearly two million dollars in the 1920s. In turn the knowledge that Woodrow Wilson had also been a managing editor of the *Daily Princetonian,* along with the interest of his fellow editors—the future diplomatic historian Foster Rhea Dulles especially—directed his attention to foreign policy during a period in which the *Daily Princetonian* carried more articles on the League of Nations and the Washington Disarmament Conference than did many American newspapers, including the *Pantagraph.* Years later Stevenson proudly commented to a friend, "Oh, what a *Daily Princetonian* was produced under my *mothering* eye!"

But as happened too often, Lewis Stevenson spoiled his son's triumph by notifying the *Chicago Tribune* that young Adlai Stevenson of Bloomington was the "highest on the paper" and that membership on the board was "the most sought after honor in Princeton literary life." "Stevenson who is not yet 21 was chosen by his fellow editors and the faculty," quoted several Illinois papers. It was not the first time that his father had used him to further his own thwarted ambitions, assuming what Adlai ridiculed as "the duties of my publicity manager. . . . As in the past, when I have strenuously objected, you have nevertheless gone ahead, and with the apparent intent of pleasing *a mere child,* put things in papers which were altogether wrong in point of fact most embarrasing [*sic*] to me. And now again; assailed from all sides with clippings from the Chi. Trib. to the effect that I am head of the Princetonian & as a matter of fact I am only second. . . . Please desist & do me a real favor." But neither Lewis nor Helen could ever resist the intrusions that other parents stopped when their children became adults, and Adlai's struggle for a private identity continued into the 1920s.

There was no confusion about Adlai's other offices. He was elected to the prestigious senior council; he was selected as a member of the Polity Club and Whig Hall, where attention was directed in debates and lectures to Wilson's trip to Paris in 1919 and to issues relating to the president's Fourteen Points; he was chosen for the class day committee and served on a special group recommending that the eating clubs "so pregnant with delightful associations and fostering desirable friendships" be retained and a university club for snubbed undergraduates added.

Supporting the League of Nations Treaty without the reservations Republicans would attach to protect national sovereignty, Stevenson participated in the Democrat James Cox's presidential campaign against Warren Harding, marching in a party parade when Cox visited Princeton in October of 1920. *Princetonian* editorials were unsigned, but as the June 14 news editor of the paper, Adlai Stevenson was the likely author of an editorial condemning Harding, in his mother's language, as a "mediocre among mediocrities." On election day he may have joined a group of students who volunteered as poll watchers in nearby Trenton, where voting was considered a boss-controlled charade.

An outsider at Princeton despite his success, Adlai Stevenson represented a minority in a bastion of Republicans opposing the League of Nations. But he was also different in irredeemable ways, coming from a small midwestern town while most of his classmates were from large eastern metropolises. Nor was he the son of a banker, businessman, or merchant, as an overwhelming proportion of his class were. But he made up for his marginality by his cheerful, untiring service.

Stevenson contributed to extracurricular activities despite, not because of, his academic record. His grades were average, occasionally marginal, although ever improving. In his freshman year he ranked in the fifth group of seven, and thereby placed in the class's lowest 15 percent of students in a category labeled barely passing. In his sophomore year he attained the fourth group, classified by the university registrar as "low standing." In his junior and senior years he joined the majority of his classmates in group three. With the exception of geology, which endowed him with a lifelong interest in mining ventures and which was considered the easiest means of fulfilling the science requirement, his courses covered the standard liberal arts program with a concentration in history and politics.

Once he endured a lecture by Professor William Starr Meyers on the failures of the Cleveland-Stevenson administration, to the amusement of his friends, who clapped and cheered. "I didn't like mathematics or the physical sciences," he explained to a biographer. "But I enjoyed geology so much—and not because it was easy. . . . But certainly my tastes were largely humanist and I loved the history and English and literature courses—*all* history and all literature."

Thirty years after he graduated, Stevenson summarized what he had studied at Princeton as "the archive of the Western mind. . . . As the keeper of Western culture, the University has an obligation to transmit from one generation to the next the heritage of freedom—for freedom is the foundation of Western culture." Still, he never forgot his other Princeton, characterizing his college years as "lots of fun and some incidental education as well." By any measure Adlai Stevenson was never an intellectual arguing philosophy and writing poetry like Fitzgerald's fictional Tom D'Invilliers in *This Side of Paradise*. Like most of the class of 1922, he read the *Saturday Evening Post*; probably voted for Tennyson's "If" as his favorite poem, and, when they played at the local movie theater, enjoyed the silent films *The Four Horsemen of the Apocalypse* and D. W. Griffith's *Birth of a Nation*—the latter one of Woodrow Wilson's favorites as well.

Stevenson also participated in Princeton's other side of paradise—the tea dances, proms, and entertainments surrounding football and baseball games. In his freshman year he was entranced by a "thé-dansant" at President Hibben's house, where he was "a receiver" introducing "the fellows to some of the girls" and making himself "generally useful," he reported to his mother. Like most of his classmates, he was self-conscious about his appearance. Gone were the heavy twill suits of his Bloomington boyhood, replaced by fashionable Duke of Norfolk–style belted jackets and small knotted ties. Now he parted his hair in the middle and slicked it down with the much advertised petroleum jelly Olequea. Popular in the 1920s, such a smart-set Rudolph Valentino style separated him from the country rubes whose hair sprouted like corn in June. Fearful of a family inheritance that rendered her father-in-law and husband bald in their twenties, his mother insisted that he have hair treatments. Obediently Adlai found time for Miss Green's weekly scalp massages. No doubt this improved physical appear-

ance brought confidence in the spring of his sophomore year when he competed with nearly five hundred others for a place in an eating club.

Certainly Adlai Stevenson would have been invited to join some club.
He came from a well-known boarding school and had achieved a campus
reputation by the spring of his sophomore year. Still, the eating clubs were
informally ranked; most students aspired for a bid to Ivy, the oldest and
first among equals. For weeks in the winter and spring of 1920, the *Princetonian* railed against any discussion before the official week when "bicker"
committees could legally extend their invitations and sophomores
responded either as individuals or as members of an "ironbound" group
accepting only a bid for all. For the class of 1922, the highest values of
loyalty, honor, friendship, and prestige seemed at stake this last week of
March 1920, "the most important week in our college world," acknowledged the *Princetonian*. Finally the invitations went out. On the second day
Adlai Stevenson and seven classmates accepted Quadrangle's invitation.

The club he joined was a relatively new one, and in the hierarchy of
sixteen clubs stood not in the first tier with Ivy, Cottage, and Cap and
Gown but in a second group with a reputation for attracting literary "fellows" from the staff of the *Princetonian, Nassau Herald,* and *Bric-a-Brac.*
Housed in a vast salmon-colored brick mansion with marble quoins, the
club's 84- by 42-foot living room afforded a view across Lake Carnegie as
well as an opportunity for dancing. Downstairs there was a billiard room
and a piano, and in the dining room members ate as they might at home—
with silver spoon and fork on linen table cloths. The enchantment of membership occasionally included the steward's home-brewed gin and beer,
after the Eighteenth Amendment, prohibiting alcohol, went into effect two
months before Stevenson joined. By his senior year Stevenson had become
Quadrangle's student representative on its board of trustees. In turn, like
Princeton itself, the club afforded a place in an alumni network of prominent writers, brokers, bankers, and lawyers.

Preeminently, Quadrangle became the staging ground for Stevenson's
social life. He played tennis on the club courts, took his dates to lunch, and
played the new male role of stag at tea dances during football weekends.
"The general concensus [*sic*] of opinion," he wrote his mother his junior
year when he had been on the bicker committee choosing new members,
"not only in Quad but on the Street in general seems to be that we undoubtedly have the second best section and needless to say it makes Cap [and
Gown] pretty sore. . . . I think we are in a fair way to resume our old prestige next to Ivy." Both Princeton and Quadrangle solidified a latent Stevenson characteristic learned from both his father and his grandfather of
privileging personal contacts and good times with wealthy notables over
solitude and associations beyond the gentry. In this attitude he differed

from George Kennan, a Princetonian of his generation who so disliked club life that he nearly resigned from Key and Seal until he realized that such a radical decision might imperil a cousin's chances for membership.

Stevenson's life was, and would forever be, punctuated by weekends of social entertainment built around athletic events. A typical fall weekend—that of November 5, 1921—began for Adlai Stevenson, and for many others of the university's gay boulevardiers, on Friday afternoon with the arrival of "many old friends from Harvard and Yale," followed that night by a dinner party at one of the clubs, after which he went to the prom. On Saturday his date arrived, and after lunch at Quadrangle he and 54,000 others watched Princeton defeat Harvard, 10–3. "In the evening we had a dance at Quad and it was a marvellous party. Don Lourie and all the heroes of the game were there and it was a veritable riot of joy." The next day the parties at the clubs continued along with ice skating on the new Hobart Baker ice rink, named after a university hero who had died in the war.

Only the humiliating arrival of his mother and Buffie spoiled Adlai's golden years at Princeton. Like Mary Pinkney MacArthur and Sara Delano Roosevelt, who followed their sons to West Point and Harvard (from her hotel Mrs. MacArthur could observe the light in her son's room), Helen Stevenson moved to Princeton, renting Dean Henry Fine's house on Library Place, a few blocks from the campus and across the street from Woodrow Wilson's former home. During his freshman year she had lived at nearby Peacock Inn. During Adlai's senior year she and Buffie returned, this time bringing to their rented house on Cleveland Place the impressive silver set bestowed on Adlai the First by the U.S. Senate. Available to entertain his friends with the icon of family prominence in view, his mother sent notes, went to her son's dormitory to pick up his laundry, and implored him to come for meals. "Is there no chance of you coming over Saturday?" she often wrote, for she knew he was busy with classes and the newspaper during the rest of the week. Helen Stevenson's presence was, he later confided to Buffie, the cruelest thing any parent could possibly do, though at the time his objections were muted by his mother's health.

When Helen Stevenson was not in Princeton, she continued to manage his life. "Remember the futility of the tobacco habit," his mother wrote when she discovered that he had begun smoking cigarettes. "What is your desire? I remind you that you had two grandfathers who didn't smoke. . . . Would you not have me believe that you had one object in life and that is to lead it as decently and uprightly as is possible and be an example of moral virtue to your fellow man?" When she heard of a worse transgression—that he had been drinking—she censured her son again. This time the charges were false, and "a miserable and thoroughly incensed" Adlai self-righteously complained of "a conscious injustice" by his own mother.

In his senior year Helen Stevenson remained his moral overseer. This time, however, when she decided to live in Princeton, Adlai stalled, refusing to find a house to rent. To his father he explained, "Received your special this morning. I don't believe you would have been so peremptory in your demands about looking for houses if you fully appreciated the exacting demands for time on an active senior in the 'two big game weeks' of his senior year. . . . Personally I can see no reason for [mother's] coming to Princeton—if you want to come at all—until after Christmas—about the first of February."

No matter how Adlai tried, he failed to break out of a maternal custody that stifled confidence and initiative. "Twenty-one years old, 21 years young, 21 years wise, 21 years beloved!" rejoiced Helen in a letter written on what she always celebrated as the "great Natal Day." "Your babyhood, your boyhood, and your young-manhood have been a natural, sweet unfolding and gradual development. . . . There are no dark, muddy spots thus far in your career. . . . You have never wanted something for nothing nor anything that was not rightfully yours. And so whatever in rewards come to you you can rejoice over Right for the sake of Right! . . . So you know how grateful and happy your little family is, on this your blessed birthday."

The next year, when Adlai sat with his classmates listening to President Hibben praise the "united purpose" of the nation and university during a war that freed Princeton "from self-seeking and suspicion and class distinctions," and the day after when in the June heat he marched down the aisle in front of Nassau Hall to claim his bachelor of arts degree, no mother surpassed Helen Stevenson's profoundly possessive love. Nor could any mother's vision of her son's future have conformed so well to that of Princeton's. As Hibben directed in his baccalaureate address, "Today the peril is not so obvious, the duty not so simple and immediate. . . . Nevertheless I call upon you in this last hour of your college course to volunteer your service for the welfare of your country and of the world. . . . The heights are still there. They fling out their challenge. They are the great objective for you to take and to hold; there to plant your banner and constantly move forward to the further point of vantage which always lies just above and beyond."

5

AFTER SIX YEARS of inspiration at Choate and Princeton, Adlai Stevenson had no idea what he wanted to do. The attraction of the university persisted, and for a time he thought about teaching in the nearby boarding school Lawrenceville or working on Princeton's alumni magazine. Ranching in the West, so distant from Bloomington, also appealed to him. He knew Wyoming from several summers spent there with friends, with Buffie, and once with a French tutor. But Stevenson needed money to buy land, and his father, either forgetting his own youth or remembering it too well, threatened that if he did not come home, he would bring him back. Certainly Adlai did not want to return to Bloomington. Nor did he want to enter what he described as "the hardest graduate school of any kind in America."

In the spring of his senior year his parents had insisted that he apply to the Harvard Law School, which, requiring nothing more in admissions materials than his undistinguished record from Princeton, accepted him. Meanwhile Lewis used his own thwarted career as a cautionary example, insisting on a law degree for his son. And Helen, by this time experienced in living nearby no matter where her laddie was, concurred.

In late September of 1922, the reluctant law student obediently began his first-year law courses of civil procedure, contracts, criminal law, property, and torts. From the beginning, Adlai Stevenson disliked both Harvard and the town of Cambridge, which, save for Harvard Yard, lacked trees and even grass. With verdant Princeton his point of comparison, he found the atmosphere uncongenial: Harvard, he reported in a revealing metaphor, "was a city club. Princeton was a country club."

For the first time in his life, Stevenson was going to school with a more heterogeneous student body. Fifteen percent of the 452 students in the Harvard Law School were Jewish. With undergraduate classes at the university one-quarter Jewish, the administration was considering quotas, as was the nation at large. President A. Lawrence Lowell had earlier encouraged a policy that "Hebrews be investigated with the nicest care." Stevenson evinced similar anti-Semitism, employing the common expression of "jewing" down a price and identifying Jews with certain characteristics of "their race." When Lewis Stevenson came to Boston and visited a class, Stevenson reported to his mother that his father "seemed very impressed with the display of erudition, not to mention the thirsty intellects of the semitic element."

Adlai Stevenson was not so thirsty. From the beginning Harvard Law School was too intense for a man of abundant sociability and restlessness whose academic abilities were average. And while Adlai Stevenson never minded hard work, he was ill equipped for sustained labor on the rigorous tasks that demanded both memorization of cases and logical thinking. With a faculty that included Austin Scott, an expert in constitutional law, Zechariah Chafee, a champion of civil rights, and several proponents of the new sociological jurisprudence that held that the law must serve the people's needs, not simply perpetuate ancient precedents, the Harvard Law School used the Socratic method in its classes. It was an approach that generated terror among often humiliated students.

"Everyone works all the time and still about 25–35% get dropped every year," Stevenson warned his mother. "The law school is sort of like being in business, not college," he concluded about training for a profession that he never saw as an intellectual discipline, a story of human conduct, a tool for social justice, or even the required lever for a political career. Always the law was a job—a mostly pleasureless way to earn money. In this attitude he parted ways with his mentor Woodrow Wilson, who once explained that the profession he chose was politics, but the profession he entered was the law.

In his years at Harvard, Adlai Stevenson alternated complaints about the monotony—"tomorrows are much like todays here"—with stories about his fear at presenting a law club brief or undergoing the "retributive vengeance" of semester exams. "The law is indeed a jealous mistress and thus far not a particularly attractive one," he told his mother, joking about the enormous books and notebooks, which some students appreciated as a symbol of their chosen career's prestige, but which Stevenson deplored as too heavy to carry back and forth to class. Always available for solace, Helen Stevenson responded that he must somehow defeat the anxiety that inhibited his best efforts. "I suppose it is natural now to get tremors over the exam, but it would be a lesson not to encourage fear. Face it and destroy it."

Yet Stevenson persisted in following a Princeton undergraduate's schedule, weekending from Friday to Sunday in Poland Springs, Lake Placid, the Massachusetts countryside, Princeton, and New York. In the midst of the late-spring exams on which most of his grade depended, he found time for golf and a visit from some Lake Forest friends. He played squash and learned to ride horseback and dated—especially Harriet Cowles, a Vassar graduate. When Cowles jilted him, ever a good loser, he had time to find a replacement, explaining to his mother that some "air castles" had crumbled. At first bewildered, after a few days "unconsciously I found myself forgetting all about it and [was] quite as merry as usual—a little mortifying to myself in my self-imposed role of the martyred lover!" Despite his social schedule, he found Harvard a hostile place where "nobody seems to know or care to know anyone else." In a word it was not friendly Princeton, or nosy small-town Bloomington, or communal Choate, or even tiny Charlevoix.

In the spring of 1924 Adlai Stevenson took his second-year exams, cramming a semester's work into ten- and twelve-hour days. Impressed with the "appalling amount of law which we are presumed to have absorbed this year," he was nervous, but that was not unusual. "Here's to lady luck, bribed with one last mighty week of Work!" he gaily informed his mother and then promptly failed two courses—on agency and on evidence, with a 51 in each. His other grades were barely passing—a 59 in equity, 62 in property, 61 in sales, and 62 in trusts. Adlai Stevenson had failed out of Harvard Law School.

Years later, when Adlai Stevenson's son wrote for his father's grades so that an authorized biographer could use them, the dean of the law school, Erwin Griswold, exploded the family myth that Stevenson could have returned and by retaking and passing his final exams removed his F's and rejoined his class. "He was not eligible to return," wrote Griswold to Adlai Stevenson III; only by a rare vote of the entire faculty could he have rejoined his class. "Your father long ago displayed the qualities that made his academic record here purely irrelevant," wrote Griswold, who sequestered his grades during the campaign of 1952. "Yes, you did better," acknowledged the dean to young Adlai, who graduated from Harvard Law School in 1957.

Like the shooting of Ruth Merwin, Stevenson's failure at Harvard became an obscure topic, mostly avoided or denied, though sometimes explained by his attention to his family's interests in the *Pantagraph*. By the early 1950s, when Stevenson was the subject of several biographies, only his graduation from Northwestern's law school two years later with respectable grades was mentioned. "Another frequent canard about Stevenson's education is that he flunked out of Harvard Law School," wrote Noel Busch in a biography that Stevenson read before publication, while according to another biographer, "he went to Harvard Law School, departing there after two years of indifferent marks." As reluctant to stain their hero as he was to be forthright, biographers continued to gloss over the fact that he was an academic casualty. Stevenson aided the confusion by explaining that he had been "obliged to return home because of the death of my uncle who managed the family newspaper. It was necessary that I go to work immediately to maintain some family continuity in management." In fact, Uncle Bert Davis died a year after Stevenson's expulsion, and his cousin Davis Merwin provided continuity.

In the summer of 1924 Adlai Stevenson returned to 1316 East Washington Street. It was, he wrote his sixteen-year-old "junior amour," "the mandate of the family that little Adlai remain unseen in Bloomington so he can familiarize his langorous faculties with the affairs of the family newspaper." More than ever enmeshed in family affairs, the twenty-four-year-old found the "prairie garden" dull. Missing football games and "happy collegiate gatherings," he ridiculed Bloomington's aspirations to society weddings and made fun of the drama company in which he briefly played. He complained about the unfashionable females who displayed bare knees between their rolled stockings and short skirts, gave up other eastern habits of "the refined and unrefined," and worried that "the simple and pleasant amenities of life in gallant Bloomington have innoculated [me] with languor and apathy."

He returned at a time of declining prosperity in McLean County and on farms throughout the United States. A bushel of McLean County corn that had brought $1.38 during the war years was worth only 65 cents in 1924. Using their new combines, prosperous farmers made up the difference by planting more acres. As production rose, prices fell, and with European markets closed off after a postwar recovery overseas, expansion only drove prices lower, with the predictable result that the farmers' share of the national income dropped. His mother's farms in Iowa and Illinois were an example, barely returning a profit in the 1920s, while his father blamed lazy workers. Meanwhile throughout Illinois the number of tenant farmers and day laborers rose.

In Bloomington, where cash-short farmers came to shop as they had for almost a century, several substantial businesses had closed, unable to compete with the mail-order houses and national firms whose advertising and lower prices loosened even the closest ties to local retailers. In 1922, the year Stevenson graduated from Princeton, both streetcar and railroad workers struck for higher wages, and anxious city fathers had requested the National Guard. More threatening in the long run than any labor unrest were the new diesel engines, seven times as powerful as steam engines. In time they would destroy the municipality's largest employer—the steam engine repair shops where skilled boiler workers, carpenters, and iron molders earned good wages. In a decade Bloomington lost nearly twenty manufacturing establishments, and a hundred wage earners left the city or joined a growing pool of unemployed. Those who stayed were plagued by the shutdowns, layoffs, and slowdowns that lowered the annual wages of Bloomington's west side workers. Meanwhile the east side Stevensons, with a steady annual income of over $50,000 from the *Pantagraph,* were never affected by the deterioration of the local economy. Nor did their son have to look for a job.

Adlai Stevenson started in the business office of the *Pantagraph* in the summer of 1924. After briefly serving as a telegraph operator, he became a reporter and then a feature writer on a paper whose managing editor, Helen Stevenson's brother, Bert, lived in California and whose local replacement was twenty-four-year-old Davis Merwin, Adlai's first cousin. Stevenson covered everything—from tornadoes in southern Illinois to the Bloomington convention of the Illinois Ku Klux Klan at which 583 robed members marched down Main Street.

He followed the epic trial of John Scopes, the Tennessee schoolteacher who refused to be gagged by a state statute outlawing the teaching of evolution. Scopes had continued to teach Darwinian theory in his biology class, and was indicted. In a test case that symbolized the differences between rural fundamentalists and urban progressives, William Jennings Bryan represented the creationists. Relying on the Bible, Grandfather Stevenson's former running mate rejected the theory of organic evolution and opposed its teaching in public schools, where children would be forced to learn something that contradicted their parents' understanding that God created the world.

Stevenson held otherwise in the pages of the *Pantagraph*, where he condemned "this mortifying recurrence of Mediaevalism." The young reporter wondered why "scholars in every field should not decide what should be taught in every field." Even as a journalist working for a paper whose motto was to make it short, Adlai Stevenson exhibited the expansive vocabulary and complex sentences that later marked his speeches. "If the children of Tennessee find the Bible any less puissant as a guide to a better and more fulsome life because they have evolved from the amoeba rather than ready-made men created by God," he informed the *Pantagraph*'s eighteen thousand readers, "it is a sad commentary on our spiritual and intellectual independence." At the time his own independence was on his mind.

In the summer of 1925 Uncle Bert died, and a great battle, not unusual in family businesses, came to divide the Merwins and Stevensons. They fought over the control of an asset that William O. Davis had expected to be shared by his three children, but managed by the male descendants of his son, Bert. Because both of Bert's sons had predeceased their father, a poorly drawn will, neglecting improbabilities, did not make clear whether the *Pantagraph* stock, now worth nearly two million dollars and left as a life estate to Davis's surviving daughters, Helen Stevenson and Jessie Merwin, before it was inherited by Davis's five grandchildren, should be halved between the two families or awarded individually. If the latter was the intention, the three Merwins rather than the two Stevensons would inherit a majority of the stock and control of the *Pantagraph*. Fired by the presence in both families of potential future editors, a controversy that involved the legal principle of inheritance per stirpes or per family drove the Merwins and Stevensons apart. Adlai, not his hot-tempered father, represented his mother's interests, as she, so poorly prepared for any controversy, raged against her sister and suffered another breakdown.

The families turned to the courts—amicably at first. The circuit court ruled for the Merwins; the Stevensons appealed and won. As lawyers from Chicago arrived, friends and neighbors took sides. Buffie remembered loud quarrels between the two sisters and their husbands on the back and side porches that now sheltered residents from the public view of strollers on East Washington Street. Characteristically Adlai tried to settle the lawsuit by proposing that Davis Merwin continue to run the paper and that the stock be divided equally. The Merwins refused; the case went to the Illinois supreme court. By the time that court in effect ruled for the Stevensons, the decision was moot. The Merwins had bought the only outstanding stock— ten shares that Davis had years before bestowed on a loyal employee.

Once again a capricious fate had intervened in Stevenson's life; once again he translated what the Merwins believed a business deal into a moral issue. Years later Stevenson reminded Davis Merwin of the Merwin family's "anxiety to get control of the paper by any means . . . when I thought we were in good faith trying to resolve our family dispute by orderly recourse to the courts." But Stevenson refused to sign an angry indictment written by his father: "[My mother's] wishes were never consulted. . . . Nothing is worth the loss of dignity, love, and friendship, and self-respect. I am going to live in such a way that my peace of mind shall not be disturbed by your ghastly act of buying stock. It was unfair, unfriendly, unethical, and secretive while we took what the fates brought forth."

No longer did Stevenson have a future in the family business. As a large stockholder he remained a director, often objecting to the Merwins' endorsements of Republican candidates and questioning the salaries his cousins bestowed on themselves. What had been a potential career now became a dependable source of income. For the rest of Adlai Stevenson's life, with the exception of four years in the late 1950s, the *Pantagraph* provided the largest proportion of his income. Yet the Merwins' control enhanced the possibilities for liberation. Now released from any responsibility for the newspaper, Stevenson moved to a bachelor's apartment in Chicago, resisted his mother's pleas that she come to Chicago and spend several nights a week, and returned to law school at Northwestern University.

Chapter Eight

TOURS OF DUTY

1

WHEN TWENTY-SIX-YEAR-OLD Adlai Stevenson boarded the Italian steamer *Conte Biancomo* for Naples in the early summer of 1926, it was his fourth trip to Europe. That spring he had graduated from Northwestern University's law school. After passing the Illinois bar, he planned a final adventure before joining the solemn professionals who earned their livelihood in the banks and law firms along Chicago's La Salle Street. Several times in the past, Stevenson had shepherded his mother and sister across the Atlantic before joining American college friends bitten by wanderlust. Once he had run into his father at Paris's spectacular Folies-Bergère, where the attractions, even of Montmartre's famous prostitutes, proved no match for his virtue. Adlai informed his mother of his "astonishment to see Father walk in all of a sudden. Of course he said he was just looking for me, but it certainly looked as if he had started out on a little party of his own. . . ."

Even after an Italian customs official insulted Buffie, Adlai shook loose from his mother and sister. Twenty-nine-year-old Buffie understood. Like her brother, she was moving beyond the family triumvirate to make her own life. After an acquaintance of three days, she became engaged to Ernest Ives, an American consul stationed in Naples. Despite her father's objections, she and the handsome, blond, Virginia-born Ives were married the next year in Naples.

While his sister found love, Adlai searched for something else. He had outgrown the conventional tourism "of seeing museums" and "wasting time in galleries and shrines," which he now discredited as having "nothing to do with the more diverting exercise of the study of peoples." Joining several friends, Stevenson traveled through eastern Europe toward the Soviet Union. But the United States did not recognize the Bolshevik regime that had come to power in 1917.

In Rome, Vienna, Budapest, Bucharest, and Sofia, Soviet officials refused a visa to the young American who flashed press credentials from the

Bloomington *Pantagraph* and the *Chicago Herald*. Discouraged, two compatriots returned home to begin their careers—the routines and staying in one place that dismayed Stevenson as "selling out to a system which makes a man intellectually and morally subservient to his natural interest in direct proportion to his degree of 'success.' " Instead, Stevenson pressed on until, after a week's wait in Constantinople, a Soviet official gruffly wondered why the young American hadn't come sooner to pick up his papers. It was Stevenson's first introduction to the mysteries of the Soviet bureaucracy.

Alone—as he had rarely been before—Adlai Stevenson set off for Moscow, intending to interview Trotsky's replacement, the elusive Soviet foreign minister Georgii Vasilievich Chicherin. No one, not even the seasoned Moscow correspondents Louis Fischer of the *Nation* and the Baltimore *Sun* and Walter Duranty of the *New York Times,* had penetrated the ministry's Siberian silence on the debt issue. During World War I the United States had extended seven billion dollars of credits and loans to its allies. Now the Americans were demanding repayment.

What had been patriotic duty to keep the world safe for democracy became, in peacetime, an interest-bearing financial arrangement. The issues surrounding repayment divided public opinion into two camps—those like President Coolidge who insisted that governments that "hired" the money during wartime must repay with interest, as much praised Finland had promptly done, and those like General Charles Dawes, soon to become ambassador to the Court of St. James, who acknowledged that the economic chaos of postwar Europe necessitated the rescheduling of payments. The hard-pressed Soviets had repudiated American wartime loans of $187 million, and denied any liability for another $89 million of private investment in railroad companies and mining ventures, on the basis that such loans had been made before their regime came to power and therefore were contracted without the consent of the Russian people.

While Wilson, Harding, and now Coolidge condemned the Soviets' refusal to abide by Western rules of international behavior, the Soviets remembered that five thousand American troops had been sent to Siberia in August of 1918 by President Wilson. The new government considered this presence on their soil as the meddling of a capitalist antagonist intent on overthrowing their regime by aiding Admiral Kolchak's White Russian Army. They refused to discuss the debt issue unless the Americans signaled some interest in extending credits and loans. Such intransigence appealed to an idealistic traveler who saw an opportunity for a journalistic scoop—and possibly the formulation of some grounds for Soviet-American reconciliation. But as it turned out, Stevenson was merely introduced to his future, which featured the frustrating differences between Soviets and Americans.

It took Stevenson nearly three weeks to get to Moscow. Papers in hand, he commandeered a rowboat in the harbor of Constantinople and then boarded an Italian freighter that plied its way along the Black Sea ports. At Batum, the first landing in the Union of Soviet Socialist Republics, Stevenson's French-Russian dictionary and his copy of Bernard Pares's *History of Russia* were confiscated. Now without papers "somewhere in Russia," he took a train to Tiflis in the Ukraine. Later he advised his flame Claire Birge in his pontifical style that she would remember that Batum was Jason's destination on his quest for the Golden Fleece and that here "East really does meet west. . . . Tiflis was a really new experience—Tartars, Kurds, Armenians, Georgians, Persians, & Russians of all kinds."

From Tiflis he traveled by train over a thousand miles to Moscow—feeling an unfamiliar sense of solitude, even as he shared crowded train cars with Russian families and once with an American socialist. "Travelling alone in this very 'furin' land is not so pleasant," he informed Birge. As it did throughout his life, the landscape held his attention: "At last yesterday we came out on the great green, smiling valley of the Don dotted with herds of cattle & in the distances the sun shining on the great domes of Orthodox churches marking the location of clusters of white-washed thatched hut-communities of the long-suffering Russian peasants. . . ."

In Moscow, the new Russia's political center, he stayed at a boarding-house run by Quakers, where he encountered journalists and private citizens intrigued with the great revolution that some concluded worked. At Princeton, Stevenson had joined an undergraduate discussion group studying socialist texts not because (as they advertised in the *Princetonian*) they were believers but because all Americans should understand the theory of Marxism and the history of the Soviet revolution. Even during a time of relative calm with the civil war ended, the drought eased, and Lenin's New Economic Plan installed, Stevenson found none of the socialist improvements that other Americans discovered.

As Sophia Tolstoy, the novelist's regal niece, guided him through the city, Stevenson observed homeless "wolf" children who somehow had survived a decade of war, colonies of adolescent boys who slept in the asphalt kettles used to repave the city's cobblestone streets, and roughly clothed, hungry-eyed peasants in their characteristic blue-and-brown moujik blouses. Years later Stevenson recalled "turbulent confusion," though there was, in his view, "little doubt that Lenin and Trotsky were remarkable organizers and inspired leaders. . . . Without adroit propaganda and a simple slogan that the simplest peasant could understand—'bread, peace and liberty'—they might never have surmounted their fantastic difficulties." Stevenson drew a comforting lesson from his experience in Russia: "[We] must view the misery and squalor with compassionate understanding but not with pain, for remember that joy is not the sole prerogative of the rich and can mask in rags as well as silks."

Day after day Stevenson took up his station outside Chicherin's office. But few saw the goateed aristocrat of the old regime who was superintending the Soviet Union's perilous diplomatic journey in the 1920s. Only on rare occasions did he emerge for the fifteen-minute walk to Red Square and the Kremlin from his office in the Foreign Ministry on Stretenka Street, where he worked and slept. Convinced that the minister was eavesdropping just beyond the guard and if he could hear his visitor's purpose would grant an interview, Stevenson presented his case insistently in French and English. Day after day Stevenson came; day after day he was refused an interview, until Russian stubbornness prevailed and the young American went home.

2

RETURNED TO THE United States, Stevenson maintained his newly established independence by leaving Bloomington and commencing his belated career as a lawyer. "I must confess," he wrote Claire Birge, "heretical and un-American as it may seem, that I view the prospect without the least eagerness. It's not laziness altogether either, but I know perfectly well that if I am to make a 'success,' sooner or later I must 'sell out'—I mean chuck most of my ideas and my acute sympathy for the less fortunates. A stony and obedient loyalty to class and vested interests seems to be the necessary adjunct of a life of hard and imagination-less work."

Like thousands of men of his generation, he fled his hometown for Chicago, an exciting metropolis of nearly four million residents and the second-largest city in the United States. In the process Adlai Ewing Stevenson completed another stage in the migration of his family—a journey that had led from Scotland to Ireland and across the Atlantic to the seaboard states of Pennsylvania and North Carolina, and then inland to Kentucky and finally Illinois. By the midnineteenth century, male Stevensons were no longer farmers working with their hands, but supported themselves and their small families as town-dwelling lawyers, politicians, merchants, and, like Adlai's father, managers. Others undertook similar journeys until by the 1920s over half of all Americans lived in cities.

Promptly Stevenson found employment at $125 a month as a clerk in one of Chicago's most prestigious law firms—Cutting, Moore, and Sidley. Earlier he had declined his father's blustering intervention that he would "fix things up," and after he was hired, Stevenson somehow dissuaded his mother from entertaining the firm's senior partners. Still, connections helped. "We were hiring Princeton that year," one partner later recalled, and Adlai knew a partner's brother-in-law. Grandfather Stevenson had helped too. In the nineteenth century when Cutting, Moore, and Sidley needed a lawyer in central Illinois—especially for its largest client, Western Union—the Chicago firm used Stevenson and Ewing in Bloomington.

As an associate, Stevenson researched precedents for the firm's probate and corporate clients; he made the rounds of real estate closings and once repossessed a defaulter's movie projector, but only after the feature film starring Jean Harlow had ended. It was the necessary work of apprenticeship, and Adlai Stevenson was remembered as conscientious and cheerful. But to Claire Birge, he acknowledged the misery "of wandering with growing assurance in [the law's] bewildering maze. . . . I can't say that I love it with a fierce passion—indeed as a profession it's rather disappointing since it's not a profession at all, but rather a business service station and repair shop." Wanting to be exceptional because he was a Stevenson and his mother's son, he came to view himself, disconsolately, as "one of the standardized earnest young men whom I used to dispise [sic] so wholesomely. In short I've given up trying to solve the mystery of life. . . ."

Instead, Stevenson concentrated on his social life as a bachelor in Chicago's smart set. A generation earlier or later, the walls of the city's four hundred were less permeable. But in the 1920s changes in ballroom dancing and the new debutante structure of "cutting in" at the huge balls organized to present the precious few to an established society required four males to every female. According to Stephen Hord, one of Stevenson's bachelor friends and later his investment counselor, the mothers of debutantes simply telephoned the number of young men they needed to obtain the proper proportion of males to females at their parties. From approved bachelor apartments, and in the summer from the rented Lake Forest cottage where Stevenson and his friends took shelter from the city's heat and enjoyed tennis and golf at the Onswentia club after work, legions of the acceptable emerged in tuxedos, tails, and belted Norfolk jackets to take their place at tea dances and formal dances, luncheons, and theater parties. "If you had a dinner coat and kept your ears and neck clean, you were invited," said one outsider, though it was not so easy without contacts. Debutantes whose status was determined by the number of their dance floor cuts called these newcomers "round-faced boys" and worried about getting stuck, while their mothers feared the worst about the unknowns' backgrounds.

In this world of "extra men," Stevenson played the role of a naive immigrant from the prairies, labeling himself "an awful bumpkin." In fact, as he migrated into another class, he was well prepared, carrying his manners, connections, and agreeable personality into Chicago's high society. Although his mother's assistance was not needed, in 1925 Helen Stevenson did her part by joining Chicago's exclusive Fortnightly Club, even as she continued to hope that her son might somehow achieve greatness in Bloomington. Soon Adlai Stevenson was an eligible bachelor, though he was not included in Chicago's *Social Register* until after his marriage.

From the East Coast, Claire Birge teased Adlai about his reputation for partying, to which the gay blade replied, "As to my alleged social desireabil-ity, I call it deliberate mendacity on the part of your informer. Tho' to be sure I have had an excellent good time here." Ever the outsider—a Demo-crat in a Republican firm that refused to hire Catholics and Jews, a lawyer who found "little moral foundation in the law," a native of Bloomington who dined on gold plates at the Chicago table of the fabulously wealthy Potter Palmers—the son of sybaritic Lewis and puritannical Helen feared what he enjoyed in the roaring twenties—the insidiousness of "losing one's values and becoming simply a reliable stuffed shirt in a place where anyone who's white, washed and reasonably mild mannered can trot around like a circus pony night after night and mislead himself into thinking that it's all worthwhile."

Expressing his "dread ennui" to Claire, he nonetheless courted the debs. Earlier, when Claire had "come out" at a fancy ball at New York's Ritz Hotel, her suitor provided some fatherly instructions to a young debutante seven years his junior. It was important to participate, but never to make too much of these festivities, advised Stevenson. "College parties," he wrote, "should be a fact of every girl's social education." Claire must be careful not to rely on the "line" developed by flirtatious debutantes or believe the smooth compliments of the stags who cut in to dance with her. Despite their perils, the seasonal Ivy League rituals of Princeton house par-ties, of June boat races in New London, and of football weekends at Har-vard, Yale, and Princeton remained essential ceremonies in any young socialite's education. At these lessons the fresh-faced Birge excelled, retaining the seriousness of purpose and interest in the "important things" her suitor treasured. But Adlai rebuked her interest in economics—"an intellectual accomplishment . . . not the most becoming for young women." Instead, "Europe is an excellent climax to your work."

Smitten, Adlai Stevenson proposed to Claire Birge after her debutante party in December 1925. But the eighteen-year-old Birge had just graduated from the exclusive Miss Porter's School in Farmington, Connecticut, and pleaded youth and inexperience as she prepared for a six-month trip to Europe. Disliking emotional disruptions, Adlai continued his affectionate paternalism: "I feel a new warmth and reality about [your] letter, more ease and facility. . . . Quite a contrast to those treasured, stiff, laborious little compositions of your school days. . . ." Birge remained, according to her suitor, "honest, clean, sincere, seeking the best in life and giving the best."

Soon another young socialite replaced Claire Birge. In the winter of 1926 Adlai Stevenson was one of five hundred Chicagoans attending the post-Christmas dance of Mrs. Waller Borden in honor of her eldest daugh-ter, Ellen, "one of the most important debs of the season," according to the columnists who gossiped that this party would be the season's supreme event. Too large for even the family's twenty-two-room mansion at 1020 Lake Shore Drive, the party was held at the Drake Hotel, where, according to the *Chicago Tribune,* "the ballroom was an intricate and effective pale green and gold of palm leaves and yellow feathers and the young debutante wore a gown of silver cloth and lace. At midnight an elegant supper was served." That season as they swirled about on the stone floor of the Drake and at the fashionable Casino Club, and whispered to each other in the hidden corners of the grand ballroom floor of the Morrison Hotel, Adlai Stevenson and Ellen Borden fell in love. To the year's hit song "Will You Love Me in December as You Love Me in May?" they answered yes.

Like Birge and all of Stevenson's other girlfriends, Ellen Borden was rich. Her father, John Borden, was one of the wealthiest men in Chicago. After inheriting the family's real estate and mining fortune, Borden invested in several profitable enterprises, including the Yellow Cab Company. Like many Americans during the 1920s, he played the stock market, often using brokers' loans to increase his holdings. Divorced in 1925 from her hard-drinking, absentee husband (Borden was a famed explorer, yachtsman, and polo player), Ellen's mother, Ellen Waller, was almost as rich from the extensive North Side Chicago holdings of her ancestors. Besides money she provided her daughter with the image of an independent woman, who even before she divorced had an affair with her future second husband, the composer John Alden Carpenter.

Like Birge, Ellen Borden had attended an exclusive boarding school—in her case St. Timothy's School in Catonsville, Maryland, where she received good grades in English, but failed math and earned the most demerits in her class. After graduation, like Birge, she spent a year in Europe, studying art and poetry at Miss Sheldon and Miss Nixon's ladies' seminary in Florence, where well-chaperoned daughters of the rich were exposed to European culture. Also like Birge, Ellen Borden was half a generation younger than Stevenson and hence available for worldly insights from an older man. She was remembered as a protected, pampered little rich girl rarely out of her governess's sight, and her romance at eighteen with twenty-six-year-old Adlai Stevenson was her first, and as had been the case with Birge, Adlai's popularity with her mother advanced his cause.

By the early twentieth century courting practices had changed. In contrast to his father and grandfather, Stevenson was not limited to formal inside-the-house calling, in the grand baroque setting of the Borden mansion. Nor, while silently observed, was he required to sit on the front porch with Ellen. Instead, the couple went out on unchaperoned dates. But her mother's approval was crucial for the romantic drives along Lake Michigan in his new Ford.

Sometime during the summer of 1928, probably at the Wallers' elaborate summer estate on Lake Geneva, the "Newport of the West," Adlai proposed and Ellen accepted. "Destiny is inevitable and can't be forced," he explained to Claire Birge, who was then teaching arithmetic to what Stevenson described as "New York Jew-boys." To Birge, whom he now tried to include in an unrealistic threesome, he described Ellen's accomplishments as a "poet . . . , a musician, a linguist, an athlete and not quite 21. And in spite of these impressive talents quite normal and need I say most attractive."

To his mother, Helen, Adlai described differently the woman whose name echoed hers. Ellen had a "quiet reassuring way," which he had at first feared was "dreamy indecision," but which in time he discovered as "ordered calmness . . . exceedingly good for an 'intense planner' like *we are*." He also recounted the traditional visit to Mr. Borden's office to seek Ellen's hand. "He's really a very pleasant man, if a little arrogant and determined. . . . Says Ellen will have about a million exclusive of what she inherits from her mother whom he says is worth probably a million. He wants E. to live on my income tho' she should be able to use some of her own income for dresses, etc."

Like all courting couples, Ellen and Adlai Stevenson found themselves reflected in their beloved's adulation during what Stevenson described as "fits of exultation and bitter despondency—all of the symptoms of adolescent heart trouble!" Later, when the couple divorced, it was hard for outsiders to see any common ground for the romantic attachment this generation required before marriage. Yet for nearly two decades Ellen confirmed Stevenson's sense of himself as a well-traveled sophisticate (she too knew Europe, having been introduced at the Court of St. James); as interested in ideas (he was proud of her recently published poems in *Poetry* magazine and the *Chicago Tribune,* which he sent home to be pasted in the family scrapbooks); as gay and especially as different (few other debs could discuss *The Education of Henry Adams*).

As he saw himself, so Ellen was charming, energetic, funny, and also an entrenched part of something that Stevenson coveted (even as he grumbled about class and vested interests)—money and society. At the same time, to a man forever skeptical about his career, Ellen Borden conveyed an appealing potential for heresy as well as an opportunity for the sculpting presence of an older man who acknowledged that he was sometimes "didactic and ministerial" with women. And, of course, romance with a woman unknown to his parents cemented his hard-fought autonomy and assured that, only briefly and in his memories, would Adlai Stevenson ever go home to Bloomington again.

To a young woman whose parents had recently divorced, whose mother had had an affair, and whose father had remarried, this time a woman who was (in Ellen's words) "disconcertingly younger and dumber" than she, Stevenson returned paternalistic reassurance. His uncertain ambitions sepa-

rated him from the social beings of her universe. To Adlai, flirtatious
Ellen—a perfect "flapper" of bobbed hair and mysterious sensuality—
offered the sexuality he had avoided in his personal campaign for morality,
while, four years older than the typical American groom, he gave back to
Ellen a presumptive experience in worldly ways. Even Adlai's name set him
apart. Through this unusual suitor from a small town whose parents were
Democrats, Ellen saw reflected her own uniqueness, earlier installed by
wealth and the symbolic grandiosity of a home that resembled a museum,
and later confirmed in a well-tended identity. Ellen Borden intended to
shape her suitor from the prairies: Adlai Stevenson intended to mold his
little rich girl. "Remember," he once informed Claire Birge, "the women
men most admire are the women they *think* (at least) their mothers were."

Years later Ellen's mother described an episode in her daughter's childhood when she walked into Lake Geneva wearing a pair of elegant new red
shoes, which she refused to take off even as she destroyed them, but gained
the attention of all on the beach. By marrying Adlai, Ellen could retain a
much desired notoriety and stand out, not only as Chicago's top debutante
and—her special innovation—as a published poet but, at twenty, as the
youngest bride of the season.

While the Bordens were pleased with Adlai (and Ellen's mother was
delighted), the Stevensons disliked Ellen. No doubt Helen Stevenson would
have found it difficult to accept any daughter-in-law, but now she threatened "Mother visits" and what the triumvirate called the "low-down conversations" of their intimacy. Her son resisted. Meanwhile Lewis Stevenson
told anyone who would listen that his son "had the wrong girl." Nor was it
long before Buffie was complaining about Ellen's immaturity and "childish-
ness." "A woman," Buffie once wrote, with her sister-in-law in mind,
"should fit into her primary job of wife . . . and stand by her man. Isn't
it enough to hold one man's love and his trust and be a compliment to
home?"

Ellen Borden and Adlai Stevenson were married in December 1928, in
the ivy-decorated chapel of the fashionable Fourth Presbyterian Church on
Chestnut Street, on Chicago's North Side. The bride wore her grandmother's ivory satin dress and an heirloom emerald necklace, and carried a bouquet of orchids. After the ceremony several hundred guests enjoyed a lavish
reception at the Borden mansion on Lake Shore Drive. Surrounded by
friends from his bachelor days, Adlai survived what he knew from his frequent appearances as an usher in friends' weddings to be "the stuff and
nonsense of weddings that generally results in a nervous breakdown for the
bride and a very bad head for the groom."

Buffie missed the wedding. She had married the year before and now
lived in Constantinople with her husband, Ernest Ives, and her six-month-
old son, Tim. Nor did Helen attend: she was visiting Buffie and her new

grandson. While previous generations had traveled miles to celebrate the ceremonies of their relatives, the modern Stevensons were often separated during important family transitions. After the wedding the couple left for a two-month honeymoon during which, in testament to their distinctiveness, they motored through Tunisia, Morocco, and Algeria instead of taking the traditional upper-class wedding trip to the Riviera.

3

WHEN ADLAI AND ELLEN returned, they rented an apartment on Chicago's North Side. In the 1920s the city had expanded northward across the Chicago River into the appropriately named Gold Coast and beyond. A building boom had produced giant skyscrapers like the glistening white, thirty-five-story Wrigley Building and the Gothic revival Tribune Tower with its flying buttresses. More than any other American city, the size of its buildings and the massiveness of their design came to symbolize Chicago's power. Sumptuous retail stores lined newly widened Michigan Avenue, which, even in the age of the automobile, retained a bridle path and promenade. Nearby the stone mansions and fashionable brick apartments like that of the Stevensons at 76 Walton Street offered glimpses of Lake Michigan for five hundred to a thousand dollars a month.

The couple's domestic life was typical of other wealthy young socialites. They hired a maid and went to the opera with the Rockefellers. Ellen decorated the apartment with the good taste that would be one of her hallmarks. Proudly, they saved money by slipcovering rather than upholstering their furniture. Attractive and entertaining, Ellen and Adlai played leading roles in Chicago's smart set. "We've been suffering from a severe attack of society—weddings, engagement parties and then just parties," the new husband wrote his mother.

Photographs of Ellen, who preferred writing poetry to the volunteer activities at the Women's Exchange or the charity balls that filled the hours of more conventional upper-class women, regularly appeared on the society page. Usually she wore a hat, the signature cloche of popular fashion that set off her pert features. Often she sported her furs, representing those disparaged by the feminist writer Charlotte Perkins Gilman as "the generation of white-nosed women who wear furs in summer [and] cannot lay claim to any real progress." Society required reciprocity, and Adlai and Ellen entertained, gaining a reputation for the annual fancy-dress party they hosted at Ellen's mother's home at 1020 Lake Shore Drive. There were quiet evenings as well, Stevenson wrote his mother, of "good reading and bitter chess & checker contests!"

A few months after Adlai and Ellen returned from their honeymoon,

Lewis Stevenson died of a heart attack, leaving his son with an ambiguous deathbed benediction that politics was a hazardous business, but that he expected his son's participation as part of an ancestral obligation. Now officially the head of the family, twenty-nine-year-old Adlai administered his father's estate of over $174,000 and arranged his father's funeral. Neither Buffie nor Helen attended. Both were in Copenhagen, where Ernest was now stationed.

Later that year the stock market crashed, though the decade-long depression that followed barely touched the young Stevensons. Some of Ellen's stocks had been purchased on margins, and a flurry of selling in her trust account to cover the broker's calls left the couple with a loss of $128,000. Yet during the worst years of the depression Ellen's income was never less than $20,000—a time in which, according to the Bureau of Labor Statistics, over half of all American families filing income tax returns earned below $1,500. But in a plummeting stock market that lost nearly three-quarters of its value in a year and a half, an overextended John Borden never recovered from the broker's calls on his margined stocks. Thereafter Ellen's father could not afford to send a set of younger children to private schools, while his son-in-law Robert Pirie (who had married Ellen's sister, Betty) fumed to Adlai that their father-in-law should do what he had never done before—"go to work." Establishing a pattern that she would try to repeat with her own children, Ellen lent her father substantial and ultimately irretrievable sums. Both Ellen and her sister also sent John Borden a monthly allowance from their trust fund accounts.

In October 1930, nearly two years after their marriage, Ellen and Adlai Stevenson became parents of a son named for his father and great-grandfather, Adlai Ewing Stevenson III, but called by his father, in testament to his size at birth, Bear and, sometimes, Big Boy. Like most American couples (and 90 percent of all professional families), the Stevensons no doubt controlled their fertility. As recommended by contemporary child-raising manuals, which encouraged brief intervals between siblings in order to establish companionship, Ellen was pregnant a year after her first son's birth. By the summer of 1932 the Stevenson family included a second son, Borden, nicknamed Squeak. (At their annual costume party that year, Adlai and Ellen appeared as Brigham Young and Margaret Sanger.) In 1936 a third son was born. Though they might have honored Stevenson's father, Lewis, the couple instead christened their last child John Fell, using part of the name of Adlai's family hero—his Republican great-grandfather on his maternal side, Jesse Fell—planter of trees, friend of Abraham Lincoln's, and founder of the *Pantagraph*. At twenty-eight Ellen Stevenson had delivered her last child; at thirty-six Adlai had completed his invented family.

Other men might have cherished Stevenson's life of easy frivolity, family privilege, and high society. Kenneth Burgess of his law firm spoke for many of Stevenson's friends: "In my own work it frequently seems to me as though I am doing little of a really worthwhile nature, and there are times when all of us get discouraged. I suppose that is a human tendency. It is given to very few people to do anything outstanding for the good of humanity; perhaps only two or three of a generation do anything that is really of permanent value. On the other hand, if we do our day's work and live a family life so that we and our children are good citizens, I suppose that is as much as we can do."

Adlai Stevenson had different ambitions. One night in January 1930 he went to the opera with Colonel Albert Sprague, who combined influence in the Cook County Democratic organization with standing in Chicago society. During the intermission Stevenson discussed the possibilities of running for the state legislature. Nothing came of it.

Next Stevenson tried, and failed, to find a place on the bottom rung of the Irish-controlled Kelly-Nash machine, which dominated Cook County politics until after World War II. When Stevenson sought an appointment as an alternate delegate to the 1936 Democratic presidential convention and was recommended by a friend as "young, active and a good speaker," Paddy Bauler, boss of the Forty-third Ward, had never heard of him. Earlier Bauler, who used his tavern as a political base, had registered voters from the wealthy East Side in a diverse ward that included slums, flop houses, and a large community of Irish and Italians in "Little Hell." But on election day Bauler discovered that few residents of the Gold Coast bothered to vote, at least not in the local elections that were his bread and butter. In Paddy Bauler's realm of favor exchanges—a vote in return for a relative's job with the city—the honor of joining the Democratic delegation belonged not to the rich lawyer from La Salle Street but to a hardworking Irish alderman whose efforts helped win elections.

Claiming indifference to this rebuff, Stevenson declared himself "far more concerned with the implication of thoughtless disregard of long range party welfare. The attitude of to hell with him and the east side of the ward is a brief and eloquent answer as to why more men . . . don't take an active part in our municipal politics. . . . My missionary work among the heathen, a familiar role in my family for several generations, can never be very useful unless the party leaders occasionally recognize and thus enlist some of these younger men in the active Dem. party." Stevenson never shed this disdain for machines and local politics, once sarcastically describing the position of state senator as "a dizzying height." Yet he did learn to work with professional politicians, endorsing Mayor Edward Kelly and, to the disappointment of his idealistic followers, emerging as one of Richard Daley's patron saints.

With local opportunities for party service blocked and the state government in the hands of the Republicans until 1933, Stevenson chose another route. During the grim fourth season of an unending depression when over half of Chicago's one and a quarter million workers were unemployed, when nearly every bank in Chicago (as well as Grandfather Stevenson's People's Bank in Bloomington) had closed, when soup kitchens and shanty-towns proliferated on the edge of the Loop and the bitter street signs in this cardboard Hooverville separated Prosperity Road from Hard Times Avenue, and when men and women fought over garbage outside restaurants, Adlai Stevenson went to Washington and joined the most progressive of all New Deal agencies—the Agricultural Adjustment Administration.

The year before, in 1932, Roosevelt had won the Democratic nomina-tion at the party's national convention in Chicago. Stevenson's preference had been Newton Baker, Wilson's internationally minded secretary of war, who he predicted to his Republican partners would win the nomination over Roosevelt. Even before Roosevelt proved him wrong, he and Ellen invited James Farley, soon to be in Roosevelt's cabinet as postmaster general and dispenser of patronage, to dinner along with some local Democrats. Stevenson was in the audience when Roosevelt, who broke tradition by flying to Chicago to accept his nomination, pledged a "New Deal." After-ward Stevenson raised money for the national ticket from Chicago busi-nessmen and worked for Henry Horner, the successful Democratic candidate for governor of Illinois.

In October, Roosevelt returned, carrying a straightforward message dur-ing an unusual presidential campaign in which a candidate who could not walk traveled 13,000 miles and delivered sixteen major addresses and sixty-seven shorter ones. In an atmosphere of crisis, to a dispirited and desperate population, New York's patrician governor offered the hope of jobs—the right of every man to make a "comfortable" living and the right not to starve. Roosevelt outlined no cohesive social or economic program, but committed himself to relief, recovery, reform, and a balanced budget. At some point Stevenson was introduced to this ever-smiling, optimistic politi-cian who, more than Al Smith, the party's contender in 1928, and Stevenson himself, merited the partisan compliment of "Happy Warrior." Roosevelt dazzled Stevenson with stories of the association of his father, James Roose-velt, with Grandfather Stevenson and his own memories of Lewis Stevenson when Roosevelt was assistant secretary of the navy during World War I. The Democratic nominee also shone his easy charm on Chicago's party regulars, who were marshaling one constellation of his emerging New Deal galaxy of urban, southern, ethnic, and labor voters.

Inspired, Adlai Stevenson traveled to Washington for Roosevelt's inau-guration and heard the new president tell a somber audience of over 100,000, "This is a day of national consecration. . . . This great nation will endure as it has always endured, will revive and will prosper. So, first of all, let me assert my firm belief that the only thing we have to fear is fear itself—

nameless, unreasoning, unjustified terror which paralyzes needed efforts to convert retreat into advance."

In the summer of 1933 Adlai Stevenson joined Roosevelt's New Deal as a special attorney and assistant to Jerome Frank in the legal division of the Agricultural Adjustment Administration. Like the National Industrial Recovery Administration, the Tennessee Valley Authority, and other programs of Roosevelt's whirlwind first hundred days, the Agricultural Adjustment Act established a new federal agency designed, in this case, to protect the farmer's declining economic status by establishing parity payments and controlling production. A friend had recommended Stevenson to the agency's head, Illinoisian George Peek. "Why, that is Louie Stevenson's boy," Peek responded. "He ought to be well backgrounded in farm problems, all right. Let's get him if we can."

Stevenson's salary was $6,500 a year, more than the $4,847 that he earned at the law firm, though subject to the administration's recent surtax of 15 percent. In Washington he joined a group of sixty-three lawyers—the "Happy Hotdogs," mostly from Harvard and Yale, who poured into the capital to be part of the "greatest law firm in the country." Until Ellen and the children came briefly in the fall, he boarded with friends, sharing with numerous other New Dealers the mutual fulfillment, not available in private practice, of patriotic duty in what this new recruit called "the Federal Service."

The Great Depression, once described by Stevenson as a time "of bread lines, muttering masses, burning corn, and smokeless chimneys," was not war, but its destructive potential was incalculable. Efforts at economic recovery held the same urgency as any battle preparations. In the spring of 1933, Iowa farmers had threatened a judge at a foreclosure hearing, dragging him from the bench and carrying him out of town, while members of Milo Reno's Farmers Holiday Association Alliance warned of a farm strike. Meanwhile the governor of Iowa placed ten counties under martial law. "For all of the loose talk in America about red revolution . . . ," warned the New York *World-Telegram*, "Americans are slow to understand that actual revolution already exists in the farm belt. . . ."

Besides public service during a crisis, other reasons brought the junior Brain Trusters to Washington. Some could not find jobs in the prestigious big-city law firms whose business had declined. Others came because they held an economic vision of government activism at odds with Herbert Hoover's leave-alone principles of rugged individualism. (During the 1932 campaign Hoover had complained that the apple selling on street corners that supported some of the unemployed was a ruse of the apple growers association.) A few New Dealers, notably the Agricultural Agency's John Abt, Lee Pressman, and Nathan Witt, were Communists, seeking more than the rehabilitation of a chronically overproductive agricultural system and the restoration of the farmer's fair share of income. Others, like Abe Fortas, envisioned the application of a legal doctrine learned at Yale Law School that emphasized, in its modernity and realism, context and social change over precedent and tradition. For these young men the early years of the New Deal were "a time when there was practically no obstacle between thinking up an idea and putting it into practice."

Some, like Adlai Stevenson, came for motives that had less to do with any legal philosophy than with personal considerations of restlessness and interest in politics. Francis Biddle, attorney general and later chairman of the Americans for Democratic Action, remembered "the deep sense of giving and sharing, far below any surface pleasure of work well-done, but rooted in the relief of escaping the loneliness and boredom of oneself and the unreality of personal ambition." Whatever their reasons, the bright young men living in un-airconditioned Washington during the steamy summer of 1933 shared what George Ball called "a yeasty and rarefied environment": "We were, all of us—to a greater or lesser extent—guided by two operational principles. We were convinced that our predecessors had made a mess of it and that nothing done up to that point in history was much good. And we had the satisfying feeling that there was nothing we could not do."

The hours were long; the writing of the contracts that established parity, arduous; the demand for their completion, immediate. With these marketing agreements establishing production quotas and minimum prices, the agency intended to raise prices, achieve a higher share of income for farmers, and thus stimulate business through the trickle-down effect of more consumer buying by the farmers, who represented a quarter of the American work force. By the time Stevenson arrived in the capital, antitrust regulations had been suspended for the duration in an arrangement that reversed the Wilsonian tradition of restoring competitive markets through antitrust legislation. But Stevenson, a dedicated Wilsonian, did not complain. Later—for Wilson, not Roosevelt, remained his hero—he criticized Roosevelt for spending too much money, not balancing the budget, extending federal control, and permitting Congress "to abdicate." He also joked that given his Republican social and professional friends, service in the New Deal made him "virtually immune to scorn and ridicule."

When the agency moved to control prices by destroying cotton and, in its most notorious exercise of managed scarcity, killing six million pigs (muttered Secretary of Agriculture Henry Wallace, "You'd think Americans had only pet pigs"), one farmer complained that the new arrangements were "more bolshevistic than any law in Soviet Russia." Four years later the Supreme Court declared unconstitutional the tax on food processors that had been used to pay farmers for the cost of removing their land from production. In the meantime the AAA had slightly improved prices and assisted some farmers, but had made little impact on the lives of tenant farmers and sharecroppers.

As Stevenson later described his work, "My first job was a marketing agreement for the fresh California deciduous tree fruit industry. The delegation from California was only a little upset when I asked what 'deciduous' meant!" Still, this gaffe was not as memorable as that of a New York lawyer who inquired what the macaroni growers wanted. "There is a lot more to the A.A.A. than wheat, corn, hogs and cotton," explained Stevenson, ". . . I negotiated with producers, processors, or handlers of everything from Atlantic oysters to California oranges and from Oregon apples to Florida strawberries."

When Adlai had time, he missed Ellen, who, save for brief visits, stayed in Chicago. "Lambkin! Think of it—I left the office at 7 P.M.—I think that's the earliest yet and I feel now as tho' I had only done a half days work!" He also shared his anti-Semitism with his wife. "There is a little feeling that the Jews are getting too prominent—as you know many of them are autocratic. . . . [Jerome] Frank has none of the racial characteristics and has done a dreadfully difficult job as well as could be hoped for—he's indefatigable & literally works most all night every night but he's brought several other Jews down who, tho' individually smart and able, are more racial."

Ellen returned his affection in frequent, exuberant letters that suggest the sexual nature of their relationship. She would come and vamp the Jews; she had not slept well: "I thought your absence might have a soothing effect—but alas—I roll and toss—and spill over into your bed—which I certainly never did before. Goodbye—My beloved Pig." He was alternately "Dear Adlai," "Assistant Agrarian," and "Adlai My Love," and she wanted to be with him. Like his mother, she urged him not to worry about all the things he worried about, even as she became preoccupied with the lessons she was learning from his absence: "I am getting very independent—I'm afraid that you will have to break me in all over again!—or raise my wages!!" Ellen signed this letter "S.M.R.A." which stood for Stevenson Matrimonial Recovery Act, an admission that shocked her so much that she crossed out the reference.

In early 1934 Adlai Stevenson moved to a different agency within the Agriculture Department—the Federal Alcohol Control Administration, a newly established division organized after Roosevelt's decision to end a decade of prohibition. Although Stevenson had been at the Agricultural Adjustment Agency only six months, his sponsor, George Peek, had lost a policy fight with the "men with their hair ablaze" who wanted to control production. Peek preferred selling American crops overseas at low prices to using acreage allotments and controlled scarcity. In the fall Roosevelt removed the rumpled, homespun Illinoisian who represented a more traditional approach to palliating the agricultural depression. Peek's comment about "the plague of young lawyers [who] settled on Washington, claiming to be friends of somebody or other, mostly of Felix Frankfurter and Jerome Frank . . . who floated airily into offices, took desks, asked for papers and found no end of things to be busy about, though no one ever knew what," revealed differences with the city-bred Jerome Frank that were more than substantive.

In his new job Stevenson got a raise and more authority. But he had also moved from the front ranks to the periphery on this tour of duty. "The Chief Attorney of the FACA," he informed his mother, "presents his compliments & advises you that he has a hell of a job! Ten or 12 hours a day will just about handle the mail—with 5 assistants—without giving me any time for the important work," which was establishing fair-competition guidelines and marketing arrangements for the industry's resurrection. Stevenson's rapid change of agencies previewed his lifelong tendency to be a transient federal appointee; it revealed as well an ambition for duty in the first circle of public significance, if not at the inner core of decision making.

The New Deal became, for Adlai Stevenson, more an administrative shift of power from the states to Washington than a rehabilitation of democratic capitalism. Describing his work in one of the longest speeches of his career, Stevenson quoted Supreme Court Justice Louis Brandeis on "the right of the state and nation, 'to remold, through experimentation, our economic practices and institutions to meet changing social and economic needs.' " But the crucial concern—and a theme of his family's politics—was to get "the best men" to serve the growing bureaucracy, thereby sustaining the power of the privileged in a new era.

"I can look forward mistily to the time when government service will be one of the highest aspirations of educated men. . . . Our economic life is being rapidly remolded and what is called the 'New Deal' in essence is little more than the use of the power of government to preserve private enterprise by regulating its abuses and balancing its deficiencies. But the machinery is personal, arbitrary and dangerous and the lawyer, the craftsman of social principle, which we call justice, must contribute his skill and experience to that remolding or the bar will have signally failed society in a great opportunity."

From his background and his unacknowledged ambitions not so much for power as for responsibility, Adlai Stevenson drew his conviction that men in private life must volunteer for public agencies. "Bad government is bad politics and . . . good government means good men." While he never specified the exact qualifications of these "good men," at the least they must share with him an elite manhood's obligations of loyalty, integrity, wisdom, and hard work. Good men responded to ingrained impulses of noblesse oblige absorbed from parents, school, and college.

In the fall of 1934, after only thirteen months in Washington (most

New Dealers stayed two years or more), Stevenson returned to his "cubicle" at Cutting, Moore, and Sidley (soon to be reorganized as Sidley, McPherson, Austin, and Burgess), where his sometimes disapproving associates grew accustomed to his departures and returns. One partner, skeptical of Adlai's playing "in both leagues" in a period before law firms became reservoirs of public servants, recommended "wholehearted" commitment to either law or government. On his part, Stevenson now aspired to the kind of clientele that established for lawyers like Charles Evans Hughes and John Foster Dulles a swinging door, as they ranged back and forth between private practice and government jobs.

In 1936 Adlai Stevenson became a partner in the firm, earning over $9,000. Still, he considered himself "the other partners' servant." Once Stevenson joked to Robert Hutchins, the president of the University of Chicago, who heard his frequent complaints about "this infernal law firm," that he would practice until he made $25,000 and then offer the money to the Democratic National Committee and say, "I want to be an ambassador." Later, when he was a famous man and it was impossible not to preach his version of life, Stevenson explained that his "fascination with public affairs—at home and abroad—must date from infancy, or almost! And in a curious inverted sort of way I have never found my own affairs quite as absorbing. Law, business, profit, *making* money, have never interested me as much as impersonal public affairs."

Marriage to a rich woman and a private income diminished any crass concern with making money, although as an unadmittedly rich man after his mother died, Stevenson speculated in the stock market. In 1936, the year he became a partner, his income surged to over $40,000 and included, in a year in which he and Ellen filed separate federal income tax returns in order to lower their taxes, $9,400 from his law practice and $23,000 from his chief asset, the ever-prosperous *Pantagraph*. When only 1 percent of all American families earned above $10,000 and most families lived on $2,500, Stevenson's income included $4,000 of gains from his successful speculations in grain futures with what his wife later insisted was her money.

Returned to the private life that soon bored him, Stevenson immersed himself in a surrogate form of service—the volunteering and good works to which businessmen and lawyers applied themselves with the objectives of good deeds, enhanced status, and fruitful contacts. Soon—for he was a diligent worker and an enthusiastic joiner—he emerged as a civic leader, serving on the board of directors of Jane Addams's Hull House, the Immigrants' Protective League, the Illinois Children's Home and Aid Society, the Library of International Relations, the Chicago Latin School, and the Illinois Legislative League, which monitored the voting records of state legislators. Despite complaints of overwork and "unremitting pressure," he found time to chair the Chicago Bar Association's Committee on Civil Rights, investigating violations of First Amendment rights. Always he was busy, too busy. No longer the "rabbit" of college days, Adlai Stevenson had become a self-proclaimed "beaver" and, revealingly, "bird-dog."

Never was his political muse stilled. Twice he was recommended for public appointments and, using Grandfather Stevenson's trick, he sent the erroneous newspaper reports that he might replace Dwight Green as U.S. attorney for the District of Illinois to well-placed politicians with the ingenious comment that the news was a surprise to him. Still, as he informed Secretary of the Interior Harold Ickes, "I would be delighted to have this appointment." Yearning for public life, he explained to a member of the Cook County organization that because of an "irresistible, congenital urge," he hoped to take an active role in politics. When Secretary of Labor Frances Perkins, the first female cabinet officer in American history, offered him the position of commissioner of naturalization and immigration, he declined, but noted, "If something comes along that interests me particularly, my excellent resolutions, which you have already enfeebled will evaporate!" During these seven years out of official civic uniform, two private associations—the Chicago Council on Foreign Relations and, in 1940, the Committee to Defend America by Aiding the Allies—claimed his attention.

4

ADLAI STEVENSON JOINED the Chicago Council on Foreign Relations in the early 1930s and found there, along with his blue-blooded friends, an education in international affairs, a road to prominence, and a podium. The intention of the council's founders was "to provide public understanding of the United States role in world affairs" among local opinion makers, who, in turn, would promote an interest in foreign policy issues among generally inattentive Americans. By 1935 Stevenson was president of this organization, whose membership quadrupled during the decade. When the Chicago papers persisted in covering the council on the society page, Stevenson complained that the "Council is not a club but an important Chicago institution—an active adult educational institution," a part of "the great American pastime of lunch and learn."

Once a week from September to May, during a lunch meeting usually held in the Palmer House in downtown Chicago, prominent authorities on international affairs addressed the council's 2,500 members. Sometimes it was an expert from the University of Chicago faculty such as Professor Samuel Harper, or a newspaper man like George Slocombe of the *London Herald,* or CBS's Edward R. Murrow. In 1938, a few weeks after the English prime minister Neville Chamberlain agreed to Hitler's demands for the Sudetenland and heralded his negotiations as achieving "peace in our time,"

Murrow criticized the conference in Munich that would forever fix the attitude of Stevenson's generation toward nations they considered aggressors.

As the council's reputation grew, national and international figures lectured. Former President Herbert Hoover came. So did William Bullitt, the American ambassador to the Soviet Union, and Eduard Beneš, the deposed president of Czechoslovakia. In 1938 Bertrand Russell, the English philosopher, shocked the council's Anglophiles by proclaiming that no matter who won the impending war, civilization would be destroyed. With the Nazis annhilating Jews, the council invited Colin Ross, a Nazi fellow traveler. When Ross denied German mistreatment of Jews amid the audience's hisses and Stevenson's gaveling for order, an aroused rabbi shouted, "Why don't you tell the truth?"

Adlai Stevenson introduced most of these notables. And like his father and grandfather, he cultivated acquaintances with the famous and powerful. His charming introductions earned him a reputation in Chicago for wit and intelligence. By this time even his briefest comments exhibited the stylistic specialties for which he later became famous—distinctive images, arresting word choice, complex sentence structure, and moralizing precepts. In return for its spotlight, the staunchly nonpartisan council taught Stevenson never forgotten lessons on the importance of a bipartisan foreign policy.

Listening intently from the head table, Stevenson heard alarming reports. From the Far East came word of the triumph of right-wing militarism within the Japanese government. In 1935 Edgar Mowrer, a *Chicago Sun-Times* foreign correspondent who had grown up in Bloomington, discussed the Italian invasion of Ethiopia and the failure of the League of Nations sanctions to accomplish an Italian withdrawal. That same year Ernest Price from the University of Chicago warned of Japanese advances into Manchuria and Outer Mongolia. In early 1936, a week after the Germans violated the Versailles and Locarno treaties by marching into the Rhineland, the council discussed the topic "Europe—New Roads to War." In 1938 Jan Masaryk, the son of Czechoslovakia's founding father, declared that if his country's sacrifice of the Sudetenland guaranteed world peace, "it was worth making." But Masaryk predicted that the decisions made at Munich were in fact only "the beginning of a chain of appeasement."

In turn, Stevenson carried warnings to other audiences about the disintegration "of the democracies of the Old World" and the risks of appeasement. Though he disclaimed any status other than that of a "simple lawyer with an amateur taste for international politics," he was now considered something of a specialist. Characteristically he began to shape global events into an apocalyptic moral struggle between authoritarian dictatorships and self-governing democracies. By the late 1930s Adlai Stevenson considered war inevitable, though the nature of American involvement remained uncertain. Otherwise "dictators would soon be shaking hands across Europe." Throughout the Chicago area, in person and on the radio, in speeches and in debates, he spoke out for the need to understand German, Italian, and Japanese aggression in the historical context of American withdrawal from world affairs. In a message that held a personal analogue, he urged Americans to get involved because "the world is on fire."

Stevenson's fire included not only acts of aggression but hostile ideas. In 1938, speaking to the American Legion, he described a "new ideology, the antithesis of liberalism and individual freedom [that] has spread through the world like wild fire. . . . My hope and my guess is that before it is too late the liberal democracies will realize that there is something worse than war—slavery!—and that fascism will retreat into history before their united front as a temporary and perhaps useful device for remaking maps and that the 20th century will be saved!" Increasingly Stevenson compared the warlike movements of the Germans and Japanese to a firestorm, a useful image that linked his public observations to his private life.

5

IN 1935 HELEN STEVENSON DIED in a Milwaukee hospital, one of the many institutions that served as her home as she moved, ever complaining, from one to another. With her only daughter overseas, Helen shadowed Adlai and Ellen. For several years she rented a suite in Chicago's Churchill Hotel, near the Stevensons' new apartment on State Street. When Helen left Chicago for treatment in sanitariums in Michigan, Florida, and Massachusetts, Adlai dutifully wrote, offering optimistic prospectuses for her health: "But most of all I think you owe it to yourself to get together and have some fun . . . be yourself for a while and then we'll plan the future." Ever cheerleading, he made up an encouraging word: "Try to discuss symptoms as little as possible and just *unlax* and be happy things are not worse." Increasingly distracted—Adlai once told Marietta Tree that his mother was insane at the end of her life—Helen claimed her son's attention. Her telephone calls were frequent and her letters thick with self-absorption, complaints, and, in the last year of her life, protests about the hated Riggs clinic in Stockbridge, Massachusetts. Consumed by her own sickness, Helen Stevenson no longer offered gratuitous advice about interior decorating to a hostile daughter-in-law.

When Helen died, Buffie was unable to come to her mother's funeral in Bloomington. Instead, Ellen made the intimate arrangements regarding flowers and even the dress in which Helen Stevenson was buried. Consoling her brother, Buffie acknowledged "the strange irony that I couldn't be there and that of all the world it should have been Ellen who had fought her and misunderstood her so pitifully in life who should do the last mortal service." Buffie remembered her mother's "strong and vital love" and closed with an unusual admission of her brother's early torments: "I know you have ugly, sad memories and much pain, but we all have."

Soon after his mother's death, Adlai and Ellen decided to build a house in Libertyville, thirty-five miles from the Loop and ten miles from Lake Forest. The location, outside the village of Libertyville along the Des Plaines River, confirmed their exceptionalism. (In 1952, during the presidential campaign, an outraged Republican complained that the Democrats' "Man from Libertyville" was using a patriotically contrived post office address, though by this time Stevenson had lived in Libertyville fifteen years.)

The couple avoided the traditional setting of suburban, upper-class Lake Forest with its elegant brick homes and several-acre lots. Moreover, as parents of three young children, they did not remain on Chicago's North Side, disliking city life with its views of "chimney pots spouting bituminous smoke." Instead, they purchased forty (later seventy) acres from the extensive Lake County holdings of Samuel Insull, the mustachioed electric power tycoon who wore spats and was Chicago's idea of a capitalist until he went bankrupt in the early 1930s. Ellen and Adlai intended to create on their "gentleman's farm" the outdoor privacy that would serve as a modern replica of the rural life that neither had experienced as a child. The image was sufficiently authentic to permit Ellen to abandon the cosmetics that more American women were using and to adopt rustic dirndl dresses that fewer were wearing. In the style of the gentry, her husband kept horses, including a massive hunter named Jeb Stuart after the Confederate cavalry commander, rode a tractor, and bought a flock of sheep.

In the summer of 1937 the house was finished, an example of the boxy Prairie style of flat squares, low roofs, and emphasized horizontals described by Frank Lloyd Wright as the Midwest's indigeneous architecture. It cost $24,976, "about twice what I anticipated," complained its proud owner, who wondered "why women seem to think that everything has to be perfect." Thereafter Ellen began her tasteful decorations of its twelve rooms—a graceful Degas original set off the bedroom's pink and gray tones. Two Diego Rivera watercolors hung in the front hall. In the huge 29- by 18-foot living room, painted yellow in a period in which green was the favorite color, Ellen placed the grand piano in one corner. There she played the sonatas and love songs of Edward MacDowell and the tone poems of her new stepfather, the composer John Alden Carpenter.

Then, one windy night in January of 1938, the steel-girded, supposedly fireproof house—"our mechanical house"—burned to the ground. As a neighbor expressed sympathy, some burning debris landed at Stevenson's feet. Picking it up, he lit a cigarette and commented, his fatalistic aplomb unshaken, "You can see, we are still using the house." Meanwhile Ellen prophesied to a bystander that perhaps she was not meant to have possessions.

The Stevensons rebuilt their home, but lost in the fire were family records, especially "the treasures" of Grandfather's Bible and his library, the electoral vote box from his vice presidency and a smaller one from his Bloomington ward, and correspondence of the Fell and Davis families, along with the family archives stored in the cellar. Lost too, along with furnishings valued at $20,000, was the couple's innocent expectation that a country farm could shelter them from misfortune. In the late 1930s the destruction of their home offered a calamitous personal parallel to global catastrophes. Stevenson acknowledged this simultaneous disappearance of two worlds he had known—one private, one public.

"Our family is vanishing rapidly," he informed Buffie after attending the funerals of several elderly cousins in Bloomington, "but I suppose it happens to everyone and we must realize that we've suddenly become the older generation now." Such bereavements were necessary losses, but along with them, instead of tranquillity along the quiet banks of the Des Plaines River, came the reality of what Borden Stevenson, after psychotherapy, called "a dysfunctional family," marred by increasing friction between Ellen and Adlai and between Ellen and her sons.

As a commuter on the Northwestern Rail system, Stevenson left home early for the fifty-minute ride to downtown Chicago. Borden remembered the gardener-chauffeur bringing his father's car around well before seven for the drive to the Lake Forest station. Some days Adlai drove the boys to the Bell Academy, a private school in Lake Forest, often not returning until they were asleep. Some weeks he saw his youngest son only on Sundays. "We didn't have a lot of contact with Dad. He was a compulsive worker," acknowledged his oldest son. Asked years later what kind of a father Adlai Stevenson was, John Fell replied "a busy one."

Meanwhile, with the help of governesses and maids (a French-speaking Austrian governess arrived in 1938, preceded and followed by Scottish, English, and American replacements), Ellen raised the children. Her strict parenting, a generation before Dr. Benjamin Spock prescribed more flexible forms of child raising, ran counter to changing modes of permissiveness and would be remembered by both her older sons as abusive. Second son Borden suffered the most, often hiding from his mother in the servants' wing over the garage. And it was Borden who years later held his father accountable for his mother's isolation and for not intervening in his own mistreatment. All three sons grew up with their father's past of an absent father and an intrusive mother, preferring, unlike their father in his youth, their father's company to their mother's.

Like those of other twentieth-century American mothers, Ellen's child-raising strategies were unconnected to any social or public purpose.

Instead, she practiced "libidinal motherhood," based on her own shadow world of feelings and anchored, according to the period's experts, in an instinctual natural love. Unlike those of previous generations of Stevenson mothers, Ellen's expectations for her children contained no external public goals of creating good American citizens or shaping competitive scholars or entrepreneurs. Rather than any civic or family goal, she located motherhood in a private psychological world inherited from her own extraordinary circumstances as a poor little rich girl.

Sharp disagreements marked the relations of a husband and wife who argued over everything from Ellen's tardiness and extravagance to Adlai's career and absences. What had been ingenious examples of distinctiveness degenerated into causes for complaint. Ellen liked cars and drove a snappy new Buick coupe with yellow-walled tires; Adlai, a drab Ford. Adlai practiced small-town frugality on an income in 1938 of $50,417, which included $33,127 of dividends, mostly from the *Pantagraph*. He was punctual and popular, while Ellen's old-money urbanity, interest in the art world, and expectations for pleasure clashed with her husband's sense of duty and interest in politics. Ellen held to the aristocrat's view that men shouldn't have to work for a living and seethed when Adlai's work claimed his time.

Remembering his mother, Adlai expected a more solicitous wife and more traditional homemaker than Ellen, although in an age of disappearing domestic servants, his wife often "ended up in the kitchen . . . with her hands full." Even with the servants that three-quarters of all American households did without and whom Ellen hired and fired, her husband had little comprehension of the traditional domestic roles she filled. He observed what he considered time-saving machines available to wash and dry the clothes and to vacuum the rugs. Once acknowledging that his wife was doing all the cleaning, cooking, and child care, "working from 7 [in the morning] to 10 each night," Stevenson described Ellen as "satisfied" and hoped that she could stand the pace with three children under six. A chagrined Ellen guessed that she was born to be a housewife.

Rising standards of cleanliness were keeping pace with labor-saving technology, with the result that twentieth-century homemakers like Ellen spent as much time completing domestic tasks as their grandmothers had. Now women did every day what other generations had left for a semiannual housecleaning. Floors must shine; children, though fewer, must have daily rather than weekly baths. Like other American housewives, Ellen offered time-consuming menus to her guests. Among America's upper-class, simple junket gave way to "perfection salad." When the head of the Democratic National Committee came for lunch in 1940, Ellen supervised a complicated meal of veal, gelatin salad, baking powder biscuits, and a French import, baba au rhum. Later she printed menus for a lunch that featured iced whole tomatoes with a special caviar dressing, halibut ring with sea-food Newburg, and crepes suzette.

While Adlai Stevenson offered public glimpses of a deteriorating marriage, none of Ellen Stevenson's letters remain to present her side of matters. In one of his introductions to the Council on Foreign Relations, Stevenson included his wife in a scatterbrained group of Chicago council members who forgot their tickets; he noted that women can never make up their minds and denounced "the effective feminine weapon of relentless reminder." Using a familiar male dismissive, he called Ellen "his war department." Several times he confided to friends that though they might remember his birthday, his wife didn't. He commented that he had seen his wife "the other day," grumbled that Ellen would write soon, "which means some day," and complained that "Ellen will have her way about how the place will be run." When a friend described Ellen as healthy and well, he responded that his wife always flourished when he was away, adding, "I must be an exhausting husband."

Unable to fathom his wife's sense of suffocation and loss of identity in what she considered a bad marriage to an unresponsive man, or even her flirtations with two neighbors, Stevenson averted his eyes. In a letter to his sister, he offhandedly included the news that while he was home in bed, Ellen had partied at a nightclub until 3:30 A.M. Like his mother and father, he and Ellen were often physically and emotionally separated. But holding no childhood image of what a happy home might be, Stevenson was surprised when Ellen threatened divorce. But after the storms, there was affection; from Mexico in 1940 Ellen wrote her husband, "This is the place for babies. Come on down."

Travel became marital therapy. In the spring of 1939, just before the Russians and Germans signed their nonaggression pact, Ellen and Adlai Stevenson left on a six-week European vacation—their last, Stevenson believed, before the "instinct to fight a bully is as strong in the mass man as the love of peace." The couple had always taken extended journeys. After the birth of each child, they traveled outside the United States—to Mexico, Scandinavia, and Bermuda—with Stevenson holding to the fiction that he took few vacations. Now amid the gathering storms of domestic and international strife, while the Germans massed their forces on the Polish border and his wife talked of a separation, Adlai and Ellen motored through England, Scotland, and Ireland.

A year later, in the spring of 1940, German divisions smashed across Norway and Denmark, moved through Belgium and the Netherlands, and crushed France. A week after the French surrendered, in late June 1940, Adlai Stevenson "reluctantly" became chairman of the Chicago chapter of the Committee to Defend America by Aiding the Allies. As he explained to his mother-in-law, Ellen Borden Carpenter, "It is in our interest to help

Britain stop or hold Hitler and . . . a rising tide of sentiment in the next few weeks could be decisive or could at least bring about ultimately a negotiated peace of which we could be a major beneficiary. I don't believe our economy or standard of living can long endure the burdens in prospect if we are really going to do the job."

Adlai Stevenson was a volunteer, but the task of sounding the alarm in the isolationist Midwest consumed him for the next year. Just as his grandfather had participated in the nineteenth century's great debate over secession, slavery, and the union and, during the 1890s, in the national deliberations over gold and silver and American colonialism in the Philippines, so Adlai Stevenson II played a role in the decisive controversy of his generation. Shaped by his background, his mother's exhortations to duty, and his desire to have a public voice, he donned the cloak of Anglophilic internationalism. In so doing, he at first ran counter to the sentiments of most of his isolationist business and social friends, earning the admiration of associates who noted how much he had to lose by such an embarrassing notoriety.

Like most of the Committee to Defend America by Aiding the Allies, Adlai Stevenson believed Britain "America's first line of defense," following the views of an administration gingerly constructing a foreign policy consensus. Stevenson argued for a repeal of the neutrality legislation whose original intention seemed archaic in a world in which "our way of life is in deadly peril from an unappeasable, dynamic, ruthless and victorious foe." As Hitler changed the map of Europe, Stevenson came to support the exchange of fifty American destroyers for English bases in the Caribbean and Newfoundland and to accept the economic warfare implied by the administration's lend-lease policy after the British could no longer pay for goods. Committed to the proposition that aid to Britain would keep the United States out of war, Stevenson was by the end of 1940 arguing for arming merchant ships and protecting them in convoys shepherded through the North Atlantic by the U.S. Navy.

During the summer of 1940, as Roosevelt prepared for his third presidential campaign, Adlai Stevenson testified before the Democratic platform committee, urging his party to resolve, in its foreign policy plank, "that our armed forces shall not be used for aggression anywhere, and that our soldiers shall fight only for defense and not in Europe." During his campaign against Wendell Willkie, Roosevelt popularized the point in an election eve speech delivered in Boston: "your boys are not going to be sent into any foreign wars."

Events overtook promises. By the fall Congress had passed, by one vote, the first peacetime draft in American history, and during the winter, with Roosevelt's encouragement, was debating lend-lease. The two-thirds of the American public that in 1939 believed that the United States should remain neutral shrank to a minority. With German airplanes bombing London and the Battle of Britain under way, Stevenson emerged as the Chicago leader of the internationalists in a battle for public opinion.

His motive was morality: "I do not believe there can ever be a new moral order in America if there is a new unmoral order in the rest of the world." His ideas were secondhand, though their expression was often riveting. His weapons were pamphlets, letters to the editors, telegrams to congressmen, senators, and the president, press releases, public speaking, and an early delineation of the domino theory. "We believe that 'isolation' is impossible; that a triumphant Nazism will make repeated inroads in the Americas," wrote Stevenson as he awaited changes in "the present state of public mind."

Meanwhile the America First Committee (two-thirds of whose members lived within a three-hundred-mile radius of Chicago), the Chicago Citizens Committee to Keep America Out of War, and Robert McCormick's isolationist *Chicago Tribune* (which daily printed George Washington's 1796 warning in his farewell address to avoid entangling foreign alliances) disputed the need to repeal neutrality legislation or to pass the lend-lease bill. Ohio's Senator Robert Taft compared the latter to lending chewing gum— "you don't want it back." These mostly Republican noninterventionists (for they were only isolationists to opponents like Stevenson) contended that Hitler had limited expansionist intentions and that the Germans posed no threat to the Western Hemisphere. Nor, according to the leaders of America First, would the defeat of Great Britain lead to a decline in American markets in Europe or German dominance in the Atlantic. Soon Stevenson, their most visible opponent, was assailed as a "war-shouter." "Why don't you go to Canada and volunteer?" wrote one angry Chicagoan.

In response, Adlai Stevenson organized an ambitious rally. He intended to carry his committee's call for aid to Britain and support of Roosevelt's preparedness program to his neighbors who, he believed, failed to comprehend the significance of the Battle of Britain. On the balmy night of September 18, 1940, after the German Luftwaffe had bombed London for twelve successive days, fifteen thousand Chicagoans filled the Chicago Coliseum to hear an all-star cast that included the actor Douglas Fairbanks and the journalist Dorothy Thompson. With a nod to his city's ethnic blocs, Stevenson arranged that a judge of German descent introduce Maury Maverick, the mayor of San Antonio, who worried about the infiltration of the Third Reich in Mexico, that a Polish baritone sing "God Bless America," that a Czechoslovakian-born Chicago school superintendent present Dorothy Thompson, and that there not be too many Jews on the platform. The evening was long; the issues were too important for brevity.

It was nearly one o'clock when Adlai Stevenson—a huge button emblazoned with the single word NOW askew on his lapel—asked that those in

A thoughtful Helen Davis in one of her muttonchop, full-sleeved gowns around the time of her marriage to Lewis Stevenson in 1893. (Princeton University Libraries)

A frail Lewis Stevenson poses in Japan after separating from Helen in the 1890s. (Illinois State Historical Library)

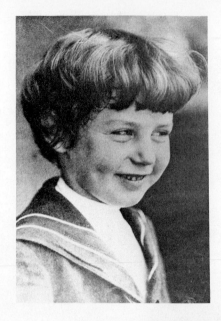

Cherubic Adlai Ewing Stevenson II during the years in which his parents moved often, probably taken at the Davis's home in Charlevoix, Michigan. (Courtesy of Buffie Ives)

Three years older than her brother, Elizabeth "Buffie" Stevenson places a protective arm around her younger brother, Adlai. It remained there throughout their lives. (Courtesy of Buffie Ives)

The Stevensons never seemed to be together as a nuclear family. Here in Charlevoix, Adlai and Buffie pose with their father. (Illinois State Historical Library)

In 1906 Helen Davis Stevenson purchased this home at 1316 East Washington Street, which remained the family home in Bloomington until Buffie Ives died there in 1994. It is now owned by the McLean County Historical Society. (McLean County Historical Society)

A street scene in Bloomington at the turn of the century, possibly of Washington Street, before cars changed the lives of the town's residents. (McLean County Historical Society)

The Washington Street school that Buffie and Adlai attended. (McLean County Historical Society)

Adlai Stevenson (first row, far right) as a member of the Choate tennis team in 1916. (Courtesy of Buffie Ives)

Adlai Stevenson appears as the character Sneer in the Choate school performance of a Sheridan play. (Courtesy of Buffie Ives)

Stevenson as he looked at his Princeton graduation in 1922. (Courtesy of Buffie Ives)

The early building housing the *Pantagraph*, the source of the Stevensons' wealth. Here W. O. Davis published a popular Illinois newspaper. (Princeton University Libraries)

Young socialites Adlai and Ellen Stevenson arrive at a party in Chicago during the 1930s. (Princeton University Libraries)

The relationship between Truman and Stevenson was a difficult one. Truman began encouraging Stevenson as a successor in the spring of 1952. (Courtesy of Buffie Ives)

In 1952 Adlai's aunt Letitia Stevenson and his sister, Buffie Ives, campaign for Stevenson in late November before television appearances replaced whistle-stopping. (Courtesy of Buffie Ives)

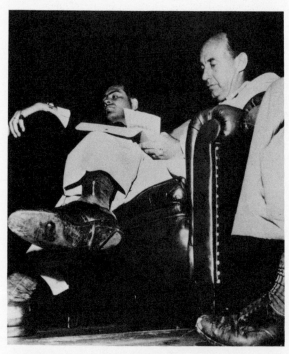

The Pulitzer Prize–winning photograph of Stevenson in 1952. Moments before he is to speak in Flint, Michigan, Stevenson is still editing his remarks in a characteristic pose. (Princeton University Libraries)

The Stevensons at the 1956 convention. To the left of Adlai and John Fell are Paul Butler, Les Bittle, and Jim Farley. For generations Stevensons attended the national nominating conventions of their party. (Photo by Cornell Capa Magnum)

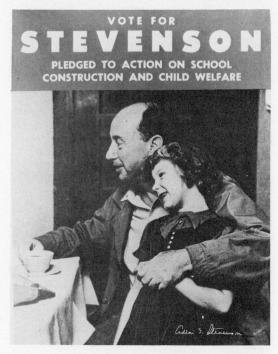

The first divorced, still unmarried candidate to run in an American presidential election, Stevenson emphasized family images in his campaign. (Smithsonian Institution)

**IF YOU STAY HOME
on Nov. 4
You *WILL* be voting**

FOR { Boom, Bust and Breadlines

Wage Slashes

Higher Rents

Tougher anti-labor laws

VOTE FOR CONTINUED PROSPERITY
VOTE STEVENSON
Labor's Committee for Stevenson and Sparkman

GEORGE M. HARRISON, Chairman   E. L. OLIVER, Secretary-Treasurer
1631 K Street, N.W., Washington 5, D.C.

A Stevenson poster in 1952 attempts to mobilize the voters who in increasing numbers were staying home. (Smithsonian Institution)

Stevenson addresses his friends and neighbors during the campaign in Bloomington's Miller Park. (Courtesy of Buffie Ives)

During the 1952 campaign, Stevenson spoke at his son Adlai's commissioning ceremonies at Quantico, Virginia. His sons Borden (*rear*) and John Fell came too. (United Press International)

Stevenson's prairie-style home in Libertyville. In the back the land sloped to the Des Plaines River. (Illinois State Historical Library)

favor of extending to Britain all possible aid "compatible with our defense requirements" rise. And with the audience standing, he offered a Churchillian peroration: "Liberty is like air. You do not notice it until it is gone. We—all of us for whom America is something more than a word—must rekindle our national passion for liberty which was *won* in danger and sacrifice and will be *preserved* in danger and sacrifice!" With the singing of the national anthem, the rally ended. Ten months later, and five months before the attack on Pearl Harbor, the man who found his public voice in a volunteer committee joined the Navy Department as an assistant to Secretary of the Navy Frank Knox and moved to Washington.

6

WARTIME WASHINGTON was like a crowded railroad station—noisy, full of arrivals and departures, and permeated by an atmosphere of surreal impermanence. In the first year of the Second World War the city's population of 700,000 grew by an indigestible 70,000, reaching over a million by the end of 1941 and nearly two million by 1945. Primarily made up of civilian government workers and military personnel, the human tide taxed housing and services.

Yet many aspects of the city soon to be the capital of the "Free World" remained as they had been in Grandfather Stevenson's day half a century earlier: the old trolleys of the Capital Traction Company, with their half-open cars, still ran up the center of Pennsylvania Avenue. Most of the city's black population of nearly 300,000 continued to live in segregated slums in the shadows of the splendid marble buildings dedicated, on their façades, to justice and freedom for all Americans. In other ways the District retained its southern atmosphere. In 1939 the Daughters of the American Revolution, over which Letitia Stevenson had presided in the 1890s, prohibited the celebrated African-American contralto Marian Anderson from singing in Constitution Hall. And as in Grandfather's day, three commissioners appointed by the president governed the District, with authority residing in the congressional committees that controlled the city's budget. Greek temples, only slightly more weather-beaten than in the 1890s, still commanded the landscape, though the Lincoln Memorial and the National Archives were twentieth-century additions.

As in Grandfather's day, there was not enough office space. Even after the federal government took over 358 buildings, including a woman's college, offices overflowed with military personnel, job-hungry citizens, and typewriter-less secretaries ("It takes 25 government girls behind typewriters to put one man behind the trigger," went a popular slogan). Before the war the Office of the Secretary of the Navy had been run by a civilian and military staff of fourteen; in a year it grew to over a hundred employees. Nor was there enough residential housing, though the District government was issuing over fifteen hundred building permits a month. Like many of his friends, Adlai Stevenson worked in a drab temporary World War I Navy Annex on the mall, as he scrambled to find a place to live—first in the Hays-Adams Hotel near the White House, next in a friend's house, and in the fall, when Ellen briefly and unhappily arrived with the children, at 1904 R Street in Georgetown. But housing was not important. Within weeks of his arrival, Secretary of the Navy Knox dispatched his personal assistant on the first of his overseas missions.

A Republican anomaly chosen to provide a bipartisan complexion to Roosevelt's wartime cabinet, Frank Knox had been a member of Teddy Roosevelt's Rough Riders, and in 1936 a Republican vice-presidential candidate on Alf Landon's losing ticket. The bluff, hard-driving publisher of the *Chicago Daily News* was well known for his sharp attacks on the wastefulness and centralization of Roosevelt's administration. Referring to Adlai Stevenson as "my New Dealer," he instructed his new assistant to deliver two messages to the president.

In his first weeks in Washington, Stevenson had already been assigned to work on a labor controversy at a Kearny, New Jersey, shipbuilding company that had refused to accept the recommendations of the National Defense Mediation Board. By late spring sixteen thousand workers at the Federal Shipbuilding and Drydock Corporation went out on strike over wages and hours, though by this time Stevenson had worked out a statement of principles by which labor would voluntarily withhold "the exercise of its right to strike." A ship-short Navy Department, faced with the demands of a two-ocean war, decided to nationalize the yard, and for a time the Navy occupied the plant. But only Roosevelt had authority to end an impasse that threatened to delay naval production, and the president had spent the last week off the Newfoundland coast. There he and Winston Churchill had signed the Atlantic Charter, a Wilsonian statement of noble intention, which included the principles of self-determination and the postwar establishment of an international organization.

Hurriedly Stevenson left Washington to deliver an executive order along with a secret (and erroneous) intelligence message that Stalin was negotiating a dictated peace with the Germans, who had invaded the Soviet Union a few months earlier. Finally Stevenson caught up with the president in Maine. Adlai described the scene to Ellen: "As I walked thru the door [the president] looked up, said, 'Hello Adlai, sorry I missed you at Rockland. Do you know all these people—Mr. Hopkins, (who remembered me), Ad. X, [etc.]'—while I stuttered something like 'Hi Folks'—explained my mission, delivered my papers—hoping he would deem it important enough to ask me to stay on the train & talk with him en route to Wash. He didn't, but took my memoranda, said he would read them tonight . . . whereupon I backed out gurgling some inarticulate sounds." In an embellished version Stevenson delivered the message orally, was asked by the president whether he believed the rumor of a Soviet-Nazi peace, and stammered in response as he bumped into the door, "Why, I don't know, Mr. President."

Both versions revealed Stevenson's habitual deference and sense of the absurd. So did his job description of himself as "legal maid servant" to Secretary Knox. Earlier Stevenson had sought several other jobs in Washington, had been turned down for some, and had refused others—once because he did not consider himself qualified. Even as he described a "restless anxiety to help in some way," his reluctance accommodated a sense of obligations fulfilled for conscience's sake, not for private ambition. Yet he obscured the aspirations that allowed him to recall, twenty years later, that in the news coverage of the Kearny strike his name appeared for the first time in the *New York Times*.

To one Chicagoan who wrote for more details than just "the plain facts of your life," Stevenson replied that there was not much to add. "I have had a good many outside interests, probably too many. For a long while I have been impressed with the necessity for a more general recognition of the growing economic and political inter-dependence of the world." And after eight paragraphs he puckishly concluded, "I like to ride, read, and rest—mostly rest—but in that respect this job has been a bit disappointing." In 1942, when a reporter asked what his duties as Knox's assistant entailed, he responded, "Odd jobs, most unpleasant. Each day I am impressed with how many wiser people there are (in Washington than I). It is good for the ego to get a little deflated and this is the right moment." Only his psyche was deflated. Now of "sparse thatch and ample girth," when Adlai Stevenson registered for the draft in 1942, he measured five feet, ten inches and weighed thirty more pounds than he had twenty-four years before as a shivering seventeen-year-old in the Princeton gym.

In December the Japanese attacked Pearl Harbor. Knox left immediately for Hawaii to assess the damage and blame for a Navy that had kept its ships in the harbor despite warnings of an impending attack. In Washington, Stevenson was left to draft a message to all naval yards, one that irritated labor unions with its cheerleading paternalism: "Speed up—it's your Navy and your Nation." Meanwhile, in Chicago, Ellen was telling her friends that "she wanted out of her marriage." That spring, when Adlai returned from another of his wartime trips, he acknowledged "the unworthy business" of cross-examining one of her male friends. "We are getting older now," he wrote in a conciliatory, patronizing letter, "and the fever of youth is subsiding—don't be alarmed by it & please don't feel that I can't understand your anxiety to find yourself and peace and the feeling of urgency."

Like his marriage, the war was a calamity. The Japanese controlled the Pacific, and their huge air base at Rabaul, on New Britain, in the Bismarck Archipelago, jeopardized shipping routes to New Zealand and Australia. Germany declared war on the United States three days after Pearl Harbor, and the president assigned priority to winning the war in Europe. By the early summer of 1942, the armies of the Third Reich had penetrated deep into Russian territory, with the Sixth German Army driving to reach the oil fields in the Caucasus Mountains near Stalingrad. Meanwhile, like a bulldozer, General Rommel had pushed British forces eastward across northern Africa into Libya, and now threatened Allied control of the Mediterranean after Greece and Yugoslavia had fallen under German authority. At no other time was the future of the Allies as bleak. In anticipation of the worst, Stevenson was sent to evaluate the readiness of the Caribbean defenses in Panama, Guantánamo, and San Juan, the critical outposts in any battle for America.

Seven months later, in January of 1943, Stevenson took a longer trip, this time accompanying Secretary Knox to the South Pacific. Warning Ellen about the need for secrecy, he began a diary, though it was more a traveler's account than an avenue for self-examination, and it lasted only as long as his trip. Excluding any secrets, he commented on his travels as a tourist might—from Pearl Harbor ("many ships in repair—all damage cases—stirring stories") to volcanic Savo (misspelled by Stevenson as Suva), an island in the Solomon chain. By this time the tide of war in the Pacific was shifting.

In June of 1942, Navy carriers and airplanes had turned back the Japanese at Midway. Two months later the First Marine Division had retaken Guadalcanal, the place nobody had heard of before, but everyone would remember after the bloody battles on its death beaches and the seesaw engagements that left the Japanese in control of the island's volcanic peaks for months. By the winter of 1943, plans for a counteroffensive in the Pacific were under way. Decisions about military strategy brought Secretary of the Navy Knox and his assistant to the South Pacific, along with Admiral Chester Nimitz. Obsessed by his "I shall return" pledge, General MacArthur argued that the quickest route to victory was a land-based offensive from New Guinea to the Philippines, while the Navy wanted to move across the central Pacific, combining air strikes from carriers with island assaults that depended on its new landing craft.

Excluded from high-level discussions in New Caledonia and Fiji (where he ran into his Princeton friend Dr. George Finney), Stevenson learned about these issues only when, on his return to Pearl Harbor, Admiral Nimitz turned "loquacious and [told] me more about the technical strategic problems in the Pacific than I've heard on the whole trip." From other officers he heard criticism of the Navy's nemesis—imperious General MacArthur, the commander of the Southwest Pacific Area Command, considered by one admiral as a "good soldier 20 years ago, [but now] egotism 'afraid of me' law unto himself, knows little of ships and the Navy." After hearing both strategies, the Joint Chiefs of Staff approved a dual-pronged attack that by 1945 had established American forces on the Mariana Islands and in Okinawa (Iwo Jima was taken by March of 1945 and Okinawa by June) and in control of the Philippines.

Returned to wartime Washington in the early spring of 1943, Stevenson served as ombudsman for the secretary's office. Unlike two of his fellow Princetonians, flinty, obsessive Undersecretary of the Navy James Forrestal and genial Assistant Secretary of the Navy Ralph Bard, he played no role in decisions on strategy, production, and war material allotment. Nor was he a part of the chain of command in a department that Forrestal modernized. Instead, Adlai Stevenson accomplished humbler tasks, representing the secretary at meetings of the Office of Facts and Figures and the Economic Defense Board. Although he was a shareholder of the Standard Oil Company, he negotiated leases in Elk Hills, California, which gave that company rights to produce petroleum. He lobbied Congress at budget time, and when the secretary asked his staff to provide a list of congressmen "with whom you are on good relations and to whom you could readily go at any time in behalf of a matter in which the Navy might be interested," Stevenson provided the longest list—eleven senators and fourteen congressmen.

In September 1943 Stevenson wrote a memorandum on the department's racial policies, recommending to a reluctant Knox that the Navy, which by this time had enrolled sixty thousand African-Americans, "commission a few negroes . . . and review the rating groups from which negroes are excluded. . . . One reason we have not had the best of the race is the suspicion of discrimination among the negroes and in the Government as well."

Meanwhile he sought a commission as a lieutenant commander in the Naval Reserve, not in order to go into combat but to have more authority in the department. Knox resisted on the grounds that his personal assistant was more useful out of uniform in his dealings with high-ranking naval officers. Again an outsider—a civilian in a military department—Stevenson cheerfully recommended acquaintances who wanted jobs or commissions. He helped fifty-year-old Paul Douglas, the University of Chicago economics professor and Chicago alderman, become a combat marine and wrote endless letters for middle-aged friends. By the time he left Washington in 1944, Stevenson carried home to Libertyville a bulky file labeled "People I helped while in the Navy Dept"—which included three hundred names, along with the service rendered. But he remained convinced that educated men—professionals in seersucker and linen suits like himself—best served the nation in Washington, not on the battlefront.

As Knox's health deteriorated, Stevenson delivered the speeches he wrote for the secretary. Many described the need to give the Navy more credit. To the Chicago Council on Foreign Relations, he noted "the gigantic development of our Navy in the last three years" and declared, "Sea power has saved us from defeat. . . ." But Stevenson also struck cautionary notes about the "disquieting degree of self-confidence" on the home front. "Many people talk and act as though it was all over but the shouting. There are stoppages and strikes; there are black markets all over the country and, what's more, people who profess patriotism frequent them." Such behavior was, according to Stevenson, "undisciplined." To the question "Can we win the war?" he answered, "Not until we have the will to win . . . not as long as the ladies say they have bought the last dress, confident they'll get another when they want it." Stevenson appropriated images from the athletic field: "We've got to clear the decks . . . and hit the ball, for we're in the finals now and it's going to be no game for the faint-hearted."

What distinguished Stevenson's message beyond his moralistic condemnation of the Germans and Japanese as "robbers" of the peace was his attention to the future. With the Soviets an ally, his earlier concerns about communism gave way to predictions of congenial relations with the Soviet Union, now referred to more amiably as Mother Russia. "Russia wants and needs a stable world more, if anything, than we do." Still Stevenson's globalism, even though based on some form of collective security, reserved a special place for U.S. power. Misguided American isolationism had blighted the League of Nations. "But tomorrow is not yesterday. . . . What we are fighting for in essence is peace—a better world in which there are no wars or, at least, fewer wars. . . . Until there is collective force to police the road to the better world, there must be individual force ready and determined to keep order until the community is organized."

With a patrician's appreciation of the differences between the rich and the poor, Stevenson predicted a postwar world of rising expectations among poor nations: "No one has enough food, enough clothing, enough anything—except in the United States of America," he informed a group of Chicago lawyers in a speech that folded domestic liberalism into Wilsonian internationalism. "And now all these people have seen our healthy boys, their clothes, their food, and their equipment. . . . Are they envious; is more and worse trouble in the making, or is there a great opportunity to improve their lot and ours at the same time? The demand is there; is the wisdom here?"

In the winter of 1943–44 Stevenson undertook a third mission overseas, this time detailed by Secretary Knox to the Foreign Economic Administration, which had begun preliminary investigations of its postwar role in Italy's rehabilitation. By this time General Mark Clark's forces had taken Sicily. But moving across the Bay of Naples into Salerno and turning northward up the coast, the Fifth Army had been stymied by the terrain and the Germans' tenacious defense. From the rubble of the tiny village of San Pietro, Adlai Stevenson watched the shelling of Mount Cassino, the formidable German-held fortress built as a Benedictine monastery on a humpbacked mountain in the sixth century. Not until June 1944 was Rome liberated, though the Italian commander Marshal Pietro Badoglio had surrendered his forces nearly a year earlier. In the interim impoverished Italy teetered between the status of a cobelligerent and that of an occupied power, while the Russians insisted that they were entitled to some role in this first liberation.

Stevenson's job was to investigate Italy's economy and politics at a time when Mussolini's successor, Marshal Badoglio, commanded little support among the people and when bread was "everyone's preoccupation." In Naples he contemplated the irony of a huge white-painted "Duce" on the rocks. In Sicily he read the Fascist slogan engraved in stone: "With a dagger in your teeth, a bomb in your hand and a sovereign disdain for danger in your heart—Il Duce." In Naples he saw the effects of the Germans' obliteration of transportation, sewer and water supplies, industry, and food sources. Privately he noted that Italians stood in line to join Togliatti's Stalinist-aligned Communist party, and because the revival of the Italian economy was critical to blocking the Communists, he lamented the Sicilian lemons rotting on the docks. Ever optimistic in hard times (as he was pessimistic in good ones), Stevenson praised the rapidity with which essential services were being restored by Allied forces.

From this trip arose a durable legend about the origins of Stevenson's political involvement, though in fact his epiphany occurred decades earlier when his family had instilled "a congenital taste for public service, politics, politicians and the public trough where my family has been nibbling frugally, albeit, for several generations." During this "ugly" Italian winter of 1943–44, he read in a public opinion poll in *Stars and Stripes* that most Americans disapproved of their sons' going into politics or public service, though they believed military service a civic duty. "From what I had already seen of the war at home, in the Pacific, in the Mediterranean and from what I was still to see in Europe, I've often thought of that morsel of news: fight, suffer, die, squander our substance, yes; but work in peacetime for the things we die for in war, no! . . . Small wonder, I thought, that our 'politics' is no better, and great wonder that it is as good as it is."

As the retreating Germans laid bare, as if skinning a rotten onion, the ruined core of devastated Europe, Stevenson's 122-page "Report of FEA Survey Mission to Italy" called for immediate aid to the Italians. "Delay . . . will only injure local morale, multiply our burdens, prolong the period during which we must feed populations, and impair our larger interest in laying the foundations of enduring peace." Criticizing Washington's ignorance and jurisdictional confusion, he emphasized the need for American assistance and planning by expert advisers in an early formulation of what later became Truman's Point Four Program. But Stevenson's was no Marshall Plan, and he wondered how the American taxpayer could be persuaded "that to help Italy is to help himself." Eight years later, during the 1952 presidential campaign, Senator Joseph McCarthy used this report to charge, outrageously, that Stevenson had supported Italian Communists.

In the spring of 1944 seventy-year-old Frank Knox died from a heart attack, a civilian casualty of the war. Now Stevenson hoped for an appointment as an undersecretary or assistant secretary in the Navy Department's hierarchy. Roosevelt was willing, but Stevenson had never impressed the new secretary, James Forrestal, who, according to George Ball, "hated Stevenson" and "made a fetish of being tough-minded, the kind of thing Adlai most abhorred." As Carl McGowan, who later served in Stevenson's gubernatorial administration, commented, "He kept waiting around to see if he'd be appointed, but . . . Forrestal . . . said 'He's too diffuse.' It's the beginning of this Eastern establishment view that Stevenson was a soft-head. Forrestal, McCloy, Lovett, and Acheson thought of themselves as sharp and sophisticated intelligences. They believe that power, not kind words, decides things. This group was always anti-Stevenson, especially in private conversation. It gets down to the idea that they can't understand a guy that started Harvard Law School and didn't finish."

There were other detractors, among his admirers. A subcommittee of the House chaired by Representative Lyndon Johnson of Texas criticized Stevenson's leases with Standard Oil as too generous to the company. James Douglas, a Princeton and Lake Forest friend who was in the Air Force, spread the word that Stevenson never commanded much responsibility as a personal assistant. John McCloy, a Washington insider who also moved between private and public life, quoted Knox as saying that he hoped to work Stevenson into other committee assignments. "But it just never worked out. I have him working on speeches."

So Adlai Stevenson went home to Libertyville in June 1944, a week after the Allied landings in Normandy. That next-to-last summer of the war, he organized a syndicate to buy the *Chicago Daily News,* Knox's paper. He promised $250,000 of his own, some from Ellen's portfolio, some from his own stocks. Wealthy friends, including the retail magnate Marshall Field, pledged the remainder. But his group's bid of $1,935,000 fell short, its ethical component of what Stevenson referred to as "local ownership, continuity of control and staff support" making little difference to the executors of the Knox estate, who sold instead to a national chain at a higher price. "The force of money took possession of the paper," commented Stevenson darkly. Ready for another tour of duty, he was "at large again to do some government work."

When George Ball, a former colleague from Cutting, Sidley, and Moore, offered Stevenson a deputy's position in the newly organized U.S. Strategic

Survey, he hesitated only a moment. Thus Adlai Stevenson's final wartime service came as part of a team evaluating the effects of World War II's saturation bombing on German munitions production, transportation facilities, and morale. In London, in Paris, and finally in Belgium, just before the Germans struck in their last offensive during the Battle of the Bulge in the Ardennes, Stevenson helped to organize, as Ball's assistant, a survey that involved over a thousand investigators.

Attempting to quantify the effectiveness of one of World War II's new offensive weapons, members of the survey assessed damage reports from Point Blank, the name given to the relentless bombing of Germany delivered by Allied B-17's and B-24's. The eventual conclusions—that raids had not broken German morale and that in some industries, such as the manufacture of tanks, they had made little impact—gathered dust on the shelves of the Pentagon and were neglected by most American policymakers. Lost to public consciousness by the time of the Vietnam War, its lessons were remembered by George Ball, who, as an assistant secretary of state in 1966, opposed the bombing of North Vietnam. Later a young Illinois senator—Adlai Ewing Stevenson III—advanced the same position as he came to oppose the war.

7

In the spring of 1945 the Germans surrendered, and Adlai Stevenson returned to his law firm, assessing his future in glum shorthand: "old, time, bench, college, DA, dull practice—don't know what it is, unhappy, have a right to come back, wouldn't be content to do . . . estates, get clients because competent—not on the basis of friendship." After promising Ellen that he would stay in Chicago, he had within months accepted the poet Archibald MacLeish's invitation to help with public relations for the U.S. delegation at the first formal United Nations conference. In San Francisco, Stevenson served as a briefing officer, officially paid by the State Department he disparaged "as the Third Circle of Hell" to conduct "an underground news leakage office for the U.S. press." His wife visited, contributing a poem in her spare style about the crowd of 285 delegates, 1,450 advisers, 2,600 accredited journalists, including the gossipist Elsa Maxwell, and uncounted onlookers, all intent on observing history in the making: "The press is here / the press is there / Free to speak / Free to stare."

By the time the fifty-nation conference had adjourned to meet in London in the fall, it had created an organizational structure based roughly on that of the League of Nations, though featuring an empowered Security Council. The conference also approved a charter that began with a noble, Stevenson-applauded preamble of hopeful intention for a war-sick world:

"We the peoples of the United Nations determined to save succeeding generations from the scourge of war and to reaffirm faith in fundamental rights and to establish conditions under which justice and respect for the obligations of others and to promote social progress and better standards of life . . ."

Adlai Stevenson had found his postwar mission, but his fellow Americans were wavering in their commitment to the United Nations. Glumly Stevenson feared a repetition of the defeat of the League of Nations treaty in 1920. Hurrying to Washington, where the U.S. Senate had begun debating the United Nations treaty, he briefed witnesses scheduled to testify before the Senate Foreign Relations Committee on how best to respond to the objections that the United Nations unfairly gave the Soviet Union two additional seats in Byelorussia and the Ukraine, that membership could undermine American regional authority in the Western Hemisphere, that American forces could be sent overseas in the name of the fictitious principle of collective security, and that the Security Council provided an undemocratic veto. But by August 1945 isolationism had dwindled, and the Senate approved the treaty by the one-sided vote of 61 to 16. That same month Adlai Stevenson was appointed an adviser to the U.S. Preparatory Commission meeting in London in the fall. Of his efforts to prepare for the first session of the General Assembly, Stevenson wrote, "I'm just a machinist helping to build the complicated machinery of the United Nations. . . ."

For the next two years, while the flesh (in Stevenson's metaphor) was added to the bones of the United Nations, he accepted "piecework," serving in London and later in the UN's first home near Flushing, on Long Island's Lake Success. To inquiring friends Ellen described her husband's positions "as an assistant something." To his law partners, as he left for six months in London, Stevenson gave his full title of Deputy United States Delegate to the Preparatory Commission of the United Nations Organization "with the rank of Minister and some thirty-five to fifty people on the United States staff to direct." To his friends he described his desire "to have a small place near the circle's edge." Though hoping for a loftier position as an alternate delegate by 1946, Stevenson instead played the lesser role of an adviser to the U.S. delegation. In a critical international arena, Stevenson's was not a front-row seat, but rather one on the second row. Still, "it was the most exacting, interesting and in many ways the most important interval of my life," he later wrote.

The United Nations and Adlai Stevenson were a perfect match. In his youth he had learned the necessity of peacemaking in an emotionally tumultuous home. Influenced by Wilson's failed League during his years at Princeton, Stevenson had always believed in some form of organization to settle international disputes through legally agreed upon, morally acceptable, noncoercive means. As he tried to negotiate an unattainable peace in his personal and professional life, Stevenson raised the public failure of the United States to join the League of Nations to a moral delinquency. Now, for a time, he found his future in its successor, acknowledging amid the "golden age of America born in the agony of Pearl Harbor . . . the responsibility that destiny has assigned the United States to bring intelligent leadership among the peoples of the world."

Not by chance did Stevenson compare the United Nations to a troubled "house with a lot of different families in it." By 1946, as Soviet-American relations deteriorated over issues such as Soviet aggression in Iran and American loans to a bankrupt Great Britain but not to the Soviet Union, Stevenson proclaimed an end to the "war-born honeymoon" with the Russians. But his 1926 journey to that nation had implanted a sensitivity to their position, and he believed that the United Nations provided insurance against war. "We must choose to live together or we must choose not to live." He described his role as "one of the jubiliant midwives of the United Nations birth and one of its anxious nurses during its infancy." Wilson, he remembered, "said that permanent peace can grow in only one soil—the soil of actual good will and understanding. He was fond of a story about Charles Lamb who said he hated a certain man. Someone said, 'Why, Charles, I didn't know you knew him.' 'Ah,' he said, 'I don't. I can't hate a man I know.' "

Stevenson was in London when Secretary of State Dean Acheson proposed a new American policy of peacetime aid to Turkey and Greece. The Truman Doctrine and the Marshall Plan were designed to forestall anticipated Russian meddling in Europe. Stevenson was in the United States struggling with the issue of a permanent site for the United Nations when Winston Churchill delivered his "iron curtain" address in Fulton, Missouri. Like most of his generation, he now became a Cold Warrior, though of a slightly different stripe than most. From George Kennan, Stevenson adopted the view that Soviet expansion represented the protective needs of Mother Russia, more than any Marxist-Leninist–inspired aggression against capitalism. Placing his faith in the United Nations as a peacekeeper (even while he privately opposed the Security Council veto used by the Russians to offset the American bloc's power in an organization that until the 1960s nearly always followed American interests), Stevenson understood as cultural difference what other policymakers considered Russian bellicosity. Still, he never wavered in his commitment to containment, a reactive doctrine that suited his style and rhetoric.

The Soviet delegation delayed, according to Stevenson, not to be difficult but because it was on a tight leash from Moscow. While Americans hammered out differences in committee, the Russians, he discovered, waited until the vote to press their objections. Throughout, he remained impressed with his antagonists' discipline. "They never look at the clock, never! They are as good at 4:00 o'clock in the morning as they are at 4:00 o'clock in the afternoon," he marveled to Chicago's Commercial Club. Understanding that the Russians wanted their share, Stevenson acknowledged that "there is no one that can deal with them but us. We must be the peacemaker." Still it was exhausting work. "I'm weary," he wrote his confidante Jane Dick in the fall of 1947, "my eyes ache & I'm still smarting under that two hours of garbage [Vyshinsky, the former prosecutor at the Stalin purge trials] hurled at us this afternoon."

In the spring of 1947 Stevenson entitled a speech to Chicago's Investment Bankers Association "Where Do We Go from Here?" The question was as much personal—for he had just completed his fourth tour of duty with the United Nations mission—as it was political. With the war ended and the creation of the United Nations completed, Stevenson's answers were introspective descriptions of the American condition. He worried not simply about Europe but about the United States and himself. He worried about America's ability to persevere. "Obviously our resources are not inexhaustible. We can't provide everything that is needed everywhere at once, if at all. How much we can spare, how to use it, where to use it, when to use it, is going to require bold, fast thinking . . . ; widespread public education . . . ; and a political courage that doesn't generally characterize national campaign years."

Like the nation and the United Nations, he wasn't sure where he was going, having agreed that his law firm had no obligation to rehire him. And like the strained postwar collaboration, his marriage seemed in danger of collapse. Nor was he certain of any future in the revolving door of government positions he had held, on and off, since 1933. Still, Adlai Stevenson believed in the United Nations, as "the organized conscience and will of the community of nations"—the last best hope of mankind. "With malice toward none," he concluded a speech in Abraham Lincoln's Springfield, "with faith and tolerance, there is nothing to fear but our own default." It would be fourteen years before Adlai Stevenson returned to the United Nations. When he did, his stature as a Democratic presidential candidate and as a leading commentator on national affairs, the latter initiated in the 1940s, had earned him the leading role.

CHAPTER NINE

TALKING SENSE:
The Presidential Campaign of 1952

1

ADLAI STEVENSON'S TERM as governor of Illinois was almost over when, in the scorching July heat, over a thousand mostly male, white, middle-aged Democratic delegates came to Chicago for their party's 1952 national convention. They traveled by train and car from every state in the Union, as well as from the expectant territories of Alaska and Hawaii, and even from those less hopeful of achieving statehood—the District of Columbia, Puerto Rico, the Canal Zone, and the Virgin Islands. Only a few party chieftains could afford to take one of Pan American's propeller planes into Midway Airport, where President Harry Truman was expected by week's end. For most this would be their only national convention, and they brought their families along to enjoy Chicago's Magnificent Mile, the Stockyards, Lake Michigan, and the spectacle of a political circus set, appropriately, in a metropolis whose horizontal expanse, vertical elevation, and massive buildings conveyed power as no other American city could. Once the proceedings began, delegates anticipated days of tedium and nights of drama in the International Amphitheater, at Halsted and Forty-third Streets.

As devoted partisans, increasingly chosen in primaries, more and more of which were binding, delegates looked forward to this Thirty-first Democratic National Convention as an opportunity to meet friends, deliberate about the affairs of their party, and follow the directives of the local and national leaders who controlled the party from the smoke-filled rooms of American imagination. By week's end they would make history by writing a platform and nominating a candidate for president and vice president. In the meantime the delegates must reconcile their differences.

Whatever their bonds as Democrats, the delegates of 1952 were divided by background and belief. One wing represented the party's traditional agrarian base. Hailing from towns and villages mainly in the South and the West, these Democrats, whose views Grandfather Stevenson would have favored, supported light governance, free trade, small enterprise, and the family farm. Another group stood for the working-class minorities of north-eastern cities, and they were more inclined to an activist state. For nearly twenty years the skill of Franklin Roosevelt and the pressures of the Great Depression and World War II had tamed the divisions between these coalitions. But in 1948, at the Democrats' first postwar national convention, disagreements had erupted that nearly demolished the party.

That year, after the passage of a civil rights plank supporting the right of racial minorities "to live and work with the protection of the government," along with pledges supporting an Equal Rights Amendment, southerners had walked out and later formed the Dixiecrat ticket. Led by Strom Thurmond, who advocated "the segregation of the races and the social integrity of each race," the Dixiecrats had terrified party leaders. For over seventy-five years the Democrats had depended on the South to provide 127 electoral votes, half of those needed to win the presidency. At the same time the 1948 platform's sternly anti-Soviet Cold War message and its threadbare extension of New Deal social programs had encouraged another insurgent group—Henry Wallace's Progressives, who sought a less confrontational approach to the Soviets and whose platform promised negotiations "through the United Nations for world disarmament," especially of atomic bombs. Neither faction had done well with the electorate, although the Dixiecrats had carried four southern states and, now established in the minds of voters, might do better in 1952.

Remembering these defections four years earlier, some Democratic leaders demanded a loyalty oath that would force state delegations to support the party's preference, no matter who the candidate and what the platform. Uncertain about their programs and anxious about Korea, where American troops under a United Nations command had been fighting for two years, Democrats in Chicago and elsewhere were also indefinite about their presidential favorite.

What the Democrats needed, the party's wheelhorses insisted as they patrolled the lobby of the newly refurbished Hilton Hotel on Michigan Avenue, was a unity ticket that would heal, not divide. Now that the Republicans had nominated the popular war hero Dwight Eisenhower and the Red-baiting California senator Richard Nixon on a platform that made voting Republican a national priority after twenty years of Democratic administrations, factionalism would destroy any chance of victory. Truman, who might have inspired harmony despite his low standings in the polls, had declined a second full term, though there was agreement that the newly approved Twenty-second Amendment, which limited to two a president's terms, did not apply to him. For the first time since 1932, there was no obvious candidate for the nomination; instead, there emerged a handful of ambitious governors and senators.

Harry Truman presumptuously intended to mandate his successor.

"The President always controls the nomination," Truman generalized, citing Jackson, Hayes, Teddy Roosevelt, Wilson, Franklin Roosevelt, and himself. Disillusioned with Stevenson, the president had tried to place his mantle on the shoulders of his vice president, but leaders of the labor movement promptly dismissed seventy-four-year-old Alben Barkley as too old and too conservative.

With growing intensity the delegates discussed other aspirants: Senator Estes Kefauver of Tennessee had won fourteen of the sixteen presidential primaries, including that in Illinois. But the handshaking senator with the coonskin cap irritated congressional leaders. After his nationally televised hearings on gambling, he had lost the support of some state bosses whose influence was often determinative, especially among delegations using the unit rule, requiring an entire delegation to vote as its majority did. Another possible contender—Senator Richard Russell of Georgia—would never be accepted by northerners. Oklahoma's Senator Robert Kerr was believed the pawn of the oil interests, while New York's ambitious Averell Harriman, who had never held an elective office, might satisfy blacks, progressives, and members of the influential postwar interest group—the Americans for Democratic Action—but southerners might defect again. No longer the harmonious constellation set in Franklin Roosevelt's orbit, the Democrats of 1952 starred interest groups and regional coalitions, as they searched through their alternatives on the eve of the convention.

From party leaders and the writers who shaped postwar opinion through their syndicated columns, delegates frequently heard the name of Adlai Stevenson, the man who said he did not want the nomination. Just two weeks before the convention, the governor had written Barry Bingham, the influential editor of the Louisville *Courier-Journal,* that he "was more anxious every day to keep out of the presidential business," acknowledging, though there was still time to do so, "[my] tragic mistake not to indicate long before this that I could accept the nomination under no possible circumstances." They read as well Alicia Patterson's column in *Newsday* about her interview with Stevenson: "I have talked to the Governor several times over the past weeks and he is a human in sore distress. He does not want the nomination; neither does he want to serve notice that if drafted he would refuse to run. 'How can I do that,' he asked me, 'when young men are dying in Korea?' "

Stevenson's supporters on the seventh floor of the Hilton Hotel insisted that he would accept a draft. A man of such distinguished Democratic credentials and cultivated sense of duty could hardly refuse the party's highest honor. Still, the governor's cause needed priming among the delegates—for no one wanted to waste a vote on a noncombatant. To make sure that he was nominated, Adlai's Amateurs, his unauthorized surrogates associated with the Independent Voters of Illinois, followed the traditional practices of other contenders. They rented hotel space for their headquarters, handed out soda pop to visitors, placed a copy of *Life's* recent complimentary article on every delegate's seat, and instructed volunteers on how to answer inquiries about their no longer dark horse. They printed a glossy folder highlighting (for Eisenhower had only military experience) their man's administrative ability. Their slogan—"A Great Governor; A Great Candidate; An Able Administrator—Experienced in Both Democratic and International Affairs"—summarized what they believed to be Stevenson's strengths.

While some party professionals were attracted to this peculiar noncandidate, others believed that the Stevenson operation displayed its inexperience, lack of money, and lack of proper respect for the professionals and their influence on the outcome. The amateurs had not rented enough phones; the rapidly disappearing red-and-white buttons hedged by carrying not the office Stevenson sought but only his last name, in case he ran for the Illinois governorship, as he ardently wished to do. More damaging, when the nominee had arrived from Springfield for the convention, he said, "I shall never be a candidate in the sense that I'll ask anybody to vote for me here. On the contrary, I'll do everything possible to discourage any delegate from putting me in nomination or nominating me." In modern electoral politics, such a statement—even though it did not rule out a draft—could be interpreted as a snobbish disclaimer of any interest in the nomination.

A member of the fifty-five man, six-woman Illinois delegation, the object of this attention took up residence during the convention on fashionable Astor Street in the brick mansion of the family of his friend and administrative assistant William McCormick Blair. In a second-floor bedroom overlooking an elegant urban garden on Chicago's near North Side (and down the block from his ex-wife's apartment) Stevenson worked and, as was his habit, reworked the welcoming address to be delivered on the first day of the convention, seemingly unaware of the uproar at the foot of the block. There cables and lights, telephone wires and electrical outlets—all the electronic paraphernalia of the media—were being installed. Democratic delegates might be uncertain about their nominee, but the press sniffed a Stevenson victory. On Sunday afternoon the governor joined the Illinois delegation at a secret caucus at Democratic headquarters in the Morrison Hotel. The press followed.

By Illinois law prospective delegates running in the state's closed party primary were required to list their presidential preference on the primary ballot, if they had one. (At-large delegates were chosen by county conventions and were bound by the unit rule.) Most had run as uncommitted, a few as Kefauver men, but even after the senator from Tennessee won the state's uncontested presidential primary, Illinois delegates were not legally bound to vote for him in the convention. Now, with the possibility of a native son as the Democratic nominee, excited party members convened to consider their choice.

Discovering a space between the floor and the sliding partition to the meeting room, eavesdropping reporters heard Adlai Stevenson deny his suitability for the presidency. "I do not dream myself fit for the job—temperamentally, mentally, or physically. And I ask therefore that you abide by my wishes not to nominate me, nor to vote for me if I should be nominated." It was Jack Arvey who responded that the Illinois delegation might not nominate him, but "you can't take away my vote in the interests of the Democratic party." If someone else nominated Stevenson—an influential party man like David Lawrence of Pennsylvania, Governor Henry Schricker of Indiana, or even the young hotspur Hubert Humphrey from Minnesota—then Illinois delegates would vote for him. Stevenson's reply was inaudible, but he instructed his alternate to vote for Harriman.

The next day Stevenson followed Chicago's mayor to a podium that extended into the audience, like a model's walkway, all the better to show off party leaders on the television cameras that for the first time were carrying the proceedings into nearly one-third of the nation's households. No orator, Mayor Kennelly woodenly welcomed the delegates to his city: "We are highly honored to have been chosen as the host city for the national nominating conventions of 1952. . . . Everything that could be done has been done to make you comfortable."

Then Governor Adlai Stevenson, dressed in a pin-striped suit, his blue silk tie decorated with tiny white donkeys, advanced to the microphone in the bos'n walk that some characterized as a waddle. Six minutes of cheering and shaking of "Stevenson for President" and "Twenty Years of Security" and "Don't Let Them Take It Away" placards by the Illinois delegation seated in front drew a quip: "I thought I came to welcome you, not you me." Clearing his throat and running his hand down his coat collar in his customary marks of nervousness, which disappeared after he began, Adlai Stevenson welcomed the Democrats to Illinois. By the time he finished, he had been interrupted by applause twenty-seven times. The man who, according to the columnist James Reston, had been trying "to talk himself out of the Democratic Presidential nomination for the last five months, talked himself right into the leading candidate's role this morning."

Nearly the last of the favorite sons and serious candidates to be nominated three days later, Stevenson was presented to delegates as a vice president's grandson, having "inherited a fine tradition of public service," "a superbly educated man with the educated man's access to the best contemporary political and social thinking," a capable governor who "has never sought public office, nor does he now." When the voting began, interrupted by the continuing squabble over the loyalty oath and the seating of four recusant southern states, Stevenson did not win on the widely divided first ballot. Instead Kefauver led. On the second ballot, Stevenson gained.

As a consensus candidate, he was attractive to liberals for his bold stand against McCarthyism and encroachments on civil liberties, to conservatives and southerners (if they could not have a distant cousin of his, Georgia's Richard Russell) for his lack of activism on civil rights for women and blacks, to labor (if they could not have New York's Averell Harriman) for his objections to the Taft-Hartley Act, and to party bosses (if they could not have Truman) for his friendship with the Illinois leader Jack Arvey and his potential as a moderate capable of keeping the party unified. Everyone admired his eloquence, his governorship, his support of New Deal programs, and his roots in a state with twenty-eight electoral votes, the fourth-largest number in the nation. The reluctant candidate had become the inevitable one.

Friday morning Adlai Ewing Stevenson was nominated on the third ballot after Harriman released his delegates. Then, with Stevenson's approval, the delegates nominated as vice president Senator John Sparkman, the son of a tenant farmer from Alabama, where the slogan "white supremacy" still appeared at the top of the party ballot above the traditional rooster.

Three days earlier Stevenson had suspected that he would win. With patrician politeness he had called Truman to inform the astonished president, who said, in his report of their conversation, "I have been trying since January to get you to say that. Why would it embarrass me?" By this time the governor had begun writing his acceptance speech. On Wednesday he remained secluded, communicating by limerick with the press: "There was an old man named Adlay / Who wanted to be Governor badly / Said he with dismay / Tho my heart's far away / I'll give a prize for a last line—gladly."

On Friday, as he left his "Blair House" to accept the nomination, Stevenson spoke from a nearby porch, apologizing to reporters for their "vigil" and acknowledging the "poor talents" he would now offer to his country. "I did not seek it. I did not want it. . . . I feel no exultation and no sense of triumph whatever." Arrived in the amphitheater amid the roars of the delegates (from the Trumans' box Buffie Ives watched a solitary Kefauver balloon drifting out of sight), after Truman's introduction of "this able, capable man . . . who hasn't made any deals with anybody," the fiscal conservative Adlai Ewing Stevenson accepted the Democrats' nomination and moderate platform. The latter neither extended the civil rights platform of 1948 nor the New Deal programs of Social Security, federal housing, agricultural parity, and public assistance. For the first time since the New Deal, similar programs had been endorsed by the Republicans.

Meanwhile, in the mountains near Fraser, Colorado, Dwight Eisenhower was fishing with his Republican friends. Someone had a radio and tuned in the Democratic convention. As they listened to Stevenson, Eisenhower was impressed, but one of the party remarked that the governor of Illinois would be easy to beat: "He's too accomplished an orator." No one would ever accuse Eisenhower of that.

While Stevenson and Eisenhower shared freshman status in national politics in 1952 as well as a personal attractiveness that had boosted their careers, they were different men. Eisenhower had grown up in a lower-middle-class family of six sons on the other side of the railroad tracks in Abilene, Kansas. His informality and simplicity made him more a native son of the Midwest than the urbane Stevenson was. Despite his humble beginnings, the general's education at West Point in the years before World War I had been technical, and he pursued his military career with single-minded determination, impressing superiors like George Marshall with his administrative abilities and reliability. Along the way he adopted from the military culture a style of intense preoccupation and long hours of work set off by periods of inactivity and leisure.

Accustomed to taking orders, familiar with the uses of public relations, and suspicious of both generalizations and rhetoric, Eisenhower had at first denied any interest in what he dismissed as "this political business." Eventually he had been persuaded by the powerful Republicans Henry Cabot Lodge and Thomas Dewey along with the publisher Henry Luce and the prominent businessmen John Hay Whitney and L. B. Maytag to leave his position as Supreme Allied Commander in Europe to save the country from the Democrats. Once launched on his first political campaign, the man with a genius for popularity, a schoolboy's grin, and a reputation as the most admired man in America fought with the determination of a hardened field commander against the entrenched forces of Ohio's senator Robert Taft to win the Republican nomination.

By any calculation, his opponent Adlai Stevenson had been drafted, though Stevenson had enrolled himself in national politics with his eloquent partisanship and covert aspirations. The governor had done little to get the nomination; on the other hand, he had not done much to prevent it, and so entered the campaign with his benighted nineteenth-century notion intact that men must be chosen for office, not seek it. In fact, activities such as giving speeches to influential Democratic audiences at fund-raisers, writing feature articles for national magazines, and refusing to deny his availability had titillated his supporters and advanced ambitions originating in a family-inspired sense of duty.

Nor had he offered a bland journeyman's speech to the delegates. Instead, his entirely partisan, up-and-to-the-polls exhortation had attacked the Republicans as deeply divided between the conservative isolationism of Senator Taft and the internationalism of General Eisenhower. To responsive delegates he had dismissed the Republican program as one of "pompous phrases . . . in search of an idea." In the past, welcoming speeches had been restrained and parochial, hardly intended to draw attention to the speaker. Now, appealing to delegates wearied of stale rhetoric, Stevenson elevated the Democrats' national contributions into "the American story, written by the Democratic Party"—"the party of the people, that of everyone."

Throughout he behaved as an activist descendant of his grandfather Adlai Stevenson I, a candidate for a presidential draft intent on escaping the memories of his father's thwarted ambitions and on restoring the tradition of Stevenson public service. In the end he had spoken to himself, quoting in his welcoming address from Justice Holmes, with whom he had once spent an afternoon. "We must sail sometimes with the wind, sometimes against it; but we must sail and not drift or lie at anchor."

Before the convention Stevenson had created for himself a personal dilemma, a moral test of his probity that must, on the moment of his nomination, be resolved by his sense of obligation. The test was not obscure. While he may have hidden from the press during the convention, through his earlier speeches he disclosed his character, his personality, and his values. In the campaign that followed, he urged the Democrats' 1952 agenda—increasing parity prices, attacking the divided Republican party, reforming the Taft-Hartley Act, and supporting Truman's version of Soviet containment through the Marshall Plan, aid to Greece and Turkey, and the war in Korea. But beyond the issues Adlai Stevenson offered himself and the American people a spiritual pilgrimage in the unusual setting of a political campaign.

For Adlai Stevenson the campaign trail became a moral test, a journey undertaken amid the constant temptation of pandering to the people and playing the demagogue in order to be elected. As he told an unsympathetic audience of American Legionnaires, who preferred more concrete expressions of martial sentiment: "The road we travel is long, but at the end lies the grail of peace. And in the valley of peace we see the faint outlines of a new world, fertile and strong. It is odd that one of the keys to abundance should have been handed to civilization on a platter of destruction. But the power of the atom to work evil gives only the merest hint of its power for good."

Stevenson did not, as he acidly informed the governor of Texas, Allan Shivers, who wanted to trade electoral support in return for Stevenson's backing of state ownership of offshore oil lands recently granted by court decision to the federal government, "*have* to win." In his acceptance speech when he called on the delegates, the party, and himself to "talk sense to the American people," to "tell them the truth," Stevenson established the paradox of the puritan in politics who would never bargain for votes despite the demands of modern electoral politics. Viewed from this perspective, the campaign became his calling. With an arrogance that irritated some professional politicians, Adlai Stevenson believed that the "single greatest diffi-culty about running for responsible public office is how you can win without, in the process, proving yourself unworthy of winning." "Better we lose the election than mislead the people," he said, warning delegates that "a responsible political party has a greater responsibility than winning votes at any price."

Surely, according to his detractors who found such Wilsonian idealism distasteful, it was possible to win the election and not deceive. And if it wasn't, then why was he in politics? Employing the spiritual idiom that marked this campaign, Stevenson found his answer to this dilemma of "the staggering task" that he had been assigned in the Book of Micah. "I shall always try 'to do justly and to love mercy and to walk humbly with my God.' "

Unlike most politicians, candidate Stevenson wore no mask, and wear-ing none he refused the performances that permitted a politician like Ke-fauver the ease of sitting on a campaign bus, pulling down his visor, putting on his sunglasses, and going to sleep between appearances, only to wake with a start and reflexively extend a handshake to hundreds, including, for the third time, his bus driver. Stevenson disdained such "Hallowe'en masks." During his odyssey no visible line extruded between his public displays of speechmaking and meeting the people and his private character-istics of wit, charm, intelligence, moodiness, and uncertainty. The Adlai of Libertyville was the same man as the Democratic nominee for president. To the dismay of Harry Truman, this Democratic candidate believed he had "full freedom of action and was uncompromising in being himself."

Considering himself a messenger of policies, positions, and visions, Ste-venson felt no need to disguise himself. Ironically—for he disapproved of personalist politics—the candidate who found posturing in others distaste-ful presented himself as himself to voters at a time of diminishing party loyalty and increasing interest in the character of leaders. As often as he drew from his hero Woodrow Wilson's New Freedom, or Franklin Roose-velt's New Deal and Harry Truman's Fair Deal rhetoric, his texts were the Bible, the Presbyterian Prayer Book, a Unitarian language absorbed in his childhood, and the evocative quotations gathered by friends and staff scrib-bled in a black notebook. His theme became a self-defined search for moral-ity that he encouraged other Americans to join; and his reference point, a personal experience burdened by his own private dilemmas.

Some observers—Harry Truman was one—believed him indecisive and compared him to Hamlet, though what he shared with the Prince of Den-mark was not uncertainty but self-disclosure. Rarely indecisive about mat-ters of policy, Stevenson publicly shared the private matters that some men told their wives and others told no one. As in his campaign for the gover-norship, he displayed himself through his speeches. By the end of the campaign, the *New Republic* had discovered "a political Peter Pan . . . a candidate who makes no distinction between his political personality and his private personality." The editors predicted such a stance would gain him "respect and stature" among a special audience.

Others, especially the clergy, also understood that there was no demarcation in this man between public display and private personality. Hearing his two addresses to the convention, the archbishop of Chicago, Samuel Cardinal Stritch, caught the references to Saint Francis, to grace and sin, to the presidency as the greatest "temporal" office on earth, to the postwar period as the "most turbulent era of the Christian age," and, more audaciously, to Christ's words at Gethsemane applied to his own conflict: "I have asked the Merciful Father—the Father of us all—to let this cup pass from me," he said in his acceptance speech. "But from such dread responsibility one does not shrink in fear, in self-interest, or in false humility. So 'If this cup may not pass from me, except I drink it, Thy will be done.' " Many Christians were outraged by the arrogance of such a comparison. Joseph Alsop was so disgusted he "was literally driven to drink." But Stritch wrote the governor a few days after the convention, "In your own charming way you unwittingly gave to the country a master portrait of yourself."

After the convention, as the delegates straggled home, Stevenson returned to Springfield. With the memories of what he dismissed as "the tumult and the shouting," he went alone to sit for several hours in Abraham Lincoln's house. The hard-boiled Alsops, who had followed the nominee to Springfield along with other members of the press, were increasingly alarmed by Stevenson's identification with Lincoln, having a "steadfast rule that when American politicians began bracketing themselves with Abraham Lincoln it was always well to send for a psychiatrist." But this was after the fact. At the time an admiring Joseph Alsop added Stevenson's acceptance speech to Roosevelt's first inaugural in 1933 and the president's stirring call to arms after the Japanese attack on Pearl Harbor in 1941 to his list of great twentieth-century speeches.

Stevenson's friends believed his unusual approach to politics a reflection of his class and status. When he spoke of the "hard road," they marveled that this old-monied aristocrat had exchanged leisurely encounters with high society at one of his five clubs (two in Chicago, one each in Lake Forest, New York, and Washington) for the harried attendance at ward meetings with politicians like Botchy Connors and Paul Powell. The Lake Forest blue bloods and postwar idealists understood that the former corporate lawyer seemed distant and aloof with the masses because of his sheltered background in prep schools, an Ivy League college, and the oldest and most prestigious law firm in the city. He had other private roads he could travel with fewer mountains to climb.

Later Stevenson acknowledged the political path as "lonely. I never met anyone coming the other way." Dean Acheson, the Groton- and Harvard-educated secretary of state, wrote the candidate a note of patrician understanding: "A hard road opens. You have answered the call of conscience and whatever rewards are internal ones," to which Stevenson replied, "The road is hard. . . . But I have loved the stars too fondly to be fearful of the night."

2

THE CAMPAIGN BEGAN immediately. Proud that he had traded no promises for convention votes, Stevenson soon learned that political independence came with a price. He had neither organization nor staff, and he liked to write his own speeches or, as time went on, edit what others had written. Meanwhile the Republicans had initiated what Eisenhower called, his military language now adopted to an adroit campaign burnishing the weapons of radio and television, "the Republican crusade." Organizing their effort to win the White House around a cohesive strategic plan, the Republicans followed two rules—"Attack, Attack, Attack" and "Negativize Stevenson and Truman."

By August, Stevenson was still dealing with matters of organization, personnel, and scheduling: he replaced the chairman of the Democratic committee, Frank McKinney, with Stephen Mitchell, another of his amateurs; he auditioned the most talented cast of political speech writers ever assembled in a presidential campaign, a group that included Arthur M. Schlesinger Jr., John Kenneth Galbraith, and John Bartlow Martin; he chose as his campaign manager Wilson Wyatt, a member of the Americans for Democratic Action and the former federal housing administrator, and as his personal campaign manager Carl McGowan, a former Northwestern University law professor, who had been in his gubernatorial administration; he picked his personal friends Barry Bingham and Jane Dick to head the Volunteers for Stevenson, the arm of his issue-oriented independents, who, inexplicably, would be delegated authority over his television appearances.

Seeking the autonomy that remained a personal requirement, Stevenson distanced himself from Truman, whom he believed unpopular and tainted by corruption. To do so he established his headquarters not in Washington or even Chicago but in a small brick house with one telephone at the corner of Cook and Fifth Streets in Springfield, marked by a tiny, 15- by 25-inch black sign with the words "Stevenson for President" barely visible above the weeds.

In a press conference in Springfield's St. Nicholas Hotel, Stevenson met with reporters after his nomination. They inquired about his baggy, ill-fitting suit (a gift from a friend in Spain), his convention floor leader, former Senator Frank Myers of Pennsylvania (who?), his position on the Taft-Hartley Act (labor's "bane" needed to be revised), and his resignation from the governorship (what had Dewey done in 1948?) and, finally, whether his divorce would affect the election. To the latter question the second divorced presidential candidate in American history replied, "I wouldn't think so." In fact, there were already rumors that Ellen Borden Stevenson would support Eisenhower and was, in the language of mental illness often applied to her by her former husband, "on the rampage." Asked if he would wage a Trumanesque campaign and "give 'em hell," Stevenson replied that he did not think that was where his talents lay.

To his friends, Stevenson acknowledged a "troubled heart," along with shudders "at what it means psychologically for me and publicly for the record," "that I cannot hope to do my writing *in toto* myself any longer." Throughout his campaign he demoted his writers to the role of researchers, "secretly and unconsciously," as one noted, "resenting us." Forever editing, he weighted his sometimes drifting oratory with long sentences that averaged over thirty words. Usually he failed to provide the morning newspapers with climactic themes for headlines. And though he attacked Eisenhower for using secondhand material, he merited similar criticism. His advisers joked that Stevenson would rather write than be president.

The famous symbol of the 1952 Stevenson campaign—the Pulitzer Prize–winning photograph of the candidate sitting on a platform in Flint, Michigan, with a hole in his shoe and no sole on his heel, intended to portray Stevenson's notorious frugality and hard work—missed the true sign: that the candidate was not smiling or waving or even looking at the audience, much less pointing at individuals in the personal salute often affected by politicians. Instead, minutes before he took the podium, his head was bowed, his eyes focused on the printed message he would soon deliver, his pencil ready for additions to, or deletions from, his text. Sometimes his last-minute changes numbered over a hundred, until the typewritten pages were difficult to read. His speeches were never final until delivered, in contrast to his opponent, who never wanted to see his speeches until he delivered them.

Bradford Jacobs, a young Baltimore *Sun* correspondent assigned to cover the Stevenson campaign, remembered a typical fly-in. On the ground below, the local crowd had assembled at the airport, the high school band ready to salute the candidate with a Sousa march or his campaign song "If You Knew Adlai." As the pilot prepared to land the four-engine propeller American Airlines plane, word came from the cabin where the secretaries were hurriedly typing the last corrections. The candidate was not satisfied with the speech. While Stevenson edited and the mimeograph machine cranked out a final version, the plane circled and circled. On the ground Stevenson's greeters slowly trickled away. By the time the adverbs and adjectives were in place, the crowd was not. When Stevenson finally stepped from the plane, only the mayor and a few fervent Democrats were on hand for the motorcade to town.

Stevenson saw this process differently: "You must emerge, bright and bubbling with wisdom and well-being, every morning at 8 o'clock, just in time for a charming and profound breakfast talk, shake hands with hundreds, often literally thousands, of people, make several inspiring, 'newsworthy' speeches during the day, confer with political leaders along the way and with your staff all the time, *write at every chance,* think if possible, read mail and newspapers, talk on the telephone, talk to everybody, dictate, receive delegations, eat, with decorum—and discretion!—ride through city after city on the back of an open car, smiling until your mouth is dehydrated by the wind, waving until the blood runs out of your arm, and then bounce gaily, confidently, masterfully into great howling halls, shaved and all made up for television with the right color shirt and tie—I always forgot—and a manuscript so defaced with chicken tracks and last-minute jottings that you couldn't follow it, even if the spotlights weren't blinding and even if the still photographers didn't shoot you in the eye every time you looked at them."

American politicians were supposed to enjoy such encounters with the populace. In his distaste for stumping, Stevenson set himself apart from what he once called "the garden variety of opportunistic politician who charges off looking for a distant pasture whenever he hears a distant bell." Many voters sensed his aloofness. John Hersey, who contributed several speeches, described Stevenson's fatal flaw as "his inability to adequately acquire the common touch so as to reach all levels of society," while a public relations expert believed that Stevenson made people feel inferior by insisting too often that he was inadequate. "The more I saw him," wrote the columnist Joseph Alsop, "the more I thought of the world he came from: the cultivated, old-fashioned only-WASP-family-in-town world where cast iron deer adorned every front lawn and ladies in white-lace dresses and lingerie hats took tea and finger sandwiches under the elms. American upper-class genteel was the note, and I had long ago concluded that one could not be a serious politician and be genteel."

Intent on creating carefully crafted political essays graced with complex vocabulary—the language of the university, the Washington-based institutes, and the nation's best writers (two of whom, Archibald MacLeish and John Hersey, were among his speech writers), Stevenson paid no attention to the important consideration of advancing himself as a future president. Always the presentation of his words was secondary to the words themselves. Immediately the Republicans created a negative image of the Democratic candidate as a wordy, indecisive, highbrow, aristocratic amateur. In cartoons he was depicted as Harry Truman's errand boy, "the Little Joker," a young child in an Eton collar and Lord Fauntleroy suit, a giggling girl in a petticoat and a spinsterish female on a couch wooing the independent voter.

Unknown to either candidate, this was the last presidential campaign in which the amount of money spent on radio exceeded that spent for television. From the beginning the Republicans had adapted their efforts to both mediums, hiring Batten, Barton, Durstine and Osborn, the largest advertising firm in the world. Outspending the Democrats by nearly three to two, the Republicans offered party propaganda as entertainment, though their version of "I like Ike" never displaced *I Love Lucy* in the affections of viewers, who complained when a Republican special cut fifteen minutes from America's favorite show. Employing short spots, martial music, and a March of Time newsreel format with scenes from their candidate's illustrious military career, the Republicans associated their candidate with heroic moments of his past. By election day they had reached more American homes than the Democrats had, in a transitional campaign that revealed how soon the set speeches the first two Adlai Ewing Stevensons preferred would be replaced by studio appearances and living room viewing.

In one program Eisenhower "answered the nation," responding to staged questions in a homespun manner. "But aren't the Democrats motives good?" inquired one woman. "Well," grinned Ike, radiating likability, "the driver of the bus may have good intentions, but if he runs you off the road, it's time to get a new driver." When another average American asked about the cost of living, Eisenhower replied, "My wife Mamie worries about the same thing. I tell her it's our job to change that on November 4th." The Republican election eve extravaganza, costing $627,000 with its songs and celebrities, presented politics as entertainment rather than edification as Stevenson intended.

Meanwhile the Democrats placed their advertising account with a small Baltimore firm that, in the spirit of Stevensonian frugality, sought to lower costs by preempting large slots of time. Accordingly Americans were most likely to see and hear Stevenson between ten-thirty and eleven at night. The man who wrote after the election that the people would be best served "if a party purchased a half hour of radio and TV silence during which the audience would be asked to think quietly for themselves" was no electronic match for the Republicans.

The Democratic election eve program revealed the difference between the parties and their candidates when Stevenson and his son John Fell desultorily made conversation on expensive prime time. Both said that they would rather watch television than appear on it, though Stevenson did not own a set at the time. Then the Democratic candidate for president turned to his running mate and asked what Sparkman, who had been campaigning feverishly in the South, had been "up to." Only then did he launch his political remarks, which characteristically ran too long.

Throughout the campaign Stevenson remained suspicious of television and film, disliking—for he must be himself—acting or dissimulation. He declined makeup, which his opponent wore under protest, though he sometimes donned blue shirts for his television appearances. He continued to wear his glasses, while Eisenhower changed to distinctive owl-like horn rims. Eisenhower was coached by the film star Ronald Coleman. Stevenson, despite his appeal to Hollywood stars like Lauren Bacall and Humphrey Bogart, refused lessons in the new art of electronic projection. Ill at ease with teleprompters, he several times abruptly halted in mid-sentence, scowling as something he disliked, but had not had time to edit, rolled by on the teleprompter.

Mostly his speeches were not available in time to be placed on the new invention that transformed stilted political oratory into smooth informal conversation with the voters. Refusing to tailor his remarks to the implacable seconds and minutes for which his volunteers had prepaid, Stevenson was frequently cut off the air when he ran out of time. Agonized by his friend's television performances, William Blair, who was congratulated on those rare occasions when Stevenson finished on time, often found himself too upset to watch.

Even the Democratic party's films seemed contrived and old-fashioned. One featured three voters caught in an elevator, with the predictable result that by the time they reached safety all supported Stevenson. Another re-created the story of a twentieth-century Rip Van Winkle who, having slept through the New Deal, awoke just in time to rally behind the continuation of its programs under Stevenson.

On August 27 Stevenson officially opened his nine-week pilgrimage with a speech before the American Legion Convention in New York. By this time he had a plan to educate the American people and especially the independent voters, who made up a quarter of the electorate. Never did he consider the campaign a tactical struggle culminating on election day; rather, it was a fall seminar for the people. Nor, though Stevenson worked hard, did he travel as much, make as many speeches, or hold as many news conferences as Eisenhower.

During September he planned to address issues relating to agriculture, regionalism, equal rights, and foreign policy, especially considering Korea, and in October he would present a close analysis of specific partisan differences on the order of the Lincoln-Douglas debates. But after the Associated Press received a schedule of Eisenhower's itinerary and asked for one of Stevenson's, his managers admitted that they didn't know *where* they would be next Saturday, only what their man stood for. Believing campaigns the measure of the man, the columnist Mary McGrory wondered what the lassitude and confusion of the Stevenson camp might portend in the White House.

The day before Stevenson's speech to the American Legion, "the great General" (never referred to by name by Stevenson and soon demoted to "general" or simply "my opponent") addressed the group, extravagantly promising to liberate Europe by somehow rolling back the advances of communism in Eastern Europe. It was an attractive appeal to millions of ethnic voters of Polish and East European heritage. The veterans of the American Legion cheered such Cold War impossibilities. Their convention had already adopted bellicose resolutions denouncing Secretary of State Acheson and calling for a military victory in Korea and a NATO-sponsored warning to the Soviets.

In his turn at the podium, Stevenson promised the Legionnaires a strong national defense and a continuation of American leadership in the world. Then, in a tactic that so persistently defined his speeches that his writers learned that the best way to get a point into a speech was to tell Stevenson that his audience would not like it, he lectured "my fellow Legionnaires" on the meaning of patriotism. Love of country must not become public irresponsibility, he advised, or "short, frenzied outbursts of emotion," or "a club for attacking other Americans," or claims for favoritism. Even Samuel Johnson's familiar complaint that patriotism—the very core of Legionnaire communality—could be the last refuge of scoundrels was quoted. "I should tell you . . . as I would tell all other organized groups, that I intend to resist pressures from veterans, too, if I think their demands are excessive," he told his now sullen Madison Square Garden audience.

The speech had been written by the poet Archibald MacLeish, but in its Stevensonian adaptation it carried the candidate's penitential style of telling audiences precisely what they did not wish to hear. In his childhood Adlai Stevenson had learned the virtues of self-criticism, and so throughout the campaign he offered the language of business to labor, remarking that "goons and violence and property damage are as wrong and as intolerable in labor disputes as anywhere else." In New Haven he promised an audience of loyal party men that he would support only worthy Democratic candidates. In New Orleans he spoke on civil rights and tidelands oil. At a town hall luncheon in Los Angeles, he informed party activists that the people got the kind of leaders they deserved. "Your public servants serve you right; indeed often they serve you better than your apathy and indifference deserve." The first presidential candidate ever to address a Harlem audience, he shelved a speech on brotherhood and desegregation written by John Martin and delivered some vague comments on the Bill of Rights. Before an audience cheering "I like Ike" in Wisconsin, he attacked the state's U.S. senator Joseph McCarthy as a "sinister figure of the Inquisition" who pilloried the innocent and made suspicions into facts. Before long Adlai Stevenson emerged as a brave idealist who asked for votes "not because I offer promises of peace and progress, but because I don't."

Stevenson even declined the obligatory Al Smith dinner in New York, at which both candidates traditionally paid homage to the Catholic archbishop Francis Spellman. "For God's sake," he exploded, "don't you believe we're going to win with such a big vote that that kind of noxious business isn't necessary?" Such independence aggravated the church's distrust of a divorced man. Meanwhile Stevenson criticized what he considered the opposition's unethical behavior: Eisenhower's "versatility" and Nixon's "flexibility" on issues on which he took only one position. To this reversal of the usual political trimming, there was one exception. In deference to the Kennedys, who had close ties to McCarthy, grounded in a shared religion and Joseph Kennedy's acceptance of the Communist witch-hunt, Adlai Stevenson did not condemn the Wisconsin senator in Massachusetts.

At the end of a West Coast campaign trip, on September 11, Stevenson was scheduled to speak in Los Angeles on political morality, hoping to ride what the *Illinois State Register* perceptively called "God's coattails." The speech was intended as a response to the Republican hammering on the second "C" of their triad—K1, C2—that is, Korea, communism, and corruption. By this time the Republicans had added a third C, with which Stevenson had some sympathy—change after twenty years of Democratic administrations. Because California was a critical state, with the third-largest number of electoral votes, the Stevenson campaign planned a whistle-stop from San Francisco to Los Angeles, the kind of traditional politicking that had been perfected by Harry Truman in 1948. At the time Ike and Mamie (the latter once viewed in curlers) were also touring the United States in a whistle-stop campaign modeled after Truman's with the candidate appearing from the last car of his "Look Ahead Neighbor" Pullman car to make a few genial comments about the mess in Washington and to invite the crowd to join his "crusade." Then he was off to the next town.

Stevenson, it was expected, would do the same—appearing from the last car, saying a few words about his California roots, recognizing the local industry or crop, asking for votes, and then inviting local leaders on board for a brief but flattering visit, after which the whistle would blow and his four-car train would inch forward as the candidate waved farewell. Eight stops of ten or fifteen minutes were planned as the train wended its way southward through central California.

His appearance of September 11 began inauspiciously with Stevenson apologizing for the early hour and the method of campaigning, which he clearly considered inferior to set speeches because of its abbreviated opportunities for instruction. By noon, as the train moved south, a surprised candidate announced that he was having a good time and was "not ashamed of it." Then he retreated into his car to rework his remarks for the next audience. While local officials fumed on the platform and once mistook his bald campaign manager, Wilson Wyatt, for the candidate, advisers told Stevenson that he must either repeat himself or speak extemporaneously. Ill at ease without a text to separate him from his listeners, he worried about making a mistake and boring his audiences, forgetting that his grandfather and William Jennings Bryan had given the same speech over and over.

Stevenson hated to speak spontaneously to groups of strangers; the chances for the meandering verbless syntax that soon characterized his opponent's press conferences were too great, though he did reuse a punch line: "I [will] make a proposition to my Republican friends. . . . If they will stop telling lies about the Democrats, I will stop telling the truth about them." Borderline Democrats in conservative Bakersfield, he dosed with bad-tasting medicine: the need to end racial discrimination and an analysis of the policy differences between conservative Republicans and liberal Democrats, which embarrassed Bakersfield's centrist Democrats. Meanwhile his writers tried but failed to produce satisfactory all-purpose whistle-stop remarks, similar to the expandable standard speech of Richard Nixon.

Calling himself a bald fat man from Illinois and wondering aloud why anyone would push through a crowd to greet him, Stevenson kept his elbows at his side and managed only halfway salutes as the train meandered through the San Joaquin Valley. (Ike waved with arms outstretched in the embracing V of his wartime salute.) Rocking back and forth, Stevenson grinned so mechanically that his smile seemed almost a facial tic. By the time he reached Los Angeles and talked about man's fulfilling his destiny as a child of God, he was exhausted.

One listener encouraged a more even pace of delivery and more emphasis on critical points. As the Hollywood producer Dore Schary later complained, the candidate should not wing away his sock points too rapidly. Stevenson's reaction was expectable: "If they don't like me as I am, *tant pis!* I won't pretend to be anything else." What Stevenson wanted was the people's ears and minds, not their eyes or hearts. Negligent in his understanding of the degree to which oratory conveyed character and motive, he continued to depend on words and appeared to voters—90 percent of whom did not know the difference between his stand on the Taft-Hartley Act and Eisenhower's—as well educated and capable. But in a postwar harbinger of the decline of heroes and parties, nearly one-half of the registered Democrats could think of nothing favorable or memorable about Stevenson or the Democratic party.

By the end of September, in the midst of a second regional tour, this time to New England, a scandal broke among the Republicans. Richard Nixon was accused of having a personal fund of over $18,000 contributed by rich Californians. Dissatisfied by his running mate's explanations that the money had been used for political expenses to maintain his Senate office and that Communist sympathizers were behind the smear, Eisenhower, who had found the corruption issue useful against the Democrats, demanded that Nixon make himself as "clean as a hound's tooth." Then the general waited as some of his advisers urged him to get rid of Nixon. Meanwhile Stevenson said little. By the time Nixon used national television (purchasing the slot after the popular Milton Berle show and reaching an audience of fifty-eight million Americans) to make his everyman's case for Pat's cloth coat, the family dog Checkers, and his mortgage to gain his way back into Eisenhower's acceptance as "my boy Dick," there were questions about a Stevenson fund.

Representing the unspent campaign money from his 1948 gubernatorial campaign along with additional money collected after he became governor, Stevenson's fund of $80,000 was both like, and different from, Nixon's. As public officials, both men were available to dispense special favors to contributors, but unlike Nixon, Stevenson spent most of his fund to increase the salaries of underpaid workers in his state administration. According to his finely calibrated moral calculator, he had destroyed any opportunity for favoritism and influence-peddling, because there was no direct association between the givers and the receivers. It went without saying that he was not available for graft, and so the press dropped the matter, though besides bonuses to his staff, the governor had used the fund for his own travel expenses, for flowers, for the orchestra at his sons' Christmas party, and for costumes for a bowling team in Springfield. In so doing, he limited his own expenses. But, argued Stevenson, his fund was not secret, though its potential unsavoriness had led Stevenson to write to Hermon Smith ("better in longhand") about the need for $20,000 a year "to enable me to do what we have talked about without robbing the children."

In Nixon's case one donor had received help from the senator's office in a tax debt owed the government by his lumber firm, but arguably this was the kind of service that a senator's office might be expected to deliver. In any event, the Internal Revenue Service never raised any claim for additional taxes from either man, though a growing body of opinion held that such gifts should be declared as income. In the future more stringent standards would make both funds illegal. The day that the Nixon scandal broke, the American Bar Association passed a resolution calling for criminal penalties for any private concern or individual guilty of giving a gratuity to a public official.

At first Stevenson refused to release the names of his donors, whose privacy, as a gentleman, he had to protect. But under pressure from reporters who treated the noble centurion Stevenson more gently than the politician soon to be labeled "Tricky Dick," a partial list without the dates of contributions was finally published. It left $13,000 unaccounted for, the result of sloppy record keeping rather than malfeasance. Then, to safeguard his reputation and to show he had not used any of these contributions for himself, Stevenson urged full financial disclosure, as he had done in Illinois in 1948.

Reiterating his desire that some more confidential means than the public disclosure of private tax returns be created—perhaps a judicial commission—to prevent the invasion of "a man's legitimate privacy," Stevenson was nonetheless resigned. "However distasteful," he explained in a radio broadcast, "public service makes you public property." Soon the world learned of the Democratic candidate's private wealth—his $46,000 of dividend income in 1951 from a portfolio valued at approximately $750,000. Diverted by such titillating information, along with the disclosures of Eisenhower's royalty income of nearly one million dollars from his best-selling book *Crusade in Europe,* monies accounted as capital gains rather than as income, along with the information that Sparkman's wife was on the senator's payroll as a receptionist, the press forgot about the Stevenson fund. The candidate did not forget the invasion of his private life, joking after the election that he had won the "bosom-bearing public stripping" of financial disclosure.

Stevenson held no more press conferences; there was no debate between the presidential candidates; the issue of the slush funds disappeared—a partisan standoff in a campaign in which the Republicans had already accused the Democrats of corruption and had linked Adlai Stevenson to the supposedly mob-connected Chicago boss Jack Arvey. For his part, Stevenson continued to charge that an Eisenhower administration would be the puppet of big-business interests, but his demonstration of the point through the Nixon fund was neutralized. Secure in his own incorruptibility and contemptuous of Nixon's, the governor remained aggrieved that the press depicted contributions to him as similar to those to Nixon.

Before long—now that his tax returns for the last ten years were available—the financial magazine *Barron's* evaluated the Democratic candidate as a financier. "He is not just the passive possessor of a tolerably large fortune; he is also an astute investor who knows much more about Wall Street than he chooses to say." Surprised by his speculative holdings, *Barron's* upgraded his reputation from a staid investor in blue-chip stocks to that of an aggressive capitalist who speculated in high-risk companies. Indeed, suggested *Barron's,* Stevenson should make "a pitch" to the nation's six million American stockholders. Stevenson proved the magazine correct about his interest in venture capital. During a campaign in which he never had enough time, on the advice of his investment counselor at Brown Brothers, who was amazed at his ability "to carry on with such small and detailed matters" after his nomination, he decided to invest in an oil company that turned up only dry wells in Acadia Parish, Louisiana.

By October the polls, still an unproven novelty to Americans, who recalled their failure to predict Truman's victory in 1948, showed Eisenhower leading by at least 10 percentage points, with 16 percent of the voters undecided. Stevenson remembered his upset victory in 1948, and his advisers, who assigned all the undecideds to their man, were heartened. But in retrospect the issue during 1952 remained not who would win but how large Eisenhower's margin would be. There was never any chance for Stevenson, who sometimes in the heat of the battle thought he might win. What was at stake was his share of the vote and his personal rating of his efforts as a Democratic messenger intent on "an educational and elevating national discussion."

In such ratings he was winning. By Stevenson's moral calculations, the Republicans were losing their souls, especially Nixon, whose speeches Stevenson despised as "McCarthyism in a white collar." Nixon was "the kind of politician who would cut down a redwood tree, and then mount the stump and make a speech for conservation." Earlier Nixon had defamed both Truman and Stevenson—calling the Democratic party of Truman responsible for "twenty years of treason" and the Illinois governor the holder of a "Ph.D. degree from Acheson's College of Cowardly Communist Containment"—"a weakling, a waster, and a small-calibered Truman" who owed his career to a machine infested with "mobsters, gangsters, and remnants of the old Capone gang."

Implying fellow traveling by association, Nixon exaggerated Stevenson's acquaintance with Alger Hiss into a suspicious friendship. The governor's deposition in the former State Department official's perjury trial, his mission to Italy, and his veto of the Broyles bill became circumstantial evidence for the charge that the Democratic candidate was a dupe of the Communists. Stevenson tried to defend himself by noting that he had only done a citizen's duty and told the truth, to which a group of Republican lawyers replied in a widely circulated advertisement that, without a subpoena, the Democratic candidate was under no obligation to say anything. Smeared, Stevenson could reply only that he did not suppose that the Hiss case exhausted "the arsenal of accusation with which the General's high command hopes to obtain victory."

In this he was correct. Led by Nixon and McCarthy, Republicans transformed Stevenson's New Deal service into companionship with left-wingers. His wartime fact-finding mission to Italy became a guilty association to aid the Communist party's rise to power under Togliatti. Even his veto of the antisubversion Broyles bill, which contained provisions for loyalty oaths, was distorted into an effort to make Illinois schools safe for the hiring of Communist teachers. After the election legal experts concluded that some of the Republican's charges were libelous, and even Nixon, who habitually placed himself above apology, acknowledged "the intensity" of a campaign that set new standards for personal vilification. Holding politics to be a testing ground of character, not a means-neutral road to power, Stevenson retreated to the commandment that one should not bear false witness, along with a piety from Matthew: "The Republicans undermine our basic spiritual values. For in the final accounting, what shall it profit a man if he shall gain the whole world, and lose his own soul?"

McCarthy was even cruder in his attacks on Stevenson. At the end of the campaign, when the senator from Wisconsin planned to smear "Ad-Ad-Ad-Lie" as a member of the State Department's "pinks and pansies," the Democratic National Committee threatened to release a letter obtained from the Pentagon files exposing Eisenhower's apparent intention to divorce his wife, Mamie, at the end of the war and marry his English driver Kay Summersby. For the time being the "Great Accuser" McCarthy deleted the reference, but in his abusive style still managed an "Alger—I mean Adlai."

By October nothing stopped the whispering campaign that Stevenson was a homosexual, not even Buffie's appearances at women's lunches, on podiums, and at the gendered activities that were a part of politics in the 1950s. In Washington it was called the "Stevenson innuendo." Everyone knew what was meant. In the rest of the United States, the gossip wove its way into telephone conversations and informal political discussions, barroom jokes and beauty shop frowns at a time in which same-sex preference was still in the closet. Delegates in Chicago heard the smear even before the convention ended.

The rumors originated in Washington, where Director of the FBI J. Edgar Hoover was intent on assuring the election of Eisenhower and Nixon. On the day of Stevenson's nomination, bureau officials prepared a nineteen-page document containing allegations of his homosexuality. In public places like the Mayflower Hotel's Town and Country Room, FBI agents could be—and meant to be—overheard, loudly discussing Stevenson's homosexuality and the file that J. Edgar Hoover kept on the Democrat's sexual preferences. After an investigation by the attorney general, the defamers denied their rumor mongering, but by this time such private recanting had little effect. Once fixed, the image was never dispelled.

In its most explicit form the gossip alleged that Stevenson had been arrested in Illinois and in New York for sexual crimes, that he and David Owen, the president of Bradley University in Indiana, were "deviates," that Stevenson went by the nickname "Adelaide" in the gay bars he frequented in Chicago, and that Hoover had placed Stevenson on the Sex Deviate index kept in his personal office. Hoover did organize such a confidential file, which contained gossip from his unauthorized investigations into the personal lives of many Americans. These materials proved useful in his blackmail of a generation of public officials. Some of Hoover's files were later destroyed by his secretary, but not before the director of the FBI had told everyone who would listen, including, much later, the Kennedys, that he had evidence that Adlai Stevenson was "a notorious homosexual."

All was hearsay, disseminated sometimes by Hoover himself and sometimes, as one student of the FBI concludes, "through a devious route which hid the Bureau's complicity," as Crime Records leaked the stories to local police, including some in Illinois who "channeled this and other derogatory information to Nixon, McCarthy, and members of the press." At least one FBI agent later said he was "absolutely appalled by [the smear of Stevenson], but Mr. Hoover was determined to elect Nixon and Ike."

During the 1950s Hoover kept alive the libels of Stevenson, until a gullible Walter Winchell announced on national television, in a confusing reference to the era's famous transsexual, "A vote for Adlai Stevenson is a vote for Christine Jorgensen and a woman in the White House." And so Adlai Stevenson joined a distinguished group of public figures who were victims of Hoover's illegal investigations and slander. Stevenson never mentioned these defamations, though they continued when Illinois's Republican senator, Everett Dirksen, identified him as one of "the lavender lads of the State Department."

Beyond the obvious libel rested a gendered smear involving popular notions of masculinity. The Cold War generation of the 1950s demanded as its heroes steely-eyed "true men" who enjoyed the centerfolds of the new magazine *Playboy,* who identified with John Wayne and Burt Lancaster, who talked tough against the Communists, and who resisted the feminizing effects of an increasingly powerful consumer culture. "As long as there were Communists anywhere," writes Barbara Ehrenreich, "there would have to be real men in America like Joe McCarthy who blustered that he'd like 'to teach patriotism to little Ad-lie with a baseball bat' to the urbane but no less belligerent John F. Kennedy."

Cold War presidents from Dwight Eisenhower to Richard Nixon (the latter's toughness displayed by a growth of whiskers beyond the control of two shaves a day and timely applications of "Lazy Shave" powder) exuded the requisite characteristics. In their carefully crafted image of the Democratic candidate, the Republicans made sure that Stevenson did not. They were aided by his pear-shaped physique, his extra pounds, and his baldness. "The idea of putting Adlai Stevenson in the ring with a man like Stalin petrifies me," said Nixon.

Stevenson was an exception to the "true man" ethic for other reasons. Not only had he never been in combat in the armed services, and been labeled an effete intellectual during an outbreak of anti-intellectualism propelled by McCarthyism, but he was divorced. In this generation men who had no wives were tainted by the suspicion of homosexuality. Such enfeebled males were, as diagnosed by contemporary psychologists, "overwhelmed by the increasing demands of masculinity." Immature and cowardly, they supposedly fled heterosexuality and marriage. One midwesterner, connecting home and Republic, expressed a common sentiment to a reporter: "If a man can't run his family, he has no business trying to run the country."

Ellen Borden Stevenson added fuel to such perceptions, announcing that she would "expose" her husband in a book of poems entitled "The Egghead and I." First proposed by Stewart Alsop, the term "egghead" had become a popular description for an unusual candidate whose bald pate resembled an egg and whose speeches were those of a remote, sometimes tentative scholar. Playing off the title of a current best-seller, *The Egg and I,* Ellen proposed satiric verse, beginning with her version of Plato's observations about men who could not govern at home. She had already embarrassed the campaign with an enigmatic statement: "If words should become more than deeds, democracy will find that the English sentence has become a sentence of death. Pocketbook principles and pinup principles are not enough. This is no time to be swayed by class hatred and party politics." Isolated from her family, determined for a revenge that increasingly placed her at odds with her sons, and invisible to those who would be her husband's friends, she offered Roger Straus, a New York publisher, letters in which she questioned her former husband's capacities as both husband and father. Diplomatically Straus delayed until it was too late, and Ellen Stevenson learned the bitter lesson of a future in which her husband held the stage.

To Stevenson his former wife was only part of a personal campaign— and the dirtiest one up to this point in American history—adopted by Eisenhower and the "primitive Republicans" who surrendered to the expediency that he intended to avoid along his "hard and unfamiliar road." In Stevenson's mind the Republican candidate was now a captive of that party's unquenchable desire for office at any price. Stevenson noted that while campaigning in the Midwest, Eisenhower shared the platform and three embraces from Indiana's extremist senator, William Jenner.

Accustomed to following orders—no matter what his private feelings— the general also endorsed, as Stevenson would not, all of his party's candidates. These included the vituperative Jenner, who had called Eisenhower's patron General George C. Marshall—the man responsible for the general's rapid advancement over higher-ranking officers in the U.S. Army—"a front man for traitors" and "a living lie." Only privately did Eisenhower assail Jenner in the soldier's language learned many years before at Fort Sam Houston, in Texas. When the Republican campaign moved into Wisconsin, Eisenhower intended to praise General Marshall. Again the party's Red-baiters prevailed. Seated on a platform with Senator Joseph McCarthy,

Eisenhower removed a complimentary paragraph about Marshall.

Late in the campaign Stevenson tried to respond to the Republicans' "systematic program of innuendo and accusation" and its "great surrender" to right-wing extremists. Stevenson hoped to debate, but Eisenhower, after consulting his media adviser, rejected what Stevenson viewed as the essence of informed electoral politics. "And that's my answer," the general was quoted as saying about a campaign feature that would not be in place until 1960.

Late in October, in Stevenson's view, the Republicans again surrendered their integrity, this time on the issue of Korea. The tangled negotiations between the United Nations command and the North Koreans had begun in July 1951 at Panmunjom, a little more than a year after the North Koreans had invaded South Korea, and nine months after General Douglas MacArthur's reckless decision to cross the 38th parallel and approach the Manchurian border had brought the Chinese into the war. While fighting continued sporadically in what had become a brutal infantry war of position, the discussions recessed when an American plan for the repatriation of prisoners of war was rejected by the North Koreans. In the midst of the presidential campaign, the UN command walked out, and any chance for an armistice was delayed. Fighting resumed near Chorwon and White Horse Hill, in the Bloody Triangle near the 38th parallel. While Truman sought international acceptance of the principle of nonforced repatriation, in Tokyo General Mark Clark cabled the Pentagon that he considered it necessary that "plans be made for the use of atomic weapons" against Manchuria and China.

Most Americans were frustrated by what had been initiated as a police action under the United Nations, but had turned into an expensive stalemate with heavy American casualties. The campaign debate centered on the past: on the Democrats' responsibility for removing Korea from the American defense perimeter and the rapid demobilization of American armed forces after World War II. Eisenhower, whose son John was a major stationed near the Imjin River, accused Stevenson, whose son Adlai was training with the Marines for a tank command in Korea, of making too many jokes: "Is it amusing that we have stumbled into a war in Korea; that we have already lost in casualties 117,000 of our Americans killed and wounded; is it amusing that the war seems to be no nearer a real solution than ever, that we have no real plan for stopping it?" chided the general. To which Stevenson later replied, referring to Eisenhower's abandonment of his benefactor General Marshall, "While the General worries about my funnybone, I'm worrying about his backbone."

Stevenson also hammered at Eisenhower's compliance with policy decisions that had led the North Koreans to invade. Earlier he considered an announcement that he would go to Korea, but quickly dropped such a suggestion as a demagogic pandering for votes. Instead, in a Louisville speech, he offered his special brand of the politics of unresolved modern dilemmas: "I promise no easy solutions, no relief from burdens and anxieties, for to do this would be not only dishonest; it would be to attack the foundations of our greatness." It was typical of Stevenson that he carefully and thoughtfully dissected the Korean War—its history, its manipulation by the Soviets (this was an era in which Americans misunderstood the tensions among Communist countries and exaggerated the power of the Soviets), and its necessary resolution by military containment under the United Nations.

Then, at the end of October, Eisenhower announced that if elected he would go to Korea. The general was accustomed to making battlefield visits, but to Stevenson's way of thinking his opponent was playing to the public. "The General has announced his intention to go to Korea. But the root of the Korean problem does not lie in Korea. It lies in Moscow. If the purpose of the General's trip is to settle the Korean War by a larger military challenge, then the sooner we all know about it, the better." Yet the dramatic, campaign-ending solution made even Stevenson's advisers suspect that what had looked like an Eisenhower victory would now become a rout. Stevenson's self-conscious wisecrack "If elected, I will go to the White House" seemed an insufficient response. The prospect of America's best-known military leader going to the battlefield at a time of national bewilderment appealed to thousands of war-weary Americans. As the campaign closed, Stevenson could only reiterate his inscrutable message of morality, speaking of evil and goodness and his design "for the American cathedral." "Let us remember that, while Christ preached the doctrine of eternal salvation, he also did the work that needed to be done in the kingdom of man."

In his final message on election eve, Stevenson ran overtime. Consequently Americans were denied his brilliant peroration of campaign memories followed by, after an encouragement to vote, these words: "If your decision is General Eisenhower and the Republican Party, I shall ask everyone who voted for me to accept the verdict with traditional American sportsmanship. If you select me, I shall ask the same of the Republicans—and I shall also ask Our Lord to make me an instrument of His peace." Instead, television viewers saw, and radio listeners heard, as the final words of Adlai Stevenson's journey of the spirit, "This has been a paid political announcement."

On election day Stevenson drove to the polling place near his home in Libertyville, where he finished his nine-week course of instruction, this time giving local children a quick lesson in civics. "What you see here is something that does not happen everywhere in the world. . . . [Your parents and neighbors] are deciding for themselves who is going to lead them— who is going to be their leader. You understand that? . . . One of the highest degrees of intelligence in the whole United States is political intelligence."

Then he returned to the governor's mansion in Springfield to await the returns.

By eight o'clock the huge CBS Univac computer projected a substantial Eisenhower victory. Two hours later the machine underestimated the general's eventual majority of 55 percent of the popular vote to 44 percent for Stevenson, in part because of the large number of stay-at-homes. Only six of ten eligible voters had cast ballots. Some did not vote because they had recently moved and did not qualify as residents of their new precincts or had not reregistered. Others, especially in the South, faced difficult registration procedures, poll taxes, and literacy tests; still others were no longer interested in a partisan system whose programs and leaders did not address their concerns. As one citizen complained, "The parties and the leaders don't really care what people like me think."

By early evening Adlai Stevenson was ready to concede. Characteristically unconcerned about the effect of such an acknowledgment on close races in the West, Stevenson wanted to surrender almost immediately— as gentlemen did after losing a match—but on the advice of professional Democrats he delayed his announcement. It was after 1:00 A.M. when he congratulated Eisenhower and offered an appropriate Lincoln quotation about the little boy who stubbed his toe in the dark and was too old to cry, but it hurt too much to laugh. Stevenson would have liked to use laughter as a solace and, the best of losers, did so later in a hilarious speech to Washington's Gridiron Club about what had happened to him on the way to the White House. But election day was a serious occasion and he had been accused of being glib. When a woman with a diamond "I Like Ike" pin complimented him for educating the American people, he snapped, "Too many people flunked the course."

Stevenson carried only nine states and lost four of the previously iron-bound Democratic southern states that had not voted Republican since Reconstruction. In the South he ran only one percentage point ahead of Truman in 1948, even without the challenge of a Dixiecrat ticket. Illinois went Republican, as Stevenson did poorly with big-city voters—the result of Eisenhower's appeal, the nonchalance of local politicians whose ties to inner-city voters were loosened by national welfare and insurance programs, and the unenthusiastic response to Stevenson by some Democrats. Even Cook County went Republican for the first time in six presidential elections.

The Roosevelt voting coalition once characterized by Stevenson as "a natural drawing together of the miserable . . . mistakenly called liberalism" shattered in 1952. Stevenson had never spoken for the poor or what Roosevelt called the dispossessed "one-third of the nation," preferring to station himself as a statesman above interest group politics. As a result workers held no strong allegiance to him. Meanwhile the traditional cliques of Protestants and the middle class continued to vote Republican in disproportionate numbers.

Stevenson overwhelmingly carried the votes of strong Democratic partisans, but he lost the independents and the growing numbers of Democrats who were less closely affiliated with the party in an increasingly nonpartisan age. In a letter to a friend after the election, Stevenson glibly explained, "We ran out of poor people and we ran into Korea and a few rather solid obstacles," the most substantial of which was the personal appeal of Dwight Eisenhower. In a notable example of the erosion of party politics and the emergence of presidential elections as personal competitions, three out of five voters in 1952 who voted for Eisenhower did not vote the party's entire ticket, as Eisenhower ran 10 percentage points ahead of many Republican congressional and senatorial candidates. Correspondingly Stevenson ran behind the national Democratic congressional vote and behind Democratic aspirants for governorships, initiating an era of divided authority between a Democratic Congress and a Republican executive.

By his moral tape measure Adlai Stevenson had won. "My dominant impression," he wrote a young student, "is that our campaign, disappointing as was its outcome, had values of its own which justify all the time and trouble and heartbreak that went into it." Believing himself a good instructor who had kept the faith during an "unsought and unwanted" campaign, he considered his journey a special kind of pilgrimage—"unique," as he called it in the collection of speeches he edited in Barbados after the election. And for weeks Stevenson's *Major Campaign Speeches* remained on the *New York Times* nonfiction best-seller list. To Alicia, whom he forgave for *Newsday*'s endorsement of Eisenhower, he telegraphed, "I've no regrets, did the best I could, didn't trim, equivocate or clasp dirty hands." He also explained his defeat by noting the swelling sentiment for change among voters in a two-party culture after two decades of Democratic governance, adding to his reasons for defeat, "the moribund Democratic organization, Korea and Truman's campaigning," the latter "raising the target again and diluting my coverage."

From his campaign Stevenson bequeathed to the American people, besides his leadership of the Democratic party, his eloquent speeches. The Democratic presidential campaign of 1952 became a symbol of what Americans always located in a previous generation's politics—that is, a dignified issue-oriented approach to public affairs, though in fact few voters absorbed the specifics of his message, and some came to assume that a man of such eloquence could not govern. Yet Stevenson invigorated an alternative style of electioneering favored by Woodrow Wilson and Charles Evans Hughes. To this tradition he added a spiritual idiom in his secular sermons.

Uncomfortable with the carnival side of elections, candidate Stevenson tried to be a man for the people, not of them; a man of reason talking sense, not manipulation or sentiment. Yet, as his hero James Madison once affirmed, reason was usually the servant of self-interest; one man's appeal to reason might be a claim for personal privilege in another's mind. Heir to an Anglo-American political culture of idealism and supposed disinterested statesmanship undertaken in the name of the public good and the status quo, the patrician Stevenson had a deficient sense of relativism. In any case, his appropriation of rectitude, as one voter commented, "left Mr. and Mrs. America chilled."

Unable to accomplish his mission of placing policy debate at the center of elections, he nonetheless remained a hero—not a prophet, but a traditionalist of honor. In his affirmation of the importance of every individual's scanning of the issues, he denied the partisan faith of his grandfather's age and so inadvertently contributed to the decline of American political parties.

The loser was comforted by a high-minded theme he had developed late in the campaign. "What is the lesson of history and of all human experience?" Stevenson had inquired of a national radio and television audience, which might have thought that it had tuned in to a religious service. "What is the primary law of life? You struggle and you survive—you fail to struggle and you perish. . . . Your salvation is in your own hands; in the stubbornness of your minds, the tenacity of your hearts, and such blessings as God, sorely tried by His children, shall give us. . . . If telling you the truth about the world as I see it should cause you to cast me down, and revile me, and with me the Democratic Party, I should still tell you the truth as I see it."

Later, liberals who wanted to expand the entitlements of the New Deal and a managed economy, and who supported Truman's civil rights program to end racial barriers in voting, education, and housing, questioned why a moderate-conservative who had run an amateur's campaign and who was committed to frugality, gradualism, and localism became their respected dean during the 1950s. In fact, Stevenson had been overwhelmingly endorsed by the Americans for Democratic Action and by the progressives of this generation, because they had nowhere to go as Roosevelt's giant footsteps faded in the political sands. They were attracted to the Illinois governor because he firmly opposed McCarthyism, a stand that earned him the allegiance of those members of his generation who, at least in 1952, believed the threat to civil liberties (which included blacks and whites) took precedence over the extension of civil rights (which arguably affected only blacks). Like all his positions, Stevenson's bold anti-McCarthyism carried the unconscious personal component that he, and all Americans, be independent and autonomous before the challenge to free speech inherent in the national version of anticommunism.

But liberals also appreciated Stevenson because of his style. A candidate who described his campaign experience as "talking to everybody in great howling halls" had clearly dissociated himself, as did many Americans, from the plebeians. Stevenson dramatized the complex feelings of educated elites, some of whom came to adore him not because he was a liberal, as Irving Howe has written, but because he was not. "Here was this remarkable man from Illinois, so charming and cultivated, so witty and so . . . well, *somewhat* weary . . . come to represent and speak for them." Stevenson also appealed because he spoke a language that set apart from average Americans an increasingly college-educated population, many the recipients of GI Bill tuition payments. His approach to voters as rational participants in a process that depended on weighing the issues attracted reformers, intellectuals, members of the growing Democratic club movement, and middle-class women with time and money—"the Shakespeare vote," joked one columnist. Or as an enthralled voter wrote, "You were too good for the American people."

Preeminently admired for a conflicted presence that seemed to embody the nation's postwar condition of power but not security, prosperity but not happiness, individualism but not community, Adlai Stevenson ended the election of 1952 with the allegiance of an adoring group of "Stevensonites." Articulate and loyal, impressed with the fragility of life in the atomic age and man's capacity for self-destruction, they would soon create the Stevenson legend and make the man from Libertyville a counterhero to Eisenhower, whom they would portray as inept and banal.

3

IN THE YEARS FOLLOWING the election, Adlai Stevenson continued, by his definition, to talk sense to the American people. He would have preferred to do so, he wrote Norman Cousins, as "a citizen at large" rather than as the leader of the Democratic party. Still, his campaign had won him a unique pulpit from which he could command attention "without the stark reality of responsibility." More than just a defeated presidential candidate, in his role as a party spokesman with over one hundred invitations to speak every week, he found himself perpetually overcommitted. Torn among dutiful efforts to speak for his party and for himself, his intention to make some money "for the boys," his need to pay off his $800,000 campaign debt, and his desire to laze in the sun with Alicia Patterson on her Florida plantation or with his friend Marietta Tree at her place in Barbados, he complained to Alicia, "The damnable 'schedule' has just been worked out. I leave here for Wash[ington] to see Ike Sept 29th. Go to N.Y. the 30th or 1st, spend the week end in the country seeing some characters and return to Chicago Mon or Tues Oct 5 or 6. I pray I won't miss you both places. . . . As for me, well its damn hard to be 'responsible' and 'helpful' and all those sweet things. But maybe I don't care enough—and certainly not enough for my more aggressive Democratic brethren."

In 1955 Stevenson opened a law office in downtown Chicago with William Blair, Newt Minow, and Willard Wirtz, three of the political advisers who had become, as his sons reached adulthood and his affairs with Alicia Patterson and Dorothy Fosdick cooled, members of an intimate circle. He had sworn that he would never return to the law and "all those debentures," but like Grandfather Stevenson he discovered that the law mixed well with public life. Political prominence brought wealthy clients, both corporate and individual, including RCA, Reynolds Metal, and Maurice Tempelsman, whose diamond business needed a skilled negotiator. Mostly because of the senior member of the firm, the partnership earned $126,528 in fees in 1955, though the leading partner's legal ambitions were muted: "I only want enough to make some money and get my foot back in the door in the law business."

As he dedicated himself to his "ambiguous role" as the party's titular leader, Stevenson clearly preferred the English model of a loyal opposition. In a parliamentary system he would have relished a congressional backbench from which to challenge the Republicans with wit and acuity. Instead, he spoke at fund-raisers in order to pay off his campaign deficit, met with party leaders to discuss the appointment of a new Democratic national chairman, and in 1954 campaigned for Democratic candidates in the off-year elections. The party provided neither staff nor funds nor speech writers nor consultants from Washington's new cottage industry. Stevenson complained to a friend, "As for party leadership, the path is thorny and filled with pitfalls, ambushes and unpleasantness."

Occasionally Stevenson attended the sessions of the Finletter National Issues Group and read the position papers developed by this brain trust on health care, poverty, civil rights, farm income, education, and foreign policy. In turn the Harvard professors Arthur M. Schlesinger Jr., John Kenneth Galbraith, and Seymour Harris, along with various government officials, including former Secretary of the Air Force Thomas Finletter, hoped to educate Stevenson up to their more liberal views by the time of the 1956 election—as Schlesinger said, "to help him overcome his upbringing" and to provide fresh initiatives for the decaying New Deal themes.

Four times between elections, Stevenson traveled overseas, disclaiming the pleasures of tourism for the "self-education" instilled in his childhood and now assimilated as a character-building exercise, because of its opportunities for learning, for slaking his restlessness and loneliness, and for its tests of what he derided as his "chronic stamina." In the spring of 1953 he journeyed around the world, commissioned by *Look* to write a series of articles for $50,000. The next year he was in Alaska, in 1955 he traveled to Africa, and in 1956 he planned a trip to the Soviet Union—everywhere acclaimed, everywhere an indefatigable sightseer, and everywhere such a popular American that he joked to his former running mate, John Spark-man, "Anywhere in the world except the Middle East, we would have had all the votes." He exaggerated. Particularly in India and Great Britain, Stevenson emerged for some as a surprisingly harsh Cold Warrior, a man who failed to speak out against Eisenhower's foreign policies and who conformed so closely to the American "popular mood" as to seem, according to the *New Leader,* "a bumbling edition of John Foster Dulles."

In the spring of 1954, as Stevenson prepared to campaign for his party's congressional candidates in the off-year elections, three events reinforced his fatalistic notion that events shaped the destinies of man, not the reverse. Quoting Brutus's words on the tides of men's affairs, he confronted the complexities of the Army-McCarthy hearings, the Supreme Court decision *Brown* v. *Board of Education,* and the defeat of the French army at Dienbien-phu. Of the three only his condemnation of McCarthyism displayed his self-defined "politics of morality."

The Army-McCarthy hearings took place in Washington, where Senator Joseph McCarthy's subcommittee of the Senate Committee on Government Operations had begun an investigation into the armed forces in the spring of 1954. At issue was more than the loyalty of the army major Dr. Irving Peress, who refused to answer McCarthy's questions about his alleged Communist involvement and his subsequent promotion and honorable discharge. Emboldened by an approval rating of over 62 percent among Republicans, McCarthy had begun his final firestorm—opposing Eisenhower's nominations for government jobs, including those of James Conant, the former president of Harvard, and William Bundy, raging against the CIA and the Department of Agriculture, and threatening to call before his committee Secretary of the Army Robert Stevens and even Sherman Adams, the president's crusty chief of staff.

Meanwhile the Democrats, who had lost the Senate to the Republicans in 1952, watched silently as McCarthy assailed the liberal wing of the Republican party. At stake was not simply the search for fantasized numbers of disloyal government employees but McCarthy's contest with Eisenhower for control of the Republican party. What had started as a national security matter and political ambition now began its fade-out as farce on the television screens of America.

Stevenson had sharply challenged Eisenhower on his tolerance of McCarthyism during the 1952 campaign. Now he did so again. The Great Crusade had become, he said in a televised speech at a fund-raising dinner in Miami, "the Great Deception." Its labeling of conscientious Democrats as traitors threatened the mutuality of a two-party system and the essential democratic understanding of opponents as a loyal opposition. An advocate of a bipartisan foreign policy, Stevenson condemned the Republican attacks on the "highly intelligent and highly successful" containment policies of Truman and Roosevelt.

In this speech—and in all that he said on the subject of McCarthyism—Stevenson raised the issue of domestic anticommunism into a struggle between good and evil. The Republican "calculated campaign of deceit . . . [and] insensate attacks on all Democrats as traitors, Communists, and murderers of our sons" became more than the efforts of "political plungers" to get power. "It is wicked and it is subversive for public officials to try deliberately to replace reason with passion; to substitute hatred for honest difference; to fulfill campaign promises by practicing deception; and to hide discord among Republicans by sowing the dragon's teeth of dissension among Americans." Not only were the Republicans lying about the evidence of disloyalty, but especially Nixon and McCarthy had lost all self-restraint, the latter an essential component of good citizenship.

During a season in which many politicians faltered before the onslaught of irresponsible anticommunism and in which Ohio's influential senator Robert Taft notified Eisenhower that he would not support any appointment challenged by McCarthy, Stevenson provided his alternative: let the professionals in the FBI search for Communists under already established programs. Let the government "push forward in developing the economic and moral strength of the non-communist world." Impressed, the *New York Times,* which had opposed him in 1952, now praised Stevenson as "more than a partisan . . . a conscientious American citizen."

By the summer of 1954 McCarthy had been unmasked, a process that Stevenson had aided. Stevenson had always believed the alcoholic senator from Wisconsin a madman and now called the Army-McCarthy hearings a "squalid, disgraceful spectacle" and "a ghastly vaudeville." After observing the senator's abuse of witnesses and his clamorous interruptions for points of order on television, many Americans were beginning to agree. Even the rejoinder of Joseph Welch to a personal attack—"Have you no decency?"—seemed grounded in Stevenson's plaintive approach to public ethics. Still, McCarthy's approval ratings remained high, and the fall of the junior senator from Wisconsin could not be accomplished without the president. Furious that McCarthy had reached into the White House with his investigation, Eisenhower stiffened his opposition. A few weeks after the hearings ended in June of 1954, the Senate formed a select committee to consider censure charges against McCarthy, which were voted in December.

McCarthyism continued to affect American foreign policy and politics for decades. But save for the victims of McCarthy's vilification, the acute phase of the battle against the witch-hunt of the 1950s was ending, though the national characterological failing that had created it was not, at least not for Stevenson. "The quality that is missing from our national life is self-confidence, the ebullient spirit that sustained us when . . . we stood up to the greatest empire on earth and fought for our independence; when we hammered together on the forge of civil war a federal union dedicated to the rights of man. . . ." In this lack of self-confidence, so much a part of Stevenson's own personality, originated, in his view, the national hysteria of Cold War McCarthyism.

In May of this same spring, the second of the events that stamped the culture and politics of postwar America occurred when the Supreme Court in the case of *Brown* v. *Board of Education* handed down its decision that racial segregation in schools was inherently unequal and therefore uncon- stitutional. For ten days Stevenson withheld public comment about what the *New York Times* called a "sociological decision," though he gave two speeches during this time, one in Meridian, Mississippi, at the National Hillbilly Music Festival, where he spoke instead about the Republican "appeasement" of McCarthyism before an audience waiting for the music. There he joked that the FBI had located only one Communist in Missis- sippi. "Even though one is too many, we can gather certain comforts that he can't call a meeting."

Returned to Libertyville, Stevenson finally commented on the inescap- able moral issue of his time, offering an equivocation that cheered southern whites. The leader of the Democratic party began by noting, "Much of the talk since the Supreme Court decision has missed the most important point: that the South has been invited by the Supreme Court to share the burden of blueprinting the mechanics for solving the new school problems of non- segregation. . . . The rest of the country should extend the hand of fellow- ship, of patience, understanding and assistance to the South in sharing that burden." Like Eisenhower and nearly all Republicans, but only a few promi- nent northern Democrats, Stevenson neither praised the decision nor made the ringing call for compliance of which he was capable and which public figures like George Meany of the American Federation of Labor and others were delivering in the spring of 1954. Both black and white activists marked Stevenson's silence and became disenchanted with the man who called for foreign aid overseas but could not speak for integration at home. "His feel- ings for the civil rights movement weren't intense, and in the movement if you weren't intense, you generally were not for it. That's not fair, but it could be true," decided the civil rights lawyer Joseph Rauh. Stevenson, who came to represent the American conscience, was, like most of the nation in the 1950s, insensitive to civil rights.

Roy Wilkins, the head of the National Association for the Advancement of Colored People, angrily telegraphed Stevenson that he had capitulated to the "go-slow boys." Like other blacks, Wilkins had heard the stories of the Democratic candidate's reaction to the plight of an African-American reporter who had been denied hotel accommodations while covering Stevenson's southern campaign in 1952. Stevenson had refused to change hotels and had been quoted as asking why the reporter "couldn't go somewhere else." Thereafter the head of the NAACP disliked Stevenson for "his Olympian liberalism so far above the fray." Meanwhile Stevenson reiterated his distaste for the activism of the NAACP and his preference for leaders like Ralph Bunche over what he called "wild men," like Adam Clayton Powell, the congressman from Harlem, and even Wilkins himself.

A year and a half later Emmett Till, a fourteen-year-old African-American from Chicago visiting relatives near Greenwood, Mississippi, was taken from his bed and brutally murdered, his offense a whistle at two white women. Despite the evidence an all-white jury acquitted the obvious murderers, even refusing to hand down an indictment for kidnapping. Promptly the Till case emerged as a symbol of racial injustice. Yet when Mrs. Till took her case to the nation, Stevenson condemned her appearances as "a spectacle of parading around the country." Again the spokesman of the Democratic party was mute save for his private exasperation: "No one can approve of the Till case, and anyone can say so, and say it over and over again." But he had not said so once in an age of shifting, fluid opinion when the views of popular leaders shaped attitudes. And when Stevenson was asked about the case in a press conference, he cut his questioner off and returned to the subject of taxes.

Preeminently Adlai Stevenson spoke for the status quo: "We must recognize that it is reason alone that will determine our rate of continued progress and guard against a reversal of the trend that has made the last three decades the period of greatest advancement for our Negro citizens on all fronts." Believing that discrimination could only be ended by individuals, that activism produced dangerous disharmony, and that the mobilization of the federal government violated individual and state rights, Stevenson opposed Congressman Adam Clayton Powell's amendment to cut off federal funds for schools refusing to desegregate. Such an amendment, he held, was unnecessary: "Any school which accepts school funds is a public school and . . . that brings it under the jurisdiction of the Court."

The Court, of course, had no regiments, and in any case Stevenson opposed the use of force to accomplish desegregation, as did Eisenhower. In 1957, after Governor Orval Faubus sent the National Guard to Little Rock with instructions to prevent integration, Eisenhower changed his mind, dispatching federal troops to Little Rock's Central High School, where they patrolled for months. Asked at the time his reaction to the Arkansas governor's flouting of the law, Stevenson replied in a television interview that he was both distressed and surprised by what "my friend Faubus has done." Many northern Democrats cringed on hearing this casual announcement of friendship with the arch-segregationist Faubus.

Throughout his life Stevenson held fast to gradualism, suggesting January 1, 1963, the hundredth anniversary of the Emancipation Proclamation, as a target date for the desegregation of schools. "So long as man remains a little lower than the angels, I suppose that human character will never free itself entirely from the blemish of prejudice, religious or racial." With an instilled predilection for harmony and an abiding distaste for disorder—the legacies of his childhood, of his class, and of his early years in communities, from Bloomington to Princeton, where African-Americans were invisible—Adlai Stevenson supported the ends of "freedom and equality for all Americans" through the unenforceable, nonspecific means of schooling, understanding, and the use of obscure "sociological resources." Later, when Senator Herbert Lehman of New York complained in a letter to Stevenson that his gradualism was the stance of apologists for segregation, Stevenson penciled *no* in the margin, but did not dispute the point. And he continued to give his personal credentials as his membership card in the civil rights movement, noting his efforts to desegregate the Navy during World War II, his commitment to desegregating some school districts in Illinois while governor, and his support for a state Fair Employment Practices Act.

Four years later, in another speech in Harlem, Adlai Stevenson endorsed the *Brown* decision and pointed out that Eisenhower had made no such endorsement, ending his remarks with a benediction that could hardly have stirred his audience: "The profound questions of our time remain questions of conscience and of will. And the answers will come, at the last, 'Not by might, nor by power, but by thy spirit.' For ours is a time of which the prophet Amos wrote: 'let justice roll down as waters, and righteousness as a mighty stream.'" To Eisenhower a man who expressed such sentiments seemed an ideal candidate for an appointment to the Civil Rights Commission, but Stevenson declined.

Like nearly all public men of his time, Stevenson did not pay any attention to the emerging civil rights movement for women, although the Democratic platform in 1952 supported an Equal Rights Amendment. His views were firmly embedded in an upper-class culture in which women were to be nonworking wives and mothers. As he told Smith College's graduating class in June 1955 (an audience that included his future daughter-in-law Nancy Anderson), their "assignment," "their homework," was "to restore valid, meaningful purpose to life in your home . . . to watch for and to arrest the constant gravitational pulls to which we are all exposed, your workaday husband especially, in our specialized, fragmented society that tends to widen the breach between reason and emotion, between means and ends." Thus he viewed home not as the haven of his grandparents' generation where men recovered from bruises sustained in the marketplace. Instead, he saw women as homemakers preserving human values at risk in the commercial society of the midtwentieth century. Home was, for Adlai Stevenson, the schoolhouse of the liberal arts.

To this message Stevenson added a darker personal touch. In his life with Ellen Borden, he had been instructed in the feminine mystique by a sometimes beleaguered, often lonely woman who had introduced her husband to poetry and the arts. "I am told that nowadays the young wife or mother is short of time for the subtle arts, that things are not what they used to be; that once immersed in the very pressing and particular problems of domesticity many women feel frustrated and far apart from the great issues and stirring debates. . . . Once they read Baudelaire. Now it is the *Consumers' Guide*." Stevenson closed with a familiar quotation from Proverbs about the woman blessed by her children and praised by her husband. Later when *Woman's Home Companion* bought the address for $1,000, Stevenson split the royalties with one of his new speech writers—the English activist Barbara Ward.

That same May of 1954, when civil rights was placed on the national agenda and Joseph McCarthy was still damaging the reputations of loyal Americans, eight thousand miles away from the nation's capital, the Vietminh surrounded the French garrison at Dienbienphu, in Vietnam. After World War II the French army had tried to hold on to the cities and towns of its colonial possession in Southeast Asia, even while forces led by General Nguyen Giap were enlarging the rural areas under their authority. Now his army was pounding the French fortress with artillery.

In Washington the French were pleading for American troops and weapons from a government that was already paying for 80 percent of the war's cost. Vice President Nixon agreed, supporting intervention through air strikes and the use of American forces. If that was the only way to stop Communist expansion, then the "executive branch of the government has to take the politically unpopular position of facing up to it," said the vice president. Meanwhile, with an international conference under way in Geneva attended by the foreign ministers of nineteen countries, Ho Chi Minh intended to show his principal allies—the Chinese—just how powerful the Vietnamese were. To make the same point to their occupiers, the night before they captured the garrison at Dienbienphu on May 17, 1954, they played the songs of the French World War II resistance on frequencies used by French troops.

Stevenson had visited Hanoi and Saigon in his 1953 trip around the world and had even lunched with Bao Dai, the feckless French puppet supported by the West. Grumbling afterward that Bao Dai had not thanked the Americans for their aid, Stevenson also talked to the American chargé d'affaires about what several observers were beginning to identify as a civil war. In his second magazine piece for *Look*, entitled "Ballots and Bullets," Stevenson laid out his own ambivalent positions about the future of "Indochina." Vietnam was essential to the security and economy of the United States, he wrote. The country was the rice basket of Southeast Asia, a cir-

cumstance that, he concluded, made what would later become famous as
Eisenhower's domino theory especially relevant. "If Viet-Nam falls, all of
Indochina is doomed. Thailand and Burma would be in mortal danger.
Malay and Indonesia would be exposed and vulnerable. If this vast area of
the world, with its 175,000,000 people, its tin, rubber, minerals and oil, is
absorbed into the Moscow-Peking empire, the still vaster nations of India
and Pakistan would quickly lose any freedom of action. All Asia would slide
behind the Iron Curtain."

For Stevenson, Indochina had become the next test, after Korea, of
Western resolve to stand against the Russians. Yet his sensitivity to ambiguity led him to see the fighting in Vietnam as simultaneously a chapter in
the Cold War, a civil war between factions in Vietnam, and a demonstration
of nationalism against French colonialism. In these judgments he was far
ahead of American understanding, which only in the late 1960s came to
acknowledge the extent to which the war was an internal one.

As a campaign issue in the congressional elections of 1954, Vietnam
became a case in point for Stevenson's indictment of Republican foreign
policy. As the principal Democratic spokesman during this off-year election, he criticized not Eisenhower's policies of material support for the
French and covert American action but rather Republican "boasts, bluffs,
and brinks"—the latter a reference to Secretary of State Dulles's comment
on the necessity of brinksmanship. The Republicans had talked liberation
and had lost half of Vietnam—"the greatest disaster to the free world since
the fall of China." As good a Cold Warrior as any, Adlai Stevenson accused
the Republicans of dangerous cuts in the defense budget, which, he argued,
led to their dependence on nuclear weapons. He also glimpsed a civil war
fueled by nationalism and poverty. "You are asking a people to save themselves who do not choose to be saved because they regard white colonialism
as a greater menace than communism." Such a position revealed a keen
appreciation of international reality and of, as he wrote in *Look,* a new kind
of war marked by "sabotage, ambush, fluidity—an enemy behind and
beside as well as in front." Somehow this perceptive tourist of 1954 forgot
these conclusions. Ten years later Stevenson refused to see his fellow countrymen as white colonialists and resisted the logical implications of his earlier discovery. But that was later. Now he faced another decision about his
role in public affairs, and again his decision required the acquiescence of
the delegates of the Democratic party.

CHAPTER TEN

ON THE ROAD: 1956

1

IN 1955 ADLAI STEVENSON decided to run again for the presidency, though his lamentations about fading out "for a bit" and trying "to recover my strength, my equilibrium and my fortunes" continued. Enigmatically ambitious as ever, he informed the Democratic National Committee in late 1954 that, "as in the past," he had no political ambitions and would now devote more time to private matters. To Stevenson's surprise no one paid much attention to what might have been interpreted as a retirement from public life. As the Democratic spokesman without official portfolio but with a national pulpit, he had intended his announcement, according to his friends, to give party leaders an opportunity to determine whether they wanted him.

But politics was not ballroom dancing. No such gracious invitation to choose another partner was needed. Three times in the past—in the cases of Martin Van Buren, Lewis Cass, and Al Smith—Democratic conventions had denied renomination to a defeated candidate. Reiterating his inadequacy, Stevenson hoped "a better man might take it." But whereas in 1952 he had not sought the nomination, in 1956 he wanted it and so seemed to dissemble.

If he had not wished to run in 1952, why run in 1956? inquired one correspondent. If, as he informed Eleanor Roosevelt, he did not like working with state politicians, why seek a position that, whatever else it entailed, demanded daunting intercessions with local leaders? If the explanation for his reluctance to run in 1952 was his desire to remain the governor of Illinois, a position he once described as "the full measure of my abilities," why not challenge his bumbling Republican successor, William Stratton, who would soon be tried (and acquitted) on charges of income tax evasion? If he had declined to seek the nomination in 1952 believing Eisenhower invincible and accepting the necessity for change after twenty years of Democratic control, then why run against the incumbent in 1956? And if Stevenson's recharged ambitions came from his disappointment in the leadership of a man he now believed a "dud," how had he been fooled earlier about the general's capacities? Had the man who described himself during these years as "an elderly moralist" and who thought power could never be wielded without guilt, because it is ultimately selfish, been bitten by ambition?

Few national politicians evoked so much concern about their intentions. Most chose a simpler path, running for office whenever they could, hoping to win and thereby advance their careers. Stevenson's political path was different. Enjoying what George Ball described as "the drama of an inner struggle," he created dilemmas, and as in 1948 and 1952, in 1956 his inspiration was propelled by private values—his determination to improve, his attachment to sacrifice, his refusal to abandon public life and with it his opportunity to set American politics on a straighter path. "Duty?" he wondered about his decision to run. "Can any impersonal, honest sense be so compelling? Vanity? I had thought not, having experienced the honor once before and having dealt with it as well or better than I shall ever be able to again. Yet vanity it must be."

As a man with a vision of civic virtue and a private sense of unworthiness, his perception of what America could be fired his ambition, at the same time that his reputation, service to the party, and the chilling effect of Eisenhower's popularity on ambitious senators like Lyndon Johnson made him the logical choice for the Democratic nomination in 1956. Stevenson was also spurred by his disappointment in Eisenhower's domestic and foreign policies—"operation bromide," as he called them in a crack at the president's nonchalance. He detested as well the surrender of the government to rich businessmen, symbolized by the cabinet's nine millionaires and a plumber, though the plumber—Secretary of Labor Martin Durkin—was gone in a few months.

Having made a decision that he wanted to do the "Democratic honors," provided the party wanted him, Stevenson retired to Libertyville and his Chicago law practice, grumbling about his life as a hermit in the country. Now was the time for the party leaders to choose another, if they wished, though as the most influential Democratic leader he was raising the question of whether he wanted himself. In the spring of 1955, when Stevenson left Washington's National Airport on his way to Africa, he told reporters that he had not made up his mind whether to run for president in 1956. By the summer he felt that "old devil 'destiny' was creeping up . . . though I still live in some light-hearted or headed hope that it may all blow away." As always Stevenson encouraged "destiny"—this time by setting up, under the direction of Newt Minow, a Stevenson steering committee, which promptly raised $11,000.

In the meantime Stevenson polled his circle of intimates and, of course,

347

his sons, all three of whom were, at one time or another during this interval between campaigns, students at Harvard. Twenty-six-year-old Adlai had returned from Korea in 1954 and was finishing Harvard Law School; twenty-four-year-old Borden, a heavy drinker at this stage of his life, had dropped out of Harvard and was serving in the Army before completing his bachelor's degree; twenty-year-old John Fell, who was recovering from a serious automobile accident, had graduated from Milton Academy and was a sophomore enrolled in an economics course taught by a Stevenson brain truster, the Harvard professor Seymour Harris. (Wrote Stevenson to Harris, "Don't spare the rod.") After they listened to their father's indictment of Eisenhower's administration, all three sons responded that he should do what he wanted. This time what he wanted was the Democratic nomination.

Stevenson talked as well with his sister, Buffie, and her husband, Ernest Ives. Retired from the foreign service after nearly fifteen years in consular posts as far-flung as South Africa and Denmark, the couple now divided their time between Southern Pines, North Carolina, and the family home in Bloomington. Since Stevenson's divorce in 1949 the Iveses had organized Christmas celebrations where blue donkey ornaments rather than red Santa Clauses decorated the tree. On such occasions Alverta Duff, who had long served the family as a cook and housekeeper, produced Adlai's—and George Washington's—favored deep-dish cherry pies. Wherever it was celebrated, Christmas—the most maternal of holidays with its rituals of shopping, cooking, and decorating—remained a "difficult interlude" for Stevenson.

As the presidential season approached, Buffie reminisced about her brother's childhood in a book intended to humanize the aloof Stevenson. Published by William Morrow and later serialized in the *Ladies' Home Companion, My Brother Adlai* began with young Adlai asleep during a William Jennings Bryan speech and ended with a sisterly prediction: "I don't know what God has in store but when anyone is as faithful to ideals as Adlai is, he's bound to wind up in a serious job." Adlai emerged from his sister's memories as an unsophisticated Penrod of small-town America who broke his nose fighting, loved animals, thought about becoming a "great minister," and held tightly to his "invincible truthfulness."

Of course, Stevenson also sought advice about his future from Alicia Patterson, who, like Buffie and Jane Dick (and in nearly the same words), urged him to be true to himself. After editing Buffie's book, he remembered his mother's motto borrowed from William James—"Let go your hold; resign yourself to your destiny"—as well as her maternal invocation that she would rather have him "physically and morally sound" than president. Stevenson spoke as well to public men, including Harriman and Truman, earning the disgust of Clark Clifford, the Missouri-born, self-professed

counsel to presidents for "enjoying the chase, and the leisurely self-indulgent, self-satisfied attitude that came as others told him what a fine President he would make." Among his counselors were three women: Eleanor
Roosevelt, his staunch 1952 supporter, who urged him to change his attitude. "Winning is hard enough even if one has the will and drive," advised
an experienced Mrs. Roosevelt. He also sought out two new confidantes,
Agnes Meyer and Marietta Tree.

Thirty-five-year-old Marietta Tree was born a Peabody, the daughter of
a distinguished Boston family whose individual members had founded the
Groton School (with the help of J. P. Morgan), counseled Franklin Roosevelt, served Episcopal parishes, marched (and would be jailed) in civil
rights rallies, and governed Massachusetts. Raised in the privileged surroundings of boarding school at Maryland's St. Timothy's School (which
Ellen Borden had also attended) and summers in Maine's Northeast Harbor,
Marietta Tree absorbed a sense of public service honed during the Great
Depression and sharpened by her family's values. She was as well a beautiful
woman of impeccable taste and with a talent for what she termed the "general conversation" that moved beyond gossip to political and intellectual
exchanges held not as debate but as lively social discourse. The last of an
era—for intelligent women of a later generation were less willing to adopt
her style of interviewing prominent men—Marietta Tree carried on a discreet love affair with Adlai Stevenson for the rest of his life. He became, as
he signed his letters, "ever yours," though he was never only hers.

They had met in the late forties after Marietta Tree returned to New
York with her second husband, Ronald Tree, a wealthy Englishman. At the
time Stevenson was in New York on United Nations business. Invited for
dinner at the Trees' Seventy-ninth Street Manhattan apartment, he proved
a dud according to his hostess—a shy, nervous guest who didn't want to
play charades, the game of the decade. A few years later Adlai Stevenson
became a hero to Marietta Tree when she entered New York reform politics
through the Lexington Democratic Club—handing out literature critical of
the New York boss Carmine De Sapio's machine, stuffing envelopes, and
doing the lowly work of this generation's party activists. She campaigned
hard as a foot soldier in the 1952 Volunteers for Stevenson. Soon Alicia
Patterson's 1,800-acre Kingsland plantation, with the black river of Adlai's
fantasy world, had a counterpart at Heron Bay, the Trees' home in Barbados.
There the casual nudist Stevenson—who often wanted "to escape myself"—
shocked several women by throwing off his clothes and plunging naked
into the soft Caribbean sea.

If Marietta Tree represented a new affair of the heart for Stevenson—
one observer remembered "his hand way below her waist during a dance at
Brooke Astor's," and her daughter Frances Fitzgerald recalled his roaming
between their rooms in a Spanish hotel—Agnes Meyer was an incarnation

of his mother, Helen Davis Stevenson. Like his mother, she became absorbed by this attractive, witty, complex man. Both Tree and Meyer noted that he rarely discussed his father, though they heard a great deal about his sister and mother.

The daughter of middle-class German immigrants, Agnes Ernst had in 1910 married the wealthy financier Eugene Meyer, who in the late 1930s purchased the bankrupt *Washington Post*. A well-informed member of "the literate liberals" of the postwar generation and an expert on Chinese art and education, Meyer was sixty-seven when she met Adlai Stevenson in 1954. Like Patterson and Tree, she was well connected, rich, and influential; like Patterson and Tree, she attracted powerful men to parties where the conversation flowed from politics to poetry and where, as one participant marveled, the affairs of the world were discussed by those who determined them. "I have to keep the Washington and Mount Kisco houses teeming with intellectual men and beautiful women, or [my husband] reproaches me for being a hermit," she once wrote. But as much as her husband, Agnes Meyer—a graduate of Barnard College and the Sorbonne—enjoyed the salon of which Stevenson now became a life member.

Smitten by the man whose speeches had first attracted her, Agnes Meyer promptly proclaimed her adoration "as a woman who loves you." It was love at first sight—the best kind, in Meyer's practiced view. Theirs was a relationship carried out through a voluminous but unbalanced (in his direction) correspondence, and, because she found the Illinois plains dull and Libertyville difficult to find, through meetings in Washington and on the Meyers' Seven Springs estate near Mount Kisco. "Careful please; I'm falling in love!" responded Stevenson with the gaiety that the woman he nicknamed Hurricane Agnes advised him to carry into his political life.

"Dearest Adlai," "Adlai my Hero," "Adlai, Adlai, Adlai," she greeted him in thirteen-page handwritten letters that acknowledged "the ecstasy" of their brief encounters and sometimes offered historical examples of the liaisons of older women and younger men. Accustomed to his wife's emotional but not necessarily sexual passions with distinguished men, ranging from Thomas Mann to Albert Schweitzer, Eugene Meyer described Agnes as in love again, to which his niece replied, when she heard who the correspondent was, that every "sensible" woman in America was in love with Adlai Stevenson.

Agnes Meyer had no difficulty fathoming the contradictions of a man so warm and loving with his friends, but cold, impersonal, and unapproachable to the outsiders whose votes he must solicit—"this bowl of contradictions . . . who wanted to be President and didn't"; "who didn't have heart and mind together"; "who had been terribly hurt by his marriage, was the kindest man in the world when he thought about it but never knew when he hurt people, was very self-centered but a man with a delicious sense of

humor." Like his mother, Agnes badgered her beloved about his disorga-
nized, cluttered speeches, his frequent gossiping about Ellen at dinner parties ("never, never let fly about your wife"), and especially his need to love
himself, which she discerned as his fundamental problem. Furious at his
languid attitude toward politics—he once wrote that he had not bothered
to listen to the primary returns from New Hampshire—Agnes Meyer complained and then apologized: "How I hate to be so hard on you," to which
the busy Stevenson responded, "Let us not argue about my frailties."

Of all the intimates who became members of his expanded family,
Meyer best sensed how Stevenson's political campaigns were psychological
journeys into his past and how his childhood had created certain demons.
"Whether you are elected to the Presidency or not, you are bound to
become the nation's outstanding leader if only you can overcome a deep
psychopathic fear of your own greatness and destiny."

Ignorant of the origins of this emotional block, Meyer continued to
probe. Soon a confessional-minded Stevenson had "dissolved." He elabo-
rated, "I suppose I needed someone to whom I could unburden without
self consciousness or affectation, someone who was wise without being
superior, and devoted without being maudlin." For the rest of his life Agnes
Meyer continued to provide, as Stevenson put it, "both feminine understanding and masculine fortification and mental provocation and moral
confidence"—along with considerable sums of money for his campaigns.

In an age before psychologists diagnosed politicians as human beings
needing special doses of adulation, Meyer concluded that Adlai was like
Woodrow Wilson—a lonely, isolated man "with a powerful need for
affection and a cramped capacity for communication." A man who had been
"cruelly treated by the fates," Meyer's Stevenson "guarded [his] emotions
from powerful overflows." The object of this diagnosis at first demurred,
explaining that his political career was determined by "genuine anxiety to
be sure the Democratic party is doing the best thing."

In August 1955 Stevenson held a strategy meeting with advisers less
concerned with his psyche. Blair, Minow, Wyatt, Dick, and Finletter, along
with the two most powerful Democrats in Illinois, Jack Arvey and Richard
J. Daley, attended. A pudgy fifty-three-year-old political dynamo, Daley had
recently won the Chicago mayoralty with Stevenson's support and was in
the process of using his chairmanship of the Cook County Democratic
Committee to create a machine whose attachment to Stevenson would compromise the candidate's high-minded political idealism. Their advice was
mixed: some thought Stevenson should run for the Senate seat currently
held by Everett Dirksen. Most agreed, however, that he was the best Democrat to challenge Eisenhower. As they plotted tactics, talked money, and
spoke of an offensive campaign focused on domestic themes, they also
encouraged more aggressiveness. "The world loves a fighter," instructed

Arvey, to which Stevenson responded mysteriously, "No one is fighting."

To dispel suspicions of indecisiveness and to close the door to other candidates, Stevenson announced his candidacy a year before the election. In the ensuing press conference he gave as his reasons the ineptness of the Eisenhower administration, the need for a return to power by the Democrats, and his personal explanation that all citizens must do what they could for a better world. He also described a "surprising degree of interest in my being a candidate again. I did nothing for it." By this time Eisenhower had suffered a heart attack, and the reporters asked if his candidacy was contingent on Eisenhower's health, to which he answered "not at all."

But other Democrats now found a run for the 1956 presidency more attractive. At a time of faltering party control over nominations, the self-anointed Estes Kefauver announced; Averell Harriman, the man likened by some to a sleepy alligator that, once disturbed, snapped with ferocity, was interested. An honor more easily bestowed on Stevenson when the popular Eisenhower was healthy became tangled in the emerging primary system that Stevenson despised. Despite his old-fashioned sense that "leaders about the country should indicate if they want me again," a reluctant Adlai Stevenson was now transformed from a public figure attacking Republican domestic policy into a candidate declaiming on the Mediterranean fruit fly in Florida and irrigation in California in order to win his party's nomination.

Having always focused (as leaders from the elite traditionally did) on national and international issues, Stevenson showed little interest in local affairs. Still, he had to establish some difference with his competitors if voters were to discriminate between candidates of the same party. Years before, Grandfather Stevenson had confirmed his distinctiveness through his name and reputation; now, half a century later, his grandson relied on attentiveness to local concerns as a means of gaining the support of Democrats.

Despising what he dismissed as a slapstick circus and uncomfortable with extemporaneous speaking that reduced public expression to "banality and irresponsibility," Adlai Stevenson complained to Alicia that Harriman was "kicking away the first chance in modern times for a major party out of office to agree on its candidate 10 months in advance and concert its effort and resources against the enemy instead of against each other." Reluctantly he began his campaign.

2

NINETEEN FIFTY-SIX WAS the busiest year of Adlai Stevenson's life. Defined by politics, it was divided into three parts—the primary season from January to June, the search for delegates from June until the Democratic convention in August, and the general campaign from August to November. It was also the year in which Adlai Stevenson celebrated his fifty-sixth birthday. Always the same age as his century, he was in fact older than the century and, past middle age, would live for only nine more years. Two years before, Stevenson had offered Princeton undergraduates his thoughts on aging. "What [a man] knows at fifty that he did not know at twenty boils down to something like this: The knowledge he has acquired with age is not the knowledge of formulas, or forms of words, but of people, places, actions— a knowledge not gained by words but by touch, sight, sound, victories, failures, sleeplessness, devotion, love—the human experiences and emotions of this earth and of oneself and other men; and perhaps, too, a little faith, and a little reverence for things you cannot see."

In 1956 he had no time for such bittersweet reflections. Nor was there a moment even for the customary birthday party. Since his divorce his intimates from Lake Forest had made February 5 into a special occasion remembered with poetry and verse, gaiety and song. Always the man they honored as the "Guv" starred at what Newt Minow called "the deflating retort, the complete squelch and the droll epigram."

The competition that took Stevenson on his unwanted odyssey began in January, intensified after he lost the Minnesota primary in March, and reached its climax in late spring with the Florida and California primaries. At first he entered only four of the nineteen presidential primaries that would choose less than half of the convention delegates. Still, reformers' complaints about the influence of party bosses on past nominations, television exposure that granted instant celebrity status to primary winners, and the nationalization of American politics that undermined the states' favorite sons pressed toward the adoption of primaries.

But primaries were not yet mandatory exercises, and Stevenson might have won the nomination without running in any. On the other hand Kefauver, a master at the informal exchanges of person-to-person campaigning that emphasized handshaking over speechmaking, might have convinced party leaders with uncommitted delegations of his preeminent popularity and therefore electability. Already the Tennessee senator had attacked Stevenson's record as an absentee governor gone from Illinois nearly 20 percent of his term, as a politician who had vetoed a bill to increase pensions, and as a corporate lawyer defending the giant monopoly RCA and therefore ill suited to represent the party of the people.

Confronted with these attacks, Stevenson began the search for delegates that irritated him so much that he threatened to write a book entitled "How Not to Elect a President." "[The presidency] is the highest temporal office on earth. There may be crazier ways of electing a president, but I can't think of any. . . . Why can't we grow up?" complained Stevenson of electioneering that required over a dozen appearances a day at Democratic meetings, at luncheons, and in the shopping malls of postwar America. "What do they think I am, a candidate for deputy sheriff?" he asked. Such a system prevented what he liked best—the development of national and international issues—and required what he despised—attacks on opponents, the glad-handing of voters, and speeches about such trivia as Mother's Day.

Primaries were also expensive. By the spring the Stevenson campaign was spending $21,000 a month and had a staff of thirty-eight on the payroll. Later Adlai Ewing Stevenson III agreed with his father: "The primaries make a candidacy into a thousand skirmishes, a welter of draining detail which plunges the candidate into a morass of dervish-like activity all largely beyond his control and comprehension."

Stevenson began campaigning ten months before the election. To Californians, his bald pate shining, blue eyes flashing, Adlai Stevenson joked, "Eggheads of the World arise. I was even going to add that you had nothing to lose but your yolks." He "confessed" that he was seeking the presidency and acknowledged the humility any presidential candidate should feel. If they didn't, they were undeserving. "I did not say that I am qualified for the presidency . . . [but] I am available." In any case, the "prize" should not be won in a popularity or endurance contest. Rather, "the important thing in our system is to continue and improve the dialogue between the two great parties in order to give our sovereign, the people, educated understanding choices between men and measures." But after hearing references to Woodrow Wilson, Charles Evans Hughes, Arnold Toynbee, and John Locke, some Democrats worried that Stevenson was too esoteric.

With civil rights issues moving into the foreground, he was asked everywhere about its episodes: the suspension of the black postgraduate student Autherine Lucy from the University of Alabama in Tuscaloosa on the grounds of "public safety"; the African-American congressman Adam Clayton Powell's proposal that segregated schools be denied federal funds; the Southern Manifesto, which committed ninety-six southern congressmen and senators to apply all lawful means to reverse the *Brown* decision; and the Virginia legislature's embrace of an anachronistic doctrine of state nullification of desegregation called interposition.

Adlai Stevenson read the complaints of African-Americans who, as a young friend of Chester Bowles's wrote, believed that his civil rights education was not complete. "[You] seem to be speaking to an audience that no longer exists. . . . [Your] approach is similar to the approach a college professor would use in a class. [You] should simply realize that a moral issue is involved which is not susceptible to the usual approaches. [The question] is how can you educate when the people to be educated are in daily contact with institutions, separate schools, railroad stations, drinking fountains, etc. which repudiate what you are trying to achieve?"

In response Stevenson offered neither a progressive's directive to push forward nor a conservative's support of the status quo. Planted firmly on narrowing middle ground, he presented placebos: he hoped that the issue would stay out of politics; he wondered why blacks were trying to embarrass him; he opposed cutting off federal aid to segregated schools on the basis that such a policy denied the very purpose of education. Persistently he placed desegregation (as he had anti-McCarthyism) within his definition of liberalism as the defense of individual interests, not as an attempt to secure equality for an entire category of people. To Agnes Meyer he complained that "all the intense young liberals want to hear about is civil rights, minorities, Israel and little else and certainly no 'vague futures.' "

To an audience at the University of Minnesota he declared, "The problem of changing a people's morals particularly those with an emotional overlay is not to be taken lightly. It is a problem which will require the utmost patience, understanding, generosity and forbearance and from all of us, of whatever race. But the magnitude of the problem may not nullify the principle. And that principle is that we are, all of us, free-born Americans, with a right to make our way unfettered by sanctions imposed by man because of the work of God."

The leader of a party that included southern segregationists, Adlai Stevenson invoked God and recommended, in light of the North's civil rights record, "no casting of stones." When the North Carolinian Jonathan Daniels, Franklin Roosevelt's former press secretary, a Truman adviser, and a family friend, urged him to stop appeasing "the arrogant Democrats from the South" and make known "we are not willing that the Ku Kluxers in pleated bloused robes run the party down here or elsewhere," Stevenson replied, "How you can write! It was a grand letter and my blood is hot." A few weeks later in his introduction of Stevenson, Florida's segregationist governor Millard Caldwell implied that Stevenson believed in white supremacy and "interposition." Characteristically busy revising his speech, Stevenson never heard the description and thanked the governor for kind words that later had to be disavowed. To Marietta Tree, who tried to educate him up to civil rights—even as he defined his role as requiring "more courage than pro–civil rights demagoguery"—it seemed that he always asked more sacrifices of blacks than of whites, a stance that led the leaders of the California NAACP to support Kefauver.

In March 1956, despite the support of state leaders such as Hubert Humphrey and Orville Freeman, Stevenson lost the Minnesota primary, the first of his contests with Kefauver. For this upset there were, as always in politics, many explanations: the Republicans had crossed over in the state's open primary and voted for Kefauver in order to embarrass Stevenson; Minnesota voters were rebels; the Democratic state organization was feuding; Stevenson had refused to endorse the farmers' favored policy of 100 percent parity; Kefauver had successfully smeared him as a captive of the Chicago bosses and a corporation lawyer out of step with regular Democrats; Kefauver, whom Stevenson considered a political huckster, was a more effective campaigner. Only the last was correctable.

For the remainder of the primary season, there was a new Stevenson. Reporters noticed, so did the campaign staff. His customary self-deprecation and cloudy forecasts of the national climate mostly disappeared. He acknowledged the need for reacting to the news in brief statements. "My long, carefully considered, painfully prepared speeches have a mighty meager audience in fact and get into the back country not at all," he informed Tom Finletter. He would abandon his efforts "to make each speech a masterpiece, a dazzling solo performance . . . and instead drive home a set of basic themes."

Harry Truman led the cheerleading of professional Democrats for the new Stevenson: "You have all the qualifications for that position [the presidency] if you will just let them come to the top. In the California and Florida primaries it began to come out." The candidate, pronouncing himself "liberated and emancipated," acknowledged that he was going to try harder than ever to "communicate with the people" and stop "pleading conclusions." There would be, he said quoting a friend but probably himself, fewer subjunctives and shorter sentences.

Less philosophical and more cogently organized, his speeches for the rest of the year contained fewer ethical appeals, fewer plays on words, and even less of the alliteration for which he was famous. After hearing one, his son Adlai joked that his father finished important speeches on time.

Now two Stevensons coexisted—the man who would be president and knew himself as an excellent governor, the leader of the Democratic party, an internationalist, and an exponent of midtwentieth-century liberalism, and the forceful politician. Gone was the charmingly ineffective candidate who got lost trying to show the farm he inherited from his mother to reporters whose names he never learned. Now he followed Arthur Schlesinger Jr.'s advice to become "more concrete, programmatic, down to earth and less rhetorical and be positive."

Distaste for the game of politics disappeared as Adlai Stevenson smiled and held lizards and stuffed alligators in Florida, donned Levis and cowboy boots in Texas, played croquet in California, and shook hands with a mannequin in Oregon. "I'm Adlai Stevenson and I need your support," said the remodeled Stevenson, advancing toward a group of old men in San Diego, one of whom groused, "I know who you are." Stevenson kissed babies and was kissed by women, though after one encounter a woman announced that she had lost her diamond ring. He no longer wore his homburg and looked much less like a history professor on his way to class, with a black loose-leaf notebook full of high-blown lecture notes. He was even photographed on his tractor with his shirt open at the neck.

By no means did this new approach to politics come easily, nor would it be sustained. In the end it would prove exhausting and drain the candidate's energy even before the general campaign began. After one meeting his speech writer Harry Ashmore advised that whatever was thrust into his hands he must not repeat his comment to a child who had presented him with the local specialty of a lizard: "For Christ's sake, what's that?" an unreconstructed Stevenson had shuddered. When he glimpsed a pregnant woman carrying a sign with the words "Adlai's the One," he told the story to everyone. In the past he might have included such a slogan in what he despised as the carnival of politics. Previously reluctant to use his children as props, he now asked his son Adlai and his pregnant daughter-in-law Nancy—the latter, in the style of Letitia and Buffie Stevenson, an effective campaigner—to come to Florida. Ruefully he informed his speech writers that he was doing his best to rise above the principles of "loving truth and despising winning."

For the first time Stevenson put on the politician's mask and became a supplicant. "I have come to New York to ask support for my candidacy for the office of president." He wandered through crowds establishing what he previously derided as the intimate relationship that emerges between "shaker and shakee." He looked on his campaigning self as another, using the third person to explain to Jane Dick that when a truck driver hailed him as "Adlai, Adlai," the driver was addressing another man, the public Adlai. Schlesinger observed that like many politicians he was developing the unreachable insulated core that protected public men from constant observation. Stevenson smiled and grinned, shamed his staff that they were not enjoying "pot-hole" politics, held a debate with Kefauver, and in the late spring won the primaries in California and Florida. As a prize, Agnes Meyer sent the victor a gilded bronze eagle from China's Han dynasty.

3

AFTER THESE VICTORIES Adlai Stevenson went home to Libertyville. In the style of nineteenth-century campaigns, party leaders now arrived to pay court—to sit on his screened porch, look at the sugar maples, and walk with their host (who was forever picking up fallen branches) to the Des Plaines River where it twisted through the back of his property. Some were invited to play tennis with a man whose game featured slices, wicked volleys, and what Marietta Tree described as "a slippery sinister forehand," but not much court coverage now that his five-foot eight-inch frame carried nearly 190 pounds.

Walter Reuther, the powerful head of the United Auto Workers, came, complaining of Harriman and curious about Nehru's India, which Stevenson had visited in 1953. George Ball and other advisers received an audience. So did the precinct captains of Lake County. At a reception for the latter, the old Stevenson briefly reemerged when the candidate wandered away from talk of local judgeships and party patronage to discuss American theater with the playwright Marc Connelly. Members of the Democratic issues group visited, heralding the 180 concerns they had identified for inclusion in the forthcoming campaign. A surprised Stevenson discovered that he had positions on only 50.

Then came the Reverend Robert Andrus, pastor of the Second Presbyterian Church in Lake Forest, which Stevenson, a Unitarian, had recently joined. Stevenson's switch to Presbyterianism offended Unitarians. The tiny denomination of fifty thousand, proud of its most famous living member, suspected that his departure to the Presbyterians was politically motivated. Agnes Meyer was also disgusted with his rebaptism: "Faith in what?" Meyer sneered, "in the value of religion as a political asset?"

Stevenson was perplexed by this interest in what he considered a personal matter. He explained his defection from the church of his mother to that of his grandparents on the basis of convenience (there being no nearby Unitarian church) rather than theology. He denied the switch had anything to do with politics and was sustained by a public letter written by three ministers. They noted that as governor, Adlai Stevenson had often sat in the Lincoln pew in Springfield's Presbyterian church, savoring the sermons of his friend the Reverend Richard Graebel, who acknowledged that Stevenson's Unitarian rearing had imbued him with the means of translating religious and ethical values into civic issues.

Adlai's friend Jane Dick had another explanation for the change. Privy to the inner Stevenson, she believed he discovered new spiritual opportunities in the Presbyterian church's emphasis on duty, guilt, and the fatalism of predestination he liked to call "his devil." He went to church more, sometimes arriving in the backseat of a friend's Oldsmobile bearing an "I Like Ike" sticker on its back bumper. Religion never disappeared entirely from his public messages—it was indeed part of his appeal—and his 1956 Christmas card brought the prayer that "nations will unite and the future will belong to those who have done the most suffering."

On July 4, 1956, Stevenson traveled to Bloomington to take part in a traditional celebration. Like his great-grandfathers Jesse Fell and John Turner Stevenson, and his grandfathers Adlai Stevenson and William Davis, he spoke to a local audience gathered in Miller Park for an afternoon picnic and, after dark, the setting off of Roman candles, sky rockets, and aerial bombs. Childhood neighbors gathered in the 98-degree afternoon heat, their fans waving like wind through leaves. By this time the celebration of a national holiday was no longer a community occasion as it had been in the nineteenth century, and so Adlai Stevenson spoke to mostly Democrats

from the stand where the Bloomington High School band played a program
of patriotic music.

He spoke of freedom and liberty throughout the world, noting as a
cause for optimism "the outbreaks of freedom from Soviet tyranny" in faraway places like Poland, East Germany, and Czechoslovakia, where spontaneous uprisings had briefly challenged Communist governments. Then he
turned to America's failings, describing a nation "adrift, leaderless in a troubled anxious world," and adding, "We are stalled in the middle of the road.
The American people have been fed a diet of sweet complacency that can
only lead to fatty degeneration." He closed with a gentle reminder to himself: "What I have learned in my travels across virtually all of the known
world is that the more we seek distant reaches, the more precious home
becomes."

Five weeks later Adlai Stevenson was nominated on the first ballot by
the 1,372 delegates of the Democratic National Convention, one-third of
whom had been in Chicago for Stevenson's first nomination. In a transitional period between the brokered conventions of the past and nomination
by primary, the delegates reflected traditional mandates: the American
attachment to states, party loyalty (delegates were allocated according to
their state's Democratic vote), and the power of the party's leaders, many
of whom were elected at large and some of whom became delegation chairmen. Reflecting the composition of the Democratic hierarchy, there were
only 295 women and probably (for no one counted) only 25 black delegates. Again the convention assembled three miles west of the Chicago
Loop in the fifty-year-old International Amphitheater, close by the stockyards, where the smell of blood and violence from a century of slaughtered
animals still seemed to permeate the air, especially around convention time.
Inside the hall delegates milled about the commercial displays of cigarettes
("Be Happy Go Lucky") and Coca-Cola ("The Pause That Refreshes") as
the national networks prepared to televise the proceedings into the 80 percent of all American homes equipped with the new electronic marvel. By
renting out the amphitheater's lobby, the chronically money-short Democrats simultaneously built their reserves and amused delegates.

After the young Massachusetts senator John F. Kennedy narrated a celebratory film that managed to absorb Abraham Lincoln into the party's pantheon of heroes, Tennessee's governor, Frank Clemens, displayed the
rhetorical gratifications of out-of-power politics. Referring to Nixon as the
"Vice-Hatchet Man," Clemens called for "decent political debate in
America," instead of Republican "double-faced debate. . . . The Vice-
Hatchet Man slinging slander and spreading half-truths while the Top Man
peers down the green fairways of indifference—will not be tolerated." For
five minutes the delegates cheered a line that signaled a theme of the forthcoming campaign.

No longer hidden away in a friend's home, Adlai Stevenson had this time rented the Hilton Hotel's Skylight Suite as well as a three-room headquarters in the Stockyards Inn. There, though he was furiously working on his acceptance speech in his law office, he also watched the proceedings on television and heard, during the long stretches of inactivity that exhausted even accomplished commentators like Edward Murrow, Eric Sevareid, Chet Huntley, and David Brinkley, what the Stevensonites called *Adlai's* songs—one from the popular musical *South Pacific* "I'm in love with a wonderful guy"; another with the 1952 slogan "I'm madly for Adlai" set to a complex melody.

This time Stevenson even suspended his chronic anxiety that he was being controlled—in the metaphor of his adult years that his mother was forever putting rubbers on him and chastising him if he misbehaved, got caught out in the cold, or failed an examination. Gone, too, was the emblem of his uncertainty—the "Ho Hum" used in his letters to convey nonchalance. Proudly he called attention to "*my* twenty-seven and a half million," referring to his popular vote in 1952. Marietta Tree, who arrived from New York to open the hospitality rooms necessary for delegate chasing, reported that "Adlai seemed quite serene and rather liked the role of being the focal figure. As who wouldn't?"

Earlier Kefauver had released his delegates. Only Harriman, whose interest surged when Eisenhower underwent intestinal surgery in June for Crohn's disease, remained in the race—with the support of Harry Truman. The wealthy New York governor had already given out baseballs signed by the Yankees at a governor's conference, and now his staff was preparing packages for delegates filled with books, china, and even aspirin. Along with the leaders of farm organizations, the former president preferred the New York governor's "fighting style." Unimpressed by claims from the Stevenson camp that the Democratic party needed a conciliator who could appeal to both North and South, Truman and Harriman supported a resolution pledging the party to implement Supreme Court decisions relating to desegregation and to pass federal legislation to secure equal opportunity for employment, voting, and the right, still uncertain for African-Americans, of "security of person."

Neither Stevenson nor his aides appeared before the Democratic Platform Committee, which spent fifty hours in hearings on civil rights. Instead, Stevenson sent a message that he would not "presume to dictate the resolutions to the committee or to the convention. I have every confidence that your conscientious labors will produce a plank that will enable us as the only national party to become the instrument of progress." There had been objections from southern delegates organized by Alabama's George Wallace when Stevenson offhandedly announced to reporters that he supported school desegregation. Instinctively antagonistic to the symbolic in politics, Stevenson declared that it was ridiculous to have to assert support for what the Supreme Court had already affirmed, thereby irritating both southern segregationists and northern supporters of civil rights. Meanwhile Stevenson's advisers prepared a memorandum of their candidate's credentials as a supporter of civil rights.

In the end the Democratic platform on civil rights in 1956 was an innocuous compromise. Southerners accepted its repetitions about the party's record in civil rights, and its assertion of fact that the Supreme Court was "one of the three constitutional and coordinate branches of the federal government superior to and separate from any political party." (The latter was a response to Nixon's partisan claim that the Republican party deserved credit for *Brown* v. *Board of Education*.) In return the liberals dropped their insistence on a strong statement supporting the Court's decision. Without any reference to implementation, the Democrats adopted Stevenson's do-nothing strategy of trying to detach white moderates from the South's extremists.

Nor, though this was less controversial, did the Democratic platform extend the party's endorsement of women's rights beyond its rhetorical approval of the Equal Rights Amendment, which had been languishing in the Senate Judiciary Committee since 1927. At least one veteran of the women's suffrage battle complained to the convention about this oversight. The disgusted Pennsylvanian Emma Guffey Miller declared that Democratic women campaigned as hard as men, and voted nearly as often as men, but were never consulted on policy or "integrated" into party affairs. "I simply want to warn every Democratic organization that if you go in for integration, gentlemen, make it true and make it real." But amid laughter—for in this era women's issues were considered trivial—the chairman commented that among the chorus of noes he heard an "attractive" woman's voice in opposition.

After his nomination a self-confident Adlai Stevenson, now his own man, beyond the partisan strings of Harry Truman, appeared before the delegates to demand a striking innovation in party tradition. Before he did so, in the moment of triumph as delegates rose, stamped their feet, clapped their hands, and cheered for Adlai Stevenson, Newt Minow encountered the Oregon congressman Richard Neuberger, another ardent Stevensonian, on the floor. The elation of the moment and the hard work that had made it possible brought tears to both men's eyes, but also, with Eisenhower as their opponent, a chagrined mutual understanding: "Brother, this is another lost cause."

Stevenson now insisted that delegates pick his running mate by ballot, using the same procedures employed for his selection. In the past personal predilection and political expediency had dictated the choice of the vice president by the nominee and party insiders. According to Stevenson, "The

American people have the solemn obligation to consider who will be their President if the elected President is prevented by a Higher Will from serving his full time." With Eisenhower's health uncertain and the despised Nixon back on the ticket, Stevenson had brought drama to the party convention at the same time that he subtly focused attention on a chink in the Republican armor—Eisenhower's health.

The next day a new generation of Democrats became national figures, as an audience measured at one-half of all American households watched the Democrats nominate a vice president. Fifty-year-old Albert Gore of Tennessee, forty-five-year-old Hubert Humphrey of Minnesota, and a candidate so young that his brother-in-law and adviser Sargent Shriver asked that his age not be mentioned, thirty-nine-year-old John Kennedy of Massachusetts, were all put forward, along with Kefauver. Stevenson expected Kennedy to win, and the Catholic senator came within thirty-nine votes of doing so. But the older, better-known Kefauver prevailed on the second ballot, as Stevenson grumbled that "the man who cost us a million dollars in the primaries" had become his running mate. The convention ended with Adlai Stevenson's second acceptance speech—in which elevation and spiritual searching were submerged in attacks on the Republicans and attention to issues like poverty and health care.

After four years of Republican "smiles and complacency," the new Stevenson proposed a "New America" to cheering delegates. "I mean a New America where poverty is abolished and our abundance is used to enrich the lives of every family. I mean a New America where freedom is made real for all without regard to race or belief or economic condition. I mean a New America which everlastingly attacks the ancient idea that men can solve their differences by killing each other"—the latter an obscure reference to both domestic crime and international tension over Quemoy and Matsu, the offshore islands claimed by Taiwan, that precipitated a crisis in 1954–55 between the United States and the People's Republic of China.

Other presidential candidates had attached the word "new" to their programs, hoping to convey inspiring vistas of opportunity. During the Civil War, Lincoln had called for "a new birth of freedom"; Theodore Roosevelt's New Nationalism had preceded his cousin Franklin's New Deal. In 1956 Stevenson found the origins of his campaign slogan as much in himself and his self-confident reseeking of office as in his hero Woodrow Wilson's New Freedom.

By the "New America" he meant to extend the depression-engendered New Deal programs (now accepted by Republicans) to areas of education, health, and poverty. In the past Democrats had organized campaign issues around easily conveyed positions of improved economic distribution to the old, poor, and unemployed, or around evocative group differences between the rich and the poor and around targets such as, in Grandfather Steven-

362

son's day, Wall Street, creditors, easterners, and corporations. Now Stevenson confronted intangible concerns relating to the quality of American life in the postnuclear "Age of Anxiety," in the phrase that coincided with the candidate's own impressive personal uncertainties.

In the New America the old Stevenson was still occasionally visible. "There is a spiritual hunger in the world today," he declaimed, "and it cannot be satisfied by material things alone—by better cars on longer credit terms. Our forebears came here to worship God. We must not let our aspirations so diminish that our worship becomes rather of material achievement and bigness."

Stevenson relied on the word "liberalism" to summarize his program. He meant by this malleable, ambiguous concept a humanistic persuasion reaching beyond the pocketbook concerns of depression scarcity (but also including some of them) to incorporate complex relationships between business and government, citizen and federal government, and especially nation and world. His views were shaped as much by the older progressive concern for individual virtue and good government as by the New Deal's attention to economic reform. Liberalism for Stevenson, beyond its "ardor for mankind" and commitment to private property, individual liberty, and sense of government as a positive agent for restrained social reform, was not so much a set of programs as "an emotional sympathy for the exploited."

Rejecting the reflexive antibusiness ethic of his father and grandfather's Democratic party, Stevenson depended on the partnership of business and government, a connection he had already developed in an article in *Fortune*. There he argued for "the frank recognition that every frontier in American progress has been, and will always be, opened by the joint enterprise of business and government."

Influenced by the message of anti-totalitarianism in Arthur Schlesinger Jr.'s *Vital Center* and, through Schlesinger, by the Protestant minister Reinhold Niebuhr, Adlai Stevenson's American liberalism was the search for what Niebuhr once called "proximate solutions for insoluble problems" in the age of the hydrogen bomb. Like Niebuhr, he believed that the goodness of man was bounded by human frailty and depravity, and he offered voters an unending struggle against evil not from a church's pulpit but from a politician's podium. As a confirmed Cold Warrior who would nonetheless "never fear to negotiate," he emphasized peace. Always more liberal in temperament than in policy, Stevenson became the spokesman for a national philosophy that, as ambivalent as the candidate espousing it, was losing its coherence. Two decades later his son would consider the doctrine of liberalism irrelevant.

Adlai Stevenson ended his acceptance speech with the hope that he would meet the delegates again "in every town and village of America." By November he had exhaustively tried to do so, three times crisscrossing the

United States until, in the plague of modern presidential candidates, his normal ruddy complexion had turned gray with weariness. In nine weeks he gave three hundred speeches and traveled 55,000 miles. (His hero Wilson delivered fifty speeches in the 1912 campaign.) At the beginning one reporter found him "the same Adlai that he was four years ago. He is somewhat thicker around the waist—his profile is vaguely ellipsoid, in fact—so that his clothes no longer achieve the sophisticated Princeton drape they once did."

In fact he was not the same. Throughout his earlier life Adlai Stevenson was notable not for talent or brilliance but for dogged self-improvement. Habitually, in everything from sports to schoolwork, he tried to get better. In his second national campaign a more confident and assured Stevenson made himself a better candidate not necessarily to beat Eisenhower—though he hoped to win—but to become a more effective agent of his views. Ironically in 1956 he shook more hands, patted more heads, and in the style of a Kefauver or Truman "humanized" himself in his contacts with the electorate, but got fewer votes. Always in touch with his message, he now made contact with his audience. While his son and his advisers insisted this was not new, reporters described a new "poised" style of mingling with crowds, greeting "humanity in the mass" in airports, posing with local dignitaries, and exchanging small talk at receptions and cocktail parties. From Agnes Meyer came the advice that Adlai Stevenson was doing his best to follow: "You must appear to enjoy politics. . . ."

Still, in this unusual repetition (since 1800 there had been only five rematches in successive elections of the same candidates), some aspects of his campaign remained the same—though now more firmly under his direction. His devoted eggheads—Schlesinger, Ball, Galbraith, and Martin—retained their influential role as "researchers." But this time Stevenson hired a veteran of Philadelphia politics, James Finnegan, as his manager, and his headquarters was in Washington, not in Springfield or in Chicago. "Last time," he wrote Dean Acheson, "I am afraid I spent too much time on texts, at the expense of politics. It's hard to do otherwise when you have some taste for responsibility and style. Evidently neither commands much of a premium in this business!" So believing, he never entirely mastered the politician's street personality, but he did improve.

A hero to many Americans, Stevenson was joined by several young admirers. Among them was Robert Kennedy, a twenty-six-year-old with a shock of unmanageable hair, a powerful father, and a brother in the U.S. Senate. Recently graduated from Duke University Law School, Kennedy had worked for the Justice Department and most recently on Senator McCarthy's subcommittee. Anticipating a political career, he rode the Stevenson trail as an apprentice, intending to take home some lessons on how to manage a presidential campaign.

Robert Kennedy was soon disillusioned. Never did these two men comprehend each other, and at no time was this truer than during the very campaign in which Stevenson altered his approach to politics. But not enough for Kennedy, who was so disenchanted that he voted for Eisenhower. "I thought it was ghastly," he said of Stevenson's effort. "It was poorly organized. More important, my feeling was that he had no rapport with his audience—no comprehension of what campaigning required—no ability to make decisions. . . . In 1952 I had been crazy about him. . . . Then I spent six weeks with him on the campaign and he destroyed it all." In turn George Ball believed the young lawyer surly and unhelpful, but after the election the ever gracious Stevenson acknowledged in a wry letter to Kennedy that he had "seldom heard sounder, more sensible and thoughtful remarks stated with better verbal conservation."

Among the differences between Kennedy and Stevenson was the latter's approach to television. After a licensing moratorium on new stations was lifted in 1953, some 80 percent of all Americans owned television sets. The implications of such figures were not lost on most politicians. But Stevenson remained suspicious of being advertised, as George Ball noted, like soap and toothpaste. He did agree to some coaching by CBS's Edward R. Murrow. He traveled to New York, where secretly—for Murrow had to be politically chaste—Stevenson discussed the possibility of a documentary that would highlight the declining prestige of the United States under the Eisenhower presidency. But when Murrow tried "to teach the candidate the finer points of speaking to the camera, [Stevenson] protested his dislike for the tyranny of the clock and the bright lights." Returned to Libertyville, Stevenson limited himself to short films. Hitting at the issue of inflation, which had risen to an annual rate of over 3 percent, he discussed the high cost of living with Nancy and Adlai, using grocery bags as props. Under the title "The Man from Libertyville," Adlai Stevenson stiffly answered questions about himself and his politics.

Swayed by his frugality at a time when half an hour of television cost $62,000 compared to radio's $200, Stevenson approved the airing on radio of some amateurish jingles. These included a barbershop quartet singing "The Democratic Party's not the party of the few / The Democratic Party is for you," used in the Midwest and the South. And as the Democratic National Committee frantically searched for a first-rate agency to take its account (many firms declined because of their Republican-controlled corporate accounts), the Republicans, adopting the innovation of five-minute spots, were completing their fiftieth short film and preparing to use television to persuade voters that their candidate was as healthy as he said he was after a heart attack and an intestinal operation.

While Eisenhower stayed in the White House until October, Stevenson was on the road. In a letter to the columnist Walter Lippmann, the Democratic candidate again employed the image of his early childhood, an echo of 1952: "The road I have chosen seems to be endless, but there can be no looking back now." And to the Schlesingers: "The road is long and full of obstacles." By this time the road was most often a flight path or a railroad track or an automobile cavalcade—the latter detested by Stevenson, who despised the police sirens and speeding limousines. Along the way the candidate's voice roughened and sometimes cracked; his face grew sunburned not from playing golf, as he liked to tell audiences in a knock at Eisenhower, but from "standing in public places delivering speeches." Everywhere he carried his battered tan calfskin bag with its three suits rumpled from his rushed inexpert packing, along with the rump-sprung briefcase filled with the coin of the campaign—manuscripts of past and future speeches.

Some thought his delivery improved this political season. A few, including a speech teacher, were not so sure. "Please, please tell our great candidate not to lower both his voice and his head at the end of each phrase or each sentence," advised one Democrat. "[His] most important words so well chosen are often lost. Better to pause before the new phrase or sentence rather than prepare for it at the end of the earlier one."

One of the governor's friends, the writer John Steinbeck, wanted improvements. Stevenson's problem, according to Steinbeck, was still his failure to communicate with audiences. "We know also that ordinarily people do not listen with their ears but with their feelings. To get to the brain we must go through the emotions," wrote Steinbeck, using as an example his popular novel *The Grapes of Wrath:* "When I wanted to pound home a harsh economic fact I was forced to open my reader by an emotional passage which left him receptive." But, according to Steinbeck, Stevenson lacked passion, referring to strontium 90—the fallout from hydrogen bomb testing—as interfering "with the procreative process. Now to an audience that doesn't mean a damn thing. If [Stevenson] had faced the camera and said right to their faces with anger 'And I mean by this you may not be able to have children and if you do they may be deaf and blind or deformed and sterile.' . . . Said that way he would have had his audience with something they could understand and feel."

4

IN THIS ELECTION YEAR of 1956 the villages, towns, and cities to which Adlai Stevenson came in his second presidential journey were as ambivalent about the future as the candidate was, and just as there were two Stevensons this electoral season, so there were two Americas. Postwar America was a fresh paradox, what Harry Truman once likened to two halves of the walnut. On the one hand, there was the prosperous, contented America of Republican advertisement, fed by continuing defense spending for the Cold War, innovative technologies and new businesses in electronics and plastics, and the baby boom. In one Republican television spot a grinning Eisenhower was introduced as a "man who looks forward toward tomorrow with confidence and excitement. And under Ike, America has begun more projects for tomorrow than ever before."

Aided by the federal entitlements of their war service, World War II veterans went to college, married the wartime Rosie the Riveters they displaced from high-paying manufacturing jobs, and bought houses in the new developments where identical ranch homes ($65 a month, $6,000 total purchase price financed by a Federal Housing Administration mortgage) faced each other on roads that curled in labyrinths through the countryside. The decade's increase in single-home ownership was greater than that in the preceding century and a half, until by 1960 nearly one-quarter of all Americans lived in planned communities, many bearing verdant rural names like Emerald Garden and Green Acres. Constructed far from the workplace, postwar suburbia made homeownership a reality for millions of Americans whose parents had rented cramped city apartments throughout their lives.

Interstate highways, new airports for jet travel, including Chicago's O'Hare and Bloomington's improved Municipal Airport, and two-car garages, soon enlarged for the longer, wider, chromier postwar car, defined a society on the move. The word "freeway" entered the vocabulary. Cities seemed to become paved parking lots overnight, and by 1956 one out of seven American workers held a job connected to the automobile industry, whose product was the symbol of the decade.

In the fifteen years after 1945, the average real income of American workers increased by almost as much as it had in the preceding half century. In the calculations of a new breed of statistically trained economists, by the 1950s nearly 60 percent of all American families could be classified as middle-class, that is, with annual incomes from $3,000 to $10,000. With money available to purchase the postwar bounty of freezers stocked with TV dinners, motor scooters with plastic seats, and electric carving knives marketed in cushioned boxes, consumers sheltered the economy from any backsliding, though there were two brief recessions in the 1950s.

The addition of thirty million people to the nation's population in fifteen years also fueled a prosperity in which the gross national product jumped fivefold. During this age of abundance—which Stevenson's adviser John Kenneth Galbraith labeled the "affluent society"—the poor, so obvious during the 1930s, seemed to have disappeared. The publisher Henry Luce dismissed poverty as merely "the habit of thinking poorly," as the editors of *Fortune* concluded that "only a million American families still look really poor."

In earlier years thrift and financial discipline had ruled the nation's economic culture; by the 1950s credit card buying challenged such an ethic. Ben Franklin, earlier enlisted for his frugality, was commandeered by advertising agencies. Reincarnated in an ad developed by the influential advertising agency J. Walter Thompson, he wondered if it is "not the hope of being one day able to purchase and enjoy luxuries that is a great spur to labor and industry."

It was the question of a newly inspired capitalism. Silenced by the economic failures of the Great Depression and by military concerns during World War II, American business began a political mobilization in the 1950s that would last for the rest of the century. Using their financial resources to extol the virtues of capitalism, along with the specific products that made consumers feel good, corporations spent millions of dollars promoting the benefits of the American system. One trade association created an economic counterpart to Virginia and Santa Claus. A widely distributed pamphlet, "The Miracle of America" ("Yes, Junior, there is capitalism"), featured a dialogue between Uncle Sam and "Junior" about what makes America great—"our economic system and all that." The answer, predictably, was capitalism, with its training in competition and its success in productivity.

When Eisenhower's secretary of commerce Sinclair Weeks assured the National Association of Manufacturers that "a climate favorable to business has most definitely been substituted for the socialism of recent years," more Americans (although not a greater percentage) purchased stock in what the Advertising Council dubbed "the People's Capitalism." Class divisions seemed to have dissipated in postwar America as labor leaders concentrated on bread-and-butter issues of hours and wages, cost-of-living adjustments and job security, rather than pressuring management for shared responsibility over the workplace or status concerns such as the closed shop and secondary boycotts. Meanwhile intellectuals who in the past had observed class struggle between warring economic groups now accepted the American future as a contest between competing power groups of farmers, business, veterans, and the aged. Adlai Stevenson agreed. In 1955 he encouraged the end of "talk about a basic antagonism between American business and government and [the replacement of] such nonsense with a recognition of the common purposes and obligations of these two cornerstones of democratic capitalism."

A "salariat" (in Daniel Bell's term) of women in pink collars and men in gray flannel suits filled expanding white-collar positions, blurring the traditional categories of labor and management, workers and owners. New categories of middle management ran personnel departments and learned how to supervise. In jobs that had not existed before the war, employees sold, advertised, and tested markets. Listening to postwar America, Walter

Lippmann concluded that Americans talked about themselves "as if we were a completed society, one which has no further great business to transact," save the continuation of personal happiness. To the chagrin of many northern Democrats who resisted this form of consensus, Stevenson picked up the theme: "It is a time for catching our breath; I agree that moderation is the spirit of the times." This America of low unemployment, of rising wages and affordable goods, of an enlarged middle-class living in suburbia, and of advertising was Eisenhower's America and the nation to which he and Nixon appealed during the 1956 campaign.

What the president called his "middle way" held as its highest ideal a classless society in which America's diverse economic interests were submerged in social harmony and stability. Believing the disunity created by "the great chasms separating economic groupings the most serious domestic threat of all," Eisenhower opposed the "unbearable selfishness of vested interests," whether of concentrated wealth, labor unions, or, as he later envisioned, the military-industrial complex. When politicians like Stevenson talk about issues, said the president, "they are often talking about those things on which they feel it expedient to make extravagant promises to various pressure groups." Adopting the philosophy of "a corporate commonwealth," Eisenhower accepted some social welfare programs of the Democrats, meanwhile promoting the interdependence of groups within the economy—a harmony of businessman, housewife, farmer, and laborer—without saying much about outsiders.

There was another America—a darker, less prosperous, more conflicted nation—about which and to which Adlai Stevenson spoke (even as he accepted parts of Eisenhower's vision of consensus) and to which some of his New America programs were directed. Stevenson's America was the nation, as he explained in a telecast from Milwaukee, where classrooms routinely held thirty-five or forty children, where many pupils attended part-time because of the lack of space, and where teachers who earned less than the average factory worker were neither fully trained nor qualified. Stevenson's America was the country in which the cost of medical care was "beyond the reach" of millions of families and where comprehensive health insurance was neither widely available nor financially attainable. Stevenson's America was the place where farm income had dropped during the Eisenhower years and farm families were losing their land to the mortgage bank, where four out of every ten households had neither running water nor inside toilets, where half of all houses lacked central heating, and where 6 to 8 percent of the labor force was unemployed. "These are the sorry facts, disgraceful facts, in this richest, most fortunate country in the world," said Adlai Stevenson in his Labor Day speech to automobile workers in Detroit's Cadillac Square.

Beyond the calm seas and prosperous voyage that the Republican ship of state sailed this campaign season, Stevenson's America included another form of destitution—the poverty of the spirit in a materialistic society "with the supermarket as our temple and the singing commercial as our litany." The Democratic candidate decried the death of civility amid "the roaring hot-rod car, teen-agers' beer cans along the roadsides, juke box blues dishing up love and religion in identical groaning tones, the rural mailbox ripped off just for laughs, a switchblade in the hands of a city teen-age gang boy." Suburban lives, according to Stevenson, were examples of "spiritual unemployment." "We need not just well-adjusted persons, not just better groupers and conformers."

Linking the emptiness of the conformist 1950s to declining national prestige during the Cold War, Stevenson initiated a theme that gained more attention in John Kennedy's 1960 campaign: how could such a meager society "fire the world with an irresistible vision of America's exalted purpose and inspiring way of life"? In a series of lectures at Harvard (where students began lining up for tickets two days before he was to speak), Stevenson had earlier summarized his persistent anxiety about his time and place in the titles of his three talks: "Ordeal of the Mid-century," "Perpetual Peril," and "America's Burden."

In these speeches and in his comments on foreign policy during the 1956 campaign, Stevenson offered Americans not solutions but rather an explication of the continuing challenges to their leadership from the Soviets. As always, he observed more than he explained or solved. More global in his orientation than were most Americans, whose newly discovered internationalism still focused on Europe, Stevenson popularized the concept of a "revolution of rising expectations" in Asia, where Americans must oppose communism but understand its attraction. At a time in which Americans believed that "when we encounter a problem in foreign policy we naturally assume it can be solved pretty quick—just pour in enough man power, money and bulldozers and we can lick it and if one diplomat can't come up with the answer fire him and hire another," Stevenson encouraged discipline and patience. "Our first job, it seems to me, is to school ourselves in cold-eyed humility; to recognize that our wisdom is imperfect and our capabilities are limited."

Stevenson's New America was by no means all-inclusive. His correctives to domestic problems overlooked large groups of Americans. Little attention went to blacks, women, migratory workers, Native Americans, and the poor in either the Republicans' three p's of peace, prosperity, and progress or the Democrats' New America. Stevenson's advisers recognized the limitations of their candidate's positions. According to John Kenneth Galbraith's later assessment, Stevenson "ran for president not to rescue the downtrodden, but to assume the responsibilities properly belonging to the privileged," a sentiment that Stevenson, who believed in Wilson's concept of capable leadership exerted by a learned class, might not have disputed.

Although blinkered to the other America of working women unprotected by fair wages or labor membership, working mothers without child care, or blacks isolated on the margins of declining city job markets, Stevenson's New America did offer concrete proposals. A few of these were strikingly new, some were awaiting action in Congress, and others were enhancements of the Democratic agenda already through the gateway separating innovative policies from conventional concerns. Viewed today, from afar, the Stevenson program seems only a slightly different hue of Eisenhower's stripes, but close up, from the vantage point of 1956, the differences between the Republicans and the Democrats were vivid to those in the electorate who found issues significant.

To older citizens Stevenson offered an office of older persons welfare in the Department of Health, Education, and Welfare, federally financed housing, and proposals to lower the retirement age for women from sixty-five to sixty-two, and to permit retired persons to earn more than $1,200 a year without losing their Social Security benefits. He recommended a variant of what later became Medicare, thereby earning the opposition of the doctors' powerful lobby group, the American Medical Association, which denounced such a plan as "socialized medicine." He promoted federal financing for school construction and teacher training. But he failed to provide any specific solution to poverty during a decade in which the share of all personal wealth held by the wealthiest 0.5 percent of Americans grew from 19 percent to 25 percent. "I believe with all my heart," he concluded lamely in Tulsa, "that we can abolish poverty."

Stung by Republican charges that his was the party of fiscal irresponsibility, waste, and overspending, Adlai Stevenson debated himself on whether his New America was affordable. A fiscal conservative by temperament, training, and conviction who once complained that his advisers were trying to convince him "that we can do all these things without taxes and I don't see how we can," he calculated that his programs would cost three billion dollars—to be financed by economic growth. Not only would the New America's programs expand productivity by maintaining full employment, and by improving health and education create a better-trained work force, but through the lever of tax policy they could achieve a stable noninflationary economy. As productivity grew, the resulting increased tax revenues would be shared by local and state governments, as well as, even after tax cuts, by private citizens who would consume more, and by corporations whose spiraling profits would permit further expansion. The New America would pay for itself, according to this partial convert to Keynesian theory.

Late in the campaign Stevenson proposed two new ideas, arguing for a moratorium on H-bomb testing in the atmosphere and for a "consideration" of replacing the draft with a professional army of volunteers. Most of his advisers—the former Connecticut governor Chester Bowles and Arthur Schlesinger Jr. were notable exceptions—opposed the introduction of such controversial policy innovations, and their caution was upheld in polls that revealed strong opposition to both ideas. Stevenson's staff insisted that he stick to the domestic issues that everyone agreed were the strength of the Democrats. But the new Stevenson, who had earlier informed the Baltimore journalist Gerald Johnson that he must campaign *his* way, did not heed the advice and marched boldly off into exposed political territory.

Both concerns fell outside mainstream politics. Neither party platform mentioned the draft or a test ban, although neither was new to Stevenson. Ever since World War II he had been preoccupied with the wastefulness of the military, and had found in the examples of the Air Force and the Navy, both of which relied on volunteers, an unrealistic model for the Army. And after the dropping of the atomic bombs on Japan, he considered atomic energy not just a military weapon or a potential source of peacetime energy but a preeminently moral, peculiarly American issue, since the United States remained the only country to have used the bomb—and on the civilian populations of two Japanese cities. For Stevenson the issue had both personal and global implications.

After 1945, Americans had temporarily shrugged off their fears of the atomic menace, only to confront renewed possibilities for a nuclear apocalypse in 1952. In November of that year in the Pacific Ocean, the United States tested its first hydrogen bomb—a fusion device that was exponentially more destructive than the World War II fission bombs dropped on Hiroshima and Nagasaki. In 1953 the Russians exploded their first fusion device, and Americans looked for protection to fallout shelters, bombers fixed on Soviet cities, missile launchers, and even pamphlets such as *You Can Survive*. In the event of a nuclear attack, this publication recommended getting in a house and rolling up the windows. "Should you happen to be one of the unlucky people right under the bomb," nothing would help. Still, if citizens knew "THE BOMB'S TRUE DANGERS," they could take steps to escape them.

In the meantime American and Russian tests continued, spraying the radioactive, bone-marrow-destroying strontium 90 over the earth. During the tests at the Eniwetok and Bikini atolls in 1954, radioactive ash had fallen on the unlucky Japanese fishermen of *The Lucky Dragon*, fifty miles away giving the world reason, as Stevenson noted, to "unfairly suspect [America] of caring precious little about Asians and peace." Later he warned, for he was acutely sensitive to the issue of American prestige, "People everywhere are waiting for the United States to take once more leadership for peace and civilization. We must regain the moral respect we once had and which our stubborn, self-righteous rigidity has nearly lost."

In the imagination of millions of Americans, fireballs and mushroom clouds came to symbolize life in what the columnist I. F. Stone called the "Haunted Fifties." Popular culture's oversized radioactive insects, best-selling fiction such as Nevil Shute's doomsday novel *On the Beach,* and everybody's dreams about the effect of radioactive fallout fueled anxiety. Polls revealed sleepless children fretting about the bomb, especially after the school drills that became a fearful memory of this generation. Meanwhile the government began constructing a reinforced bunker for important officials underneath a mountain in West Virginia. And Adlai Stevenson acknowledged to a friend that the possibility of a nuclear holocaust gave him nightmares.

In the spring of 1956 Stevenson unveiled his proposal for a moratorium in a speech to newspaper editors. "I believe we should give prompt and earnest consideration to stopping further tests of the hydrogen bomb. . . ." He returned to the issue in a speech to the American Legion, arguing amid boos that there could be neither peace nor serenity during an arms race when the "earth's atmosphere is contaminated from week to week by exploding hydrogen bombs." In Minneapolis at the Democratic-Farmer-Labor Bean-Feed in September, he reiterated, "We don't want to live forever in the shadow of a radioactive mushroom cloud." At first these were only fugacious inserts in his speeches on a topic that needed comprehensive elaboration.

In a nationally televised speech from Chicago in the middle of October, Stevenson presented his case at length: the United States had already stockpiled enough bombs; atmospheric testing of H-bombs over a quarter of a megaton in size could be monitored without on-site inspections, which the suspicious Russians would not permit; an end to testing might begin the process of negotiation and treaty writing that would end nuclear weapons proliferation; and, finally, a halt in testing would stop the spread of strontium 90 fallout, "the most dreadful poison in the world." On the eve of the election, he released a statement that offered expert testimony from a St. Louis surgeon to establish the point that the Eisenhower administration had lied about the levels of strontium 90 and that "growing children are the principal potential sufferers."

In response an angry Eisenhower—for this was his terrain, not the layman Stevenson's—placed the issue beyond the citizenry's understanding by demanding an acceptance of the authority of his experts. In the future such an approach would mark public discussion on many issues, until by the 1960s the removal of foreign policy concerns from the people had devastating effects during the Vietnam War. In 1956 the president established the pattern: "This specific matter is manifestly not a subject for detailed public discussion—for obvious reasons," said Eisenhower, thereby creating an image of the Democratic candidate as simultaneously weak and dangerous. Many citizens, even those supporting Stevenson, came to think that only government experts were capable of taking a position on security and foreign policy matters. "Can you imagine," said a snobby Stevenson volunteer, "Mayor Daley's Chicago precinct workers walking up and down the street wearing sandwich boards imprinted with big type 'Down with Strontium 90'?"

Although the Republicans considered it a matter for specialists, the experts disagreed about the limits of permissible exposure, some fearful of continued atmospheric testing, others supporting *Meet the Press*'s Lawrence Spivak's flip dismissal that present accumulations were equal to the radioactivity of a luminous wristwatch dial worn for a lifetime. Eisenhower announced that he would say no more, but later did. With the White House mail running in favor of a suspension, Nixon pummeled Stevenson's idea as "catastrophic nonsense," "the height of irresponsibility and absurdity." Stevenson "does not have the experience and the judgment that President Eisenhower does."

Then, in one of those rare interventions in American elections by outsiders, the Soviet premier Nikolai Bulganin, who had earlier proposed a twenty-year treaty of mutual cooperation and friendship with the United States, approved of Stevenson's idea for a ban, along with the "public figures who are calling for a ban." Immediately Eisenhower accused the Russians of interfering in the election. The political benefit was clearly to the Republicans, who inaccurately portrayed Stevenson as pledging to stop all research on atomic weapons and supporting unilateral cessation of all testing—not just of H-bombs in the atmosphere. Eisenhower gained support from those who could imagine Stevenson as foolish and ignorant, a naive mouthpiece for the Russians.

Rebuked, Stevenson was unrepentant. "I am sure I am on sound ground here and that the administration is unspeakably culpable in its failure to do anything whatever about the most terrible thing on earth," he wrote his English speech writer Barbara Jackson. And he was. Unsuspected by most Americans, Eisenhower had begun discussions with his national security advisers about the possibility of some kind of ban. Despite the pressure of senior-level administration figures who believed that the Soviets would cheat, two years later Eisenhower agreed to a suspension of all atmospheric testing. By 1963 the United States, the United Kingdom, and the Soviet Union were ready to sign a treaty outlawing nuclear tests in the atmosphere, in outer space, and under water, along with underground tests if they resulted in spreading radioactive debris outside the territorial limits of the testing state. Stevenson's initiation of public discussion on arms limitation was prescient.

As part of his New America, Stevenson proposed another innovation that, like his idea for a ban of H-bomb atmospheric testing, hurt him politically but was later accepted by Republicans and Democrats alike. Believing

~~the Republicans~~ incapable of any policy initiatives, Stevenson informed hostile members of the American Legion, "We can anticipate the possibility—hopefully but responsibly—that within the foreseeable future we can maintain the military forces we need without the draft." Again Stevenson shocked Americans who preferred hard-line militarism over any suggestion of weakness; again—for he had earlier accused the administration of cutting military spending for ballistic missiles—he appeared inconsistent. And again he introduced a complicated policy change that required explication and development in a lecture hall or policy paper, rather than in a paragraph in the harried political setting of a partisan rally.

Ahead of his time—for Richard Nixon would campaign on the issue of ending the draft in 1968—Stevenson saw modern armies as different from the foot soldiers of the past, who needed only a few days' drill and a rifle before taking the field. In the 1950s the three and a half million Americans in the military required expensive training in order to use the sophisticated weapons of modern warfare. Of this point there was no better example than his son Adlai, who had trained for over four months for his tank command in Korea.

Support for a volunteer army was a natural expression of Stevenson's elite liberalism. He opposed the draft because it unnecessarily disrupted the educational plans of young Americans like his sons Adlai and Borden, as they embarked on "life's ordained course." In peacetime, according to Stevenson, an army of draftees was extravagant, authoritarian, and inefficient, sweeping up those who lacked the education or commitment for professional soldiering. He also opposed the draft on economic grounds, because it encouraged an expensive turnover of nearly a million men a year. But as the campaign neared its end, he could not bring himself to adopt Chester Bowles's dramatic suggestion for a $25,000 tax-free bonus for those who stayed in the army ten years. Nor did he accept Bowles's idea that both his draft and his moratorium pledges appear in a comprehensive New America for Peace. Meanwhile the general in the White House dismissed the idea: "We cannot prove wise and strong by hinting that our military draft might soon be suspended. . . . This—I state categorically—cannot be done under world conditions of today."

5

THE PRESIDENTIAL CAMPAIGN of 1956 was shorter than most because of Eisenhower's health and because both conventions were held in August. Still, there was time to develop this contest's plot—its villains, heroes, conflicts, and fateful occurrences—though given the president's popularity its resolution was known from the beginning. The prosperity of the early fifties made another Republican victory easy to accomplish, as Americans separated "that nice guy Ike" from those things they disliked about his party, his policies, and his administration. The cries of "I like Ike" that greeted the president (and Stevenson) expressed affection for a popular leader.

Meanwhile Stevenson's reputation declined. Voters paid more attention to his divorce, and he surrendered the one personal advantage he had over Eisenhower—his administrative experience as governor of Illinois. Polls revealed that negative comments about Stevenson had tripled from 1952. Later Carl McGowan noted the agony of this campaign: "We went into 1956 with more research effort and thought than 1952. 1956 was heartbreaking. We were wrestling with jelly. The country was very complacent. Though the war hero had been shown wanting, there was no indication that was going to affect the voters." It didn't. Never did Stevenson come within ten points of the president in the polls.

The only dramatic element in the campaign was the president's health. If Eisenhower died during the campaign, could Richard Nixon beat Adlai Stevenson? Several polls showed Nixon losing to Stevenson. And even if the president survived the election, would he live through his second four-year term? Was a vote for Eisenhower a vote for a Nixon presidency—the man whom Stevenson accused of having "no standard for truth but convenience and no standard of morality except what will serve his interest in an election"? Could Americans "imagine putting Richard Nixon's hand on the trigger of the H-bomb"?

From Stevenson's perspective 1956 offered possibilities for a reprise of the moral tests of his childhood. He must be virtuous and so refused to consider victory as an end in itself. Such a view made Adlai Stevenson the last presidential candidate to avoid the excesses of image making—as Dean Acheson once said of the Kennedy administration, "of looking at oneself rather than the problem. How will I look fielding this hot line drive to shortstop? This is a good way to miss the ball altogether." With Stevenson there was never any doubt that once in the game, he would field the ball no matter how he would look. Moreover, in his calculations an error was an acceptable, even honorable badge of penitence.

As he informed the undergraduates of Yale during the campaign, "Victory is, after all, not an end in itself. Yet I often think that the single greatest difficulty about running for responsible public office is how you can win without, in the process, proving yourself unworthy of winning. . . . But the perception that you can pay too great a price for victory—that the means you use may destroy the principles you think you cherish—is fundamental to Democratic responsibility." Such idealism was good preparation for the role of noble loser, and it also raised victory, as in 1948 in Illinois, into triumph.

Meanwhile, through their creation of a mythic Eisenhower, the American people created a figure of authority and competence for the trials of the nuclear age. Stevenson accepted parts of this representation. But to him, fatherhood, the relationship he had endured in the household of Lewis Green Stevenson, conveyed mixed images—not so much of superintendence and benign authority but of absenteeism, indifference, and neglect of duty, the very components of Eisenhower's failed presidency. The Stevenson portrayal of his opponent may not have won votes, but for two decades it helped to shape a durable view of the Eisenhower administration. With Nixon's jowls and heavy brows providing grist for cartoonists, Eisenhower's bridge playing, golfing, and frequent absences from the White House reinforced Stevenson's image. Still, as a gentleman-politician, the Democratic candidate placed off-limits discussions of the president's health, as he had even before the campaign began. (Offspring must never anticipate a sire's death.) To one audience Stevenson offered a son's indictment of a neglectful father that relied on a fairy tale: "The Republican candidates can't say with much vigor and enthusiasm what they want to do—because they don't want to do very much. Hans Christian Andersen has already written the story of this campaign. He called it 'The Emperor's New Clothes.' All that Estes Kefauver and I have been doing is to tell people what they already know: that the emperor really doesn't have any clothes on at all."

Throughout the campaign Stevenson assailed the president's complacency: "The President doesn't run the store"; "Negligence is precisely what we have been getting." "On February 17, he played golf. On February 18, he shot quail. On February 22, . . . the President shot eighteen holes of golf," during a week in which there were significant developments in the Middle East. Like Lewis Stevenson, Eisenhower "huffed and bluffed, threatened and didn't deliver." Much like his father, who had let the Stevenson heritage of public life atrophy, this part-time president was responsible for a "paralysis of action . . . a calamitous decline of American power and diplomacy, false promises of liberation [of Eastern Europe], bungling in the Suez."

To this indolent, paternal Eisenhower, Adlai Stevenson played the son—an active, hardworking, bumptious adolescent anxious for respect and authenticity in a style that led Eisenhower to refer irreverently to his opponent as "that monkey." After the voting, when Eisenhower had won and Stevenson was reading his gracious concession speech, the president refused to watch, telling others to accept "the surrender": "I haven't ever watched him. Why should I start now?" Later, after Eisenhower suffered a stroke, his advisers rarely mentioned Stevenson's name, understanding that to do so would raise the president's blood pressure.

Stevenson had a different relationship with Nixon, who, to his representation of the good citizen, played the contemptible bully—a reincarnation of the schoolboys who fought dirty and who three times broke his nose in boyhood fights in Bloomington. Mutual contempt between Adlai Stevenson and Richard Nixon emerged from differences of class, personality, ambitions, and ethics. Stevenson's 1952 campaign manager, Wilson Wyatt, remembered Nixon as one of the few who earned the oath—"that son of a bitch"—from the rarely profane Democratic candidate. And years later Stevenson's oldest son vividly remembered his father's dislike for the vice president.

For Stevenson, Nixon was an ambitious, unprincipled partisan who craved winning, the exact personification of what was wrong with the modern form of American politics that made the achievement of power rather than the education of the people the purpose of campaigning. Nixon wore many masks, while only in his second presidential campaign did Stevenson begin to separate his private and public selves. An early practitioner of the late-twentieth-century political style in which the candidate became whatever was necessary to win, Nixon was an entirely plastic politician. Harshly denigrative in 1952, the vice president sweetened in 1956 on orders from Eisenhower and his advisers. He "has put away his switchblade," said Stevenson, "and now assumes the aspect of an Eagle Scout." The Democratic candidate hoped that *this* Nixon would repudiate the "irresponsible, vindictive, malicious words so often spoken by the impostor who has been using his name all these years."

Graced with none of the characteristics Stevenson believed those of civilized man—that is, courage, irony, humor, integrity, style, and grace under pressure—Nixon was Stevenson's complete villain. Others sensed the potential for immorality that led to Nixon's humiliating resignation in 1974, but Stevenson was among the first. Although Eisenhower had reservations about giving the vice president a second opportunity on the Republican ticket, offering him instead a cabinet post, it was Adlai Stevenson who first warned the nation of the perils of "Nixonland"—a place of "slander and scare; the land of sly innuendo, the poison pen, the anonymous phone call and hustling, pushing, shoving; the land of smash and grab and anything to win."

Finally—for by election day Adlai Stevenson had been on the road nearly a year—the end of this second journey was in sight. On October 29 an exhausted Stevenson was in Boston, where he issued two position papers—one on the hydrogen bomb and the other on the economy. The candidate had already given six speeches that day, including a telephone message to Democratic state chairmen predicting that the election of 1956 would follow the pattern of Harry Truman's 1948 upset victory. Then the news came that the Israelis had invaded Egypt.

The Israeli advance into the Sinai Peninsula followed by three months the announcement by Egypt's General Gamal Abdel Nasser that he had nationalized the Suez Canal. The day after the Israeli invasion, the French and British bombed Egypt, prepared to land troops near Port Said on the Mediterranean, and called for Anglo-French control of the Suez. The former allies hoped for American support, but instead received Eisenhower's call for a withdrawal of their troops, his outright rejection of any American troop involvement, and his support of a United Nations resolution for troop withdrawal, which was vetoed by the British and French. In a rare Cold War coalition, the Americans and Russians voted together on the General Assembly resolution calling for Israeli withdrawal.

And behind the Iron Curtain first the Poles and then the Hungarians had begun contesting Soviet power in the streets of Warsaw and Budapest. Premier Imre Nagy of Hungary denounced the Warsaw Pact and sought what was not to be—his nation's neutrality and autonomy. On the night before the American election, Soviet troops assaulted Budapest and put a bloody end to Hungarian efforts to achieve independence. Nagy was seized as Russian tanks and infantry stormed the parliament building.

These two events, taking place so far from the placid towns and cities of the United States, testified to the effect of global developments on postwar elections. In Washington, according to the *New York Times,* "the White House presented the country with the image of a veteran Commander in Chief putting politics aside to stay at the helm in a time of gravity." Stevenson saw the crisis as a confirmation of his earlier criticism that the president had given the Russians an unnecessary "toehold in the Middle East."

Earlier Stevenson had spoken against the inconsistency of first offering Nasser aid to build the Aswan Dam on the Nile and then withdrawing the offer when the Egyptian leader accepted aid from the Soviets. Events had, to Stevenson's way of thinking, validated his indictment of Republican foreign policy. And because Stevenson saw issues rather than men as the key to public affairs—"who leads us is less important than what leads us"—he calculated that these international crises would gain him votes. Clearly the Republican's seductive promises of rolling back the Iron Curtain, broadcast by the CIA's Radio Free Europe into Eastern Europe, had stimulated tragic uprisings against the Soviets. But when liberation movements began, support from the United States had never materialized. The Republicans, in Stevenson's moral indictment, had broken their promises.

Granted equal time on television in one of the first applications of the Federal Communications Commission's "fairness doctrine," Stevenson spoke to the nation about the "bankruptcy" of U.S. policy that had given the Soviet Union "two great victories": "the establishment in the Middle East of Russian influence [and] . . . the breakdown of the Western Alliance," the latter a reference to the division between the Americans and their Cold War allies, the French and British. As election day approached, Stevenson denounced the Republicans for their secrecy and complacency, offering a four-point program to secure Israel's borders, to oppose any unilateral control over the Suez, to resettle Arab refugees, and to improve economic conditions in the Middle East. Eisenhower did not disagree with such proposals. On the other hand Stevenson did not oppose Eisenhower's refusal to send military forces. The differences between the two men rested in Stevenson's criticism of past policy and his pledge that under his administration the United States would do better.

Three days before the election, amid the frenzy of this international crisis, Nancy Stevenson delivered her first child and named him Adlai Ewing Stevenson. "I hope this child will make its parents as happy as my boys have made me," said the grandfather. Once again private affairs intersected with public destiny. Changing his plans, Stevenson flew to Boston, where newsmen agreed that the baby resembled its grandfather, but was surely more handsome. In a family alert to public events, the timing of the birth on the eve of a presidential election in which the grandfather was the Democratic candidate seemed especially auspicious.

Returned to private affairs at the end of his year-long public exposure, Stevenson recalled in a television broadcast from Boston the values that he had learned from his family and had tried to convey to his children: "to distinguish right from wrong, to be disciplined, to be stalwart and dependable. These are old-fashioned virtues, but they are not, I pray, outdated." As a new grandparent, Adlai Stevenson remembered, "It was twenty-six years ago since I sat at the bedside of my eldest son and when he cried out in the night, sat there to assure him he was loved, that he was safe, that he was home. And during those hours and in so many small dark hours since I have asked myself as all of you parents have surely asked yourselves, have I done enough?"

Between visits to the hospital, Stevenson broadcast his last speech as a national candidate. Vintage Stevenson in the beginning, he eloquently invoked memories of the campaign and prophecies of the future. "We Democrats see in 'the people' the strong young man at the loom or the press or the drill in the clatter of earning a wage, and we want for that young man fair work laws and a steady job. . . . Or we see the grandmother with a broken hip or a heart attack or cancer, sitting in the sun on the porch in the thin workless evening of life, and for her we want security and medical care and some sort of bulwark against loneliness. Or we see the mother pushing a wire cart in the grocery store, anxious whether she can buy enough for the children. . . . And for this mother we want prices within reach and a good life of her own and high hopes for her kids."

Just before he came to the responsive reading "Methought I saw a nation arise in the world / And the strength thereof was the strength of right," Stevenson abandoned the high ground to announce that "every piece of scientific evidence we have, every lesson of history and experience, indicates that a Republican victory would mean that Richard M. Nixon would probably be president of this country within the next four years. I say frankly, as a citizen more than a candidate, that I recoil at the prospect of Mr. Nixon as custodian of the nation's future, as guardian of the hydrogen bomb, as representative of America in the world, as commander in chief of the United States armed forces." Hatred for the bully Nixon had overcome moral scruple; the prophet with honor of American politics had aired a judgment on Eisenhower's health that he had promised never to introduce into the campaign. Adlai Stevenson's spiritual journey in the guise of a political campaign ended with a personal attack.

The next day Americans reelected Eisenhower and Nixon with a larger majority than in 1952. Improving their popularity to 57 percent of the vote to Stevenson's 42, the Republicans carried five southern states, including, for the first time since Reconstruction, Louisiana. Stevenson lost over a million votes from his total in 1952 and ran behind his party, as the Republicans failed to displace the Democrats in the Senate or the House. The popular incumbent carried Democratic strongholds like Chicago, Jersey City, Milwaukee, and Baltimore.

The leaders of machines, never attracted to Adlai Stevenson, had not worked hard for his election. City wards, previously teeming with Democratic voters, were losing population as expressways, urban renewal, and the appeal of the suburbs ripped the heart out of political organizations. Stevenson's support among blacks dropped, as some voters agreed with Adam Clayton Powell that "Negroes who voted for Stevenson were traitors to their race." In 1956 more voters lived in the suburbs, making the older methods of door-to-door campaigning difficult. The split ticket, the declining party, the independent voter, and the nonvoter had become permanent features of American politics.

Believing that the international crisis at the close of the campaign would help his candidacy, Stevenson in his postmortem decided that it had cost him three million votes. As he explained to his cousin Julia Scott Vrooman: "All the evidence indicates that probably five or six million people rushed to find refuge with Eisenhower. . . . Let us pray that the consequences are not as disastrous as the Russian entry into the Middle East for the first time in centuries." To another supporter he acknowledged "the irony of the people rushing by millions to take refuge *with* Eisenhower *from* Eisenhower's disastrous mistakes in the Middle East." Eventually the Suez crisis and the Soviet invasion of Hungary became the rationale for his defeat in an impossible campaign against a man who had become a national good-luck piece.

The election of 1956 shattered Stevenson's faith in the electorate's ability to listen and to respond to his brand of politics. Still, a victory that narrowed the distance between what the candidate once called the "respectable and privileged" and the people might have been more difficult than a defeat. For his devoted partisans such an outcome would have demonstrated that the American public was not as foolish or ill informed as the Stevensonites believed. Or as Stevenson wrote Senator Herbert Lehman of New York four days after the election: "I am profoundly alarmed by the massive ignorance of our people about the situation abroad, and the extent to which the Administration has successfully contributed to this delinquency. To ratify failure is bad enough, but the ignorance it discloses is more serious." The candidate's adherence to the Wilsonian view that the rational citizen could understand objective truth (and that he was presenting it) was shaken, and references to the sheeplike tendencies of the electorate crept into his postmortems.

Stevenson's perspective offered little room for any understanding that public affairs, campaigning, and getting elected were inextricably linked in a democracy. Or that the process was changing because of technology, though he had tried to offer "a new Stevenson" to accompany his programs for the New America. In politics competitors were never supposed to believe that their campaign had a monopoly on truth. Stevenson, however, located his voters in his grandfather's time when "to hear the candidates discuss the great issues of an earlier America, people rode all day by buggy or wagon; they waited for hours for the candidate's train; they stood in the sun and rain and listened." But as Adlai Stevenson I knew and his grandson evidently had forgotten, this generation reflexively voted the party line.

Four years later, testifying before a congressional committee considering the replacement of the equal-time rule with debates between the Republican and Democratic nominees, Stevenson argued for substantive debates that would restore "democratic dialogue . . . what we seem to have lost— our sense of great national purpose." By this time he had become a hero in defeat to those who accepted his vision of politics as a crusade against pandering to the voters—"a civilized man's search of power," wrote Hans Morgenthau in the *New Republic*. In his case the search was always conditional, as Adlai Stevenson made it clear that the party needed him more than he needed it or the supreme prize of the presidency. But what would be remembered about his two campaigns were not his public programs and ideas for the New America but, ironically, the private man—his character and personality, his wit and charm, his efforts to negotiate and keep the peace within the Democratic party, his elegant speeches and the grace with which he accepted defeat.

No loser was ever more poised. While his supporters wept and required weeks to recover, Stevenson described himself as "beaten but not bruised," and opening a jeroboam of champagne, he invited reporters to partake in "post-mortems on toast." (By comparison an angry Nixon snarled at reporters after his defeat in 1962 for the California governorship that the press would no longer have him "to kick around any more.") After his second defeat Adlai Stevenson said farewell to his followers "with a full heart and a fervent prayer that we will meet often again in the liberals' everlasting battle against ignorance, poverty, misery and war. Be of good cheer. And remember, my dear friends, what a wise man said—'A merry heart doeth good like medicine, but a broken spirit dryeth the bones.' As for me, let there be no tears. I have lost an election but won a grandchild."

In the coming years he would try to keep the merry heart developed in childhood, when he first discovered, as Arthur Schlesinger Jr. once described, "that life wasn't going to work out the way he hoped."

PART THREE

ECHOES

Stevenson in the limelight at the 1956 convention, with Kennedy in the background. Later their positions were reversed. (Illinois State Historical Library)

Stevenson wanted to be secretary of state, but Kennedy, in an announcement made from his Georgetown home, offered him the ambassadorship of the United Nations. (Collection of the Library of Congress)

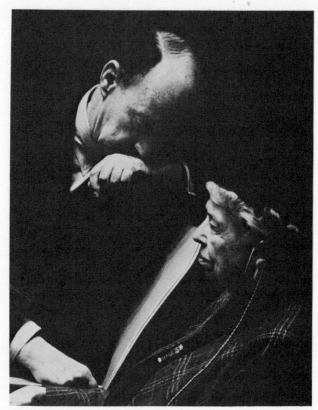

A pensive Stevenson at the United Nations with his friend and ally
Eleanor Roosevelt. (Courtesy of Buffie Ives)

Buffie Ives and Adlai Stevenson hold the great icon of Stevenson
public service—the pen and ink set given by the Senate to Vice
President Stevenson in 1897. (Princeton University Libraries)

With a stern John McCloy in the background, Stevenson confronts the Russians during the Cuban missile crisis of October 1962 at the United Nations. (Princeton University Libraries)

The UN was transformed during the Stevenson's tenure by the admission of new countries in Africa. Here Stevenson meets with the ambassador from Guinea. (Princeton University Libraries)

In Dallas, weeks before Kennedy was assassinated in November 1963, radical right-wingers beat Stevenson on the head with their signs. Note the reference to Hiss and the woman who has just spit on the ambassador. (Princeton University Libraries)

Stevenson expected an improvement in his position when Johnson became president, but soon found otherwise. Here the two men hold an unusual conference. (Courtesy of Buffie Ives and the Lyndon Baines Johnson Library)

Among Stevenson's diversions during his final years was his social life. Here several women cluster around him at a United Nations party. (Princeton University Libraries)

Stevenson arrives at the opera with First Lady Jacqueline Kennedy and the wife of a German official. (Collection of the Library of Congress)

Marietta Tree in her capacity as a United Nations representative confers with Stevenson. The two had an intimate relationship for several years. (Princeton University Libraries)

"Bear," as he was called by his father, and his parents at Libertyville in the 1930s. The two Adlai Stevensons remained close, and the younger Adlai gave his father advice about politics. (Princeton University Libraries)

In 1964 Adlai Stevenson III was elected on the bed-sheet ballot to the Illinois legislature. Here the new legislature is sworn in. (Illinois State Historical Society)

Anger and division at the 1968 Democratic National Convention. (Collection of the Library of Congress)

Richard Daley was an important figure in the lives of both Stevensons. Here he and Adlai Stevenson II share the political stage at a Democratic picnic. (Courtesy of Adlai Ewing Stevenson III)

Stevenson III and Daley were at odds during the 1968 convention, especially after Daley used the police against war protesters in Chicago. (Collection of the Library of Congress)

The last Libertyville picnic, in September 1969. Democrats met to reform the party, when news came that Everett Dirksen had died. Mayor Daley attended, as did Jesse Jackson. (Illinois State Historical Library)

Adlai Stevenson was elected to the U.S. Senate in 1970 and served there for ten years. (Illinois State Historical Library)

Three Adlai Ewing Stevensons. The bust is of Vice President Adlai Ewing Stevenson I (1835–1914). (Illinois State Historical Library)

At home on the farm in Jo Daviess County he loves so much, Senator Stevenson with his four children and wife, Nancy. (Illinois State Historical Library)

The Stevenson glare. During the 1980s Stevenson lost twice in his bid for the governorship. Some said his inability to relate to voters was a reason. (Illinois State Historical Library)

Buffie Ives, Adlai Stevenson, and a grandchild continue a family tradition on Stevenson's last visit to Bloomington, in 1964. (Courtesy of Tim Ives)

CHAPTER ELEVEN

IN THE SHADOWS

1

IN 1960 TWO MEN stepped from a fashionable house in the Georgetown section of the nation's capital. The younger—tan, boyish, restlessly running his hands through his thick hair—moved quickly to the microphones. The older man was bald and fat; even a double-breasted suit could not disguise his girth. Frowning into the slanting December sun, he took his place before an impatient corps of reporters accustomed to waiting for news in front of this red brick house on N Street. Behind the press a group of Georgetown University students paraded to and fro, holding aloft hand-lettered placards reading "Stevenson for Secretary of State" and "America Needs Stevenson."

The younger man, the barely victorious president-elect, began, "I can think of no American who would fill this responsibility [of ambassador to the United Nations] with greater distinction. . . . I regard this as one of the three or four most important jobs in the entire Administration . . . and it is my hope that if Governor Stevenson accepts the position, he will attend Cabinet meetings and will serve as a strong voice in foreign policy over its entire range. He has always answered the call of duty on every occasion in his life. . . ."

Politely Stevenson thanked the president-elect for his confidence. The United Nations, he agreed, was at the center of American foreign policy. Then he uttered the words that transformed his host's smile into an icy glare: "While I have not sought this assignment, I want to be helpful. I have some matters both of the organization of the work and of ways and means of strengthening it that I want to consider and discuss with him further." Did this mean, a reporter asked, that he had not accepted the ambassadorship to the United Nations? Yes, but he hoped to soon, "pending a further talk."

Furious—for other presidential appointees had shown no such insulting hesitation at the prospects his administration offered, and he had even met certain conditions for this one—the president-elect stalked back inside muttering, "I hope it will be before the middle of next week." In response, Stevenson turned his back and walked along N Street, gathering, like a pied piper, crowds of applauding students, one of whom thrust a copy of Thucydides at him for an autograph. "I've never gotten so close to greatness," he enigmatically murmured, insisting to the trailing reporters that he would do "his duty."

The differences between John Fitzgerald Kennedy and Adlai Ewing Stevenson, so obvious in this exchange, haunted both men during the early 1960s. Because of Stevenson's international reputation and national following, their barbed relationship was more than a minor irritation for the president. For Adlai Stevenson, serving in the administration of a man who "never said please or I'm sorry" became another in a lifetime of dilemmas. Friends noted how in each other's company they became their exaggerated selves—Kennedy more ruthlessly ironic, Stevenson more verbosely prim.

Believing that Stevenson acted like "an old woman" when he refused to say whether he was a candidate for the 1960 Democratic nomination, Kennedy once placed the sixty-year-old former governor in the bow of his sailboat in the choppy waters off Hyannis Port, watching wickedly for any signs of seasickness from a man he described as an "idealistic weeper." Disparaging even Stevenson's reputation as an intellectual, Kennedy told friends that he read more books in a week than Stevenson did in a year. From Stevenson's perspective, Kennedy had become "very self-confident and assured and much tougher and blunter than I remembered in the past." Later he would complain of the "boy commandos running around down there in Washington."

On the surface Kennedy and Stevenson shared circumstances that might have nourished mutual respect. Both came from families that had trained them for political careers. Both were wealthy; both were graduates of Choate and Ivy League colleges (Kennedy had briefly attended Princeton before enrolling at Harvard); both were articulate Democratic leaders who inhabited that wing of the party considered liberal on social issues and internationalist on foreign policy. Harshly anti-Eisenhower, both had moved beyond the bread-and-butter issues of Roosevelt's New Deal to confront national malaise—what Stevenson identified as "the decline of moral purpose . . . [in a nation] that prefers the political status quo, business profits and personal comforts." Practitioners of the postwar policy of containment, both focused on foreign affairs.

But their personalities, sculpted in different family politics, set them apart, especially in their attitudes toward power. While Stevenson, according to his friend George Ball, "hated to think in power terms but rather dealt in aspirations and the relations of people," Kennedy followed his adviser McGeorge Bundy's dictum that "the center of the concern of the man who takes an active part in government is the taking and using of power itself." Intensely competitive, Kennedy believed the presidency conferred an authority that he could use to shape history and gain, as in a touch football game, victory. Stevenson, on the other hand, considered no man worthy of the office's demands. Still, if he were summoned, he would dutifully serve. Remembering his own relationship with the heroes of the New Deal and later Secretary of the Navy Frank Knox, Stevenson expected Kennedy to behave as a deferential apprentice. But the son of Joseph Kennedy needed no paternal surrogate.

Their differences emerged in 1956 when, at the Democratic National Convention, Stevenson opened the vice-presidential nomination to the vote of delegates, hoping that Kennedy, then a thirty-nine-year-old Massachusetts senator, would win. Like elephants, the Kennedys never forgot—or forgave—what followed, believing that Stevenson had withheld support for Kennedy, who nearly won a nomination that, only in retrospect, might have hindered his triumphal march to the White House. Stevenson viewed the train of events differently. "I have felt that I launched [Kennedy]," he said, remembering that he had given a little-known senator the honor of nominating him. Such a privilege had spotlighted Kennedy, who had returned the favor, his eyes on his own prize, with the encouragement that Democrats "think beyond even the election in November or the four years that lie ahead."

When Stevenson lost his second presidential election, in 1956, he denied any interest in another. "I will not seek the nomination," he repeated in the intervening years. "It would be presumptuous of me to claim squatter's rights or to seek a third nomination," explained the two-time loser who had redefined the word "candidate" to apply only to those who "go after" nominations. "However if nominated, I will accept a draft." It was a renunciation, given an unlikely draft, that resounded through the upper echelons of the Democratic leadership, especially since Stevenson encouraged his friends "to work for the avowed candidate of your choice." Meanwhile Kennedy was courting delegates.

In January 1960 Senator Kennedy announced his candidacy for the Democratic nomination, entered the now essential presidential preference primaries in the spring, and defeated Senator Hubert Humphrey of Minnesota in the Protestant state of West Virginia, thereby demonstrating his electability as a Roman Catholic. By the summer he was, in the language of the columnists, the front-runner. Still, the field of contenders was large, and favorite sons might suck up enough first-ballot convention votes to prevent a victory, even by one who counted a quarter of the necessary votes by late spring. Kennedy wanted a Stevenson endorsement. After the Oregon primary in May, he traveled to Libertyville for a horse trade. The young senator, if he won the presidency, could offer the secretaryship of state in return for Stevenson's support, though Stevenson's lieutenants encouraged Kennedy not to be so crass. Their man would never accept anything that smacked of a deal.

Later there were conflicting reports about what happened in Stevenson's study, but certainly Kennedy did not get what he wanted. As a result Stevenson did not either. In a phone call to George Ball, Stevenson described the confrontation: "He said to me, 'Look, I have the votes for the nomination and if you don't give me your support, I'll have to shit all over you.' . . . I should have told the son-of-a-bitch off but, frankly, I was shocked and confused by that Irish gutter talk."

Two months later the Democratic convention met in Los Angeles—Stevenson territory, where the graduates of the independent club movement and devoted followers led by Hollywood's Dore Schary still supported their 1950s hero. Stevenson's neutrality fitted into the ambitions of another contender—Lyndon Baines Johnson, the Senate majority leader. Johnson and a fellow senator, Missouri's Stuart Symington, hoped an anti-Kennedy coalition could stalemate the convention to their benefit on later roll calls. But as they plotted, all the contenders noted the persistence of the draft-Stevenson supporters, bankrolled by the noncandidate's rich friends, especially Agnes Meyer, and organized in forty-two states under the direction of Oklahoma's Senator Mike Monroney. Hoping to make history repeat itself, these faithful tried to sign up delegates for a two-time loser who refused to participate.

By the time of the convention, they had gathered a million signatures on a draft-Stevenson petition. Still, their task was frustrating, especially as the night of decision approached. "You have overdone your hands-off policy," complained Agnes Meyer, who was paying William Attwood to write Stevenson's speeches and now in her midseventies took up the role, reminiscent of Helen Stevenson's, of an admonishing mother. "I demand that you rise to your greatest self. . . . My demand [is] that you now become the great leader you are."

Others despaired as well. "Isn't it about time you did something to help us?" wrote one dispirited volunteer who did not understand, as the Kennedys forthrightly cajoled and promised, the intricate dilemma that Stevenson was fashioning for himself. But this time the predicament was not the governor's alone. Members of his inner circle were struggling with their allegiances—a future with Kennedy or loyalty to the man who had first fired their political impulses. Few were as diplomatic as the party's grande dame and fervent Stevenson admirer Eleanor Roosevelt, who eventually proclaimed herself "nostalgically for Stevenson, ideologically for Humphrey, and realistically for Kennedy."

Before the Stevenson inner circle, likened to "a curious religious order," defected, most followed the Harvard professor and former speech writer

Arthur Schlesinger Jr.'s lead in asking Stevenson whether he was going to run. When he airily maintained that he wasn't "personally a candidate," John Galbraith, James MacGregor Burns, Arthur Goldberg, and even Stevenson's law partner Willard Wirtz moved into Kennedy's camp. Torn, Schlesinger acknowledged that Stevenson was "a much richer, more thoughtful, more creative person" than the cool, measured Kennedy. The latter demonstrated an "intelligent concern with action and power," whereas Stevenson conveyed an "odd sense of unreality . . . a certain frivolity, distractedness, an over-interest in words and phrases."

When Stevenson arrived at the Los Angeles airport for the convention, over five thousand enthusiasts cheered and waved the familiar signs—"Stevenson for President"; "We Believe in Steve"; "Adlai Is a Moral Man." It stirred the noncandidate's partisan blood, even though he promptly isolated himself in a Beverly Hills hotel cottage scented by orange trees, far from the sweaty, smoke-filled convention hotels where the Kennedys were signing up delegates and consulting files crammed with the names of seventy thousand Democrats. His faithful supporter Eleanor Roosevelt pressed him to announce—as she had earlier in her newspaper column—but he merely grumbled that he should have stayed home. When Bobby Kennedy demanded that Stevenson place his brother's name in nomination and threatened, according to one report, "I warn you—you are through if you refuse," Stevenson ordered him from his room. "Your guy must be out of his mind," hissed Joseph Kennedy, who had been working for his son's nomination for four years and whom Stevenson despised.

On the second day of the convention, Stevenson took his place among the Illinois delegation. By this unusual appearance, he intended to end any confusion about his candidacy. That candidates did not take their place on the floor had remained a fixed protocol from Grandfather Stevenson's time. But just as Stevenson was out of step with the nominating process of the 1960s, which required intense campaigning in the primaries, sophisticated polling, and attention to individual delegates, so again he miscalculated. As Democrats glimpsed the man from Libertyville, an uncontrollable ovation arose, a moment of spontaneous nostalgia for many delegates and for the galleries, where hundreds of Stevensonites were packed, their orchestrated hope for the future. Half carried to the podium amid cries of "We Want Stevenson," the noncandidate of covert ambition was asked to address the convention. Waiting for silence, his admirers anticipated the soaring rhetoric of 1952, which might, as Eleanor Roosevelt hoped, swing the convention to him. Someone glimpsed a scowling Bobby Kennedy crouching in the audience. A poster with the old rhyme "Madly for Adlai" floated past the television cameras.

Like Grandfather, Stevenson customarily began his speeches with an anecdote. Such was his public version of what in private was his specialty—

gracious self-deprecatory small talk. Now he began with a lackluster wise-crack, joking that this convention's nominee would be the one who survived the crowds. What followed—a brief attack on the "listless" Republicans and a pedantic recital of Cold War issues—was no better. Soon the man of the golden words was addressing a convention stilled not by his eloquence but by the certainty that Adlai Stevenson must not lead the party into the 1960s. Most likely nothing could have shaken the delegates' commitment to Kennedy, but having risen through the force of his words, Stevenson now fell through their banality. Some believed his performance intentional; others noted that the man who depended on written texts was unprepared. Eleanor Roosevelt explained that it would have been "un-Stevenson-like" to prime any draft.

But later that night Adlai Stevenson abruptly began working for the nomination, soliciting votes from the delegations of California, Pennsylvania, Minnesota, and his own crucial state of Illinois, which must serve as a beachhead. Within hours he became, even by his own strict definition, a candidate, though he declined to admit such a heresy. After he consulted Monroney about possible nominators, Stevenson explained to those solicited that he was not a candidate. "But my incorrigible friends have made me a candidate and insist that I be placed in nomination." When the moment came for presidential nominations, Senator Eugene McCarthy eloquently begged the delegates not "to reject the man who has made us proud to be Democrats. Do not leave this prophet without honor in his own party."

The next day the delegates shook off a losing hand and on the first ballot chose Jack Kennedy, who rode to the convention with clenched fist muttering, "Go—Go—Go." In the voting that followed, Adlai Stevenson received 79½ votes of 1,521, running behind Johnson and Symington. Only 2 came from Illinois's 68 votes. That delegation was on the firm leash of Cook County's boss, Richard Daley—the man whom Stevenson had appointed director of the Illinois Department of Finance in 1949. And Daley had switched to Kennedy months before the convention.

Stevenson's behavior at the convention was characteristic. In an act of principled realism, he initially removed himself from the presidential race so that others might have a chance and so that he might avoid the possible humiliation of becoming, along with William Jennings Bryan, a three-time presidential loser. Then, subverting his neutrality, he never silenced the coterie of enthusiasts who continued to work for him until Kennedy was nominated. To do so would have been to manipulate the people's voice, though in the end he had no compunction about appealing to party leaders.

From the perspective of a man who believed democracy's survival depended on attracting the best men to politics, the electorate might, if left alone, recognize his virtue and call him to power—especially since the despised Richard Nixon was the likely Republican candidate. "It never occurred to me," Stevenson wrote John Kenneth Galbraith, who reminded him of his disclaimers, "that anyone would doubt I was available if wanted." To the political scientist James MacGregor Burns, he explained his refined partisan manners: "If I said I would support a draft, I'd be courting it. If I said I would not, I'd be a draft evader." His imagined past as a "political accident" made it easy to overlook the usual reality that conventions (and society) gave nothing to those who asked for nothing. Operating from different premises, Kennedy interpreted Stevenson's behavior as demonstrating his craving for a nomination he sought without having to work for it.

There was this time, as there had been in 1952, evidence for Kennedy's point. Until the second day of the convention Stevenson had honored his pledge not to work for the nomination, but he made certain that no avenues toward its advancement were blocked. He had drawn attention to himself through speeches during the spring of 1960, some written by a paid member of the draft-Stevenson movement. He had agreed to edit a volume of his collected speeches entitled *Putting First Things First,* which appeared in January and sold out in Los Angeles during the convention. He had published articles in national magazines and newspapers such as *Life* and the *New York Times,* and in May had written an article for *Harper's* called "The New Africa." After his return from a trip to Latin America, he chose the timely subject of leadership for a major address at the University of Virginia, where he claimed Thomas Jefferson as a fellow egghead. To the Americans for Democratic Action, he declared, with a glance at Kennedy, that integrity must be the essence of presidential leadership. As the convention approached, Stevenson gained attention with his stinging criticisms of Eisenhower's administration, especially after the Russians shot down a U-2 plane in May 1960, and Eisenhower took cover in the fiction of a lost weather plane. Yet before the Democratic convention Stevenson never wavered from his position that he would let his forlorn hopes run their course without his encouragement, even briefly removing a speech writer paid by the draft-Stevenson movement.

Then, in a moment of self-deception during the convention, he contradicted himself by advancing his cause, justifying his reversal by the necessity of loyalty to the friends who had worked for his nomination and whom he had never discouraged. Perhaps no mortal could have withstood the pandemonium of the convention, but his devotees expected either more or less of him. Indeed, Stevenson expected more of himself, though he retained the consoling fiction, as he informed Agnes Meyer, that if he had wished, he "could have taken it away" from Kennedy.

That fall, as Kennedy had worked for him in 1956, so Stevenson dutifully campaigned for Kennedy, especially in California. With his special audience—"the Stevenson people, the young and those interested in foreign policy"—he intended to "talk of course about civil rights. I'm completely in sympathy to the sit-ins, as long as they are respectfully handled as they have been so far." Earlier he had been irritated by northern liberals who pushed for desegregation of schools "in terms solely of racial justice instead of education. Don't pull down whites to raise the blacks." When, in October, Martin Luther King Jr. was arrested in Atlanta on trespass charges after a sit-in and later sentenced to four months hard labor in a maximum security jail for driving with an expired Alabama license, Stevenson refused to console King's pregnant wife, Coretta, by telephone—as Kennedy later did—because he had not been introduced to her. It was another example of Stevenson's wariness in racial matters.

With the despised Nixon as his target, Stevenson delivered seventeen major speeches in October, heatedly attacking an administration he called lackluster and a candidate he dubbed "Revolving Richard, who has changed so many times he doesn't know whether he's coming or going. Well, we do. He's going." In Sacramento after a torrid condemnation of Nixon, a voice in the dark stung: "Governor, since when have you become Jack Kennedy's hatchet man?"

Throughout the campaign Stevenson rued his bad luck, for in 1960 the Democrats no longer faced the supreme hero of postwar America. Self-consciously Stevenson compared Cicero and Demosthenes. When Cicero finished his orations, Stevenson told an audience that may have missed the point, the people said how well he spoke, but when Demosthenes finished, they said let us march. It was a difference revealed in another exchange when Stevenson and Kennedy campaigned together in California. The conversation flagged, and to fill the silence that often separated two otherwise talkative men, Stevenson complimented Kennedy's tan. The handsome Democratic nominee replied that his sunburn came from waving at the crowds from the back of convertibles. "I would never do that," Stevenson replied. "It's awful, the sun in your eyes and the dust. You can't see for hours afterward."

Seldom in his speeches did Stevenson mention Kennedy's name, a practice initiated when he introduced John Kennedy to the Democratic convention for his acceptance speech and in a five-minute introduction named the nominee only once. In Scarsdale, New York, Stevenson's omission was so egregious that the local head of the former draft-Stevenson club, Dean Rusk, felt compelled to mention Kennedy by name. Meanwhile, using Stevenson's campaigns as disastrous examples of bad politics, Robert Kennedy reminded his brother never to give "elaborate speeches on world affairs to twenty-five miners" or work a county without advance notice to local politicians. By November the effect of Stevenson's effort was uncertain.

Nixon carried California, but in an election in which less than one-tenth of a percentage point and 113,000 votes separated the candidates, it certainly did no harm.

After the election Adlai Stevenson expected John Kennedy to appoint him secretary of state. He believed himself best qualified; he had delivered over twenty campaign speeches and had swallowed his earlier reservations that he "could not go to work for such an arrogant young man." Not only had he served, along with Chester Bowles, as Kennedy's foreign policy liaison to Eisenhower during the campaign, but appealing to Agnes Meyer for financial support, he had persuaded George Ball to write a comprehensive survey of foreign policy admired by Kennedy. (Later Ball complained that he could hardly get Stevenson to read the 123-page report.) Then, in December, Stevenson heard the shattering news that he was being considered for the lesser posts of attorney general, ambassador to Great Britain, and ambassador to the United Nations. "Why should he appoint you to State?" his former assistant William Blair explained to a chagrined Stevenson. "He doesn't owe you anything."

There were other reasons for the decision besides Kennedy's personal distaste for the man he believed had tried to derail his nomination. Stevenson, according to the president, was too controversial. His sympathy for a two-China policy in the UN compromised his usefulness as secretary of state for a president with a scant majority who needed good relations with Congress. The State Department "will chew him alive. They'll call him an appeaser, a Communist." "Poppycock" was Stevenson's response delivered through his emissary Blair. The close election was the very reason to appoint him: "[I] would bring the confidence [the president] needs," along with the support of the Stevensonites, many of whom had supported Kennedy only reluctantly. Besides, wrote Stevenson to a friend, "Kennedy's orientation is to neither Europe nor Asia, just to Washington."

The president-elect considered other possibilities for secretary of state—Arkansas's Senator William Fulbright, Connecticut's former governor Chester Bowles, Ambassador David Bruce, and the unknown from Cherokee County, Georgia, who was currently president of the Rockefeller Foundation, Dean Rusk. Meanwhile an FBI clearance contaminated Stevenson by reviewing his innocuous associations during the 1930s with two groups on the attorney general's list of subversive organizations during the McCarthy era—the Institute of Pacific Relations and the Southern Congress on Human Welfare.

Stevenson further irritated the agency's director by "uncooperatively" dismissing two agents checking on his law partner Newt Minow, soon to be appointed director of the Federal Communications Commission. In retaliation Hoover repeated to a Kennedy emissary the lie that Stevenson was a notorious homosexual. Stevenson remained on the bureau's "restricted" list, and the top bureaucracy of the FBI included in his file a report that he "had made a point of visiting pornographic statues" in Lima, Peru—the latter among the artistic treasures of that nation.

While Stevenson glorified the unattainable secretaryship of state despite the warnings of a friend, the writer John Steinbeck, that "any strong president is his own state minister and the titleholder is an errand boy," he had few illusions about the position Kennedy eventually offered him. Pondering a future as United Nations ambassador, Stevenson drew up a balance sheet. On the debit side, besides the lack of authority over policy, which was set by the State Department, was the risk to his "tranquil old age and reputation" and an anxiety that he believed "evidence of incompetence." Still unsure of himself as he sought a role in public life at a time when self-effacing modesty was no longer a virtue, Stevenson told an English interviewer that he used to be afraid he was going to fail his examinations: "I would wake up in the night and worry about that, and I sometimes still do. I'm still taking those examinations, over and over again." He recalled as well a Roman emperor who "everyone agreed was fit to rule until he did."

On the other hand, propelling him toward the ambassadorship was his family-inculcated, itchy sense of public service and what his friends knew was a reluctance to retire to the sidelines. By no means intoxicated by power, Stevenson had nevertheless discovered that applause compensated for the emptiness of his private life. "Would I feel more frustrated out than in?—If after year could retire if not being effective and have subordinated my own interests—been good soldier as usual. If say no, not prepared to take less job—bad sport? If say no—6 months may feel frustrated—something may jeopardize the whole UN."

The final decision was agonizingly arrived at, though predictable. At first Adlai Stevenson insisted that he would decline. William Blair, soon to be appointed ambassador to Denmark, responded that the governor would never be happy practicing law in Chicago "after all you've done." When Stevenson regally replied that he would continue as "*we* are—speeches . . . articles," his law partner warned, "Instead of front page news you'll get three lines on page forty-six of the *New York Times*." The United Nations was, after all, a conspicuous stage and a continuation, now that he had lost the leadership of the Democratic party, of his public forum.

Over brandy George Ball advised Stevenson that he was "incapable of taking himself out of public life" and that he should not play Agamemnon. "He always had an enormous capacity for dramatizing himself. . . . The thing that fascinated me about Adlai was that he accepted so easily the idea that he was a great historical figure. . . . I think he had Abraham Lincoln on his mind a great deal."

Persuaded, Stevenson added conditions that included a congenial secretary of state—for example, he would not work with McGeorge Bundy, who had twice voted against him and was, he believed, hostile to the United Nations. He must have a veto over staff appointments, a voice in foreign policy matters beyond the United Nations, and Kennedy's agreement to the platitude "Our policy is to end the Cold War as soon as possible." On December 11, three days after Kennedy had offered him the position, Adlai Stevenson accepted.

His ambassadorship at the United Nations would be the longest period of his public service, and he would die in office. Unlucky in love and politics, Stevenson never looked back after he became ambassador, sharing with Alicia Patterson his hopes for the future: "Waste no tears upon the blotted record of lost years / But turn the leaf and smile / Ah, smile to see the four white pages that remain to thee and me."

Adlai Stevenson joined an administration whose members were chosen to reverse what the new president had described during his campaign "as a dangerous slide downhill, into dust, dullness, languour and decay." Such a message held a Stevensonian ring. In his suggestions for Kennedy's inaugural address, Stevenson warned that "no nation in all history from the days of Greece and Rome has survived the poison which creeps into its lifeblood when the pursuit of ease and comfort becomes its goal." The president did not use Stevenson's words, only some of his ideas about the United Nations. But he did turn the lamentation into a call for national service.

Providing a symbol of the nation's aspirations, as presidents invariably do, Kennedy added little philosophical content to the aging principles of Democratic liberalism, offering instead a nonexistent missile gap to fire up a nation more preoccupied with the Cold War than with minimum wage rates and Social Security. To catch up with the Russians (when the Americans were already ahead) required a tenacious zeal, and the president surrounded himself with young successes under fifty—Robert McNamara, his brother Robert, Stewart Udall, McGeorge Bundy, Orville Freeman, and J. Edward Day, the last Stevenson's former insurance commissioner. Steeliness became a prized trait among those whom the journalist Theodore White called the "Action Intellectuals."

As he had been in college, as a LaSalle Street lawyer, and even as a Democrat in the age of Eisenhower, Adlai Stevenson was again an outsider—in but not of the administration, a songbird amid the lions and foxes. Only Luther Hodges, the secretary of commerce, was older than Stevenson in a cabinet that averaged forty-seven years of age. Flaccid, bald, and soft compared to the new frontiersmen's lean, hirsute hardness, Stevenson's marginality rested on more than physical difference. No matter how often Kennedy proclaimed the importance of the United Nations, everyone knew that Stevenson's position was that of a bit player. As Kennedy talked about catching up with the Russians, second-strike capacity, and soon Secretary of Defense McNamara's counterforce–no cities nuclear strategy (the latter posited reserving some nuclear forces with which to threaten Soviet cities after the initial counterattack on Soviet missile sites), Stevenson preached blithely vaguer themes of harmony and negotiation in an age with the potential for global suicide. A proponent of both the military and the economic containment of the Soviets, Stevenson mixed these principles with hopes for disarmament, advocating an expanded role for the inconsequential United Nations Disarmament Committee.

Most members of the Kennedy cabinet offered, in the rare cabinet meetings of this short administration, crisp directives for action presented in declarative sentences, studded, especially in McNamara's case, with impressive statistics. Stevenson preferred abstractions—what one State Department official described as "the rhetorical side of things . . . rather than the mechanics of multilateral diplomacy which Kennedy was interested in." The UN ambassador's comments instead meandered into the contrarieties and antonyms that wasted the time of young activists employing "almost wise-guy language."

He had other failings, appearing to National Security Adviser McGeorge Bundy to be in a hurry to leave meetings and "never seem[ing] to have the government on the top of his mind." According to Undersecretary of State Richard Gardner, "Stevenson was a disappointing administrator. . . . Too often he was pushed by the flow of events. . . . JFK loved details, but Adlai got off at a certain depth. He was not interested in detail. If it could be certified as liberal or helping world order, then it was all right. He didn't probe too deeply." Soon in the Georgetown living rooms and around the water coolers of the State Department, Adlai Stevenson became the butt of derisive jokes.

The president was among the few who appreciated "the searing destruction of self-confidence after two defeats," observing to his adviser Walt Rostow that "Stevenson wouldn't be happy as president. He thinks that if you talk long enough you get a soft option and there are very few soft options as president." To Robert Kennedy, Stevenson came to represent "the discredited liberals . . . who were more or less in love with death . . . and who like a cause more than a course of action. Action or success makes them suspicious. That's why they think Stevenson is the Second Coming. He never quite arrives there. He never quite accomplishes it."

Amid these tough guys of undaunted self-confidence, Stevenson quickly learned the degree of his obsolescence. When he attended the inauguration, on a memorably cold day in January 1961, he heard the president proclaim, "The torch has been passed to a new generation of Americans born in this century, tempered by war, disciplined by a hard and bitter peace. . . ." After the inaugural address "the brightest and best . . . the sons of the morning"—a phrase from a nineteenth-century hymn used by Sargent Shriver to describe the talent this administration sought—flocked to the waiting limousines for the ride to the White House, some like the president with neither coat nor hat. But there was no car designated for Adlai Stevenson. So the future ambassador to the United Nations trudged down the hill and along Pennsylvania Avenue, warmed by the applause of a crowd gathered to watch the pageantry.

2

IN THE FOURTEEN YEARS since Adlai Stevenson had served as an alternate delegate, the United Nations had grown from a small tentative club of fifty-one nations housed in temporary quarters on Long Island. Now the buildings along New York's East River displayed the organization's permanence—the glass tower of the Secretariat, where since 1953 the Swedish diplomat Dag Hammarskjöld had served as an activist secretary general from his office on the thirty-eighth floor; the General Assembly Building with its large auditorium, where what Stevenson called "the agenda of mankind" was discussed; and across the street the new multimillion-dollar U.S. mission for its UN staff of 117.

Here, on the fifteenth floor, Adlai Stevenson, who preferred to be called governor because there were so many ambassadors at the United Nations, presided over a staff that included three others with ambassadorial rank—Charles Yost, an experienced foreign service officer, Francis Plimpton, his friend and former roommate at Harvard Law School, and Philip Klutznick, the wealthy Chicagoan soon to become the mission's expert on the UN debt. Criticized by black leaders for failing to hire more African-Americans and by members of Kennedy's staff who found him unwilling to accept blacks, Stevenson did find room for two friends—Jane Dick and the woman whom he called "dearly beloved" and might have married, Marietta Tree. Anxious to attract the State Department's best men, the new ambassador sought, with limited success, to turn the UN into a training ground for young foreign service officers.

During his four and a half years as UN ambassador, fifteen nations—mostly from Africa—joined an organization that swelled to 115 members by 1964. Such a tangible expression of colonialism's demise became the principal story of Stevenson's tenure, just as his appointment signaled to the international community his nation's recognition of a world beyond Europe. Flagstaffs, it seemed, were always going up in front of what Stevenson called the home of "the family of nations," made up, in this nuclear age, of "the whole human race. . . . We have to learn to live in this great family of the world. It is a complicated family and as the house gets smaller, the family gets larger."

To Stevenson's chagrin, Soviet-American conflicts remained beyond the

reach of an organization whose charter upheld two contradictory principles: the territorial integrity of the nation-state and the need for collective
security. As the UN deteriorated into a theater for Cold War propaganda,
Stevenson frequently played the role of an American nationalist. In June
1962 he assailed the Russians' hundredth veto and the Soviet abuse of their
voting privilege in the Security Council, thereby reinforcing hostility
toward the Russians. But mostly, as he admitted, "the balls are going over
our heads."

Still, he dutifully maintained an optimistic view of the organization's
possibilities, variously describing it as a perpetual peace conference, a listening post to the human race, a policeman, a Solomonic judge, an American vision, a humanitarian Red Cross, a moral lesson, and a debating
society where "we beat plough shares into words." In Washington the
United Nations was viewed as a field post, but to Stevenson it remained, in
his paraphrase of Lincoln, "the last best hope of peace." Its problems were
those, according to Stevenson, of an adolescent. Applying his habitual
domestic metaphors, he likened Woodrow Wilson's League of Nations to a
stillbirth and the organization he had served in the late 1940s to an infant.
Whatever it was, the UN was no longer the handmaiden of the U.S. State
Department, as Stevenson searched for voting coalitions beyond European
allies in order to defeat resolutions for the admittance of Mao's China, sanctions against South African apartheid, and, after the Bay of Pigs invasion,
its own censure.

Stevenson lived in an eighteen-room Manhattan apartment rented by
the U.S. government with a dining room that seated forty on the forty-
second floor of the Waldorf Astoria Hotel. From his eagle's nest, the horizon
stretched across Long Island and northward into Westchester County and
southern Connecticut. A man who had spent his early years in a small
midwestern city on the Illinois plains lived his last years in a hotel with
room service, surrounded by original French Impressionist paintings on
loan from the Metropolitan Art Museum or from the collections of rich
benefactors like Mary Lasker. Stevenson did find space for some Americana,
hanging letters by George Washington, Thomas Jefferson, and Abraham
Lincoln in an apartment that cost the United States $30,000 a year.

In such a setting midwestern plainness gave way to a gourmand's indul-
gences. His other half reemerged—the side of Stevenson that in the past
had enjoyed college weekends and vacations in Jamaica and Chicago deb
parties—as if private excesses and a celebrity's perquisites might somehow
compensate for a diminished public role. He was "going to seed," according
to his friend George Ball, surrounded by "those rich females, this odd
harem who gave him the best food in New York." A rich man whose outside
income from his portfolio, the *Pantagraph,* and his $25,000 annual retainer
from the *Encyclopaedia Britannica* as a member of the board dwarfed his

$27,500 salary as ambassador, Adlai Stevenson departed from the thrift and discipline he encouraged for the nation.

Always in the company of beautiful women, he escorted the movie stars Joan Crawford, Lauren Bacall, and Marlene Dietrich, along with Jacqueline Kennedy—once complaining that the first lady indiscreetly discussed her marriage. Now a social trophy, the ambassador attended Broadway openings, nightclubs, restaurants, and parties with his harem, cruised on friends' yachts in the Caribbean and Mediterranean, where he enjoyed the public's adulation, and rested during the summers at Buffie's rented villa outside of Florence. Even the energetic Lady Bird Johnson wondered how Stevenson "can work and think all day in the tense arena he's in and go to parties all night."

Once Stevenson joked that he got along best with the wrong kind of people—married women and intellectual men, though he was considered intellectual only by those who were not, and some of his female friends, including twenty-seven-year-old Sarah Plimpton, the daughter of his friend and UN associate Francis Plimpton, were single. Aware of his restless search to surround himself with celebrities in what William Blair called "Stevenson's Hotel," Buffie recognized his loneliness and disgustedly listed eight of his "intimates" in her diary. Some of these relationships were platonic, but others were not. Earlier, when Agnes Meyer had diagnosed him as a poor prospect for marriage, Stevenson had agreed, though it was not easy to dismiss the idea: "I've been so busy all my life with impersonal things and still am [that] I'm not a fit candidate for marriage."

His signature recipe—an artichoke and shrimp casserole—was replaced now by soufflés and French cooking, graced by California wines. He painted his bedroom his favorite deep blue, and reinstalled the gold silk dining room curtains considered too ornate by his predecessor Henry Cabot Lodge. Although Stevenson had given up smoking after the 1956 campaign, he began again, adding to this intemperance of two packs a day more drinking and eating than his friends remembered. Both Lauren Bacall and Marietta Tree noticed his compulsive gorging on hors d'oeuvres and plates of after-dinner chocolates, consumed as if he were filling an emptiness. Wilson Wyatt was disturbed by the incessant twitching of his eye, and his surrogate mother Agnes Meyer cautioned an unattainable "calmness for the long haul." Buffie, who correctly believed that both she and her brother had better nerves than their parents, forwarded Helen Stevenson's maxims and one of her own: "Never be in a rush"; "Be true to yourself ever and in all ways"; "Be merciful to those boys and to us of your own blood."

Temptation was everywhere. "Here," Stevenson wrote his friend and speech writer Lady Barbara Jackson in 1962, "things swirl along at the usual ridiculous intensity and pace. I fight off the smoked salmon and creamed chicken and alcohol, but surrender to too many engagements and too little sleep. I even went to Princeton to celebrate the dedication of a memorial for Foster Dulles," the latter a reference to Eisenhower's secretary of state, whom he had criticized during his 1956 campaign.

Stevenson traveled constantly, though visits to Libertyville became infrequent. Instead, the United Nations became his home; the family of nations his family, for he saw little of his sons: thirty-one-year-old Adlai, a lawyer in Chicago; twenty-nine-year-old Borden, mostly unemployed in New York; and twenty-six-year-old John Fell, a real estate developer and oil investor in San Francisco. "Too much of my life and travels," Adlai Stevenson complained, "have been spent alone without kith or kin." Honored as the American father of 1961, he signed his letters to his sons "with much, much love from a wandering Father" and lamented to Borden, who shared his apartment, "how hard it seems for us to get together."

In his capacity as ambassador, Adlai Stevenson not only represented the United States at the United Nations; he also served as an advocate of the UN to the United States. In the former capacity he had to be—and was—a dependent. Policy came from Washington and was delivered through the State Department's Bureau of International Organization Affairs. As its assistant secretary Stevenson had chosen Harlan Cleveland, a graduate of Andover and Princeton. But the two men's personal compatibility never changed the reality that as an ambassador he "was a messenger boy—always on the end of a telephone being told what to do," in circumstances that mimicked his childhood in their erosion of his independence.

At least one member of the administration, Dean Rusk, felt that despite his complaints Stevenson was relieved when his orders came from the State Department. "I never saw anyone happier to get them." Others agreed that he was "no great fighter with [the State Department] on policy" and that he made "many fewer proposals for action or initiatives" than his successor Arthur Goldberg. Shut out by Kennedy and overworked at the mission, his appearances in Washington dwindled.

Even his jewels—the speeches that featured so prominently in his career—came from Washington. Though they were colored by his evocative expression, only their delivery was his. Disingenuously, he complained, "They are holding me in too tightly—even changing words in my speeches," although he had not written most of his speeches for years and more than ever depended on his friends, especially the English writer Lady Barbara Jackson, to provide complete texts. Later Harlan Cleveland could remember only two speeches Stevenson had drafted in four years.

In the beginning Stevenson described his labors as "the most exhilarating work done by man," undertaken with his high-minded resolve "to do something indispensable to human welfare and the welfare of one's country . . . and to leave the world better than [I] found it." It was also work that adhered to the Stevenson tradition of traveling the main highways of history. Like the family's migration, Grandfather's engagement in nineteenth-century party politics, and even his own governorship at a critical time in the emergence of state governments, Adlai Stevenson's service at the UN summarized significant themes—in this case of the American assumption of world power and a newly discovered internationalism. Not by chance did Stevenson entitle a volume of his speeches *Looking Outward.*

Adlai Stevenson was also the voice of the United Nations to the United States at a time when right-wing zealots like the former Army general Edwin Walker (who with impunity flew the American flag upside down in front of his Dallas home as a sign that the nation was in peril) accused the United Nations of being a Communist-dominated conspiracy that controlled American foreign policy. (On the contrary, though neither Walker nor Stevenson knew this, Secretary General Trygve Lie had so capitulated to McCarthyism as to permit the FBI to investigate American employees of the UN for subversive activities.) The Daughters of the American Revolution were as vehement as General Walker, resolving that the UN was an anti-Western institution undermining national sovereignty. Such a stance led Buffie Ives to resign from the organization her grandmother Letitia had founded. The Daughters had no regrets: "We don't want pinks in the DAR," responded one.

Though he was attacked by conservatives for his supposed lack of patriotism, Stevenson's internationalism in fact never strayed from an abiding faith in American exceptionalism, which he expressed in the moralistic language of the Cold War. In his messages on *Adlai Stevenson Reports*—a bimonthly Sunday radio and television program—he described the United Nations as a national export, a by-product of the Republic's idealism. "The UN is to America," he enthused, "as a novelist approaching some universal theme." Not only was its structure a replica of that of the government, with its one-nation, one-vote mechanism in the General Assembly mimicking that of the U.S. Senate, so that tiny Luxembourg with a population of 316,000 had the same vote as the United States; but the UN charter, modeled on the preamble to the U.S. Constitution, "expresses our deepest philosophical traditions." From this nationalistic perspective developed Stevenson's view that the United Nations would be the birthplace of a code of ethical international behavior. Implicit in his understanding was Wilson's legacy that democratic constitutional governments provided the most rational responses to crises in any system of collective security.

When he took his place at the horseshoe table of the Security Council in early February of 1961, Ambassador Stevenson was warmly applauded at his first meeting, shaking hands with his principal antagonist from the USSR, Valerian Zorin, and apologizing for laryngitis. With gay eloquence, he responded to his introduction with the disclaimer that "flattery is all right if you don't inhale." In the following weeks the uninhaled flattery gave way to insults by Zorin and the Cuban foreign minister Dr. Raúl Roa, postcolonial turmoil in the Congo, and even a protest in the galleries when black nationalists from Harlem shouted "Congo Yes—Yankee No" after the murder of Patrice Lumumba, the Congo leader who had become their hero.

Other issues crowded the ambassador, an agenda he once described as "a virtual compendium of the ongoing problems of the modern world. Listen to this list of trouble spots and sore spots: the Congo . . . the Gaza strip . . . Southern Rhodesia . . . South West Africa . . . the Portuguese African territories . . . Kashmir . . . Yemen . . . West New Guinea . . . and the Arab refugee camps. Mark this string of contentious issues: Chinese representation . . . North Korea . . . Hungary . . . colonialism . . . Troika . . . and sovereignty over natural resources. Consider, if you will, this list of universal concerns: disarmament . . . nuclear testing . . . outer space . . . world food . . . world trade . . . world science . . . and the training of manpower for economic and social development." Typically—for he never wallowed in despair and often buried the unpleasant—Stevenson omitted Cuba, whose conflicts with the United States twice nearly led to his resignation.

On April 8, 1961, three months after Stevenson became ambassador, Arthur Schlesinger Jr., Stevenson's former speech writer and now his liaison with the White House, and Tracy Barnes of the Central Intelligence Agency, traveled to New York to brief Stevenson and his staff about a forthcoming operation by Cuban exiles designed to overthrow Fidel Castro. Several times Foreign Minister Roa had complained to the Security Council about "American adventurism." Now, just before the Cuban complaint was to be discussed by the council, according to Francis Plimpton, "we were told that a lot of refugees wanted to go back and overthrow Castro and that they were financed by rich Cuban refugee money and that no U.S. property was involved save an abandoned army site in Louisiana. . . . We got the idea of a lot of muffled-oared boats landing on a dark shore and going up into the hills as Castro did. . . ." A misinformed Stevenson, who was assured that the action would not take place during discussion of the Cuban complaint, was chagrined that he had not been given an opportunity to voice his instinctive opposition.

The extent of American sponsorship was strikingly different from what Schlesinger and Barnes represented. Persuaded by Allen Dulles, whom Kennedy retained as head of the CIA, and Dulles's chief lieutenant, Richard Bissell, Kennedy had ordered one of Eisenhower's planned covert operations to go forward. On April 14 the Cuban brigade of fourteen hundred, which had been training in Guatemala under the auspices of the CIA, left Nicaragua on boats previously owned by the United Fruit Company. In the early hours of April 17, they landed on the western shore of Cuba at the Bay of Pigs, jumping into the coral-studded waters; the first man on the beach was a CIA agent. The brigade members' intention was liberation of their homeland, and they anticipated, in a mortally damaging miscalculation nurtured by the CIA, that their fellow Cubans would rise up against the repressive Castro government that had driven them into exile.

The brigade also expected American planes piloted by Cubans to destroy Castro's modernized T-33's. If the United States controlled the airspace, the men on the beaches would be protected as they moved inland to face Castro's army of 20,000 and a national militia of 200,000. Eight American B-26's had been painted with the insignia of Castro's air force. In a carefully arranged fraud, a Cuban pilot flew on April 15 from a base in Nicaragua and landed in Miami to tell the world of the rebellion against Castro.

In New York at an emergency meeting of the Security Council called by the Cubans, Adlai Stevenson followed his instructions, speaking on April 15 and 17 and delivering to the Security Council the CIA cover story: "The United States has committed no aggression against Cuba and no offensive has been launched from Florida. . . . No Americans were involved. We are opposed to the use of our territory for launching of a military attack against any foreign country." Using a pointer, the ambassador tapped the wing of the supposedly Cuban planes on the grainy enlargements of photographs wheeled out to demonstrate American veracity. "These two planes, to the best of our knowledge, were Castro's own air force planes."

Within hours of its landing, the brigade had been hemmed in on the rocky beaches along the Bay of Pigs; Kennedy had refused more than one sortie of naval air force cover from the carrier *Essex*; and a reporter, discovering the metal nose of the plane in Miami (Cuban planes had plastic noses), had scratched through a recent coat of paint to find American insignia on what the ambassador to the UN had described as a Cuban plane.

Adlai Stevenson had lied to the world, unknowingly at first but with full knowledge of his distortions two days later. The ambassador who had struggled since childhood for moral rectitude was exposed, and the president who had earlier commented that Stevenson's credibility and integrity were a national asset, began calling Stevenson, with relished irony, "my official liar." When awareness of his sin dawned, an ashen Adlai Stevenson walked in a daze, according to Jane Dick, who met the distracted ambassador on the elevator and followed him to his apartment. "You heard my speech today? Well," he told his friend from Lake Forest, "I did not tell the whole truth; I did not know the whole truth. I took this job at the President's request on the understanding that I would be consulted and kept fully informed on everything. . . . Now my credibility has been compromised and therefore my usefulness. Yet how can I resign at this moment and make things worse for the President? I've got to resign. . . . There's nothing I can do but resign. But I can't resign [when] the young president and the country are in trouble."

The Bay of Pigs confirmed Stevenson's misgivings about the president's morality. "I believe in on-the-job training, but not for Presidents." As he told his biographer Kenneth Davis, the mistakes that Kennedy made during "this foolish escapade" were not the kind that "honorable" men make. "How could any man of moral sensitivity, with power to control the event, have permitted so criminal a violence to proceed in so soiled and tattered a cloak of lies?"

While he judged Kennedy, Stevenson's own behavior raised questions. Would Stevenson have resigned if he had known the extent of American involvement? Would he have delivered the misleading but technically accurate distortion that there was no invasion from Florida and that the United States had nothing to do with the operation? Why, when he learned the truth that the United States had trained and armed the Cuban brigade, did he violate his personal rule that nothing he said at the UN would be less than the truth? How much, in this late-life conflict between wanting to be onstage and wanting to be upright and virtuous, did Adlai Stevenson treasure his post on the margins of power?

In time the sting of "that Cuba trick they played on me" faded, rubbed off by a staff that encouraged him to stay and the devotion of backers who showered him with messages of support. At the same time representatives from other countries were sympathetic to a man they respected. They too were often called to the bank of phones just outside the General Assembly auditorium to receive their orders. No one knew better than UN delegates the habitual prevarications of the modern nation-state. Ironically Adlai Stevenson served an administration that believed, according to a paraphrased comment of Secretary of Defense McNamara's press secretary, "the government has the right to lie."

Stevenson also did not resign, because if he resigned and went public with his criticism of the operation, he would damage the president. As a result the Kennedys spent "no little amount of time keeping Stevenson happy," especially when, again a political tease, Stevenson briefly considered running for the Democratic nomination for Illinois senator. In time Kennedy and his brother Robert intended to move Stevenson, the man they considered to be of another generation, to political oblivion as ambassador to Great Britain, their father's former post. But it was time they did not have.

A year and a half later, in the fall of 1962, another Cuban crisis tested Adlai Stevenson as it brought the United States and the Soviet Union to the brink of nuclear war. During a summer in which Stevenson spent several weeks cruising off the Dalmatian coast, the Russians began building launching sites for nuclear missiles in Cuba; they also sent crated MiG jets to Cuba, along with ground forces numbering over 42,000 men. En route to the Caribbean were nuclear warheads and launchers. On October 16 Kennedy learned from photographs taken by U-2 surveillance planes of the preparations for offensive missiles in Cuba.

The White House believed that the Russians intended to use the 1,500-mile-range missiles as bargaining chips, perhaps to deny the American government a free hand in Latin and South America or, as Bobby Kennedy said, "to squeeze us on Berlin." Yet Defense Secretary Robert McNamara acknowledged that the weapons represented no shift in the strategic balance and were a political rather than a military problem. A missile fired from Cuba was no different from one launched from the Soviet Union. Still, Dean Rusk declared, "I don't think we can sit still."

The president agreed. A man who had condemned British appeasement during the 1930s in his notorious Harvard thesis and to whom assertive masculinity, sexual and otherwise, was a prized virtue, viewed the missiles as a provocative challenge to his manhood. The deployment also undermined his credibility, for as recently as September, Kennedy had denied that there were any offensive ground-to-ground missiles in Cuba. And the missiles threatened his political image of standing tough against the Russians on the eve of the November elections. "He can't do this to me," said Kennedy of Khrushchev. "He's putting this out in a way that's caused maximum embarrassment."

Few members of the administration had heeded earlier signals from both Khrushchev and Castro that they would respond to American plans to assassinate Castro and invade Cuba. After the Bay of Pigs, Cuba, which posed no threat to American security, had become Kennedy's—and the CIA's—obsession. They had launched Operation Mongoose, the code name of a bungled operation in 1962 to kill Castro and sabotage his regime, and ordered an American invasion force of 40,000 into training along the east coast from North Carolina to the Caribbean island of Vieques. Aware of these efforts—even if the American public was not—the Russians and Cubans defined their weapons as defensively deployed to resist the forthcoming invasion. Permitted under the United Nations charter, such arms were no different from American missiles installed in the NATO countries of Turkey and Italy.

At a three-to-one disadvantage in operational intercontinental missiles and a larger disadvantage in delivery systems, Khrushchev remained apprehensive of the Americans' counterforce capability, which after a first strike destroyed most Soviet strategic weapons could theoretically retain the capability to block retaliation. In such circumstances the Russian chairman, according to Aleksandr Alekseev, the Soviet ambassador to Cuba, "was looking for a way to talk to the Americans equally." From the Soviet leader's perspective Cuba—a country that had become Communist without the help of the Red Army—must not become his domino.

On Tuesday, October 16, the same day the deployment was recognized, the president designated a group of men (dubbed, appropriately, Elite, and later ExComm as the Executive Committee of the National Security Council) to consider his options. In the Indian summer days of mid-October, with the weather an ironic counterpoint to their dismal thoughts of armaggedon, Robert McNamara, Robert Kennedy, Dean Rusk, McGeorge Bundy, Roswell Gilpatric, and occasionally Adlai Stevenson and Dean Acheson, among others, considered, in ninety-six hours of meetings, how to get the missiles out. Kennedy's alternatives never included doing nothing, though everything from an invasion of Cuba to air strikes and a blockade was considered. "We must," said McGeorge Bundy early in their discussions, "try and imagine to think what the world would be like if we do this and what it will be like if we don't."

On Wednesday, October 17, and again on Saturday, October 20, Adlai Stevenson joined the tense discussions that lasted for two weeks and continued for Stevenson at the United Nations until January 1963. Sometimes the president attended, though it was believed that more free-ranging options could be developed in his absence. Although the Cuban missile crisis was the most dramatic confrontation of the Cold War—the nightmare of superpower nuclear brinkmanship dreaded by Stevenson—the business of the United States must go on. The government had stolen a march on its adversaries, who remained unaware the missiles had been discovered. Stevenson must return to the United Nations, where the topic of the day was the seating of Mao Tse-tung's China. The president must go on a scheduled campaign trip with the off-year congressional elections only three weeks away. Secrecy must accompany the discussions of ExComm until the president chose to act.

Before Stevenson returned to the United Nations on Wednesday, he left a hasty summary of his thinking for the president. At the time the advocates for an invasion and bombing (the latter, a surgical air strike that on second presentation turned out not to be so surgical) were carrying the day, and Stevenson was reacting to what he considered a calamitous approach that would lead to Soviet reprisals in Turkey and Berlin, the violation of American ideals of self-determination for all nations, and the possibility of a nuclear war. In the Olympian rhetoric of his last years, he reported to Philip Klutznick, a member of the American UN mission, that he would "insist for history we make one last day's effort to avoid a clash."

Arguing for the traditional diplomatic method of sending personal emissaries with messages to Castro and Khrushchev in order to negotiate the crisis, Stevenson wrote, "It should be clear as pikestaff the US was, is and will be ready to negotiate the elimination of bases and anything else. . . . *The existence of bases anywhere is NEGOTIABLE before we start anything.*" Kennedy promptly dismissed the advice as Stevensonian ambivalence, because the ambassador had also written, "We can't negotiate with a gun at our head." Sharing the memo with Sorenson, the president said, "Tell me which side he's on."

By the time Stevenson had returned to the ExComm meetings on Saturday, the proponents of a blockade had increased. Encouraged by McNamara and Robert Kennedy, this strategic option called for a quarantine—so called because a blockade by international law was an act of war—to be established by the U.S. Navy to stop, board, and turn back Russian ships bringing offensive weaponry to Cuba. At this meeting Stevenson proposed, along with the quarantine, an exchange, based on the dismantling of the Jupiter missiles in Turkey and Italy and the abandonment of the American base at Guantanamo in return for the "neutralization" of Cuba. The latter would have accomplished what the quarantine did not—the removal of the missiles under the supervision of a United Nations force. "Neutralization and demilitarization would immediately and drastically remove the troublemaking capability of the Cuban regime, and would probably result in its early overthrow," argued Stevenson, using postwar Austria as his model. But the hard-liners of ExComm, especially Douglas Dillon, the Republican investment banker who was Kennedy's secretary of the treasury, Robert Lovett, the Republican in-and-outer who had served in Truman's administration, and John McCone, Allen Dulles's replacement as head of the CIA, who was noted for his resistance to any nuclear test ban, scorned Stevenson's proposal.

From the beginning of the ExComm meetings, the now obsolete Jupiter missiles had been an issue, and Stevenson, often portrayed as heretical in his approach to the crisis, was not alone in considering them. While the president remained insistent, inaccurately, that he had ordered their dismantling earlier, several members of ExComm worried that Khrushchev might demand an exchange unacceptable to this administration. Hardliners denied any correspondence, viewing the American missiles targeted on Russian cities from Turkey as defensive and Soviet missiles in Cuba as offensive. When Stevenson, ever the outsider, objected to this double standard and advanced the importance of UN involvement, "everyone," according to Arthur Schlesinger Jr., "jumped on him." Unchastened, Stevenson told the presidential aide Kenneth O'Donnell as he left the White House, "I know that most of those fellows will probably consider me a coward for the rest of my life for what I said today, but perhaps we need a coward in the room when we are talking about nuclear war."

To the crisis managers of the New Frontier who favored risky military confrontation over negotiated political solutions, Stevenson had begun with the concessions they hoped to avoid. In their mind he overemphasized the importance of world opinion and diplomatic alternatives. Secretary of State Rusk recalled how he often withheld the department's fallback positions from the ambassador, convinced "that Stevenson would reach that point in the first five minutes of negotiation." Even his associate Francis Plimpton acknowledged that Stevenson was not "always as tough a bargainer as some of us would have wished."

Disgusted, Robert Kennedy advised his brother that Stevenson "was not strong or tough enough to be representing us at the UN at a time like this." "Get him off the reservation" became the refrain of State Department officials who feared that the ambassador would make too weak a case for the quarantine. When Stevenson returned to New York, he was accompanied by John McCloy, the former Wall Street lawyer admired for his unyielding positions as high commissioner in Berlin. Yet Stevenson's ignominy also brought presidential respect. To his brother, John Kennedy confessed admiration at the way "Adlai sticks to his position even when everyone is jumping on him." McCloy, who sat behind Stevenson at the Security Council, soon reported that the administration need not have worried: "Stevenson was a hopping mad hawk."

On Monday night, October 22, along with most Americans, Adlai Stevenson watched the president practice Cold War confrontation by television. While some private avenues of negotiation remained open—most initiated by the Russians—a somber president announced the unilateral American quarantine. The next day in the Security Council, while Kennedy watched the televised meeting from the White House, Stevenson presented a resolution calling for the immediate removal of the missiles and requesting that Secretary General U Thant send UN observers to ensure compliance. At the following meeting of the Security Council, Stevenson lashed into the Soviets, receiving, as he spoke, word of the unanimous resolution by the Organization of American States (from which the United States had orchestrated Cuba's expulsion in 1962) calling for "the immediate dismantling and withdrawal from Cuba of all missiles and other offensive weapons." Meanwhile, at the United Nations, a harried U Thant sought a delay of the blockade, which Kennedy refused.

As the world trembled and twenty-five Soviet ships approached a line of American naval vessels off the Cuban coast, Stevenson returned to the Security Council, where both the Cubans and the Russians were asserting that the weapons were defensive and that the United States had only "fake evidence." Reluctantly—for he remembered the doctored evidence from the Bay of Pigs—but finally with great finesse, Stevenson pointed to the photographic evidence of concrete bunkers, retaining walls to shelter vehicles and equipment from rocket blast-offs, fuel tanks, missile trailers, and the construction of launching sites for medium-range missiles near San Cristóbal. In the hall of world opinion, Stevenson attempted to convince the Security Council—and the watching world—of Soviet treachery and American rectitude, even arguing that there was a "vast difference between the long-range missile sites established years ago in Europe and the long-range missile sites established by the Soviet Union in Cuba during the last three months. . . . In our passion for peace we have forborne greatly. There must, however, be limits to forbearance if forbearance is not to become the diagram for the destruction of this Organization."

In the exchange that briefly transformed him into an unlikely Cold War hero, Adlai Stevenson argued with Zorin. "Do you, Ambassador Zorin, deny that the USSR has placed and is placing medium and intermediate-range missiles and sites in Cuba? Yes or no? Do not wait for the interpretation. Yes or no?" To this the Soviet ambassador replied that he was not in an American courtroom. "You are in the courtroom of world opinion," responded a prosecutorial Stevenson, then uttering the famous words (on his own), "I am prepared to wait for my answer until Hell freezes over." Later Kennedy acknowledged that while Stevenson's performance was very good ("I never knew Adlai had it in him"), in fact "the one thing we were not prepared to do was wait till hell froze over. We wanted action from the Soviets fast."

Kennedy got quick action. On October 28, as the Soviet ships remained near the quarantine line established by the U.S. Navy five hundred miles from Havana, a complex series of negotiations and exchanges between the Americans and the Russians ended in an informal exchange—an American pledge not to invade Cuba and to remove its missiles from Turkey and Italy for the Soviet removal of their missiles from Cuba.

Overnight the man taunted for being soft on communism since his Hiss deposition in 1949 entered American living rooms as a stalwart spokesman for "standing up to the Russians." Stevenson, of course, might rather have been recognized as the architect of a nuclear test ban or the statesman who had inspired men of quality to enter public life. By late fall the administration claimed victory; the Cuban missile crisis became its hard-nosed restitution for the Bay of Pigs. According to Dean Rusk, "We were eyeball to eyeball and I think the other fellow just blinked." Left unsaid was what the Americans had secretly traded: the Jupiter missiles in Turkey and Italy and a pledge not to invade Cuba.

As it turned out, Stevenson's heroic reputation did not last as long as the negotiations with the Soviets to dismantle the missiles, which continued into 1963. In a *Saturday Evening Post* article entitled "In Time of Crisis" and written by Stewart Alsop and the president's friend Charles Bartlett, Stevenson was described as an appeaser. According to one caption, "An opponent charges, 'Adlai wanted a Munich. He wanted to trade U.S. bases for Cuban weapons.' " From sources present in the supposedly secret meetings of ExComm—perhaps even the president himself—Alsop and Bartlett had learned incorrectly that only Stevenson had dissented from the quarantine. "At first," the journalists quoted a member of ExComm as saying, "we divided into hawks and doves, but by the end a rolling consensus had developed, and except for Adlai, we had all ended up as dawks and hoves."

In fact, there were several doves in the White House, if trading the Turkish missiles was the criterion, and the "untough" ambassador believed that Kennedy had given up the bases and not achieved the neutralization of Cuba. The difference between the Kennedys and Stevenson was the ambassador's reliance on negotiation, preferably in the collective setting of the Organization of American States and the UN, his reformulation of the crisis in general international terms rather than in the national specifics often discussed at ExComm, and his inability to see the political implications of giving up the American base at Guantanamo.

Enamored of the administration's "wizards of Armageddon," Alsop and Bartlett ignored the extremists who favored a sneak air strike on Cuba (where, unknown to the Americans, some missiles with nuclear warheads were already operational), followed by an American invasion that, after the Cuban missiles were fired on East Coast cities, as surely they would have been, would have inevitably led to a nuclear war. Conveniently they made Stevenson into a scapegoat who set off Kennedy's bold resolve. In fact, the administration's "victory" was based on terms of agreement with the Russians that followed, save for Guantanamo and the neutralization of Cuba, those of Stevenson. Few Americans knew this until fifteen years later.

Instead, the derision of Kennedy insiders and warrior journalists, and the labeling of the missile crisis as a Kennedy triumph for the very reason that it did not follow Stevenson's proposals, trailed Stevenson. He was even held responsible for the failure of Kennedy to order a second air strike during the Bay of Pigs, and for Fidel Castro's survival after the Cuban missile crisis. In 1964 Barry Goldwater, along with Admiral James Van Fleet and Congressman Walter Judd, hinted that Kennedy himself had informed them that if he had not prevented follow-up air strikes, Stevenson would have told the UN that the United States was responsible for the Bay of Pigs. Stevenson's denial never caught up to the inaccuracies, although in the 1980s he received a posthumous vindication when, at a conference of Russian and American policymakers, Kennedy's trades in the endgame of the missile crisis became public knowledge. "Life," he acknowledged to Agnes Meyer, "has been unkind. . . ."

Now Stevenson faced his own crisis. The friendship between the president and Bartlett suggested that Kennedy had approved the article, perhaps even contributing as one of its unnamed sources. "If the President wanted me to go," Stevenson told Schlesinger, "he did not have to go about it in this circuitous fashion." The barbed relationship between the ambassador and the president led to disavowals, Alsop's assertion that the president had indeed read the piece, and continuing speculation as to the source who had made of Stevenson a convenient target for the right-wing as well as for Kennedy's inner circle.

Still, Stevenson could not resign. He wrote Barbara Jackson in early

December, "I have now had to face—once again—the assaults of malicious—with overtones of White House—conspiracy that have excited the
press and agitated my friends. The latter have quickly converted a hatchet
into a boomerang—and the President has been forthright and noble in his
responses. But the incident leaves some bad scars—the suspicion among
the working press of favoritism and news management, the insecurity of
the President's most secret discussions . . . and the impression that there
are many people in the higher councils of government who really wanted
an invasion of Cuba and maybe still do, with all the risks of reprisal and
escalation."

Practiced in hiding his feelings, a demoralized Stevenson made no mention of his own humiliation, even to his sister. "I'm afraid if I don't stay in
the picture I'll feel terribly lost. I've been in the heart of things so long. . . .
I don't think I could stand it in Libertyville writing a book." He confessed
to Archibald MacLeish that "the troubles come close, the joys recede." His
Christmas card carried a poignant message from Robert Louis Stevenson:
"Give us grace and strength to persevere. Give us courage and gaiety and
the quiet mind. . . . Give us the strength to encounter that which is to come,
that we may be brave in peril, constant in tribulation, temperate in wrath
and in all changes of fortune, and down to the gates of death loyal and
loving to one another."

Six months later, in June 1963, Stevenson traveled to Moscow with the
American delegation for the signing of a limited test ban treaty that out-
lawed atmospheric nuclear testing, but not, as Stevenson had proposed in
the 1956 presidential campaign, nuclear tests under water. He had taken
no part in the negotiations with the Russians, and Kennedy, fearing his
presence might be the catalyst for the Senate's rejection of the treaty,
refused to include him in the American delegation. Stevenson pressed his
case, reminding the president that he had been the first public figure to
argue for a test ban, which Nixon had assailed in 1956 as "catastrophic
nonsense." Now Kennedy was describing his ideas to the nation as a way
to lessen radioactive pollution and a step toward "reason." Yet only when
Khrushchev encouraged Secretary General U Thant's presence did the president agree to include Stevenson.

A few supporters remembered Stevenson's pioneering efforts for nuclear
disarmament and congratulated him. John Steinbeck wrote that Stevenson
suffered because he was ahead of his time. Like so much else in these last
years, the celebration turned sour in Moscow when a needling Khrushchev
hectored Stevenson about what had happened to him since he "started
working for the United States government. We don't like to be interrogated
like a prisoner in the dock." The chairman, Stevenson lamented, no longer
believed him "objective," though it seems unlikely that Khrushchev ever
had.

3

TRAPPED IN A LABYRINTH where the path to public prominence was obstructed by personal humiliation and perpetual work, Stevenson remained in the United Nations through its stormiest times. Overall his performance disappointed some UN professionals, who found him unsure of himself, despite his reputation, and too much given to wisecracks, such as his favorite about work at the UN as one-third protocol, one-third alcohol, and one-third Geritol. Still, he retained his popularity among delegates, who appreciated his unfailing courtesy and ability to listen. Ranking him among the ten most admired men in the world, Americans also approved of his performance at the UN. But polls were frivolous exercises for Stevenson. Instead, peace amid change—in his personal life, in the UN, and on earth—became the vision of his final years, the cue word of the unofficial speeches he tirelessly delivered.

Peace was expensive. By 1963 the UN faced bankruptcy, mostly the result of its expensive military operation in the Congo against Moise Tshombe and his supporters, who threatened to secede from a UN-supported government. An enthusiast in that he promoted the importance of the United Nations (as he had his school, college, and political party), Adlai Stevenson was active on Congo matters and on the debt issue that a UN force of twenty thousand in Katanga Province had spawned.

To some extent the matter of the Congo offered Stevenson a rare opportunity for autonomy, for the State Department was divided on the issue. Europeanists opposed the sending of UN forces against Tshombe and his army of South African and Belgian mercenaries. Stevenson, with eighteenth-century American history as his guide, argued for the preservation of a central regime in Léopoldville in order to protect the territorial integrity and political independence of a former Belgian colony in danger of chaotic fragmentation. As the representative of the "first anticolonialist nation in the world," the ambassador played the Cold War card linking the disintegration of the Congo to Soviet adventurism. In his pithy aphorisms: "The only way to keep the cold war out of the Congo is to keep the United Nations in the Congo. . . . " "Are we to abandon the jungles of the Congo to the jungles of internecine warfare and of international rivalry?"

But after the Congo leader Patrice Lumumba's murder in 1961, the Russians condemned the UN peacekeeping force as favoring the West and refused to pay their share of the accumulating expenses. By the end of 1963, as problems in the Congo simmered on, the Soviets owed the UN over $52 million. After two years of delinquency, under article 19 of the UN charter, they would be expelled, and Adlai Stevenson's "last best hope of peace" would be destroyed.

Anxious for harmony in "the family of man," Stevenson struggled to end the impasse. Perhaps the defaulters could pay part of their debt in return for an acknowledgment that in the future nations did not have to pay for specific UN peacekeeping operations of which they disapproved. Perhaps the Soviets could make a voluntary contribution. But all his proposals floundered, at the same time that Congress passed a resolution calling on Stevenson, in the words of Gerald Ford of Michigan, "to demand that these nations make their payments as they are required to do under the Charter and the World Court decision. This is not a negotiable issue in the UN. Payment is to be made or else."

Opposed to what he considered a rigid application of article 19, Stevenson disobeyed his instructions, meeting with his counterpart, the Soviet ambassador Nikolai Fedorenko, to discuss the possibility of postponing the expulsion by dispensing with voting in the General Assembly. By violating his instructions Stevenson hoped, according to Francis Plimpton, to give more time to the Russians to make a voluntary contribution. "Unfortunately we were wrong."

State Department officials flinched at such an unauthorized change in American policy. Undersecretary of State Richard Gardner considered the department's policy of "flexibility and firmness" on the verge of forcing a Russian capitulation until Stevenson's bumbling interference. The anomalous relationship between the State Department and the U.S. mission at the UN prevented any reprisal against the ambassador, and eventually Stevenson's successor Arthur Goldberg disengaged the United States from its position on sanctions. In the meantime the voteless General Assembly was weakened, its decisions reached for nearly a year by informal ballots taken in the Secretary General's office. And the Russians never paid, their policy later serving as a precedent for the United States.

The incident revealed Stevenson's priorities. "What if the Assembly should falter in the exercise of its own authority? . . . I have no prophetic vision . . . —for this would be a step down a dark, down an unfamiliar path. . . . And so our world would become not a safer but a more dangerous place for us all . . . ," he observed in January of 1965. Harlan Cleveland later identified the ambassador's intentions: "He gave away some debating points for the sake of comity. . . . What was important was the UN itself, the success of the charter, the UN's prestige, influence and operational capacity." But it was hard work, and he began brooding over his retirement from the UN.

Caught in the controversies of "the family of man," Adlai Stevenson faced turmoil in his own splintered family. During the early 1960s ironic parallels emerged between the problems he encountered in his private and public lives. "The house is battered. It resounds endlessly with family quarrels. There are cracks in the walls and quite a few tenants are behind in the rent," he commented about the debt issue, at the same time that he was receiving ominous messages from his son Adlai about his former wife's financial affairs. Eventually the Stevenson family's Cold War reached the Illinois supreme court.

After her divorce in 1949, Ellen Borden Stevenson had become a local celebrity as a board member of *Poetry* magazine and the organizer of the Chicago Arts Club, housed in her childhood mansion at 1020 Lake Shore Drive. Like other American women during this decade, she was discovering a purposeful autonomy beyond the boundaries of domesticity. By 1956 forty-nine-year-old Ellen Stevenson presided over a dues-paying membership of over two thousand, ran a dining café praised by local food critics, organized art exhibits, and entertained the nation's premier poets, sometimes serving, as for the Pulitzer Prize–winning Karl Shapiro, as the subject of their poems. "Cadillac," Shapiro entitled a poem about the intense, hazel-eyed Ellen, "Your luna moths bring poems to my eyes / Your oriflamme brings banners to my slum." But neither art galleries nor poetry magazines were self-supporting enterprises, and, equally damaging, she continued to confront her husband's notoriety in reporters' questions and anonymous calls that held her responsible for his presidential defeats.

Familiar with two extremes of handling money—her former husband's frugality and her father's extravagance—Ellen Stevenson chose the latter and invested in both the club and a newly renovated home on Chicago's expensive Gold Coast. In a period when only the best-managed beef cattle farms were profitable, she took out a $41,000 mortgage on a 180-acre cattle farm and eighty head of pure-bred Angus cattle in northern Illinois.

Then, in 1962, during one of its periodic fibrillations, the stock market lost nearly a fourth of its value. Like John Borden in 1929, Ellen was heavily margined in speculative stocks, having borrowed $160,000 from two banks in order, she said, to remake the squandered Borden fortune. She was also carrying several loans to pay for the improvement of the arts club and her home. A now insufficient collateral was liquidated. Irreplaceable Borden capital disappeared, until in the early 1960s Ellen Stevenson faced a mechanic's lien for the renovations of her new home and an Internal Revenue claim for back taxes. Her former husband was reminded of her father: "I seem to remember going to the [Borden] plantation in Mississippi to haul away a lot of family possessions to provide [John Borden] with some cash," wrote Stevenson to Ellen's aunt.

As the crisis deepened, Ellen sold off family heirlooms—the emerald ring her father had given her, the emerald necklace from her mother's family that she had worn at her wedding to Adlai Stevenson in 1928, the Millet original that had hung in Libertyville, and even the Steinway grand piano. Sometimes her son Adlai purchased family treasures. But nothing seemed to stop the money hemorrhage, and Ellen kept the black Cadillac that became a symbol of her excesses. Her mother lent her $34,000, and her sons created a lifetime trust of various speculative oil and gas leases worth $12,000, but with vast, eventually unrealized potential. At one point they offered to put her on family welfare by paying her debts and providing her with a place to live and a $500-a-month allowance.

Ellen refused. What she wanted was a no-strings loan without family supervision. She wrote her eldest son, Adlai, who because of his name, his proximity, his political ambitions, and his personality drew most of her fury, "You betray me. . . . I am losing my honor. I was your mother. Remember I loved you once." The telephone became Ellen Stevenson's weapon as she harangued her children and mother, sometimes, as her son Adlai testified under oath, calling as many as eight times a day. In one taped conversation, Ellen told her son to leave her alone. "If I go broke, I'll go broke on my own. I don't want to be on a dole." She swore at young Adlai, whom she called "my most evil son," threatened her daughter-in-law, and once hurled an ashtray at her mother. Behind the anger lay growing instability and a dawning awareness that, under the commanding influence of her ex-husband, those she loved were abandoning her.

By 1964 her former husband—referring to "Ellen's tale [as] sad, sadder, saddest"—was making gifts to his sons, who in turn passed along a monthly stipend to their mother. With dogged intransigence, both sides refused to compromise—the sons and grandmother unable to cut Ellen loose, and Ellen unable to accept control over her assets and an allowance, but also unable to end the appeals for money. In New York, Adlai Stevenson contemplated the further severing of family bonds. There matters stood until, amid acrimonious conflicts among the sons as to the amount of their monthly contributions to their mother, and with her ex-husband paying the legal fees, the ascending and descending generations of Stevensons—her mother and three sons—went into probate court to have a conservator appointed.

On the very day in May 1964 when Ambassador Stevenson arrived in The Hague for discussions with the leaders of NATO, the Cook County court took action on the family complaint against Ellen Borden Stevenson, appointing the Continental Illinois Bank as her conservator. (Ellen later charged a conflict of interest because her son Adlai's Chicago law firm represented the bank.) Illinois had no provision that the defendant be notified or even in court during conservatorship proceedings. Due process for the largely female defendants would not become a part of state law until the late 1960s. Judge George Dunne, the son of the Illinois governor who had appointed Lewis Stevenson to a state job, waived notice to the defendant "for the protection of the estate." Driving to Chicago from her farm, Ellen Stevenson learned from the radio that she had "an imperfection of mentality and suffered from a mental and emotional disturbance rendering her incapable of managing her estate." Henceforth the bank controlled her portfolio of stocks and bonds, her home on Bellevue Place, and her farm in Boone County. She would never forgive her sons, as with this court action—itself a parody of the litigious modern American family—the Stevensons entered into a protracted battle that continued until Ellen Stevenson's death in 1972.

4

IN THE FALL OF 1963 Adlai Stevenson traveled to California for the celebration of United Nations week. At the time polls revealed that over a third of all Americans distrusted the organization, and no one was more skilled than Adlai Stevenson at the celebratory speeches that made citizens warm to the notion of an international organization dedicated to peace, not as some Republicans were insisting, to the end of their national sovereignty. The ambassador told an audience in Los Angeles, "I believe the cause of peace and freedom has a glorious future in the world. And in that future the United Nations will play a mighty part. Let none of us mock its weakness, for when we do, we are mocking ourselves. It is the hope of the world and our country's pride that we stand by the United Nations, the meeting house of the Family of Man, in its time of hardest trial."

Stevenson's next stop was Dallas, where supporters of the recently resigned major general Edwin Walker's National Indignation Convention packed the auditorium. Outside, angry pickets chanted and waved placards with pictures of Kennedy and Stevenson over the inscription "Wanted for Treason." Stevenson's speech was interrupted; the police removed one protester. In the ensuing confusion he remarked, "I believe in the forgiveness of sin and the redemption of ignorance." But this crowd didn't laugh.

So threatening were they that after his speech, his hosts hurried Stevenson out the back door. The mob followed. Several spat in his face. Then someone hit him on the head with a placard bearing the words "Down with the UN." "Is she animal or human?" muttered Stevenson as he was hustled into a car. In Washington, Kennedy was impressed with the ambassador's coolness, but Stevenson worried about Kennedy's future trip to a city where he had found "something ugly and frightening." Though he shared his concerns with the president's advisers, Stevenson could not overdo his apprehension lest, according to Arthur Schlesinger Jr., "it convict him of undue apprehension in the president's eyes." Three weeks later John Kennedy was assassinated in Dallas, and in the city Stevenson had found ominously hostile, schoolchildren cheered their president's murder.

In Washington at Lyndon Johnson's first cabinet meeting, four days after the assassination, a composed Adlai Stevenson read a statement:

"While we cannot obscure our loss, we are, I know, mindful, too, that there is only a moment's pause in the nation's business and that the brutal burden of leadership has suddenly fallen on your shoulders. To share as best we can that crushing burden is our task now."

Stevenson expected that his task would be made easier by a new president who would assign him more authority at the UN and who, because of their closeness in age and their previous associations, would move him out of the shadows. Although Kennedy had warned that Johnson was "a chronic liar," Stevenson fell for the Johnson treatment—that unique combination of coercion, obsequiousness, cajolery, and manipulation—which began with the new president's telling Stevenson, "You should be sitting here. You carried the banner when the going was hard." "You'll be my expert on foreign policy." Such buoying flattery included an office in the White House. Arthur Schlesinger Jr. noticed that Stevenson could not suppress "his glee. There was a smile on his face. It was a half smile." Schlesinger commented, "I loved Stevenson but I never felt the same way about him after that."

As it turned out, Stevenson had less of a voice in this new administration, remaining, as he plaintively put it, at the wrong end of the telephone. Within weeks his relationship with Johnson deteriorated, as an insecure president came to depend on an inner circle nudging him toward the Americanization of the Vietnam War. Stevenson rarely attended Johnson's informal Tuesday lunches, where policy was discussed. "I have the impression that my views seldom come to the President's attention," he grumbled to one of Johnson's inner circle. Again he was remaindered as a custodian, not a creator, of foreign policy by a vulgarian who referred to him as that "fat ass Stevenson" and in an allusion to the never stilled rumors of his homosexuality, "the kind of man who squats like a woman when he pees." Soon the president was entertaining White House insiders and reporters with unflattering imitations of his UN ambassador. At the celebration of the UN's twentieth anniversary in San Francisco in June of 1965—a significant celebration for Stevenson—Johnson ordered Stevenson out of his room, and not for the first time.

As Kennedy had been obsessed with Cuba, now Johnson became fixated on a small country in Southeast Asia, even calling the White House situation room for reports in the middle of the night. And Vietnam brought to Stevenson a final dilemma. Like most Americans in 1963, both he and Lyndon Johnson—the latter often telling his advisers, in a reference to Munich, that he would be "no Chamberlain umbrella man"—accepted the Cold War rationale for American involvement. Faced early in his administration with deteriorating military and political conditions in South Vietnam—at Ap Bac in 1963 the Vietcong confronted the South Vietnamese and their American advisers in a fixed battle—Johnson ended the pretense of any partnership with the "brave people who are under an attack controlled, that is directed from outside the country." By the end of 1964 a president who hated to hear bad news increased the number of American ground troops to 26,000, expanded the bombing raids, implemented a naval plan to monitor North Vietnamese coastal installations, and gained congressional agreement to take "all necessary measures to repel any armed attack against the forces of the United States and to prevent further aggression" without a declaration of war.

In the United Nations the Soviets hammered Stevenson about American aggression, which the ambassador deflected as the response to "the armed conspiracy which seeks to destroy the Government and the very society of the Republic of Viet-Nam itself." In his gentleman's code, "there is something both grotesque and ironic in the fact that the victims of this incessant terror [who] are the accused before this Council are defending themselves in daylight while terrorists perform their dark and dirty work by night throughout their land." Believing all Communist activity directed from China and Russia, Stevenson cast aside the possibility of civil war, which he had astutely observed during his 1953 visit.

In August 1964 Stevenson complained to the Security Council of "deliberate aggression by the Hanoi regime against naval units of the United States." The American version of events placed two naval vessels—the *Maddox* and the *Turner Joy*—in international waters thirty miles off the North Vietnamese coast, not, as was the case, electronically eavesdropping in rough seas sixteen miles from land during a coordinated American and South Vietnamese assault on islands off the North Vietnamese coast. Instead, as the ambassador informed the Security Council, the attack from Hanoi was deliberate, justifying "limited aerial strikes on North Vietnamese torpedo boats." More skeptical after the Bay of Pigs, when first informed of the Tonkin Bay incident, Stevenson asked Harlan Cleveland, "But are our hands clean? What the hell were our ships doing there in the first place?"

In the coming months, as the United States expanded the war in strategic offensives dubbed Operation Flaming Dart and Rolling Thunder, Stevenson continued to question, but never to challenge, the government's policy. Too long a mouthpiece for the State Department, he merely rehearsed the arguments on both sides in a growing national debate over Vietnam. Viewing the country as a legitimate security interest similar to Greece and Turkey, he extended containment in Europe to Asia, in order to "establish a tacitly agreed frontier between Communist and non-Communist areas of influence on the understanding that neither side will use force to change the status quo." Adlai Stevenson held the conventional view that the "loss" of Vietnam might ripple across Asia, bringing the waves of communism into the Middle East, although he was aware that the Chinese Red tides had had little effect on contiguous India.

Preeminently Stevenson considered American involvement a just cause. To protect South Vietnam from aggression was a morally correct enterprise, of the same order as American aid to Britain in 1940 and to South Korea in 1950. Embracing the Munich analogy, the ambassador recalled his struggle against midwestern isolation in the 1930s, and because he believed in American exceptionalism, he held his nation to be the guardian of the weak against a bully. For Stevenson, in the ultimate prideful contradiction of his generation, American war making was both required and explained by the nation's peace-loving instincts. Without prejudice he quoted Johnson during the UN debates over the Tonkin Bay attack: " 'We will seek no wider war.' . . . Our mission in South-East Asia is peace."

Behind his support of official policy, Stevenson pondered the president's escalation. Clearly the war violated collective agreements such as the Geneva accords of 1954 and the United Nations charter, the latter a linchpin, in Stevenson's view, of world order. When Pauline Frederick, the United Nations correspondent for ABC, pressed Stevenson on *Meet the Press* in June 1965 about American willingness to meet with the National Liberation Front (the Vietcong) and to accept a UN-sanctioned cease-fire, he stammered that the question was "properly addressed to the Saigon government." His response prompted an exasperated Frederick to ask whether the United States wasn't a party to the conflict.

By 1965 some Americans, including public figures like Senators William Fulbright and Frank Church, recognized the deception of the administration's positions. A few now turned Stevenson's moral arguments upside down. Dissenters who paraded outside the U.S. mission with antiwar chants and placards and who sometimes followed Stevenson back to the Waldorf, contested the ambassador's position. They pointed to the barbarity of the jellied petroleum napalm, which, mixed with phosphorus, burned its victims at 1,000-degree temperatures, to the chemical agents that decimated vegetation, along with the health of American soldiers and Vietnamese citizens, and to the relentless saturation bombing of North Vietnam. Some wondered if the ambassador's duty to uphold the UN charter did not transcend his obligation to the United States.

Pointedly, Senator Wayne Morse sent Stevenson a speech in which he opposed U.S. military action in Vietnam as violating international law. A few weeks later Morse criticized Stevenson for failing to fulfill his responsibilities to the UN. Stevenson begged the question, replying, "It goes without saying that the questions you have raised are serious and thoughtful and deserve a thoughtful answer"—at some future time.

Johnson, after February meetings with a group of advisers that did not include Stevenson, decided to use bombing as a strategy to pummel Hanoi into "leaving its neighbors alone." In response Stevenson expressed his admiration for the president's "prudent and careful approach to Vietnam," though he was, perhaps remembering evidence from the World War II strategic-bombing survey, suspicious of bombing as a military tool. In a meeting with the president, he expressed concern that the new bombing policy was a dangerous escalation. Yet, in a memorandum to Johnson the next week, the ambassador encouraged "all necessary military measures to stop the aggression, [including "limited" bombing] and . . . a readiness to explore the willingness of the Communists to accept a peaceful solution." Jostled by contradictions, in March the ambassador acknowledged what the administration did not: the United States could not anticipate concessions from the Vietcong, because "they have for some time been winning in South Vietnam." Earlier he had supported Secretary General U Thant's peace initiative, intended to begin direct negotiations between the Americans and North Vietnamese in Rangoon.

Hanoi was reported as interested, but in 1964 Johnson was in the midst of a presidential campaign against the Republican hawk Barry Goldwater. After the election the North Vietnamese attacked Pleiku, a provincial capital in the central highlands, at the same time that policymakers who had "won" the Cuban missile crisis believed that they could defeat General Giap's army. "The very word negotiation had become anathema," said one White House aide of an administration exhilarated by the prospects of a victorious confrontation against an evil enemy.

No one in Washington paid much attention to the U Thant proposal or to its messenger Adlai Stevenson, until in February 1965 the frustrated secretary general offered a prophecy: "I am sure that the great American people, if only they knew the facts and the background to the events in South Vietnam, will agree with me that further bloodshed is unnecessary. The political and diplomatic method of discussions and negotiations alone can create conditions which will enable the United States to withdraw gracefully from that part of the world. As you know, in times of war and of hostilities, the first casualty is truth."

The president was furious at the indictment. Denying the initiative's significance, Secretary of State Rusk informed the secretary general that the United States had many channels of negotiation and believed none worthwhile. The Americans also objected to bilateral talks without the Saigon government. Which government? U Thant acidly retorted—pointing up the weakness of any position based on protecting a South Vietnam that tumbled chaotically through the regimes after Diem, of Minh, Khanh, Suu, Quang Tri, and now Quat. What stung Johnson and Rusk was U Thant's criticism of the American government. "The U.S. Government informs its people fully and more than most governments involved," bristled Rusk. U Thant held his ground: "Frankly most Americans don't know the true facts about the war in Vietnam."

From this murky affair, Stevenson emerged, again, as a scapegoat for an administration that paid scant attention to his efforts to initiate negotiations, but which, in the face of U Thant's embarrassing revelations, had to appear conciliatory. Now Rusk accused Stevenson of exceeding his instructions by not keeping channels open. In reality, officials in the State Department had chilled any idea of talks, let alone a UN-directed effort, but Rusk based his criticism of Stevenson on the fact, as he informed Eric Sevareid, that he never told Stevenson "not to pursue the U Thant probes."

In his dealings with an administration that considered the UN no more than a compliance officer for insignificant international quarrels, Stevenson had not pressed negotiations. He filed few memos and decided on his own that the election season of 1964 justified postponement of any peace initiative. "Part of the problem," according to one official, "was that Adlai talking over the telephone was vague and imprecise about this matter"—so imprecise that Johnson denied that he had ever heard of the proposals, and State Department officials later insisted that they never received any memorandum from Stevenson.

Now casting about for a leader of national prominence, antiwar activists located Adlai Stevenson, a man identified with idealism, morality, and restraint in American foreign policy. They remembered Stevenson as a man whose views on the limitations of power ("we must not put too much faith in power") reflected his personal hesitation in the grasping of it. "If weak, developing nations want to try communism, let them learn the hard way," he argued in June 1965, holding that some countries could not be "saved" from communism. "Direct intervention against creeping revolutions is perilous. . . ." Mindful of his words, a delegation of New York writers and intellectuals came in that month to persuade Stevenson to end "his complicity in the persistent misstatements of facts by this government and by you as a representative."

Led by Paul Goodman, Kay Boyle, Dwight Macdonald, Nat Hentoff, and David McReynolds, the group read a "Declaration to Ambassador Stevenson," which called on Stevenson to resign and become a "spokesman again for that which is humane in the traditions and people of the United States." They had chosen Stevenson because of his previous "commitment to a world of law and to an honest, compassionate search for peaceful solutions to conflict." Accordingly they surmised that this was "a time of deep inner conflict" for him.

After an exchange that lasted an hour and a quarter, Stevenson politely thanked them for coming. Then he defended the administration's position, acknowledging only that he was not "secure" about the American invasion of the Dominican Republic, where Johnson had dispatched 23,000 troops three months before. Insisting that he would never resign, Stevenson resorted to schoolboy metaphor. "I would never take advantage of my political position to resign for political reasons. That's not the way we play the game."

Later Stevenson (or Barbara Jackson) drafted a response found in his briefcase after his death. In it he reiterated the basic arguments of containment, but these he characteristically matched with his hopes for a more "creative" initiative to "seek a negotiated peace in Vietnam based upon the internationalization of the whole area's security.... I don't impugn the good faith of those who hold different views. I would only ask them, in the name of the courtesies and decencies of a free society that they should equally refrain from impugning mine." For now he would stay in the UN and "act for you." In the final weeks of Adlai Stevenson's life, duty triumphed over idealism; obedience overcame dissent; the ambiguity of principles choked off action.

Stevenson's letter raised questions about what he meant and what, as the war continued, he might have done. Later his sons Adlai and John Fell recalled several conversations in which their father had supported American involvement in Vietnam and had opposed what he called these "protestants." But how long would Adlai Stevenson have remained Johnson's ambassador? He had already joined the New York bar and given several unmet dates, including January 1, 1965, for his return to his law firm. Many of the Kennedy circle had departed. But Adlai Stevenson stayed on, confounding, even as the best and brightest were stumbling, his historic opportunity to be a voice of national conscience.

And as the dissent of outraged citizens rumbled across the United States, eventually forcing Johnson's withdrawal from the 1968 presidential race, would Stevenson's sense of duty and his need for prominence—for it was not power that he had at the UN—have submerged the scruples of the nation's supreme postwar moralist? Would he, overestimating his effect on events, have stayed because he believed his resignation would be a blow to the UN he cherished? Did the fact that there was no American tradition of resignation over principle among the president's officers (William Jennings Bryan and later Cyrus Vance being notable exceptions) chill his determination? Or did Adlai Stevenson no longer believe himself one of those, as he described to the graduating class of Colby College in June 1964, required in every age "to redeem the time by living with a vision of things that are to be"?

5

ON FEBRUARY 5, 1965, Adlai Stevenson celebrated his last birthday at New York's River Club with sixty of his friends. Many traveled long distances from Bloomington, Springfield, Lake Forest, Chicago, and Washington, the places that marked the episodes of his life. Buffie and Ernest Ives came from Southern Pines. Borden, now living in the Waldorf apartment with his father, attended, the only son present. Of course, his beloved Marietta Tree was there, along with three other women with whom he had at one time or another been romantically linked. But the ranks of Adlai's friends were thinning; Alicia Patterson had died in 1963; Eleanor Roosevelt had succumbed the year before. At Roosevelt's funeral, Stevenson, as eloquent a eulogist as his grandfather, noted that he seemed to be forever saying "farewell in this world, always standing at the edge of loss and attempting to retrieve some memory, some human meaning, from the silence."

Still, as the sixty-five-year-old object of affection reported, "the party was riotous as usual—if not more so—enriched with wit, humor, verse, song, food, and drink! Somehow the familiar faces from far and near looked no older." Several guests thought Stevenson himself looked much older—the blue eyes as vivid as ever, but his eyebrows white, his once ruddy face now sallow and puffy. Friends and even his sister urged him to retire, or at least end the speechmaking and fund-raising for the Field and Roosevelt Foundations that sent him on exhausting journeys of uncertain purpose to give his trademark speeches on uplifting topics. In 1964 he had delivered twenty-one speeches outside New York, in cities ranging from Bloomington to Little Rock, despite what he described as his "palsied lips." In 1963 Stevenson flew twenty-four times to Washington, ten times to Chicago, three times to Europe, once to Africa, twice to the West Coast, and once to Antigua (with Sarah Plimpton), while in the first six months of 1965 he had already given fifteen addresses, in places as far-flung as Canada and the West Indies.

Everywhere he went, against doctors' and Agnes Meyer's orders, he ate. The slender 131-pound "Rabbit" of the 1920s had ballooned into more than 200 pounds of what George Ball likened to a fat slug. Intermittently Stevenson took medicine for his high blood pressure and sleeping pills—Seconal and scotch, he joked—for the insomnia he had suffered since his days as governor.

Sometimes Adlai Stevenson thought he would retire, telling his birthday guests that he wanted to prune trees in Libertyville and "sit on the ground and talk to the people." He craved a vacation, exaggerating that he had taken only about eleven days of vacation since he went into the UN job. Admitting to a UN associate that he hadn't read a book in five years, he hoped to enjoy what he dubbed "the leisure of the theory class"—to read, to spend time with his grandchildren, and, in the special image of the restless Stevensons, "unpack for keeps." As he searched for equanimity, poetry became the vehicle for sentiment: "I fold my hands and wait / Nor care for wind nor tide nor sea / I have no more against time or fate / For lo mine own shall come to me." But still a prisoner of family inheritance, he also embraced duty: "My first responsibility is to the President and to this job. . . . I've been so involved with affairs of my own generation I'd be a little bereft if I were *not* involved."

But how much time was left? Just after his birthday, Stevenson reported to his son Borden a "bad" electrocardiogram followed by "heart flutters." Several times in 1964 he complained of dizziness, once gripping a table to stay upright, and staggering as he clutched at chairs and walls in what friends and family mistook for fatigue, but what was more likely a symptom of his arteriosclerotic heart disease. Along with his sense of fatalism, the latter was a family inheritance. "My father died at the age of sixty; my mother at sixty-five. I am sixty-five now; that will be enough for me," he told his doctor.

In July 1965 Stevenson traveled to London after the annual meeting of the UN's Economic and Social Council in Geneva. Earlier he had delivered a long speech on the theme of global interdependence, which ended with his majestic phrase making, in this case borrowed from Barbara Jackson: "We travel together, passengers on a little space ship, dependent on its vulnerable reserve of air and soil; all committed for our safety to its security and peace; preserved from annhilation only by the care, the work, and I will say, the love we give our fragile craft. We cannot maintain it half fortunate, half miserable, half confident, half despairing, half slave. . . . No craft, no crew can travel safely with such vast contradictions."

In London, Stevenson discussed Vietnam with British officials, visited friends, including Prime Minister Harold Wilson, and talked to the CBS commentator Eric Sevareid about his and the world's need for peace—his failed public and private agenda of the 1960s. "For a while," Sevareid later quoted Stevenson as saying, "I'd really like to just sit in the shade with a glass of wine in my hand and watch the people dance." The next day, July 14, Marietta Tree arrived, and the lovers strolled together, searching for the house he and Ellen had rented during the war on Mount Row, not far from Grosvenor Square.

As they walked along, Stevenson suddenly paled and fell behind, complaining of faintness. "Hold your head high," he muttered as he crashed to the pavement, dead from a massive coronary, the pink confidential State Department papers sprung loose from his briefcase and now flying in the breeze. The sentiment, one of his mother's classic prescriptions for good health, was a perfect epitaph for a man who had seldom had things go his way, but who had endured gaily and without despair.

The manner of Adlai Stevenson's death—so sudden and dramatic—contradicted his life. With impeccable timing, like that of his grandfather, who had died on the eve of World War I, and that of his father, who succumbed months before the Great Depression, Stevenson's death came at the end of the American century, those special years of national optimism, ascendancy, and power. By July 1965 the war in Vietnam had begun to rip the United States apart. And to die at sixty-five, the full season of a man's life, the proper year for a man born in 1900 to die, walking in London on a warm sunny afternoon with the woman whom he might marry and to whom he had once written, "But if I expire today / Let it be in sight of thee," seemed, in some measure, destiny's atonement.

After his death Adlai Stevenson was remembered in many places—in London, where they read his grandfather's favorite lesson from Ecclesiastes ("Let us now praise famous men"), in Washington at the National Cathedral, where only a requiem mass was lacking from the service he once told Marietta Tree he wanted, in Springfield, where his casket rested in the Illinois Capitol Building, which he had avoided during his term as governor, and finally in Bloomington, at the simple Unitarian church, where Lyndon and Lady Bird Johnson sat in the front row with the Stevenson sons and Buffie.

Everywhere he was eulogized for his public accomplishments, though he was never an architect of his nation's affairs. Instead, despite the overblown rhetoric of his friends who heralded him as more important than Eisenhower, he would remain an attractive literate symbol of possibility for Americans disenchanted with politics and Democrats committed to Wilsonian images of government run by worthy men. Mostly it was the complex private man who emerged as friends recalled his gentlemanly conduct of politics, his gallant failures, and especially the pleasure of his company. "His great achievement was the enrichment of his time by the nature of his relationships with his time," said Archibald MacLeish with Stevensonian ambiguity. Carl McGowan, who had served in Springfield, noted that Stevenson seemed fated to move through "personal disappointments to the very center of the problems that assail all people." After the services Adlai Ewing Stevenson joined his father and mother, aunts and uncles, grandfathers and grandmothers, and four of his eight great-grandparents in Bloomington's Evergreen Cemetery, where after a family battle over its design and size, a simple slab of granite marks his grave.

CHAPTER TWELVE

LAST HURRAH

1

Six months before he died, Adlai Stevenson II visited Bloomington before traveling to Libertyville to celebrate Christmas with his sons, daughters-in-law, and grandchildren. Remembering things past in his childhood home on East Washington Street, he sought from his sister some explanation of his father's tempers, his mother's illness, and his parents' unhappiness. And when Buffie Ives asked how her brother felt about "coming back," Stevenson replied, "There's nothing here any more, is there? It's all changed." Certainly Bloomington—now an insurance town of 35,000 served no longer by family-owned shops around courthouse square but by malls on interstate highways—had been transformed, though the Stevenson home remained as it had been fifty years earlier. That night brother and sister made their obligatory calls on a dwindling circle of cousins and friends.

Change—in his private life, in the United States, and in the world—had been on Adlai Stevenson's mind all year. He had considered it in a poem to Marietta Tree:

> We have changed since, but the remembered spring
> Can change no more, even in the autumn smokes
> We cannot help the havoc of the *heart*,
> But my *mind* remembers half the spring,
> And shall—'till winter falls.

In his public life—in that small room of his own beyond the State Department directives—Stevenson had contemplated other kinds of transformations: "the ongoing agricultural revolution, the march of automation, the potentials of computer technology, nuclear energy, satellites communication, and the whole thundering impact of science upon society," which made, because of their augmented power both to create and to destroy, "our moral load . . . heavier than before."

439

Throughout the year Stevenson considered his future—whether to leave the United Nations and return to a law firm, whether to run for the senatorial nomination in New York (probably against Bobby Kennedy), and whether to press a claim for the vice presidency that Lyndon Johnson eventually denied to all his cabinet officers. With clamoring unctuousness the president had persuaded Stevenson of his indispensability at the UN, and so the ambassador stayed. He was accustomed to tension between hard duty and easy leisure—what he described to his friend Mary Lasker as "midnight reveries of life" that caused him to wonder if he had "lived two different lives." But which would he lead in the afternoon of his life?

Earlier Adlai Stevenson had written a love letter to Marietta Tree filled with a young man's passion. "The skies have cleared; the moon is high, full and brilliant over the silver sea. . . . You won't step out on the balcony to wonder at the beauty of the night for fear of prying eyes. . . . So we stand in the shadow just inside the door—very close. Breath is short and the heart fast in the struggle between looking and wondering, lying and wondering. Now I will go to sleep and dream of July days and nights. . . ." Was it time for Adlai Stevenson to marry again?

As he slept in his boyhood room at 1316 East Washington Street that December of 1964, the telephone interrupted his reveries, and he was called back to the UN. A crisis had erupted in the Congo, where rebel forces in Stanleyville had seized a number of hostages. It was late Christmas Eve before he returned to Libertyville. "House lovely—tree—whole family— Granny Carpenter joined us for Christmas dinner. Afternoon nap and cleaning up the mess," he reported. The next day he went hunting with Adlai, Borden, and John Fell, thinking of their future, rather than the past of Buffie's Bloomington. Throughout the year Stevenson thought of his sons when several times he quoted Goethe in his public addresses: "What you have inherited from your fathers, earn over again for yourselves, or it will not be yours."

One change was already confirmed for a self-described "weary old politician quietly receding into the shadows." There would be another Adlai Ewing Stevenson in public life. The Stevenson presence—the inheritance influencing his public career—was assured. But given the status of the Stevensons as a political aristocracy, the changes in campaigning and party politics and the personality of his son, what would be the relationship of Adlai Ewing Stevenson III to his times? How would he convey the legacy of elite service, independence from party, focus on the issues, and meaningful expression that represented the family's contribution to national life? And would he be lucky or unlucky in politics?

2

SIX WEEKS BEFORE Adlai Stevenson II visited Bloomington for the last time, the Stevenson torch had passed to a new generation, when thirty-four-year-old Adlai Ewing Stevenson III won a delegate's seat in the Illinois state legislature. Earlier his father had advised against politics until young Adlai established his law practice and, like father, like son, might be slated for some impressive state or national office. But after the U.S. Supreme Court decided that districts must be apportioned according to the rule of one man, one vote and the Illinois legislature proved unable, in that most fratricidal of tasks, to redistrict its lower house, all candidates for the 177-member assembly ran at large. Even in a state accustomed to political excess, an orange ballot with the names of 236 candidates was extraordinary. Two feet in length, the "bed sheet ballot" served as a tangible expression of the absurdity of late-twentieth-century politics. In such circumstances a recognizable name would be a priceless asset.

Sixteen years after the Chicago political leader Jack Arvey offered Adlai Stevenson II the Democratic organization's support for the 1948 Illinois gubernatorial nomination, Richard Daley—the powerful king of Chicago politics, now in his third term as mayor and eleventh year as chairman of the Cook County Democratic Central Committee—bestowed on Adlai Stevenson III one of 118 Democratic nominations for state delegate. It was the first of several echoes of his father's political career. This time there was less hesitation. What Stevenson might not have won in a district election could easily be attained statewide. After accepting, Stevenson asked Daley for advice and was told not to change his name. Two days before the Republicans had nominated Earl Eisenhower, the general's brother and the owner of an Illinois newspaper, who had displayed no previous interest in politics.

Stevenson's ambitions were different. "I can never remember being interested in any other line of work. It was never a question of if I would enter politics, only when and how," he explained. Like his father, he campaigned, exhaustively but diffidently, on a good-government, anti-Republican platform in every one of the state's 102 counties. He began in an African-American church in Chicago. In July he traveled to Metamora, the tiny town in central Illinois where his great-grandfather had lived. Afterward Stevenson described, to Aunt Buffie, the short speech in which he mentioned that Adlai Ewing Stevenson I "had started his political career there exactly 100 years earlier. The meeting was covered by the *Pantagraph*. Characteristically they did not say a thing about me or Dad."

Stevenson spoke as well in Bloomington, where four generations of his family had tried to educate friends and neighbors gathered around the courthouse. In that perpetually Republican community, he attacked Republicans in general as having "small minds and small faiths" and this year's Republican presidential nominee, Barry Goldwater, in particular: "We dare not entrust the power to destroy all human life to a self-admitted hip-shooter, a man with no faith in the ability of his country to survive and win the peace competition with the communist world."

Accustomed to more outgoing politicians, the press noted an aloofness about this one. Adlai Stevenson III seemed reluctant even to get out of his car to shake hands with voters. One reporter glimpsed him hunched over in the front seat. When he did leave his station wagon caravan, he sometimes marched awkwardly into beauty parlors, confronting startled patrons in curlers. Later a friend explained that this most private of men hesitated to intrude on the privacy of others, though in time the politician's salutation "I'm Adlai Stevenson and I'm one of 118 Democratic candidates running for the legislature" came more easily. But his guardedness remained. To a sympathetic reporter he described progress: "I am no longer hiding under the dashboard and have even waved a few times, but it takes a lot of effort."

In New York his father solicited contributions. "You have," wrote William Benton, the former Connecticut senator and publisher of the *Encyclopaedia Britannica,* who enclosed a check, "a powerful money raiser in your father who while lunching with me and Averell Harriman whipped out your letter. . . ." In this letter the younger Stevenson had complained about the expense of a statewide contest. Certainly a district or even a congressional campaign would have been cheaper at a time when some legislators could still win a delegate's seat with expenditures of under a thousand dollars. But with a voting population of over five million, Illinois elections were costly undertakings, especially in the media-dependent politics that bothered the frugal Stevenson and his father. "The expense," he complained to a friend, borrowing a word of his father's, "is appalling."

Even President Johnson sent a requested endorsement to be read at a fund-raising dinner, along with a private message congratulating the younger Stevenson "for crossing the threshold." This year Johnson was himself campaigning for reelection against the snowy-haired Cold Warrior from the right flank of the Republican party, Senator Barry Goldwater of Arizona. The latter's attacks on the 1963 nuclear test ban treaty and on big government—Goldwater proposed automatic tax cuts for five years to deny the government revenue for any new welfare measures—seemed dangerously retrograde notions to most Americans, as did his loose talk about giving NATO commanders authority over nuclear weapons. To encourage voters' perception of Goldwater's extremism, Democrats, whose understanding of television had sharpened since the Stevenson presidential campaigns of the 1950s, ran an advertisement featuring a young girl plucking petals from a daisy, amid a countdown that ended in an atomic explosion. In the voice-over Johnson proclaimed, "These are the stakes. We must either make a world in which all God's children can live or go in the dark." The electorate understood, even without the mention of Goldwater's name, and returned Johnson to the White House with 61 percent of the vote.

Swept along by the popularity of the national ticket, 118 Democrats won election to the Illinois legislature along with 59 Republicans. Adlai Stevenson, the newcomer with the magic name, led the bed sheet ballot with nearly two and a half million votes. Earl Eisenhower ran second. Finally, exulted father and son, a Stevenson had defeated an Eisenhower. To his friends in New York, a proud father displayed clippings of the triumph in Illinois, which, after his own lopsided defeats, represented a family victory.

In the next twenty-two years Stevenson's political career drew him from Springfield to Washington and then back to Illinois. In elective positions longer than any other family member, he served six years in state office and another ten years as a U.S. senator. Whatever his enthusiasm at the beginning of these terms, by their end he was, along with many Americans, disenchanted with politics.

Like his great-grandfather, whose indefatigible search for office had been shared by a generation captivated by party politics, and like his father, who had spoken for a generation of educated liberals seeking a postwar politics of meaning, Adlai Stevenson III was representative of his time. He displayed the alienation of Americans in a period in which parties no longer held the people's allegiance and in which politicians were more likely to be independent entrepreneurs than organizational loyalists. In time Stevenson's distrust clashed with the necessity for public service—the latter interpreted, in the family tradition, as sacrificial duty and never examined for the personal benefits it bestowed on any of the Adlai Ewing Stevensons. Amid this tension, Adlai Ewing Stevenson III emerged as a thoughtful, if unrealistic, critic of modern public life.

Like that of his ancestors, his political career ended with a withering defeat from which, as Stevensons often managed, he gained moral stature. He was an unlikely politician throughout, a loner in a joiners' game, a wealthy patrician of independent principles with a distinguished Democratic name in an antiparty age, a mistimed candidate interested, as his father had been, in the education of the public amid thirty-second sound bites. Driven by the media, celebrity-watching citizens of this generation paid close attention to the personal lives and looks of their candidates, and the habitually formal, usually frowning Stevenson was out of step. Not only was his family life exemplary of the nation's ideal—two sons, two daughters, and an attractive wife—but, mostly bald by his midthirties, he was unavailable for hair styling.

His father acknowledged his differences with his son. "At 34 I was working in the FACA [Federal Alcohol Control Administration] in Washington, as Assistant General Counsel," he wrote to Adlai III before the 1964 election. "My father was dead, my mother was an invalid, my father-in-law was in deep and perpetual financial trouble; I had two children, no home in Chicago, a meagre income, an insecure base as a lawyer and a compelling interest in public affairs on the liberal, democratic side, and we were in the depths of a depression. . . . I am sure you are way ahead on most counts and surely in self-confidence and purpose. Bless you!" To Otto Kerner, the newly elected governor of Illinois, the senior Stevenson eased his son's way with an ingratiating letter: "Adlai looks forward to his service in the legislature with an eagerness I had little expected in that much beset young man who has already had such a surfeit of politics and public life. I hope he will have some opportunity to be of service to you. I am sure he wants to, but he inherits a diffidence and shyness which may inhibit him at first."

This third Adlai Stevenson had learned the politics of the past generation too well and was ill prepared for new arrangements, having been tutored by one of the twentieth century's most idiosyncratic practitioners. He despised primaries, shunned any massaging of voters, stood with his back turned to potential contributors, was awkward on television, insulted other politicians by challenging their customary ways of doing things, publicly scorned Jimmy Carter, the first Democratic president in a decade, and heretically searched for long-term solutions to America's economic woes at a time when social issues were predominant. Freed from any obsessive necessity for self-creation as the wealthy son of a famous father, he had no need to strive for offices, most of which, once attained, he promptly found unsatisfying. Yet it was not easy to abandon the Stevenson mantle of public service.

In time Stevenson became a harbinger of a new group of Democratic politicians labeled neoliberals. Eventually these Democrats, who included Senators Gary Hart and Bill Bradley and Governor William Clinton, presided over the return of their party to the White House in 1992. By that time, when he might have been appointed to office by a Democratic administration, Adlai Stevenson had abandoned politics. Like other family members, his public career was shaped by his personality and upbringing. From his father and great-grandfather he inherited his drive to be in political office; from his circumstances as an eldest son with the proper name, he encountered what he characterized as "the extraordinary environment of early associations with great men"; and from his persistently difficult relationship with his mother, he drew the need for a self-defining aloofness and his apprehensiveness of being controlled—whether by party or by electoral expediency.

Adlai Stevenson III was born in 1930, the second year of the Great Depression, though it was less economic hardship than his status as an eldest child of an erratic mother and famous father that shaped his early years. He was, in the manner of eldest sons, a dutiful youngster of special significance, an admitted introvert who emerged as a family caretaker even before his father's death. With a claim to leadership as the eldest of three brothers, he was susceptible from his family position to the politician's necessity of knowing what was good for others. Like other Stevensons in this nomadic clan, he lived in many places as a child—first in Chicago, then twice in Washington, where he briefly went to two schools; in London for six months, where he attended Harrow, the exclusive English boarding school, while his father worked at the UN. Once he went to three schools in three years, and his father held these changes in teachers and curriculum to be the cause of his lackluster academic performance.

Like other scions of wealthy families, Stevenson's education was advanced by his summer travel to resorts, to dude ranches in the West, or to his maternal grandmother's estate on Cape Cod and, at sixteen and again during college, to Europe and Mexico. When he was older, he traveled with his father, and it was the personal observation of great historical figures—from Albert Schweitzer and Jean Monnet to Andrei Gromyko and Harry Truman—that he held as important a training ground as "any genetic or inherited tendency toward politics."

Adlai Ewing Stevenson lived mainly in Libertyville, where he gained an abiding appreciation for country living despite his loneliness. Years later he recalled his seclusion on a farm ten miles from Lake Forest, where, along with his younger brothers, Borden and John Fell, he attended private school. There were few playmates along the deserted banks of the Des Plaines River, only the tangled elms and roots of weed trees that hung precariously over the stream bed. "I guess," Stevenson acknowledged later, "we weren't very happy as children. There was the terrible discipline, few friends, living on the farm which we loved but which made us feel isolated." Remembering him as a solitary child sprawled on his father's bed reading or fishing for bullheads, Aunt Buffie later claimed he had few friends.

Yet as crown prince he shared with his father a name and a special relationship that replaced friends. What other children learned about civic power and authority from outsiders—perhaps from a policeman or a teacher or from a televised appearance of the president—Adlai Stevenson gained firsthand from the father who adored him and whom he adored. As a young child, Adlai proudly whispered to his governess that the father who called him Bear long after he was grown had shared secrets with him about a forthcoming trip. When his father ran for governor, he and his cousin Tim Ives drove the candidate from town to town, handed out campaign literature at each stop, and sat in the audience during Stevenson II's speeches, trying to fathom the partisan affections of the crowd. "God bless you," his father wrote on his twenty-first birthday. "No son ever gave a parent more satisfaction, more pride, and less cause for concern."

Thereafter he absorbed politics as part of family life, spending his vacations in the governor's mansion, where on New Year's Day he stood in line greeting the people of Illinois, and increasingly after his parents' divorce, serving as his father's counselor. His mother's hostility cemented his identification with his father, just as his closeness to his father further aggravated his mother. "We were in such symbiosis," he once said about his father, "that there was very little to discuss as far as career decisions were concerned." It was young Adlai who advised his father not to run for the U.S. Senate in 1962. And in 1952 it was young Adlai who counseled his father to "be wary of sacrificing a good chance of being reelected governor . . . for the uncertainty and work on a presidential campaign in a tough year."

On the other hand, his relationship with his mother was acrimonious, and it was she, along with various French governesses, who, with his father often absent, presided over his development. As an adult, Stevenson came to believe his mother abusive, but such labels—and understandings—were not available in the 1930s and 1940s. Knowing nothing different, he endured Ellen Stevenson's mercurial moods, spankings, and insistent regimens—that he speak only French at meals, that he eat only vegetables, that he take cold showers, that he not listen to the radio or watch the movies his classmates enjoyed, and that he avoid the evils of the world so that he not be "infected." "We *never* demonstrated affection in our family. We were not a demonstrative family. We were not a close family. Dad was in London or somewhere. . . . He never felt confident that he had done a good job with his own children," an awareness sharpened by the chasm between his mother Helen's child raising by suffocation and his wife's harsh discipline.

Withdrawal was the best means to avoid what Stevenson III later described in court as his mother's violent temper and "merciless slappings," the latter, in time, centering on his younger brother Borden, as the youngest son, John Fell, became the maternal favorite. Years later a psychiatrist advised Adlai against confrontations with his mother: "Take the abuse, don't answer back. It will merely make your mother more violent." Such advice reinforced what he had been practicing for years, but the resulting behavior shaped a personality ill suited to the gregariousness of elective politics or the consensual coalition building of lawmakers.

Like his father, he was destined for boarding school in the East and for the same reasons. Since the elder Stevenson had attended Choate before World War I, eastern boarding schools had gained in appeal for wealthy parents ambitious for their sons' education, contacts, and admission into an Ivy League college. In the fall of 1944 Adlai Stevenson climbed onto the Twentieth-Century Limited en route to Milton Academy, outside of Boston. It was his mother's choice and one over which he had no control: "I was just sent there."

Before he enrolled, his father offered, to the Milton registrar, an assessment of his eldest son. Adlai was weak in Latin ("an hereditary failure"), interested in shooting, and possessed of good health and strength, though not much athletic skill. "Adlai is a conscientious, diligent boy, quite self-reliant I think but perhaps a little immature. He is somewhat reserved and finds his own company not uncongenial. . . . His habits are normal, with a taste for reading which has not been well-organized and some tendency toward solitude. I think he is something of an introvert, but there is nothing solemn about him and he has a lively sense of humor and comedy."

Except for his name and the fact that his father was running for governor of Illinois during his senior year, he was an average boy, but also, in his own memories, a lonely and unhappy one. Neither at school nor at college did he display any interest in the student government or clubs, though, perhaps by way of preparation, he was for three years a member of the debating society. By his senior year his classmates had begun calling him "Guv," though they did not pick him for either insult ("thinks he is") or praise ("most likely to succeed") in their class poll.

After Milton his father intended that his son enter Princeton, but the school registrar cautioned that he was not ready. Princeton, his first choice, agreed, putting him on a waiting list because of his standing in the fourth quarter of his class. "Adlai has plenty of ability. His school reports that he once made an I.Q. grade of 137 which is considerably above average. He also did very well indeed in three out of his five College Board tests. . . . I have never met Adlai," offered the director of admissions at Princeton, "but this record would seem to indicate immaturity or at least an immature attitude toward the important problem of education."

Even during the frenzy of his 1948 gubernatorial campaign, the elder Stevenson, unwilling to abandon his ambition that his eldest son walk in his footsteps, contacted influential alumni to intercede. He also offered additional reasons to the admissions director why Princeton, then struggling with large postwar classes, should accept his son. "I am anxious for him to go to Princeton where my family have been educated since the 18th century." He exaggerated, for in fact neither his father nor his grandfather or great-grandfather had attended. Perhaps he exaggerated as well his son's "exceptionally broad worldly experience and mature sense of responsibility and judgment."

Unmoved, the director responded with a lacerating comment: "Adlai is immature and might easily do badly and exert very little influence for good on others. . . . He needs to punish himself. . . . I think that it should be impressed upon him that he has done poorly at Milton and stood low in his class simply because he has not chosen to apply himself." With the door to Princeton closed, Adlai benefited from Milton's close ties to Harvard and was accepted there as a freshman in the class of 1952.

In fact, Harvard was a more suitable environment for a reserved eighteen-year-old than smaller Princeton, where social life along the club row of Prospect Street still flourished and gave primacy to the gregarious, as it had during his father's time. At Harvard, the nation's training ground for ruling elites, Stevenson's privacy was assured—even though his father was governor of Illinois and his parents' divorce was well publicized—on a non-chalant university campus with forty-five hundred undergraduates. At Harvard what had been opaque for so long to his father became clearer to Stevenson III, as he saw what during his so-called immaturity had been only an unconscious sense of his future in politics. His grades improved; his interest in academics deepened; he joined the Harvard Liberal Union and during one election "went out and rang doorbells, but I wasn't too good at it." Knowing his destiny, he even got in a fistfight with another freshman about Harry Truman.

Choosing government as his major, Stevenson concentrated on political theory. Most students in a popular department that described itself as focus-ing on "problems of power" and that included academic stars like Arthur Holcombe, V. O. Key, and Carl Friedrich (the last a government adviser on postwar Germany) studied the mechanics and structure of the American government or international affairs; Stevenson had his own mentor for those topics. "I thought I'll never have another chance to study political theory," and so he read Friedrich, Montesquieu, Locke, Tocqueville, and Calhoun "to get the grounding in political theory for the political career I knew would come." With his background, any study of practical politics or Democratic party history only repeated what he had learned firsthand from his father.

In June 1952, the month before his father's nomination for the presi-dency, Adlai Stevenson graduated from Harvard and tried to join the Marine Corps. At first he failed the eye test for a service offering, after six weeks of officer candidate's training, a commission in the toughest, most prestigious service. It was the beginning of the third year of a stalemate between the United Nations forces and the North Koreans; it was the second year of stalled negotiations between the belligerents that simmered on, even as the war did, during a truce that did not end the fighting. With American casual-ties reaching over 25,000, nearly every young graduate in 1952 knew some-one who had died in the rugged land halfway around the world.

But Stevenson's generation had grown up with the Cold War, absorbing from their fathers the Munich analogy that made American involvement and their participation an unthinking decision. "I volunteered from a sense of duty. There was never any question to me of the right or wrong of Korea," Stevenson later explained of an experience that built his confidence and enhanced his understanding that he might be, as he had not been in either school or college, a leader.

His selection of the Marine Corps was more calculated. "It was a politi-

cal decision," he acknowledged forty years later, remembering the fate of a
politician of his father's time. "In 1948 when the Democrats wanted a candidate [for the Senate], they turned to Paul Douglas, who had been wounded
as a Marine." So intent on joining the Marines was this Harvard graduate
that, changing identities with a friend who took his eye test while he took
a failed blood pressure test for his friend, he was accepted, the first Stevenson since the Revolution to serve in the military.

Stationed in Quantico, Virginia, he heard his father accept the 1952
Democratic presidential nomination, hunched over a car radio in the dark.
Weeks later Adlai Stevenson II, on his way south during a campaign tour,
addressed at commissioning ceremonies a spit-and-polish corps of new
officers that included his son. The elder Stevenson connected a personal
theme to an international one: "In one way or another each generation has
to fight for its freedom in the conditions of its time. Our times are hard—
as hard as any in our history. We, your fathers, have asked you to make
ready to fight so that you and your children may walk upright and unafraid.
. . . The fighting in . . . Korea is fighting which must inevitably have been
faced, somewhere in the world, so long as the Soviet Union pressed its
purpose to subjugate the free peoples of the earth. . . ." In October, Eisenhower delivered his dramatic promise to go to Korea if elected president,
and a few weeks later Adlai Stevenson lost the presidential election.

By the time the younger Stevenson arrived in Korea, in early 1953, the
deadlock over the return of prisoners had been resolved, and his unit did
not face combat. The following July an armistice was signed at Panmunjom,
establishing a permanent cease-fire and a demilitarized zone of separation
between North and South Korea at the 38th parallel. The Korean War,
which had interrupted Stevenson's career and had hurt his father's presidential chances, was over.

In the fall of 1954 Adlai Stevenson began the next stage of an ordained
life course when he entered Harvard Law School, home of the most
demanding and prestigious program in the country. A law degree with its
training in public speaking, in the analytic dissection of arguments, and
in the exposure to civic controversies was still the union card for most
officeholders. His father encouraged his son to avoid competitive Harvard;
"it is better if you have political ambition to be in Illinois," either at the
University of Illinois or at Northwestern. But he was admitted to Harvard
and, unlike his father, graduated. Years later, searching for the truth about
his father's dismal record in that institution in the 1920s, he received the
dean's confirmation that he had indeed done better than his father.

In 1957, law degree conferred, Adlai Stevenson III began a clerkship
with Walter Schaefer, the chief judge of the Illinois supreme court and the
former Northwestern University professor whom his father had appointed
to that bench in 1952. A year later Stevenson joined the firm of Mayer,

Friedlich, Spiess, whose sixty lawyers were "more various in religious, social and political background" (than those in other well-known Chicago firms) and which made "a genuine effort to give young lawyers broad experience." Described by his wife as working eighteen hours a day, he shared his father's distaste for the practice of corporate law, as he awaited a political opportunity.

3

IN JUNE 1955 the Anderson family of Louisville was preparing for the wedding of twenty-four-year-old Adlai Stevenson III to their daughter Nancy. The couple had met when Second Lieutenant Stevenson was stationed at nearby Fort Knox, and Nancy forever remembered her future husband reading Mark Twain under a piano at a party. For over a year they corresponded, often daily. The circumstances of their marriage were ideal: an outdoor wedding and reception at the home of the bride's parents, a lovely smiling bride dressed in the traditional satin and lace wedding dress, and a handsome groom attired in the upper-class marriage uniform of a cutaway, vest, and cravat.

During the 1950s similar introductions to domesticity were commonplace in the United States, as advertisements, television situation comedies like the *Donna Reed Show* and *The Adventures of Ozzie and Harriet,* magazines, and popular opinion placed relentless pressure on young middle-class women to undertake promptly their allotted future as wives, mothers, and housewives. In the postwar period women were expected to find fulfillment in domesticity. Marriage was universally praised as the first step, with the formation of a home and family necessary for the contentment of both partners, not just a comfortable haven for hardworking breadwinners as it had been during Great-Grandfather Stevenson's day.

During the 1950s the marriage age fell in the United States, until nearly 70 percent of all white women were married by the age of twenty-four, and the average age of marriage declined to twenty-two for women and twenty-four for men. At twenty and twenty-four Nancy and Adlai Stevenson were representative of this rush to the altar, though Nancy Anderson did not follow the usual female course, as two-thirds of her classmates did, of dropping out of college. She had graduated from Smith College in Northampton, Massachusetts, a few weeks before her wedding, and at her graduation had listened to her future father-in-law deliver his version of the 1950s instruction that educated women serve as the bearers of culture and the healers of the hearth for busy men who did not have time to keep up with the arts. With characteristic diplomacy she had complimented Stevenson after his address. "The speech meant different things to different people and gave each person a challenging boost."

Yet, just as there was a dark side to the mythic, polished façade of companionate family life in the 1950s, so Nancy Anderson's wedding contained ugly features. For months Ellen Borden Stevenson had sought some role in the wedding, opposing her former husband's suggestion for two rehearsal dinners, assailing Nancy as a social climber and schemer, and repeatedly calling the Andersons to complain. Caught in the middle, young Adlai walked a tightrope between his father's patronizing advice to "butter up [his mother] so she will purr like a kitten," his future father-in-law's concern for his daughter and belief that Ellen Stevenson should not be "appeased" by her son, his future wife's agony at her treatment, his anger at his mother's "haranguing," and the demands on a first-year law student.

He wrote his father, "Mr. Anderson really is beside himself. . . . I think that Nancy may break down if she has to go through much more. Her faith in me conflicts with her respect for her father I think. . . . I'm getting some professional advice about mother—I refuse to try to live a married life exposed 24 hours a day to her vindictiveness and she's getting worse." The elder Stevenson intervened, informing Nancy's father, "Ellen is a hazard that Nancy and Adlai will have to face. . . . I wonder if you would have more respect for Adlai if he had behaved with less compassion and consideration for his mother. After all she is his *mother*."

As it turned out, Ellen Borden Stevenson did not disrupt the wedding, though she did wear black and carry a pistol in her purse. There was never any need for the plainclothes detective hired by the bride's parents to remove the mother of the groom. Yet she did grumble audibly (and accurately) during the service that her son's name was not Adlai Stevenson Junior but the Third. And by the time Ellen Stevenson complained about the photographers and threw the orchids her son had sent on the ground, she had reduced her daughter-in-law to tears. It was a bad beginning to a strong marriage of an older brother to a younger sister that endured through a period in which nearly one-half of all American marriages ended in divorce.

Nancy explained to her father-in-law, "Ad and I have, I think, a very deep calm loving underneath. . . . I understand many things about Mrs. Stevenson. I hope you won't worry about my feelings. Mine are more easily protected than Ad's." Recalling his own honeymoon in North Africa and Europe, the elder Stevenson offered unheeded advice that the newlyweds' plans to camp out across the United States and Canada might not be a proper beginning. Yet on this trip the couple discovered their paradise in the hilly country of Jo Daviess County, in the northwest corner of Illinois, along the Mississippi River, where they later returned to build a home.

In the fall the Stevensons settled in Cambridge while Adlai finished law school. To her father-in-law Nancy described "these days of reading, eating, laughing and talking [which] may spoil us for the 9–5 life ahead." In the pro-family decade of the 1950s, Nancy was typical of other American women, delivering her first child seventeen months after her marriage, propitiously on the eve of the 1956 presidential election. At less than two-year intervals three other children were born—Lucy in 1958, Katherine in 1960, and Warwick, named after Nancy's father, in 1962.

The elder Stevenson was surprised by four grandchildren arriving in less than six years, and sought on more than one occasion to recruit domestic help for his daughter-in-law. "It seems all I have to do is glance at Nancy and she starts swelling up," Adlai confessed to his father. In fact, the younger Stevensons were no different from thousands of other parents in this child-centered decade. Having married in their early twenties, these couples created a baby boom during their long reproductive lives. Whereas during the Great Depression the birthrate in the United States dipped to 18.4 per 1,000, in 1958, the year Lucy Stevenson was born, the birthrate stood at 25.3 per 1,000. Consequently the birthrate for third children doubled between 1940 and 1960, and that for fourth children tripled. "Most of us did not decide whether to have children, but when to have them," Nancy Stevenson later acknowledged as she testified to the revolution in birth control, which in the form of oral contraception began to be available in the late 1950s.

Dr. Spock provided the child-raising directives for this generation. From his best-selling *Baby and Child Care,* mothers of the 1950s and 1960s received comforting practical advice ("You know more than you think you do") and more permissive instructions ("He doesn't have to be sternly trained") than had shaped a previous generation's rigid understandings about how to superintend a child's journey from infancy to adolescence. No doubt Nancy Stevenson would have created a child-oriented, companionate household even without Dr. Spock. As it was, her outgoing, flexible temperament reinforced his injunctions to listen to children and abandon the schedules and constraints of Ellen Stevenson's generation.

Adlai Stevenson II was tolerant of the palpable changes in child raising in a household where romping replaced regimens. Nancy Stevenson later acknowledged her father-in-law's reaction: "I think there were lots of things [of which her father-in-law didn't approve] about the way we raised the children—loose and easy because of having no help and constantly there and never dressed nicely, [but rather] in holey blue jeans and dirty shirts."

Returned to Chicago after their student days, Nancy and Adlai Stevenson did not follow other young couples to the suburbs, choosing instead to buy, on Chicago's North Side, a three-story brick home described as "on the edge of the slums" by Adlai Senior, who surmised that his son might be "thinking about politics as well as saving money." Later they moved to a more fashionable address, closer to the children's schools. In the summers they drove to Libertyville, where Nancy became the housekeeper for her father-in-law's home and its many guests, organizing meals, picking fresh vegetables, and supervising four young children. "We'd get a call on Thursday that would say the governor was arriving home on Friday. And I'd fly out [from Chicago] and clean that huge house and make the beds and buy the food and cook the dinner, balancing a salad on the one hand and a baby on the other."

Rarely did Nancy Stevenson succumb to what Betty Friedan described as a difficulty "that had no name." With a husband and a father-in-law in politics, she avoided the isolation and boredom common to homebound middle-class mothers of this period, but not the incessant tasks of domesticity in two houses—her father-in-law's and her own. Like Letitia and Buffie, though not Ellen, she was recruited into the family business of campaigning, providing a female presence in her father-in-law's 1956 campaign as well as in his Libertyville home, where she posed with bags of expensive groceries to reinforce his anti-inflationary message. Years later, when her husband was under consideration as a vice-presidential nominee in 1976 and she had participated in four of his campaigns, Nancy Stevenson scribbled a note to her husband: "Our family life has not been damaged in the least by your public life, because you have separated the two so thoughtfully." But this separation closed off the political training that for so many years had characterized the Stevenson family.

4

IN JANUARY 1965, when Governor Otto Kerner, a Democrat, convened the Seventy-fourth Illinois Assembly, Adlai Stevenson joined 176 other delegates in the state capitol well known to four generations of his ancestors. Like other Stevensons, he had benefited from a century of family contacts with Illinoisians, along with his own service in local organizations like the Committee on Illinois Government and Hull House. More formal than those of his great-grandfather's time, these organizations were no less useful. As he wrote his father, whose own reputation had grown in the Chicago Council on Foreign Relations, "I'm embroiled as ever in extralegal activities."

Stevenson found his desk next to another newcomer—forty-two-year-old Harold Washington, who represented the emerging force of African-Americans in Cook County politics. Seated on the Democratic side of a legislature in which his party held twice as many seats as the Republicans, and in which there were only five women and six African-Americans, he took the oath for an office he soon dismissed as "not important and . . . a great deal of work." Soon Stevenson was working on anticrime and ethics bills, along with proposals to control guns and lobbyists. But as they had his father's proposals, legislators weakened these reforms and dismissed Stevenson's efforts to limit the power of special-interest groups as an effort to "repeal human nature."

For Stevenson the session provided a case study in bad government. "The legislature is inadequate to its task," he darkly informed Illinoisians. "Times change, but the legislature hasn't. In the haste and chaos which characterize the whole session, the Legislature makes many mistakes— most of them fortunately minor. And each session devotes much of its time to correcting the mistakes of past sessions." Irreverently Stevenson disputed the power of the party to control his vote—"the slavish deference of some legislators in both parties to every whim, real or imagined, of their political leaders [which] is not the stuff of good government or strong political parties."

Lacking public confidence because of its deficiencies, the Illinois legislature, in the view of this freshman, did not attract the best-qualified men and women. Granted that some delegates were "patient, able men and women," most were nonetheless deficient in that Stevensonian essential of independent judgment. From his father's famous black book of quotations, he drew George Bernard Shaw's dictum "Democracy is a device that ensures we are governed no better than we deserve."

Even the reformers—a group of legislators including Abner Mikva and Harold Katz, with whom Stevenson was associated—had failed: "Some of the 'blue ribbon' members were driven, not so much by fear as by a craving for respectability and acceptance in the ruling establishment to forsake all idea of reform." With his name and money Stevenson was freed from any need for such approval. When Stevenson voted against the party's orders, Harold Washington leaned over once to whisper that he wished he could afford the same autonomy.

Mostly Stevenson stayed at his desk (for it was one of the inadequacies of the legislature that it provided neither office nor staff), surrounded by mounds of bills that by May numbered 3,500. Never joining the after-hours social gatherings in Springfield's hotel bars for the arm grabbing and shoulder hugging familiar to most lawmakers, he was considered, in an evaluation that he would never shake, aloof and snobby: "a bit pompous and stiff and not very articulate," concluded a fellow delegate. "I never could get close to him. I doubt anyone could," said another. Meanwhile his comments on the floor were measured not so much by what he said as by how he said it. Some found his voice thin and reedy, lacking in projection. Soon the joke circulated that while Earl Eisenhower couldn't think, Adlai Stevenson couldn't talk. More generous legislators appreciated his diligence and intelligence.

In the summer of 1965, two weeks after the tumultuous end of a legislative session in which the clock had been turned back several times, Adlai Stevenson's father died. At the time his mother, armed with a Republican lawyer, was intensifying her efforts to overturn the conservatorship, threatening as well to sue her sons. Meanwhile Borden Stevenson was planning to open a nightclub in Chicago—"the worst possible time so far as my fortunes are concerned," wrote Stevenson to his father's friend Ruth Field in 1966. "We'll just grin and bear it. There's probably a sufficient psychological explanation for it."

Often at odds, Adlai and his brothers disagreed about the monuments to their dead father, as they sorted through proposals for international institutes, a biography, and a lecture series at Illinois State University in their great-great-grandfather Fell's hometown of Normal. As family custodian, Adlai administered his father's estate and in an act of symbolic separation butchered his father's sheep—the latter the emblem of the senior Stevenson's life as a country gentleman. With their father dead and their mother an emotional and legal adversary, the brothers were drawn together less by bonds of family affection than by discussions of oil and real estate investments and, until her death in 1972, by the turmoil of their mother's circumstances.

Six months after his father's death, Adlai Stevenson summarized his father's legacy at Illinois State University. Characteristically he would not, perhaps could not, relay his private feelings. "The words come slowly. Emotion envelopes thought." Even those who "really knew him not at all can better express themselves than can the son of a father deeply loved." In his private mourning he established a distance between himself and his audience that became a permanent feature of his public speech—and his personality. Such a separation of the private and the public led to controversies with his father's biographer John Bartlow Martin over the inclusion of material relating to his father's affairs and earlier anti-Semitism. "I can't for the life of me understand [Martin's] interest in all these peripheral and personal matters. To the average reader it would be intensely boring. It prolongs the book, obscures the history and all in all does no one credit. . . . I just regret he had access to so much stuff. Fortunately we took precautions to eliminate some of the most damaging material," said a man who believed personality peripheral to the issues on which he intended to concentrate.

In his speech at the university in Normal, Stevenson discussed his father's commitment to morality in politics, to education, and to world peace through the United Nations, which now required fighting in Vietnam "to end an unprovoked aggression." Then he concluded with a self-directed platitude. "Thus he has left the fulfillment of his goals to us. We are the richer for his words, for his wisdom. The path is clearer for his having walked along it."

Three months later, during a week in which Adlai Stevenson spent three days testifying in his mother's competency trial about her abusive telephone calls and threatening behavior, Adlai Stevenson was slated as the Democratic nominee for state treasurer. It offered, he informed his eighty-eight-year-old great-aunt Letitia—"a fair chance for public service and a great opportunity for political advancement." Like his father, he made certain that everyone knew that he had not sought the office. "I am up for state treasurer and often wonder why. It really wasn't of my choosing, but it does give me an opportunity for service and advancement," he wrote Dr. Carl Binger, a psychiatrist whom he had consulted about his mother.

Like other Stevensons, he had responded to obligation and an opportunity levered as much by who he was as by what he had done. His vote-getting ability in the 1960s, the power of his name as Illinoisians mourned his father, and his inherited—and now earned—reputation as a principled lawmaker chosen by the Independent Voters of Illinois as one of the state's best legislators, attracted Democratic leaders, especially Richard Daley, who held a sensitive regard for reformers. But Stevenson's independent endorsements of candidates disliked by Daley and his support of a graduated state income tax irritated more orthodox party members.

In 1966 Stevenson began his second statewide campaign in two years, this time for a technical executive office that he dismissed as "dull" at a Washington fund-raiser. This widely reported gaffe, his confusion of black-eyed peas and beans at a local state fair, and the persistent playing of "Brother, Can You Spare a Dime" as his caravan pulled into towns and shopping malls, received as much attention as his ideas about modernizing the treasurer's office by ending the system of pet banks for state deposits and streamlining the office's functions. In this election Stevenson confronted the electorate's indifference to the policy concerns he and his father embraced as crucial to the survival of the Republic. Perhaps for self-inspiration, his campaign messages turned apocalyptic: "The office of state treasurer is important because the future of state government is at stake in this election. It's vitally important that we elect the kind of men in legislative and administrative offices who will welcome the responsibilities that forward-looking service demands," he informed an audience in Perry County.

Like other children of famous parents in a society with ambivalent feelings about dynasties of any kind, he was measured against his father. Some Illinoisians complained that, still too young, he was traveling on his father's name. When his Milton classmate Senator Edward Kennedy spoke at a Democratic fund-raiser, Kennedy joked that Stevenson had asked him for advice. "I told him I could not give him advice. I had a different problem. He's running on his name." To one correspondent who believed that "hardly anyone can measure up to your dear father's gracefulness of language and wit," Stevenson acknowledged, "It is hard following after my father but I try not to think about those footsteps. I can only be myself which isn't enough." Usually Stevenson offered a standard reply: "Of course my name had something to do with it. I hope not everything. After a time I am on my own. Besides while I inherited his friends, I inherited his enemies as well." This latter observation infuriated Aunt Buffie, whose son Tim Ives was running, unsuccessfully, for state senator without the magic designation.

In this campaign Stevenson and his followers continued the Libertyville picnics—those rallies at his late father's home that conformed to the family's love of nature and the great outdoors. Organized as family events with pony rides and a steam calliope along with a 1960s "big beat band," such affairs displayed the differences and similarities between his great-grandfather's campaigns a century earlier and his own. In order to mobilize his followers, Great-Grandfather Adlai Stevenson had used torchlight parades of marching loyalists in a pageant that climaxed with a long windy speech; Adlai III's rally featured entertainment and a few short remarks. For a contribution of five dollars the political consumers of the 1960s—many of whom were not Democrats but rather independents—ate hot dogs and cotton candy, enjoyed the clowns and pony rides, and played catch with the baseball celebrity Leo Durocher.

As the rituals of Stevenson I characterized a Democratic army going off to war, those of Stevenson III (for Ill. Treasurer, in his campaign logo) appealed to modern consumers through an amusing circus. Yet such entertainment clashed with Stevenson's avowed determination to run campaigns that instructed the people "so that they can make informed decisions at the polls," just as his family-instilled belief in elite leadership contradicted his rhetorical commitment to rule by the people. In any case, his ideas of using state funds as levers to encourage open housing were often lost.

In November 1966 Stevenson led the off-year Democratic ticket with more than 1.8 million votes and 52 percent of the vote. Still in his thirties, Adlai Stevenson III had emerged as a rising star whose self-described "creative treasurership" included tripling the return on the state's investments, cutting the employees in the treasurer's office, and putting state deposits to work as seed money for low-income housing and other public needs. Characteristically—for it required no coalitions for implementation—Stevenson remembered his position as state treasurer as his favorite office because he "could accomplish something." At the time it seemed a platform to higher office. "My only aspiration," he told a reporter in 1968, "is to remain in public office. And you know you can't succeed yourself in the treasurer's office." Still, as a proud Stevenson who knew his political worth, he would accept "no lateral movements."

5

ELLEN BORDEN STEVENSON never joined her son in his campaign appearances or even before the microphones of victory. Instead, she became an adversary in a brutal family fight. In 1966 the case for a conservator to manage Ellen Borden Stevenson's assets was finally heard and decided in favor of the plaintiffs—her three sons and mother. Ellen Stevenson had refused the court's injunction to be examined by two Illinois psychiatrists. She had instead chosen New York's Dr. Thomas Szasz, a frequent critic of medical psychiatry, who had found her "competent to manage her affairs." But having not cooperated with the process of discovery, she lost her legal right to conduct a defense and a jury found her incompetent. A few months later Ellen Stevenson was evicted from her home on Chicago's North Side, and in 1968 after being accused of harassing another woman, she fled to Indiana.

Ellen Borden Stevenson died of cancer in Gary, Indiana, in 1972 at the age of sixty-four. Her voice has been expunged from the Stevenson record, but this is what she said and wrote in the 1960s:

Now they say I have an imperfection of mentality—whatever that is. But I'm sane enough if I'll just sign an agreement with them. They have destroyed my independence and the bank has sold off my priceless Black Angus cattle. I was not represented at the hearing. But how can I live? All I want is a loan and they are so unreasonable. For years their father infected . . . brainwashed them, especially Adlai—that crazy little bastard—with scurrilous information about me. He says I'm insane. He's the insane one. My lawyers say my family is hopeless when all I want is a loan, and they have driven me to bankruptcy . . . put me on the dole so they can control me. God damn them!

I am dangerous, I am so God damn dangerous that I told young Adlai on the phone he'll probably end up in jail or worse. And when he asked why, I told him about the conspiracy—the lawyers in cahoots with them because they think they are so rich and powerful, and the judge whose father was a friend of the family. But all I have to do is call up the FBI and Adlai [III] will be through. He's evil. If they don't help me, there will be a great national scandal. I have friends everywhere. If it's between you and me, Adlai, you killing me and my killing you, boy I'm going to kill you. I'm going to slaughter you.

My lawyer says I haven't been properly represented and that there was never any medical evidence that I was crazy. And Adlai taping our phone conversations. Is hanging up the phone a sign I'm crazy? Are business losses a measure of mental incapacity? Since when have human problems become medical illnesses? What they have done is force me to choose between a cookie-a-day and a court-administered incompetence under a system that should be changed to give women like me more rights. I have been given fewer rights than criminals. Some day my full story will be known.

And now they are after me again with that woman who says I hit my friend Jim Ingram's mother. Jim's the only one who has ever helped me. That neighbor Rita Warren who got a court order to detain me involuntarily in a mental ward at Presbyterian–St. Luke's works for the Health Department and that little creep Adlai's friend is the legal counsel. I will not be taken to be examined by a psychiatrist and locked in an institution. I will never see my son again. He has no mother. I will move out of state where the summons is not valid. I will appeal.

Now they tell me I have a grapefruit of cancer in my belly and Jim tells me the Illinois Supreme Court has ruled against me in my appeal. But I will go on to the U.S. Supreme Court. The nurses tell me how courageous I am even if I can't walk or control what Jim calls my evacuations. My sons telephone and John Fell is here in the hospital—but I will never see Adlai again. For once will they do what I say and when I am dead scatter my ashes over the farm they stole from me.

6

IN 1967—BEFORE the disgrace of Vietnam cost Lyndon Johnson a second term—Richard Daley persuaded the president, who preferred Houston for his anticipated second nomination, that Chicago should be the site of the next Democratic convention. His city, in Daley's advertisements, had avoided race riots such as those in Watts and Detroit. The mayor did not mention a municipal policy of segregated housing, or the four nights of street fighting in 1965, or Martin Luther King Jr.'s rallies in the Loop for open housing and jobs for blacks.

More to the point, Daley could deliver more than one hundred Democratic delegates and, as he had in 1960 and 1964, twenty-seven electoral votes. "I would say," said the bulldog of Illinois politics, "that it is an important sign of faith to the American people for this national convention to be held here not in some resort center [the Republicans were meeting in Miami], but in the very heart of a great city, where people live and work and raise their families, and in one of the biggest neighborhoods in Chicago—my neighborhood." The president agreed with the Democrats' powerful political boss.

The sixty-four-year-old Daley, born into an Irish Catholic blue-collar family in the south Chicago working-class neighborhood of Bridgeport, educated in a second-rate three-year commercial high school, and grown to maturity during the New Deal as a clerk in the city government, perfectly represented the traditional supporters of the Democratic party. He also ran one of the most effective machines in American politics, his political career having accelerated after Governor Stevenson appointed him director of finance in 1949 and then supported Daley in his first mayoral campaign in 1955.

In early 1968 Adlai Stevenson III, eager to move up the political ladder as his father had done, appeared before Daley and the Democratic slating committee for its endorsement. Noting his accomplishments—his electability as the party's leading Illinois vote getter in 1964 and 1966, and his reputation both as state treasurer and as a legislator—Stevenson argued that he deserved one of the party's largest prizes. Usually in the inquiry that followed a prospective candidate's presentation, questions centered on how a potential nominee expected to finance his campaign and whether the candidate would pledge loyalty to the entire party ticket.

But in 1968 divisions over race and war, apparent throughout the United States, intruded. Committee members peppered Stevenson with questions about his loyalty to a president who had sent 45,000 more troops to Vietnam in the preceding summer and whose policy of intensive bombings disgusted Democratic liberals. Would Stevenson support the president's policy in Vietnam? Stevenson equivocated: he would support the president as far as his conscience would allow. Again the question was asked, this time broadened to include Democratic nominees who sought the continuation of Johnson's escalation in Vietnam.

The fifty loyal partisans of the Democratic Central Committee gathered in the ornate Gold Coast Room of the Sherman Hotel stiffened as they considered the audacious independence of young Stevenson. It reminded them of his father. The oldest among them might have also recalled stories of his great-grandfather who had wandered off from party orthodoxy over the currency issue. Finally State Senator Paul Powell, one of his father's antagonists, erupted: Does this mean that you would not support all Democrats? Would you take the ticket from the top to the bottom? "You have your loyalties and I have mine," replied Stevenson as he stalked from the room, amid some applause but generally indignant murmurs of "what that young man lacks is loyalty." It was Richard Daley who rose to remind the slate makers "that Adlai is a Stevenson. Generations of Stevensons have supported the Democratic ticket." But this year Stevenson would not be endorsed for governor or senator, and only the foolish and the brash ran in the primary without the central committee's approval.

A month later Martin Luther King was assassinated, Daley's Chicago erupted, and the mayor became famous for his shoot-to-kill directive. Meanwhile Lyndon Johnson's hopes for a second term slipped away amid increasing opposition to his failed war policies. As the Democratic convention approached, 1968 was already, in Adlai Stevenson's description, "a tragic and troubled year."

Like most state officials, Adlai Stevenson was a member of the Illinois delegation, but unlike many of them, he was not attending his first convention. Since those boss-brokered, cigar-filled assemblies to which Great-Grandfather had taken his son, Lewis, to which Lewis had brought his son, Adlai, and in turn Adlai had introduced his son Adlai III, the Stevensons had used conventions as a partisan schoolhouse. In the years before nominations left the conventions for the personal competition of presidential primaries, such assemblages introduced young Stevensons to party leaders and issues, to the pageantry of life as a Democrat, and expectantly to the next president of the United States. This year's convention taught conflict and chaos to eleven-year-old Adlai Stevenson IV.

Disagreeing about Vietnam, delegates were angrily divided among those who favored the disgraced incumbent president and his surrogate Hubert Humphrey, those who accepted George McGovern as a replacement for their slain hero Robert Kennedy, and those who gave their allegiance to the insurgent, poetry-writing, antiwar candidate Senator Eugene McCarthy. A final group of white southern Democrats held ties to George Wallace, the populist, segregationist governor of Alabama, who would run as a third-party candidate in 1968.

By the middle of August, Chicago had become a microcosm of the nation's conflicts. More than a thousand radical yippies and political hippies led by Abbie Hoffman and Jerry Rubin were threatening to float nude in Lake Michigan and to lure Democratic delegates into fake taxicabs, releasing them after the convention was over, in Michigan. More than four thousand antiwar advocates had arrived to make their case to the Democratic party through action in the streets: parades, rallies, and the now familiar tactic of teach-ins. Activists for racial justice were organizing as well. Daley, inflating to 100,000 the numbers of those who might defy his calls for law and order, refused permits to march down State Street—the city's traditional parade grounds—and instituted an eleven o'clock park curfew intended "to keep unpatriotic groups and race agitators out of the park." When the protesters refused to leave, Chicago police waded into the students, reformers, and hippies, swinging their clubs and hurling their tear gas canisters amid cries of "Pigs, pigs." Thereafter assaults by what Stevenson called "storm troopers in blue" occurred throughout the city.

Besides the parks, the mayor intended to protect both the Democrats and the city from "outside agitators." Around the convention site at the Chicago Amphitheatre, protected during the convention by fifteen hundred policemen, stretched a quarter-mile chain link fence seven feet high and topped with barbed wire. But no security could prevent the catastrophic

schisms both inside and outside the convention. As police marched on protesters outside the Hilton Hotel with tear gas and clubs, inside the convention a split occurred over the party's plank on the war. On a floor vote
delegates accepted a resolution approving the president's policy and urging
eventual withdrawal over an alternative calling for an immediate unilateral
halt to the bombing and the withdrawal of American troops. In response,
antiwar delegates with black bands on their sleeves paraded around the hall
singing "We Shall Overcome" and chanting a refrain that echoed throughout America: "Stop the War. Stop the Bombing. Bring American Troops
Home."

Soon Daley's treatment of protesters outside the amphitheater became
an issue inside, as Democrats rose to condemn his brutal treatment of dissenters numbering at most five thousand. From his front-row seat the
mayor, never one to turn the other cheek, retorted to the Connecticut senator Abraham Ribicoff's charges of Gestapo tactics by shaking his fist at the
podium and shouting, "Fuck you. You Jewish son-of-a-bitch"—or so, amid
the bedlam, the lip-readers translated.

In the pandemonium that followed, Adlai Stevenson tried to organize
delegates into an anti-Daley protest march inside the convention hall, while
the New York delegate Allard Lowenstein urged a postponement of the
proceedings. But in the white working-class neighborhoods of Daley's Chicago, citizens marched with placards reading "Chicago Loves Daley." On
the night that Vice President Hubert Humphrey received the Democratic
nomination on the first ballot and the leader of the antiwar movement,
Eugene McCarthy, refused to appear on the platform in the traditional sign
of party unity, acrid smoke from tear gas drifted through downtown Chicago. The stench testified to the wounds within the Democratic party, as
well as those in the nation.

Adlai Stevenson had supported the peace plank and Hubert Humphrey,
taking the candidate over the issue because, he argued, peace negotiations
had already started. With the high-minded rhetoric associated with his family's politics, Stevenson condemned Daley's inability "to take into consideration a rather long American tradition of resistance to being pushed around
and being told where, when and how to walk on a public street." Such a
public attack was audacious for a high-ranking Democrat who wanted
another posting. Its ferocity was imbedded in Stevenson's own antiauthori-
tarian refusal to be controlled by the party, a legacy, in the manner of the
personal as the political, of a harsh maternal upbringing that made the
affirmation of autonomy important.

Daley's city, Adlai Stevenson asserted, had refused "to tolerate dissent
realistically. . . . Force is met by force, and violence escalates. . . . It leads to
a closed political system where 'the outsider' is disruptive. And how many
outsiders—outsiders who are Democrats—do we have today? I am, I guess,

an outsider, as my father was. . . . More than ever before, Illinois Democrats are restless within the confines of a feudal structure which exists by paying homage with jobs and favors. Chicago, the Democratic Party, indeed all our institutions must open up to new ideas and forces, rewarding idealism and energy and innovation—either that or they will not command the allegiance of the people."

It was a declaration of war against Richard Daley and his organization delivered in the Stevenson idiom. It was also a reflection of the social strains within a party whose identification with blacks, women, and war dissenters—Stevenson's outsiders—placed its liberal wing in opposition to its white working-class base and led to disastrous electoral losses for the party in the 1980s. These divisions among Democrats might be traced to his father's indifference to middle-class culture and his association, however exaggerated, with dovish foreign policies.

Thirty-eight-year-old Adlai Stevenson, born to a wealthy Unitarian Lake County family, Harvard educated, and grown to maturity in the household of a Democrat who had won his only elective office by appealing to independents willing to break free of a Republican machine, perfectly represented the new forces of the Democratic party. Yet in the past his father and Daley had been strange but congenial bedfellows locked in a mutually gratifying embrace.

Now Stevenson threatened to form an insurgent local party. His warning reached Washington, and in a conversation overheard by the future Chicago mayor Jane Byrne, Daley shouted over the phone to Lyndon Johnson, "Don't worry about young Adlai. He's not going to form any third party, Mr. President. I explained to him that you don't desert the party in bad times; you take the ticket from the top to the bottom. . . . Why I even told him how we all supported his father twice for the presidency, even though we knew he was a loser."

The hostility continued with Daley proclaiming himself a liberal and Stevenson working for more flexible voting procedures and "an open party and open political processes, a progressive Democratic party responsive to the issues on the American agenda." Understanding politics as power in a manner that his father never had, he mobilized the Citizens for Stevenson Committee and supported reform candidates for alderman in Daley's urban fiefdom of Chicago. To further the cause, Adlai Stevenson arranged another fund-raising picnic at his father's home in Libertyville—the last, for the estate had been sold. "We'll have barbecue, beer, pony rides and bands. . . . [This is] a time to take a good hard look at our own party and where we go from here."

On a warm sunny day in September 1969, more than ten thousand Illinoisians gathered by the banks of the Des Plaines River, along with Senator George McGovern of South Dakota and Senator Fred Harris of Oklahoma, the chairman of the Democratic National Committee. Jesse Jackson, the young black leader of Operation PUSH, who had been working with Stevenson to place state funds in black-owned and operated banks, also attended. (Earlier Jackson had criticized Stevenson: he was too honest, and he didn't speak in parables.) As the crowd ate hamburgers, drank beer and soft drinks, and listened to a reading of the Libertyville Proclamation "for an end to the purchased loyalties of patronage," speculation centered on the chief dispenser of these "purchased loyalties." Would Daley make a historic pilgrimmage to Libertyville, the symbol of antimachine politics?

Then a latecomer brought the startling news that Illinois's senator Everett Dirksen had just died. On the platform inside the huge tent, McGovern was eulogizing the dead senator when a black limousine drew slowly down the quarter-mile driveway. From it emerged, along with his retinue of Dan Rostenkowski and others (like pallbearers at a funeral, someone joked), the short, squat figure of Richard Daley. In a symbolic moment of reconciliation, the boss who always followed power and the Stevenson who wanted another nomination shook hands.

It was Jesse Jackson who hushed the crowd when the mayor took the podium amid hisses and shouts of "Let him sign the Libertyville Proclamation. . . . How does he stand on more women and black convention delegates?" Finally, after prayers by Jackson for a dead Republican, a church choir launched into "Battle Hymn of the Republic" and "We Shall Overcome," as the crowd—young and old, black and white, partisan and independent, Adlai Stevenson and Richard Daley—linked arms, swaying to the music.

Six months later the Cook County Central Committee slated Adlai Stevenson as the Democratic candidate to fill the remaining four years of Senator Dirksen's term. With Nixon in the White House, questions of party loyalty seemed irrelevant. Like his father, Stevenson had merged his reformist ideals for good government with political reality. Daley wanted a winner and this Stevenson in Washington, just as, even when delivered by the man he had condemned in 1968, Stevenson wanted a national office that had eluded his father in 1948.

In the negative campaign that followed during the fall of 1970, Stevenson's Republican opponent, Ralph Smith, tried to transform a centrist Democrat into one of the president's and Spiro Agnew's fictions—a "rad-lib" sympathetic to drug use. "Extremists need a Stevenson/Illinois Doesn't" read Republican fliers in a campaign full of the kind of personal attacks that soon became a hallmark of American politics. Smith used the slurs of the past: "Somehow when I think of Ad-A-Lay, I see red. You can take that any way you like." On the orders of a president who remembered the taunts of Stevenson's father, Vice President Spiro Agnew traveled to Illinois dispensing what Stevenson called "political pornography." In four speeches in

Springfield and Chicago, Agnew used his fool's language against "those who moan endlessly about what is wrong with their country . . . and who offer a pusillanimous pussyfooting on critical issues of law and order."

In response Stevenson—an acknowledged "introvert in transition"—put an American flag in his lapel, mentioned his service in Korea, adopted the unexciting slogan "No Hate, No Fear, Just Hard Work and Harmony," and concentrated on the state's sagging economy and his opposition to violence, whether by Weathermen, young people, criminals, or state troopers. Stevenson wrote more of his material than his father ever had, but noted, "Somehow I don't get the results my father did."

Glumly sober, blandly unmetaphorical, and deeply informed, he encouraged Democrats to mobilize. To a Decatur audience in an age when direct mailings and television had ended the people's participation in electioneering, his remarks had no definable beginning or end: "We are not going to solve our problems by ignoring them—or by calling each other names. . . . My real hope, then, lies with the people. . . . There is nothing the people cannot do, but it takes hard work. It takes work in the precincts. It takes shoe leather and doorbells and postage stamps. . . . It is not too late to work for government from the courthouse to the White House which we can all trust."

Indefatigably Adlai Stevenson, a self-proclaimed "willing victim of hereditary politics," traveled through the state, remembering his first political campaign with his father in 1948, when they ate catfish in the river bottom towns along the Mississippi and Ohio. Now it was fried chicken everywhere. Some things hadn't changed as the candidate wondered whether he "shouldn't stay home and think through the issues and what you should be saying to the people that's useful to *them*." Despite his doubts, in November of 1970, Adlai Stevenson won his third statewide election, with 57 percent of the vote, only 40 percent of which, in a harbinger of electoral change, came from Daley's Chicago.

7

AFTER THE ELECTION, when the forty-year-old senator arrived in Washington for his swearing-in ceremony, he noticed Great-Grandfather Adlai's bust—the one that Letitia liked to hug while it was being sculpted—just outside the Senate chamber, and in the deferential way of the Stevensons, he wondered why it was in such a prominent place. Family ties seemed everywhere as senators who had known his father offered congratulations. With Aunt Buffie's consent, he brought to the vice president's room Adlai I's silver pen and ink stand, the Senate's gift to their retiring presiding officer in 1897 and the family's icon of public service. Then, during a session in which Adlai Stevenson was presiding—as freshmen often did—Senator Sam Ervin of North Carolina quoted his great-grandfather on the "great evils of hasty legislation" and the importance of Senate rules grounded "in human experience and tireless effort." It was ancestral advice counter to Adlai's intentions.

Beyond the U.S. Capitol the new senator observed transformations in a city where he had lived during the early 1930s and briefly during World War II. Capitol Hill and the area along Independence Avenue were studded with indistinguishable marble buildings housing the offices of the nation's civil servants. During Stevenson's ten-year tenure in Washington a new Senate building of over a million square feet with gymnasium and pool (which Stevenson labeled "a monstrosity with too many frills") was no sooner dedicated then filled with some of Congress's 25,000 employees.

By the 1970s physical changes mirrored political ones, as Washington accommodated trade associations and single-interest lobbying groups anxious for proximity to legislators. Consulting firms and think tanks spread along Massachusetts Avenue. Providing information for senators, congressmen, and the federal bureaucracy, lawyers and lobbyists—often the same—occupied lavish buildings along Connecticut Avenue, near Du Pont Circle, and along K Street in sleek downtown Washington, areas only thinly developed during Great-Grandfather's time.

Great-Grandfather had lived in a boardinghouse on the northeastern edge of the city while his family remained in Bloomington during his congressional years in the 1870s; a hundred years later the Stevensons came as a family, buying, after three months, a red brick $125,000 home on Foxhall Road across the street from Nelson Rockefeller, in a fashionable section near Rock Creek Park. Echoing his father's frugality rather than his mother's extravagance, Stevenson called the house "pretentious," as he continued to wear clothes one reporter described as "second-hand from the coroner's office." Still, parsimony did not extend to education, as his younger children attended private schools; by this time Adlai IV, following the well-established family tradition, attended boarding school in New England.

Nancy Stevenson, helped by an au pair, played the companionate role of this generation's political wives, organizing breakfast meetings, participating in the children's school organizations, and, after the Republicans left town in early 1977, visiting the White House. In an era in which the Equal Rights Amendment, supported by her husband, led to a national discussion of feminist issues, Nancy promoted her version of equal rights: "The woman of this day can play the part as she wishes . . . yet we political wives are put down for enjoying supporting our husbands. But ERA is about choice." Serenely comfortable in her role as political helpmate, she told a reporter, "I've never felt my husband's position has restricted me. I don't feel my life would have been very different for me if I hadn't married Ad." It was a perspective her mother-in-law had rejected.

The Stevensons were never part of the social scene, avoiding even Carter's inaugural ball. The junior senator from Illinois worked too hard to have time for Washington's perpetual parties, though he later wished that he had made more friends rather than eat lunch at his desk and work at home every night. "I think there's a great value in getting to know people well and talking intimately with them and exchanging information with them. I think I'd have been a more effective senator if I'd done more of that." Such isolation reflected the emotionally contained, self-assured personality of a man who enjoyed solitude.

It also reflected the ease of jet travel, which made camaraderie difficult as senators flew home on weekends, transforming the Senate, even as it increased its annual days in session, into a hectic Tuesday–Thursday Club. "I try to spend as much time as I can on weekends with Nancy and our children, but many of my weekends must be spent in Illinois, speaking at a luncheon meeting of the United Nations Association in Chicago or addressing the Peoria Association of Commerce, meeting with staff members and constituents and making stops in three or four towns to maintain my political fences." Like most senators, he spent a quarter of his time in his home state.

The first Stevenson in elected national office for nearly a century, he echoed family themes. "I owe [the people] my conscience," he declared with an Olympian Stevenson ring that irritated some observers. While his positive ratings by the Americans for Democratic Action, the Democratic party, and antiwar and consumer groups revealed the direction of his votes, these measures tabulated outcomes only between two positions. Preeminently, he was a policy activist rather than an ideologue, and his unsuccessful efforts to create a joint House-Senate committee on national priorities directed to shaping an industrial policy displayed the futuristic instincts of an introvert worrying not about the present but about the future. A rarity in his nonchalance about polls and celebrity appearances, Adlai Stevenson kept his legislative compass set on internal reform of the Senate so that it might undertake the necessary improvements in the ways in which the United States did business with the rest of the world.

At first other issues intruded. As the Vietnam War had been one of his father's last considerations, so it became one of his first. And because freshmen senators no longer were seen and not heard, in the spring of 1971 Stevenson rose six times to complain about Nixon's support of President Thieu's reelection campaign in South Vietnam. Similarly he supported Congress's efforts to undo the Gulf of Tonkin resolution his father had defended in the United Nations. But beneath the substantive difference lay philosophical similarities. Echoing his father's and grandfather's suspicions of power and the ability of government to change attitudes and behaviors, he dismissed the impact of any bill requiring congressional oversight of executive warmaking: "It gets back to the naive attitude that by passing a law you can solve a problem. . . . There is no easy answer."

As the war simmered on and Stevenson's contempt for both Richard Nixon and "the terrible leadership" of Secretary of State Henry Kissinger grew, another conflict between Congress and the presidency erupted. Stevenson was hardly surprised by the Watergate scandal; he had inherited his father's vast contempt for a man "who corrupts everything he touches." As Senator Ervin's Judiciary Committee investigated the "third-rate burglary" that was in fact a systematic effort to undermine the independence of government agencies and to cover up illegal activities ranging from wiretapping to the use of campaign funds, Stevenson drafted various technical powers for the new office of independent prosecutor.

Then, in a Democratic caucus considering Congressman Gerald Ford as a replacement for the bribe-taking, resigned Vice President Spiro Agnew, Stevenson predicted the fall of Nixon—and hence the significance of the Ford appointment: "The people are left to conclude that government of the people, by the people, for the people has given way, in Mr. Nixon's Washington, to the politics of wealth and stealth. And they are left to conclude that the era of the New Deal and the era of the Fair Deal have given way to Mr. Nixon's era: The Era of the Deal."

Stevenson was in the midst of his second successful senatorial campaign in August 1974 when Richard Nixon, amid tearful bathos, left the White House. The legacy of Watergate and Vietnam became the context for Stevenson's anticorruptionist senatorial agenda and for his pessimism about contemporary politics. Government, he believed, must be—but wasn't—accountable in Vietnam and Watergate. In one abuse of power, he had himself been the subject of a secret Defense Intelligence Agency surveillance of civilians.

For the next six years a devoted son sought to legislate his father's rhetoric. Having absorbed the lofty view "that politics is the means by which a people make the moral decisions which determine their welfare," Stevenson sought to limit individual campaign contributions "to lessen the power of the very rich in elections." Arguing for full public disclosure ("then leave it to the public to decide accordingly whether your votes are influenced by your interests"), he and only sixty other members of Congress released accounts of their assets, which, in Stevenson's case, amounted to $776,784. The latter placed the senator with the dog-chewed briefcase and rumpled clothes close to the Ninety-second Senate's millionaire's circle. By 1979, with an income of over $100,000, he was included in a list of thirty-four members of the senate's millionaire club. When the *Pantagraph* (and its parent company, Evergreen Communications) was sold in 1982, his net worth soared to over $5 million.

Yet Stevenson's legislation had little effect on the individual lawmaker's necessity, now that parties were slender reeds, to raise money in a political system of permanent campaigning. By the 1970s Senate business was routinely interrupted from five-thirty to seven-thirty so that senators could attend fund-raising events with large donors and lobbyist groups.

Under pressure from Democratic leaders who recognized his integrity but also the distance from colleagues that made him beholden to no one— neither party nor lobbyist nor friend—as chairman of the Senate Ethics Committee, Stevenson presided over the investigation of Senators Herman Talmadge and Edward Brooke, who were accused of misusing campaign funds. "It's been an agony. It's not what I came here to do," he complained, having come to set the agenda of the future. Instead, he was balancing the demands of constituents, evaluating how much shrimp staffers could accept before any largesse was considered sufficient to influence a vote, serving on committees and subcommittees, and overseeing a staff of thirty-five. Such demands left little time for the Stevenson mandate of thinking about the issues.

The pace quickened; the nights of study lengthened; his pessimism deepened. Like his father, he spent hours on his speeches. "I think we are going to celebrate the bicentennial by marking time. . . . Congress is adrift," he told the journalist Elizabeth Drew. "The U.S. isn't putting its house in order." That same year Stevenson (along with Charles Mathias of Maryland) tried to streamline a tangled committee process that held senators to service on as many as eighteen different committees and subcommittees, often with overlapping jurisdictions. Subcommittees had developed as a means of democratizing the choke hold that senior, usually southern senators had exerted on the legislative process, and by the mid-1970s 174 subcommittees provided a mechanism for those beyond the inner club to influence policy. Yet the reform was another example of the ways in which intended improvements only spawned more resistant forms of corruption.

In January 1977, as chairman of the Temporary Select Committee to Study the Senate Committee System, Stevenson appeared before the Rules Committee to recommend a reduction of committees from 31 to 15 and subcommittees from 174 to 100. He proposed as well lightening the committee loads for harassed senators, who often found themselves scheduled for two meetings at the same time. Immediately there was grumbling about the "rush of the thing" and "the restricted access of citizens with particularized interests to the legislative branch." There was also intense lobbying from veterans and small-business men because Stevenson had intrepidly abolished their committees. Unsympathetic to compromise, he now faced determined resistance. "This is a fight about power. . . . If this committee wants reorganization, this is where you make the decision right now." And so the Rules Committee did, but by scaling down his recommended shrinkage and by reinstating committees on Veterans Affairs and then Small Business and next Aging and Nutrition, as according to Senator Claiborne Pell, a melancholy "Senator Stevenson sat patiently watching his creation slowly deteriorate."

By the mid-1970s Stevenson himself chaired a "special" subcommittee on oil and gas production and distribution. As the great energy crisis of the 1970s choked an unprepared nation, the country's lifeblood congealed amid 500-car lines at gas pumps. Energy came to symbolize a new age for Americans—that of shortages and declining power. Growing demand, an overreliance on oil as an energy source, intermittent supply and distribution problems, an antiquated pricing system, limited natural gas supplies because of various regulations, and the emerging power of the Organization of Petroleum Exporting Countries—all contributed to what President Carter called "a deep resentment [by Americans] that the greatest nation on earth was being jerked around by a few desert states."

The junior senator from Illinois saw energy policy as part of a larger need for an integrated industrial and trade policy that would install a comprehensive national approach to global competition. The scant attention given to a coherent energy program characterized, for Stevenson, the obsolescence of a contemporary Democratic agenda mired in Roosevelt's economic liberalism of the 1930s and Johnson's social liberalism of the 1960s. He was glad to bury his party's ancient faith. "The Democratic party is in danger of losing its identity," Stevenson predicted. "The politicians of both parties are turning backward—either to the conservatism of the 1950's or to the social welfarism of the 1960's. . . . The country must face the future," he preached as he coauthored a bill to set up federally funded technology research centers at universities. "For decades the American economy thrived on cheap money, cheap labor, cheap land, cheap fuel and materials. Now all that has changed," became a modern Stevenson lamentation.

Such a vast problem could not be approached piecemeal, as in the classic liberal mandate of the Humphrey-Hawkins bill of 1976, which set acceptable levels of unemployment at 4 percent and which Stevenson, to the anger of labor unions and Democrats, at first opposed as inflationary. "Far from providing action," he wrote Leon Keyserling, the president's economic adviser, "Humphrey-Hawkins looks to me like an excuse for a congressional failure of leadership." Instead, Congress must shape the nation's economy through the encouragement of space technology, through incentives for investments, through export strategies, and through a national development bank, which he proposed in 1978.

"We are not little Hubert Humphreys," Gary Hart once said of a new class of senators more interested, like Stevenson, in policies of cooperation among business, labor, and government and improving the nation's deteriorating economic status, undermanaged economy, and low rates of capital investment than in traditional party themes of civil rights and poverty. "Such questions as national health insurance and public housing in the order of magnitude are secondary," concluded Stevenson, whose consciousness of family history encouraged a concentration on long-range issues in a nation that he complained had "no trade strategy, no industrial policy, no food policy." "What I've been trying to aim for are real influences and forces that shape the welfare of the people and nation."

To Stevenson's chagrin, the Carter White House paid no attention to his ideas for a government-owned energy company and energy bank, although the senator's complex legislation on how to price natural gas became the first bill Carter signed when he took office in January 1977. But when the president crafted his own energy policy, he did not consult with Stevenson—or in fact any other Democratic senators. "I've laid out ideas to President Carter, but I still detect little interest in new directions and a great preoccupation with reorganization . . . in other words with methods of government, not ends."

Stevenson's struggle for a new industrial policy continued throughout Carter's administration. Earlier he had voted against the corporate bailouts for Lockheed and Chrysler, on the grounds that failing corporations should not get government support and, at the least, government aid should come with requirements for corporate restructuring and the retraining and relocation of workers. "Mr. Iacocca could get a job somewhere making pizza," joked his (and his father's) speech writer John Martin. And then, worried that the ever-candid Stevenson might use the line, he cautioned, "For God's sake don't use that last line. I couldn't resist it, but you should." Instead, the senator introduced a bill to establish an American trading company for smaller "sunrise" companies to band together to sell their products overseas. But no one seemed to be listening to his pleas that "we can not ignore long-term economic interests."

At first Stevenson's disillusionment centered on President Carter, whom he dismissed as "embarrassingly weak." The public expression of such a heresy shocked regular Democrats; they remembered that Stevenson had been one of eight Democrats considered by Carter for the vice presidency in 1976. Interviewed by *People* magazine in early 1979, Stevenson complained to a vast audience that the Democratic president had "little interest in new directions" and that he might start a third party to jolt Carter. "My interest is in getting attention for some new ideas, getting the country moving again. . . . [Carter's] a wonderful listener who leaves you feeling good and helpful. But I'm not feeling that way any more."

In Illinois the columnists and the reporters, the politicians and the citizens speculated. Would Stevenson do the partisanly unthinkable: resign an office to which he could easily win reelection in 1980? Propelled by family images as he approached fifty—the age at which his father had been governor—would he return to Illinois and run for the governorship? "Adlai's Aspirations—Presidential or Identity?" headlined the *Pantagraph,* still published by his cousins the Merwins. Or would he simply retire to practice law and supervise his 1,000-acre commercial beef cattle operation in the rolling wooded hills near the Mississippi River outside of Hanover, where, according to his wife, he spent "many thousands of hours" removing stumps, chopping down trees, taking away debris, and planting other trees. In the past this often impenetrable subject had informed reporters who sought personal information, "We have been farming for six generations. I don't think people really understand that the Stevensons are farmers." And he wrote John Martin that the Senate was not the only place to serve.

Then Stevenson's disapproval turned inward to include the Senate. For years the occupational hazard of being a responsible senator had made him feel impatient—in a hurry, aggravated, fragmented but fulfilled. Once describing a day that had begun with an early morning breakfast with a cosponsor of a NATO proposal and that had ended at 11:29 P.M. when the Senate finally adjourned, he concluded with a Boy Scout's enthusiasm, "Each hectic day brings a measure of satisfaction if I know that in some way—however small—we have served the public interest."

By the late 1970s pessimism overrode any sense of fulfillment, and Adlai Stevenson decided to give up his senatorship—not because he was tired or wanted to move on but because the Senate had deteriorated. He had not lost interest in politics; instead, the system—American politics and public life—was no longer compatible with the Stevenson way of doing things. "The Senate used to be the greatest forum of free people. It is no longer. . . . Senators rarely debate the great questions before the country. There is a continuing preoccupation with everything *except* the ends of government." Certainly his own efforts to restrain campaign spending had not influenced the need for senators to put together four-million-dollar campaign chests spent mostly on negative television advertising; the sunshine laws, the efforts at gun control, the ethics codes, and even the streamlined committee system intended to strengthen the hand of the public had only fortified the interest groups. The reforms he had helped to spawn had produced few results.

"It's no longer possible to represent the public; we have to go behind closed doors," he bleakly informed a reporter. "When we opened the doors, it wasn't the American people who came in, it was all those interest groups. The American people aren't here, but the National Rifle Association is. . . . The 70's were hard years for activists in the Senate. I recognize now in a way that I didn't when I came here, that Congress does very little," he concluded as he packed his bags, gave up his notions of a third party, and, after a brief time in Washington as a lawyer, went home again. "If I were here as a senator in the '40's and '50's, I'd be running for reelection enthusiastically. But politics has changed. It's not the politics I was raised for." In fact, the public life for which he had been trained—that civic entity that all Stevensons believed existed a generation earlier—had already shattered.

Along with Adlai Stevenson five other senators chose not to run for reelection in 1980. The rate of voluntary turnover in Congress increased during this decade, in part because the success of incumbents assured long tenures for congressmen and, to a lesser extent, for senators. Yet most of those who retired were older than the fifty-year-old Stevenson. None did so to form a new party or to run, as Stevenson first intimated, against an incumbent president of his own party. On the other hand, few congressmen held such boundless (and often progressive) ideas for change, and surely none had as great nostalgia for the way American politics never was and certainly would never be again. Nor did these other lawmakers display such reluctance to adjust to the present—the state of public affairs and politics in the late 1970s marked by a powerful and increasingly snide press in a constitutional and political system designed not for efficiency but to protect liberty by fragmenting power.

Asked about a possible 1980 presidential campaign, Stevenson responded, "I'm not going into the primaries. I'm not running for sheriff," using a line of his father's about the primary system more important in 1980 than it had been in 1956, when his father was so offended by it. "I'm going to purchase 15 minute spots and explain the issues. It's been twenty-five years since a presidential candidate talked sense to the American people." Questioned who that was by some historically illiterate reporters, he answered, "My father."

8

IN THE FALL of 1981 Adlai Stevenson returned to politics (for with the Republicans in the White House he had no chance at an appointive job) and was nominated for governor. By this time Richard Daley was dead, missed by Stevenson, who had found him, unlike many politicians with better reputations, concerned with programs and policies and not just the favors of his stereotype. Disenchanted with primaries, Stevenson looked backward to praise the system of bosses "that had worked pretty well when my father was nominated." With the Cook County organization in disarray after the boss's death in 1976, Stevenson had no difficulty winning the nomination to run against a popular two-term incumbent—the ambitious Republican James Thompson, who had his eyes on Washington, even as

Stevenson looked homeward to Springfield, where "I could make Illinois a model of some of the economic programs I stood for in Washington." As governor he would be assured a degree of independence and authority not possible in a legislative body.

Thompson and Stevenson were mirror images of each other. At six-feet six and over two hundred pounds—the slim Stevenson once called him a "big blubbering whale"—the fleshy forty-five-year-old governor had worked his way up the educational and political ladder—first, two years at the University of Illinois, and a year at Washington University, followed by law school at Northwestern. Unlike Stevenson, he had no partisan inheritance or wealth. His father had been a physician working by day at the Municipal Tuberculosis Sanitarium and at night on his practice in a middle-class section of Chicago; his mother was a housewife from De Kalb who told her son that if "he wanted to get into politics, he should think about studying law."

In an electorally competitive state, Thompson had used the highly politicized U.S. Attorney's Office to bring some questionable indictments of Democrats, including former Governor Otto Kerner. In 1976 he was well known when he ran for, and won, his first term as governor, with strong support from the Chicago suburbs. Thereafter Thompson excelled at campaigning and at the creation of an efficient personal machine that Stevenson dubbed "a pin-striped spoils system."

With the exception of his antiques collecting, which became a campaign issue, Thompson's tastes remained plebeian. He drank beer with students and peppermint-flavored schnapps from a toilet plunger, rode a horse inside the state capitol, and donned the obligatory hats, from the headgear of belly dancers to that of Native Americans. An effective self-publicist who campaigned in denim and T-shirts, Thompson in Stevenson's view took a reactive, passive approach to the process of governing. In turn Thompson charged that Stevenson had been asleep in Washington for ten years. A perfect example of what Stevenson decried as "a packaged politician," the governor had a skill Stevenson lacked: he was a successful fund-raiser. And while Thompson was a masterful arm-twister, Stevenson described himself as "not having sharp elbows."

Even on the hottest days of the 1982 gubernatorial campaign, the patrician, frowning Stevenson wore a long-sleeve shirt and tie and what his Washington staff described as "his typical blah-Brooks Brothers suit." Asked by a reporter about the governor's campaign, Stevenson answered, "He's trying to make me into a wimp." Thereafter the self-constructed image of a wimp became an albatross, even as Stevenson tried to draw attention to "all the pioneering work" he had done in Washington. "But is anyone following up?" Stevenson promised active leadership to solve the state's economic problems. With an inherited inability to fit message to audience, he talked about sanctions against the Soviets and trade with China to a dwindling audience of workers on Springfield's south side, never once mentioning what was foremost in their minds: the closing of an auto plant. Stevenson had difficulty raising the two million dollars both candidates believed necessary for their campaigns. And after the election his running mate for lieutenant governor echoed the postmortem reviews of his father's presidential campaigns: "You have to be available and willing to say what you think. Sometimes I got the feeling our campaign headquarters hid. . . ."

In the 1982 election Thompson defeated Stevenson by 5,000 of over 3.5 million votes cast, the closest vote ever recorded in Illinois history, in a contest that pollsters thought would be an easy Thompson victory. Election day had been rainy, and Stevenson discovered a sufficient number of damaged ballots, missing precincts, and misplaced tally sheets in especially the Republican areas of southern and central Illinois to petition for a court-ordered recount. "Find a suitable court," advised Robert Strauss, the Democratic national chairman, from whom Stevenson sought advice. The challenger petitioned the Illinois supreme court, on which, although supposedly cleansed of any partisanship when they donned their black robes, four former Democrats and three former Republicans sat. With a stroke of adversity that his father would have understood, Stevenson had withheld an endorsement from one of these Democratic judges for a position on the federal bench, and this same judge had a son-in-law on the Illinois payroll. By a four-to-three decision, the court ruled against Stevenson, striking down as unconstitutional the election law that set up recount procedures. Thereafter the election of 1982 became, for Stevenson, another example of the modern vagaries that kept good men out of politics. "I see," he glowered, "very serious defects in the elections system in Illinois. . . ."

Four years later, in a replay of his father's campaigns against Eisenhower, Stevenson returned to politics, as the 1986 Democratic gubernatorial candidate against Thompson, who was seeking an unprecedented fourth term. None of the Stevensons, with their sense of partisan noblesse oblige, ever paid much attention to primaries, considering this means of extending democratic participation to be a "mindless, endurance contest." This year proved no exception after Stevenson's principal Democratic rival, Neil Hartigan, withdrew. Beset by factional fights in Chicago, the Cook County Democratic party saw little reason even to include the names of Stevenson's running mates on their sample ballots, especially after Stevenson labeled Chairman Edward Vrdolyak's leadership as "disastrous." As usual the primary came in early spring before the newspapers began covering the election. Stevenson himself had done almost no campaigning and had been out of the state in the weeks before the vote. "You were lecturing in China; you were on LaSalle Street; you were on the farm," taunted Thompson.

On primary election night an astonishing example of the follies of contemporary politics was revealed to a man who held a good chance to defeat
Thompson. Two followers of Lyndon LaRouche had upset Stevenson's
hand-picked candidates for lieutenant governor and secretary of state. La-
Rouche's incomprehensible, often anti-Semitic platform, conveyed to voters
at malls and airports and through megaphones at street corners, featured
attacks on Henry Kissinger and Queen Elizabeth as KGB agents and drug
runners, support for the development of weapons in space, and universal
testing for AIDS. No doubt only a few of the over 200,000 Illinoisians who
had voted for the followers of Lyndon LaRouche's National Democratic Policy Committee supported the positions of candidates who wanted to send
tanks down State Street to end drug trafficking and who thrust a pound of
raw liver into the hands of Chicago's Catholic archbishop. Some confused
the LaRouches with libertarians; others were attracted to the LaRouche
assertion that "people are sick of the lies and corruption of the Democratic
party and its establishment leaders." But most, in this apartisan age, followed only national elections and celebrity candidates and knew not for
whom they voted.

Rather than a LaRouche victory, the Democratic primary of 1986 was a
Stevenson defeat. The candidate of issues and meaningful politics found
himself cobbled on the Democratic ballot with two extremists. Stevenson
had been penalized by his own—and his fellow Illinoisians'—indifference
to primaries, a democratic system of participation that over the years had
eroded party organization. By the end of the twentieth century, what could
not have happened in Adlai I's time of strong political parties or even in
Adlai II's time of powerful state leaders like Richard Daley had ruined Adlai
III's chances for election. But this was a partially self-inflicted wound, the
result of Stevenson's disdain for party politics.

Only a quarter of the more than six million registered Illinois voters
had cast ballots on the rainy March primary day; the antiseptic, Anglo-
Saxon names of the LaRouche supporters, which came first on the ballot—
Mark Fairchild and Janice Hart—appealed to some downstate voters more
than those of the regulars Aurelia Pucinski and George Sangmeister. Democrats in all the counties where the Stevensons had lived—McLean, Lake,
and Jo Daviess—favored the LaRouches, in a catastrophe beyond imagining
in Richard Daley's time. Vowing that he would never run on a ticket with
"neo-Nazis," Stevenson struggled to find a way to run for the job that "I
have in my bones. I've been training for it all my life."

Some Democrats suggested that, if he won, Adlai Stevenson could simply abolish the post of lieutenant governor. Others, including Congressman
Dan Rostenkowski, urged Stevensons's resignation from the ticket so that
the party could nominate another candidate. "He has no right to put himself
above the party," complained leaders whose primary allegiance was still to

the party, as it had never been for the Stevensons. Meanwhile, during a season of setbacks as Stevenson probed the possibilities of running as an independent (and found he had missed the filing date) and finally settled on running as a third-party candidate on the newly created Illinois Solidarity ticket with two new running mates, he suffered other injuries—a cracked vertebra in a fall from a horse and, in a later accident, a broken foot. While the press made much of his gentleman's recreation of horseback riding and noted that he lived so far from Chicago that he had been taken in an ambulance to a hospital in Iowa, Stevenson acknowledged that he drove a Japanese pickup truck. "That truck saved me $1500. I've got four vehicles all American except one. If I had known I was running then, I wouldn't have done it."

As Stevenson hobbled about the state in the blazing hot summer of 1986, yearning for "the peace and tranquillity that I knew as a tank commander in Korea," he was not bringing the message of economic reform to the state. Nor on the fly-arounds that now took candidates by air from town to town was he accomplishing what he considered the campaign's purpose: "I really don't consider the object of a campaign is winning. I think the object is informing the people so that they can make sensible decisions." Instead, he was trying to get the 25,000 signatures necessary to get on the ballot as a third-party candidate. Still lacking a campaigner's common touch, he was once observed eating lunch in Belleville without attempting to greet other customers.

"Good public servants are known by their enemies" had long been a Stevenson commandment, and by 1986 these enemies included major donors such as the American-Israeli Political Action Committee, and the Illinois AFL-CIO and United Mine Workers, who for the first time in Illinois history supported a Republican. "If [Thompson] were a woman, he'd be pregnant all the time," charged Stevenson of the governors' relationship with special-interest groups such as labor, thereby infuriating feminist voters who remembered that though Stevenson had supported the Equal Rights Amendment, he had earlier refused to have a female running mate on his ticket because "a woman couldn't be aggressive enough without being shrill and strident." By the summer the National Organization of Women withdrew its endorsement. And as the only Democratic senator to vote against limiting the age of mandatory retirement to seventy, he lost the votes of senior citizens. Then he made hometown enemies by opposing the incentives Thompson had offered the Japanese auto maker Mitsubishi to attract it to job-hungry Bloomington.

Having lost his straight ticket advantage, the man who despised pollsters and party tyranny—because "I'm no good if I don't know what's on the minds of the people of Illinois"—compromised. He hired political consultants and public relations specialists, one of whom acknowledged that

Stevenson made his own judgments regardless of political pressure. "It's one of the things that makes him admirable as a public official, but [it] can be problematical for a candidate," concluded David Axelrod. Stevenson lent $150,000 of his own money to his faltering campaign, the sum then doubled by a wealthy commodities broker; he ran a thirty-second negative ad that began with Thompson's face superimposed on a light bulb that came on only in election years and another with a tap-dancing governor. "When it comes to song and dance, nobody's better than Thompson," read the caption.

When Stevenson debated the governor, his ideas for improving the state's banking and educational system were lost amid invective. "I don't like getting involved in personal attacks. . . . I'm just responding to his attacks. I'm not going to let them pass. I'm going to hold him accountable," said Stevenson. Meanwhile Thompson mispronounced Adlai, called the senator "frantic and bobbled" and accused him of what was indeed a family way of politics—disappearing.

It was no surprise that this last hurrah ended in defeat, though Stevenson's Solidarity party got 40 percent of the vote. On election night Stevenson told his workers that they had been through "the political ordeal of the century." A graceful loser bred to good manners, he warmly stroked the hands and the morale of his defeated band "who had passed the test of friendship," and proclaimed a moral victory. "I am proud of what we have done. We fought back against every conceivable adversity. We can hold our heads high. We did what was right. We ran a straight race." Asked whether he would run again, Stevenson replied that whatever he did, it would "serve the public."

He soon found mostly private ways to serve the public in a system corrupted by "cheap and easy popular answers, unfunctioning government— at risk of producing a gray, shapeless mediocrity." In his political obituary, he condemned "professional politicians [who] have surrendered to the media and to public relations experts, and cosmeticians . . . the actors and managers who have taken over from the statesmen." Like his father and his grandfather, he believed that a morally degraded political system had left him, not he the system. And as the season of an American family's political life drew to a close, Adlai Stevenson III represented a son who had learned the family business too well. "The object of our leaders today is not the exercise of power, but the acquisition of power." In possibly the Stevenson family's last effort to exercise power, Stevenson had been forced to ask Illinoisians to vote not for the Democratic ticket of his heritage but for a third party with an unfamiliar and transitory title.

Adlai Ewing Stevenson III currently runs a merchant banking company that focuses exclusively on "helping business firms of different nationalities do business with those of another nationality." His partners are Mexican-

American and Japanese, and the firm gravitates to "fast-moving areas like East Asia." Meetings of the eighteen-member Asia Pacific Economic Cooperation Forum, which represents a giant trading zone from China to Chile, have replaced those of the Democratic party. He remains gloomy about our democracy, which "as we practice it, is not conducive to a candidate's cerebration—or the people's confidence. . . . To succeed, Democracy must inform and exhort the public to some high and common purpose. . . . Now it seems paralyzed by timidity and partisan bickering."

Nancy Stevenson represents thousands of Americans whose public involvement is no longer focused on political parties but rather on associations with specialized interests that seek to solve community problems. Having worked on the Illinois Humanities Council, Nancy Stevenson is currently active in Voices for Illinois Children. None of the next generation of Stevensons is at present in public life. In the summer of 1994 Buffie Ives died shortly before her ninety-seventh birthday, in the Stevenson home in Bloomington, surrounded by the artifacts of her brother's political career and convinced that "the Lord has left me here to do what I could for Adlai's memory." Adlai Ewing Stevenson IV, having predicted as a ten-year-old that he would be Adlai the Last, not as some said Adlai the Next, has worked in communications, the field, his father notes with some bitterness, that has replaced politics as the way to influence public opinion and educate the public.

In the fall of 1994 Adlai Ewing Stevenson V was born. Although the Stevensons will go on, the habit of politics has been lost in a family whose cumulative relationship to its times is more significant than any of its individual accomplishments. With the perspective gained from an ingrained sense of the family history, Adlai Stevenson III recently left a pallid benediction to the students of Indiana University: "Every generation has its turn. At the risk of sounding like a civics teacher, the choice is yours. It's your turn to make the machine run. Nothing is holding the country back, except its politics and that's something you can change for the better."

NOTES

ABBREVIATIONS

AES	Adlai Ewing Stevenson II
AES III Papers	Adlai Ewing Stevenson III Papers, Illinois State Historical Society
ASOH	Adlai Stevenson Oral History Collection, Columbia University
Bulletin	Bloomington *Daily Bulletin*
CHS	Chicago Historical Society
Family Folders	Stevenson Family Folders, 1316 East Washington Street, Bloomington, Illinois
Governor's Papers	Adlai Ewing Stevenson II Papers, Illinois State Historical Society
HDS	Helen Davis Stevenson
IC	Elizabeth Stevenson Ives Collection, Illinois State Historical Society
IGAOH	Illinois General Assembly Oral History Program, Sangamon State University
IRAD	Illinois Regional Archives Depository, Illinois State University
ISHS	Illinois State Historical Society, Springfield, Illinois
ISU	Illinois State University, Normal, Illinois
JFKL	John F. Kennedy Library, Boston
Johnson Papers	Walter Johnson Papers, Milner Library, Illinois State University, Normal, Illinois
LC	Library of Congress
LGS	Lewis Green Stevenson
Martin, *Illinois*	John Bartlow Martin, *Adlai Stevenson of Illinois: The Life of Adlai E. Stevenson* (1976)
Martin, *World*	John Bartlow Martin, *Adlai Stevenson and the World: The Life of Adlai E. Stevenson* (1977)
MCHS	McClean County Historical Society
NA	National Archives, Washington, D.C.
Pantagraph	Bloomington *Daily Pantagraph*
Papers	Walter Johnson, ed., *The Papers of Adlai E. Stevenson,* 8 vols. (1972)
PUL	Seeley Mudd Library, Princeton University
SSU	Sangamon State University

LIST OF INTERVIEWS

William McCormick Blair	Jane Dick	Dr. Nicholas Fortuin
Barbara Bruns	Dr. William Fitzpatrick	Jane T. Gilbert

Dr. Paul Green	Michael Maher	Arthur Schlesinger Jr.
Mrs. Paul Graebel	Edward Maumanee	Adlai Stevenson III
Lawrence Hansen	Senator Charles Mathias	Borden Stevenson
Robert D. H. Harvey	Mary Jane Masters	Nancy Stevenson
J. Stuart Ingram	Margaret Munn	John Taylor
Elizabeth Stevenson Ives	Michael Murphy	Vlada Tolley
Timothy Ives	Steve Neall	Marietta Tree
Kathryn Allamong Jacob	Dr. Emmet Pearson	Harriet Welling
Greg Koos	Joseph Rauh	Wilson Wyatt
Dr. Paul McHugh	John Regan	

CHAPTER 1: POSTWAR DILEMMAS

PAGE

3   *"If you don't"*: Hermon Smith Oral History, Jacob Arvey Oral History, Adlai Stevenson Oral History Collection, Columbia University, hereafter ASOH.

3   *Arvey and Illinois politics:* Milton Rakove, *We Don't Want Nobody Nobody Sent: An Oral History of the Daley Years* (1979), 3–19; Arvey Oral History, ASOH. The term "clout" is an especially Chicagoan idiom for political influence. See Len O'Connor, *Clout: Mayor Daley and His City* (1975); John Martin, typescript on Chicago, 1960, in AES Papers, Box 793, Seeley Mudd Library, Princeton University, hereafter PUL. See also Milton Rakove, *Don't Make No Waves: Don't Back No Losers* (1975), 142–47.

3   *Idealism of postwar period:* Paul Fussell, *Wartime: Understanding and Behavior in the Second World War* (1989), 165, 172.

4   *End of ethnic leaders:* Stephen Erie, *Rainbow's End: Irish-Americans and the Dilemma of Urban Machine Politics, 1840–1985* (1985), 140–86; David Fremon, *Chicago Politics Ward by Ward* (1988), 159.

4   *The new independents:* James Wilson, *Amateur Democrats: Club Politics in Three Cities* (1962); Fremon, *Chicago Politics,* 158.

4   *"without any scars"*: Arvey Oral History, ASOH.

5   *"I never fancied myself"*: Walter Johnson, ed., *The Papers of Adlai E. Stevenson,* 8 vols. (1972), 2:26, hereafter *Papers.*

5   *"I am bothered"*: Smith Oral History, ASOH.

5   *Purging New Dealers:* Chester Bowles, *Promises to Keep: My Years in Public Life, 1941–1969* (1971), 176.

5   *"father's admonition"*: AES to "Aunt Julia," 11 Dec. 1947, Walter Johnson Papers, Milner Library, Illinois State University, Normal, Illinois, hereafter ISU.

5   *"Poor Adlai"*: *Life,* 24 March 1952.

5   *Information on Brooks and Douglas:* "Campaign Materials, 1948," AES Papers, Illinois State Historical Society, hereafter cited as Governor's Papers.

6   *"Why don't I"*: 20 Jan. 1947, Stevenson Diary, AES Papers, PUL.

6   *"Am forty-seven today"*: 5 Feb. 1947, ibid.

6   *Ellen's demand for divorce: Chicago Daily News,* 20 Aug. 1952.

6   *"all was well"*: Diary, 4 Feb. 1947; Kenneth S. Davis, *The Politics of Honor: A Biography of Adlai E. Stevenson* (1967), 201–5.

6   *All he'd "known of love"*: AES to Alicia Patterson, 23 Feb. 1949, Johnson Papers. On Alicia, see "The Case of the Hot-Tempered Publisher," *Saturday Evening Post,* 12 May 1951; Robert Keeler, *Newsday: A Candid History of the Respectable Tabloid* (1990), 139–55.

7   *"I marvel at you"*: AES to Alicia Patterson, n.d., Folder 136, Johnson Papers.

PAGE

7   *The Stevenson movement:* Edward Doyle, ed., *As We Knew Adlai: The Stevenson Story by Twenty-two Friends* (1966), 28–29, 50–52, 67.

7   *"most ardent backer":* Papers, 2:361.

7   *"party activity":* Arvey Oral History, ASOH.

7   *Kohn's support:* Lou Kohn Oral History, ASOH.

8   *Description of Stevenson acceptance:* Smith Oral History, ASOH.

8   *"Well, I guess"* and *"I didn't ask to be":* Papers, 2:462–63, 465.

8   *"finally surrendered":* AES to Sir Louis Spears, 27 Feb. 1948.

8   *Ellen's reaction:* Jane Dick to AES, n.d. (copy), Box 441, John Bartlow Martin Papers, LC.

8   *Ellen agrees not to divorce:* Porter McKeever, *Adlai Stevenson: His Life and Legacy* (1989), 113; Arvey Oral History, ASOH.

8   *"I am in it":* AES to Buffie and Ernest Ives, 1 Jan. 1948, AES Papers, PUL.

9   *"I have a bad case":* Speech to Democratic State Central Committee, 7 Jan. 1948, 1948 Speeches, AES Papers, PUL.

9   *"noblesse oblige":* Paul Douglas, *In the Fullness of Time: The Memoirs of Paul A. Douglas* (1971), 129, 131, 136;

9   *"Four counties":* Papers, 2:548.

9   *Campaign descriptions:* Jack O. Brown, *Early Days and Late Hours with Adlai Stevenson* (1956), 4, 8, 11, 12.

10   *"Attaboy, Professor":* Interview with William Blair; Campaign Folders, 1948, Governor's Papers.

10   *Stevenson on Centralia:* Papers, 2:526; James Mulroy Folder, Governor's Papers; *Chicago Daily News,* 28 Feb. 1948; Patricia Harris, *Adlai: The Springfield Years* (1975), 14.

10   *Stevenson positions:* Campaign Folders, Governor's Papers.

10   *"Striped pants":* Harris, *Springfield Years,* 8.

11   *One-liners:* Papers, 2:509, 544.

11   *"Ananias":* Ibid., 527, 545.

11   *"too painfully eager":* Harris, *Springfield Years,* 12–13.

11   *"Keep your talks":* James Mulroy to AES, 17 Oct. 1948, Governor's Papers.

12   *"the illusive business":* Papers, 2:471.

12   *Attitude toward radio:* James Mulroy File, Governor's Papers.

12   *"Enormously insecure":* Interview with Borden Stevenson.

12   *"The good of the whole":* Papers, 2:572.

12   *"Not so much":* Ibid., 570.

12   *Acting as if off-duty:* O'Connor, *Clout,* 68.

13   *"the way I tie":* Papers, 2:493.

13   *"our intimate family":* Ibid., 480.

13   *"I can readily":* Ibid., 529.

13   *"You can't have":* Ibid., 557.

13   *"Our nation is very sick":* Speech to Young Democrats, Speech File, 1948, AES Papers, PUL.

13   *"Must we forever":* Papers, 2:494.

13   *"Broken hearts":* Ibid., 541.

13   *"and so on and on":* AES to Alicia Patterson, May 1948, Johnson Papers. The letters from Stevenson to Alicia Patterson were lent to Walter Johnson, while he was editing AES II's papers, by AES III. All citations to Stevenson letters to Alicia Patterson are to copies of these letters in the Johnson collection.

14   *"an amateur's pilgrimage":* AES to Glen McHugh, 1 July 1948, AES Papers, PUL.

PAGE

14 *Description of Bloomington rally: Pantagraph*, 16 Sept. 1948; Campaign Folders, Governor's Papers.

14 *Ellen during the campaign:* Interview with Elizabeth Ives.

15 Pantagraph *information:* Douglas, *Fullness*, 136.

15 *"friendliness, belief in the Republic": Papers*, 2:558–60.

16 *"You are asking":* Jane Dick to AES, 18 June 1948, AES Papers, PUL.

16 *Campaign financing:* Campaign Materials, Governor's Papers.

16 *Raising money:* AES to Hermon Smith, 8 April 1948, *Papers*, 2:490–91.

16 *Press reaction to Stevenson: New York Times*, 31 Oct. 1948; *Newsweek*, 15 Nov. 1948.

17 *"golden nugget":* The term, in reference to AES, was coined by Secretary of State James Brynes. See Doyle, *As We Knew Adlai*, 50.

17 *"Command me": Papers*, 3:34.

17 *"He might have been":* Harris, *Springfield Years*, 12.

18 *"I carried":* AES to Alicia Patterson, 6 Nov. 1948, Johnson Papers.

18 *Stevenson on election night:* O'Connor, *Clout*, 68.

18 *The trip:* George Marshall to AES, 26 Nov. 1948; AES to Eleanor Roosevelt, 6 Nov. 1948, AES Papers, PUL; "dream of this," AES to Alicia Patterson, 22 Nov. 1948, Johnson Papers.

18 *"Is it really":* AES to Alicia Patterson, 22 Nov. 1948, Johnson Papers.

18 *Descriptions of inauguration:* Inauguration Folder, Jan. 1949, Governor's Papers.

19 *Ellen's ideas for the inauguration:* Smith Oral History, ASOH; Inauguration Folder, Governor's Papers.

19 *References to the mansion as confining:* AES to Alicia Patterson, n.d., Folder 132; AES to Alicia Patterson, 22 Jan. 1949, Johnson Papers.

19 *"I am marooned":* AES to Ralph Hines, 1 July 1949, AES Papers, PUL.

19 *AES's frugality:* Elizabeth Ives, *My Brother Adlai* (1956), 221–23.

20 *On Artie:* Interview with Elizabeth Ives.

20 *"who considered us":* Harris, *Springfield Years*, 32.

20 *"Work has been my refuge":* AES to Alicia Patterson, n.d., Johnson Papers.

20 *"I found Adlai":* Quoted in John Bartlow Martin, *Adlai Stevenson of Illinois* (1976), 471, hereafter Martin, *Illinois*.

21 *"I love him so much":* AES to Alicia Patterson, 11 April 1949, Johnson Papers.

21 *"Did I ever":* AES to Alicia Patterson, 14 Sept. 1951, ibid.

21 *"that the boys":* Ellen Stevenson to "Ad," 25 Nov. 1949 (copy), Box 388, Martin Papers, LC.

21 *Spending time with their mother:* John Fell Stevenson Oral History, ASOH.

21 *"100,000 circulation":* AES to Alicia Patterson, 8 March 1949, Johnson Papers.

21 *"self-management":* AES to Alicia Patterson, 19 Oct. 1950, ibid.

21 *"Dearly beloved":* AES to Alicia Patterson, n.d., 16 July 1951, ibid.

21 *"I think I behaved":* AES to Alicia Patterson, n.d., ibid.

21 *"Very well":* AES to Alicia Patterson, 16 July 1951, ibid.

22 *"Certainly to seek":* AES to Alicia Patterson, 16 July 1949, ibid.

22 *"Nobody's ever":* Martin, *Illinois*, 449, 453. The Fosdick correpondence has been withdrawn by the family, although it was made available to John Bartlow Martin for his biography of Stevenson in the 1970s.

22 *"Donald Duck":* AES to Alicia Patterson, 9 Nov. 1950, Johnson Papers.

22 *"How can you":* AES to Alicia Patterson, 28 Oct. 1949, ibid.

22 *"bear to be":* AES to Alicia Patterson, (summer) 1949, 20 Feb. 1951, ibid.

23 *"the fairy land":* AES to Alicia Patterson, 4 Jan. 1950, 12 Nov. 1948, ibid.

PAGE

23   *On public men and their distaste for intimacy:* ~~Myra McPherson, The Power Lovers~~ (1975), 17.

23   *"I will be in":* AES to Alicia Patterson, 1 July 1951, Johnson Papers.

23   *"Soft, fat and bald":* AES to Alicia Patterson, 5 April 1949, ibid.

23   *"Write guarded letters":* AES to Alicia Patterson, 3 Jan. 1949, ibid.

23   *"that strong scent":* AES to Alicia Patterson, n.d., ibid.

23   *"Oh Lord":* AES to Alicia Patterson, 15 Feb. 1949, ibid.

23   *"Where there":* Newsday, 6 Nov. 1948.

23   *"I stood":* AES Collection, Box 1401, Cards, PUL.

24   *"this Ellen business":* AES to Alicia Patterson, 10 July 1949, Johnson Papers; telegram to Borden Stevenson, Governor's Papers.

24   *"Ellen is getting":* AES to Alicia Patterson, 7 July 1949, Johnson Papers.

24   *"Ellen wants":* Box 388, Martin Papers, LC.

24   *Ellen's position:* Ellen Stevenson to AES, 20 Dec. 1960 (copy), in possession of J. Stuart Ingram, Evanston, Ill.; William Boyden to Richard Bentley, 7 July 1949; memo in Divorce Folder, Box 388, Martin Papers, LC.

24   *Divorce statistics:* Alexander Plateris, *Divorce Statistics Analysis* (1967), 4.

25   *"I am deeply distressed":* Papers, 3:154; also Box 388, Divorce File, Martin Papers, LC.

25   *"Your wife":* Lady Spears to AES, 8 Nov. 1949, Elizabeth Stevenson Ives Collection, Illinois State Historical Society, hereafter IC.

25   *"trouble and triumph":* Buffie Ives to "Adlai dear" Stevenson, n.d. (copy), Divorce Folder, Martin Papers, LC; interview with Elizabeth Ives.

25   *"the problem":* Betty Friedan, *The Feminine Mystique* (1963), 15.

26   *portrayal of Ellen's domesticity:* Campaign Materials, Governor's Papers.

26   *"not the girl":* Interview with Elizabeth Ives.

27   *McGowan on the divorce:* McGowan Oral History, ASOH.

27   *"I never really thought":* AES to Jane Dick, 2 May 1949, copy in Martin Papers, LC.

27   *"of the first volume":* AES to Alicia Patterson, 15 Sept. 1949, Johnson Papers.

27   *Reading on paranoia:* John Fell Stevenson Oral History, ASOH.

27   *"the end of what":* AES to Alicia Patterson, 26 Sept. 1949, Johnson Papers.

27   *Ellen's comments after divorce:* Chicago Herald American, 18 Dec. 1949; Chicago Daily News, 13 Dec. 1949.

28   *"Perhaps Ellen thinks":* AES to Alicia Patterson, 9 Oct. 1949, Johnson Papers.

28   *"attention and the limelight":* Buffie Ives to AES, n.d. [1948], AES Papers, PUL.

28   *"I've failed":* Davis, *Politics of Honor*, 206.

CHAPTER 2: CLEANING HOUSE

29   *New breed of American governors:* Larry Sabato, *Goodbye to Good-Time Charlie: The American Governorship Transformed* (1983). Stevenson's cabinet and upper-level patronage appointments were entirely male, though he did appoint, as his predecessors had, some women inspectors to the women and children's division of the state labor department, one of the few patronage positions available for women. Later his friend Jane Dick served on the Board of Public Welfare. See AES to "Dear Dicks," 15 July 1949, AES Papers, PUL.

29   *"I will have no reluctance":* Papers, 3:27.

29   *"We can set":* Ibid., 14. See also ibid., 2:525; AES, "The Challenge of the New Isolationism," *New York Times Magazine,* 6 Nov. 1949.

PAGE

29   *"I want to do"*: Peoria speech, 5 May 1948. Governor's Papers.

30   *"Good government"*: Papers, 3:429.

30   *"It is a good"*: John Fribley Oral History, Illinois General Assembly Oral History Program, Sangamon State University, hereafter IGAOH; see also Leland Kennedy and Donald O'Brien Oral Histories, IGAOH; Kenneth S. Davis, *The Politics of Honor* (1967), 199.

30   *Reaction to Stevenson as governor*: Martin, *Illinois*, 390–92.

30   *"I am not one"*: Stevenson speech to the Decatur Association of Commerce, 30 Nov. 1949, Governor's Papers; also in Michael Maher, ed., *An Illinois Legacy: Gubernatorial Addresses of Adlai E. Stevenson* (1985), 36.

31   *Diversity in Illinois*: Jeremy Atack, "The Evolution of Regional Economic Differences within Illinois, 1818–1950," in Peter F. Nardulli, ed., *Diversity, Conflict, and State Politics: Regionalism in Illinois* (1989), 61–91.

31   *Materials on Springfield*: *Saturday Evening Post*, 27 Sept. 1947; Springfield Public Library, Vertical Files.

31   *"In Springfield"*: *New Yorker*, 24 June 1950.

32   *Partee incident*: Cecil Partee Oral History, IGAOH; *Papers*, 469–71.

33   *"Our foreign policy"*: Speech to Illinois Educational Association, Governor's Papers. For examples of foreign policy comments, see Speech at Centre College, 7 Feb. 1950, Governor's Papers; Maher, *Illinois Legacy*, 96–97. For AES's interest in international affairs, see *Papers*, 3:160, 165, 175, 306, 336, 362–63.

33   *"As I have said"*: AES to Porter McKeever, 30 Sept. 1950, AES Papers, PUL.

33   *Illinois constitution*: *Illinois State Review*, 10 March 1949.

33   *"grotesque parodies"*: Sabato, *Goodbye*, 59.

34   *"In the remote"*: AESI comments on the constitution, Stevenson Family Microfilm, ISHS.

34   *"the people [who]"*: Comments in Radio Address, March 1949, Governor's Papers.

34   *Arvey's importance*: Martin, *Illinois*, 394.

35   *Preference for talking to Childs*: Marquis Childs Oral History, ASOH; Leland Kennedy Oral History, IGAOH.

35   *"Stevenson was not"*: Abraham Marovitz Oral History, IGAOH. See also Martin, *Illinois*, 292; interview with Mary Jane Masters; Mary Jane Masters Oral History, SSU.

35   *"a legislative liaison"*: *Papers*, 3:312.

35   *Blair and Democrats*: Edward Doyle, ed., *As We Knew Adlai* (1966), 67.

35   *"How am I going"*: Martin, *Illinois*, 394

35   *Strategy of constitutional reform*: Constitutional Reform Folder, Governor's Papers.

36   *Gateway amendment delays reform*: Jeff Broadwater, *Adlai Ewing Stevenson* (1994), 90.

36   *Stop-gap measure*: Memo to Walter Schaefer, 25 April 1949, Governor's Papers. On the reaction of Samuel Witwer, a Chicago lawyer who fought for constitutional reform, see Elmer Gertz and Edward Gilbreath, *Quest for a Constitution: A Man Who Wouldn't Quit* (1984).

36   *Votes on constitutional reform*: Martin, *Illinois*, 394. For Stevenson's reaction, see *Papers*, 3:89.

36   *Stevenson on personnel*: *Papers*, 3:295, 4:123;

36   *Replaces Republicans*: Carl McGowan to John B. Martin, 6 March 1966, Martin Papers, LC; Willard Wirtz Oral History, ASOH; Appointment File, Governor's Papers.

PAGE

37   *"louses up"*: Papers, 3:314.

37   *"Who am I to be"*: AES to Alicia Patterson, 5 Nov. 1950, Johnson Papers.

37   *Need for more responsible men:* Maher, *Illinois Legacy*, 63.

37   *"The public takes"*: McGowan Oral History, ASOH.

37   *"business and government"*: Meeting with law clerks, Governor's Papers.

37   *"a politician pays"*: AES to Sherlock Swann, 26 May 1952, AES Papers, PUL.

37   *"We had a good time"*: Interview with William Blair.

37   *"He was a wonderful"*: Margaret Munn Oral History, SSU; interview with Margaret Munn.

37   *"too often"*: Papers, 3:18.

38   *"for some small service"*: Mrs. Emmons Blaine to AES, 18 July 1949, Governor's Papers.

38   *"I find"*: AES to Mrs. Emmons Blaine, 21 July 1949, Governor's Papers.

38   *Contributors to fund:* Martin, *Illinois*, 695–97, appendix A, 766–68; Boxes 268–70, AES Papers, PUL. Also Box 442, Martin Papers.

38   *An example of contributions:* Kenneth Burgess to AES, 24 Jan. 1950, AES Papers, PUL.

38   *Press account of fund:* New York Times, 28 Sept. 1952.

38   *"None ever"*: Papers, 4:122–23.

39   *"so-called personal"*: Ibid., 3:47.

39   *"If [Dad] had"*: Martin, *Illinois*, 509.

39   *Douglas-Stevenson disagreement:* AES to Paul Douglas, 10 March 1952, AES Papers, PUL.

39   *Mulroy incident:* Martin, *Illinois*, 448; Mulroy Folder, Horsemeat Folder, Governor's Papers.

39   *AES disappointment:* Masters Oral History, SSU.

40   *Truman scandals:* Andrew Dunar, *The Truman Scandals and the Politics of Morality* (1984), 136, 138, 144–45.

40   *Graft as AES's greatest problem:* Tom Matthews, "Portrait with Scratches: Adlai Stevenson," *Vogue*, May 1966, 238.

40   *"corruption is treason"*: Article in the *Columbian*, 29 Feb. 1952, Box 233, AES Papers, PUL; also Maher, *Illinois Legacy*, 63.

40   *"Green promised"*: Speeches Folder, Box 252, PUL. See also comments in *Chicago Daily News*, 24 Feb. 1948.

40   *Stevenson's response to mining disaster:* Martin, *Illinois*, 502–3; Mining Folder, Governor's Papers; John B. Martin, "The Mine Disaster No One Stopped," *Harper's*, March 1948, 193–220.

41   *"What a job"*: AES to Alicia Patterson, n.d. [1951], Johnson Papers.

41   *"Nothing has exasperated"*: Speech to Regional Conference of the Civil Service Assembly, May 2, 1950, in Maher, *Illinois Legacy*, 68.

42   *Stevenson's assessment of his governorship:* Papers, 3:589.

42   *Hoover and AES:* Curt Gentry, *J. Edgar Hoover: The Man and the Secrets* (1991) 192; "Adlai Ewing Stevenson," FBI materials, Files 94-40154; Bureau Memo, M. A. Jones to Mr. Nichols, FBI Archives, Washington, D.C. Some Stevenson material is still classified.

42   *Stevenson comments on FBI:* Chicago Sun Times, 12 Jan. 1949.

42   *Hoover material on the incident:* Files 94-49154.

43   *"the dropping of a"*: AES, "Who Runs the Gambling Machines?" *Harper's*, Feb. 1952, 36–38.

PAGE

43 *"beneath a monster": Papers,* 3:225.

43 *Gambling in Illinois:* Vertical File, Springfield Public Library, Springfield, Ill.; Carl Whittemore Oral History, IGAOH.

44 *"a terrible mistake":* Donald O'Brien Oral History, IGAOH; Gambling Folders, Governor's Papers.

45 *"public indifference"* and *"In ordering these raids":* Speech to American Bar Association, Sept. 1950, AES Papers, PUL.

45 *Criticism of Stevenson's gambling initiative:* Gordon Schendel, "Illinois Shakedown: The Little Guys Lose," *Collier's,* 15 April 1950, 13–15, 79–80; ibid., 22 April 1950, 16–17, 77–99.

45 *"You knew":* Louis Ruppel to AES, 15 May 1951, Governor's Papers.

45 *"No major":* Kefauver Committee Hearings, "Chicago," 98–95, 88–85, copy in Governor's Papers.

46 *"morality of government":* Speech to the Association of American Law Schools in 1953, *Papers,* 4:309. See Rodney Sievers, *The Last Puritan? Adlai Stevenson in American Politics* (1983), 34.

46 *Gubernatorial contributions:* Mimeograph memorandum by J. Edward Day, "The Stevenson Administration—The First Three Years," 7 May 1952, Governor's Papers; Martin, *Illinois,* 508.

46 *"If we can do":* AES, "New Isolationism."

46 *The Red scare:* M. J. Heale, *American Anticommunism: Combatting the Enemy Within, 1830–1970* (1990), 165, 167.

47 *"This is the Anxious Age": Papers,* 3:241.

47 *Questioning about Hiss:* "Direct Interrogations on Behalf of Defendant Alger Hiss," Hiss File, Box 267, Governor's Papers.

48 *"To damn and impugn":* AES to Alicia Patterson, 25 Sept. 1950, Johnson Papers; Martin, *Illinois,* 407.

48 *Stevenson I and Knights of the Golden Circle:* Clippings, Governor's Papers; *Papers,* 3:445; Martin, *Illinois,* 498; AES to "Voice of the People," *Chicago Tribune,* 27 Aug. 1951.

48 *Broyles bill:* E. Houston Harsha, "Illinois—The Broyles Commission," in Walter Gelhorn, ed., *The States and Subversion* (1952), 54–139.

48 *"I know full well. . . . Does anyone":* Veto message, 26 June 1951, Governor's Papers. See also *Papers,* 3:413–18.

48 *Overriding vetoes:* Coleman Ransone, *The Office of Governor in the United States* (1956), 182.

48 *Interpretation of Truman:* Barton Bernstein, "The Ambiguous Legacy," in Bernstein, *Politics and Policies of the Truman Administration* (1970), 269–304.

49 *"He felt":* McGowan Oral History, ASOH.

49 *Not lobbying:* Broadwater, *Stevenson,* 90–91.

49 *AES's reputation on civil rights:* R. M. Westcott to James Mulroy, 3 July 1949, Governor's Papers. On Eisenhower's position, see Richard Dalfiume, *Desegregation of the U.S. Armed Forces: Fighting on Two Fronts, 1939–1953* (1969), 101–2, 158–59.

49 *"Whatever our personal prejudices": Papers,* 3:507.

50 *"We have learned":* Ibid., 458.

50 *Chicago race relations:* Charles Abrams, *Forbidden Neighbors: A Study of Prejudice in Housing* (1955), 102–6.

51 *"introducing into a neighborhood":* Ibid., 102.

51 *Description of Cicero:* Ibid., 102–6. *Bunche congratulations:* Ralph Bunche to AES,

PAGE

2 Aug. 1951; AES to Ralph Bunche, 4 Aug. 1951, AES Papers, PUL; Cicero File, Governor's Papers.

51   *"Deep beneath the"*: Papers, 3:458–59.

52   *"I need not"*: TV program, 4 Nov. 1951, transcript in Governor's Papers.

52   *"I get frightfully irked"*: AES to Ralph Bunche, 5 Aug. 1952, PUL.

52   *Opposition to NAACP in Illinois*: Interview with Joseph Rauh.

52   *"by events and spacing"*: AES to Alicia Patterson, 4 Jan. 1950, Johnson Papers.

52   *"No one has done"*: Papers, 3:389.

53   *"I live in a gold-fish"*: Interview with Elizabeth Ives.

53   *"I'm alone"*: AES to Jane Dick, 8 March 1949, Johnson Papers.

53   *"I cannot agree"*: Message of 23 April 1949, *Veto Messages of Adlai Ewing Stevenson* (1949), 8–9.

53   *AES's health*: Interview with Dr. Emmet Pearson.

53   *"no good and sufficient"*: AES to Alicia Patterson, 19 Dec. 1951, Johnson Papers.

54   *"I've been in fiendish"*: Ibid.

54   *"combat politics"*: AES to Letty Bromwell, 26 Dec. 1951, IC. For articles on Stevenson, see *Collier's*, 19 April 1952; *Life*, 24 March 1952.

54   *"Our society is becoming"*: Speech to Illinois Retail Equipment Association, 3 Dec. 1949, Governor's Papers.

54   *"After long and prayerful"*: Papers, 3:492.

55   *"If I were Ike"*: AES to Alicia Patterson, 19 Dec. 1951, Johnson Papers. For other comments on 1952 politics, see ibid., 18 April 1951.

55   *"coy and backward"*: Robert Ferrell, *Off the Record: The Private Papers of Harry S. Truman* (1980), 246. 554–57; Jacob Arvey, "The Reluctant Candidate," *Reporter*, 24 Nov. 1952, 21–21.

55   *AES and the Truman announcement*: Martin, *Illinois*, 548–49.

56   *"I do not want"*: AES to Charles Murphy, 17 March 1952, AES Papers, PUL.

56   *"wriggled out again"*: AES to Jane Dick, 15 March 1952, Johnson Papers.

56   *"I can't or don't"*: AES to Alicia Patterson, 27 June 1952, ibid.

56   *"Illinois has been"*: AES to Edward Murrow, 23 Feb. 1952, AES Papers, PUL.

56   *"This summer"*: Papers, 3:552.

56   *"I'm not qualified"*: Martin, *Illinois*, 524.

56   *"I never overestimate"*: AES to Porter McKeever, 2 Aug. 1951, Governor's Papers.

57   *"altogether too young"*: AES to Charles Murphy, 17 March 1952, AES Papers, PUL.

57   *"Women don't leave"*: Mrs. Marie Fuchs to AES, 11 April 1955, Governor's Papers.

57   *"on a rampage"*: AES to Alicia Patterson, 11 June 1952, Johnson Papers; AES to Robert Pirie, 21 Feb. 1952, AES Papers, PUL; interview with Borden Stevenson.

57   *Information on Ellen Stevenson*: Karl Shapiro, *Reports on My Death* (1990); Clippings and Cook County Court Records, Ingram File, in possession of the author.

58   *"mentally, temperamentally"*: Quoted in Herbert Muller, *Adlai Stevenson: A Study in Values* (1967), 80.

58   *"You know, I've got"*: Steven M. Gillon, *Politics and Vision: The ADA and American Liberalism, 1947–1985* (1987), 84.

58   *"ultimately be available"*: Arvey, "Reluctant Candidate."

58   *"I refuse to speculate"*: Chicago Daily News, 2, 4 May 1952. See also *Papers*, 3:563 n.

58   *Issuing a "General Sherman"*: AES to Alicia Patterson, 15 May 1952, Johnson Papers.

PAGE

59   *"If one has to be"*: Porter McKeever to AES, 3 April 1952, AES Papers, PUL.

59   *"noose . . . tightening"*: *Papers*, 3:536. On the conceit necessary to be president and presidency as a Golgotha, see ibid., 562, 563.

59   *"my wretched predicament,"* AES to Adolf Berle, 3 April 1952.

59   *"I'll shoot myself"*: Martin, *Illinois*, 578.

59   *"Do you really"*: AES to Jane Dick, April 1952 (copy), Martin Papers, LC, partly cited in *Papers*, 3:551.

59   *"We glory in tribulations"*: Handwritten memo, n.d., Box 263, AES Papers, PUL.

59   *"full measure"*: "From the Governor's Office, Transcript," Box 26, ibid.

60   *Call to Reston*: Martin, *Illinois*, 524.

60   *"I would not accept"*: Memoranda, Box 26, AES Papers, PUL.

61   *"If there's a touch"*: AES to Alicia Patterson, 27 June 1952, Johnson Papers.

61   *"I had thought"*: Truman, *Memoirs*, 562.

61   *"The Stevensons must be"*: *Chicago News*, 3 Oct. 1949; Transcript of *Meet the Press*, 30 March 1952, Box 24, AES Papers, PUL.

61   *"shadows gathered"*: *Papers*, 3:578.

CHAPTER 3: "OUR FATHERS IN THEIR GENERATIONS"

62   *Description of Stevenson migration*: Interview with Elizabeth Ives; "Memories," Family Folders, 1316 Washington Street, Bloomington, Ill., hereafter Family Folders.

63   *Stevenson in charge and details of journey*: AES I, "Personal," Family Folders. For a description of similar migrations, see Hazel Dicken-Garcia, *To the Western Woods: The Breckinridge Family Moves to Kentucky in 1793* (1991), 34–37.

64   *"Instead of asleep in"*: Duane Meyer, *The Highland Scots of North Carolina* (1963), 16.

64   *Bad economic conditions and Stevenson as a gravedigger*: Henry Grey Graham, *Social Life of Scotland in the Eighteenth Century* (1899), 1:146–48.

64   *Religious oppression*: Ian Graham, *Colonists from Scotland: Emigration to North America, 1707–1783* (1956), 34.

65   *"how so small"*: Raymond Gillespie, *Colonial Ulster: The Settlement of East Ulster* (1985), 35.

65   *"undertaking" and relation of Scots to Ireland*: H. G. Graham, *Social Life*, 146; Gillespie, *Colonial Ulster*, 47–50, 87–89; Raymond Gillespie, "The Transformation of the Borderlands, 1600–1700," in Gillespie and O'Sullivan, *The Borderlands* (1989), 75–105.

65   *Power of the MacDonnels*: Gillespie, *Colonial Ulster*, 16.

65   *Settlement patterns*: I. Graham, *Colonists*, 110, 122.

65   *Dance called America*: David Hackett Fischer, *Albion's Seed* (1989), 608; Gillespie, *Colonial Ulster*, 66, 143–45, 182.

65   *Stevenson apprenticeship and family history*: Rev. Samuel Harris Stevenson et al., *A History and Genealogical Records of the Stevenson Family from 1748 to 1979* (1979); Andrew Phelps McCormick, "Scotch-Irish in Ireland and America" (typescript in possession of the author).

65   *Apprenticeship*: Ibid., 180.

65   *Descended from a Belfast hatter*: AES to Ed Austin, 2 Feb. 1943, AES Papers, PUL.

66   *The fourth migration*: Fischer, *Albion's Seed*, 611.

PAGE

66   *Difficulty of migration:* Ibid., 612; Donald MacDougall, *Scots and Scots Descendants in America* (1917), 21–22.

66   *"a swarm of people":* Fischer, *Albion's Seed,* 605, 633; Meyer, *Highland Scots,* 18; Solon Buck and Elizabeth Buck, *The Planting of Civilization in Western Pennsylvania* (1939), 152–54.

66   *Renting in Chester County:* Jack Greene, *Pursuits of Happiness: The Social Development of Early Modern British Colonies and the Formation of American Culture* (1988), 129.

66   *Family names: Commemorative Biographical Record of Washington County, Pennsylvania, Marriages, 1780–1857* (1976).

67   *Scots settlements in North Carolina:* Forrest McDonald and Ellen Shapiro McDonald, "The Ethnic Origins of the American People," *William and Mary Quarterly,* 3rd ser., 37 (1980): 179–200; Thomas Purvis, "European Ancestry of the U.S. Population, 1790," ibid., 41 (1984): 85–101.

67   *Concept of "derbfine":* Fischer, *Albion's Seed,* 663.

68   *Land opportunities and prices in western North Carolina:* Homer Keever, *Iredell, Piedmont County* (1976), 43.

68   *Wars in West:* Robert Ramsey, *Carolina Cradle* (1964), 193.

68   *Description of Rowan County:* John C. Campbell, *The Southern Highlander and His Homeland* (1927); Keever, *Iredell,* passim; Jethro Rumple, *A History of Rowan County* (1881), 3; McCormick, "Scotch-Irish," 44–45.

69   *Location and description of Stevenson land: The Landmark,* 28 Oct. 1913, clipping in IC; U.S. First, Second, and Third Decennial Census, North Carolina, Rowan and Iredell Counties, 1790, 1810, 1820; Family Folders.

69   *North Carolina architecture:* Hugh Lefler and Albert Newsome, *The History of a Southern State: North Carolina* (1973), 107–8.

69   *"the house is gone":* AES I to "my dear mother," 28 May 1876, IC.

70   *"a pleasant savanna":* Rumple, *History,* 25; C. L. Hunter, *Sketches of Western North Carolina* (1877), 125–50.

70   *Place naming and agricultural system:* Keever, *Iredell,* 35–48; Terry Jordan and Matti Kaups, *The American Backwoods Frontier: An Ethnic and Ecological Interpretation* (1989), 118.

70   *Value of household production:* Lewis Gray, *The History of Southern Agriculture* (1933), 2:92.

70   *Tobacco production:* Ibid., 92, 122; Keever, *Iredell,* 120.

71   *Cousin marriage:* Fischer, *Albion's Seed,* 665–66. For other families in the community, see Keever, *Iredell,* 45–48; Stevenson, *History,* intro.

72   *Distribution of Scottish highlanders:* Harry Merrens, *Colonial North Carolina in the Eighteenth Century* (1964), 58.

72   *"We resolve":* John Wheeler Moore, *History of North Carolina from the Earliest Discoveries to the Present Time* (1880), 36.

72   *"the African trade":* Rumple, *History,* 25.

72   *Story of Tommy Stephenson: The Landmark,* 28 Oct. 1913.

73   *Cornwallis campaign:* Lefler, *North Carolina,* 233–38. I. Graham, *Colonists,* 157–61; Hunter, *Sketches,* 200.

73   *Stevensons and the Revolution: Charlotte Observer,* 31 March 1953, Clipping in IC.

73   *"God made me":* Lefler, *North Carolina,* 237.

74   *Information on William Stevenson:* Dr. P. F. Langenour, "William Stevenson," Genealogical Society of Iredell County, N.C.; Stevenson, *History.*

PAGE

74 *William's religiosity:* Samuel Stevenson to Jane Vikry, 8 Dec. 1894, Genealogical Society of Iredell County.

74 *Map of parish:* Keever, *Iredell,* frontispiece.

75 *Whitefield:* Arnold Dallimore, *George Whitefield: The Life and Times of the Great Evangelist* (1970), 2:383; Langenour, "William Stevenson"; McCormick, "Scotch-Irish," 48–50; Stevenson, *History,* 4–7; Frank Lambert, "Peddler in Divinity: George Whitefield and the Great Awakening," *Journal of American History* 77 (1990): 812–37.

75 *"first there was":* AES I, *Something of Men I Have Known* (1909), 232–33.

75 *"number of exercised persons":* Charles Johnson, *The Frontier Camp Meeting: Religious Harvest* (1955), 55–58.

75 *William's epiphany and contributions to the church:* Keever, *Iredell,* 186–87; Stevenson, *History.*

76 *William as Little Gabriel:* Stevenson, *History,* 5–6.

76 *"was conferred":* Fischer, *Albion's Seed,* 693–94.

76 *Will of William Stevenson:* A copy is in IC.

76 *"Getting out of the omnibus":* AES I to "Dear Mother," 18 May 1876 (copy), Family Folders.

77 *Information on Stevenson farms:* Stevenson, *History,* 3–6; Second Census of the United States, 1800, North Carolina, Iredell County, Burke County, NA.

77 *Figures on migration:* Hugh Wooten, "Westward Migration from Iredell County, 1800–1850," *North Carolina Historical Review* 30 (Jan. 1953): 61; Hugh Wooten to AES, 12 April 1951, Governor's Papers.

77 *Kentucky as the American Eden:* Wooten, "Westward Migration," 69–72.

77 *Death of Adlai Osborne's son:* Rumple, *History,* 55–58.

78 *Western great road:* Merrens, *Colonial North Carolina,* 162; John C. Campbell, *Southern Highlander and His Homeland* (1921).

78 *"so wild and horrid":* Archer Hulbert, *Boone's Wilderness Road* (1902), 118, 127.

78 *"One nag got a little lazy":* AES I, "Personal," Family Folders.

78 *Routes to Kentucky:* P. P. Karnan, *Atlas of Kentucky* (1977); Samuel Allen, "Observations of Travellers in Kentucky, 1750–1850" (M.A. thesis, University of Kentucky, 1950).

78 *"We arrived in good health":* Moses and Annie Ewing Stevenson to David Hampton, 25 March 1817, IC.

79 *James Bell Stevenson's health:* Moses and Annie Ewing Stevenson to "Dear Brothers and Sisters," 25 March 1817, IC.

79 *"More bags of coffee":* Moses and Annie Ewing Stevenson to "Dear Brothers and Sisters," 17 July 1817; Annie and Moses Ewing to ?, 17 July 1817, IC.

79 *"I would not begrudge":* Adlai Ewing to ?, July 1818, IC.

79 *"These of our kindred":* AES I to "my dear mother," 18 May 1876, IC.

80 *Information on Christian County:* U.S. Bureau of the Census, Seventh Census of the United States, 1850, Population and Slave Schedules, First District, Christian County, Kentucky.

80 *Information on early Stevensons:* Louisville *Courier-Journal,* 8 Aug. 1892, clipping in IC; Stevenson, *History.*

80 *Ewings and militia:* W. Henry Perrin, *Christian County History* (1884), 289.

80 *"Death has made":* Sophia Wallis Ewing to "dear sister," 1 Sept. 1822, IC.

81 *Family genealogy:* Stevenson, *History.*

81 *Eliza's inheritance of Maddison:* Will of Nathaniel Ewing, 4 Nov. 1822, IC.

81 *"anything he pleases":* Eliza Stevenson to Jane Stevenson, 6 Aug. 1837, IC.

PAGE

82   *Description of Stevenson home:* Stevenson, *History,* 5; AES I, "Personal," typescript in Family Folders. On early North Carolina homes, see Fischer, *Albion's Seed,* 658–61.

82   *"All I had to do":* Julia Hardin, "Remembrances," Family Folders.

82   *Stories of his youth:* AES I, "Personal"; AES I, *Something of Men,* 321–28; AES I to Hunter Moss, 25 Nov. 1911, IC.

83   *Kentucky education:* Charles Petrie, "The History of Education in Christian County" (M.A. thesis, University of Kentucky, 1939).

83   *Description of school and father's funeral:* AES I, "Personal."

83   *"the boys making their":* AES I, *Something of Men,* 324.

84   *Information on the school:* St. Louis Post Dispatch, 8 Aug. 1892, clipping in IC.

84   *Schools as agents of social learning:* David Tyack, "The Tribe and the Common School," *American Quarterly* 24 (March 1927): 3–19; Jean H. Baker, *Affairs of Party: The Political Culture of Northern Democrats in the Mid-Nineteenth Century* (1984), 77.

84   *Statistics on Kentucky school attendance:* John Folger and Charles Nam, *Education of the American Population* (1960), 3–4.

85   *Conditions in Christian County:* George Meacham, *A History of Christian County* (1930), 720.

85   *Statistics on inequality in Kentucky:* Fischer, *Albion's Seed,* 752; U.S. Bureau of the Census, Fifth, Sixth, and Seventh Census of the United States, 1830, 1840, 1850, Population and Slave Schedules, Kentucky, Christian County; James Oakes, *Slavery and Freedom: An Interpretation of the Old South* (1990), esp. 40–135.

85   *Problems of tobacco growing:* Leland Smith, "A History of the Tobacco Industry in Kentucky from 1783–1860" (M.A. thesis, University of Kentucky, 1950).

86   *"We are surprised":* Hopkinsville Gazette, 16 Jan. 1836.

86   *"Tell the boys":* Albert Ewing to Mary Jane, 29 May 1851, Ewing Papers, MCHS.

86   *Information on early Bloomington:* Interview with Greg Koos; local materials in MCHS; Family Folders; Vernon Syfert, "The Naming of Bloomington," *Journal of Illinois State Historical Society* 29 (July 1936): 161–67.

87   *Description of professions:* Milo Custer, *The First Directory of Bloomington* (1855).

87   *"overcrowded with emigrants":* Sherman Wakefield, *How Lincoln Became President: The Part Played by Bloomington* (1936), 26.

87   *"how to manage":* Mary Ryan, *The Cradle of the Middle Class: The Family in Oneida County, New York, 1790–1865* (1981), 153.

88   *Native Americans in county:* Joseph Herring, *Kenekuk: The Kickapoo Prophet* (1988).

88   *Competition between towns and loss of population:* Don Doyle, *The Social Order of a Frontier Community* (1982), 71.

88   *Early maps of railroads:* William Ackerman, "Early Illinois Railroads" (paper presented before Chicago Historical Society, 1883), 39, 42, CHS.

89   *Advertisements of land:* Charles du Puy, *Illinois Central Railroad Offers for Sale* (1885), 4, pamphlet in LC.

89   *Description of celebration:* Jacob Hasbrouck, *The History of McLean County, Illinois* (1879).

89   *"out west of Bloomington":* Greg Koos, *Illustrated History of McLean County* (1982), 79.

90   *Schools:* "School Record of McLean County and Other Records," *Transactions of the McLean County Historical Society* 2 (1903): 20–23, 34.

90   *"no enemies, many debts":* Elmo Watson, *The Illinois Wesleyan Story, 1850–1950* (1956), 22.

PAGE

90   *Multiple parties: Pantagraph,* 6 Sept. 1854; Wakefield, *How Lincoln Became President,* 60–83.

91   *"politics was in the air":* William Gienapp, "Politics Seems to Enter into Everything: Political Culture in the North, 1840–1860," in Stephen Maizlich and John Kusma, eds., *Essays on American Antebellum Politics, 1840–1862* (1982), 15–69.

91   *Memories of early politics:* AES I, *Something of Men,* 6–11, 381–82, 386–412.

91   *AES I and Douglas:* Chicago *Inter Ocean,* 20 Sept. 1908.

92   *Illinois Wesleyan: Transactions of the McLean County Historical Society* 2 (1903): 128–51; Watson, *Wesleyan Story.*

92   *"any people have the right":* "Kossuth," 22 May 1853, Rolfe Collection of Stevenson Family Papers, LC.

92   *Kossuth:* Donald Spencer, *Louis Kossuth and Young America* (1977).

93   *"It gives me great pleasure":* AES I to "my dear mother and father," 10 Nov. 1856, IC.

93   *"standards as high as those":* Centre College Archives, Danville, Ky.; *New York Times,* 3 July 1892; William Strode, *Centre College* (1985); *General Catalogue of Centre College,* 1850–60, 1890, Centre College Archives; Hardin Craig, *Centre College of Kentucky* (1967), 33.

94   *Riots in colleges and demand for professional training:* Burton Bledstein, *The Culture of Professionalism* (1976), 229.

94   *"If rents, interest and profits":* Will of John Turner Stevenson, April 1857, McLean County Courthouse, Bloomington, Ill.

95   *"What a tremendous question":* Bledstein, *Culture of Professionalism,* 159.

95   *Lists of lawyers: Metamora Sentinel,* 9 Dec. 1858. On the culture of the profession, see William P. Johnson, "Education and Professional Life-styles," *History of Education Quarterly* 74 (Summer 1974): 175–85; Michael Grossberg, "Institutionalizing Masculinity: The Law as a Masculine Profession," in Mark Carnes and Clyde Griffen, eds., *Meanings for Manhood* (1990), 133–52; Mark Granfors and Terence Halliday, "Professional Passages: Caste, Class and Education in the 19th Century Legal Profession" (American Bar Foundation Working Paper 8714).

95   *AES I's life in Metamora:* AES I to Lewis Stevenson, 29 Nov. 1868, IC; Annual Lists, Income, Record Group 101, Roll 34, 1864 Metamora, NA; documents signed by AES I, 1863, Metamora County Land Records, Woodford County Historical Society, material in Illinois Regional Archives Depository, hereafter IRAD.

96   *AES I's public career:* Stevenson Clippings, MCHS; Woodford Country Tax Judgment Record, ISU; Land Records, Woodford County, IRAD.

97   *"War is upon us":* Quoted in Koos, *History,* 84.

97   *Teachers' regiment: Transactions of the McLean Country Historical Society* 2 (1903): 162–63.

97   *"Recruitment in Illinois:* Aretas Dayton, *Recruitment and Conscription in Illinois during the Civil War* (1940), 1–10.

98   *Meetings in McLean Country:* Koos, *History,* 85; *Transactions of the McLean Country Historical Society* 2 (1903): 162; Victor Hicken, *Illinois in the Civil War* (1966). The figure of 259,000 is somewhat inflated by reenlistments and the inclusion of some men from other states who served in Illinois units.

98   *Material on Woodford Country: Woodford County, Past and Present* (1878), Eureka Country Historical Society; Enrollment Books, Woodford County, Record Group 301, Adjutant General Endorsement Books, Military Census, IRAD.

98   *Material on AES I's war status:* Woodford County Militia Reserve, 1861–62; Provost Marshal Records, Record Group 109, 8th District, "Enrollment," NA; ibid., "Medi-

PAGE

cal Exemptions": Woodford County, Record Group 301, Adjutant General Endorsement Books, Military Census, IRAD; Robert Sterling, "Civil War Draft Resistance in the Middle West" (Ph.D. diss., Northern Illinois University, 1974), 166. For attitudes of Union officials, see *Official Records of the Rebellion*, ser. 3, 1:18, 159, 289, 316–18, 324, 360, 688, 700, 4:148–53, 221–22.

99 *AES I charged with copperheadism:* Joseph Medill to E. B. Washburne, 14 Jan. 1863 (copy), IC; *Chicago Tribune*, 12 Aug. 1892; *Pantagraph*, 21 Oct. 1874. On the exaggeration of copperheadism, see Frank Klement, *Dark Lanterns: Secret Political Societies, Conspiracies, and Treason Trials in the Civil War* (1984), 1–6, 12–33.

100 *"How cleverly Adlai":* "Aunt Julia" to "Buffie" Ives, 1 April 1952 Family Folders.

100 *AES I's income:* Income Tax Records, 1864, Woodford County, Record Group 58, NA. Careful studies in Ohio reveal that the profile of soldiers matched the 3 percent of the population who were professionals, and there is no reason to suspect that the enrollments were skewed by class in Illinois. See Eugene Murdock, "Was It a Poor Man's Fight?" *Civil War History* 10 (1964): 241.

100 *"Now Tommy, I want you":* AES I to "Tommy," 1865, AES Papers, ISU.

CHAPTER 4: CALLINGS

101 *Stevenson scrapbooks:* Stevenson File, MCHS and IC.

101 *"I love my scrapbooks":* *Pantagraph*, 1, 9 Jan. 1911; *St. Louis Globe Democrat*, 8 Jan. 1911, clippings in IC.

101 *"the great legend of the grandparents":* Elizabeth Stevenson Ives Oral History, ASOH.

102 *"Ah, under this tree lies":* Folder on Joshua Fry, Family Folders.

102 *Material on Lewis Green:* L. Halsey Jones, *Memoir of the Life and Character of Lewis Warner Green; Addresses Delivered at the Inauguration of Rev. Lewis W. Green* (1856); Julia Stevenson Hardin, "Remembrances," IC; *Washington Post*, 7 July 1892.

102 *Letitia's education:* *Washington Post*, 7 July 1892; Early family history, Stevenson Microfilm, ISHS; also in Stevenson Scrapbooks, MCHS.

102 *Death of Lewis Green and housing arrangements:* Trustee Minutes, 1862, 1863, Centre College Archives, Centre College, Danville, Ky.

103 *"I have loved":* AES I to Mary Peachy Green, 15 Sept. 1866, IC.

103 *"at once, but":* *New York Times*, 7 July 1892; *St. Louis Globe Dispatch*, 8 Jan. 1911.

103 *Victorian courting:* Karen Lystra, *Searching the Heart: Women, Men and Romantic Love in 19th Century America* (1989).

103 *"grandfather courted":* *Papers*, 4:115.

103 *"This is to invite you":* AES I to "my dear cousin," 5 Nov. 1866, IC.

104 *Letitia's appearance:* Margaret Gibbs, *The Daughters of the American Revolution* (1969), 60; Wallace Evans Davies, *Patriotism on Parade* (1955), 97; *San Francisco Examiner*, 23 July 1893.

104 *"It was the coldest":* Letitia Stevenson, "Sketches," Stevenson Microfilm, ISHS.

105 *Rating of Stevenson and Ewing:* Illinois, vol. 5, pp. 156, 389, R. G. Dun and Co. Collection, Baker Library, Graduate School of Business Administration, Harvard University.

105 *"If all goes well":* AES I to Lewis Green, 29 Nov. 1868, IC.

106 *"The welfare of the household":* Letitia Green Stevenson, "Sketches." The Duchess of Buccleuch is a reference to the ducal title and lands near Edinburgh owned by a favorite southern author—Sir Walter Scott.

PAGE

106 Butcher story: Chicago Journal, 13 March 1896.

106 "He has never": Clipping in Scrapbooks, MCHS.

106 Servants: U.S. Bureau of the Census, Ninth, Tenth and Eleventh Census, 1870, 1880, 1890, Population Schedules, Bloomington, Ill., entries under Adlai Stevenson.

106 "By a fair division": Henry McCormick, Women of Illinois (1913), 120–23.

106 "But establishing a home": Ibid., 121.

107 "the deeper sense": St. Louis Globe Democrat, 8 Jan. 1911.

107 "criminals against": Theodore Roosevelt, Presidential Addresses and State Papers (1910), 3:282–91.

107 "I was one of those": 1911 clippings, IC.

107 Letitia on birth control: Letitia Green Stevenson to the Bloomington Women's Club, AES I Papers, ISU; Letitia Green Stevenson, "Joys of Motherhood," IC. For background on birth control, see Linda Gordon, "Birth Control and Social Revolution," in Nancy Cott and Elizabeth Pleck, eds., A Heritage of Her Own (1979), 445–70.

108 "I have no doubt": AES I to "my darling wife," 16 Oct. 1897, IC.

108 Oyster story: "Aunt Julia" to AES II, 7 Dec. 1949, Governor's Papers.

108 "I suppose Papa": Julia Stevenson to "my own Ange," 15 Oct. 1890, IC.

108 "The home is": "Commencement Address," Stevenson Microfilm, ISHS.

109 "Never let your mother": Clippings, Scrapbook, IC.

109 "Would you have": AES I to Lewis Green Stevenson, Nov. 1868, IC.

109 "to gratify mama": Matthew Scott to "Letty," 17 Feb. 1889, Scott-Hardin Papers, Cornell University.

109 "Opportunity rarely": Bulletin, 12 Feb. 1899.

109 "making home": McCormick, Women of Illinois, 120–21.

109 "Do you remember": AES I to "Lewis, my blessed Toh and JuJu and Ange," 6 Feb. 1876, IC.

109 "I am thinking": AES I to "my dear children," 16 Feb. 1876, 15 Feb. 1875, IC.

109 "an active member": Lulu Winters, "Waiting for Uncle Adlai" (typescript), ISHS.

110 George Washington story: AES I to "my darling Bub," 14 Dec. 1875, 6 Feb. 1876, IC.

110 Bloomington organizations: Interview with Greg Koos.

110 "Never forget": AES I to "my darling wife," 29 April 1913, IC; Julia Stevenson Hardin, "Memories," Family Folders. On Sophia Wallis's death, see Eliza to my dear son, 4 May 1896, IC.

110 "What a wonder," "when papa talked," and "She was not": Julia Hardin, "For my Grandchildren," Ives Collection; Julia Stevenson Hardin, "Remembrances."

111 "A few days": AES I to S. S. Jack, 1883, IC.

111 American health: Edward Shorter, From Paralysis to Fatigue: A History of Psychosomatic Illness (1992), 220–29, 277–78, 294.

111 Female responsibility for health: Richard Meckel, "The Awful Responsibility of Motherhood: American Health Reform and the Prevention of Child Mortality" (Ph.D. diss., University of Minnesota, 1980).

112 Letters about Lewis: Letitia Green Stevenson to "my darling child," 17 Nov. 1890; Letitia Green Stevenson to "my darling people," 5 Oct. 1890, IC.

112 On sanitariums: Barbara Bates, Bargaining for Life: A Social History of Tuberculosis, 1876–1938 (1992), 350. For narratives of tuberculosis, see Sheila Rothman, Living in the Shadow of Death: Tuberculosis and the Social Experience of Illness in American History (1994).

PAGE

112   *Progressives' agenda:* Thomas R. Pegram, ~~*Partisans and Progressives: Private Interest*~~ *and Public Policy in Illinois, 1876–1922* (1992), 7–8.

113   *"He expands and":* Boston Herald, 6 Oct. 1908, clippings in Scrapbooks, MCHS.

113   *"A valuable contribution":* Champ Clark to AES I, 22 Jan. 1910, IC; other reviews, IC.

114   *"history of their country":* "Eulogy at Metamora, July 4, 1861," IC.

114   *"witness following":* AES I, *Something of Men* (1909), foreword.

114   *"The latch-key":* Undated clippings, Scrapbook, IC.

114   *"Contrary to all precedents":* T. E. Nash to William Vilas, 13 Aug. 1885, William Vilas Papers, Wisconsin Historical Society, Madison, Wis.

114   *"stayed awake":* Julia Hardin to Buffie, 27 March 1946, IC.

114   *Clay story:* AES I, *Something of Men,* 54.

114   *Forgetting issues:* Ibid., 250. For other examples of stories, see ibid., 156, 182, 190, 288.

115   *Vance story:* Ibid., 291–92.

115   *Hamlet:* Ibid., 45.

115   *Naming the mountain:* Clipping from *Takoma Daily News,* 26 July 1893; AES *Major Campaign Speeches* (1953), 83.

115   *AES I admires stories by Page:* Letters in John Rolfe Collection and Thomas Nelson Page Papers, Duke University.

115   *"Yes sah, but den":* "Stevenson Visits Cleveland," clipping in Scrapbooks, IC.

116   *"Father had":* Julia Hardin to Buffie, 27 March 1946, IC.

116   *Newspapers publish personal letter:* Leonard Schlup, "The Political Career of the First Adlai Ewing Stevenson" (Ph.D. diss., University of Illinois, 1973), 25, 53.

116   *"a public man":* House Document, no. 176, 44th Cong, 1st sess., serial 1706, June 1876, 107.

116   *City and state machines:* Raymond Wolfinger, "Why Political Machines Have Not Withered Away and Other Revisionist Thoughts," *Journal of Politics* 34 (1972): 365–98; Harvey Wish, "J. P. Altgeld and the Background of the Campaign of 1896," *Mississippi Valley Historical Review* 24 (1938): 512. On Cox, see Jean H. Baker, *Affairs of Party* (1984), 133–34.

117   *Community spelling bees:* Pantagraph, 14 March 1875; Jacob Hasbrouck, *History of McLean County, Illinois* (1879), 875–76.

117   *Lawyers' camaraderie and mock trials:* AES Scrapbook, MCHS; *Pantagraph,* 2 July 1874.

117   *Stevenson speeches:* Pantagraph, 8 July 1872, 5 July 1883.

118   *Illinois Independent Reform party:* Appleton's Annual Cyclopedia, 1874, s.v. "Illinois."

118   *Reform movements:* Pegram, *Partisans,* 31.

119   *Railroad issues:* Ernest Bogart and Charles Thompson, "The Industrial State, 1870–1893," in *The Centennial History of Illinois* (1920), 4:91–93; Joanne Wheeler, "The Origins of Populism in the Political Structure of a Midwestern State: Partisan Preference in Illinois, 1876–1892" (Ph.D. diss., SUNY at Buffalo 1976).

119   *Politics as mobilizing armies and the "politics of education":* Michael McGerr, *The Decline of Popular Politics: The American North, 1865–1928* (1986), 69–91.

119   *"some statistics":* Speech of Hon. Adlai Stevenson, De Witt County, 1878; AES I Scrapbook, MCHS; also in Stevenson Microfilm, ISHS.

120   *Stevenson banner:* Pantagraph, 11 Oct. 1880.

120   *campaign of 1874:* William Roger Scott, "General John McNulta" (M.A. thesis, Illinois State University, 1951).

497

PAGE

120　*Firing of the cannon: Pantagraph,* 24 Oct. 1874, 11 Oct. 1880; Scott, "McNulta," 6.

120　*Campaign financing:* Political File, Democratic Committee, Democratic State Central Committee: Cyrus McCormick Papers, Wisconsin Historical Society.

121　*Scott's contributions:* Matthew Scott notebooks, "Democratic Canvass," Scott-Hardin Papers, Cornell University.

121　*"Republican monied interests":* Speech of Hon. Adlai Stevenson, Scrapbook.

121　*Story of murderer:* AES I, *Something of Men,* 38.

121　*Accusations of copperheadism:* Clippings, Stevenson File, MSHS; *Pantagraph,* 21 Oct. 1874.

121　*Description of voting: Pantagraph,* 5–8 Nov. 1874.

122　*"Let every man": Bulletin,* 16 Oct. 1882.

122　*"all men have won": Pantagraph,* 6 Nov. 1874.

122　*Democratic overturn:* Albert House, "The Speakership Contest of 1875: The Democratic Response to Power," *Journal of American History* 52 (1965): 252–74.

122　*Description of Washington:* Kathryn Allamong Jacob, *Capital Elites: High Society in Washington, D.C., after the Civil War* (1995) 157–61, 171–75, 125–30; Isabel Duffield, *Washington in the 1890s* (1929); George Townshend, "The New Washington," Columbia Historical Society, Washington, D.C.; Carl Abbott, "Dimensions of Regional Change in Washington, D.C." *American Historical Review* 95 (1990): 1378; Pamela Scott and Antoinette Lee, *Building of the District of Columbia* (1993), 39–40.

123　*Description of Forty-fourth Congress:* Terry Seip, *The South Returns to Congress* (1983), 13, 35–36, 145.

123　*"Nothing is more"* and *"The Democratic caucus":* James Garfield, *The Diary of James Garfield* (1975), 3:192, 4:184.

123　*Party loyalty and congressional behavior:* Michael Les Benedict, "The Party Going Strong: Congress and the Elections in the Mid-19th Century," *Congress and the Presidency: A Journal of Capitol Studies* 9 (Winter 1981): 37–60; Margaret Thompson, "Corruption or Confusion: Lobbying and Congressional Government in the Early Gilded Age," ibid., 10 (Autumn 1983): 170.

124　*"We have a murderous": Congressional Globe,* 44th Cong., 1st sess., 1700.

124　*Blue jeans in the House:* AES I, *Something of Men,* 33.

124　*Corruption:* Thompson, "Corruption," 169–89; Jerome Sternstein, "Corruption in the Gilded Age Senate," *Congress and the Presidency: A Journal of Capitol Studies* 6 (1978): 13–37; Everett Wheeler, *Sixty Years of American Life* (1917), 214; R. F. Pettigrew, *Imperial Washington: The Story of American Life* (1927).

125　*"seat assignments":* AES I to "my dear mother," 8 Dec. 1874, IC; AES I to Tommy, 8 Dec. 1875, AES Papers, ISU.

125　*"the terrible possibilities":* Woodrow Wilson, *Congressional Government: A Study in American Politics* (1956), 149.

125　*"You had to":* Quoted in David Rothman, *Politics and Power: The U.S. Senate, 1869–1901* (1966), 155.

125　*"It has been my intention": Congressional Record,* 44th Cong., 1st sess., 1275.

126　*"with its indigent":* Ibid., 2930–33.

126　*"The time, sir":* Ibid., 2nd sess., appendix, 80.

126　*"Mossback Bourbon": Pantagraph,* 25 Aug. 1880.

126　*"Who will Mr. Stevenson":* Ibid., 25 Oct. 1876.

127　*1880 campaign:* Ibid., 21 Oct. 1880.

127　*Coverage of AES I:* Ibid., 25 Aug. 1880; 12 Aug. 1876.

PAGE

127 *Election returns:* Howard Allen and Vincent Lacey, ~~Illinois Elections, 1818–1990~~ (1992), 16–22.

127 *"I will pillow my head":* Pantagraph, 25 Aug. 1880.

127 *"Mr. Stevenson takes":* Ibid., 4 Nov. 1878.

127 *"the Great straddler":* Ibid., 4 Oct. 1876; Schlup, "Political Career," 46.

127 *Redistricting and the Thirteenth District:* Pantagraph, 30 March, 8 April, 26 May 1881.

127 *The law firm:* Illinois, vol. 5, pp. 156, 389, R. G. Dun and Co., Baker Library. School of Business Administration, Harvard University.

128 *Attacks on AES I:* Pantagraph, 28 Feb., 7 March 1881.

128 *"Mr. Stevenson and his brothers":* Ibid., 15 March 1881.

128 *Stevensonville: Leader,* 17 Aug. 1881; Clipping in Stevenson File, MCHS.

128 *Workers and the community:* Pantagraph, 9 March, 10 March 1881, 18 April 1883, 10 July 1885. For other examples of industrial towns, see Bridget Meakin, *Model Factories and Villages* (1905); John S. Garner, *The Model Company Town* (1885); Janice Reiff, "Manufacturing a Community: Pullman Workers and Their Towns" (unpublished paper, Case Western Reserve University).

128 *Concept of civic capitalism:* Sally Griffith, *Home Town News: William Allen White and the Emporia Gazette* (1989); interview with Greg Koos.

129 *Community fears:* Pantagraph, 20 June 1881; *Bulletin,* 10 Aug. 1881; Timothy Mahoney, "Provincial Lives: A Social History of Regional Urbanization in the American Midwest, 1820–1880" (unpublished paper, Newberry Library Seminar, 1992).

129 *"pitched into the defense":* Pantagraph, 3 Oct. 1881.

129 *"This act of lawlessness":* AES I Scrapbook, Newberry Library.

130 *"no question of conscience":* AES I to William Vilas, 15 Nov. 1884; also 6 June 1892, William Vilas Papers; Schlup, "Political Career," 75.

130 *"dreadful self-inflicted penance":* Allan Nevins, ed., *Letters of Grover Cleveland, 1850–1908* (1933), 48.

130 *Personal strife and "self-assertion":* Leonard Schlup, "Vilas, Stevenson and Democratic Politics," *North Dakota Quarterly* 44 (Winter 1976): 44–53; H. Wayne Morgan, *From Hayes to McKinley: National Party Politics, 1877–1896* (1969), 411.

130 *AES I campaign on the tariff:* Bulletin, 17 Oct. 1884; AES Scrapbook, MCHS.

130 *Earlier press coverage of Halpin:* Buffalo Evening Post, 21 July 1880.

130 *"moral victory of the age":* AES I to William Vilas, 15 Nov., 12 Dec. 1884, Vilas Papers; Schlup, "Political Career," 50.

131 *"partisan zeal":* Nevins, *Letters,* 47.

131 *Washington and patronage:* Morgan, *Hayes to McKinley,* 74.

131 *Pendleton civil service and spoils:* Ari Hoogenboom, *Outlawing the Spoils: A History of Civil Service Reform Movement, 1865–1883* (1961), 1, 39, 279.

131 *The fourth-class post offices:* Official Register, 1885; Post Offices, Record Group 46, NA.

131 *"It is a better":* David Davis to AES I, n.d., James Rolfe Papers.

131 *Length of time spent on patronage:* Robert Wiebe, *The Segmented Society: An Introduction to the Meaning of America* (1975), 34.

131 *"Therefor I say":* David Locke, *Swinging around the Cirkle* (1888), 298.

132 *"begging like dogs":* Nevins, *Letters,* 78–79, 88–89.

132 *"Father's lambent humor":* Julia Stevenson to AES, 30 April 1948, IC.

132 *Cleveland and the silverite conspiracy:* Nevins, *Letters,* 78–79, 88–89.

PAGE

132 *AES I as postmaster:* Schlup, "Political Career," 55–60. On the post office and patronage, see Dorothy G. Fowler, *The Cabinet Politician: The Postmaster General, 1829–1909* (1967), 182–97.

132 *"a man who uses":* Clippings, AES I File, MCHS.

132 *"great attention":* Melville Stone to AES I, 28 May 1889, IC; *Pantagraph,* 10 July, 5 Sept., 12 Oct. 1885.

133 *"It is a reflection":* AES I to H. Butterworth, 17 March 1886, IC, Stevenson Scrapbooks; *Pantagraph,* 22 March 1886.

133 *List of female clerks: Official Register,* 1886. See also Mary Clemmer Ames, *Ten Years in Washington* (1884), 364.

133 *"that he [Stevenson] might think":* Nevins, *Letters,* 156.

133 *Nomination to the court:* (Peoria) *Morning National Democrat,* 1 Feb. 1888, Stevenson Scrapbook; Schlup, "Political Career," 64; 50th Cong., Senate, 50-B-A3 Papers Re Nominations, Record Group 46, NA; AES I to Joseph Fifer, 11 Feb. 1889, IC.

133 *"Father is infatuated":* Lewis to Helen, 20 Feb. 1889, IC.

133 *"severe blow":* William Springer to Mrs. Springer, 1 Oct. 1893, Springer Papers, CHS; *Pantagraph,* 13 Feb. 1889.

133 *On rooms:* Lewis to Helen, n.d. [1887], IC.

134 *"a resort for":* Pantagraph, 7 June 1885.

134 *Description of home:* Interviews with Elizabeth Ives and Greg Koos.

134 *"was sometimes replaced":* Bulletin, 12 Feb. 1899, Clippings, MCHS; "Grandmother Stevenson," Governor's Papers.

134 *Stevenson request for papers:* AES I to Grover Cleveland, 2 Oct. 1891, Cleveland Papers, microfilm edition.

134 *Life on Franklin Park:* Julia Hardin, "For my Grandchildren"; Julia Hardin to Buffie, 10 Feb. 1955, IC.

135 *"taffy for revenue only":* Letty Stevenson to Mr. Kinney, 3 Oct. 1952, IC.

CHAPTER 5: LEGACIES

146 *Description of convention:* New York Times, 24 June 1892; Everett Wheeler, *Sixty Years of American Life* (1917); *Chicago Tribune,* 21–24 June, 1894.

146 *The vice presidency and preference for senatorships:* David Rothman, *Politics and Power: The United States Senate, 1869–1901* (1966); Michael Nelson, *A Heartbeat Away: Report on the Twentieth Century Fund Task Force on the Vice Presidency* (1988); Paul Light, *Vice Presidential Power: Advice and Consent in the White House* (1994).

146 *"four years of rest":* Lucius Lamar, *His Life, Times and Speeches* (1896), 204–5. A succession act was passed in 1886 which provided that, in the event of death or removal or resignation or inability of both president and vice president, the heads of executive offices should succeed to the duties of the president.

147 *Stevenson and Democratic National Committee: Official Proceedings of the 1892 National Convention* 21–24 June 1892, 105, 128, 163.

147 *Stevenson's attraction:* Charles Morris, *A Sketch of the Life and Services of Adlai Ewing Stevenson* (1892), 360; Allan Nevins, ed., *Letters of Grover Cleveland* (1933), 289–90.

147 *Cleveland's reaction to campaigning:* H. Wayne Morgan, *From Hayes to McKinley: National Party Politics, 1877–1896* (1969), 411.

PAGE

147   *"had a jolly"* and *AES I's reaction:* Henry Clendenin, *Autobiography: The Story of a Long and Busy Life* (1926), 203; *Proceedings of 1892 Convention,* 229.

148   *"unnecessary appointments":* Whitelaw Reid to Benjamin Harrison, 8 Aug. 1892; Whitelaw Reid to Frank Millikan, 10 Aug. 1892, Whitelaw Reid Papers, microfilm edition, LC.

148   *"Converts one warm":* Whitelaw Reid to General Felix Angus, 15 Sept. 1892, ibid.

148   *"opinions be known":* Nevins, *Letters,* 189.

148   *"I can not bring myself":* Horace Merrill, *Bourbon Leader: Grover Cleveland and the Democratic Party* (1957), 159. On the use of Mrs. Cleveland's name, see Nevins, *Letters,* 291.

149   *Cleveland's campaign:* George Parker, *Recollections of Grover Cleveland* (1909), 170–71. For a general study of presidential campaigning and Cleveland's 1892 campaign, see Gil Troy, *See How They Run: The Changing Role of the Presidential Candidate* (1991), 98–101.

149   *Strategy of campaign:* Daniel Hickey to William Whitney, 10 Sept. 1892, William Whitney Papers, LC; Parker, *Recollections,* 170–71; George Knoles, *The Presidential Campaign and Election of 1892* (1942); Leonard Schlup, "The Political Career of the First Adlai Ewing Stevenson" (Ph.D. diss., University of Illinois, 1973), 53.

149   *"Politics I believe":* Frank Jones to William Whitney, 1 July 1892, William Whitney Papers, LC.

149   *"The one point":* AES I to Grover Cleveland, 12 Sept. 1892, Grover Cleveland Papers, microfilm edition, LC. On the South, the Democratic party, and the Populists, see Dewey Grantham, *The Life and Death of the Solid South: A Political History* (1988), 15; Albert Kirwan, *Revolt of the Rednecks: Mississippi Politics, 1876–1925* (1964).

149   *Family connections and Stevenson's campaigning:* Clippings on 1892 campaign, Stevenson Microfilm, ISHS; Stevenson Folder, MCHS.

150   *Stevenson speech: Review of Reviews* 6 (1892–93): 205.

150   *"Men of Alabama":* *Birmingham Herald,* 19 Oct. 1892; Leonard Schlup, "Adlai Ewing Stevenson and the 1892 Campaign in Alabama," *Alabama Review* 29 (1976): 3–16.

150   *"I fear [Stevenson] is":* Frank Jones to William Whitney, 1 July 1892, William Whitney Papers, LC; Bingham Duncan, *Whitelaw Reid: Journalist, Politician, Diplomat* (1975), 155; Whitelaw Reid to Frank Millikan, 8 and 10 Aug. 1892, Whitelaw Reid Papers, LC. On worries of leaders about Stevenson, see Carl Schurz, *Speeches, Correspondence and Political Papers* (1913), 5:121.

150   *"power to bring":* AES I to Grover Cleveland, 12 Sept. 1892, Grover Cleveland Papers.

151   *"You will play":* Letitia Stevenson to Frances Cleveland, n.d. [1892], Stevenson Family microfilm.

151   *"to manage the colored voters":* *Davidson College Monthly,* Jan. 1893.

151   *Herndon meeting:* *New York Times,* 3 Sept. 1892; Stevenson Clippings, MCHS.

151   *"heavy responsibility":* *Review of Reviews* 6 (1892–93): 205.

151   *Stevenson storytelling:* Andrew Dickson White, *Autobiography of Andrew Dickson White* (1905), 2:127.

151   *"With my eyes":* *Hopkinsville Kentuckian,* 2, 6 Sept. 1892, University of Kentucky Library, Lexington, Ky.

152   *"taxed for the purpose":* Stevenson Scrapbook, MCHS.

152   *"he can do":* Stevenson Clippings, MCHS.

PAGE

152 *"he always spoke"*: Champ Clark, *My Quarter Century of American Politics* (1920), 1:261.

152 *Stretching to shake hands*: Review of Reviews 6 (1892–93), 205; *San Francisco Examiner*, 18, 23 July 1893, in Stevenson Clippings, MCHS; White, *Autobiography*, 2:126.

152 *"Should it please"*: Proceedings of 1892 Convention, 230.

152 *"partisan passions"*: "Speech at Bloomington," Stevenson Scrapbook.

153 *"lips touched with"*: AES I, *Something of Men I Have Known* (1909), 37; *Proceedings of 1892 Convention*, 230; *New York Times*, 21 July 1892.

153 *Women's voting*: Steven Buechler, *The Transformation of the Woman Suffrage Movement: The Case of Illinois, 1850–1920* (1986), 149–54.

153 *"I remember"* and *election day*: Pantagraph, 4 Nov. 1892; *Crimson Crest*, 9 Nov. 1892, clipping in Stevenson Scrapbooks, MCHS.

154 *Description based on photograph*: Family Folders. For Washington in the Gilded Age, see *Washington, D.C. with Its Points of Interest* (1894); James Goode, *Capital Losses: A Cultural History of Washington's Destroyed Buildings* (1979).

155 *Society in D.C.*: Kathryn Allamong Jacob, *Capital Elites: High Society in Washington, D.C., after the Civil War* (1995), 124–27.

155 *"a man's domestic"*: Sunday Eye (n.d.), Family Folders; *Boyd's Directory*, 1893–97.

155 *"were antagonistic to"*: Mrs. Jane Keim, *Handbook of Official and Social Etiquette*, 9, Columbia Historical Society, Washington, D.C.

155 *Family doings and descriptions*: Stevenson Clippings, MCHS; Stevenson Family microfilm; *Plymouth Reporter*, 26 July 1892; *St. Louis Post Dispatch*, 8 Jan. 1911, in IC.

155 *Phrenology*: John D. Davies, *Phrenology: Fad and Science: A Nineteenth Century Crusade* (1955).

155 *"lofty, earnest, loyal"*: Stevenson Scrapbooks.

155 *The Stevensons' activities*: Kate Field's Washington, 4, 31 Oct., 15 Nov. 1894.

155 *Stevenson's social life*: Rolfe Papers, LC; Visitor's List, Grover Cleveland Papers, ser. 3, microfilm ed.; Scrapbook, IC.

156 *"I can't shake"*: Kate Field's Washington, 19 July 1893.

156 *"People love to say"*: Chicago Journal, 13 March 1896, in Family Folders.

156 *Letitia and the DAR*: Wallace Davies, *Patriotism on Parade: The Story of Veteran's and Hereditary Organizations* (1955), 58. On DAR principles, see Mary Lockwood et al., *Story of the Records of the Daughters of the American Revolution* (1906), 24–27.

156 *"being limited"*: Mary Desha, *The True Story of the Daughters of the American Revolution* (1892), 6. For general issues of women's associations, see Anne Firor Scott, *Natural Allies: Women's Associations in American History* (1992).

156 *"It became apparent"*: Mrs. Adlai Stevenson, *A Brief History of the Daughters of the American Revolution* (1913), 10–13; Margaret Gibbs, *The DAR* (1969), 37–38.

156 *DAR succession and nativism*: American Monthly Magazine 2 (1893): 450; 6 (1895): 250; Davies, *Patriotism*, 82.

157 *"My ancestors had always"*: Julia Scott to Mrs. Watson, n.d., Genealogy Folder, IC; Gibbs, *DAR*, 20–21. On genealogy in the late nineteenth century, see T. Jackson Lears, *No Place of Grace: Antimodernism and the Transformation of American Culture, 1880–1920* (1981), 188.

157 *Descent from Washington*: Interview with Elizabeth Ives; Scott King to Buffie, 21 Oct. 1953; Fielding Fry to Elizabeth, 8 Feb. 1955, Family Folders.

PAGE

157   "to build up": Charlotte Observer, 28 Feb. 1893.

157   "Ladies, there is": American Monthly Magazine 8 (1896): 430, 639.

158   Controversies: Washington Post, 22 Feb. 1894; Gibbs, DAR, 63.

158   Trials of presidency: Letitia Green Stevenson to Mrs. Lindsay, 9 June, 2 July 1897, 16 Feb. 1898, William Lindsay Papers, University of Kentucky Library.

158   Letitia and the NCM: Letitia Green Stevenson to Mrs. Lucas, 18 Aug. 1962, Personal Folder, Governor's Papers.

158   "inculcating the love": David Rothman and Sheila Rothman, eds., National Congress of Mothers: The First Proceedings (1987), 273.

159   "it is to the mothers": Stevenson, "Joys of Motherhood," Stevenson microfilm; also IC.

159   "The hand that": Rothman and Rothman, National Congress, 14. For other examples of pronatalism, see ibid., 198, 255; Jan Lewis, "Mother's Love: The Construction of an Emotion in Nineteenth Century America," in Andrew Barnes and Peter Stearns, eds., Social History and Issues in Human Consciousness (1989), 209–29.

159   "destiny of nations": Rothman and Rothman, National Congress, 271–73; New York Journal, 20 Dec. 1896.

159   Letitia on suffrage: Clippings, IC; Bulletin, 16 Jan. 1910.

159   "less need of": Stevenson, "Joys."

159   "for their future": Alice McClellan Birney, Childhood (1905), 91; Rothman and Rothman, National Congress, 5, 27, 208–19, 240; Kate Field's Washington, 7 Nov. 1893.

159   "The most wonderful": Stevenson, "Joys."

160   Contemporary theories of women's education: Edward H. Clarke, Sex in Education: Or a Fair Change for Girls (1873).

160   "Every woman ought": San Francisco Examiner, 23 July 1893, Stevenson scrapbooks, ISHS; Richard Meckel, "Save the Babies": American Public Health Reform and the Prevention of Infant Mortality (1990).

160   "Motherhood is the only": Stevenson, "Joys."

160   Letitia's recruiting: Davies, Patriotism, 66.

161   "thorough knowledge": San Francisco Examiner, 23 July 1893.

161   Continuing in DAR: AES I to Letitia Green Stevenson, n.d., IC.

161   "fatigues and excitements": Letitia Green Stevenson to Mrs. Whorton, 3 Oct. 1892, IC.

161   Chicago's relation to Bloomington: William Cronon, Nature's Metropolis: Chicago and the Great West (1991), 31.

161   Description of the fair: Lloyd Wendt, The Chicago Tribune: The Rise of a Great American Newspaper (1979), 299; The Columbian Exposition and World's Fair Illustrated.

161   Chicago's radicalism: Bruce Nelson, Beyond the Martyrs: A Social History of Chicago's Anarchists, 1870–1901 (1988).

162   Women's Building and the fair: Bessie Pierce, A History of Chicago (1937–57), 2:244, 263.

162   "This is the first time": World's Columbian Exposition Manuscripts, Women's Building, 1893, CHS; Martha Banta, Imaging American Woman: Idea and Ideals in Cultural History (1987), 134, 509.

162   "mission to discuss": American Monthly Magazine 2 (1893): 173, 337, 596, 650, 656; 3 (1893): 173.

162   Visitors to the fair: World's Columbian Exposition Manuscripts, CHS.

PAGE

162 *Stevenson at the Fair:* Family Clippings, IC; Carter Harrison, *Growing Up with Chicago* (1944), 21. *"an old-fashioned": Chicago Journal,* 16 June 1893.

163 *"Why not Stevenson?": Baltimore Sun,* 4 April 1892.

163 *AES I past and challenge to Letitia's presidency:* "Lettie" to "Julia," 2 Feb. 1912, IC; *American Monthly Magazine* 4 (1895): 350; 8 (1899): 639; 9 (1900): 647, 660.

163 *Depression of 1893:* Douglas Steeples, "Five Troubled Years: A History of the Depression, 1893–1897" (Ph.D. diss., University of North Carolina, 1961); Richard Welch, *The Presidency of Grover Cleveland* (1988), 116–18.

164 *"The lessons of paternalism":* Grover Cleveland, *Messages and Papers of the President* (1897), 9:390.

164 *"You boys will":* AES I to reporters, Clippings, IC; *Bulletin,* 4 March 1893. The description of the vice president's room and the Wilson desk is based on an interview with Kathryn Allamong Jacob.

165 *"Adlai's silver cabinet":* Nevins, *Letters,* 370.

165 *Cleveland operation:* John Stuart Martin, "When the President Disappeared," *American Heritage* 6 (Oct. 1957): 10–11; Grover Cleveland to Richard Gilder, 12 Oct. 1894, Cleveland Papers, microfilm edition, LC. On Stevenson's ignorance of the operation, see Julia Stevenson Hardin, "Remembrances," IC.

165 *"the office of dignity":* AES I, "The Vice-Presidency," *Collier's,* 1 Sept. 1900, 2.

165 *"He is to preside": Congressional Record,* 44th Cong., 2nd sess., 1014.

166 *Silver in the 1890s:* Sean Cashman, *America in the Gilded Age: From the Death of Lincoln to the Rise of Theodore Roosevelt* (1993), 311.

166 *Interpretation of* The Wizard of Oz: *New York Times,* 20 Dec. 1991.

166 *"We are in the midst":* AES I to Letitia Green Stevenson, 16 Oct. 1893, IC.

166 *"Stevenson lacked":* Harry Peck, *Twenty Years of the Republic, 1885–1905* (1908), 347.

166 *Coxey's army:* Carlos Schwaites, *Coxey's Army: An American Odyssey* (1985).

167 *"If Adlai": Pantagraph,* 9 Jan. 1896; Stevenson speeches, Stevenson Family microfilm, ISHS.

167 *"a good many people": Brooklyn Daily Eagle,* 30 June 1896.

167 *"There is no mark": Washington Star,* 9 April 1896; *Raleigh News and Observer,* 5 June 1896; Melville Stone to General Stevenson, 18 May 1886, Grover Cleveland Papers, LC.

167 *"He always left":* Schlup, "Political Career," 205, 210–20. See also Leonard Schlup, "Adlai Ewing Stevenson, Gilded Age Politician," *Journal of the Illinois Historical Society* 82 (Winter 1989) 218–30. For background on politics in 1896, see Harvey Wish, "John Peter Altgeld and the Background of the Campaign of 1896," *Mississippi Valley Historical Review* 24 (1938): 503–18; Schlup, "Political Career," 224; *Chicago Daily Tribune,* 11 Oct. 1894.

167 *Issues of Gilded Age:* Cashman, *America,* 224.

168 *Stevenson as a presidential candidate:* "Stevenson for President," 1896, Clippings, Stevenson Family microfilm, ISHS.

168 *"The Vice President": New York Times,* 3 June 1896; *New York Herald,* 6 July 1896.

168 *Bryan's background:* Paolo Coletta, *William Jennings Bryan* (1964), 1:100, 102, 125, 137.

168 *"the moneyed interests":* Ibid., 137.

168 *Hearing Robespierre:* Ibid., 139.

169 *Cross of gold speech: Official Proceedings of the Democratic National Convention, 1896,* 233–34.

169 *"The question of silver":* William Jennings Bryan, *The First Battle: A Story of the*

PAGE

Campaign of 1896 (1923), 577. On the Bloomington meeting, see *Bulletin,* 4 Oct. 1896.

169 *"our friend Stevenson"*: Grover Cleveland to William Eckard, 19 March 1897, Cleveland Papers.

169 *"I am grieved"*: AES I to Jonathan Daniels, 13 July, 3 Aug. 1896, Daniels Papers, Duke University Library.

170 *"a representative"*: AES I, *Something of Men,* 242–45, 315; *Brooklyn Daily Eagle,* 30 June 1896.

170 *Analysis of election:* Duncan MacRae and James Meldrun, "Critical Elections in Illinois, 1888–1958," in Jerome Clubb and Howard Allen, eds., *Electoral Change and Stability in American Political History* (1971), 45–71; Gilbert Fite, "The Election of 1896," in Arthur M. Schlesinger Jr., ed., *History of American Presidential Elections,* vol. 2 (1971), 1822–23; Paul Kleppner, *Continuity and Change in Electoral Politics, 1893–1923* (1987).

170 *"My political career"*: AES I to "my dear mother," n.d. [1897], IC; Schlup, "Political Career," 235; AES I to John Lewis, 30 Oct. 1897, IC.

170 *"What remains"*: AES I to "my dear son," 30 Oct. 1897, IC.

170 *"prompt decision"*: *Congressional Record,* 54th Cong., 2nd sess., 27 Feb. 1897, 2399; ibid., 3 March 1897, 2931.

170 *Controversy over the silver set:* Elizabeth Stevenson Ives to AES III, n.d., AES III Papers, ISHS; *New York Times,* 28 Feb. 1897.

171 *"First it was"*: AES I to "my dear mother," 20 June 1894, Rolfe Collection.

171 *Description of Bloomington:* Greg Koos, *Illustrated History of McLean County* (1982), 114, 138–44; oral histories of Bloomington, MCHS; *Pantagraph,* 4 March 1896; interview with Greg Koos.

171 *"There is no"*: Letitia Green Stevenson, Stevenson Clippings, MCHS.

172 *"I am not a club woman"*: Stevenson Family microfilm, ISHS. For Letitia's reading see, *St. Louis Globe,* 8 Feb. 1911, in Stevenson Scrapbook, MCHS.

172 *Significance of dining room:* Clifford Clark, "The Vision of the Dining Room," in Kathryn Grover, ed., *Dining in America* (1987), 147; Koos, *History,* 179–80.

172 *Spencer Ewing's brougham:* W. O. Davis to Lewis Stevenson, 20 Dec. 1898, W. O. Davis Letters (bound copy), Family Folders.

172 *Stevenson's knickers:* John Hay to William McKinley, 16 July 1897, William McKinley Papers, LC.

172 *"Father disdained"*: Julia Hardin, "Remembrances."

172 *Crawford family: Pantagraph,* 21 Aug., 21 Oct. 1874.

172 *Changes in Bloomington:* Koos, *History,* 228–34; James Spencer Ewing, "No Mean City," pamphlet, MCHS. On the decline in population, see Cronon, *Nature's Metropolis,* 365.

173 *"the return of all"*: AES I, "Speech in Miller Park," 15 June 1907, Family Clippings, Stevenson Family microfilm.

173 *"No man can"*: AES I, *Something of Men,* 415.

174 *American perceptions of aging norms:* Howard Chudacoff, *How Old Are You? Age Consciousness in American Culture* (1989), 45, 53, 59.

174 *"The tender grace"*: Scrapbook, 23 Oct. 1875.

174 *"mementoes of long ago"*: AES I, *Something of Men,* 74, 219–21, 228; Julia Hardin, "Remembrances"; AES I to "my dear sister," 15 March 1899, Ewing Papers, MCHS.

174 *Stevenson on his nomination: Pantagraph,* 5 and 7 July 1900; *Louisville Courier-Journal,* 7 July 1900; Schlup, "Political Career," 296, 304.

174 *Stevenson commended for party loyalty: New York World,* 7 July 1900.

PAGE

175 *Delegates on Stevenson: Official Proceedings for 1900,* 159, 169. On other issues, see ibid., 162, 236.

175 *Stevenson on bimetallic commission:* Memorial booklet of Bimetallic Commission, W. O. Wolcott to Henry White, 20 April 1897, Wolcott Papers, Colorado Historical Society.

175 *Campaign:* Walter LaFeber, "Campaign of 1900," in *Presidential Campaigns,* 5:1906.

176 *Stevenson campaign in 1900:* Schlup, "Political Career," 327–35.

176 *"If you want to see":* Pantagraph, 11 July, 1 Nov. 1900.

176 *"to guerrillas who":* LaFeber, "Campaign of 1900."

176 *"the greedy spirit"* Stevenson Acceptance Speech, *Official Proceedings for 1900,* 236.

177 *"the sure pathway":* Mr. Stevenson's Speech of Acceptance at Military Park, Indianapolis, Ind. *Official Proceedings for 1900,* 237, 239–240. On the seriousness of the Philippine war, see Brian Linn, *The U.S. Army and Counter-Insurgency in the Philippine War, 1899–1902* (1989).

177 *"I guess I can":* Clark, *My Quarter Century,* 2:196.

177 *Disappearing voters:* Walter Dean Burnham, *The Current Crisis in American Politics* (1982), 44.

177 *"I should have kept":* LGS to HDS, 6 July 1908, IC.

178 *"old times are":* Pantagraph, 20 Sept. 1908; interview with AES I in *Chicago Journal,* 12 Oct. 1908. See also AES I, *Something of Men,* 5, 6, 228.

178 *"riding in the common cars":* Pantagraph, 30, 31 July 1908.

178 *Primary: Chicago Tribune,* 15 July 1908.

178 *Strategy meeting: Bulletin,* 18 Oct. 1908.

178 *"I stand as a nonpartisan":* Pantagraph, 9 Sept. 1908. For other examples of his nonpartisanship, see ibid., 6, 20, 21 Oct. 1908; Leonard Schlup, "Adlai Stevenson and the Gubernatorial Campaign of 1908," *International Review of History and Political Science* 13 (1976): 74–88.

179 *"a political Hessian":* Pantagraph, 20 Oct. 1908.

179 *Stevenson strategy:* AES I to Carter Harrison, 8 March 1908, Harrison II Papers, Newberry Library.

179 *"He does not need":* Bulletin, 6 Nov. 1908.

179 *Springfield riot:* Roberta Senechal, *The Sociogenesis of a Race Riot* (1990), 130.

179 *Stevenson speeches:* Stevenson Family microfilm, ISHS;

179 *"I am told":* Pantagraph, 30 Oct. 1882, 11 July 1908; John McBride to editor, AES I Papers, MCHS; Folders, 1908 campaign, CHS; Schlup, "Political Career," 81–83.

179 *Deneen on Stevenson:* Pantagraph, 9 Sept., 3, 6 Oct. 1908.

180 *"He appeared":* Mt. Sterling *Democratic Messager,* 26 Aug. 1908; clipping in Governor's Papers. On his father's campaign, see LGS to HDS, typescripts, Family Folders.

180 *Results:* Schlup, "Political Career," 374, 388–91; *Pantagraph,* 6 Nov. 1908; Stevenson Family microfilm, ISHS.

180 *"quite so anxious":* LGS to "Aunt Jule," 1 Oct. 1912; LGS to "Aunt Jule," n.d.; Julia Scott to Carl Vrooman, 15 April 1913, Scott-Hardin Papers.

180 *Sunday lunches:* Clippings, Stevenson Family microfilm, ISHS.

181 *Stories:* AES I, *Something of Men,* 386–412; AES II, "Grandmother Stevenson," Governor's Papers. The term "yellow-dog" refers to Democrats who would vote for yellow dogs over Republicans.

181 *Health: Chicago Journal,* 16 June 1914.

181 *Obituaries: New York World,* 27 Nov. 1914; *New York Times,* 17 June 1914.

PAGE

181   *Stevenson will:* Copy in Family Folders, original missing from the McLean County Court House. AES I to "my darling wife," 29 April 1913, IC.

181   *"we were part":* Julia Stevenson Hardin to Tim Ives, 20 Dec. 1943, IC.

181   *"if the sons":* Pantagraph, 27 Nov. 1914.

CHAPTER 6: AFFLICTIONS AND AFFECTIONS

185   *The Stevenson-Davis wedding:* Pantagraph, 22–26 Nov. 1893; Bulletin, 22–26 Nov. 1893; clippings in Family Folders.

186   *Secular ceremony and courting:* Ellen Rothman, *Hearts and Hands: A History of Courtship in America* (1984).

186   *List of gifts and description of wedding:* "Love in the Prairies," Bulletin, 21 Nov. 1893; Pantagraph, 24 Oct., 18, 21 Nov. 1893; clippings, Family Folders.

186   *Consulting S. Weir Mitchell:* HDS to "Folkses," n.d. [1893], HDS typescript, Family Folders.

187   *"Maple Lane's lover lanes":* LGS to HDS, 26 July 1889; LGS to "my sweetheart," 1892, IC.

187   *Dean Academy:* HDS to "my dear papa," 1 Sept., 16 Oct. 1885, AES Papers, ISU.

187   *"overdoing brings nervousness":* William O. Davis to HDS, 4 Nov. 1886, bound typescript, Family Folders.

187   *"a dandy place":* LGS to HDS, n.d. [1887], IC.

187   *Lewis at Exeter:* LGS to HDS, n.d., typescript; Roll Books, Exeter Academy Archives, Exeter, N.H.

188   *John Wesley Powell expedition:* LGS to HDS, n.d. [1886]; John Terrell, *The Man Who Discovered America: A Biography of John Wesley Powell* (1969), 234; Wallace Stegner, *Beyond the 100th Meridian: John Wesley Powell and the Second Opening of the West* (1954).

188   *Lewis on the expedition:* U.S. Department of the Interior, *Official Register* (1888), 1:588; (1889), 1:645.

188   *Lovers' long-distance world:* LGS to HDS, n.d. [1888], 11 Nov. 1886, 2 June 1888, IC.

188   *"You say you will":* LGS to HDS, n.d. [Jan. 1887], IC.

188   *Professionalization of the law:* Michael Grossberg, "Institutionalizing Masculinity: The Law as a Masculine Profession," in Mark Carnes and Clyde Griffen, eds., *Meanings for Manhood: Constructions of Masculinity in Victorian America* (1990), 133–52; William R. Johnson, *Schooled Lawyers: A Study in the Clash of Professional Cultures* (1978), 58–95.

189   *"He flew off the handle"* and *"Lou is very vindicative":* Bert Davis to HDS, 2 Feb., 24 Sept. 1892, Family Folders.

189   *Lewis's anger at failure to support his father:* LGS to HDS, 24 Aug. 1892, IC.

189   *"other boys suffer":* LGS to "my darling," n.d. [1887].

189   *"I prefer business":* LGS to HDS, 20 Nov. (n.y.), IC.

189   *"had better take":* LGS to HDS, 6 Feb. 1888, IC.

189   *Lewis's failed businesses:* LGS to HDS, 4 Feb. 1892, 30 Dec. 1887, 26 July 1889, IC.

189   *Taking time before beginning work:* LGS to "my darling," 25 Dec. 1887, IC.

190   *Nervousness in late nineteenth century:* Tom Lutz, *American Nervousness* (1991), 25.

190   *"There is scarcely anything":* HDS to LGS, 29 Sept. (n.y.), IC.

190   *"Retire within [herself]":* HDS to LGS, 4 Oct. 1890, bound typescript, Family Folders.

PAGE

190   *"If you were here"*: LGS to HDS, 3 Aug. 1887, IC.

191   *Advice of Davis to his daughter*: William O. Davis to HDS, 9 June 1888, 20 Jan. 1889, 23 Oct. 1892, IC. See also "The Autobiography of William O. Davis," *Journal of the Illinois Historical Society* 39 (1946): 345–50.

191   *Davis corrects his daughter's spelling*: William O. Davis to HDS, 9 June 1888; 20 Jan. 1889, 23 Oct. 1892; Davis typescript, IC.

191   *Helen's advice to Lewis*: HDS to LGS, Sept. 1890.

191   *Lewis's omission from list of Bloomingtonians*: LGS to J. H. Hudson, 16 Jan. 1915, IC.

192   *The short-circuit theory*: Barbara Sicherman, "The Uses of Diagnosis: Doctors, Patients, and Neurasthenia," *Journal of the History of Medicine and Allied Sciences* 32 (1977): 36–38.

192   *Women at risk of neurasthenia*: Lutz, *American Nervousness*, 31; S. Weir Mitchell, *Fat and Blood and How to Make Them* (1899), 40–50. *"America seems little better"*: William Dean Howells, *Suburban Sketches* (1878), 96.

192   *The malady of nerves*: Frances G. Gosling, *Before Freud: Neurasthenia and the American Medical Community, 1870–1910* (1987), 9–13; Anita Fellman and Michael Fellman, *Making Sense of Self: Medical Advice Literature* (1981); George Beard, *Sexual Neurasthenia* (1884); idem, *A Practical Treatise on Nervous Exhaustion and Neurasthenia* (1888).

193   *"my arm hurts"*: LGS to HDS, n.d. [1889], IC.

193   *"I wonder if there"*: LGS to HDS, 4 Feb. 1904, IC.

193   *"resulted in headaches"*: Julia Stevenson to "Miss Helen," 3 July 1891, IC.

193   *"house of horrors"*: LGS to "sweetness," n.d. A fictional depiction of bed rest therapy appears in Charlotte Perkins Gilman's short story "The Yellow Wallpaper." See also Beard, *Sexual Neurasthenia*.

194   *"my dear boy"*: HDS to LGS, Sept. 1890, IC.

194   *"the strenuous life"*: Lutz, *American Nervousness*, 78–79; Peter Filene, *Him / Her Self: Sex Roles In America* (1975).

194   *"I haven't felt so well"*: LGS to "my darling," n.d. [1887], IC.

194   *"I believe that I am not"*: LGS to HDS, n.d. [1889], LGS typescripts, Family Folders.

194   *Lewis's cures coincide with political season*: Eliza Fell Davis to "dear Husband," 22, 27 March 1899, Family Folders.

194   *"failing always to"*: HDS to LGS, 21 Oct. 1890, IC; Loren Baritz, *The Good Life: The Meaning of Success for the American Middle Class* (1988), 55–58.

194   *"suffered the same ordeal"*: HDS to LGS, n.d. [Sept.], IC.

195   *Helen's membership in the Women's History Club*: Obituary, clipping in IC; Davis's habits: William O. Davis typescript. See also William O. Davis to Fannie Fell, 2 Dec. 1888, IC.

195   *"You are better"*: HDS to LGS, Oct. 1890, IC.

195   *"You are not an invalid"*: LGS to "dearest Helen," n.d. [1888], IC.

195   *"You simply must not be"*: LGS to HDS, 13 Aug. 1889, IC.

195   *"weary days"*: LGS to HDS, n.d. [1906], IC.

195   *"dangerous beginning"*: LGS to "my darling Helen," n.d. [1888], IC.

195   *"But how selfish"*: HDS to LGS, Oct. 1890, IC.

196   *"Knowing the great"*: LGS to HDS, n.d. [1892], IC.

196   *"You have caused us"*: LGS to HDS, n.d. [1888], IC.

196   *"It's hard for me"*: LGS to HDS, 19 Jan. 1892, IC.

196   *Description of Mitchell*: Ernest Earnest, *S. Weir Mitchell, Novelist and Physician* (195); Lutz, *American Nervousness*, 31–34.

PAGE

196   *"I was never more interested"*: HDS to "folkses," n.d., IC.

197   *Attraction of the Orient*: T. J. Jackson Lears, *No Place of Grace: Antimodernism and the Transformation of American Culture, 1880–1920* (1981), 101, 142–43, 175–77, 228–31; John Ashmead, *The Idea of Japan, 1853–1895* (1987).

197   *Lewis comments on his trip*: San Francisco Call, 18 Oct., 1 Nov. 1895, clippings in IC; *Pantagraph*, 7 April 1896.

197   *Trip to Canton*: LGS to HDS, 14, 17 Feb. 1896, IC.

197   *"our troubles"*: LGS to HDS, 5 Dec. 1895. For other comments on the marriage, see LGS to HDS, 14 Feb. 1896, IC.

197   *"of blissful happiness"*: LGS to HDS, 17 Feb. 1896, IC.

197   *Stevenson solicits work for his son*: AES I to Henry Watterson, 6 Jan. 1903, Family Folders.

197   *Family migrations*: Herman Steen to Mrs. Ives, 13 Aug. 1971, Family Folders.

197   *Lewis's travels*: LGS typescript, Family Folders.

198   *"when you are with"*: HDS to LGS, 22 July 1899; "Our Family Homes," notes of Elizabeth Stevenson Ives, Family Folders.

198   *Lewis's wanderings*: HDS to LGS, 22 July 1899, IC.

198   *"Lewis can hardly stand"*: HDS to "Papa," 14 Sept. 1897, IC.

198   *"good business ability"*: HDS to William O. Davis, 12 Dec. 1898, IC.

198   *"you know as well"*: LGS to William O. Davis, 22 March 1899, LGS typescript, Family Folders.

198   *Lewis's jobs*: LGS to HDS, 16 July 1900, IC.

198   *Lewis's tribulations*: Eliza Fell Davis to "dear husband," 27 March 1899, Davis typescript, Family Folders. See also the same to the same, 22 March, 1899, Family Folders.

198   *Son's credentials*: AES I to Henry Watterson, 6 Jan. 1903, Family Folders.

198   *"We live in a flat"*: Pantagraph, 16 July 1880.

199   *"I never was in better"*: HDS to "Dear Mama," 9 March 1898, IC.

199   *"ugly, third-rate"*: HDS to "Dear Mama," 9 March 1898, IC.

199   *Life in New Mexico*: HDS to "folks," 1897, IC.

199   *"Up the road"*: HDS to "folks," n.d. [1898], IC.

199   *"It is a horrible"*: HDS to "folks," Feb. 1899, IC.

199   *"Helen does not want"*: Eliza Fell Davis to William O. Davis, 27 March 1899, Davis typescript, Family Folders.

199   *Move to Fort Bayard*: LGS to HDS, 30 Aug. 1898, IC.

199   *Description of houses*: HDS to "Dear Mama," n.d. [1898], Feb. 1899, IC.

200   *"brain-jogging"* and *"attaining the joy"*: LGS to HDS, 23 Nov., 24 Dec. 1906, LGS typescript, Family Folders.

200   *"continued effort"*: William O. Davis to LGS, 20 Dec. 1898, Davis typescript, Family Folders.

200   *"I doubt if"*: William O. Davis to HDS, 4 Feb. 1904, ibid.

200   *"I expect you"*: William O. Davis to HDS, 29 May 1904; also 18 Feb. 1902, 6 June 1904; Davis typescript, Family Folders.

200   *Treatment in Switzerland*: Dr. Roger Vittoz, *Treatment of Neurasthenia by Means of Brain Control* (1911).

200   *"You must recall"*: LGS to HDS, 4 April [1910], Family Folders.

201   *"Producing an heir"*: HDS to William O. Davis, March 1900, Davis typescript, Family Folders.

201   *"the successful launching"*: William O. Davis to HDS, Feb. 1900, Davis typescript, Family Folders.

PAGE

201 *"a young father's"*: LGS to William O. Davis, n.d. [July 1898], IC.

201 *"Your father is gone"*: LGS to HDS, n.d. [1911], IC.

201 *HDS's maxims*: HDS to "my darling," Feb. 1916, n.d. [1917], 25 Jan. 1924, Family Folders.

202 *"If mother had had"*: Interview with Elizabeth Ives; Kenneth S. Davis, *The Politics of Honor* (1967), 34–44; HDS to "Dear Laddie," March 1923, IC.

202 *Suffocating mothering*: Laurie Ashner and Mitch Meyerson, *When Parents Love Too Much* (1990); interviews with Elizabeth Ives.

202 *Nicknames*: HDS to William O. Davis, 22 March 1900; William O. Davis to HDS, Feb. 1900; HDS to "Dear Laddie," n.d. [1917], IC; Elizabeth Stevenson Ives Oral History, ASOH.

202 *Buying no. 1316*: Deed in McLean County Courthouse, Oct. 1906, no. 1480.

202 *Helen's activities*: Elizabeth Stevenson Ives to Jean H. Baker, 9 Oct. 1989; interviews with Elizabeth Ives.

202 *Early-twentieth-century domestic life*: Margaret Marsh, *Suburban Lives* (1990).

203 *Music and middle-class consumer culture*: Craig H. Roell, *The Piano in America, 1890–1940* (1989).

203 *Display of family wealth*: Bloomington City Directories, 1855, 1870, 1893, 1910; Bloomington Oral Histories; Augusta Parke, "Memories of East Grove St.," MCHS.

203 *Bloomington's culture*: Evocative introductions are Stephen Sears, *Hometown U.S.A.* (1975); Richard Lingeman, *Small Town America* (1980). For specifics, see Louise Large, "The Social and Economic History of Bloomington, 1870–1874" (M.A. thesis, University of Illinois, 1959).

203 *"With the home begins"*: HDS to ?, 1909; HDS to "Papa," 1905, IC.

203 *Rules at home*: HDS to "dearest lad," n.d. [1922], IC.

203 *Connection of moralism and good home*: Gwendolyn Wright, *Moralism and the Model Home* (1980).

205 *Lewis and guns*: Davis, *Politics of Honor*, 43.

205 *"And [I] stood the work"*: LGS to "my precious chicks," 3 July 1908, IC.

205 *Hard work*: LGS to Julia Scott, 23 Sept. 1910, Scott-Hardin Papers, Cornell University.

205 *midwestern tenancy*: Paul Gates, *Landlords and Tenants on the Prairie Frontier* (1973), 86–90, 181; Jacob Hasbrouck, *History of McLean County, Illinois* (1924), 1:218–21.

206 *Illinois agriculture*: Donald Tingley, *The Structuring of a State: The History of Illinois, 1899 to 1928* (1980), 40–41.

206 *Families and sons' move out of tenancy*: Frank Yoder, "Rethinking Farm Tenure: A Cultural Perspective" (unpublished paper, Newberry Library, fall 1991).

206 *Descriptions of tenants*: Hub to "my lover," n.d., LGS typescript; contract between LGS and Julia Green Scott, 1919, Scott-Hardin Papers.

206 *"shiftless and utterly"*: LGS to Julia Scott, 25 March 1911, Scott-Hardin Papers.

206 *The lien system*: Agreement between Julia Scott and LGS, July 1910, Scott-Hardin Papers.

206 *"to secure better tenants"*: LGS to Julia Scott, n.d. [1915], Scott-Hardin Papers.

207 *Efforts to set up a dairy farm*: LGS to Julia Scott, 1910, Scott-Hardin Papers.

207 *"no partnership"*: Julia Scott to LGS, n.d. [1910], Scott-Hardin Papers.

207 *Exchanges between Aunt Julia and Lewis*: Julia Scott to LGS, 5 Feb. 1910, 4 Feb. 1915, Scott-Hardin Papers.

207 *"I begin to realize"*: LGS to Julia Scott, 26 Sept., Scott-Hardin Papers.

207 *"You can't have tenants"*: LGS to Julia Scott, 15 Nov. 1910, ibid.

PAGE

208   *"under my hard work"*: Julia Scott to LGS, n.d. [1915], Scott-Hardin Papers.

208   *"so utterly preposterous"*: Lyman Graham to J. Ford, Ford Collection, MCHS.

208   *"to put aside"*: Julia Scott to LGS, 5 Feb. 1910, Scott-Hardin Papers.

208   *Call for more accurate forecasts*: Julia Scott to LGS, 3 Oct. 1910, 12 Dec. 1912, Scott-Hardin Papers.

208   *Midwest agriculture*: John Shover, *Cornbelt Rebellion* (1965), 102–13, 140–44, 160–62.

208   *"take the cure"*: "Aunt Julia" to LGS, 10 Nov., 1910, Scott-Hardin Papers.

209   *"Please just believe this"*: LGS to Julia Scott, n.d. [1915], Scott-Hardin Papers.

209   *LGS's venture*: LGS to Mayor Thompson, 3 June 1921, IC.

209   *"It's just barely possible"*: LGS to Julia Scott, 24 March 1912, IC.

210   *Illinois politics*: Hasbrouck, *History*, 1:929.

210   *Need for city liberals*: John Buenker, *Urban Liberalism and Progressive Reform* (1973), 31–37, 65; Richard Allen Morton, "Edward Dunne, Illinois, Most Progressive Governor," *Journal of the Illinois Historical Society* 83 (1990): 238–34.

210   *Theories of parole*: Vincent O'Leary, *The Organization of Parole Systems in the United States* (1973); Illinois State Reformatory, 12th Bureau Report, July 1912–14; Charles Meyer, "A Half-Century of Federal Probation," *Journal of Criminal Law, Crime and Policy Science* 42 (1952): 348–52.

210   *LGS as Illinois secretary of state*: Folder 50, IC.

210   *LGS presiding*: *Illinois House Debates* (1915), passim; *Chicago Herald*, 15 Jan. 1915.

211   *Single-issue lobbying*: Thomas Pegram, "The Dry Machine: The Formation of the Anti-Saloon League of Illinois," *Journal of the Illinois Historical Society* 83 (1990): 173–86.

211   *"the legislature's low-down wrangling"*: LGS to Julia Scott, 25 Jan. 1915, Scott-Hardin Papers.

211   *"I'm too sick"*: LGS to Julia Scott, 21 May 1920, Scott-Hardin Papers.

212   *"My experience has not"*: LGS to B. G. Green, 4 April 1916, IC.

212   *"No one is more"*: LGS to G. M. Evert, 28 Aug. 1916, IC.

212   *"I want you to know"*: LGS to Jonathan Daniels, 14 Dec. 1916; also LGS to Carl Vrooman, 27 Dec. 1916, IC. See Leonard Schlup, "Lewis Green Stevenson and the 1928 Vice-Presidential Question," *Illinois Quarterly* 40 (Spring 1928): 49–61.

212   *Leaves for the East*: LGS to "Aunt Julia," 11, 26 Aug. 1916; "Use Sense" and other campaign documents, Folder 58; Folder 61, IC.

212   *Clippings on Lewis*: *Metamora Herald*, 27 Oct. 1916; Chicago *Examiner*, 29 June 1916.

212   *"I was defeated"*: LGS to AES, 8, 9 Nov. 1916, IC.

213   *"of father's vindication"*: HDS to Elizabeth Stevenson, 23 Jan. 1924; HDS to AES II, 24 May 1924; HDS to "Buffie," March 4 1928, IC.

213   Helen's interior voice is reconstructed chronologically and mostly verbatim from her letters and from those of her family, contained in the Ives Collection, and the Family Folders at 1316 E. Washington St. There are no departures of consequence from her actual words. See HDS to LGS, n.d., Aug. 1899, n.d. [1908], Dec. 1908; LGS to HDS, Oct. 1908; HDS to "my darling," 4 Feb. 1916, 17 June 1918; HDS to "blessed chicks," 1920; HDS to "my darling child," n.d.; HDS to William O. Davis, 27 Nov. 1885, n.d. [1916]; HDS to "my darling Buffie," 2 May 1916; HDS's letters in 1912, Family Folders; LGS to Julia Scott, 7 Feb. 1913; AES to "Father," 24 June, Scott-Hardin Papers; LGS to Aunt Julia, 17 Oct. 1916; HDS to "dearest Adlai," 1917; HDS to AES, 1917, HDS typescript; HDS to "my precious boy," 5 Feb. 1921, 1 May 1924; HDS to "Buffie," 4 Feb. 1916, 4 Oct. 1935; HDS to "Buffie," 8 May

PAGE

1916; HDS to Jessie Merwin, 10 Jan. 1930; Elizabeth Stevenson Ives, "What I Remember," 10 June 1950, Family Folders; HDS to AES, 12 June 1918; HDS to "my darling Buffie," 22 Nov. 1920; HDS to "Dearest Buffie," 1915; HDS to "my dear lad," 1917, 3 Oct. 1920, typescript; on her son's hair, *Papers,* 1:100; LGS to HDS, 1920; HDS to LGS, n.d. [1927]; HDS to "my precious babes," n.d., IC; HDS to "darling boy," 24 March 1934; HDS to "Darling one," n.d. [1927]; HDS to "dearest," 23 Jan. 1924, IC; HDS to "darling good boy," n.d. [1933]; 1 Oct. 1935; HDS to AES, 1932, 4 Dec. 1920; Buffie to HDS, 23 March, n.d. [1935], Elizabeth Stevenson Ives typescript; HDS to Jessie Merwin, 18 Feb. 1930, IC.

219 *LGS's death:* "Notes for Adlai Ewing Stevenson in Case of my Death," March 1924, Box 213, PUL.

219 *"Observe your mother":* "Father" to "Buffie," Feb. 1929, Family Folders; obituaries, *Pantagraph,* 17 Nov. 1935; *New York Times,* 6 April 1929; also clippings in IC.

220 *Helen's sickness and Adlai's reaction:* Martin, *Illinois,* 34, 39–40.

CHAPTER 7: FAMILY CLAIMS

221 Unless otherwise noted, all personal letters in this chapter are in the Ives Collection of the Adlai Ewing Stevenson Papers at the Illinois State Historical Society.

221 *AES as a traveler and collector:* Elizabeth Ives, *My Brother Adlai* (1956), 37. Train whistles: Kenneth S. Davis, *The Politics of Honor* (1967), 23.

221 *Early letters:* AES to "Dear father," *Papers,* 1:7; undated letters, IC.

222 *"anxious little son":* AES to "Dear Father," 1 Jan. 1907.

222 *AES and early relation with father:* C. Eric Sears, "Adlai Ewing Stevenson and the Early Cold War" (Ph.D. diss., University of Hawaii, 1976), 23; Martin, *Illinois,* 34.

222 *"Remember, I have loved you":* HDS to Elizabeth Stevenson, 16 Nov. 1935.

222 *"Darling one":* HDS to AES, n.d. [1922].

222 *Readings of women's club:* Bloomington Women's Club Records, ISU.

222 *Maternal manuals:* Emma Marwedel, *Conscious Motherhood: The Earliest Unfolding of the Child in Cradle, Nursery, and Kindergarten* (1889).

222 *School attendance, child labor laws, and reformers:* Edith Abbott and Sophonisba Breckinridge, *The Administration of the Aid-to-Mothers Law in Illinois* (1921); Rosalind Rosenberg, *Divided Lives: American Women in the Twentieth Century* (1992), 46–50; Ellen Fitzpatrick, *Endless Crusade: Women Social Scientists and Progressive Reform* (1990), 187–92.

222 *Figures on working children:* U.S. Dept. of Commerce, Bureau of the Census, *Children in Gainful Occupations,* 14th Census, 11–12.

223 *"with the mother [as]":* Mrs. Emma Angell Drake, *What Every Parent Should Know* (1901) 45, 212.

223 *"the moral curriculum"* and *"oldest steadiest profession":* Mary Lillian Read, *The Mothercraft Manual* (1916), 1–2, 4, 248; Felix Adler, *The Moral Instruction of Children* (1892); William Byron Forbush, *The Character-Training of Children* (1919), 1:288.

223 *New interpretations of child raising:* Glenn Davis, *Childhood and History in the United States* (1976), 91–119.

223 *Masturbation:* L. Emmett Holt, *The Diseases of Infancy and Childhood* (1897); Joseph Howe, *Excessive Venery, Masturbation and Continence* (1907).

PAGE

223   *"clean living habits":* Margaret Sangster, *Child Study for Mothers and Teachers* (1901), esp. the chapter "Habit-Forming and Habit Breaking."

223   *"Watch your impulses":* HDS to "dearest and best," 19 Dec. 1923; HDS to "my blessed chicks," n.d.

223   *Stevenson's continence:* Marietta Tree to Ken McGregor, 12 Feb. 1975, Box 322, John Bartlow Martin Papers, LC; Martin, *Illinois,* 62.

223   *"history has never":* HDS to Jessie Merwin, n.d.

224   *"Get the right habits":* HDS to AES, n.d. [1917]. For other advice, see HDS to "Dear Laddie," 3 Oct. 1917, 5 May 1926.

224   *"Character is better":* HDS to "my darling," n.d.

224   *A genius in its midst:* HDS to "My Darling," n.d. [1917].

224   *"Our Mother is too":* Elizabeth Stevenson to "Dear Brother," 16 Nov. 1935, AES Papers, PUL.

224   *Relation of Adlai to Lewis:* Interview with Bethia Currie, cited in Sears, "Stevenson and the Cold War," 16, 31, 36, 118.

224   *"I will remove you":* LGS to AES, 20 July 1915.

224   *Changes in fatherhood and the development of a boys' culture:* Robert L. Griswold, *Fatherhood in America: A History* (1992), 2–5, 29–33, 93.

224   *"tranquil and phlegmatic":* Papers, 1:181. On life in small cities at the turn of the century, see Stephen Sears, *Hometown U.S.A.* (1975); Clara Kessler, "Hometown in the Cornbelt," MCHS.

225   *Stevenson composition:* "My Pet Bunny," *Papers,* 1:8.

225   *"highly developed lingual":* Ibid., 183.

225   *Set apart from peers:* Interview with Bethia Currie, in Sears, "Stevenson and the Cold War," 23.

225   *Parents as snobs:* Martin, *Illinois,* 31, 35; interview with Elizabeth Ives.

225   *Reaction to Democrats:* Kessler, "Hometown," 112; Kindergartens, Bloomington Directory, 1910.

225   *Illinois school attendance:* Peter De Boer, "A History of the Early Compulsory School Attendance Legislation in the State of Illinois" (Ph.D. diss., University of Chicago, 1968).

226   *"natural currents":* HDS to AES, 3 Oct. 1917; HDS to Elizabeth Stevenson, 4 Sept. 1920.

226   *Washington Street School:* Bloomington School Records, MCHS; Kessler, "Hometown"; Edith Muxfield, "Bloomington Schools, 1900–1950" (unpublished paper, MCHS).

226   *Schooling for immigrants and changes in teaching:* Lawrence Cremin, *American Education: The Metropolitan Experience, 1876–1984* (1988), 171–74; "Rules of the Board of Education and Sextennial Report," MCHS.

226   *"grabbing their hats":* Interview with Elizabeth Ives.

226   *Physical punishment in schools:* Jean H. Baker, *Affairs of Party* (1982), 101.

227   *"Adlai was a very good":* Elizabeth Stevenson Ives Oral History, ASOH; Buffie Ives, "What I Remember."

227   *New ways of controlling children:* Peter Stearns and Timothy Haggerty, "The Role of Fear: Transitions in American Emotional Standards for Children, 1850–1950," *American Historical Review* 96 (1991): 63–95.

227   *Physical punishment and AES's schooling:* "Rules of Board of Education," MCHS; Vertical Files in Bloomington Public Library.

227   *"till it is done perfectly":* Ives, *My Brother Adlai,* 7; Buffie Ives, "The Childhood Home," in Kessler, "Hometown."

PAGE

227 *Joseph Bohrer recollections:* Martin, *Illinois*, 40; Folder 4, IC.

227 *Family travels:* Ives, "Childhood Home"; interview with Elizabeth Ives; Ives, "What I Remember," typescript, Family Folders.

227 *Family trip:* HDS to "Lew," n.d. [1912].

227 *Helen's reservations about trip:* Ives, *My Brother Adlai*, 65–66.

228 *Nurses when young:* AES to Mrs. R. L. Hallam, 2 April 1948, AES Papers, PUL.

228 *Stevenson grades: Papers*, 1:13; AES Vertical File, Bloomington Public Library; Folder 6, Johnson Papers, ISU.

228 *Metcalf Training School and University High: Annual Catalog and Course of Study, Illinois State Normal University*, 1912–15, Charles Harper Collection; Helen Marshall, *The Grandest of Enterprises: Illinois State University, 1857–1957* (1956); David Felmley Papers, ISU; Alice Eikenberry, "The University High School," *Teacher Education* 20 (Dec. 1957): 52–71.

229 *Visit to Woodrow Wilson:* Davis, *Politics of Honor*, 45.

229 *Posting Wilson signs:* Ives, "What I Remember"; Ives, *My Brother Adlai*, 70–71.

229 *Wilson's campaign:* August Heckscher, *Woodrow Wilson* (1991), 236, 253–63.

229 *The shooting of Ruth Merwin:* Interview with Elizabeth Ives; materials in Box 321, Martin Papers, LC; *Pantagraph*, 30 Dec. 1912, 2 Jan. 1913.

230 *"all due precautions": Pantagraph*, 31 Dec. 1912.

230 *"too prostrated by grief":* Ibid., 1 Jan. 1913.

230 *"pop corn balls":* AES to "Dear Father," 20 Jan. 1913.

230 *"was determined to face":* LGS to "Aunt Jule," 7 Jan. 1913, Scott-Hardin Papers.

230 *Ellen's ignorance of shooting:* Interview with J. Stuart Ingram.

231 *AES tells the story:* Davis, *Politics of Honor*, 47.

231 *"A thing like this":* Ibid., 322.

231 *LGS jokes with son about hunting:* LGS to AES, 14 June 1911.

231 *"[My brother] had an accident":* Buffie Ives to John Martin, n.d., Martin Papers, LC. See also Buffie Ives's compilation of errors in John Martin's *Adlai Stevenson of Illinois*, copies in PUL.

231 *Effect of shooting on Stevenson:* Martin, *Illinois*, 43: Davis, *Politics of Honor*, 48; Porter McKeever, *Adlai Stevenson* (1989), 31; interview with Dr. Paul McHugh.

232 *Guilt as a form of selfishness:* AES to "dear mother," n.d. [1924], Family Folders.

232 *Stevenson at University High:* University High Materials, ISU.

232 *Recollections of childhood:* Elizabeth Stevenson Ives to "Sweetest Mother," 15 Sept. (n.y.); Kessler, "Hometown."

232 *"girl in the pink tights": Papers*, 1:521.

232 *Majestic Theatre:* Greg Koos, *Illustrated History of McLean County* (1982); Sidney Lawrence to Francis Knipp, 11 Jan. 1967, Martin Papers, LC.

233 *Hides under bearskin rug:* Davis, *Politics of Honor*, 44.

233 *Hiking trip:* AES to "Dear Maw," 16 Aug. 1915; Memorabilia, University High, 27 May 1916, Box 1526, AES Papers, PUL.

233 *Tries to keep mother away:* AES to "Dear Mother," 25 July 1915.

233 *"Please, Please! please":* AES to "Dear Mother," 15 Sept. 1913.

233 *Changed studies:* AES to "Dear Mother," 18 Sept. 1913.

233 *"Please telegraph":* Ibid.

233 *Father adjudicates athletics:* LGS to George St. John, 25 Sept. 1917; Ives, "What I Remember."

233 *"All doctors haven't":* AES to "Dear Mother," n.d.

234 *Being mediocre:* HDS to "my darling Buffie," 16 Jan., 2 April 1916.

234 *"Don't waste time":* HDS to "Dear Laddie," March 1923.

PAGE

234   *"With hard summer work"*: George St. John to Mr. and Mrs. Stevenson, 18 May 1916, Choate School Archives, Wallingford, Conn.

234   *"It is clear"*: HDS to Elizabeth Stevenson, 16 Jan. 1916.

234   *"Let Adlai spend"*: LGS to George St. John, 4 Feb.; see also LGS to George St. John, 4 March, 23 Nov. 1917.

234   *"It troubles [Adlai]"*: George St. John to Mrs. Stevenson, 24 March 1917, Choate Archives.

234   *"My ten days"*: AES to "Dearest mum," n.d. [Friday evening], 2 April 1918.

234   *Information on Choate*: Interview with Lee Sylvester; Peter W. Cookson, *Preparing for Power: America's Elite Boarding Schools* (1985); Nelson Aldrich, *Old Money: The Mythology of America's Upper Class* (1988), 38–39, 42–43; Choate Catalog, 1917.

235   *"a lot more than books"*: LGS to Buffie, 24 Feb. 1916.

235   *New England boarding schools train gentlemen and leaders*: James McLachlan, *America's Boarding Schools: A Historical Study* (1970), 5–16, 189–299.

235   *"the capacity to distinguish"*: AES, introduction of George St. John in Chicago, 1935, James Oakes microfilm of AES speeches, ISHS.

236   *Choate's history and culture*: Peter Prescott, *A World of Our Own: Notes on Life and Learning in a Boys' Preparatory School* (1970).

236   *"We invite you"*: *Choate News,* 27 Oct. 1916.

237   *Slack school spirit*: *The Brief,* 1917.

237   *"If one has a vision"*: Choate Catalog, 1917.

237   *Stevenson's grades and performance* and *"is a delightful fellow"*: George St. John to Mr. and Mrs. Stevenson, 22, 27 Oct., 18 Nov. 1916, Johnson Papers; also AES Folder, Choate School.

237   *Stevenson in* The Critic: *Choate News,* 27 Oct. 1916.

237   *Parents' worries*: LGS to George St. John, 2 Jan., 16 May 1917.

237   *"not remain for"*: HDS to George St. John, 16 June 1918, Johnson Papers.

237   *"The boy should have"*: LGS to George St. John, 1 Feb. 1917. For other complaints, see LGS to George St. John, 4, 12 May, 25 Oct. 1917.

237   *St. John's responses*: George St. John to LGS, 6, 9 May 1917, Johnson Papers.

238   *Issue of a single room*: HDS to George St. John, 9 Feb. 1917; LGS to George St. John, 2 Jan., 25 May 1917; George St. John to Mr. and Mrs. Stevenson, 14 June 1917.

238   *Never "to room alone"*: AES to "Dearest Mum," 30 Sept. 1917.

238   *"the second biggest thing"*: AES to "Dear Father," n.d.; undated correspondence in Folder 31, Johnson Papers.

238   *"The news of your singles"*: HDS to "Dearest Laddie," 12 June 1918.

238   *"pretty big dude"* and *"It's nice to be"*: AES to "Dearest Mum," 7 Oct. 1917, 20 June 1918.

238   *Kennedy at Choate*: Nigel Hamilton, *John F. Kennedy: Reckless Youth* (1992), 33–34, 88–101, 119–27.

239   *"Evidently you don't"*: AES to "Dearest Mum," n.d. [fall 1917], 14 Oct. 1917.

239   *Fight over Spanish*: LGS to George St. John, undated letters, Folder 3, Johnson Papers.

239   *"unable to see how Spanish"*: LGS to George St. John, 25 May 1917.

239   *Wilson and war declaration*: David Steigerwald, *Wilsonian Idealism in America* (1994), 33–38; Thomas Knock, *To End All Wars* (1992), 120–22.

239   *Bloomington mobilization*: Council of Defense Folder, World War I, MCHS.

240   *Choate mobilizes*: *Choate News,* May–June, Sept.–Dec. 1917, Feb.–June 1918, passim.

PAGE

240　*"the brief paradise of America"*: Max Eastman, *The Enjoyment of Living* (1948), 586.

240　*"our last time of daydreams"*: AES, *Major Campaign Speeches* (1953) 222.

240　*"If a Christian is"*: Choate News, 24 Nov. 1917.

240　*encouragements to public service*: Ibid., 8 June, 8 Dec. 1917, 10 April, 11 June, 1918.

240　*"we have 136"*: AES to "Dearest Mum," 12 May 1918.

241　*"I have fought"*: Choate News, 8 June 1917.

241　*"Also Dr. [St. John]"*: HDS to George St. John, n.d. [1917].

241　*"Once more I beg"*: AES to "Dearest Mum," 12 May 1918.

241　*"The country needs"*: Choate News, 11 May 1917.

241　*Registration in Bloomington*: Harold Sinclair, *The Daily Pantagraph, 1846–1946* (1976), 191.

241　*"desire and are eligible"*: Choate News, April 1917.

242　*Princeton tuition*: James McLachlan, *Princetonians, 1748–1768: A Biographical Dictionary* (1976). *Princeton requirements*: Princeton Catalogue, 1918, 1919.

242　*Argument over classics*: Daily Princetonian, 7, 25 Feb. 1919, Princeton University Archives.

242　*Helen's "unceasing care"*: AES to "Dearest Mother," 27 Sept. 1918.

242　*AES's measurements*: AES to "Dearest Mother," 23 Sept. 1918, AES Papers, PUL.

242　*Buffie and John Harlan*: Interview with Elizabeth Ives.

243　*"There are quite a few"*: AES to "Dearest Mother," 27 Sept. 1918.

243　*"slow developer"*: John Harlan Oral History, ASOH; Mrs. Harold Hochshild Interview, ibid.

243　*Fitzgerald on Princeton*: F. Scott Fitzgerald, *This Side of Paradise* (1920; Bodley Head ed., 1960), 45–55.

243　*Information on class of 1922*: Nassau Herald, 1918, 1919, Princeton University Archives.

243　*Importance of prep schools*: Papers, 1:69–70. Thomas McEachin, "History of the Class of 1922," Princeton University Archives.

244　*"What we know as the Princeton"*: Daily Princetonian, 7 Oct. 1918, 12 March 1919; "Princeton's War Class" and "The Daily Life of the Student-Sailor," *Princeton Alumni Weekly*, 16 Oct. 1918.

244　*"The difference between"*: AES to "Dearest Mum," 27 Oct. 1918.

244　*"hot looking 'Jack' "*: AES to "Dearest Mum," 22 Oct. 1918.

244　*"I'll probably stay"*: AES to "Dearest Mum," 27 Oct. 1918.

244　*Lack of spirit at University*: Daily Princetonian, 5 April, 1 May 1919.

245　*Princeton as "lazy beauty,"* Fitzgerald, *This Side of Paradise*, 50; E. Digby Baltzell, *The Protestant Establishment: Aristocracy and Caste in America* (1987), ix.

245　*Wilson and Princeton*: Steigerwald, *Wilsonian Idealism*, 18–20, 26–28.

245　*Princeton's coverage of sports*: Daily Princetonian, 6, 21 April 1921, 9 Jan. 1922.

245　*"Princeton provides"*: Princeton Alumni Weekly, 5 Oct. 1921. For similar inspirational rhetoric, see Daily Princetonian, 22 June 1922, and, for a class officer's version, Nassau Herald, 1919.

246　*"some of the wise serenity"*: AES, *What I Think* (1956), 180; *Princeton Alumni Weekly*, 5 Oct. 1921.

246　*AES at Princeton and class poll*: Edward Doyle, ed., *As We Knew Adlai* (1966), 17–19; Nassau Herald, 1922.

246　*Issues of which AES was editor*: Daily Princetonian, 11 Dec. 1917, 7, 28 Jan., 2 March, 8, 13 May, 4 Oct. 1920.

246　*Interest in League of Nations*: Ibid., 4 Oct. 1919.

246　*Princeton spurs his interest in foreign affairs*: Princeton Alumni Weekly, Oct. 1952.

PAGE

246   *"Oh, what a* Daily Princetonian": Quoted in Davis, *Politics of Honor,* 71 (italics added).

247   *"duties of my publicity":* AES to "Dear Father"; *Papers,* 1:98.

247   *Materials on AES at Princeton:* Scrapbook, 1407, PUL.

247   *"so pregnant with delightful":* Report of the 1921 Subcommittee on Eating Clubs, Correspondence, Upper-Class Clubs, Princeton Archives.

247   *Support of clubs:* Daily Princetonian, 11 Jan. 1919.

247   *AES and the 1920 election:* Ibid., 14 June 1920.

247   *Information on classmates:* Princeton Alumni Weekly, 5, 17 Oct. 1921; Daily Princetonian, 29 Oct. 1919, 14 June, 30 Oct. 1920.

247   *AES's grades at Princeton:* Papers, 1:61–63.

248   *Princeton system of grading:* Daily Princetonian, 15 April 1919.

248   *"I didn't like math":* AES to Kenneth Davis, 28 Jan. 1957, Papers, 6:438–39.

248   *"the archive of the Western mind":* Princeton Alumni Weekly, 17 Oct. 1952.

248   *College life:* Nassau Herald, 1922, 447.

248   *Wilson admires* Birth of a Nation: Arthur Link, ed., *The Papers of Woodrow Wilson,* vol. 32 (1980), 267 n. 1; Stockton Axson, *Brother Woodrow: A Memoir* (1993), 202.

248   *AES at Princeton:* AES to "Dearest Mum," 24, 28 Jan., 7 Feb. 1919.

248   *"generally useful":* AES to "Dearest Mum," 1 Feb. 1919.

248   *Hair treatments:* AES to "Dear Mother," 21 April 1921.

249   *Club selections:* Daily Princetonian, 22–25 March 1920; Frederic Rich, *The First Hundred Years of Ivy, 1879–1979* (1979).

249   *Quadrangle:* Quadrangle Club Records, Club Folder, University Archives; Informal records kept at Quadrangle; Samuel Schreiner, *A Place Called Princeton* (1984), 171; interview with Robert Harvey.

249   *"The general concensus":* AES to "Dear Mother," 21 April 1921.

250   *Kennan and clubs:* Walter Isaacson and Evan Thomas, *The Wise Men: Six Friends and the World They Made* (1986), 77.

250   *AES November weekend:* AES to "Dear Mother, Father, and Buff," 6 Nov. 1921; "Captain Hobart Baker," *Princeton Alumni Weekly,* 15 Jan. 1919.

250   *Mother gets his laundry:* T. S. Matthews, "Portrait with Scratches," *Vogue,* May 1966, 238.

250   *Cruelest thing a parent:* Ives, My Brother Adlai, 127.

250   *Mothers at college:* William Manchester, *American Caesar: Douglas MacArthur* (1978), 48; Rita Kleeman, *Gracious Lady: The Life of Sara Delano Roosevelt* [1935], 221. David McCullough, "Mama's Boys," *Psychology Today,* March 1983, 32–38.

250   *Coming for lunch:* HDS to AES, 17 Oct. 1918, 3 Oct. 1920; AES to "Dear mother," n.d. [Sunday], Family Folders.

251   *"Received your special":* AES to "Dear Father," 14 Nov. 1921.

251   *"Twenty-one years old":* HDS to AES, 5 Feb. 1921.

251   *Hibben remarks:* Princeton Alumni Weekly, 18, 22 June 1922; Daily Princetonian, 19–21 June 1922.

251   *Indecision on career:* Davis, Politics of Honor, 78–79.

252   *Father coming to get him:* Ibid.

252   *"the hardest graduate school":* AES to "Dearest Mother," 26 Sept. 1922.

252   *Harvard Law School:* Arthur Sutherland, *The Law at Harvard: A History of Ideas and Men, 1817–1967* (1967), 240–49.

252   *"was a city club":* AES to "Dearest Mother," 8 Oct. 1922.

252   *Harvard and Jews:* Nitza Rosovsky, *The Jewish Experience at Harvard and Radcliffe*

PAGE

(1986); Marcia Synnott, *The Half-Opened Door: Discrimination in Admission at Harvard, Yale, and Princeton, 1900–1970* (1979), 16, 58–84, 97.

252 *Stevenson's references to Jews:* AES to "Dearest Mother," n.d. [1924].

252 *"seemed very impressed":* AES to HDS, 26 Sept., 29 Oct. 1922.

253 *"Everyone works":* AES to "Dearest Mother," 26 Sept. 1922.

253 *"law school is sort of":* Ibid., 13 May 1924.

253 *"Law is indeed a jealous":* AES to Claire Birge, 11 May 1924, Johnson Papers.

253 *"I suppose it is natural":* HDS to "Dearest," 5 May 1924.

253 *"air castles":* AES to "Dear Mother," n.d. [1924].

253 *"appalling amount of law":* AES to "Dear Mother," 18 May 1924.

254 *"He was not eligible":* Dean Griswold to AES III, 24 April, 24 May 1967; also materials in Box 31, which include a copy of AES's application to Northwestern Law School, Martin Papers, LC. For evidence that AES argued that his course of study at Harvard was interrupted by the confusion at the *Pantagraph*, see James Ruhl to John Martin, 17 July 1975, Box 329, ibid.

254 *Interpretations of law school episode:* McKeever, *Adlai Stevenson,* 47, 50; Noel Busch, *Adlai E. Stevenson of Illinois* (1952) 51.

254 *"Departing . . . two years":* Alden Whitman, *Portrait: Adlai E. Stevenson: Politician, Diplomat, Friend* (1965), 17.

254 *"obliged to return home":* AES to Dean Griswold, 25 Jan. 1952, AES Papers, PUL; interview with Elizabeth Ives. "He did not fail, but at the end of his second year his standing had fallen below the level of his class," wrote Walter Johnson, the editor of the AES Papers, *Papers,* 1:111.

254 *"the mandate of the family":* AES to Claire Birge, 15 Feb. On returning to Bloomington, see AES to Claire Birge, 15 Aug., 23 Nov. 1924, 24 Jan. 1925, and, on his reaction to Bloomington, 23 Nov. 1924, 25 Sept. 1925, Johnson Papers.

255 *Agricultural prices:* Donald Tingley, *The Structure of a State: The History of Illinois, 1899–1928* (1980), 40.

255 *Strikes in Bloomington:* Greg Koos, ed., *Bloomington's C and A Shops: Our Lives Remembered* (1987).

255 *Bloomington's loss of jobs:* U.S. Department of Commerce, *Census of Manufacturers, Statistics for Industries: States and Cities* (1927), 6:177, 298.

256 *AES on the Scopes trial: Papers,* 1:161–63.

256 *Legal fight between Merwins and Stevensons:* Sinclair, *Pantagraph,* 218–20; Folder 11, IC; William O. Davis Will, Bloomington County Court House; Martin, *Illinois,* 1:76–78.

257 *Evaluation of will:* Thomas Washburne to Jean Baker, 18 Dec. 1991; Merwin vs. Stevenson, 246 Ill. App. 342; Oglevee and Franklin to Morrissey, Sullivan and Rust 24 May 1926, AES Papers, PUL; draft letter by LGS for AES, *Pantagraph* file, ibid.

257 *"anxiety to get control":* AES to Davis Merwin, 20 Dec. 1945, AES Papers, PUL.

CHAPTER 8: TOURS OF DUTY

258 *"astonishment to see Father":* AES to "Dearest Mum," 1 Aug. 1920, IC.

258 *Buffie's romance:* Elizabeth Ives, *My Brother Adlai* (1955), 194–95.

258 *"wasting time in galleries":* AES to Claire Birge, 8 March 1927. Subsequent references to letters to Claire Birge are to copies of Birge letters in Johnson Papers.

259 *"selling out to a system":* AES to "Dearest Claire," 4 Jan. [1927].

PAGE

259 *War debts:* Harold Moulton and Leon Pasvolsky, ~~War Debts and World Prosperity~~
(1933); Thomas Bailey, *A Diplomatic History of the American People* (1948), 700–
704.

259 *Reasons for U.S. intervention in Siberia:* William Graves, *America's Siberian Adventure, 1918–1920* (1971).

260 *"East really does meet"* and *"travelling alone":* AES to Claire Birge, 11 Sept. 1926.

260 *Undergraduate discussion group: Daily Princetonian,* 7, 14 Nov. 1920.

260 *Conditions in postwar Soviet Union:* Interview with Vlada Tolley.

260 *"turbulent confusion": Papers,* 1:388.

260 *"[We] must view the misery":* AES to Claire Birge, 2 April 1927.

261 *"I must confess":* AES to Claire Birge, 27 Oct. 1926.

261 *Hiring of AES:* Ed Austin Oral History, Robert Diller Oral History, ASOH; Austin
Interview, John Bartlow Martin Papers, PUL.

262 *"wandering with growing assurance":* AES to Claire Birge, 1 March 1928.

262 *"one of the standardized":* AES to Claire Birge, 19 April 1928.

262 *"If you had a dinner":* Stephen Hord Oral History, ASOH.

262 *"Cutting in" and freer courting practices:* Beth Bailey, *From Front Porch to Back Seat:
Courtship in 20th Century America* (1988), 3–5, 16–18, 31–34.

262 *Chicago society:* Arthur Meeker, *Chicago, with Love* (1955), 128–37; Fortnightly
Records, CHS.

262 *"an awful bumpkin":* AES to Claire Birge, 8 May 1925; *Chicago Social Register,
1926–1930,* LC.

262 *AES as a country boy:* Interview with Harriet Welling; interview with Jane Dick.

263 *"As to my alleged":* AES to Claire Birge, 2 Feb. 1927.

263 *"little moral foundation":* AES to "Dear Mother," 12 Oct. 1922, IC.

263 *"losing one's values":* AES to Claire Birge, 19 Jan. 1928.

263 *"dread ennui":* Ibid.

263 *Birge's coming-out party: New York Times,* 21 Dec. 1925.

263 *"College parties" and Claire's education:* AES to Claire Birge, 8, 27, 31 May 1925.

263 *Not to study economics:* AES to Claire Birge, 23 Oct. 1923.

263 *"Europe is an excellent climax":* AES to Claire Birge, 19 March 1924.

263 *Claire's education:* AES to Claire Birge, 27 May 1927.

263 *"I feel a new warmth":* AES to Claire Birge, 17 May 1927.

263 *"honest, clean, sincere":* AES to Claire Birge, 26 June 1925.

263 *Ellen's coming-out party: Chicago Tribune,* 28, 29 Dec. 1926; Meeker, *Chicago;* Fortnightly Records, CHS.

264 *Popularity of "Will You Love Me":* Michael Parrish, *Anxious Decades: American Prosperity and Depression, 1920–1941* (1992), 147–52.

264 *Information on John Borden:* Folder on John Borden, CHS; interview with Jane Dick;
interview with Harriet Welling.

264 *Ellen Waller Borden's affair:* Conversation with Howard Pollack.

264 *Ellen's academic record:* St. Timothy School Archives, St. Timothy's School, Stevenson, Md.

264 *Unchaperoned dating:* Bailey, *From Front Porch,* 3–5, 19, 22, 31.

265 *"Destiny is inevitable":* AES to Claire Birge, 3 Sept. 1928.

265 *"New York Jew Boys":* AES to Claire Birge, 19 April 1926.

265 *"Poet . . . , a musician":* AES to Claire Birge, 28 April, 3 Dec. 1928; *Papers,* 1:202;
AES to "Dearest Mother," 31 June, 2 July 1928, IC.

265 *Ellen's poetry:* Ellen Borden, "Songs I–IV," *Poetry: A Magazine of Verse* 32 (1928):
320–21.

PAGE

265 *"didactic and ministerial"*: AES to "Claire dearest," 31 May 1925.

265 *"disconcertingly younger"*: Ellen Stevenson to AES, quoted in Martin, *Illinois*, 108.

266 *"Remember, the women"*: AES to Claire Birge, 26 June 1925.

266 *Incident of red shoes*: Mrs. John Alden Carpenter Oral History, ASOH. For background on twentieth-century marriage, see John Modell, "Normative Aspects of American Marriage since World War II," *Journal of Family History* 5 (1980): 212–21.

266 *The Stevensons' reaction to Ellen*: Interview with Elizabeth Ives.

266 *"A woman should"*: Buffie Ives to AES, Sept. 1943, Family Folders.

266 *Reactions to Ellen and Adlai's romance*: Martin, *Illinois*, 87; Jane Dick Oral History, Harriet Welling Oral History, ASOH. *Ellen's age*: The year of her birth is variously given as 1907 and 1910, but the correct date is 1907.

266 *"the stuff and nonsense"*: AES to Claire Birge, 4 June 1926.

267 *Chicago development*: Harvey Zorbaugh, *Gold Coast and Slum: A Sociological Study of Chicago's North Side* (1929).

267 *"We've been suffering"*: AES to "Dearest Maw," 1 Feb. 1929, IC.

267 *Efforts to save money*: Ibid.

267 *Photographs of Ellen*: Scrapbooks, Box 1407, AES Papers, PUL.

267 *"the generation of"*: Quoted in Parrish, *Anxious Decades*, 149.

267 *"good reading"*: AES to HDS, 15 Feb. 1930, IC.

268 *Lewis's last words to his son*: Kenneth S. Davis, *The Politics of Honor* (1967), 106; *Papers*, 1:218; interview with Elizabeth Ives.

268 *Ellen's financial arrangements*: Ellen Borden Stevenson to "Dear Father," Box 225, AES Papers, PUL; Box 388, John Bartlow Martin Papers, LC; income tax returns, Box 1560, AES Papers, PUL; Robert Pirie to AES, 2 Feb. 1939, ibid.

268 *Borden's losses*: Elizabeth Ives Oral History, ASOH.

268 *Family planning and contraception*: Robert Lynd and Helen Lynd, *Middletown: A Study in Contemporary American Culture* (1929), 123–26; *Middletown in Transition* (1937), 166–69; Carl Degler, *At Odds: Women and the Family in America from the Revolution to the Present* (1980), 222.

269 *"In my own work"*: Kenneth Burgess to AES, 10 July 1934, AES Papers, PUL.

269 *Efforts to go into politics*: AES to "Dearest Maw," 23 Jan. 1930, IC.

269 *His contacts with Sprague*: AES to "Dearest Maw," 1 July 1934, IC.

269 *Talking to Democratic bigshots*: AES to "Dearest Maw," 23 Jan.. 6, 18 Feb. 1926 (copy), AES Papers, PUL; AES to Robert Dunham, n.d. [Feb. 1936], AES Papers, PUL; *Papers*, 1:317; Mathias Bauler to Robert Dunham, 18 Feb. 1936 (copy), AES Papers, PUL.

269 *"far more concerned"*: AES to Robert Dunham, 26 Feb. 1936, ibid.

269 *Support of Kelly*: AES to Edward Kelly, 18 March 1935, AES Papers, PUL; *Papers*, 1:294.

270 *AES's prediction on Roosevelt*: Austin Oral History, ASOH.

270 *AES's political maneuvering*: Martin, *Illinois*, 100–101.

270 *AES and Roosevelt*: Ives, *My Brother Adlai*, 112.

270 *Roosevelt's campaign*: Alonzo Hamby, "The Democratic Moment, FDR to LBJ," in Peter Kovler, ed., *Democrats and the American Idea* (1992), 250–53; Hamby, *Liberalism and Its Challengers: From FDR to Bush* (1992), 13–19, 22–23.

271 *AAA*: Arthur M. Schlesinger Jr., *The Coming of the New Deal* (1958), 40–45.

271 *"Louie Stevenson's boy"*: *Papers*, 1:240.

271 *"greatest law firm"*: Laura Kalman, *Abe Fortas: A Biography* (1990), 27, 28; idem, *Legal Realism at Yale, 1927–1960* (1986).

PAGE

271   *"bread lines, muttering masses"*: Speech at Carleton College, 1936, AES Papers, PUL.

271   *Hoover on apple selling*: Herbert Hoover, *Memoirs: The Great Depression, 1929–1941* (1952), 195.

272   *"a time when there was"*: Kalman, *Fortas*, 28.

272   *"the deep sense"*: Schlesinger, *Coming of New Deal*, 19.

272   *"yeasty and rarefied"*: Edward Doyle, ed., *As We Knew Adlai* (1966), 138.

272   *AES's criticism of FDR*: Speech at Carleton College.

272   *"virtually immune to scorn"*: *Papers*, 1:266.

272   *AAA policies*: Schlesinger, *Coming of New Deal*, 36–51.

273   *"My first job"*: Speech to Legal Club of Chicago, James Oates Microfilm, ISHS; *Papers*, 1:267.

273   *"Lambkin, think of it"*: *Papers*, 1:248.

273   *Letters to Ellen*: Martin, *Illinois*, 105–9.

273   *"men with their hair ablaze"*: Quoted in Schlesinger, *Coming of New Deal*, 46.

274   *"plague of young lawyers"*: Quoted ibid., 16. See also ibid., 16–18.

274   *"The Chief Attorney"*: AES to "Dear Madam," 13 Feb. 1934, IC.

274   *AES's Interpretation of New Deal*: *Papers*, 1:266–78.

274   *"I can look forward"*: Ibid., 278–79.

274   *"Bad government is bad politics"*: Ibid., 278. For other examples of elite manhood and its practitioners from the establishment, see Walter Isaacson and Evan Thomas, *The Wise Men: Six Friends and the World They Made* (1986), 32–35, 72–73, 736–41.

275   *In and outers*: David Stanley et al., *Men Who Govern: A Biographical Profile of Federal Political Executives* (1967), 45–46, 57.

275   *"in both leagues"*: Edward Austin to AES, 6 Sept. 1945, AES Papers, PUL.

275   *Hutchins story*: *Papers*, 1:284.

275   *"fascination with public affairs"*: AES to Kenneth Davis, 19 March 1957, AES Papers, PUL.

275   *Income tax returns, 1933–40*: Boxes 1434, 1560, PUL. For Ellen Stevenson's finances, interview with J. Stuart Ingram.

275   *"unremitting pressure"*: AES to Buffie Ives, 27 March 1937, IC.

276   *Working like a "beaver"*: AES to "Dear Buff," 11 Aug. 1937, IC.

276   *AES's interest in being U.S. attorney*: AES to Victor Rotnem, 6 March 1935, AES Papers, PUL.

276   *"I would be delighted"*: AES to Harold Ickes, 19 March 1935, ibid.

276   *"If something comes along"*: AES to Frances Perkins, 4 May 1937, ibid.

276   *The council*: *Papers*, 1:332.

276   *"Council is not a club"*: AES to Mary Welsh, 2 Oct. 1936, AES Papers, PUL.

276   *"lunch and learn"*: *Papers*, 1:361.

277   *AES and his style*: *Papers*, 1:310–12, 405–14; James Oates microfilm, introductions, ISHS.

277   *Ross incident*: Kenneth T. Jackson, *Chicago Council on Foreign Relations* (1963), 21; *Sixty Years of International Understanding: The Chicago Council on Foreign Relations, 1922–1982* (1982), 1–10.

277   *European situation and Masaryk*: Jackson, *Chicago Council*; *Papers*, 1:322, 326, 334–37; James Oates microfilm, ISHS.

277   *"simple lawyer"*: *Papers*, 1:376.

278   *"dictators would soon"*: Handwritten notes to 1938 speech, Council of Foreign Relations File, AES Papers, PUL; *Papers*, 1:376–82.

PAGE

278 *"the world is on fire":* James Oates microfilm. *Fire images: Papers,* 1:376.

278 *"new ideology":* Ibid., 394, 398.

278 *Helen's health:* Interview with Elizabeth Ives.

278 *"But most of all":* AES to HDS, n.d., IC.

278 *"unlax":* AES to "Dear Maw," Sept. 1934, IC.

278 *Tells Tree he thought mother insane:* Martin, *Illinois,* 118. *Diagnoses of Helen:* Ibid., 122, 131.

278 *"the strange irony":* Buffie to AES, 2 Dec. 1935, typescript of Elizabeth Ives letters, Family Folders.

279 *"chimney pots spouting":* AES to "Buff," 27 March 1937, IC; Michael Ebner, *Creating the North Shore* (1988). On Ellen's rusticity, see Jane Dick Oral History, ASOH; Martin, *Illinois,* 155. On American women and cosmetics, see Parrish, *Anxious Decades,* 15.

279 *"our mechanical house":* Martin, *Illinois,* 145.

279 *Story of fire:* Noel Busch, *Adlai E. Stevenson of Illinois* (1952), 4; *Papers,* 1:382.

280 *Lost "treasures":* AES to John Brown, 20 Jan. 1938, AES Papers, PUL. Income tax returns are in Box 1560, PUL, as are inventories of St. Mary's Road insurance claims.

280 *"Our family is vanishing":* AES to "Buffie," 20 Feb. 1937, IC.

280 *"a dysfunctional family":* Interview with Borden Stevenson.

280 *Sees John Fell once a week: Papers,* 1:350.

280 *A compulsive worker:* Martin, *Illinois,* 151.

280 *A "busy" dad:* John Fell Stevenson Oral History, ASOH; written comments by John Fell Stevenson to Jean H. Baker.

280 *Ellen's parenting and AES's reaction:* Interview with Borden Stevenson; interview with Adlai Stevenson III.

281 *Concept of "libidinal motherhood":* Barbara Ehrenreich, *For Her Own Good: 150 Years of the Expert's Advice to Women* (1979), 219.

281 *"ended up in the kitchen":* AES to "Dear Buffie," Sept. 1945, AES Papers, PUL.

281 *"working from 7":* AES to "Dear Buffy," 10 Oct. 1945, AES Papers, PUL.

281 *Ellen described as satisfied:* AES to "Dear Buff," 31 Jan. 1945, AES Papers, PUL.

281 *AES's social popularity:* AES to "B & E" [Buffie and Ernest Ives], 9 Jan. 1937, AES Papers, PUL.

281 *born to be a housewife:* Martin, *Illinois,* 230.

281 *Changing food standards:* Laura Shapiro, *Perfection Salad* (1986), 219. For Ellen's lunch menu, see Martin, *Illinois,* 155.

282 *Deteriorating marriage:* AES to Jane Dick, n.d. Martin Papers, LC.

282 *Ellen forgets her ticket:* AES introduction of Ernest Price, 25 Oct. 1935, AES Papers, PUL.

282 *"effective feminine weapon of": Papers,* 1:348.

282 *"the other day":* Ibid., 324.

282 *"I must be an exhausting husband":* Ibid., 2:449.

282 *"Ellen will have her way":* Diary, 25 Jan. 1947, AES Papers, PUL.

282 *"his war department":* Martin, *Illinois,* 150.

282 *Ellen's partying:* AES to "Dear Buffie," 10 July 1937, AES Papers, PUL.

282 *"This is the place":* Ellen Borden Stevenson to AES, n.d., postcard, Box 1367, AES Papers, PUL.

282 *"instinct to fight a bully":* AES to Charles Dawes, 18 Jan. 1939, AES Papers, PUL.

282 *An ideological battle: Papers,* 1:427–28.

282 *"It is in our interest":* AES to "Tonnie" [Mrs. John Alden Carpenter], 27 June 1940, AES Papers, PUL.

PAGE

283   AES's position on defense: Papers, 1:457.

283   "our way of life": Michael Prosser, ed., An Ethic for Survival: Adlai Ewing Stevenson
      Speaks on International Affairs (1969), 41, 49, 51.

283   Testimony to convention: Papers, 1:461.

283   "your boys are": New York Times, 30 Oct. 1940.

284   Argument over American position: James Schneider, Should Americans Go to War?
      The Debate over Foreign Policy in Chicago, 1939–1941 (1989).

284   "I do not believe there": Papers, 1:537.

284   "the present state of public mind": AES to Edward Ryerson, 8 July 1940, AES Papers,
      PUL.

284   "We believe that 'isolation' ": Papers, 1:457.

284   America Firsters: Wayne Cole, America First: The Battle against Intervention (1953);
      David Brinkley, Washington Goes to War (1988), 51; Schneider, Should Americans,
      35.

285   Materials on the rally: Box 1407, AES Papers, PUL.

285   Time devoted to CDAA: AES to Scott Lucas, 9 Sept. 1940, ibid.; Papers, 1:489.

285   Issue of Jews on platform: AES to William Hale, 18 Dec. 1940; Papers, 1:525–26.

296   "Liberty is like air": Scrapbooks, Box 1407, AES Papers, PUL.

296   Wartime Washington: Brinkley, Washington Goes to War, 18–23.

297   Knox: Paolo Coletta, American Secretaries of the Navy (1980), 2:685.

297   Kearny expedition: Secretary of Navy File, 42-1-24, Record Group 80, NA.

297   Delivering messages to FDR: Martin, Illinois, 192–93.

298   "legal maid servant": AES to Davis Merwin, 26 July 1941, AES Papers, PUL.

298   AES's efforts to get a wartime job: AES to Thomas Woodward, 4 June 1941; AES to
      Oscar Cox, 27 June 1941; AES to Herbert Emmerich, 27 June 1941, AES Papers,
      PUL.

298   "restless anxiety to help": AES to Kenneth Burgess, 17 July 1941, AES Papers, PUL.

298   AES "autobiography": AES to Newton Rogers, 11 Sept. 1941, AES Papers, PUL.

298   "odd jobs": Washington Times-Herald, 14 April 1942.

298   "sparse thatch and ample girth": AES to Charles Shipway, 15 May 1941, AES Papers,
      PUL.

298   "We are getting older": Martin, Illinois, 197.

298   Ellen wants to end marriage: Ibid.

299   Caribbean trip: AES diary, 24 June–5 July 1942, AES Papers, PUL.

299   "loquacious and [told] me": AES diary, 28 Jan. 1943, AES Papers, PUL.

300   "good soldier twenty years ago": AES diary, 23 Jan. 1943, AES Papers, PUL.

300   AES's list of congressmen: Papers, 2:64; Frank Knox to AES, 10 Nov. 1942 (copy),
      Martin Papers, Box 231, LC; Julius Furer, Administration of the Navy Department
      in World War II (1959), 46–55.

300   Memorandum on racial policies: AES to Frank Knox, 9 Sept. 1943, Secretary of
      Navy Files, Frank Knox, File 54-1-50, Record Group 80, NA.

300   Douglas commission: AES to Paul Douglas, 1 Jan. 1942, AES Papers, PUL.

300   Obtaining a commission: Frank Knox to AES, 26 April 1942, AES Papers, PUL.

300   Files taken from Washington: Martin, Illinois, 223.

301   "Sea power saved us from defeat": Papers, 2:139.

301   "disquieting degree": Ibid., 119.

301   "Many people talk": Secretary of Navy Correspondence, File 29-2-27, Knox memo-
      randum, 25 July 1943, Record Group 80, NA.

301   Views on Russia: Papers, 2:145–46.

301   "But tomorrow is not yesterday": Ibid., 143.

PAGE

301 *"No one has enough"*: Speech to Decalogue Society of Lawyers, March 1944, AES Papers, PUL.

301 *background on Italy*: Carl Friedrich, *American Experiences in Military Government in World War II* (1948), 111–47.

302 *FEA mission*: *Papers*, 2:165–205; Report of FEA Survey Mission to Italy, 2 Feb. 1944, AES Papers, PUL.

302 *"a congenital taste"*: *Papers* 2:253.

302 *"From what I had already"*: AES, *Major Campaign Speeches* (1953), xviii.

303 *"that to help Italy"*: Diary, 23 Dec. 1944, AES Papers, PUL.

303 *Forrestal's attitude toward AES*: George Ball Oral History, ASOH; James Douglas Oral History, Martin Papers, PUL; Martin, *Illinois*, 222.

303 *Johnson on leases*: Rowland Evans and Robert Novak, *Lyndon B. Johnson: The Exercise of Power* (1966), 16n.

303 *"The force of money"*: AES to Hermon Smith, 19 Oct. 1944, AES Papers, PUL.

304 *AES on other wartime jobs*: AES to Abbot Low Moffatt, 30 June 1944, AES Papers, PUL.

304 *Ball and strategic bombing survey*: AES to George Ball, 6 Oct. 1944, AES Papers, PUL; *Papers*, 2:216–17; Wesley F. Craven and James L. Cate, eds., *The Army Air Forces in World War II*, vol. 3, *Europe: Argument to V-E Day* (1951), 789–92.

304 *No evidence that bombing broke morale*: George Ball, *The Past Has Another Pattern* (1982), 406, 421.

304 *"old, time, bench"*: Notes, 1945, Box 1407, AES Papers, PUL.

304 *"An underground news"*: *Papers*, 2:237.

304 *Ellen's poem*: Cited in speech to Chicago Bar Association, 28 June 1945, AES Papers, PUL.

305 *AES at conference*: U.S. Department of State, *Foreign Relations of the United States*, vol. 1, *General: The United Nations* (1945), 830, 977; U.S. Department of State, *U.S. Foreign Policy Documents*, U.S. Delegation to the U.N. Conference on International Organization, San Francisco (1945), 34.

305 *"I'm just a machinist"*: *Papers*, 2:279.

305 *Accepted "piecework"*: AES to Kenneth Burgess, 24 Sept. 1945, AES Papers, PUL.

305 *"with the rank of"*: AES to Edwin Austin, 4 Sept. 1945, AES Papers, PUL.

305 *"to have a small place"*: AES to Archibald MacLeish, 25 Jan. 1945, AES Papers, PUL.

305 *"It was the most exacting"*: AES, *Major Speeches*, xx; *Papers*, 2:295.

306 *"golden age of America"*: *Washington Times-Herald*, 14 April 1942.

306 *"house with a lot of"*: Michael Prosser, ed., *An Ethic for Survival: Adlai Stevenson Speaks on International Affairs* (1969), 63.

306 *"We must choose"*: Ibid., 62. The other quotations in this paragraph are from *Papers*, 2:145, 322, 360, 370.

306 *AES's reactions to UN*: Speech to Commercial Club, 9 March 1946, AES Papers, PUL; *Papers*, 2:296–314.

306 *"They never look"*: *Papers*, 2:301.

307 *"I'm weary"*: AES to Jane Dick, 12 Sept. 1947, AES Papers, PUL; *Papers*, 2:413. On the development of Cold War policy, see Isaacson and Thomas, *Wise Men*.

307 *"Obviously our resources"*: *Papers*, 2:405.

307 *"Where do we go"*: Speech of 20 May 1947, *Papers*, 2:397–406.

307 *"the organized conscience"*: Ibid., 381, 382.

CHAPTER 9: TALKING SENSE

PAGE

308   *Division in Democratic party:* Alonzo Hamby, "The Democratic Moment, FDR to LBJ," in Peter Kovler, ed., *Democrats and the American Idea* (1992), 248–50.

309   *Civil rights platform: Official Report of the Proceedings of the 1952 Democratic Convention,* 274.

309   *Wallace movement:* Curtis MacDougall, *Gideon's Army* (1965), 2:541.

310   *"The President always controls":* Harry Truman, *Memoirs,* vol. 2, *Years of Trial and Hope* (1956), 491–92; Robert Ferrell, *Off the Record: The Private Papers of Harry Truman* (1980), 245.

310   *"more anxious every day":* AES to Barry Bingham, 4 July 1952, AES Papers, PUL.

310   *"I have talked":* Newsday, 21 July 1952. For background on Patterson's coverage, see Robert Keeler, *Newsday: A Candid History of the Respectable Tabloid* (1990), 182.

311   *Convention:* Paul T. David et al., *The Politics of National Party Conventions* (1960), 189, 195, 242–52, 317.

311   *Article on AES: Life,* 21 July 1952.

311   *Activities by amateurs:* Walter Johnson, *How We Drafted Adlai Stevenson* (1955), 4, 10, 72.

311   *"I shall never": Papers,* 4:10.

311   *AES's behavior:* John Bartlow Martin, 1952 Journal, Box 51, John Bartlow Martin Papers, LC.

311   *Illinois delegates:* William Blair Oral History, ASOH.

312   *"I do not dream": Papers,* 4:11.

312   *Description of caucus:* Clarence Berdahl et al., *Democratic Presidential Politics in Illinois,* (1952), 37.

312   *Background on convention: New York Times,* 21–26 July 1952.

312   *"We are highly honored": Proceedings of 1952 Convention,* 4.

312   *"I thought I came":* "Welcoming Speech to 1952 Democratic Convention," AES Recordings, ISU.

312   *"to talk himself out": New York Times,* 22 July 1952. For a description of Stevenson, see Martin, 1952 Journal, Martin Papers, LC.

312   *nominating speeches for Stevenson: Proceedings of 1952 Convention,* 318–25.

313   *"I have been trying":* Truman, *Memoirs,* 2:496.

313   *"There was an old man": Papers,* 4:15.

313   *"I did not seek it":* Martin, *Illinois,* 600; *New York Times,* 22 July 1952.

313   *Kefauver balloon:* Elizabeth Ives, *My Brother Adlai* (1956), 264.

314   *"He's too accomplished":* Stephen Ambrose, *Eisenhower: Soldier, General of the Army, President-Elect* (1983), 545.

314   *Description of Eisenhower:* Emmet John Hughes, *The Ordeal of Power: A Political Memoir of the Eisenhower Years* (1963), 18; Peter Lyon, *Eisenhower: Portrait of the Hero* (1952), 439–52. On his early life, see ibid., 33–39; Kenneth S. Davis, *The Politics of Honor* (1967), 257; Ambrose, *Eisenhower,* 529–45.

314   *"pompous phrases," "an American Story,"* and *"We must sail": Papers,* 4:12, 13.

315   *"The road we travel":* AES, *Major Campaign Speeches* (1953), 22.

315   *"have to win":* Edward Doyle, ed., *As We Knew Adlai* (1966), 107.

315   *Concept of puritan in politics:* Rodney Sievers, *The Last Puritan? Adlai Stevenson in American Politics* (1983). On guilt in politics, see AES, *Major Speeches,* 9.

PAGE

316   *"Single greatest difficulty"*: Papers, 6:259; AES, *What I Think* (1956), 37.

316   *"the staggering task"*: Papers, 4:19.

316   *"I shall always try"*: Ibid. Sievers, *Last Puritan*, 44–45, 126; Gordon Keller, "The Political Ideas and Ideals of Adlai Ewing Stevenson in Two Presidential Campaigns" (Ph.D. diss., Syracuse University, 1968); idem, "Adlai Stevenson: The Moral Responsibility of Power," *Humanist* 27 (May–June 1967): 91; Stevenson, *What I Think*, 36.

316   *"full freedom of action"*: Truman, *Memoirs*, 2:562.

316   *On using the Bible*: Campaign Materials, Box 102, 30 Oct. 1956, AES Papers, PUL.

317   *"political Peter Pan"*: New Republic, 8 Dec. 1952.

317   *"I have asked the Merciful"*: Papers, 4:16.

317   *"literally driven to drink"*: Joseph Alsop, *I've Seen the Best of It* (1992), 340.

317   *"in your own charming"*: Cardinal Stritch to AES, 26 July 1952, AES Papers, PUL.

317   *"A steadfast rule"*: Alsop, *I've Seen the Best*, 340.

317   *AES's as a great speech*: Joseph Alsop to Carl McGowan, 31 July 1952, AES Papers, PUL; Kathleen Jamieson, *Packaging the Presidency: A History and Criticism of Presidential Campaign Advertising* (1984), 60.

318   *The road theme*: Lloyd Garrison to AES, 29 July 1952, AES Papers, PUL; Martin, Speech in Baltimore, Box 53, Martin Papers, LC.

318   *"A hard road opens"*: Dean Acheson to AES, 30 July 1952, AES Papers, PUL.

318   *"The road is hard"*: AES to Dean Acheson, 31 July 1952, AES Papers, PUL.

318   *Republican campaign strategy*: Document X, Robert Humphreys Folder, 1952, Eisenhower Presidential Library, Abilene, Kan.; Douglas Paul Slaybaugh, "Adlai Stevenson and Political Public Relations, 1952–1956; or, The Yoke Was on Him" (Ph.D. diss., Cornell University, 1981), 7–15.

318   *Appointments and the Springfield headquarters*: Wilson Wyatt, *Whistle Stops* (1985), 95, 99–100, 106–7; interview with William Blair; interview with Wilson Wyatt. On Wyatt as manager, see AES II to "Dear Bear" (AES III), 2 Aug. 1952, letter in possession of AES III.

318   *Press conference*: Box 263, AES Papers, PUL; Slaybaugh, "Political Public Relations," 31.

319   *reports about Ellen*: AES to Robert Pirie, 21 Feb. 1952; AES III to "Dear Bear," 7 June 1952, letter in possession of AES III. James Cox, the Democratic candidate in 1920, had a brief first marriage, but had remarried by the time of the campaign in 1920.

319   *"troubled heart"*: AES to Archibald MacLeish, 14 Aug. 1952, AES Papers, PUL.

319   *"at what it means psychologically"*: Papers, 4:41, 43; AES to Irving Dilliard, 19 Sept. 1952, AES Papers, PUL.

319   *AES on speech writers*: George Ball, *The Past Has Another Pattern* (1982), 124.

319   *"secretly and unconsciously"*: Martin, 1952 Journal, Martin Papers, LC.

320   *Grand Rapids meeting*: Bradford Jacobs to Jean H. Baker, 15 Dec. 1990.

320   *"You must emerge"*: Stevenson, *Major Speeches*, xii (italics added).

320   *AES and television*: Jamieson, *Packaging the Presidency*, 58–62.

320   *"The garden variety"*: Doyle, *As We Knew Adlai*, 144.

320   *Hersey's comment*: AES File, 1960, FBI File 94–40154, FBI Archives, Washington, D.C.

320   *"The more I saw him"*: Alsop, *I've Seen the Best*, 341.

321   *Cartoons and images of AES*: Slaybaugh, "Political Public Relations," 86, 93; Stevenson Scrapbooks, Box 1446, AES Papers, PUL.

PAGE

321   *Eisenhower and TV:* Jamieson, *Packaging the Presidency,* 81–85; Ernest Barnouw, *Tube of Plenty: The Evolution of American Television* (1975), 137.

321   *AES and television:* Jamieson, *Packaging the Presidency,* 58–60, 63–64; Slaybaugh, "Political Public Relations"; Wyatt, *Whistle Stops,* 106.

321   *Eisenhower Answers America:* Jamieson, *Packaging the Presidency,* 82–85, 87–88. On the reaction to preempting *I Love Lucy,* see ibid., 44.

321   *Eisenhower and spontaneity:* Louis Galambos, ed., *The Papers of Dwight David Eisenhower,* vol. 13, *NATO and the Campaign of 1952* (1989), 1282 n. 3, 1286 n. 12; Ambrose, *Eisenhower,* 531–32, 550; Wyatt, *Whistle Stops,* 106.

321   *"if a party purchased":* AES, *Major Speeches,* xxiv.

322   *AES on television:* Tapes of 1952 campaign, Milner Library, ISU; Jamieson, *Packaging the Presidency,* 58–60, 63–66, 88; Andy Schlesinger, *Adlai Stevenson: The Man from Libertyville,* distributed by Films for the Humanities, Princeton, N.J.; Slaybaugh, "Political Public Relations," 86–95, 331; Doyle, *As We Knew Adlai,* 125–26.

322   *AES and the teleprompter:* Jamieson, *Packaging the Presidency,* 64; Blair Oral History, ASOH.

322   *AES advertisements:* Box 51, Martin Papers, LC.

322   *Eisenhower campaigns harder:* Ambrose, *Eisenhower,* 551.

323   *Campaigns as measure of the man:* New York Times, 18 Sept. 1952. On Eisenhower's detailed itinerary, see Martin, *Illinois,* 625.

323   *Speech to Legionnaires: Papers,* 4:49–53; AES, *Major Speeches,* 17–22.

323   *"I should tell you": Papers,* 4:51.

323   *AES as a Cold Warrior:* C. Eric Sears, "Adlai Ewing Stevenson and the Early Cold War" (Ph.D. diss., University of Hawaii, 1976), 44–50.

323   *AES in New Haven:* John Brademas Oral History, ASOH.

323   *"goons and violence":* Speech in Evanston, Ill., 1952 Speeches, AES Papers, PUL.

323   *tidelands oil:* AES, *Major Speeches,* 101, 235,

323   *In Harlem:* Martin, *Illinois,* 744.

323   *"Your public servants serve":* Los Angeles Meeting, Box 53, Martin Papers, LC; Civil Rights Folder, 1952 Campaign, AES Papers, PUL.

324   *"For God's sake":* Martin, 1952 Journal, Martin Papers, LC, also quoted in Ball, *Another Pattern,* 130.

324   *Ignores Spellman dinner:* Martin, *Illinois,* 762.

324   *Doesn't criticize McCarthy in Massachusetts:* Ibid., 743; Sears, "Early Cold War," 110; David Koskoff, *Joseph Kennedy* (1974), 78.

324   *"God's coattails":* Illinois State Register, 18 Sept. 1952.

324   *Whistle-stopping in California:* John Robert Greene, *The Crusade: The Presidential Election of 1952* (1985), 199–201; Martin, 1952 Journal, Martin Papers, LC.

324   *AES's whistle-stopping:* U.S. News & World Report, 17 Oct. 1952. On Ike and Mamie whistle-stopping, see Ambrose, *Eisenhower,* 551.

324   *Pantagraph's nonendorsement:* Bud Merwin to "Ad," 12 June 1952; Davis Merwin to "Ad," 20 July 1952, AES Papers, PUL; *Pantagraph,* 12 June 1952.

325   *Wyatt mistaken for AES:* Martin, 1952 Journal, Martin Papers, LC.

325   *Dislike of repeating himself:* Wyatt, *Whistle Stops,* 100–107. AES overlooked historical examples of duplicated speeches, including Bryan's often delivered "Prince of Peace" speech and AES I's tariff speech.

325   *"I [will] make a proposition":* Martin, *Illinois,* 673–74.

325   *Speech in Bakersfield:* AES, *Major Speeches,* 226; 1952 Campaign Materials, AES Papers, PUL.

PAGE

325 *Organization of whistle-stopping:* Martin, 1952 Journal, Martin Papers, LC; Wyatt, *Whistle Stops,* 106.

325 *Even pace of delivery:* Harvey Koizim to AES, 19 Oct. 1952, AES Papers, PUL.

325 *Not wing away: Papers,* 6:28; Gil Troy, *See How They Run: The Changing Role of the Presidential Candidate* (1991), 201.

325 *"If they don't like":* Doyle, *As We Knew Adlai,* 149.

325 *Nearly one-half of the electorate:* Angus Campbell et al., *The American Voter* (1960), 23–26.

325 *The Nixon fund:* Stephen Ambrose, *Nixon: The Education of a Politician, 1913–1962* (1987), 278–95; Richard Nixon, *Six Crises* (1962), 126.

326 *Differential press coverage of funds:* Arthur Rowse, *Slanted News: A Case Study of the Nixon and Stevenson Fund* (1957).

326 *AES fund:* Martin, *Illinois,* 694–98, 700–703, 766–68, appendix; AES Fund Accounts, Boxes 268–70, AES Papers, PUL.

327 *"However distasteful":* AES, *Major Speeches,* 190. For AES's explanation of the presents he gave his associates, see ibid., 189–91; Greene, *Crusade,* 192–95.

327 *AES's investments:* Rufus Brent to AES, 26 June, 21 Aug. 1952, AES Papers, PUL.

327 *"He is not just":* "Adlai the Investor," *Barron's,* 13 Oct. 1952.

328 *AES thinks he might win:* AES to "Dear Bear," 5 Oct. 1952, letter in possession of AES III.

328 *"an educational and elevating":* AES, *Major Speeches,* 269.

328 *"McCarthyism in a white collar":* Martin, *World,* 129.

328 *"cut down a redwood":* Porter McKeever, *Adlai Stevenson* (1989), 230.

328 *Lawyers on AES's obligation:* New York Times, 19 Oct. 1952.

328 *"arsenal of accusation":* AES, *Major Speeches,* 274; Ambrose, *Nixon,* 297–98.

328 *AES on Hiss case:* AES, *Major Speeches,* 269; AES file on Nixon, Box 271, AES Papers, PUL. On campaign libel, see Willard Pedrick, "Senator McCarthy and the Law of Libel," *Northwestern University Law Review,* 135–85, copy in Governor's Papers.

329 *Nixon regrets campaign's intensity:* Richard Nixon, *R.N.: The Memoirs of Richard Nixon* (1978), 110–11; Sears, "Early Cold War," 246.

329 *Not bear false witness:* AES, *Major Speeches,* 272.

329 *"The Republicans undermine":* Ibid., 275.

329 *Eisenhower and divorce:* Marquis Childs, *Witness to Power* (1975), 67–68; Kay Summersby Morgan, *Past Forgetting: My Love Affair with Dwight Eisenhower* (1976), 146–47, 155, 160; Merle Miller, *Plain Speaking: An Oral Biography of Harry S. Truman* (1973), 339–40; McKeever, *Stevenson,* 238–40; materials in Boxes 51, 65, Martin Papers, LC.

329 *AES as a homosexual:* "Adlai Stevenson," FBI Files 94-40154, FBI Archives; Mr. Rosen to Mr. Ladd, 22 Aug. 1952; Re: Information on AES, 25 Aug. 1952; Athan Theoharis, "How the F.B.I. Gaybaited Stevenson," *Nation,* 7 May 1990; Curt Gentry, *J. Edgar Hoover: The Man and the Secrets* (1991), 402–3.

330 *"notorious homosexual":* Gentry, *Hoover,* 445.

330 *"through a devious route":* Ibid., 402.

330 *"A vote for Stevenson":* Ibid., 445; Neal Gabler, *Winchell: Gossip, Power, and the Culture of Celebrity* (1994), 498–99.

330 *"lavender lads":* New Republic, 18 Aug. 1952.

330 *Republican attacks on Stevenson:* Slaybaugh, "Political Public Relations," 95.

330 *"As long as there were":* Barbara Ehrenreich, *The Hearts of Men: American Dreams*

PAGE

and the Flight from Commitment (1982), 22–26, 104; Campbell, *American Voter*, 25; Troy, *See How They Run*, 205.

331 *"overwhelmed by increasing demands"*: Quoted in Ehrenreich, *Hearts of Men*, 24.

331 *"If a man can't"*: Personal communication from Dr. Woodford Howard.

331 *Ellen's project for "The Egghead and I"*: Interview with J. Stuart Ingram; clipping in Ingram File, in possession of author; Martin, *Illinois*, 647; Keeler, *Newsday*, 179.

331 *Ellen announces for Eisenhower*: *New York Times*, 18 July, 5 Nov. 1952.

331 *"if words"*: Clipping (n.d, n.p.) in Ingram File.

331 *Republican characterization of AES as weak*: Slaybaugh, "Political Public Relations," 165; Marquis Childs, *Eisenhower: The Captive Hero* (1958), 150–55.

331 *Eisenhower and Marshall*: Ambrose, *Eisenhower*, 564–67; Forrest Pogue, *George C. Marshall* (1989), 497–98.

331 *AES on civil liberties*: Irving Howe, "Stevenson and the Intellectuals," *Dissent* 1 (1954): 18.

332 *"systematic program of innuendo"*: AES, *Major Speeches*, 269.

332 *Possibility of debate*: Kathleen Jamieson and David Birdsell, *Presidential Debates: The Challenge of Creating an Informed Electorate* (1988), 92–93, 103; AES, *Major Speeches*, 269.

332 *"plans be made"*: John Toland, *In Mortal Combat: Korea, 1950–1953* (1971), 548. The issue involved North Korean soldiers who wanted to stay in South Korea and the North Korean claim that the United Nations was forcing their retention.

332 *"Is it amusing"*: Childs, *Captive Hero*, 157; Ambrose, *Eisenhower*, 569.

332 *"While the General"*: Speech in Milwaukee, 10 Oct. 1952, AES Papers, PUL.

333 *"I promise no easy"*: AES, *Major Speeches*, 188.

333 *Effect of Eisenhower's visit to Korea*: Martin, 1952 Journal, Martin Papers, LC: Martin, *Illinois*, 741–42.

333 *"The General has announced"*: Speech in Boston, 26 Oct. 1952, AES Papers, PUL; Martin, *Illinois*, 741–42.

333 *"for the American cathedral"*: AES, *Major Speeches*, 312.

333 *"Let us remember"*: Ibid., 284.

333 *Final message*: Campaigning with Stevenson, Museum of Broadcast Communications, Chicago.

333 *"If your decision"*: AES, *Major Speeches*, 316.

333 *"What you see here"*: Martin, 1952 Journal, Martin Papers, LC; AES, *Major Speeches*, 317–18.

334 *Analysis of election results*: Walter Dean Burnham, *The Current Crisis in American Politics* (1982), 31, 55, 153–55.

334 *"The parties and the leaders"*: Michael Avey, *The Demobilization of American Voters* (1989), 11.

334 *Woman with diamond*: Martin, *Illinois*, 759.

334 *"Too many people"*: Ball, *Another Pattern*, 130.

334 *"a natural drawing together"*: AES to Stuart Brown, 27 Jan. 1956, AES Papers, PUL.

335 *"We ran out of poor people"*: Martin, *Illinois*, 762.

335 *Analysis of Democratic vote*: Campbell, *American Voter*, 278; Martin, *Illinois*, 760–65; Burnham, *Decline*, 55, 153, 155.

335 *"My dominant impression"*: AES to John Milder, 29 Dec. 1952, AES Papers, PUL.

335 *"I've no regrets"*: AES to Alicia Patterson, 6 Nov. 1952, Johnson Papers.

335 *"moribund Democratic organization"*: Quoted in Raymond Yeager, "A Rhetorical Analysis of the 1952 Presidential Campaign Speeches of Adlai Ewing Stevenson" (Ph.D. diss., Ohio State University, 1956), 186.

PAGE

335 *Suspicion of eloquent speakers: New York Times,* 27 Dec. 1994.

336 *"left Mr. and Mrs. America":* Joseph Casey to Arthur Schlesinger, 2 Oct. 1952 (copy), Box 51, Martin Papers, LC.

336 *"What is the lesson":* AES, *Major Speeches,* 197–98.

336 *The progressive endorsement:* William Stevenson Oral History, ASOH.

336 *ADA support of AES:* Steven M. Gillon, *Politics and Vision* (1987), 83–85.

337 *"Here was this remarkable":* Howe, "Stevenson and the Intellectuals," 13.

337 *AES's appeal to postwar liberals:* Sievers, *Last Puritan,* 7.

337 *"You were too good":* Jean McDonald to AES, 12 Nov. 1952, Box 385, AES Papers, PUL.

337 *"a citizen at large":* AES to Norman Cousins, 10 Dec. 1952, AES Papers, PUL.

337 *"without the stark":* Quoted in Jeff Broadwater, *Adlai Stevenson* (1994), 131.

337 *"The damnable schedule":* AES to Alicia Patterson, 19 Sept. 1953, Johnson Papers; *Papers,* 4:273.

338 *"I only want enough":* Martin, *World,* 157.

338 *AES as party leader:* AES, *What I Think,* ix–x.

338 *"As for party leadership":* AES to Herbert Lehman, 26 Nov. 1952, Lehman Papers, Columbia University Library; AES to Frank Altschul, 29 Dec. 1956, AES Papers, PUL.

338 *Issues group:* AES to Tom Finletter, 14 March 1956, AES Papers, PUL; Martin, *World,* 83, 87.

338 *Hoped to educate him:* John Galbraith to AES, 23 Oct. 1953, Box 377, Martin Papers, LC, interview with Arthur Schlesinger Jr.

338 *"chronic stamina":* AES to Alicia Patterson, 20 Aug. 1951, Johnson Papers.

339 *"Anywhere in the world":* AES to John Sparkman, 10 Aug. 1954, AES Papers, PUL.

339 *Criticism of AES:* Howe, "Stevenson and the Intellectuals," 20; *New Republic,* 1, 15 June, 3 Aug. 1953.

340 *"calculated campaign":* Quotations from speech in Miami: *Papers,* 4:327–33.

340 *"more than a partisan": New York Times,* 14 March 1954. On Eisenhower and McCarthy, see Fred Greenstein, *The Hidden-Hand Presidency: Eisenhower as Leader* (1982), 202–13.

340 *"squalid, disgraceful":* Martin, *World,* 129.

340 *"a ghastly vaudeville":* Stevenson to John Paulding Brown, 3 May 1954, AES Papers, PUL.

340 *"The quality that is missing":* AES, *What I Think,* 207; AES, "What I Believe," Box 151, AES Papers, PUL.

341 *"Even though one is":* Meridian, Miss., speech, Box 63, AES Papers, PUL. See also *New York Times,* 18 May 1954; Martin, *World,* 122–24.

341 *"Much of the talk":* AES statement, 27 May 1954, AES Papers, PUL.

341 *"His feelings for the":* Interview with Joseph Rauh.

341 *"go-slow boys":* Roy Wilkins, *Standing Fast: The Autobiography of Roy Wilkins* (1984), 232.

341 *"wild men":* AES to Ralph Bunche, 7 Aug. 1952, AES Papers, PUL.

342 *AES's comment on Till:* Martin, *World,* 238.

342 *"Why can't they go":* Quoted in John Frederick Martin, *Civil Rights and the Crisis of Liberalism: The Democratic Pary, 1945–1976* (1979), 139, 36, 115.

342 *AES cuts off questioner: Papers,* 4:605. (To put AES's attitude in context, it is worth remembering that John Kennedy did not want to go to a NAACP dinner in

the late 1950s, because he thought it would be interpreted as a ploy for black votes.)

342 *"We must recognize"*: Official Report of the Proceedings of the Democratic National Convention, 418.

342 *Materials on Civil Rights*: Civil Rights, Box 272, AES Papers, PUL; Martin, *World*, 131.

342 *AES and Faubus: Face the Nation* transcripts, 8 Sept. 1957, AES Papers, PUL.

343 *"So long as man"*: AES, *Major Speeches*, 155; Herbert Lehman to AES, 2 Feb. 1965; AES to Herbert Lehman, 11, 20 Feb. 1965, AES Papers, PUL.

343 *AES on civil rights: Papers*, 5:605, 6:64–67.

343 *"The profound questions"*: Ibid., 6:257; Martin, *World*, 116, 264; Martin, 1952 Journal; Civil Rights Folder, Box 62; "Harlem," 27 Oct. 1952, Box 62, Martin Papers, LC; Civil Rights Folder, Box 58, AES Papers, PUL.

343 *Their "assignment," "once immersed"*: AES, *What I Think*, 182–89; Nancy Anderson to "the gov," 6 June 1955, AES Papers, PUL.

344 *AES splits royalties with Ward*: AES to Barbara Ward, 6 July 1955, AES Papers, PUL.

344 *"executive branch"*: Ambrose, *Nixon*, 344–45.

345 *"If Viet-Nam falls"*: AES, "Ballots and Bullets," *Look*, 2 June 1953.

345 *"boasts, bluffs, and brinks"*: AES speech in Omaha, 7 Aug. 1954, AES Papers, PUL.

345 *"You are asking"*: AES, "Ballots and Bullets."

CHAPTER 10: ON THE ROAD

346 *"to recover my strength"*: AES to Michael Kirwan, 2 Nov. 1954, AES Papers, PUL; *Papers*, 4:428.

346 *No political ambitions*: Ibid., 439.

346 *"a better man might"*: AES to Agnes Meyer, 12 Aug. 1955, AES Papers, PUL. (All AES-Meyer correspondence cited in this chapter is in AES Papers, PUL.)

347 *"an elderly moralist"*: Speech at Vassar commencement, 14 June 1954, AES Papers, PUL.

347 *Issue of renomination*: Paul T. David et al., *The Politics of National Party Conventions* (1960), 115; letters to AES, Box 263, AES Papers, PUL.

347 *AES's view of Eisenhower*: Interview with AES III; Elizabeth Stevenson Ives Oral History; William Blair Oral History, ASOH; AES to Jimmy Sheean, 14 July 1952, AES Papers, PUL.

347 *Willing to step aside*: Herbert Parmet, *The Democrats: The Years after FDR* (1976), 121.

347 *"the drama of an"*: George Ball Oral History, ASOH; see also Ball, *The Past Has Another Pattern* (1982), 115, 130.

347 *"Duty? Can any impersonal"*: AES to Agnes Meyer, 19 Dec. 1955, AES Papers, PUL.

347 *"operation bromide"*: *Papers*, 6:111, AES to Jimmy Sheean, 14 July 1952, AES Papers, PUL.

347 *"old devil 'destiny' "*: AES to Lady Mary Spears, 15 June 1955, AES Papers, PUL.

347 *AES steering committee*: Edward Doyle, ed., *As We Knew Adlai* (1966), 87. See also Newt Minow File, Box 461, AES Papers, PUL; AES to Alicia Patterson, n.d. [1955], Johnson Papers.

348 *"Don't spare the rod"*: AES to Seymour Harris, 6 Dec. 1955, AES Papers, PUL.

PAGE

348 *AES polls sons:* Interview with Borden Stevenson.

348 *Christmas decorations:* Patricia Harris, *Adlai: The Springfield Years* (1975), 152–55; Elizabeth Ives, *My Brother Adlai* (1956), 1, 62, 74.

348 *"a difficult interlude":* AES to Buffie Ives, 12 Dec. 1955, AES Papers, PUL.

348 *"I don't know what":* Ives, *My Brother Adlai,* 308.

348 *"Let go your hold":* C. Eric Sears, "Adlai Ewing Stevenson and the Early Cold War, 1941–1954" (Ph.D. diss., University of Hawaii, 1977), 53.

348 *Reminded of mother's motto:* AES to Alicia Patterson, 8 Feb. 1956, Johnson Papers.

349 *"enjoying the chase":* Clark Clifford, *Counsel to the President* (1991), 284.

349 *"Winning is hard enough":* Eleanor Roosevelt to AES, cited in Parmet, *Democrats,* 121.

349 *On Tree:* Marie Brenner, "Marietta Tree: Aristocratic Democrat," *Vanity Fair,* Dec. 1991, 210–20, 288–300; interview with Marietta Tree; Marietta Tree Oral History, ASOH.

349 *Casual nudity:* Jane Dick Oral History, ASOH: interview with Borden Stevenson.

349 *"escape myself":* AES to John Paulding Brown, 20 July 1955, AES Papers, PUL; Martin, *World,* 30.

350 *"I have to keep":* Agnes Meyer to AES, 10 July 1955.

350 *Meyer's relation to AES:* Interview with Dr. Edward Maumanee; interview with Jane T. Gilbert.

350 *Meyer bored with Illinois:* Martin, *World,* 190.

350 *"Careful please:"* AES to Agnes Meyer, 14 June 1955.

350 *"Adlai my Hero":* Agnes Meyer to AES, n.d. [1955], 2 Nov. 1955.

350 *Niece's reaction:* Agnes Meyer to AES, 3 June, 7 July 1955.

350 *"who didn't have heart":* Agnes Meyer to AES, 9 Sept. 1955.

351 *"never let fly":* Agnes Meyer to AES, 16 June 1955.

351 *"How I hate":* Agnes Meyer to AES, 24 Sept. [1955].

351 *"Let us not argue":* AES to Agnes Meyer, 8 Aug. 1955.

351 *"Whether you are elected":* Agnes Meyer to AES, 3 Aug. [1956].

351 *"feminine understanding":* AES to Agnes Meyer, 9 Sept. 1955.

351 *Meyer's diagnoses:* Agnes Meyer to AES, 3, 16, 20 June, 7, 26 July, 2 Aug., 9 Sept. 1955, 16 July, 1 Aug. 1956; *Papers,* 6:43–44.

351 *"The world loves a fighter":* Martin, *World,* 195–96.

351 *Arvey describes AES as a politician: Time,* 16 July 1956; Ashmore memorandum, 12 Sept. 1955, AES Papers, PUL.

352 *"surprising degree": Papers,* 4:591–94.

352 *Despises extemporaneous speaking:* AES to Agnes Meyer, 8 Feb. 1956.

352 *"kicking away":* AES to Alicia Patterson, 11 Oct. 1955, Johnson Papers.

353 *"What [a man] knows: Papers,* 4:339.

353 *"the deflating retort":* Doyle, *As We Knew Adlai,* 183.

353 *Kefauver's primary campaign:* Charles Fontenay, *Estes Kefauver: A Biography* (1980), 235.

353 *"[The presidency] is":* AES to Herbert Agar, 24 Feb. 1956, AES Papers, PUL.

354 *"What do they think":* Ball, *Another Pattern,* 135.

354 *"The primaries make": Washington Post-Dispatch,* 9 Dec. 1985. For an analysis of conventions, see James W. Davis, *National Conventions in an Age of Reform* (1983), 172–81; Elaine Kamarck, "Delegate Allocation Rules in the Presidential Nomination System," *Journal of Law and Politics* 4 (1987): 277–81; Kenneth S. Davis, *The Politics of Honor* (1967), 323–26; AES to "Dear Bear," 26 May 1956, AES Papers, PUL.

PAGE

354   *"Eggheads of the world"*: Martin, Journal, Martin Papers, LC; Martin, *World*, 254–55.

354   *Quotes Locke:* AES, *The New America* (1957), 257.

354   *"[You] seem to be"*: Frances? to Chester Bowles, 29 Feb. 1956; AES to Chester Bowles, 14 March 1956, Chester Bowles Papers, Yale University.

355   *"intense young liberals"*: AES to Agnes Meyer, 8 Feb. 1956.

355   *"The problem of changing"*: AES speech at University of Minnesota, 2 March 1956, AES Papers, PUL.

355   *"How you can write"*: AES to Jonathan Daniels, 8 April 1955, *Papers*, 4:466.

355   *Caldwell story:* John Frederick Martin, *Civil Rights and the Crisis of Liberalism: The Democratic Party, 1945–1976* (1979), 141–42.

355   *Tree's comment:* Martin, *World*, 122; AES to Agnes Meyer, 15 June 1956.

355   *Educating AES on civil rights:* Interview with Marietta Tree; AES to Eleanor Roosevelt, 15 June 1956, Roosevelt Library, Hyde Park.

355   *AES's emphasis on party unity:* Parmet, *Democrats*, 136.

356   *AES hates campaigning against Kefauver:* Ball, *Another Pattern*, 135.

356   *A new AES: Papers*, 6:106.

356   *"My long, carefully considered"*: AES to Tom Finletter, 14 Feb. 1956, Bowles Papers; Memo to "J.B.M." [John Bartlow Martin], Box 64, AES Papers, PUL.

356   *Truman's reaction:* Robert Ferrell, *Off the Record* (1980), 262.

356   *Analysis of AES speeches:* Russell Windes, "The Speechmaking of Adlai Ewing Stevenson in the 1956 Presidential Campaign" (Ph.D. diss., Northwestern University, 1959).

356   *AES III on father's speeches:* Martin, *World*, 316.

356   *"become more concrete"*: Schlesinger, "How to Win the Campaign," Aug. 1956, Box 441, AES Papers, PUL; *Papers*, 6:95.

356   *"I'm Adlai Stevenson"*: Martin, 1956 Journal, Martin Papers, LC.

357   *Description of primary:* Charles Thomson and Francis Shattuck, *The 1956 Presidential Campaign* (1974), 44, 48, 55. See also Martin, 1956 Journal, Martin Papers, LC.

357   *"For Christ's sake"*: Doyle, *As We Knew Adlai*, 229.

357   *"loving truth"*: AES to John Hersey, 11 July 1956, AES Papers, PUL.

357   *Two Adlais:* John Brademas Oral History, ASOH; Doyle, *As We Knew Adlai*, 283.

357   *AES hides himself:* Interview with Arthur Schlesinger.

357   *Gift of an eagle:* Agnes Meyer to AES, 7 July 1956.

357   *"A slippery sinister forehand"*: Tree Oral History, ASOH.

358   *Episode with Marc Connelly:* Martin, *World*, 25.

358   *"Faith in what"*: Agnes Meyer to AES, 9 Dec. 1955.

358   *Shift to Unitarianism: Papers*, 617–18.

358   *AES's ethical values:* Richard Graebel to AES, 12 Dec. 1955, AES Papers, PUL.

358   *Dick on AES's religiosity:* Jane Dick Oral History, ASOH.

358   *AES's speech in Miller Park: Pantagraph*, 5 July 1956.

359   *Changing patterns of choosing delegates:* David, *National Party Conventions*, 226–35, 325–35. Over 2,500 delegates were certified, but most had half a vote.

360   *"Adlai seemed quite serene"*: Martin, *World*, 347.

360   *Fight over civil rights platform:* David, *National Party Conventions*, 101; *Official Report of the Proceedings of the Democratic National Convention* (1956), 323–30.

360   *AES on civil rights:* Box 63, Martin Papers, LC; Martin, *World*, 348.

361   *Liberal versus conservative struggle over civil rights: Official Proceedings*, 322; Steven M. Gillon, *Politics and Vision* (1987), 99; John Frederick Martin, *Civil Rights*, 146–52.

PAGE

361   *"I simply want"*: Proceedings, 311, 524.

361   *Meeting of Minow and Neuberger*: Martin, *World*, 349.

362   *AES's reaction to Kennedy*: Wilson Wyatt, *Whistle Stops* (1985), 127.

362   *AES's proposal for selecting vice president*: Proceedings, 420.

362   *"I mean a New America"*: AES, *New America*, 4.

363   *"There is in the world"*: Ibid., 8.

363   *Liberalism*: Alonzo Hamby, *Beyond the New Deal: Harry Truman and American Liberalism* (1973), xiii; Gary Gerstle, "The Protean Character of American Liberalism," *American Historical Review* 99 (1994): 1043.

363   *Changes in liberalism and Democratic ideology*: Parmet, *Democrats*, 114–16; E. J. Dionne, *Why Americans Hate Politics* (1991), 31–109; AES, *What I Think* (1956), 10–12; AES, *New America*, 257–60.

364   *"The same Adlai"*: Alden Whitman, *Portrait: Adlai E. Stevenson* (1965), 154.

364   *"You must appear"*: Agnes Meyer to AES, 17 Aug. 1956.

364   *"Last time"*: AES to Dean Acheson, 26 Aug. 1956, AES Papers, PUL.

365   *Robert Kennedy story*: Robert F. Kennedy Interview, Martin Papers, PUL. See also Robert Kennedy interview, John F. Kennedy Oral History Program, JFKL; Martin, *World*, 234–35; Arthur M. Schlesinger Jr., *Robert F. Kennedy and His Times* (1978), 133–36; *Papers*, 6:355.

365   *Campaign advertising*: Ball, *Another Pattern*, 143.

365   *Murrow story*: A. M. Sperber, *Murrow: His Life and Times* (1986), 500.

365   *AES and television*: Campaign Films, Milner Library, ISU; Kathleen Jamieson, *Packaging the Presidency* (1984), 97–98; Craig Allen, "Peace, Prosperity and Prime Time Television: Stevenson and Eisenhower and T.V. Politics of 1956" (Ph.D. diss., Ohio University, 1989).

366   *"The road I have"*: AES to Walter and Helen Lippmann, 8 June 1956; AES to Marian and Arthur Schlesinger, 8 June 1956, AES Papers, PUL.

366   *Description of AES's suitcase*: Whitman, *Portrait*, 162.

366   *"Please, please"*: Isabel Watkins to Democratic National Committee, Box 63, 1956, AES Papers, PUL.

366   *"We know also"*: John Steinbeck to Fred Hoehler, 16 Oct. 1956, Hoehler Papers, University of Minnesota Library.

367   *"man who looks forward"*: Citizens for Eisenhower-Nixon, 1956, Box 6, Young and Rubicam Papers, Eisenhower Library, Abilene, Kan.

367   *Culture of the 1950s*: Benita Eisler, *Private Lives: Men and Women of the Fifties* (1986); Martin Mayer, *The Builders: Houses, People, Neighborhoods, Governments, and Money* (1978), 312; John Diggins, *The Proud Decades: America in War and Peace, 1941–1960* (1988), 177–78, 348–50; Douglas Miller and Marion Nowak, *The Fifties: The Way We Really Were* (1977), 105–22.

367   *"only a million American"*: Quoted in William Chafe, *The Unfinished Journey* (1991) 111; Henry Luce, "Speculation about A.D. 1980," in *Fortune: The Fabulous Future* (1956), 186.

368   *Use of Franklin*: Miller and Nowak, *Fifties*, 119.

368   *Business advertises capitalism*: Robert Griffith, "The Miracle of America," in Robert Griffith, ed., *Major Problems in American History since 1945*, 200–205.

368   *Labor issues*: Chafe, *Unfinished Journey*, 94.

368   *"a basic antagonism"*: AES, "My Faith in Democratic Capitalism," *Papers*, 4:566.

369   *"as if we were"*: Quoted in Chafe, *Unfinished Journey*, 111–12; *New Republic*, 21 May 1956.

369   *"It is a time"*: AES, *What I Think*, 110.

PAGE

369 "the great chasms": Robert D. Griffith, "Dwight D. Eisenhower and the Corporate Commonwealth," *American Historical Review* 87 (1982): 87–122, quotations on 89–91.

369 "These are the sorry": Labor Day speech, Cadillac Square, Detroit, Mich., 1956 Speeches, AES Papers, PUL. For AES on schools, see AES, *New America*, 118; on "health security," ibid., 134; on farm life, ibid., 164. See also Miller and Novak, *Fifties*, 116, 122–23.

370 "The roaring hot-rod": AES, *New America*, 119.

370 "Ordeal of the Mid-century": AES, *Call to Greatness* (1954).

370 AES and Wilson: David Steigerwald, *Wilsonian Idealism in America* (1994), 204–7. See also Irving Howe, "Stevenson and the Intellectuals," *Steady Work* (1966), 209–13.

370 "when we encounter": AES, *Call to Greatness*, 95–96.

370 "[Stevenson] ran for president": John Kenneth Galbraith, *A Life in Our Times: Memoirs* (1981), 289.

371 AES's programs for elderly and health care: AES, *New America*, 135–57.

371 AES and paying for programs: Interview with Wilson Wyatt; Davis, *Politics of Honor*, 320.

371 AES on the economy: AES, *New America*, 85–101.

371 Learning to be a Keynesian: Seymour Harris to AES, 24 May 1956, 20 July 1956; AES to Seymour Harris, 15 April, 6 Dec. 1955, 31 July 1956, AES Papers, PUL.

371 Proposals for ending the draft and a test ban: Speech to American Society of Newspaper Editors, 21 April 1956; television broadcast, 15 Oct. 1956, Milner Library, ISU; AES, *New America*, 17–27, 44–58, 59–63.

372 campaigning his way: AES to Gerald Johnson, 26 Aug. 1955, AES Papers, PUL.

372 "unfairly suspect": *Papers*, 6:115. On hydrogen bomb testing, see *New York Times*, 16, 17 March 1954.

372 "People everywhere": AES, *New America*, 48–49.

373 Atomic popular culture: Miller and Nowak, *Fifties*, 56.

373 "I believe we should": AES, *New America*, 24. For materials on nuclear issue, see also "Atomic Power," Box 68, Martin Papers, LC.

373 "earth's atmosphere . . .": AES, "Statement regarding Strontium," Hydrogen Bomb folder, 1956, AES Papers, PUL.

373 Support from a surgeon: A. Evarts Graham to AES, 27 Oct. 1956, AES Papers, PUL; AES, *New America*, 46–48; *Papers*, 6:283–84.

373 "This specific matter": Quoted in Stephen Ambrose, *Eisenhower*, vol. 2, *The President* (1984), 348.

374 "Can you imagine": Wyatt, *Whistle Stops*, 131.

374 Nixon's comments on Stevenson: Stephen Ambrose, *Nixon*, 418–19.

374 "I am sure I": AES to Barbara Jackson, 13 Oct. 1956, AES Papers, PUL.

374 Eisenhower and the test ban: Martin, *World*, 366–78,

375 "We can anticipate": Speech to American Legion, Speeches, Box 63, 1956, PUL; AES, *New America*, 59–66.

375 "life's ordained course": AES, *New America*, 63.

375 Bowles's comprehensive plan: Chester Bowles to AES, 10, 13 Oct. 1956, Bowles Papers.

375 "We cannot prove wise": Quoted in Martin, *World*, 367.

375 Eisenhower on AES's proposal: Ambrose, *Eisenhower*, 2:350. On Eisenhower as a leader, see ibid., 17; Fred Greenstein, *The Hidden-Hand Presidency: Eisenhower as Leader* (1982), 97–98.

376 "We went into 1956": McGowan interview, Martin papers, PUL.

PAGE

376   *Reactions to AES in surveys:* Angus Campbell et al., *The American Voter* (1960), 51, 57–63, 527–28.

376   *"imagine putting Mr. Nixon":* Papers, 6:307.

376   *"of looking at oneself":* Quoted in Alan Brinkley review of David McCullough's *Truman*, in *New York Times*, 21 June 1992.

376   *"Victory is, after all":* Papers, 6:259.

377   *"The Republican candidates":* Ibid., 258.

377   *"President doesn't run":* AES, *New America*, 39; Martin, *World*, 142.

377   *"that monkey":* Porter McKeever, *Stevenson* (1989), 259; Ambrose, *Eisenhower*, 2:370.

377   *Eisenhower's blood pressure:* Richard M. Nixon, *RN: The Memoirs of Richard Nixon* (1978) 111.

378   *AES's reaction to Nixon:* Interview with Wilson Wyatt; interview with AES III.

378   *"has put away his":* Papers, 6:316.

378   *"irresponsible, vindictive, malicious":* Speech to New York Liberal Party, 1956 Speeches, Box 63, AES Papers, PUL.

378   *Eisenhower offering Nixon a cabinet post:* Ambrose, *Nixon*, 292–93.

378   *"Nixonland":* AES, *New America*, 249.

378   *Israeli, British, and French attack:* Diane Kunz, *The Economic Diplomacy of the Suez Canal* (1991); *New York Times*, 4 Nov. 1956; Papers, 6:302–4.

379   *AES's proposals for Middle East:* Box 99, AES Papers, PUL; Martin, *World*, 388; *New York Times*, 31 Oct. 1956.

379   *"bankruptcy of U.S. policy":* Papers, 6:311.

380   *"I hope this child":* Interview with Elizabeth Ives.

380   *"to distinguish right":* Boston Folder, 1956, Box 101, AES Papers, PUL; Martin, *World*, 389.

380   *"We Democrats see":* Papers, 6:322–23.

380   *"Me thought I saw":* Papers, 6:324–25.

381   *Powell's switch:* Charles Hamilton, *Adam Clayton Powell: The Political Biography of an American Dilemma* (1991), 270–74.

381   *"All the evidence indicates":* AES to "Aunt Julia," 16 Nov. 1956, Scott-Hardin Papers, Cornell University. See also AES to Albert Greenfield, 16 Nov. 1956, AES Papers, PUL.

381   *Analysis of election:* Campbell, *American Voter*, 239–49, 280–90.

382   *"I am profoundly alarmed":* AES to Edith and Herbert Lehman, 9 Nov. 1956, AES Papers, PUL.

382   *"Sheep-like qualities":* AES to Agnes Meyer, 14 Oct. 1955.

382   *"democratic dialogue":* Gil Troy, *See How They Run* (1991), 207, 208.

382   *Party identifications:* Gerald Pomper, *Elections in America: Control and Influence in Democratic Politics* (1973), 85–89.

382   *"a civilized man's search":* New Republic, 7 Aug. 1965.

382   *"to kick around":* Ambrose, *Nixon*, 671.

383   *"with a full heart":* Papers, 6:327.

383   *"that life wasn't going":* Interview with Arthur Schlesinger.

CHAPTER 11: IN THE SHADOWS

398   *Description of meeting with Kennedy:* New York Times, 10 Dec. 1960.

398   *"I can think of no American":* Ibid., 9 Dec. 1960.

PAGE

398 *"While I have not sought"*: Ibid.; Porter McKeever, ~~Adlai Stevenson (1989), 474;~~ *Washington Post*, 9, 13 Dec. 1960.

398 *AES's conditions:* "Conditions Given to J.F.K.," Dec. 1960, AES Papers, PUL.

398 *Kennedy's recruiting of cabinet:* Theodore Sorenson, *Kennedy* (1965), 254–56.

399 *"never said please"*: Eward Doyle, ed., *As We Knew Adlai* (1966), 178; AES to Arthur Schlesinger, 21 May 1960, AES Papers, PUL.

399 *"an old woman"*: Robert Kennedy Oral History, I, JFKL.

399 *AES sailing with Kennedy:* Michael Beschloss, *The Crisis Years: Kennedy and Khrushchev* (1991), 466–67. On JFK as an intellectual, see ibid., 466, 467.

399 *Kennedy thinks AES prissy:* David Halberstam, *The Best and the Brightest* (1969), 37.

399 *"idealistic weeper"*: Thomas Paterson, ed., *Kennedy's Quest for Victory: American Foreign Policy, 1961–1963* (1989), 19.

399 *"very self-confident and assured"*: Arthur M. Schlesinger Jr., *A Thousand Days: John F. Kennedy in the White House* (1965), 25.

399 *"boy commandos"*: AES to Agnes Meyer, 14 May 1961, AES Papers, PUL; Martin, *World*, 634.

399 *"the decline of moral purpose"*: *Papers*, 7:457.

399 *"hated to think"*: George Ball Oral History, ASOH.

400 *"the center of the concern"*: Henry Fairlie, *The Kennedy Promise: The Politics of Expectation* (1973), 175. On Kennedy's toughness, see Paterson, *Kennedy's Quest*, 14.

400 *Kennedy nominating speech: Official Proceedings of the Democratic National Convention*, 1956, 343–45.

400 *"I have felt that I launched"*: AES to Arthur and Marian Schlesinger, 7 June 1960, AES Papers, PUL.

400 *"I will not seek"*: AES Committee Materials, 1960, Box 809, AES Papers, PUL; Bill Attwood to AES, 17 June 1960, AES Papers, PUL.

400 *"to work for the avowed"*: Martin, *World*, 457; AES to Harvey C. Webster, 21 June 1960; AES to Gerald Johnson, 12 June 1960, AES Papers, PUL.

400 *Kennedy announces:* Sorenson, *Kennedy*, 122.

400 *Kennedy visit to Libertyville:* Newton Minow Oral History, ASOH; Stuart Gerry Brown, "Notes on a Conversation with Adlai Ewing Stevenson," 29 March 1961, AES Papers, PUL; Schlesinger, *Thousand Days*, 4–25.

401 *"He said to me"*: George Ball, *The Past Has Another Pattern* (1982), 158; William Blair Oral History; Newt Minow Oral History, ASOH.

401 *Draft Stevenson committee:* 1960 Campaign Materials, "In Support of Stevenson Nomination," Box 787, Box 804, AES Papers, PUL. (Box numbers are included for clarification.)

401 *"You have overdone"*: Agnes Meyer to AES, n.d. [1960], AES Papers, PUL.

401 *"Isn't it about time"*: John Forbes, "The 1960 Democratic and Republican National Conventions," Box 787, AES Papers, PUL.

401 *"nostalgically for Stevenson"*: Stuart Brown interview with Eleanor Roosevelt, 1956, Box 804, AES Papers, PUL.

401 *"a curious religious order"*: Mary Bancroft to AES, 12 Aug. 1960, AES Papers, PUL.

402 *Not "personally a candidate"*: Face the Nation tapes, 10 July 1960, LC.

402 *"a much richer, more thoughtful"*: Arthur M. Schlesinger Jr., *Robert F. Kennedy and His Times* (1978), 203.

402 *Description of convention:* Forbes, "1960 Democratic and Republican Conventions."

402 *AES at convention:* Stuart Gerry Brown interviews and memo, Box 804, AES Papers, PUL; Theodore White, *The Making of the President, 1960* (1961), 162–67.

PAGE

402   *"Your guy must be"*: Blair Oral History, ASOH; Martin, *World*, 522.

402   *AES's dislike of Joseph Kennedy*: Thomas Matthews, "Portrait with Scratches: Adlai Stevenson," *Vogue*, May 1966, 240.

402   *AES at the convention*: New York Times, 13 July 1960.

402   *Demonstration for AES*: Schlesinger, *Thousand Days*, 38–39; Gerald Strober and Deborah Strober, *"Let Us Begin Anew": An Oral History of the Kennedy Presidency* (1993), 11–13.

403   *AES's speech: Official Proceedings of the Democratic National Convention, 1960*, 61.

403   *Disappointment with speech*: Stuart Brown interview with Eleanor Roosevelt, 1960, AES Papers, PUL; Lawrence Fuchs Oral History, JFKL; Robert Benjamin Oral History, ASOH.

403   *Disappointment with AES*: Agnes Meyer interview, John Bartlow Martin Papers, LC: Robert Nathan Oral History, JFKL.

403   *Kennedy asks for a nominating speech*: Martin, *World*, 527; McKeever, *Stevenson*, 460; Robert Kennedy Oral History, Martin Papers, PUL.

403   *"But my incorrigible friends"*: Forbes materials on 1960 campaign; interview with Eugene McCarthy, Box 804, AES Papers, PUL.

403   *McCarthy's speech: Proceedings of the 1960 Convention*, 140–42.

403   *Kennedy says "Go—Go"*: Alonzo Hamby, *Liberalism and Its Challengers* (1985), 193.

403   *AES's behavior at convention*: Strober, *"Let Us Begin Anew,"* 6–10.

404   *"It never occurred to me"*: AES to John Kenneth Galbraith, 18 Aug. 1960, AES Papers, PUL.

404   *"If I said": Papers*, 7:450.

404   *"political accident"*: AES Diary, 3 March 1960, South America Notebook, comment to Fernando Belaunde-Terry of Peru, AES Papers, PUL.

404   *AES's activities before convention*: Speeches, 27 Jan. 1960, Box 120, AES Papers, PUL; *Papers*, 7:453–60.

404   *U-2: Papers*, 7:495, 497.

404   *"could have taken it away"*: AES as quoted by Meyer in Agnes Meyer to AES, 16 Sept. 1960, AES Papers, PUL.

405   *"the Stevenson people"*: AES to Lady Barbara Jackson, 29 July 1960, AES Papers, PUL.

405   *AES and the Kings*: Taylor Branch, *Parting the Waters: America in the King Years, 1954–1963* (1988), 360.

405   *AES won't call King*: Harris Wofford, *Of Kennedys and Kings: Making Sense of the 1960's* (1980), 17, 51.

405   *Intransigence of South and impatient northern liberals*: AES to Agnes Meyer, 25 Aug. 1957, AES Papers, PUL.

405   *"Revolving Richard": Papers*, 7:534.

405   *Voice in the dark*: William Attwood, *The Reds and the Blacks: A Personal Adventure* (1967), 10.

405   *Cicero and Demosthenes*: Murray Kempton in *New York Post*, 2 Nov. 1960; Kempton Folder, Box 788, AES Papers, PUL.

405   *"I would never do that"*: Mary McGrory in Doyle, *As We Knew Adlai*, 177–78.

405   *AES introduces Kennedy: Official Proceedings of Democratic National Convention*, 236–37.

405   *Rusk adds Kennedy's name*: Thomas Schoenbaum, *Waging Peace and War: Dean Rusk in the Truman, Kennedy, and Johnson Years* (1988), 16.

PAGE

405   *Kennedys use AES campaigns as negative examples:* Kenneth O'Donnell et al., *Johnny We Never Knew You: Memories of JFK* (1960), 124, 126.

406   *AES expects to be appointed secretary of state:* AES to "Dear Martha" [Mrs. T. S. Matthews], 28 July 1960; AES to Robert Hutchins, 15 Aug. 1960, AES Papers, PUL.

406   *"could not go to work for":* AES to Agnes Meyer, 10 Jan. 1961, AES Papers, PUL.

406   *Report on foreign policy:* "Report to John Fitzgerald Kennedy—Draft on Foreign Policy," Box 789, AES Papers, PUL.

406   *Ball draft of report:* Schlesinger, *Thousand Days,* 155.

406   *AES won't read it:* George Ball Oral History, ASOH.

406   *"Why should he appoint you":* Blair Oral History, ASOH; interview with William Blair; *New York Times,* 17 July 1961; Attwood, *Reds,* 7.

406   *Kennedy thinks AES too controversial: Papers,* 8:594; Strober, *"Let Us Begin Anew,"* 118–19, 122–26; Edwin Guthman and Jeffrey Shulman, eds., *Robert Kennedy in His Own Words* (1988), 6.

406   *Kennedy needs consensus:* John Martin interview with Walter Lippmann, Martin Papers, PUL.

406   *"will chew him alive":* Beschloss, *Crisis Years,* 48.

406   *"[I] would bring the confidence":* AES to Robert Hutchins, 15 Aug. 1960, AES Papers, PUL.

406   *FBI reports on AES in 1960:* FBI Reports, Main File, 94-40134, File 1, Special Inquiry, 1960, 161-138, FBI Archives, Washington, D.C.; Guthman and Shulman, *Robert Kennedy,* 6; Branch, *Parting the Waters,* 402; Curt Gentry, *J. Edgar Hoover* (1991), 403, 478.

407   *FBI on AES visiting pornographic exhibits:* Clyde Tolson to the Director, 30 April 1962, Stevenson File, 94-40154.

407   *"any strong president":* John Steinbeck to William Blair, 24 May 1960, AES Papers, PUL.

407   *Taking exams:* Interview on BBC, 27 July 1959, AES Papers, PUL.

407   *Balance sheet on joining the UN:* AES notes on the UN, n.d., Box 801, AES Papers, PUL.

407   *"after all you've":* Blair Oral History, ASOH.

407   *continue as "we are":* Minow Oral History, ASOH.

407   *"incapable of taking himself":* John Martin interview with George Ball, Martin Papers, PUL.

407   *AES's job description for UN:* "Some Miscellaneous Paragraphs," 30 Dec. 1960; "Conditions Given to JK by Phone," Box 789, AES Papers, PUL;

407   *AES won't work with Bundy:* Martin, *World,* 561; Strober, *"Let Us Begin Anew,"* 124–25; Harlan Cleveland Oral History, JFKL.

408   *"Waste no tears":* AES to Alicia Patterson, 1 Jan. 1960, Johnson Papers.

408   *"as a dangerous slide":* Fairlie, *Kennedy Promise,* 64.

408   *"no nation in all history":* Memorandum for John Kennedy, n.d. [1960], Box 789, AES Papers, PUL.

408   *False missile gap:* Richard Walton, *Cold War and Counterrevolution: The Foreign Policy of John Kennedy* (1977), 6–8; Theodore White, "The Action Intellectuals", *Life,* June 1967, 43; Fairlie, *Kennedy Promise,* 103–7.

408   *The Kennedy team:* Halberstam, *Best and Brightest,* 50–54; Robert Kennedy Interview, JFKL; Schlesinger, *Thousand Days,* 127–45.

408   *Counterforce–no cities:* Deborah Shapley, *Promise and Power: The Life and Times of Robert McNamara* (1993), 138–44.

PAGE

409   *"almost wise-guy language"*: Beschloss, *Crisis Years,* 3.

409   *"never seem[ing]"*: Cleveland Oral History, JFKL; McGeorge Bundy Interview, Martin Papers, PUL; "Reflections on the New Frontier," Oral History with members of JFK staff, Richard Donahue, JFKL.

409   *"Stevenson was a disappointing"*: Richard Gardner Oral History, JFKL.

409   *Jokes about AES:* Halberstam, *Best and Brightest,* 32.

409   *"Stevenson wouldn't be happy"*: Paterson, *Kennedy's Quest,* 19.

409   *"the discredited liberals"*: Robert Kennedy Oral History, JFKL.

409   *"The torch has been"*: Fairlie, *Kennedy Promise,* 68–75, 103–7.

409   *"the brightest and best"*: Shapley, *Promise and Power,* 92.

409   *Story of AES walking:* Strober, *"Let Us Begin Anew,"* 177; interview with AES III.

410   *AES wants a professional staff:* AES to Wilson Wyatt, 28 Aug. 1962; AES to Charles Noyes, 27 Aug. 19622, AES Papers, PUL.

410   *AES doesn't appoint African-Americans:* Chuck Stone to John Seigenthaler, 16 July 1964 (copy), AES Papers, PUL; transcripts of ABC radio and television program "Adlai Ewing Stevenson Reports on the UN," 29 Oct. 1961, Box 129; 21 May 1963; miscellaneous material in Box 864, AES Papers, PUL; Baltimore *Afro-American,* 25 Feb. 1961; Charles Hamilton, *Adam Clayton Powell* (1991), 30, 333–34; "Reflections on the New Frontier," Oral History with members of JFK staff, JFKL.

410   *Increase in size of UN:* United Nations, Security Council, *Official Records,* 22 June 1962, 21–33.

410   *UN and family images:* Michael Prosser, ed., *An Ethic for Survival* (1969), 355, 470–83; AES to Harlan Cleveland, 8 May 1962, AES Papers, PUL; *Papers,* 8:822.

411   *AES describes the UN:* Remarks on 9 May 1963, Box 867; Harlan Cleveland interview, JFKL.

411   *Changes in the UN:* Leland Goodrich, *The United Nations in a Changing World* (1974), 47–51; Arnold Beichman, *The "Other" State Department: The United States Mission to the United Nations—Its Role in the Making of Foreign Policy* (1968).

411   *AES's apartment:* Kenneth S. Davis, *The Politics of Honor* (1967), 449.

411   *$25,000 retainer from Field Foundation:* Ruth Field to AES III, 10 Dec. 1963, Box 861, AES Papers, PUL.

411   *Retainer from* Encyclopaedia Britannica: Martin, *World,* 149. *AES's social life:* Lady Bird Johnson, *A White House Diary* (1970), 146–48; Beschloss, *Crisis Years,* 466.

412   *AES affairs:* Betty Beale, *Power at Play: A Memoir of Parties, Politics, and Presidents in My Bedroom* (1993), 131; Maria Riva, *Marlene Dietrich* (1993), 652–53; income tax returns, 1960–63, Box 1562, 1563, AES Papers, PUL.

412   *Intellectual men and married women:* AES to Marietta Tree, 2 July 1958, Johnson Papers.

412   *Romance with Sarah Plimpton:* Martin, *World,* 759–60.

412   *"Stevenson's Hotel"*: William Blair to "Guv," 11 Feb. 1964, AES Papers, PUL.

412   *AES "intimates"*: Elizabeth Stevenson Ives Diary, 1962, 1965, Family Folders.

412   *AES's compulsive eating:* Interview with Marietta Tree; Lauren Bacall Oral History, ASOH.

412   *"calmness for the long haul"*: Agnes Meyer to AES, 15, 28 Feb. 1961, AES Papers, PUL.

412   *Buffie's advice:* Elizabeth Stevenson Ives to AES, n.d., Feb. 1960, Family Folders.

412   *"Here things swirl"*: AES to Barbara Jackson, 16 May 1962, AES Papers, PUL.

413   *"Too much of my life"*: AES to "Ernest and Buff," 21 June 1957, AES Papers, PUL.

413   *"with much, much"*: AES to "Dear Boys," 6 June 1957, AES Papers, PUL.

413   *Trouble seeing boys:* AES to Mary Lasker, 30 Aug. 1962, AES Papers, PUL.

PAGE

413   *"how hard it seems"*: AES to Borden Stevenson, 6 July 1965, AES Papers, PUL.

413   *AES as errand boy*: Ronald Steel, *Walter Lippmann and the American Century* (1980), 548.

413   *Other end of telephone*: Carl McGowan Oral History, Martin Papers, PUL.

413   *"I never saw"*: Dean Rusk, *As I Saw It* (1990), 155–56.

413   *"no great fighter"*: Cleveland Oral History, JFKL. See also Beichman, *"Other" State Department*, 145, 159 nn. 6, 7.

413   *AES doesn't write speeches*: Cleveland Oral History, JFKL.

413   *"they are holding me in"*: Barbara Ward File, Box 835, AES Papers, PUL.

413   *"The most exhilarating work"*: AES, *Looking Outward* (1961), 142.

413   *"to do something"*: AES to George Meany, 7 Sept. 1961; "Adlai Ewing Stevenson Reports," Box 129, AES Papers, PUL.

414   *Walker*: Clippings on Edwin Walker, AES Papers, PUL; *New York Herald*, 13 April 1962.

414   *FBI investigates UN employees*: Shirley Hazzard, *Defeat of an Ideal: A Study of the Self-destruction of the United Nations* (1973).

414   *Buffie resigns*: Elizabeth Stevenson Ives, DAR Folder, Family Folders.

414   *UN and ethical international behavior*: Dorothy Jones, *Code Of Peace: Ethics and Security in the World of the Warlord State* (1991).

414   *"The UN is to America"*: AES, *Looking Outward*, 120; AES to UN Security Council, 23 Oct. 1962, *Papers*, 8:308.

414   *AES on the charter*: *Papers*, 8:310; AES review of Wilder Foot, *Dag Hammarskjöld: Servant of Peace: A Selection of His Speeches and Statements*, in *New York Times*, 14 April 1963; AES, "The United Nations, Guardian of Peace," *Department of State Bulletin* 44 (1961): 410–14.

414   *"flattery is all right"*: AES at the UN, 1961, audio tape, LC.

415   *Disruption by black nationalists*: *New York Times*, 16 Feb. 1961.

415   *"a virtual compendium"*: AES, *Looking Outward*, 122.

415   *Schlesinger briefings*: Schlesinger, *Thousand Days*, 271.

415   *"we were told"*: Francis Plimpton Oral History, ASOH.

416   *AES and the Bay of Pigs*: Cleveland Oral History, JFKL; Folder on Cuba, Box 830, AES Papers, PUL.

416   *"the United States has committed"*: USUN Press Release, 3704, 18 April 1961.

416   *AES's presentation*: Cleveland Oral History, JFKL.

416   *Kennedy on AES's integrity*: Schlesinger, *Thousand Days*, 271.

416   *"my official liar"*: Alden Whitman, *Portrait: Adlai E. Stevenson* (1965), 267.

416   *"You heard my speech"*: Doyle, *As We Knew Adlai*, 286. Jane Dick Oral History, ASOH.

416   *AES and the cover story*: Richard Walton, *The Remnants of Power: The Tragic Last Years of Adlai Stevenson* (1968), 32; Mary McAuliffe, *CIA Documents in the Cuban Missile Crisis 1962* (1993).

417   *"I believe in on-the-job"*: McKeever, *Stevenson*, 491.

417   *"How could any man"*: Davis, *Politics of Honor*, 458.

417   *"that Cuba trick"*: AES to Eugene McCarthy, 6 May 1961, AES Papers, PUL.

417   *"the government has a right"*: Quoted in Shapley, *Promise and Power*, 183.

417   *Partial briefing of Stevenson*: Pierre Salinger, *With Kennedy* (1966), 287.

417   *"no little amount of time"*: Beschloss, *Crisis Years*, 465.

417   *Moving AES to ambassador*: Cleveland Oral History, JFKL.

418   *Cuban missiles as no shift in power*: Shapley, *Promise and Power*, 169; McAuliffe, *CIA Documents*, 139, 157–59.

PAGE

418 *"I don't think we"*: Cuban Missile Crisis Meetings, Presidential Recording Transcripts, 16, 27 Oct. 1962, Presidential Office Files, Papers of JFK, JFKL. The description of the Cuban missile crisis is based on Barton Bernstein, "Reconsidering the Missile Crisis: Dealing with the Problems of the American Jupiters in Turkey," in James Nathan, ed., *The Cuban Missile Crisis Revisited* (1992), 56–67, and Barton Bernstein, "A Jupiter Swap?" in Robert Divine, ed., *The Cuban Missile Crisis* (1971), 251.

418 *"He can't do this*: Paterson, *Kennedy's Quest,* 142; USUN Press Release, 3704, 18 April 1961.

418 *Administration's obsession with Cuba*: Thomas Paterson, "Fixation with Cuba: The Bay of Pigs, the Missile Crisis and the Covert War against Castro," in Paterson, *Kennedy's Quest,* 123–55.

418 *Possible U.S. strike on Cuba*: James Hershberg, "Before 'The Missiles of October': Did Kennedy Plan a Military Strike against Cuba?" *Diplomatic History* 14 (1990): 163–98; Bernstein, "Reconsidering the Missile Crisis," 65.

418 *"was looking for a way"*: *Newsweek,* 26 Oct. 1992.

419 *"We must try and imagine"*: Cuban Missile Crisis Meetings, Presidential Recording Transcripts, 16 Oct. 1962, Presidential Office Files, Papers of JFK, JFKL.

419 *Business as usual*: O'Donnell, *Johnny,* 312.

419 *"insist for history we make"*: Philip Klutznick Oral History, ASOH; Bernstein, "Reconsidering the Missile Crisis," 72.

419 *Administration reactions*: Paterson, *Kennedy's Quest,* 140–55.

419 *"It should be clear as pikestaff"*: AES memo to "Dear Mr. President," 27 Oct. 1962, AES Papers, PUL; Klutznick Oral History, JFKL.

420 *"Tell me which side"*: John Martin interview with Sorenson, cited in Beschloss, *Crisis Years,* 449; Sorenson, *Kennedy,* 695; Sorenson Oral History, JKFL.

420 *"Neutralization and demilitarization"*: "Why the Political Program Should Be in the Speech," "What Neutralization Would Mean," 21 Oct. 1962, AES Papers, PUL.

420 *Hard-liners' reactions*: Bernstein, "Reconsidering the Missile Crisis," 60–65.

420 *"everyone jumped on him"*: Schlesinger, *Thousand Days,* 835–38; Sorenson, *Kennedy,* 696 (AES is the "advisor" Sorenson refers to); Bernstein, "Reconsidering the Missile Crisis," 63–67.

420 *"I know that most"*: O'Donnell, *Johnny,* 326.

420 *"that Stevenson would reach"*: John Martin interview with Dean Rusk and Robert Kennedy, Martin Papers, PUL; Beschloss, *Crisis Years,* 466.

421 *Robert Kennedy's obfuscations of U.S.-Soviet deal*: Robert Kennedy, *Thirteen Days: A Memoir of the Cuban Missile Crisis* (1969).

421 *Not "always as tough"*: Plimpton Oral History, JFKL.

421 *AES thought weak-kneed*: Rusk, *As I Saw It,* 236.

421 *McCloy and AES's toughness*: John McCloy to Walter Johnson, 24 July 1967, cited in *Papers,* 8:307 n. 222.

421 *Favoring military confrontation*: James Nathan, "The Heyday of the New Strategy: The Cuban Missile Crisis and the Confirmation of Coercive Diplomacy," in Nathan, *Cuban Missile Crisis,* 1–10; Bernstein, "Reconsidering the Missile Crisis," 74; John Martin interview with Dean Rusk and Arthur Schlesinger, Martin Papers, PUL.

421 *Kennedy understands AES's wounds*: Beschloss, *Crisis Years,* 466.

421 *"Adlai sticks to"*: O'Donnell, *Johnny,* 322–323.

421 *"Stevenson was a hopping mad"*: Walter Isaacson and Evan Thomas, *The Wise Men: Six Friends and the World They Made* (1986), 630.

PAGE

421 *"the immediate dismantling"*: Papers, 8:323.

421 *"vast difference between"*: Papers, 8:319, 322.

421 *AES's reluctance to use props*: Plimpton Oral History, JFKL.

422 *"Do you, Ambassador Zorin"*: United Nations, Security Council, *Official Records*, 25 Oct. 1962, 16–17.

422 *"I am prepared to wait"*: Papers, 8:331.

422 *"I never knew Adlai"*: Beschloss, *Crisis Years*, 506; O'Donnell, *Johnny*, 334.

422 *"We were eyeball"*: Dino Brugioni, *Eyeball to Eyeball: The Inside Story of the Cuban Missile Crisis* (1991).

422 *U.S. trade*: Bernstein, "Reconsidering the Missile Crisis," 75, 98–101.

422 *"An opponent charges"*: Saturday Evening Post, 2, 8 Dec. 1962.

422 *"At first we divided"*: Ibid., 8 Dec. 1962.

423 *Father's reaction*: AES III to John Martin, 29 April 1974, Martin Papers, LC.

423 *Reevaluation of hard-liners*: Bernstein, "Reconsidering the Missile Crisis," 94–107; Fred Nathan, *Wizards of Armageddon* (1983).

423 *Accusations against AES*: AES to Walter Judd, 20 Oct. 1961, AES Papers, PUL; Barry Goldwater to AES, 26 Nov. 1962, ibid.; "Some Lessons on Cuba," 23 April 1961, Box 830, ibid.; AES to the editor of *New York Daily News*, 16 Sept. 1964; AES to Barry Goldwater, 13 Nov. 1962, Folder on Goldwater, Box 844, AES Papers, PUL; *Tampa Tribune*, 31 Oct. 1961, Box 830, ibid.; Barry Goldwater with Jack Casserly, *Goldwater* (1988), 136–38; Beschloss, *Crisis Years*, 149.

423 *"Life has been unkind"*: AES to "Dearest Agnes," 15 Dec. 1962, AES Papers, PUL. There is some evidence that AES, along with other members of ExComm, suffered from "crisis-induced stress." See Alexander George, "The Impact of Crisis-Induced Stress on Decision-Making," in Frederic Solomon and Robert Marsden, *The Medical Implications of Nuclear War* (1968), 541; Paterson, *Kennedy's Quest*, 149–50.

423 *"If the President wanted me"*: Schlesinger, *Thousand Days*, 837.

423 *AES and Alsop*: James Wechsler, "The Brothers Alsop and Adlai Ewing Stevenson," *Progressive* 27 (March 1963): 14–17.

424 *"I have now had to face"*: AES to Barbara Jackson, 8 Dec. 1962.

424 *"I'm afraid if I don't stay"*: AES to "Buffie," 12 Aug. 1962, AES Papers, PUL; Ives Oral History, ASOH.

424 *"the troubles come"*: AES to "Dear Ada and Archie," 5 March 1963, AES Papers, PUL.

424 *Christmas card*: Papers, 8:361.

424 *The treaty signing*: Beschloss, *Crisis Years*, 629–30; Schlesinger, *Thousand Days*, 479.

424 *AES reminds the president*: Memo for the President, 8 Aug. 1961, 30 July 1963, AES Papers, PUL; Schlesinger Memorandum for the President, 29 July 1963, Schlesinger Papers, JFKL; Rusk, *As I Saw It*, 411–12.

424 *AES wants to go*: Martin, *World*, 769.

424 *AES is praised for nuclear disarmament*: John Steinbeck to AES, 24 May 1960, AES Papers, PUL.

424 *"started working"*: Dean Rusk Oral History, JFKL.

425 *"one-third protocol"*: Brian Urquhart, *A Life in Peace and War* (1987), 192. On AES's short-comings as UN ambassador, see Walton, *Remnants*, 224–25.

425 *Issues of the Congo*: Andrew W. Cordier and Max Harrelson, eds., *Public Papers of the Secretaries-General of the United Nations*, vol. 6, (1976), *U Thant, 1961–1964* 299.

425 *AES on the Congo*: Walton, *Remnants*, 77.

425 *"The only way to keep"*: Papers, 8:36, 39.

PAGE

426 *The debt crisis:* Edna Kelley and William Maillard, "United Nations in Crisis," 88th Cong., 2nd sess., Jan. 1964, copy in Box 862, AES Papers, PUL.

426 *AES on debt issue:* Walton, *Remnants,* 84–87, 94–98.

426 *"to demand that these nations":* Congressional Record, Aug. 1964, H19884–86.

426 *"Unfortunately we were":* Plimpton Oral History, JFKL.

426 *Issues over debt crisis:* AES's statement quoted in *Department of State Bulletin* 51 (1964): 891. For an analysis of the debt problem, see Beichman, *"Other" State Department,* 149–58.

426 *Gardner's reaction:* Richard Gardner, "The Article 19 Crisis: A White Paper" (copy), Box 322, Martin Papers, LC; Walton, *Remnants,* 70–103.

426 *"What if the Assembly":* Papers, 8:683–84.

426 *"He gave away":* Harlan Cleveland to John Martin, 2 May 1966, Martin Papers, LC.

426 *"The house is battered":* AES, *Looking Outward,* 133.

427 *AES III on problems with his mother:* AES III to "Dear Dad," 7 July, 2 June 1962, 22 May, 1 Oct. 1963, AES Papers, PUL.

427 *Ellen Borden Stevenson:* Ingram File clippings in possession of author; Karl Shapiro, *Reports of My Death* (1992), 49.

427 *"Your luna moths":* Karl Shapiro, *Selected Poems* (1940), 306–7.

427 *"I seem to remember":* AES to Mary Spears, 27 Aug. 1962, AES Papers, PUL.

427 *Family quarrel:* "In the Supreme Court of the State of Illinois," Abstract of Record, no. 40029, Sept. 1969, in possession of author.

427 *AES III buys his mother's things:* AES III to AES II, 2 June, 4 July 1962, AES Papers, PUL.

428 *"You betray me"* and *"If I go broke":* Taped conversations of Ellen Borden Stevenson, Abstract of Illinois Supreme Court Proceedings.

428 *"Ellen's tale":* AES to Jane Dick, 16 Aug. 1962, AES Papers, PUL.

428 *Arrangement with son:* AES II to AES III, 23 Jan. 1963, AES Papers, PUL.

428 *"for the protection of the estate":* "Appeal from the Circuit Court of Cook County Probate Division"; interview with J. Stuart Ingram.

428 *Sons fight about contributions to their mother:* John Fell Stevenson to "Dad, Borden, and Adlai," 30 Jan. 1963, AES III Papers, ISHS.

429 *"I believe the cause of peace":* AES Speeches, 23 Oct. 1963, AES Papers, PUL.

429 *The climate in Dallas:* Stanley Marcus, *Minding the Store* (1974), 250–55; *New York Times,* 25 Oct. 1963.

429 *"I believe in the forgiveness":* Folder "Dallas," Oct. 1963, AES Papers, PUL.

429 *Kennedy's reaction:* Schlesinger, *Thousand Days,* 1020–21.

429 *AES's reaction:* Walter Johnson interview with Harlan Cleveland, cited in *Papers,* 8:461.

430 *"While we cannot obscure":* Papers, 8:474–75.

430 *"a chronic liar":* Martin, *World,* 509.

430 *Johnson's flattery of AES:* Interview with Arthur Schlesinger.

430 *AES hopes for new administration:* Charles Yost to John Martin, 3 April 1974, Box 322, Martin Papers, LC; Philip Geyelin, *Lyndon B. Johnson and the World* (1966), 230–32.

430 *"You should be sitting here":* McKeever, *Stevenson,* 540.

430 *"There was a smile":* Arthur Schlesinger interview cited in Beschloss, *Crisis Years,* 676.

430 *Importance of Tuesday meetings:* Henry Graff, *The Tuesday Lunch: Deliberation and Decision in Peace and War under LBJ* (1970).

430   *"I have the impression"*: AES to William Moyers, 14 June 1965, AES Papers, PUL.

430   *"fat ass"*: Quoted in Beschloss, *Crisis Years,* 464.

430   *Imitations of AES*: Stewart Alsop, *The Center: People and Power in Political Washington* (1968), 52.

430   *Johnson throws AES out*: Urquhart, *Life,* 202.

430   *Background on Johnson's foreign policy*: John Galloway, *The Tonkin Bay Resolution* (1970); Paul Hammond, *Lyndon B. Johnson and the Presidential Management of Foreign Relations* (1992), 181.

430   *"no Chamberlain umbrella man"*: Quoted in Isaacson and Thomas, *Wise Men,* 642.

431   *"brave people"*: David Levy, *The Debate over Vietnam* (1991), 36–37; see also ibid., 42.

431   *"the armed conspiracy"*: Papers, 8:553.

431   *"deliberate aggression"*: and *"But are our hands"*: Martin, *World,* 808–9; *Papers,* 592–93; United Nations, Security Council, *Official Records,* 21 May, 7 Aug. 1964, 1119, 1141.

431   *"establish a tacitly agreed frontier"*: AES to Paul Goodman, n.d., AES Papers, PUL.

431   *AES fears ripple effect*: Geyelin, *LBJ and the World,* 232.

432   *"We will seek no wider"*: Papers, 8:594–95.

432   *U.S. presence in the world*: Levy, *Debate,* 8–11, 38.

432   *"properly addressed"*: Meet the Press tapes, 27 June 1965, LC.

432   *Morse on AES's resignation*: Wayne Morse to AES, 17 May, 11 June 1964, AES Papers, PUL.

432   *"It goes without saying"*: AES to Wayne Morse, 27 May 1964, AES Papers, PUL.

432   *U.S. public opinion on sending troops*: Gallup Political Index, Report no. 1, June 1965; Levy, *Debate,* 103.

432   *"leaving its neighbors alone"*: Geyelin, *LBJ and the World,* 218.

432   *"prudent and careful approach"*: AES to "Dear Mr. President," 17 Feb. 1965, AES Papers, PUL.

432   *Dangerous escalation*: David Barrett, *Uncertain Warriors: Lyndon Johnson and His Vietnam Advisers* (1993), 18.

432   *Limited air strikes*: "Negotiations on Vietnam," 1 March 1965, *Papers,* 8:722–24.

432   *AES and U Thant initiative*: "Chronology of U Thant Suggestions that DRV and U.S. Representatives Meet in Rangoon," declassified sanitized version, United Nations, National Security Files, Agency File, Box 71, LBJ Library, Austin, Tex.; Walter Johnson, "Peace Initiatives in the UN, 1964–1965," *Diplomatic History* 1 (1977): 295.

432   *"The very word negotiation"*: Notes of a conversation of Walter Johnson and Harlan Cleveland, 24 May 1971, Johnson Papers.

432   *U Thant initiative*: Charles Yost to Walter Johnson, 18 Sept. 1968, Johnson Papers; David Kraslow and Stuart Loory, *The Secret Search for Peace in Viet Nam* (1968), 91, 94–101; June Bingham, *U Thant: The Search for Peace* (1966), 225; Mario Rossi, "U Thant and Vietnam: The Untold Story," *New York Review of Books,* 17 Nov. 1966; Brian VanDeMark, *Into the Quagmire: Lyndon Johnson and the Escalation of the Vietnam War* (1991), 116–18; Tom Wells, *The War Within: America's Battle over Vietnam* (1994), 10–12.

432   *"I am sure"*: New York Times, 24 Feb. 1965; Cordier and Harrelson, *Public Papers of the Secretaries-General,* 6:741–42, 61.

432   *"The U.S. Government informs"*: Declassified phone conversation between Rusk and U Thant, 24 Feb. 1965; AES to Dean Rusk, 7 July 1965, National Security File,

PAGE

Agency File, Box 71, LBJ Papers, printed in *Papers*, 8:664–65; Memorandum of conversation of AES with U Thant, 16 Feb. 1965, Agency File, Box 71, LBJ Papers.

433 *Rusk's reaction:* Rusk, *As I Saw It*, 463–65. For Rusk's view on AES and the peace initiative, see John Martin interview with McGeorge Bundy; Dean Rusk Oral History, 11, sanitized version, JFKL; Dean Rusk to John Martin, 15 Dec. 1971, Martin Papers, LC.

434 *AES's conversation with Eric Sevareid: Papers*, 8:841.

434 *"Part of the problem":* Quoted in Kraslow and Loory, *Secret Search*, 98.

434 *"we must not put":* "Some Lessons on Cuba," 13 April 1961, in Cuba Folder, Box 830, AES Papers, PUL.

434 *"If weak, developing nations": Papers*, 8:779.

434 *"his complicity in":* "A Declaration to Ambassador Stevenson," June 1965, AES Papers, PUL.

434 *AES's meeting with Goodman et al.: Papers*, 8:807; Walton, *Remnants*, 172–77; Nat Hentoff, in *Village Voice*, 22 July 1965.

434 *"I would never take advantage": Papers*, 8:807.

435 *"seek a negotiated peace":* AES to Paul Goodman, n.d. [1965], AES Papers, PUL; Walton, *Remnants*, 178. The letter to Goodman was probably drafted by Barbara Jackson; her original bears notations by AES.

435 *Retiring from law practice:* AES to Simon Rifkin, 27 March 1964, AES Papers, PUL; McKeever, *Stevenson*, 561.

435 *"to redeem the time":* Address at Colby College, 7 June 1964, AES Papers, PUL.

436 *"farewell in this world": Papers*, 8:345.

436 *AES birthday:* Carl McGowan Oral History; Stephen Hord Oral History, ASOH; Birthday, 1965, Box 903, AES Papers, PUL.

436 *"palsied lips":* AES to Richard Gardner, 5 Jan. 1965, AES Papers, PUL.

436 *AES is tired:* John Martin interview with Elizabeth Stevenson Ives, PUL.

436 *AES's commitments:* Robert Sager to AES, 2 Aug. 1961, AES Papers, PUL.

436 *Speeches in 1965:* Prosser, *Ethic for Survival*, appendix, 520–24; Clayton Fritchey to AES, 31 Aug. 1964, AES Papers, PUL.

436 *AES as a slug:* George Ball interview, Martin Papers, PUL. On AES's overcommitment, see Martin, *World*, 755, 807.

436 *hadn't read a book:* John Martin interview with Philip Klutznick, JFKL.

436 *"the leisure of the theory class":* Quoted in *Chicago Daily News*, 20 Feb. 1963.

436 *"unpack for keeps":* Martin, *World*, 816.

436 *"I fold my hands":* Fragment, Box 903, AES Papers, PUL.

437 *"My first responsibility": New Yorker*, 24 Oct. 1965.

437 *AES's heart disease:* Interview with Dr. Nicholas Fortuin.

437 *"My father died":* Henry Lax to John Martin, 25 April 1972, Box 328, Martin Papers, LC.

437 *"We travel together": Papers*, 8:828.

437 *"For a while":* Conversation with Eric Sevareid, *Papers*, 8:835–45.

437 *"Hold your head high":* Marietta Tree Oral History, ASOH; Marietta Tree to John Martin, 4 Jan. 1972, Box 328, Martin Papers, LC.

438 *"But if I expire today": Papers*, 8:360.

438 *AES's funeral:* Family Folders; Elizabeth Stevenson Ives to "Adlai, Borden and John Fell," 3 Sept. 1965, Folder on Funeral Services, Box 897; Clippings, Box 1406, AES Papers, PUL.

CHAPTER 12: LAST HURRAH

PAGE

439 *"There's nothing here"*: John Martin interview with Elizabeth Stevenson Ives, Dec. 1964, Martin Papers, PUL.

439 *"We have changed since"*: Quoted in Martin, *World*, 812.

439 *"the ongoing agricultural revolution"*: *Papers*, 8:604.

440 *"midnight reveries of life"*: AES to "Dearest Mary" [Lasker], 14 Aug. 1964, AES Papers, PUL.

440 *"The skies have cleared"*: Quoted in Martin, *World*, 805.

440 *"House lovely"*: AES schedule [1964], Martin Papers, LC.

440 *"What you have inherited"*: AES commencement address at Colby College, 7 June 1964, AES Papers, PUL.

440 *"weary old politician"*: AES to "Dearest Barbara" [Jackson], 10 Sept. 1964, AES Papers, PUL.

440 *Supreme Court and districting*: The rulings in *Baker* v. *Carr* and *Reynolds* v. *Sims* held that unequally populated congressional districts violated the equal-protection clause of the U.S. Constitution. This ruling reversed an earlier one in which the Court held in an Illinois case during the 1940s that it was not for the judicial branch to decide a question so "political in character."

441 *AES III and Eisenhower in the election*: *New York Times*, 7 June, 13 Dec. 1964.

441 *On campaign in Chicago*: Corneal Davis Oral History, IGAOH.

441 *"had started his"*: AES III to "Dear Aunt Buffie," 9 July 1964, AES III Papers, ISHS.

441 *Changing names*: Milton Rakove, *Don't Make No Waves* (1975), 301.

441 *I can never remember"*: Interview with AES III.

442 *"small minds and small faiths"*: Speech at Bloomington, 22 July 1964, Box 866, AES Papers, PUL.

442 *"I am no longer"*: AES III to Tom Mehan, 3 Aug. 1964, Box 7, AES III Papers, ISHS.

442 *Description of campaign*: Boxes 7, 8, AES III Papers.

442 *AES as a private man*: Interview with John Taylor; interview with Lawrence Hansen.

442 *"You have a powerful"*: William Benton to AES III, 17 June 1964, Box 1, AES III Papers.

442 *"The expense is appalling"*: AES III to Peter Danniman, 16 Oct. 1964, Box 1, AES III Papers; AES III to AES II, 15 June 1964, Box 886, AES Papers, PUL. See also AES III to "Aunt Buffie," 28 July 1964, AES III Papers; Paul Randolph and Leland Kennedy Oral Histories, IGAOH.

442 *"for crossing the threshold"*: Lyndon B. Johnson to "Dear Adlai," 24 June 1964, Box 879, AES Papers, PUL.

442 *AES's letter asking for an endorsement*: AES II to Lyndon Baines Johnson, 17 June 1964, Box 879, AES Papers, PUL.

442 *Johnson-Goldwater campaign*: Allen Matusow, *The Unraveling of America: A History of Liberalism in the 1960's* (1984), 143–52. This is an example of a growing number of "false choices" presented to voters, because NATO commanders already had the authority Goldwater would give them.

443 *AES II's reaction to his son's victory*: Martin, *World*, 815.

443 *The nonpartisan present*: Joel H. Silbey, *The American Political Nation, 1838–1893* (1991), 237–51.

443 *The new breed of politician*: Burdett Loomis, *The New American Politician: Ambition, Entrepreneurship and the Changing Face of Political Life* (1988).

PAGE

443   *Disappearance of party politics:* David Broder, *The Party's Over: The Failure of Politics in America* (1972).

443   *"At 34 I was":* AES II to "Dear Bear," 12 Oct. 1964, AES Papers, PUL.

444   *"Adlai looks forward":* AES II to Otto Kerner, 13 Jan. 1965, AES Papers, PUL.

444   *Politics of 1970s and 1980s:* E. J. Dionne, *Why Americans Hate Politics* (1991).

444   *AES at a fund-raiser:* Interview with William Blair; interview with Lawrence Hansen.

444   *Families and self-creation:* Nelson Aldrich, *Old Money: The Mythology of America's Upper Class* (1988).

444   *The neoliberals:* Randall Rothenburg, *The Neoliberals: Creating the New American Politician* (1984).

444   *Personality of eldest sons:* Edith Neisser, *The Eldest Child* (1957); Walter Toman, *Family Constellation* (1993); Lucille Forer, *The Birth Order Factor* (1976).

445   *"any genetic or inherited":* Interview with AES III.

445   *"I guess we weren't":* Quoted in Martin, *Illinois,* 152.

445   *A solitary child:* Interview with Elizabeth Ives; Buffie Ives Diary, Family Folders.

445   *AES as a child:* Elizabeth Ives, *My Brother Adlai* (1955), 234.

445   *Whispering to governess:* Martin, *Illinois,* 152; Mrs. J. Gillespie to AES II, July 22, 1942, AES Papers, PUL.

445   *Advice to father:* Kenneth S. Davis, *The Politics of Honor* (1967), 305; AES III to "Dear Dad," 10 Sept. 1961, AES Papers, PUL.

445   *"God bless you":* AES II to AES III, 8 Oct. 1951, letter in possession of AES III.

445   *Process of absorbing politics:* Norman Adler, *The Learning of Political Behavior* (1970); Roberta Sigel, ed., *Learning about Politics* (1970).

446   *"We were in such symbiosis":* Interview with AES III.

446   *"be wary of sacrificing":* AES III to AES II, 13 Feb. 1952, letter in possession of AES III.

446   *"We never demonstrated":* Martin, *Illinois,* 90.

446   *Ellen Borden Stevenson's mothering:* AES III Oral History, ASOH; Martin, *Illinois,* 152.

446   *AES's description of his mother:* "In the Supreme Court of the State of Illinois, in the Matter of the Conservatorship of Ellen Borden Stevenson," no. 40229, 1351.

446   *John Fell became favorite:* Interview with Borden Stevenson; interview with Elizabeth Ives.

446   *"Take the abuse":* AES III Oral History, ASOH; interview with AES III.

446   *"I was just sent":* Martin, *Illinois,* 226.

447   *"Adlai is a conscientious":* AES II to Merritt Hewett, 6 Sept. 1944, AES Papers, PUL.

447   *"Guv" to his classmates:* Interview with AES III.

447   *AES III at Milton:* Martin, *Illinois,* 226–27; Milton Academy, *Orange and Blue Review,* 1945–48, Milton Archives, Milton, Mass.

447   *"Adlai has plenty of ability":* Quoted in Martin, *Illinois,* 321–22; AES II to Mr. Heermance, 5 May 1948, AES Papers, PUL.

447   *"I am anxious for him":* AES to Arthur Perry, 18 Feb. 1947, AES Papers, PUL.

447   *"Adlai is immature":* Radcliffe Heermance to ASE II, 24 May, 8 June 1948, Box 440, Martin Papers, LC.

448   *On Harvard:* Harvard Yearbooks, 1948–51; Harvard Catalogs; Harvard University, *Report of the President, Reports of Departments,* 1948–52, Harvard University Archives; Richard Norton Smith, *The Harvard Century* (1986).

448   *Harvard Liberal Union and electioneering:* New Yorker, 11 Oct. 1952.

448 *The fistfight:* Martin, *Illinois,* 346.

448 *"I thought I'll never":* Interview with AES III.

448 *"I volunteered from":* Ibid.

448 *"It was a political":* Ibid.

449 *"In one way or another":* Papers, 4:104–5.

449 *Importance of Marines in his career:* Interview with AES III; interview with Lawrence Hansen.

449 *"It is better if you":* AES II to AES III, 3 May, 3 June 1954, letters in possession of AES III.

449 *AES II's record at Harvard Law School:* Dean Griswold to AES III, 24 March, 12 May 1967 (copy), Box 181, AES III Papers.

450 *"more various in religious":* AES to William Benton, 12 April 1961, AES Papers, PUL.

450 *Working eighteen hours:* Nancy Anderson Stevenson to "dearest Guv," Jan. 1963, Box 867, AES Papers, PUL.

451 *"The speech meant different":* Nancy Anderson Stevenson to AES, 6 June 1955, AES Papers, PUL.

451 *Women during the 1950s:* Wini Breines, *Young, White and Miserable: Growing Up in the 1950's* (1992).

451 *Ugly features of the wedding:* AES III to "Dear Dad," April 1955, AES Papers, PUL.

451 *"purr like a kitten":* AES II to "Dear Bear," 6 April 1955, AES Papers, PUL.

451 *"Mr. Anderson really is beside":* Martin, *World,* 171.

451 *"Ellen is a hazard":* AES II to Warwick Anderson, 8 April 1955, AES Papers, PUL.

451 *The wedding:* Nancy Stevenson Oral History, ASOH.

451 *Older-brother marriage to younger sister:* Helene Arnstein, *Brothers and Sisters, Sisters and Brothers* (1979); Forer, *Birth Order Factor.*

451 *Pistol:* Interview with Borden Stevenson.

451 *"Ad and I have . . .":* Nancy Anderson Stevenson to "Dearest Guv," 30 Jan. 1955, Johnson Papers.

451 *Honeymoon, and Jo Daviess County:* Interview with AES III.

452 *"these days of reading, eating":* Nancy Anderson Stevenson to "Dearest Guv," Oct. 1955, AES Papers, PUL.

452 *"It seems all I":* AES III to "Dear Dad," 7 Nov. 1961, AES Papers, PUL.

452 *Birthrate statistics:* Stephanie Coontz, *The Way We Never Were: American Families and the Nostalgia Trap* (1992), 24; William Chafe, *The American Woman: Her Changing Social, Economic, and Political Roles* (1986), 217.

452 *"Most of us":* Clipping from Nancy Stevenson Folder, commencement address, Barat College, AES III Papers.

452 *A new generation of child rearing:* Benjamin Spock, *The Common Sense Book of Baby and Child Care* (1961), 11, 20; *Dr. Spock Talks with Mothers* (1961), 128.

452 *"I think there were lots":* Nancy Stevenson Oral History, ASOH.

452 *"On the edge of the slums":* AES II to E. J. Ryan, 23 Oct. 1957, AES Papers, PUL.

453 *"We'd get a call":* Nancy Stevenson Oral History, ASOH.

453 *The problem that has no name:* Betty Friedan, *The Feminine Mystique* (1963).

453 *"Our family life has not":* Nancy Stevenson to AES, n.d., Vice-Presidential Folder, Box 184, AES III Papers.

453 *"I'm embroiled as ever":* AES to "Dear Dad," 15 Feb. 1961, AES Papers, PUL.

454 *"not important and":* AES III in *New York Post,* 12 June 1964, clipping in Box 886, AES Papers, PUL.

454 *"repeal human nature":* *Chicago Daily News,* 23 June 1966, 12 Sept. 1964. For his

PAGE

bill to require lobbyists to report their monthly compensation, see *New York Times,* 30 June 1964.

454 *"The legislature is inadequate": Chicago Sun Times,* 25 July 1965. Also *Washington Post,* June 12, 1964.

454 *Father's black book:* AES III to AES II, 15 June 1964, AES Papers, PUL.

454 *"some of the 'blue ribbon' ": Chicago Sun Times,* 25 July 1965.

454 *Harold Washington's comment:* Interview with AES III.

454 *Views of AES as diligent but aloof:* John Parkhurst; Carl Wittmond Oral History, IGAOH.

454 *Evaluation of his voice:* Brian Thompson to AES III, 10 Sept. 1964, Box 7, AES III Papers.

455 *Borden's Cheetah nightclubs: Time,* 3 June 1966; *Chicago Tribune,* 17 May 1966.

455 *"the worst possible time":* AES III to Ruth Field, 9 May, 1 June 1966, Box 17, AES III Papers.

455 *Divisions among Stevenson sons:* Interview with Borden Stevenson.

455 *On the sheep:* Edward McDougall to AES III, Jan. 1966, Box 16, AES III Papers; Martin, *Illinois,* vi.

455 *"The words come slowly":* AES III speech in Normal, 7 Jan. 1966, Box 70, AES III Papers; copy in Martin Papers, LC.

455 *"I can't for the life":* AES III to Warwick Anderson, 8 May 1974, Box 15, AES III Papers.

455 *AES sanitizing his father's career:* John B. Martin, *It Seems Like Yesterday* (1986), 194–202.

455 *"to end an unprovoked":* AES III speech in Normal.

456 *"I am up for state":* AES III to Dr. Carl Binger, 3 Oct. 1966, Box 16, AES III Papers.

456 *On the trial:* AES to Robert Pirie, 16 March 1966, ibid.; court records, in possession of the author.

456 *Campaign for state treasurer:* Box 7, AES III Papers.

456 *Differences with party and AES's independence: New York Times,* 6 March 1966.

456 *Treasurership as dull: Chicago Tribune,* 17 May 1966; Harris Rowe Oral History, IGAOH; Rev. R. C. Hartnett to AES III, 5 Nov. 1966, AES III Papers.

456 *"The office of state treasurer":* Newsletter, Box 7, AES III Papers.

457 *"It is hard":* AES III to Rev. R. C. Hartnett, 8 Nov. 1966, Box 15, ibid.; clipping from *Boston Globe,* 10 Nov. 1966; material on fund-raiser, 22 Aug. 1966, Box 15, ibid.

457 *Buffie's reaction:* Interview with Elizabeth Ives; Buffie Ives, "Reflections on Election," Nov. 1966, Family Folders.

457 *"so that they can make":* AES III, country rally, Box 7, AES III Papers.

457 *On use of state funds: New York Times,* 7 May 1966.

457 *"creative treasurership":* AES, "Some Random Thoughts on Improving the Quality of State Government in Illinois," AES III Papers; San Francisco *Examiner,* 1 April 1966, clipping in Box 7, ibid.

457 *Treasurership as his favorite office:* Interview with AES III.

457 *"My only aspiration":* Quoted in *New York Times,* 25 Jan. 1968.

458 *On lack of due process in conservator hearings:* Denise Topolnicki, "The Gulag of Guardianship," in *Money,* March 1989, 140–48; interview with John Regan, professor of law at Hofstra University.

459 *"Now they say":* The interior voice of Ellen Stevenson is taken from letters and court records in the possession of the author. It is also based on several interviews

PAGE

with J. Stuart Ingram, her friend and financial adviser. For changes in conservator law, see *Illinois Revised Statutes,* chap. 110, 1963, par. 109.

459   *"I would say":* Quoted in Mike Royko, *Boss: Richard J. Daley of Chicago,* 134, 172.

460   *AES's presentation:* "Adlai Ewing Stevenson III Notes to Slatemakers," 25 Feb. 1968; memorandum, 29 Feb. 1968, Box 194, AES III Papers.

460   *The slating process: Chicago Daily News,* 21 Feb. 1968; *New York Times,* 28 Feb. 1968; interview with AES III.

460   *"what that young man":* William Furlong, "The Adlai III Brand of Politics," *New York Times Magazine,* 22 Feb. 1970.

460   *Daley comment:* Melvin Kahn, *The Winning Ticket: Richard Daley, the Chicago Machine and Illinois Politics* (1984), 212. For AES III's description, see AES III to John Martin, 29 Feb. 1968, Box 321, Martin Papers, LC.

461   *"a tragic and troubled year":* AES III to "Dear Friends," 17 Sept. 1968, Box 4, AES III Papers.

461   *Daley's policy and police riot:* Daniel Walker, *Rights in Conflict* (1968); *New York Times,* 22 Aug. 1968; David Farber, *Chicago '68* (1988).

461   *"storm troopers in blue":* FBI Main File, Folder on Adlai Stevenson III, 94-40154, memo to A. Jones from Mr. Bishop, 4 Nov. 1970.

461   *AES at convention:* Telephone interview with AES IV.

462   *Description of convention:* Matusow, *Unraveling,* 417–20; Milton Viorst, *Fire in the Streets: America in the 1960's* (1979), 459.

462   *AES III's plan for protest:* Interview with AES III; Victor de Grazia Oral History, IGAOH.

462   *Lowenstein urges a postponement:* William Chafe, *Never Stop Running: Allard Lowenstein and the Struggle to Save American Liberalism* (1993), 301–4.

462   *Daley's popularity in Chicago:* Norman Mailer, *Miami and the Siege of Chicago* (1968), 114. *The choice of Humphrey: New York Times,* 25 May 1968.

462   *"to take into consideration"* and *"to tolerate dissent realistically":* AES III to "Dear Friends," 17 Sept. 1968, AES III Papers. See also AES Post-Convention Statement, Box 4, AES III Papers.

463   *"Don't worry about young Adlai":* Jane Byrne, *My Chicago* (1992), 197.

463   *"open party and open"* and *"We'll have":* Sept. 1969, Box 68, AES III Papers.

464   *Jackson's advice to AES:* Interview with AES III.

464   *Description of picnic:* Interview with Steve Neall; materials in Box 68, AES III Papers.

464   *The appearance of Daley:* Interview with AES III; Furlong, "Adlai III Brand"; *Chicago Tribune,* 27 April 1986; Ralph Nader, "Citizens Look at Congress—Adlai Ewing Stevenson" (1972), in Springfield Public Library.

464   *"political pornography":* Campaign materials, Box 70, AES III Papers.

465   *"Those who moan":* Spiro Agnew, *Collected Speeches of Spiro Agnew* (1971), 193, 268; *New York Times,* 25 Oct. 1970.

465   *"We are not going to":* AES III speeches, Decatur Rotary Club, 12 June 1970, Box 70, AES III Papers.

465   *Coverage of campaign: New York Times,* 3 Nov. 1970.

465   *"willing victim of hereditary":* Fletcher Farrar, "Liberal to Neoliberal," *Illinois Times,* 23 Oct. 1982.

465   *"shouldn't stay home":* Furlong, "Adlai III Brand."

465   *New voting patterns:* Lawrence Hansen, "Suburban Politics," Office for Urban Affairs, 1979.

PAGE

466 Ervin quotes Grandfather's support of filibuster: Congressional Record, 1 Feb. 1971, S642; AES III, "A Freshman in the Senate," Box 180, AES III Papers.

466 On transformations in Washington: Jeffrey Birnbaum, The Lobbyists: How Influence Peddlers Get Their Way in Washington (1992); Charles Lipsen, Vested Interests (1977); Haynes Johnson, In the Absence of Power: Governing America (1980).

466 "a monstrosity with too": Box 221, AES III Papers.

466 AES and house on Foxhall Road: William Furlong, "The Son Also Rises," Chicago, June 1979, 116.

466 "The woman of this day": Clippings, Box 221, AES III Papers.

467 "I think there's a great value": Fletcher Farrar, "From Liberal to Neo-Liberal," Illinois Times, 23–29 Sept. 1982.

467 Effect of air travel on Senate and House: Richard Fenno, Home Style: House Members in Their Districts (1978); interview with AES III.

467 AES's voting record and ratings: Michael Barone et al., The Almanac of American Politics (1974), 261; (1976), 224.

467 Changes in U.S. Senate: Interview with Senator Charles Mathias.

467 "I try to spend": AES, "Freshman in the Senate"; World Book, 1971.

467 "I owe [the people]": AES III, "Freshman in the Senate".

467 AES III and plans for industrial policy: AES III to Larry Fishman, 16 Oct. 1970, Box 70, AES III Papers.

468 "It gets back to the naive": Nader, "Stevenson."

468 AES III on Vietnam: Congressional Record, 2 April 1971, S4449.

468 "the terrible leadership" and criticisms of Kissinger: New York Times, 8, 13, 22 Feb. 1975.

468 AES's III distrust of Kissinger: James Sundquist, The Decline and Resurgence of Congress (1981), 285n.

468 Provisions for an independent prosecutor: New York Times, 19 Jan. 1973; interview with AES III.

468 "The people are left": New York Times, 3 Oct. 1972; interview with AES III.

468 Reports of surveillance of AES III: New York Times, 17, 19 Dec. 1970, 8, 18, 25 Feb. 1971, 17 May 1976.

468 "that politics is the means": Nader, "Stevenson."

468 AES III's wealth: Chicago Tribune, 19 May, 31 July 1979.

468 Sale of Pantagraph: Chicago Tribune, 11 July 1982.

468 Materials on campaign contribution act: Box 281, AES III Papers. On the concept of permanent campaigning, see Sidney Blumenthal, The Permanent Campaign (1980).

469 Fund-raisers: Interview with Senator Mathias. On AES III's idea for an independent electoral commission and contribution cap, see New York Times, 10 May, 29 July, 22 August 1973.

469 "It's been an agony": Nader, "Stevenson."

469 Congressional hearings: Congressional Record, 8 Feb. 1972, S13570; New York Times, 22 Oct., 19 Dec. 1978. Lowell Weicker so disliked AES III's "bureaucratic handling" of the bribe scandal that he quit the ethics committee. See New York Times, 15 April 1978.

469 AES III's attention to writing speeches: Interviews with Barbara Bruns and Lawrence Hansen.

469 "I think we are": Elizabeth Drew, American Journal: The Events of 1976 (1976), 14–15.

469 The subcommittee issue: Congressional Record, 22 June 1971, S9719, 9720, 9415;

PAGE

Sundquist, *Decline*, 430–35; AES III to Frank Moss, 22 Nov. 1972, Box 286, AES III Papers.

470   *"This is a fight"*: New York Times, 24 Dec. 1976.

470   *Coverage of committee restrictions*: Ibid., 10, 18, 25, 26 Jan., 5 Feb. 1977.

470   *Lobbying by veterans*: Ibid., 10 Feb. 1977.

470   *The energy crisis*: Daniel Yergin, The Prize: The Epic Quest For Oil, Money, and Power (1991).

470   *"A deep resentment"*: Jimmy Carter, Keeping the Faith (1982), 92.

470   *AES III on energy policy*: "Senator Adlai Ewing Stevenson Upset by U.S. Decline"; Stevenson-Wydler Bill; Box 221, AES III Papers.

470   *On U.S. decline*: Katherine Neuman, Declining Fortunes: The Withering of the American Dream (1993); Wallace Peterson, Silent Depression: The Fate of the American Dream (1993).

470   *"The politicians of both parties"*: Speeches on Trade Policy, Box 221, AES III Papers.

470   *AES's proposals for change*: AES III, "Removing the Obstacles to American Exports," Business America, 14 July 1980, 3.

470   *"For decades"*: AES III, "Dusting Off Old Values," Design News, 7 July 1980. For AES III on the end of social liberalism, see New York Times, 1 Nov. 1982.

470   *Humphrey-Hawkins bill*: Otis Graham, Losing Time: The Industrial Policy Debate (1992).

470   *"Far from providing action"*: AES III to Leon Keyserling, 7 June 1976, Box 286, AES III Papers.

470   *"We are not little Hubert"*: Quoted in Steven M. Gillon, The Democrats' Dilemma: Walter Mondale and the Liberal Legacy (1992), 153.

471   *"Such questions as"*: AES III to John Martin, 5 Sept. 1979, Box 41, Martin Papers, LC.

471   *"No trade strategy"*: Congressional Record, 5 Oct. 1979, S14173.

471   *AES's energy plan*: 1979 clippings, Box 221, AES III Papers.

471   *Carter and AES III on energy*: New York Times, 23 Feb. 1975; Johnson, In the Absence of Power (1980), 188.

471   *"I've laid out ideas"*: Illinois Times, Sept. 1982; People, 19 Feb. 1979 clippings, Box 221, AES III Papers.

471   *Carter's relation with Congress*: Johnson, Absence of Power, 188.

471   *On trading companies*: New York Times, 7 April 1988.

471   *AES III's proposals for a new industrial policy*: Congressional Record, 18 Dec. 1979, S19000; AES III, "Detente and Dollar Diplomacy" International Lawyer (copy), Box 180, AES III Papers; New York Times, 30 March, 11, 18 June, 20 Dec. 1974.

471   *"Mr. Iacocca could get"*: John Martin to AES III Aug. 1979, Box 42, Martin Papers, LC.

471   *"little interest in new"*: People, 19 Feb. 1979; Washington Star, 28 Jan. 1979. *"Adlai's Aspirations"*: Pantagraph, 3 Jan. 1979.

472   *"We have been farming"*: Chicago Tribune, 22 Nov. 1981, 2 Nov. 1986.

472   *AES removing stumps*: Interview with Nancy Stevenson.

472   *Senate not only place to serve*: AES III to John Martin, 18 Dec. 1978, Martin Papers, LC.

472   *"Each hectic day"*: AES III, "Freshman in the Senate."

472   *"The Senate used to"*: People, 19 Feb. 1979; Furlong, "Son Also Rises"; Chicago, June 1979, 116.

472   *"It's no longer possible"*: New York Times, 16 Dec. 1992.

PAGE

472   *"When we opened the doors"*: People, 19 Feb. 1979. On the quirks of reform, see Burton Sheppard, *Rethinking Congressional Reform: The Reform Roots of the Special Interest Congress* (1985).

473   *"If I were here"*: Chicago Tribune, 12 Oct. 1980.

473   *Median service and term limits*: George F. Will, *Restoration: Congress, Term Limits and the Recovery of Deliberative Democracy* (1992), 73, 76, 89. See also New York Times, 28 April 1994.

473   *"I'm not going into"*: New York Times, 31 March 1979; Chicago Tribune, 30 June 1979.

473   *On future plans*: Chicago Tribune, 9 Feb. 1980.

473   *"that had worked pretty well"*: Interview with AES III.

473   *Thompson's ambitions and background*: Richard Hartley, *Big Jim Thompson of Illinois* (1979).

474   *"I could make"*: Chicago Tribune, 7 Sept. 1986.

474   *"big blubbering whale"*: Ibid., 15 June 1986; New York Times, 12 Aug. 1986.

474   *"he wanted to get"*: Hartley, *Thompson*, 154.

474   *"pin-striped spoils"*: Chicago Tribune, 26 Sept. 1986; AES III, Debates, Box 4, AES III Papers.

474   *Thompson's career as U.S. attorney*: Jane Bone, *The Thompson Indictment* (1978).

474   *no "sharp elbows"*: Illinois Times, Sept. 1982. On Thompson's campaigning, see Hartley, *Thompson*, 15, 150, 152; New York Times, 9 Sept. 1986.

474   *Reactive passive governorship*: Illinois Times, 10 Sept. 1981; Chicago Tribune, 14 Feb. 1982;

474   *"He's trying to make"*: Chicago Tribune, 23 Aug. 1985. See also ibid., 9 Oct. 1981, 15 Aug. 1986.

474   *"all the pioneering work"*: Speech in Springfield, 11 Oct. 1982, Box 4, AES III Papers.

475   *AES's campaigning in Springfield*: Interview with Michael Murphy.

475   *"You have to be"*: Chicago Tribune, 13 Jan. 1983.

475   *AES on the Illinois court and finding the right court*: Interview with AES III.

475   *Recount and court procedures*: New York Times, 4 Nov. 1982, 8 Jan. 1983.

475   *"I see very serious"*: Chicago Tribune, 8 Jan. 1983; Recount File, Box 6, AES III Papers.

475   *On Seymour Simon, the key Democratic judge*: Chicago Tribune, 15 Jan. 1983. Stevenson later claimed that his issues and campaign were responsible for closing the gap, while the press credited the Chicago machine of Edward Vrdolyak. Both interpretations overlook a get-out-the-vote registration drive and a surge in black voting. See William Grimshaw, *Bitter Fruit* (1992).

475   *AES III criticizes Vrdolyak*: Chicago Tribune, 2 Sept. 1985.

475   *AES III criticizes primary*: Speech at Indiana University, 2 April 1992.

475   *"You were lecturing"*: Chicago Tribune, 12 Sept. 1986.

476   *Activities of the LaRouches*: New York Times, 20, 21 March, 25 June 1986.

476   *LaRouche positions*: The New Federalist; Lyndon LaRouche, *What Every Conservative Should Know* (1980); idem, *The Power of Reason* (1988); Dennis King, *Lyndon LaRouche and the New American Fascism* (1989), 85–104.

476   *"I have in my bones"*: Chicago Tribune, 15 April 1986.

476   *"He has no right to"*: Chicago Tribune, 15 May 1986.

476   *Injuries and trucks*: New York Times, 27 June 1986; interview with AES III.

477   *"the peace and tranquillity"*: Chicago Tribune, 29 Oct. 1986.

PAGE

477   *"I really don't consider"*: AES III to Sam Vaughan, 17 Jan. 1986, Box 328, Martin Papers, LC.

477   *Struggle to get signatures:* Campaign Materials, Box 212, AES III Papers.

477   *Alone in Belleville:* Campaign Materials, Box 328, AES III Papers.

477   *"That truck saved me":* New York Times, 27 June 1986.

477   *"Good public servants":* Chicago Tribune, 12 Oct. 1980.

477   *"If [Thompson] were a woman":* Ibid., 9 July 1986.

477   *"a woman couldn't":* Ibid., 7 Sept. 1986. On women, see *New York Times,* 12, 19 Sept. 1986.

477   *Loss of Democratic base support:* Ibid., 28 Sept., 5 Oct. 1986.

477   *"I'm no good if":* Interview with AES III.

478   *"It's one of the things":* Chicago Tribune, 2 Nov. 1986.

478   *Self-financing of campaign:* Ibid., 1 Nov. 1986.

478   *Negative ad:* Ibid., 26, 27 Sept., 9 Oct. 1986.

478   *"I don't like":* Ibid., 14 Oct. 1986.

478   *Analysis of election results:* Howard Allen and Vincent Lacey, *Illinois Election Results, 1818–1990* (1992), 553–55. Six percent of the vote went to the Democratic ticket that had no candidate for governor.

478   *"I am proud":* Chicago Tribune, 5 Nov. 1986.

478   *"cheap and easy popular":* Speech at Indiana University, Northwest, Gary, 1 April 1992, letter in the author's possession.

478   *"Professional politicians":* Chicago Tribune, 12 Oct. 1980.

478   *"The object of our":* Speech at Indiana University; interview with AES III.

479   *"as we practice it":* Interview with AES III.

479   *Adlai the Last:* AES III to Arthur Schlesinger, 3 Aug. 1964, Box 882, AES Papers, PUL.

479   *"the Lord has left":* Interview with Elizabeth Ives.

479   *"Every generation has":* Speech at Indiana University.

INDEX

557